Human Sexualities

"When I use a word," Humpty Dumpty said, in rather a scornful tone, "it means just what I choose it to mean—neither more nor less."

"The question is," said Alice, "whether you can make words mean so many different things."

"The question is," said Humpty Dumpty, "which is to be master— that's all."

—Lewis Carroll, *Through the Looking-Glass*

Human Sexualities

John H. Gagnon

Professor of Sociology and Psychology
State University of New York at Stony Brook

Scott, Foresman and Company   **Glenview, Illinois**

Dallas, Tex.   Oakland, N.J.   Palo Alto, Cal.   Tucker, Ga.   Abingdon, England

The photographs that open each chapter in this book were not chosen
to fit the content of the chapter they introduce. They were arranged
independently of the text. The arrangers will take credit
for any reader's interpretation of the order that the arrangers like.

Illustration Acknowledgments

John Pfahl: Cover, pages 0, 22, 40, 58, 258, 276
James Ballard: 78, 96, 116, 140, 190, 214, 294, 320, 340, 364, 382
Charles Whitman: 164, 234
Sandy Rothberg: 406

Further acknowledgments are given at the end of the book.

Library of Congress Cataloging in Publication Data
Gagnon, John H., 1931 –
Human sexualities.
Includes bibliography and index.
1. Sex.   2. Sex customs.   3. Sex (Psychology)
4. Sex research.   I. Title.
HQ21.G2338   612.6   76-51453
ISBN: 0-673-15033-X

1 2 3 4 5 6-RRC-84 83 82 81 80 79 78 77 76

For Patricia A. Gagnon

FOREWORD

UNTIL VERY RECENTLY, SEX WAS A TABOO RESEARCH TOPIC. SEVENTY-FIVE YEARS ago, Sigmund Freud (in Austria), Havelock Ellis and Marie Stopes (in England), and Margaret Sanger (in the United States) ventured into the forbidden territory, but they were rudely pushed back.

Recently, everything changed. The bold work of Kinsey . . . Masters and Johnson . . . the President's Commission on Obscenity and Pornography . . . and the recent *Playboy, Psychology Today,* and *Redbook* surveys, have given university researchers the courage to hack their way into the unknown and begin to study the physiology, anatomy, psychology, and sociology of sex.

The fact that it has been so difficult to study love and sex has had a peculiar effect on the early texts, magazine articles . . . and talk shows . . . designed to disseminate what little we did know about sex. Scientists who were brave enough to enter the foray were usually zealots: they entered the foray with their minds closed, their teeth clenched, plunging on to prove a point. The Sexual Radicals insisted that the new humanism would solve all of man's problems. The Sexual Conservatives insisted that the old ways are the best.

In contrast with much of what came before, John H. Gagnon's book on *Human Sexualities* is a delight. John Gagnon is an exceedingly rational man. He poses provocative questions. He explains how scientists go about answering sexual questions . . . and how one can evaluate their research. Finally, he presents the wealth of information that the new research has yielded about sexual behavior.

Students will like this book.

Elaine Walster
University of Wisconsin
Madison, Wisconsin

PREFACE

"HUMAN SEXUALITIES" MAY SEEM TO BE AN ODD TITLE. IT IS NOT AS EASY TO classify as "An Introduction to . . . ," or "Fundamentals of . . . ," or even just "Human Sexuality." The choice of the plural centers on my belief that there are many ways to become, to be, to act, to feel sexual. There is no one human sexuality, but rather a wide variety of sexualities. Had it been possible, I would have made the word "Human" in the title plural as well. Just as there are many sexualities, there are many humanities, different ways of being sexual, different ways of being human.

I do not view how people become sexual as a process of unfolding, or maturing, or going through a sequence of stages. Our bodies do get larger in a somewhat orderly sequence, but the psychological meanings given to those changes are not fixed or eternal; each culture has different patterns of giving meaning to the processes of human development. We assemble our sexuality, picking and choosing and rejecting the ideas, beliefs, feelings, and practices offered to us in our own society. Although we are not merely passive reflections of our culture, we cannot totally transcend it. Life is a constant tension between scripts and improvisation, between ritual and innovation.

My interest does not lie in finding the "best" way to be sexual along any dimension. I do not know, except in terms of the values of individual people in individual cultures, how to judge mature sexuality, healthy sexuality, moral sexuality, joyful sexuality. Such judgments are local, contingent upon time and place, and upon the social interests of the person making the judgment. The fact that I choose not to make such judgments for anyone else expresses my own interests, for choosing not to judge is to make another kind of judgment.

As an academic I have certain intellectual commitments. I am intrigued by variety in human experience, and view the sociological and psychological enterprise not as discovering the laws of nature, but as perspectives on the contemporary and transitional regularities in the conduct of people living in a given time and place. My intent and hope, even if I do not succeed, is to increase the understanding of people as cultural-historical creatures, not to substitute the "laws" of sociology or psychology for the laws of government or nature. I have no interest in imposing a social-science view on the world as if that view were immutable.

Finally, I would like this book to offer some pleasure to the reader, to be sufficiently stimulating intellectually and lucid in style that the reader can have a good time with it. I hope it is a serious book, without being a solemn one.

Even though I do not share the conventional view of human development as continuous and unfolding, with the past dominating the future, I have chosen a life-cycle perspective to organize the materials of the book. This is because human beings accumulate their lives, assembling and changing their senses of self against a backdrop of historical time and personal experience. The life-cycle perspective organizes the sequence of experience and allows us to weigh the significance of new experiences throughout a lifetime. In some cases the past is controlling; in others the present is of greater importance in determining what the future will be. The biological, the psychological, and the social are in a constant interplay, with one and then another set of processes taking the lead in producing change or stability. Thus the biological changes of puberty must be understood in terms of an already active and organized human being with existing preferences and goals.

While the book is organized in terms of a life-cycle perspective, it can be read and taught from a topical point of view. Certain chapters contain more information about the biology of sex, others about the history and technique of research, others about specific patterns of sexual conduct, and still others have a greater emphasis on the social and cultural aspects of sexuality. The book has a perspective, but it can be taught in a variety of ways and reorganized to meet the needs of specific teachers and students.

The intellectual debts of an author are manifold. The first of mine is to my friend and collaborator of nearly a decade, William Simon, of the University of Houston. In many cases I no longer recognize the margin between our ideas, and I would count this book a success if he can find in it extensions of the work that we have done together.

Two friends who have shaped my general intellectual outlook through books I wished I had written, and who have talked with me in freedom and warmth, are George Steiner of Churchill College, Cambridge, and Morse Peckham of the University of South Carolina.

My Danish friends and colleagues, Berl Kutchinsky of the Institute of Criminology, the University of Copenhagen, Susie Haxthausen of Foraeldre og Fodsel, and Nini Praetorius of the University of Copenhagen have provided me with ideas and affection in equal measure.

My friends and colleagues in psychology, Gerald Davidson and James Geer, of the State University of New York at Stony Book, and Raymond Rosen, of the Department of Psychiatry at the State of New Jersey Medical School, have increased my knowledge of sexuality and psychology.

Cathy Stein Greenblat, of Douglass College, Rutgers University, is a co-author of a chapter in this book, and has read all of the chapters with care and insight.

Elaine Walster of the University of Wisconsin and Gene Starbuck of Mesa College, Colorado, have read the manuscript carefully and helpfully.

Early in its development Alix Nelson and I talked about most of the aspects of this book and she was and is a source of many ideas.

My editor at Scott, Foresman, Robert Runck, has untangled my prose and talked with me about this book from outline to type so that my ideas would be clear. He has been far more than an editor in this process.

I also wish to thank Barbara Frankel and Mary Ann Lea of Scott, Foresman for their contributions to the process of selecting the photographs and illustrations for this book, and for its design and layout.

During the sabbatical year when this book was written, I received support from Population Education, Inc. I owe thanks to the President of that organization, Elizabeth Roberts, as well as to Joan Dunlop, Associate of John D. Rockefeller III, and Michaela Walsh of the Rockefeller Brothers Fund.

John H. Gagnon   Morton Grove, Illinois

CONTENTS

8 MASTURBATION   141

9 LEARNING HETEROSEXUALITY   165

10 MARITAL SEXUALITY   191

SOURCES OF SEXUALITY

We are what we pretend to be, so we must be
very careful about what we pretend to be.
Kurt Vonnegut, *Mother Night*

MANY OF US FIND IT DIFFICULT TO TALK ABOUT OUR SEXUALITY. EVEN IN A SOCI-
ety such as the United States, which appears to place a premium on being open and
honest about emotions and feelings, sexual self disclosure—talk about our hopes
and fears, successes and failures, secrets and fantasies, even with a sexual partner,
even with those we love—is surprisingly rare. This is not to say that there is not a
lot of talk about sex; however, it is talk that rarely expresses authentically what we
have done and what we would like to do.[1] We need only think of the kind of sex
talk that occurs in men's locker rooms, mostly gossip of sexual success and exploitation. Similar false talk occurs when women get together, gossip with different
themes, distinguishing between good women and bad, tales of sin and exploitation.
Our private sex talk, distorted by desire and anxiety, is echoed in the mass media.
There our secret wishes and fantasies are made into visible and audible tales, and
surrounded by advertisements which urge consumption by attaching it to sexual
desirability.

Sometimes we do talk about sex more authentically, when we are with trusted
friends or when we are talking just to ourselves. These are times when we can assess our feelings, doubts, and pleasures—when we can try to make sense of our
experiences. These are the times when we feel that our sexual lives have been less
than what we expected or wanted them to be, or we find that having sex with someone has not turned out to make us more loving, or intimate, or richer, or wiser. We
can say at such times that our sports car, or stereo, or makeup, or hairdo has not
made us more desirable, that the implicit promises of the advertisers have not been
fulfilled. When we are being most reflective, we may conclude that sexuality has
turned out to be a great deal more complex than we thought or were taught—and
what has been important is not what we have done, but how we *feel* about what we
have done.

The search for understanding our sexual conduct takes us down many paths,
branching and doubling back, sometimes getting us lost for a while. What we find
is that there is no easily accessible and reliable guide to *what* people should do
sexually; *who* they should do it with; *when* they should do it; *where* they should do

---

1. Sexuality is not the only aspect of life in which our personal experience is systematically falsified
when we talk about it publicly. We might consider other forbidden topics such as money, power, death,
and hatred.

it; and most importantly *why* they should do it. Each of these Ws—what, who, when, where, why—is a potential source of conflict, ranging from mild debates to bitter dissension—conflicts that occur not only between people, but within them as they try to decide what they should do and be.

Perspective of This Book

This book is an attempt to offer an understanding of sexual conduct from a social learning and developmental perspective. This point of view can be briefly described in the following proposition:

In any given society, at any given moment in its history, people become sexual in the same way they become everything else. Without much reflection, they pick up directions from their social environment. They acquire and assemble meanings, skills, and values from the people around them. Their critical choices are often made by going along and drifting. People learn when they are quite young a few of the things that they are expected to be, and continue slowly to accumulate a belief in who they are and ought to be throughout the rest of childhood, adolescence, and adulthood. Sexual conduct is learned in the same ways and through the same processes; it is acquired and assembled in human interaction, judged and performed in specific cultural and historical worlds.

One of the advantages of a social learning and developmental perspective is that it allows us to look at sexuality not as a force or instinct given to us when we are born, but as something each of us acquires as he or she goes along, often in different ways, at different rates, with different outcomes. It becomes important then to examine how we learn to be sexual; how place and time affect our attitudes toward sexuality; what and how children learn about it; how adults handle their own sexuality; how sexuality may change over a person's life cycle. It becomes important, too, to inquire into types of sexual behavior that are labeled "different" and the reasons the label is used. Since women and men are allocated such different roles in U.S. society, we must inquire into what causes the human organism to assume a gender identity, and what factors lead to the emergence of gender-role behavior, the behavior labeled "masculine" or "feminine," in a culture.

The view in this book is that sexuality can be best understood as a pattern of learned human conduct, a set of skills and feelings—and that part of that understanding can come from using the tools of psychology and sociology. The study of sex is best realized not through the creation of a special discipline called sexology and special scientists called sexologists, but rather by using the same theories and methods that are used to study other aspects of human conduct. Thus any theory of sexual conduct must be part of a larger theory of human conduct. Taking a less dramatic view of sexuality by focusing on its commonality with other conduct is difficult, given the society and culture in which we live. Many people, because of what they have learned and how they have been raised, believe that sexual experience is different from the rest of social and psychological experience—that it is more natural or more primordial, more dangerous or more wonderful, more sacred or profane. Therefore they believe we could not have learned how to be sexual in the same mundane ways that we have learned how to play tennis or to bowl, to become a doctor or airline pilot, to like pizza or snails.

Sexuality in Contemporary America

In the United States, sexual behavior has a very special status, partly because of our puritannical cultural history, partly because we believe sex is very important, and partly because most people learn about sex in covert ways. Among adults, discussions of sexuality are commonly tainted with self-interest, tainted with anxiety and guilt, tainted with fears about seeming either too naive or too jaded. As a consequence most people feel that they carry around a great many sexual secrets, and they experience sexual activity as very special, as something quite different from the nonsexual.[2]

The fact that people experience sex as something special is a result of its special status in the culture. However, that does not make the processes by which they acquire sexuality "special," or different than the processes by which they acquire other forms of conduct. They learn it in the same ways they learn those things they experience as mundane, and the conditions of learning the special and the mundane can be understood by the usual techniques of behavioral science.

In the past fifty years, scientists in the United States have led the world in research into human sexuality; however, sex research and sex researchers have remained largely at the edge of the U.S. cultural mainstream. Every decade or so there may be a scientific sex spectacular—a Kinsey Report, a book by a Masters and Johnson—and some new information is fed into our individual and collective views of sexuality. However, the work of even acclaimed researchers usually has limited influence on the daily sex lives of people in the society. Often the new knowledge is used not only to debunk old myths but to create new ones, as a tentative finding, a single kernel of evidence, is exploded into a mass of popular articles. Regardless of such intermittent blizzards of paper and the talk of "sexual revolution," most contemporary adolescents still feel like strangers to their sexuality as they grow up. This sense of sexual estrangement extends to the bodies and minds of others, and continues for many people all through their lives.

Only recently has U.S. society begun to build public bridges from the sexual to the rest of life. In the late 1940s, *The New York Times* refused to accept advertising for Alfred Kinsey's *Sexual Behavior in the Human Male.* The very existence of a college course in human sexuality would have been unthinkable fifteen years ago. Since then, the pace of change—at least in the erotic character of our society—has been very rapid, as a visit to almost any newsstand or a look at movie listings will show. However, the fact that people can see a movie like *Deep Throat* does not mean that their ideas about sex have changed a great deal, or that they conduct their private lives differently. The connections are still very tenuous between the mass merchandising of the sexual and the way people live inside their sexual relationships.

Where we are right now, it seems, is not in some moral "crisis" or "sexual revolution," but somewhere on a continuum of change in the ways we think and deal with the sexual. This process of change has been going on for more than seventy years, its beginnings recorded (and promoted) by Freud and other sex researchers of the late nineteenth century who began to talk about sex in novel ways. What

2. What most people think are dreadful secrets turn out to be very common acts or fantasies—it is the secrecy that creates the fear.

they did by their work was to bring sex "in from the cold," to use the phrase of novelist John Le Carré, describing the experience of a spy brought home from a foreign land. As we might expect, sexuality has been offered a mixed and fearful reception. Like any underground agent recently returned, it may be working for the "other" side—a double agent.

In late nineteenth-century Western societies, as typified by Victorian England, sex was somewhere outside, something not talked about in polite company. It was a world in which the sexual was something "out there." For "respectable" people, most sexuality was viewed as an almost antisocial activity. When people did it, they had the sense of guilt that always accompanies trespassing on the forbidden, and for some people that guilt heightened the importance and excitement of sex. Now, U.S. society seems to be cutting some of its links with Victorian attitudes, moving into an era where guilt and the forbidden may be less potent in defining and intensifying the meanings given to sexual experience.

Consequences of Change

In the past three decades, a whole series of developments in the United States and other Western societies has accelerated the trend of sexuality from "outside" to "inside." Sex is more warmly treated, both culturally and personally. Forces of social change, such as the feminist movement, are closely linked with redefinitions of sexuality. Conventional ideas of what sex involves—not only what the relationships among men and women ought to be, but also what kind of sex they ought to engage in—have been undermined.

Whether these developments will create better people and a better social order is difficult to say. Every social order, every design for arranging human life, has both costs and benefits. The judgment that this social or cultural design is better or worse than another is easy to make, but difficult to demonstrate.

For instance, there are societies where children's genitals are caressed by their parents in order to put the children to sleep. Everyone in that culture accepts it. People in other societies cannot imagine focusing children's attention on their genitals through genital caressing by a parent.[3] There is a small tribal society in India where premarital intercourse is encouraged for all young people from ages thirteen to sixteen. All the adolescents live in a common hut and all of the young people are expected to have sex (without passion or romantic love) with nearly everyone else. In the United States we covertly promote and overtly repress premarital sex ("We are not too young to love") and in some parts of the Mediterranean world (both Moslem and Christian) a girl's virginity is constantly guarded until marriage.

Such differences in how people in different cultures deal with sex (and there are many more just as striking) suggest the great variety of ways for including sexuality in human life. In each design again in one area may be countered by a loss in another. Implicit in each social design is a system of trade-offs. If the design calls for

---

3. We *do not know* the consequences of genital touching for the future social, psychological, or sexual adjustment of children. It seems to help put them to sleep, but there is no evidence that it makes them more or less sexual.

one type of behavior to the exclusion of another type, what is the cost or benefit of the choice? Even awareness of cross-cultural differences and viewing them as choices is part of the resources of a modern cultural design. Such an awareness itself can cause people to question the values of their own society. What are the costs and benefits of the ability to reflect on our own and other cultural designs? The lesson of such reflections may be somewhat disheartening: It is that there is no way of building a utopia, a perfect way to live for everyone, and that all societies are sets of compromises which are the result of reflective and unreflective human preferences.[4]

As our sense of the sexual changes, as we see it as part of a chosen design and as culturally relative, we become more self-conscious about sexuality. We begin to ask questions, to argue, to observe how we suppress and promote different points of view. The more we know about and reflect on sexuality, the more we see how it is linked to other forms of social conduct. When there is a variety of sexual options available and no clear guidelines for decisions, we begin to wonder about the role that sexuality plays, not only in the world around us, but in our own lives as well. We begin to ask such questions as: What has sex meant to me? How do I make choices about what to do sexually? Have I lived my sexual life all right, or all wrong? What does it mean to me, and what will it mean to my children? What can I do to help my own children sexually? Once this process of questioning is set in motion, it is very difficult for anyone to return easily to conventional responses to the sexual, to accept and experience them unreflectively.

Sexual Script:
Who, What, Where, When, Why?

In most Western societies, puberty and the physical changes that occur during it are the signal to the surrounding social world that the former child is now potentially a sexual person. The physical changes are cues that the young person must now be regarded and treated in very different ways and with very different expectations. It does not matter that heterosexual activity can be delayed for very long periods of time (through rules which link sex to marriage and property ownership) or even permanently (through vows of celibacy, in the case of priests or nuns, or through a lack of appropriate marriage partners, in the case of spinsters or bachelors). In U.S. culture, an adult sexual status is conferred or begins to be acquired at puberty.

In some cultures the movement into an active sexual status occurs in a rapid and orderly fashion. A well-informed young person can know before puberty what to do sexually, with whom, when, where, and for what social and psychological reasons. He or she can, after puberty rites, take up an adult sex role with ease and skill. But in the more typical fashion of modern societies, the young person at puberty is usually largely ignorant of adulthood sexuality, and must use the period of adolescence to build up skill in adult sexual conduct. One of the important uses of adolescence in the United States is the acquisition of sexual scripts, and at least some practice in what to do sexually in a range of specific situations.

4. This is not meant to imply that there are not better and worse ways for people to live, from a given point of view. But we must recognize that we are choosing not only for ourselves, but for others as well.

The idea of a *script*, a device for guiding action and for understanding it, is a metaphor drawn from the theater. Viewing conduct as scripted is a way of organizing our thinking about behavior. Scripts are the plans that people may have in their heads for what they are doing and what they are going to do, as well as being devices for remembering what they have done in the past. Scripts justify actions which are in accord with them and cause us to question those which are not. Scripts specify, like blueprints, the whos, whats, whens, wheres, and whys for given types of activity. As we act, we think about what we are doing, the people we are doing it with, the places where we do it, the times when it is done, and the reasons why we—and the persons we are with—are doing it. We use scripts to choose courses of action, to check our behavior against our plans, and to recall the prior concrete steps in our behavior through thinking about the elements in the script.

A script is simpler than the activity we perform, often more limited and schematic.[5] It is like a blueprint or roadmap or recipe, giving directions, but not specifying everything that must be done. Regardless of its sketchiness, the script is often more important than concrete acts. It is our script that we carry from action to action, modified by our concrete acts, but not replaced by them. Scripts do change, as new elements are added and old elements are reworked, but very few people have the desire, energy, or persistence to create highly innovative or novel scripts—and even fewer people can convert a private idiosyncrasy into a socially or culturally important event; that is, create a really new script that becomes a part of the social code.

All social behavior is scripted. All cultures have scripts, or perhaps levels of scripts. There are official public scripts (law and religion); the scripts of various subgroups; and the idiosyncratic and variable scripts of individuals. The less complex the society, the fewer are the scripts and the less variability there is among individuals. The less stable and more complex and heterogenous the society, the more scripts there are which may have some public support, and the greater is the variety of individual scripts and conduct.

Sexual scripts are a subset of social scripts, formulated in the same ways and with the same purposes. However, no individual's sexual script or actual pattern of sexual activity is an exact replica of the sexual script that is offered or preferred by the culture. Just as there is no personality type which can be identified with everyone in the United States, France, or England (not all people in the United States are generous, not all French people are penurious, not all English people are reserved), there is no one sexual script or type that can be identified with a given culture. We may identify scripts with cultures by examining various aspects and activities of their institutions, but the scripts do not have a one-to-one relationship to the activity of individuals. All individuals have sexual scripts that vary from their cultural scripts, and vary even more when they put these scripts to use in concrete sexual situations.

---

5. The scripts we use for the analysis of behavior are far more simple than the behavior of persons in a concrete situation. The five Ws are often recommended by textbooks as a way to analyze stories. They usually work rather well for the analysis of simpler texts, perhaps those by Mickey Spillane and Irving Wallace, and less well for complex works, such as those by James Joyce and Marcel Proust. The continued utility of this relatively simple concept for the analysis of human behavior rests on the notion that most human lives work more like simple fictions than they do like great works of art.

From comic books to pop art, who is being looked at tells about who is doing the looking. We believe in our own cliches.

What then are the components of a sexual script?

Who one does sex with is defined. The range of "whos" emerges from the social order itself. Most people do sexual things with a restricted number and kinds of other people, usually members of the opposite sex who are about the same age. There are limits set by blood relation, by marital status, and more distantly but nevertheless powerfully by race, ethnicity, religion, and social class. There are certain categories of people with whom sex is or is not allowable. And there are people one fantasizes doing sexual things with, some of whom are on the "approved list" and some who are not.

What one does sexually is also important. Of the whole range of sexual acts that people can perform, most are classified as right or wrong, appropriate or inappropriate. The thought of hugging and kissing is fairly comfortable to most people, if they can specify with whom. Vaginal intercourse seems all right to most experienced heterosexuals, and it is part of the usual marital sexual script. Oral sex and anal sex fit into a script in more complex ways, requiring careful specification of when they occur and with whom, and requiring a complex set of reasons. What is to be done and the order of doing it are learned in fragmentary ways from a variety of social sources.

When is sex appropriate? In the United States, among married couples with children, it is usually after the children have gone to bed or are out of the house. That is, sex is for private times, when no one is likely to knock on the door, and when others do not have to be cared for. In societies whose members generally believe in sexual privacy, but where there is no privacy, people may have intercourse in irregular places (automobiles) and at irregular times (two in the afternoon).

"When" can be construed in a number of ways—the day, the week, the year, or a person's age. Most societies tend to see sex as more or less appropriate at one age, one phase of the human life cycle (e.g., reproductive adulthood), than at another. Thus, the society shapes responses to many age-related questions. When is it appropriate for people to have intercourse the first time? When do people stop being sexual? For many young people, it is a great shock to learn that people over sixty continue to have sex. Their reaction is, "How can they! They're old and not attractive anymore! How can they continue to do such things?" This reaction implies, of course, a judgment that sex is only good between two young people, and that older people cannot be sexually attractive to others. That judgment has no basis in any biological fact, but emerges from social definitions of when it is appropriate to be or not be sexual.

Where does the society approve of doing sexual things? As with "when," the notion of privacy is very important here, at least in U.S. society and the societies, present and past, most closely linked to it. These are societies where the bedroom door is closed. When Sigmund Freud concluded that it would be terrible for a child to see his parents having intercourse, he was quite possibly making the mistake of thinking that all of history had been like middle class, nineteenth-century Vienna: a door on every bedroom and no more than two people to a room. For most of human history, however, most families have slept in the same room, hut, cave, or tent, and when there were beds, in the same bed. Historically, in western European rural and urban societies, a child learned about intercourse by being in the same bed with parents when they did it. One of the inadvertent consequences of the rising affluence of Western societies is that parents' and children's sleeping quarters are separate and private. As late as the seventeenth century, a high official in the court of Louis XIV complained that the people of France were growing effete: they wanted more than one bed in their houses. Notions about the importance—even the necessity—of privacy represent a cultural adaptation that is relatively recent.

Why, finally, do people have sex? That is, not "why" do human beings have the ability to reproduce or put organs together, but what are the culturally appropriate explanations for doing sexual things that people learn? How do individuals explain, both to themselves and others, why they do approved and disapproved sexual things?

The why of sex is its rhetoric. Sex is for: having children; pleasure; lust; fun; passion; love; variety; intimacy; rebellion; degradation; expressing human potential/nature/instincts/needs; exploitation; relaxation; reducing tension; achievement; service. Whatever reasons people offer for doing anything else they use for sex. Some reasons are approved, some disapproved; some we share with others, some we conceal; we may tell others one thing, and tell ourselves another. We acquire the whys in the same ways we acquire our sexual techniques and sexual preferences. They fit into our scripts, they are substitutable and revisable. "I do it because I love her/him." "I was carried away by passion." "I was being used." "I was just horny at the time." "I feel emotionally closer to the people I have sex with."

"Why" raises the most complicated and perplexing questions of all: questions about which societies and individuals are the most ambivalent; questions that carry with them the greatest potential for confusion, detachment, and alienation as well as clarity, attachment, and innovation. Again and again, from various angles, we will be looking at "why" in the following pages, because understanding human sexuality involves understanding why we do it, why we (and others) *think* we do it, and why we (and others) *say* we do it.

Who, what, when, where, why: under these headings, the *sexual scripts* of any society can be organized. From society to society, of course, the specific prescriptions will vary, but the headings remain the same. Learning a sexual script and how to apply and manipulate it is part of growing up in any society. The scripts we accumulate and our ability to apply and manipulate them are rarely the outcome of a systematic and conscious learning process, but rather an accumulation of responses to the multiplicity of cues and hints that are provided by the social world around us.

Cross-Cultural Variations in Sexual Scripts

For most of us, even those who consider themselves liberal and enlightened, it is difficult to realize how much our sexual attitudes and behavior have been influenced by our own moment in history and place in a culture. We tend to think of the scripts we have as the only sensible and proper ones. Before we make that kind of judgment, we ought to look more closely at the markedly different social designs for handling sexuality that can be found in both past and present cultures, designs which provide both historical and contemporary alternatives to our own scripts.

Making such comparisons amounts to a kind of intellectual exercise or adventure. It also can give a sense of detachment from one's own culture, almost as if one were an anthropologist or a sociologist from another planet. Here is an example. Have you ever gone to a party and suddenly felt detached from what is going on? (Perhaps because you were sober and everyone else was stoned, or vice versa.) You watch rather than listen and participate. You feel like a stranger, because you are not participating in the action. This same sense of cultural detachment can happen to you as you learn more about social life, because your unreflective participation is tempered by your increasing knowledge and awareness of what is going on.

Similarly, as we examine the sexual conduct of other cultures we may be at first disgusted or surprised or shocked, depending on how different the conduct is, but if we can quell these feelings and cultivate a sense of detachment and the particular kind of understanding that comes from that detachment, we can observe the role of sexuality in our own culture through the prism offered by alternative sexual scripts.[6] Reinterpretation of our own sexual scripts by comparing them with those of other cultures can distance us from our own experience with sexuality. It can make the way in which we go about doing sexual things seem less natural or right, and also make us question why we are doing these particular sexual things in these ways with these people in these places and at these times. Such cultural relativism is often one of the intended or unintended results of learning about how other peoples have arranged their lives with apparently successful results.

We can highlight cultural differences in sexuality by contrasting the ways in which two island cultures have organized their sexual conduct. We must keep in mind, however, that sexuality is related to the nonsexual components of a cultural life in complex ways. A discussion which focuses on the sexual tends to overstate its importance, and tends to minimize the role that the rest of life has in creating the sexual. Also, sexual conduct is usually more important to the observer than to the observed.

Among the islands of Polynesia, there is one called Mangaia, where the majority follow a sexual script very different from our own. It is a society in which there is no structure of courtship like ours, with its extended social and psychological buildup to sexuality. On Mangaia, the most casual signal between a young man and woman can result in coitus. From a Western view, the suddenness and ease with which intercourse can occur seems to represent either unrestrained lust or a marvelous sexual freedom. To many observers, a script unlike their approved ones appears to be no script at all. However, in examining this case more closely, the observer finds that ease and directness is the result of a particular history of sexual learning, and is bound into other aspects of social organization.

On Mangaia nudity among the young is common, and it appears that most young males masturbate frequently (the data for females is apparently unavailable). "Night-crawling" in the society is a practice where young men come into the hut of a family and have intercourse with one of the appropriate daughters (her parents politely ignore it). Clearly, much practical sexual information is being given to the younger children present. These younger children will be engaging in this practice when they get older, and therefore anticipate their own participation. At about age twelve to fourteen there is a male puberty ritual in which the upper flap of the foreskin is cut (superincision), making the young man ready for an adult sexual career (he has a "clean" penis). During this rite, a great deal of sexual instruction occurs: the young man is told about cunnilingus and the importance of orgasm to the female, as well as other social and sexual techniques. Within a few weeks he has his first coitus with an older, sexually experienced woman.

After this rite he enters a period when he works at sex like a young bull, going from woman to woman at night, attempting to satisfy her sexually by extended intercourse (fifteen to thirty minutes, with a great deal of thrusting), trying to bring her to climax a number of times before a mutual climax at the end. Both partners are active and vigorous during intercourse, with a commitment to mutual pleasure. It is

6. It must be pointed out that not all understanding depends on psychological or social detachment from the events under study. Other forms of understanding can result from being intensely involved with or intensely opposed to what we are learning about. Understanding that comes from the "objectivity" of Western science is particularly valued at the present time, but does not exhaust the kinds of understanding available.

important that the male perform well, since the young woman will discuss his sexual competence with other young women, and will describe to him the sexual prowess of other young men.

The pattern of sexual activity after marriage varies. At age eighteen, men usually have sex every night, and climax about three times per night. By age twenty-eight, they have orgasm twice a night and intercourse five to six times per week. By age forty-eight, they have intercourse two or three times a week and one climax per night. The women on this island all learn how to have orgasm, and apparently do so with considerable ease and a number of times during each coital act.[7]

In sum, the learning conditions and sexual script for this culture produce high rates of coital activity among adults, with vigorous sexual contacts, and involving comparisons of male sexual prowess and frequent orgasm on the part of the women. Obviously, in most particulars of who, what, when, where, and why, the sexual script of this Polynesian island differs from the script currently prevailing in the United States and the industrial nations of western Europe.

Let us look, now, at another island society whose sexual script is also different from ours. The island is Inis Beag, off the coast of Ireland. Its inhabitants are Roman Catholic; the men are mostly fishermen, some are farmers. It is a place where knowledge of sexuality is so controlled that women usually learn about menstruation and menopause only when they happen, and men believe that the sexual act will reduce their bodily energy. Nudity is so taboo that it is a serious breach of etiquette for a man to have his shoes off in front of another man's wife. Sexual intercourse takes place at night: the husband opens his nightclothes under the covers; the wife raises her night-gown; and they do it as quickly as possible. Women are taught merely to endure the sex act, and the possibility of female orgasm appears to be practically unknown to men or women. The frequency of intercourse is unknown—the investigators could not even ask about it.

The majority sexual script of Inis Beag stands as an example of a script with many limitations, a script that was probably more important in the history of Western societies than it is today. It is a sexual script historically linked to forms of land holding, with sex supposed to occur only in marriage, and marriage takes place only when a man inherits his property, perhaps in his late thirties or early forties. Both men and women come to sex untutored and unpracticed, coitus is infrequent, the women are unlikely to experience pleasure, and sexuality is clouded by both ignorance and guilt.

Rush to Judgment: The Victorian Experience

The islands of Mangaia and Inis Beag offer two contrasting sexual scripts: one relatively expansive and complex; the other relatively restrictive. Which is better? On what basis can one make a judgment of that kind? Right now, for some young people (particularly males?) in the United States, Mangaia may seem better because it

---

7. It is not clear whether this is multiple orgasm in Masters and Johnson's sense, or a sequence of single orgasms produced in extended intercourse.

appears less sexually restrictive than either Inis Beag or the United States. Yet, however much we may fantasize privately about an island sexual paradise when we measure our own or our culturally approved sexual scripts against those of other people or cultures, it is those that emphasize similar aspects that we usually judge to be "better." In other words: "The way we live is clearly better, and everybody else would be better off if they lived our way."

Throughout history, an attitude of moral superiority has been typical of all societies, but is especially dangerous in those enjoying a spell of world power. In the late nineteenth century, the Victorian English controlled most of the world by one means or another. Important segments of that society were utterly convinced that their proclaimed ways were appropriate, right, correct—the only way all people ought to live. As a consequence, they exported aspects of their religion, their economics, and their sexual scripts (backed up with gunboats and soldiers) all around the world.

The scripts that they exported contained a male-dominated, Christian view of sexuality, a view that was imposed in a variety of ways on the members of many other cultures. Clothing to cover the body, positions for coitus, the suppression of alternative forms of sexuality were offered or imposed on local populations. At the same time, colonial economic and political activity disrupted native society, and the prostitution of women that grows around military camps and seaports became an unacknowledged aspect of imperialist intervention.

In England, however, sexuality was not the tidy moral package that the religious representatives of the Victorians were exporting with such fervor. In the 1880s, there were some 40,000 prostitutes on the streets of London; and children were bought from their parents and sold to the European prostitution markets that flourished in Ostend and other brothel capitals across the Channel.

The prevalence of prostitution was a measure of the way in which women were divided into two worlds: the first a world of respectable women meant for marriage; the second a world of "bad" women, drawn from the population of female servants and working class women. The first world was virtuous and not expected to be sexual; the latter world was sexual and not expected to be virtuous. The English or French or German gentleman of the nineteenth century varied in the degree to which he had sex with women outside his social class (prostitutes and otherwise), but there appears to have been considerable restraint on the sex he had with his wife. Some men were "kind" to their wives sexually, using them only on occasion. Good women were not supposed to have sexual desires; they were expected to provide sexual service without evidence of pleasure. The good women complied with this script, viewing a brutal man not as violent, but as sexually demanding. Both good women and bad women were the objects of male sexual scripts, objects whose participation was defined by their relationship to men. This male-dominated view of the sexual is not gone, and the confusion between good women and bad women, good reputations and bad reputations, the madonna and the whore, still exists in the relations between many men and women.

As the nineteenth century came to a close, the deep contradictions in Victorian sexual scripts, not only in England but all over Europe, began to come under scrutiny. It was scrutiny from within, linked to rising class aspirations and the aspirations of women. Criticism of the economic and moral inequities of European societies appeared, largely from the socialists, who saw sexual equality and the end of sexual exploitation as part of their economic and social program. At the same time, anthropologists and sociologists began to point out the dangers of Christianizing the world, and that imperialist economic, political, and social intervention was destroying the integrity of other ways of life.

These criticisms of the ways in which sex was organized promoted a greater moral relativism. As the moral and political bases for imposing life styles on other peoples came under attack, questioning of moral judgment itself emerged. This relativism, which resulted in a weakening of the moralistic belief that we can freely impose our views on others, has led to a steady erosion of confidence in making judgments about how other people ought to live their sexual lives.

It has become increasingly difficult to decide which sexual life style is better and which is worse. On what basis does one make judgments about right or wrong, good or bad, healthy or unhealthy? And if it is difficult to judge how other societies should arrange the sex lives of their members, how much more difficult must it be to judge subcultures, or ethnic groups, or even individuals within our own society?

Historical Variations in Sexual Scripts

There is an absolutely foolproof method of misreading history. It goes like this: *What* a certain people did in the past looks much the same as what we do today. Therefore, *why* those people did it must be the same as why we do it. Consequently, they judged the "what" the same way we do now.

Consider some of the "whats" and "whos" of human sexuality: penis in vagina, penis in anus, mouth to mouth, mouth to genitalia; female and male, female and female, male and male; adult and adult, adult and child, child and child; masturbation, male or female; and so on through many combinations and variations. Today, we would judge each of these acts and the people who do them as "healthy," "perverted," "natural," "oversexed," "emotionally disturbed," "kinky," or whatever. The tendency is to assume that all people who ever lived — particularly in those cultures which we admire — made identical judgments.

This is hardly a new attitude. Each culture recreates history in its own image — in its literature, art, entertainment, and institutions. For example, ancient Greek democracy and contemporary U.S. democracy probably have about as much in common as the island cultures of Mangaia and Inis Beag described above. But ancient Greece has often been remade into the All-American Yankee model of egalitarian, participatory democracy. Another, more specific example: Movies in the historical-epic genre purport to show people of the past as they really were, but actually show them as *we* are — or like to think we are.

What might be called the "Charleton Heston syndrome" is always at work. In the 1960s and 1970s, Mr. Heston (before him, Errol Flynn, Douglas Fairbanks, John Barrymore, and others) was "our character" — our Moses, our El Cid, our Michelangelo, our General Gordon at Khartoum, our representative on the Planet of the Apes. When we go to the movies, we like to see ourselves; so Hollywood gives us Moses, for example, as a twentieth-century statesman-hero in Egyptian dress — not as the leader of a tiny tribe that had different habits, had strange religious beliefs, and who were no doubt regarded as both unruly slaves and difficult neighbors by nearly all contemporary Egyptians. The way Moses falls in love, his attachment to his wife and children and contemporaries, all the relationships and social priorities that make up a culture, are transformed into *our* culture.

It is sometimes hard to spot such transmutations. It is quite common in our current historical fiction, for example, for one or the other parent to go to pieces when a child dies. From all the historical evidence such a response is remarkably modern in character. Children have only recently become the center of our emotional lives, and are probably so only in Western and other societies with low infant mortality rates and small families. There is considerable evidence that child care in the past was fairly capricious, and that high infant mortality rates resulted in a low emotional investment in very young children. No one wanted to see a child die, but since death was a constant companion of the very young, emotional responses to their deaths were commonly unexpressed or in many cases unfelt.

In all this, what is at work is cultural imperialism. We make the past look like the present because it makes us comfortable, or because we are ignorant, or because we think that is the way it should be. It gives us a sense of linearity between then and now, a conviction that all history has been leading up to us.

In the realm of sexuality, the meanings of specific forms of sexual conduct and the emotions attached to that conduct have also changed substantially. As with nonsexual events, we usually forget these changes and make the same errors of interpretation described above. Two examples suggest how acts, and the meanings and feelings associated with acts, have shifted over time.

Our society reserves some of its harshest judgments for homosexual acts between a mature man and an adolescent boy. Yet, in ancient Athens, among certain elite groups, a homosexual relationship between a thirty-year-old man and a fifteen-year-old boy was not a "crime against nature," but something that was more or less expected and morally sanctioned. In the Athenian view, such relationships between men of different ages were educative in character; they were a pathway for learning. The sexual and emotional attachment was a way of heightening and supporting the intellectual and cultural exchange across generations.

Athenians did not view education as chasing a degree, they viewed education as changing the self. Therefore, bringing to bear the most powerful emotional tools and relationships, including shared sexuality, was entirely appropriate. Defined that way, the meaning of homosexuality was fundamentally different from the way we view it here and now, even though the organs, the acts, and the sex of the actors are the same. (Plato espoused this view in the *Symposium*, and it is the original meaning of a "Platonic" relationship.) It is very hard for us even to think about homosexuality between younger and older men in these terms. We often put people in prison for such behavior. We worry about the boy scout leader, the little-league coach, the male teacher—all who have the opportunity for such relationships.

"Love" is another category that every culture tends to recreate in its own image, which is then superimposed on the past. For us, the word has a certain set of meanings, and we talk about it as if people have always felt about love and loving the way we do. That is a mistake. Today, when somebody says "I love you" to someone else, the obligations are different then they were a hundred years ago. In a

Love will overcome all restraints.
"Why did you do it?"
"Because I was in love."

practical sense, what a word means is what it obligates the speaker or the listener to do after he or she has used it. If those obligatory activities are different now than they were in the past, then all we have is a word that lasts forever for activities that change or simply disappear.

Like the cross-cultural evidence on sexuality, the only clear "lesson" of history is that people have created many very different designs for arranging human life and putting sexuality into human life. If we are to learn anything significant or helpful from this evidence, we must focus on *why* people did and do sexual things—what sexual things meant and mean to them. It is what goes on in the heads of people, the *meaning* they give their own sexual behavior, that is of major importance, not the behavior itself.

Biology, Darwin, and the Sexual Script

What can a biological perspective tell us about human sexuality? What can we learn about our own sexual behavior from studying nonhuman primates, such as apes and monkeys, and other mammals?

One of the great moments in intellectual history was Charles Darwin's decision to link human beings with the rest of the species on this planet. *Animal* evolution was beginning to be widely accepted in Darwin's time; but special creation was still in vogue to account for the origin of human beings. That is, evolution was fine to explain nonhuman speciation and fossil evidence. Human beings were different. They had been specially created for special purposes by the Almighty at some single moment in time; therefore, a different set of rules and principles governed human organization and behavior. Darwin's contribution was to make humans and animals subject to the same evolutionary principles, to place humanity in the great chain of being.

As with Freud, so with Darwin: The ultimate rightness or wrongness of their specific formulations is only one aspect of their importance from a historical point of view. What is also important about great thinkers is that they have new ideas for reorganizing what is already known, and therefore what is knowable. They take the phenomena of the world and put those phenomena in a new context offering a different perspective. It is very much like Gestalt tests: an observer is asked to look at a picture and first sees, say, a swan, and then something clicks in the observer's head and the picture becomes the face of a woman in a hat. Great thinkers do the same thing for the human intellect. They push a cognitive switch in our heads; it goes "click" and, all of a sudden, nothing ever appears quite the same again. Darwin's decision arranged the evidence in different ways, opened the way to entirely new classes of questions, and put whole groups of scientists to work in developing new theories and finding new evidence.

The Darwinian revolution continued the process of rationalizing and secularizing the world by placing humankind into the order of nature. This meant that human beings could be studied as other species were studied, and that the scientific view could be extended to most aspects of human behavior. This was a powerful and revolutionary idea, but like all such ideas, it contained a hidden danger. By bringing human beings into the mainstream of evolution, Darwin created a situation in which easy inferences could be made from animal species about our own: for example, looking at primates (our closest animal relatives) and asking what their behavior might reveal about the organization of human conduct.

In the political and economic realm of the late nineteenth and early twentieth centuries, corrupted versions of evolutionary theory were used to justify the most oppressive aspects of the contemporary social order as well as imperialist incursions into the lives of other cultures. Evolution was thought to justify the nineteenth-century social class system, as well as the imposition of European values on other societies, since the rich people of Europe and European civilization were thought to be the pinnacle of evolution. Societies and people lower on the evolutionary scale should be (if they had the native ability) raised up to the European standard. To many nineteenth-century race theorists, the evolutionary inferiority of the poor and the foreign was biological and unchangeable—they were only fit for the less complex and simpler tasks of carrying and hauling. A similar vulgar version of evolutionary theory was used to justify economic and social oppression within Europe and the United States by arguing that the fittest were those who were running the society and the less fit (the poor, the black, the Irish, the women) deserved to be commanded by their evolutionary betters.

In the realm of sexuality, similar easy applications of evidence from the behavior of nonhumans to humans are made. One argument is that in every nonhuman group sexual behavior is governed by biological forces. As a consequence it is possible to reason that the same biological forces govern human activity, and therefore that the social and psychological aspects of human sexuality can be understood through the study of similar mechanisms in nonhuman animals, especially primates.

There is no evidence, for example, that the hormonal processes which trigger sexual receptivity in primate females *(estrus)* and the cues that elicit sexual interest in male primates (odors produced by the female in heat) have anything in common with the causes of human sexual arousal or interest. Further, there is no strong evidence that sexual interest in human females is increased at any moment in the menstrual cycle, such as ovulation. Moreover, recent studies of different primate groups (chimpanzees, gorillas, orangutangs) reveal great variety in behavior, and have found that differences occur as a function of habitat and other non-biological factors. The more closely we examine the primates, the greater the variety and complexity we see in their behavior, and we find that it is even difficult to apply what we know about one primate group to another, much less to humans.

The evolutionary lineage we have created between other species and humans may be too smooth. The jump between humanity and our closest surviving animal relatives, the great apes, may be so great that we can really infer very little or nothing from what the apes do. Although humans possess a body, they have broken away from what can be viewed as the natural order of things. By the creation of language, culture, and history — the creation of human purposes — the gap between humans and primates is now so large that we reason only by analogy and metaphor. Our biology can kill us, or set limits on our behavior of the widest kind, but it cannot explain the variety and complexity of human conduct. In this sense those who argued for special creation may have been more nearly correct than those who came after Darwin — humanity might as well have been specially created.

What we *can* learn from the primates exists only at the neurological and hormonal levels. We can experiment with their biology and see the ranges and variations produced in their behavior. We can study the mechanistic aspects of their "wiring diagrams" — but we cannot *predict* from their behavior to that of humans.

A second aspect of this biological argument begins with the "facts" of human evolution. It says that humans lived as hunters and gatherers for many thousands of years and had a division of labor between males and females. It then assumes that as a result of evolutionary forces (natural selection), male/female division of labor and the sexual scripts associated with them must be natural to humans today. But even if a long history of hunting and gathering has produced human males who are larger and stronger than human females, there is no evidence that physical strength is a factor in learning how to be sexually active or interested. The fact that women have cared for children is not necessarily connected with the nature of female sexual interest. Differentiating male physical strength and female reproductive roles reveals nothing about the evolution of sexual response, potential levels of sexual activity, or the cultural meanings given to various kinds of sexual conduct.

One of the great dangers of biological-evolutionary views is that they are often used for justifying contemporary gender role differences between men and women, which are related to differences in power, status, opportunities, and resources. The social and psychological aspects of masculinity and femininity in the twentieth-century United States are seen as rooted in some basic biological difference (evolution, hormones, the organization of the brain). That is, it is assumed that there is something about human female biology that makes women more passive, more receptive, more interested in raising children, and more likely to possess the whole range of traits included in our lexicon of female gender roles.

On the sexual level, such biological arguments promote the idea that women have weaker (or stronger) sex "drives," that they are naturally less interested in erotic materials, or that they take longer to be aroused sexually because of biological processes. As evidence accumulates, such views become less and less tenable, but they are still serviceable to those interested in defending the current arrangement of social and sexual relationships between men and women.

The argument of this book is that the social-psychological conduct of human beings is rarely explainable through the use of ideas derived from biology, or through direct appeal to biological processes. Alone among species, human beings can create their own purposes. And these purposes may, in fact, be anti-biology; that is, anti-survival and anti-evolutionary. Consider just two religious groups, the Shakers, of which there were still a few in the 1970s, and the Cathars, who lived in late medieval Europe. In both the Cathar and Shaker religious scripts, the flesh is evil. Therefore, having children is evil because it creates more spirits embedded in the flesh. Neither sect believed in redemption. The only choice was to stop having children and die out. No other species is capable of making that kind of decision. It suggests a gap of great magnitude between humans and all other species. Only human beings can invent reasons for doing something that goes against their own survival.

Human Life Cycle and Sexual Scripts

Most modern societies are highly age stratified. That is, they divide up a human life, not just into infancy, youth, adulthood, and old age, but into many subdivisions of those life periods. Age stratification is probably more pronounced in the United States than it is in any other society in the world: newborn, infant, crawler, toddler, preschooler, nursery schooler, kindergartner; elementary, middle, junior-high, and senior-high schooler; college student, postgraduate student; preteen, teen, young adult, young single, young married; and on through senility to death.

Each of these life moments varies in the sexual conduct that is approved, merely tolerated, or disapproved. Children are treated by most parents as essentially asexual, even by those parents who are most liberal. While they may interpret the genital touching of infancy or the sex play of childhood as "sexual," parents or other adults rarely do anything to foster such activities or give them a more than transitory meaning. Most parents ignore, and others suppress what appears to them to be precocious demonstrations of sexuality. As a result, children remain largely asexual because they do not live in environments that create sexual meanings and sexual scripts. In U.S. culture children do not possess a sexual dimension because there is no structure of rewards, meanings, or techniques that could be converted into a coherent domain of action called the sexual. This does not mean that children are not offered gender roles—the basic frameworks for masculinity and femininity that will shape their future sexual adaptations—but sexual adaptations are uncommon until adolescence.

Adolescence is a testing ground where socio-sexual experimentation is possible, perhaps partly supported, especially for males. In liberal families masturbation may be expected, and perhaps among the very liberal, some adolescent homosexuality. In young adulthood we expect to settle down, selecting a future marital and sexual partner—there might be a spell of living together or premarital sex with love. In early marriage, we expect to behave heterosexually with spouses, with greater or lesser experimentation and pleasure—and hope there will be children. As we approach the middle years there may be some extramarital sex, mostly for men, some for women in the script—perhaps we grow dissatisfied and supplement our sex lives with *The Joy of Sex.* As we grow older, sex is supposed to grow less important, and we should move on to more mature pleasures suited to our years.

People vary from these expectations—they divorce, they have sex between marriages, they masturbate while married, they continue or develop homosexual interests and concerns—but the model exists, supported not only by sexual prescriptions and values, but by other aspects of the social order as well. The heterosocial, heterosexual, monogamous pattern is supported by housing arrangements, economics, the legal system, older people policing the behavior of the young, children policing their parents. Variations on the script require energy, time, and desire. Some people manage them well and others poorly or not at all.

Life-cycle complexity offers opportunities to experiment—there are more things to do and be—but also offers a new set of opportunities to conform. The life cycle is played out with a changing set of sexual scripts designated for each age as well as each sex, and the content of each stage differs at different historical moments and in various cultures and subcultures.

Summary

One way of thinking about sexual conduct is to use the notion of script to examine the "official" sexual doctrines of a given culture, and the relationship between those doctrines and the scripts that guide the sexual thinking, talking, and activity of individuals in particular situations.

One fruitful place to look for scripts in societies with highly developed media systems is in the stories offered to people which contain sexual or proto-sexual events. Such narratives often contain both the approved script and cautionary tales about the consequences of violating what is approved. To take just one example: Between 1937 and 1947, Hollywood produced some fifteen movies about the joys and sorrows of the middle-class Hardy family in a small midwestern U.S. town. The teenage son was Andy Hardy. *Who* he did sexual things with was an occasional chaste and sparkly girl in his own high school class; *what* he did sexually, if he did anything beyond hold hands, was a single kiss; *when* was saying goodnight after a malted; and *where* was at the girl's family's front door.

Why Andy Hardy did all these things is relatively unspecified. Perhaps there was nothing else to do. Perhaps he wanted to be popular. Perhaps it was fun. Perhaps he was practicing social relations with females. More secretly perhaps he was bragging to his male friends—"How far did you get, Andy?" "To first base" meant he kissed her, to "second" that he touched her breast. But this is not known or shown. Apparently the *why* was so obvious that it did not need to be told us. All of the meaning was in the who, the what, the when, the where, as well as in the other elements specified—the time in history, the place in culture, the social class, the age of the participants. All these elements may in fact make the meaning at a cultural level.

What is missing from this depiction, but does occur in some contemporary films, is the turmoil, the fear, the sweaty-palmed character of most sexual experimentation. That is, even if we add all of the culturally approved components together, some real person has to perform the acts, to initiate, to respond, to fear failure, and to wonder what the other is thinking. It is sometimes unclear how young people manage their earliest sexual experimentation—nose in the way when kissing, braces entangled, the fumbling of the first sex between inexperienced partners.

As people get older, they tend to forget how inept they were in their first sexual experiences, just as most people forget how inept they once were at tying their shoes: those awful two or three months when the laces get tied backwards, left shoe gets on right foot, fingers get tied into laces, and bows turn into incredible knots; the sense of utter frustration, incompetence, and despair. Sexual competence comes no more "naturally" than tying shoes. No kind of "drive" or "instinct" or "prepared program" takes over a person's mind and body, sweeping him or her gracefully and inevitably to glorious climax.

Scripts and the sexual conduct that they guide do not emerge fully formed either at birth, or at puberty, or at the moment of marriage—there is no automatic connection between the penis and the vagina, between the man and the woman, between love and sex. Rather there is the acquisition of both nonsexual and sexual responses, sometimes accumulated rapidly, sometimes slowly, sometimes directed, sometimes accidental, in simple and in complex circumstances. From these sources we build our scripts, what goes with what and in what order (the cognitive schemes that we carry in our heads) *and* our actual sexual conduct, in situations with real people and with real consequences.

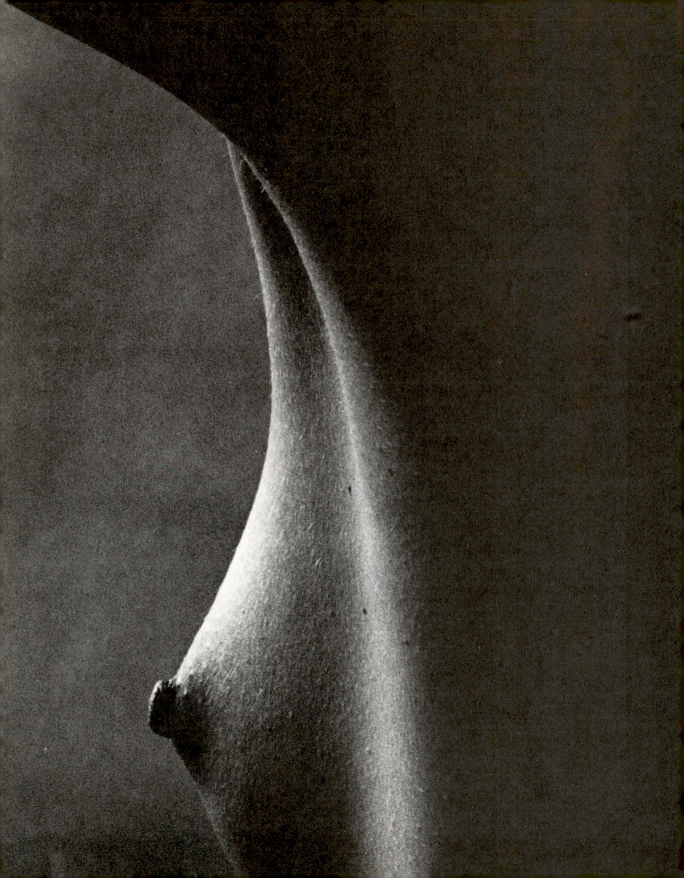

CHANGING PURPOSES OF SEXUALITY

2

One thing only do I know for certain and that is that man's judgments
of value follow directly his wishes for happiness — that, accordingly,
they are an attempt to support his illusions with arguments.
Sigmund Freud, *Civilization and Its Discontents*

CULTURES ARE CHARACTERIZED BY SEXUAL SCRIPTS (FOR BOTH APPROVED AND disapproved sex) transmitted from generation to generation. Embedded in those scripts are the purposes of sex — the reasons given for one kind of sexual conduct rather than another, or for even being sexual at all. Behind these purposes are justifications or sources of appeal used to support one or another set of purposes, one or another sexual script. The creation of purposes for conduct, and the invention of justifications for these purposes, are peculiarly human. People submit themselves to the purposes they have invented and give the purposes a life of their own. Further, people usually find that their purposes are both worth teaching (particularly to children) and worth imposing on other adults who appear not to believe in them.

A purpose is the answer to the question, "Why should (or did) I (or you) do that?" It can be asked in a forward sense, toward the future as explanation of a plan, or in a backward sense, toward the past as explanation of a prior action. We ask such "why" questions all of the time, and we get more or less satisfactory (culturally appropriate) explanations for them. The demand that people explain what they have done, a demand we often place on ourselves, is one of the most powerful forms of behavior control. The capacity to generate acceptable answers is a mark of proper socialization, even when the answers may be nonconformist.

We not only explain the right things that we do, we also explain the wrong things. We excuse, we apologize, to satisfy others and ourselves. Such explanations are part of the scripts we give children; they tell children why they should do this and not that; and we continue to use such explanations to discriminate between approved and disapproved conduct as we grow up.

People also have the capacity for saying that their purposes come from somewhere else or someone else; that is, they justify their purposes by appeals to a higher and often transcendental source. The parent questioned by a child, "Why do I have to go to bed?" gives the answer, "Because God wants you to," or "If you don't the bogeyman will get you," or "Don't you want to be a good little boy (girl)?" or "Don't you want to grow up to be big and strong?" Such appeals to God, to the spirit world, to virtue, or to a possible future are the higher justifications of our purposes. Few parents tell their children that bedtime is a parental convenience, thus admitting that they themselves are the source of purpose.

Important purposes usually emerge from the struggle and stife of human history.[1] As we come closer to modern times, the ways in which purposes are chosen become more evident. We need only note that the Declaration of Independence and the Constitution of the United States — justified by appeals to the Almighty and the nature of man — converted treason (the British view) to patriotism (the Revolutionary view) and created a new nation-state. Such written manifestos of purpose characterize the history of sexuality as well, and occur with increasing frequency as we approach the present time.

History of Legitimation

The last two hundred years may be viewed as a period during which there has been an intermittent but often intense struggle over justification of sexual purposes, and what sexual conduct is approved or disapproved. This struggle has had a number of stages, and there have been periods of rapid as well as slow change.

SACRED AND SECULAR

Prior to the end of the eighteenth century, nearly all justifications of sexual purposes, even radical sexual appeals, were based on religious values. From the point of view of conservative religious values, humanity had been made into flesh, and the doings of the flesh, especially the sexual doings, could be considered moral and right only in wedlock and for purposes of reproduction. The day-to-day impact of this doctrine on the sexual lives of peasants and the people who lived in the small villages or rural regions of Europe was probably slight. The traditional sexual values and scripts of regional cultures coexisted with Christianity well into the twentieth century. The sexual conduct of people who lived outside the urban centers of European life (and even most of the people who lived in the urban centers) probably varied a good deal from the limited sexual scripts offered by official doctrine. However, it was official doctrine, hardened by the Reformation, and a doctrine that would become more widespread and coercive as the technologies of social control improved in the nineteenth century and have culminated in the mass-media systems of the twentieth.

Radical religious opposition to such conservative sexual values occurred a number of times during European history. For instance, in England during the seventeenth century, dissident religious sects preached that "to the pure all things are pure," a doctrine used to justify sex as pleasure — obviously, they said, God would not have made sex a pleasure if he did not expect people to do it and enjoy it. Such sects supported celebratory sexuality, until the dominant religion, with the support of a secular army, restored sexual as well as political order.

Secular alternatives to various aspects of the religious or sacred world view had been emerging since the Renaissance: first from astronomy and the physical

---

1. This may account for the tenacity with which purposes are defended and imposed. If you have to pay a lot for them, they had better be true.

We are comfortable with the reproductive purposes of sexuality since they involve so many other valued symbols: loving mothers, beautiful babies, and the institution of the family.

sciences, and from theories of government, society, biology, and the individual. Major sources of secularization were the emerging new sciences of geology, biology, sociology, political science, and psychology. Each of these emerging sciences was used as support for the limited sexual scripts offered by religious doctrine, or (in the twentieth century) as alternatives to religious doctrine. What was or was not approved sexually did not actually change a great deal until the turn of the century, when the emergence of new sources and competing sources of justification offered new purposes for sexuality, and new and wider scripts for sexual conduct, in the twentieth century.

During the nineteenth century, the purposes of sex, still limited to reproduction and therefore to heterosexual intercourse in marriage, were justified by appeals to the needs of the nation, the needs of the society, the needs of the species, or the requirements of being a healthy person, physically and mentally. Rarely were these new justifications, except in the hands of political radicals, used to argue for changes from the sexual *status quo*. More frequently, a divine plan could be discerned behind the king or the prime minister or the president; or God was viewed as a master biologist, sociologist, or psychologist who had created the organism or social order which obeyed the laws of conduct. The new sciences and the *status quo* marched hand in hand.

COLLECTIVE AND INDIVIDUAL

Along with a movement from the sacred to the secular, there has been a movement from collective justifications of sexual conduct to personal justifications. This movement, which developed a major impetus in the early twentieth century, has accelerated during the last thirty years. As secular explanations detached themselves from the sacred, they became new sources for collective justification of sexual practices: Sexuality should have specific purposes because it was good for the nation-state ("The hand that rocks the cradle rules the world"); or it was good for the society (because of the family); or it was good for the species or the race; or it was good for mental health.

These collective plans seem to have less appeal now, except in times of crisis, in part because they usually attempt to limit the sexual activity of the majority. These limitations on sexual scripts fall far short of what people are actually doing. It is likely that people have always done more things sexually than have been legitimate, but what has happened historically is a recent reversal in the weight given to rules as opposed to actual conduct. In the past, the rules were eternal; the fact that people did not obey them did not mean that the rules should change. At present, there is an interaction between rules and conduct, with some people insisting that sexual rules that do not conform to sexual conduct can and should be changed, and many people simply ignoring rules they do not like. What is observable in this process is the recognition that people make the rules, even the ones they do not obey. In addition, there is a new belief that violations of the sexual rules are not nearly as important as they were in the past.

What has happened in the last few years, beginning perhaps in the 1950s, has been a far more individual perspective on sexuality. It is not sexuality in the service of some larger set of purposes, but rather sexuality in terms of individual preference. Sex is justified by appeals to what an individual wants to do. The purposes of sex as play, joy, love, intimacy, or recreation are all popular now. The largest social group to which we appeal seems to be the couple, usually (but not always) married and heterosexual. Such a radical shift in the level of appeal or justification has had serious consequences, if not on the rates of sexual activity, then on the ways in which people perceive the purposes of sex, and the kinds of scripts available that can be followed not only in secret, but in public.

Labels for Approval and Disapproval

As we have moved from sacred to secular justifications, from collective to individual purposes, from procreative scripts to recreative scripts, the words we use to describe the approved and the disapproved have changed. The religious traditions used the words *good* and *evil, virtue* and *vice* to discriminate between approved and disapproved sex. These are words of considerable power and significance, which focused on the importance of sexual behavior for moral acceptability in this world and salvation in the next. When the enforcement of differences between approved and disapproved sex was transferred to the nation-state and its criminal justice system, approved sex was *law-abiding* and disapproved sex was *criminal*.

In moments of national crisis, approved sex was *patriotic* and disapproved sex *unpatriotic*. During World War II, wives who had extramarital sex while their husbands were in the military were having unpatriotic sex. In the movies of the time, this betrayal was viewed as so serious that most unfaithful wives had to die in a flaming car crash, or in some other unseemly manner. This view of extramarital sex during wartime was echoed in the criticisms of the Kinsey female research, which reported that a quarter of the women interviewed had had extramarital coitus. Since the Korean war was going on at the time of publication (1953), members of Congress suggested that such information would lower morale in the military, and was therefore unpatriotic. Whether or not the husbands having extramarital sex during wartime were unpatriotic was rarely discussed.

The church and the nation-state were agreed on which sexual scripts were approved and which were not, and the weight of the nation-state (or at least some institutions in it) was put into the battle against disapproved sex. The "sex control" actions of the nation-state have always largely centered on pornography, birth-control information, prostitution, occasionally male homosexuality, and the rights of women in general. Private sex remained largely in the control of personal conscience rather than the police.

Biology and biologists, usually the guardians of what is "natural," were called upon in the nineteenth century, to define the margin between good sex and bad sex. The biological language of approval and disapproval had two separate bases. The first was the health and preservation of the species. Sex which went against the survival of the species or the health of the individual was *degenerative* or *maladaptive* — approved sex was *species-enhancing* or *adaptive*. This distinction produced a collection of people called sexual degenerates; some argued that they should be sterilized since they might contaminate the genetic inheritance of the race. The policemen of these biological sex standards were commonly members of the medical profession, who at the beginning of the twentieth century attained a monopoly as the health experts of the society. As part of this role they helped set the limits on what constituted sexual health.

Biology, in an alliance with the new science of psychology, was also used to justify certain sexual purposes because it had knowledge about the normal processes of human development, both physical and psychological. The line between good sex and bad sex could be drawn by justifying patterns of conduct which would make people healthy adults. This merging between the biological and psychological produced such distinctions as *normal* and *abnormal, healthy* and *perverse* or *pathological*. As the psychological tradition emancipated itself from the biological, it retained such distinctions as *mental health* and *mental illness,* and opposed "healthy" with a range of terms — *neurotic, immature,* and *aberrant* — as labels for bad sex.

Keeping the society together has also been a justification for various sexual purposes; people immune to appeals by the state or even the divine are often moved by images of the society collapsing around them. Sociologists and politicians usually speak on behalf of Society. Sociologists are very interested in the family, so many of their distinctions between good sex and bad sex have to do with what is good for the family. Up to and during the 1920s, sociologists, influenced by the idea that the society could be talked about as if it were a biological organism, tended to use such words as *social disorganization* or *social pathology* to describe sexuality which they did not approve. Later they developed a wider range of terms: good sex was *functional,* bad sex was *dysfunctional;* good sex was *conforming,* bad sex was *nonconforming* or *deviant.*

    If we cumulate all of these words (as in Figure 1) we can see two major facts. First, every term, no matter how neutral at the beginning, can become a negative

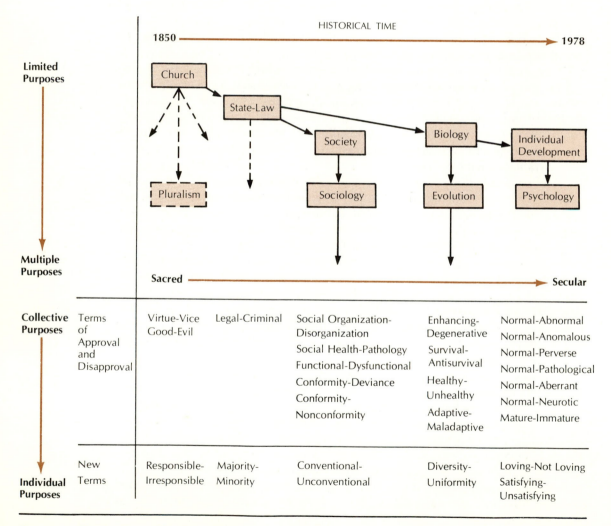

Figure 1.   Changes in Justifications, Purposes, and Labels for Sexual Conduct, over Time.

word in particular social circumstances. *Perverse, anomalous, deviant* all began their careers as detached objective words; by association with the disapproved, they became as pejorative as *sinful* and *degenerate.* Second, the trend appears to be weakening, particularly if we look at the new words which link to individual versus collective purposes. *Unconventional* and *conventional, unsatisfying* and *satisfying* — it is hard to see how these words could have any direct negative connection with a particular sexual activity; or how we could care much about them if they did. For instance, at the turn of the century there was no question in anyone's mind but that homosexuality was a sin, a vice, and a crime. Then psychiatry and psychoanalysis came along and it became abnormal, perverse, and pathological. Later still the sociologists called it only deviant, and then others labeled it merely unconventional. Now there is a definite effort afoot to move it across the barrier from disapproval to approval, to call it innocent, normal, conforming, and conventional.

As another example, masturbation has been successively called sinful, criminal, maladaptive, abnormal, dysfunctional, and deviant. The judgment keeps getting less and less powerful; now we tend to say of masturbation that it is conventional — although we seem not yet ready to label it satisfactory. The same process is happening to many forms of sexual conduct, for the variety of approved or tolerated acts increases with the general liberalization of society. The last seventy years have seen this process affect many aspects of sexuality — homosexuality, adultery, pornography, premarital sex — and as a result our responses to these forms of sexual conduct have become less extreme.

The declining potency of collective labels does not mean that individuals cannot imprison themselves quite effectively in using contemporary individualistic distinctions between good sex and bad sex. Thus women's magazines and psychological counselors have helped make the purpose of sex to express love (good sex is loving sex) or to produce orgasm (women should have it; men should induce it). However, no one will call the police if sex is not loving, as they might if they label it criminal.

Diversity of Purpose

At the present time there are many different purposes and justifications for sexuality, many contending public voices about the purposes and justifications we should hold, and finally, many positions about how we should react to people who act out different sexual scripts than are approved. One reason for the current label is that none of the traditional justifications or purposes of sex has disappeared, even in advanced industrial societies. A substantial part of the population still firmly believes in a divine plan for sexuality, and wants that divine plan enforced by government.

A second large group proposes a set of mixed purposes and justifications, or certain purposes and justifications for one kind of sex and others for another kind of sex. They may say that sex is both for reproduction and for pleasure of a husband and wife, but unmarried people should not do it. Or they may say that sex for love and affection between a young man and woman who are going to get married is acceptable, but nonmarital sex under any other circumstances is not. Still others

The erotic and recreational are now legitimate purposes of sexuality, at least in the mind's eye.

say that married heterosexual sex is the best kind; homosexuality is tolerable only when two people are not curable and they love each other.

Such mixtures of sexual justification and purposes are common, but without a great deal of consistency. There are now a number of options in purpose and justification, options which layer the society into various religious, political, and social groups. Sex has become a serious issue in the political life of the society, as what sex should be approved and disapproved have become part of the political platforms of major parties and the stances of major politicians.

As the bases of what sex is approved and what is disapproved have moved to an individual level, particularly as a result of the mental health movement and sex research, people who tell us the purposes of sex have become more visible. The priest has given way to the politician, to the professional counselor, to the advice columnist. The idealistic, one-to-many pronouncement has given way to the pragmatic, one-to-one instruction. The new justifiers of sexual conduct are social and behavioral scientists. They have no direct power of enforcement, but they share with their predecessors the function of telling us how we ought to shape our lives. The difference is that because they have performed "research" they may issue their instructions through textbooks on health, psychology, or sociology.

What the social scientists say affects how the state and church behave. Their views often become the basis for the behavior of social institutions (schools, police, and hospitals); as a result, laws and dogmas become less restrictive about the who, what, when, where, and why of sexuality. As an example, about fifteen years ago a CNAC (Council of North American Churches) conference discussed what sexual techniques were appropriate between husband and wife. The consensus was that anything sexual they could do with each other—oral-genital contact, anal inter-course, anything—was acceptable, as long as ejaculation occurred inside the va-gina. The conferees approved any arousal technique that leads to the "good" goal of getting sperm into the approved place.

In the movement away from traditional purposes, some people have stopped at different points along the way, but the general tendency has been to talk about specific forms of sexual activity and different kinds of sexual actors in less disap-proving ways. And talk is *not* cheap. What we call something has profound conse-quences. If we call homosexuals sinful, vicious criminals, which is what they were nearly universally called until 1948, we will treat them differently than if we call them unconventional.

If we argue that sex is really part of a divine plan, and that people who do not obey that plan are doomed forever, then we can do nearly anything we want to stop them from doing it. If we believe that we have a divine mandate, we can behave toward other people in very punitive and controlling ways. We know "the truth," and whether we know it from religion, law, or biology, we find it easy to justify coercion. As we move toward more individual images of sexuality, however, it becomes more difficult or complex to justify controlling other people's behavior.

One of the powers of a divine plan is that it is relatively clear-cut; it says what the rules are, even though they must be interpreted and enforced by people. It may be that they seem clear-cut because the people who enforce them seem so sure of themselves. In plans based on individualism, it is difficult to decide what is right or correct, not only for other people but also for the self; this situation is typical of the 1960s and 1970s. All of this does not mean that the older rules or standards have disappeared. They remain, and at the moment we have a crisis which exists largely on the issue of how to justify our conduct. Since society exists in layers, and there are multiple points of view, conflict is inevitable.

Models of Sex and Social Control

Another dimension of how we think about sexuality is whether we believe in sexual instinct or drive, whether we believe that that sexuality is good or bad, and what we believe the relationship is between cultural agents of control and the expression of sexuality.

TRADITIONAL CONTROL-REPRESSION MODEL

The traditional Western religious belief was that sexuality is an impulse of the flesh, a flesh that had resulted from the human fall from grace. The flesh was animal as opposed to spiritual, and the sexual impulse was prime evidence of the potential evil nature of the sinful flesh. It was assumed that in the absence of control people would do sexual things (most of which were sinful), a tendency that could be aggravated by temptation and bad example. This theory results in what might be called a pure control model, in which people should be (1) kept innocent of sexual knowledge if possible, (2) informed of its evil potential in order to strengthen their conscience, and (3) punished if they disobey. The sexual impulse is believed to be very powerful, and if not controlled would result in social disaster.

FREUDIAN CONTROL-REPRESSION MODEL

The Freudian model takes many of its features from traditional Christianity: sexuality is a powerful drive, opposed by its very nature to civilization. It is the function of the family to take the barbaric infant, interested only in its own pleasure, and train it to meet the demands and needs of society. Parents are to instill the reality principle (the Freudian superego, which equals Christian conscience) in the child, to control its sexual impulses. Freud was committed to the notion that the true "nature of humanity is opposed to civilization, and it is only through repression and control that sexual energies can be used in civilized work. The Christian tradition is committed to political and social repression of the sexual; Freud was more concerned with its psychological repression.

SOCIOLOGICAL CONTROL-REPRESSION MODEL

A belief in the anarchic and "natural" character of sexuality is reflected in modern sociology, particularly in its functionalist tradition, in which there is—at least by implication—a natural sexual person, at birth a barbarian, who must be "socialized" into accepting society's mandates.

The development and maintenance of a stable competitive order with respect to sex is extremely difficult because sexual desire itself is inherently unstable and anarchic. Erotic relations are subject to constant danger—a change of whim, a loss of interest, a third party, a misunderstanding. Competition for the same sexual object inflames passions, and stirs conflicts; failure injures one's self-esteem. The intertwining of sex and society is a fertile ground for paranoia, for homicide and suicide.[2]

Social and sexual order is thus maintained by socialization, institutional control, and the criminal justice system.

THERAPEUTIC TRUTH MODEL

From the Freudian tradition emerged a series of sexual radicals, many of whom are affected by the political values associated with Marxism. They wished to wed the

2. Kingsley Davis, "Sexual Behavior," in *Contemporary Social Problems* eds. R. K. Merton and R. Nisbet (Harcourt Brace Jovanovich, 1971), p. 317.

work of Freud and Marx, and consider the repression of sexuality as unnecessary. Their program was to let sexuality flourish by allowing children and adults the opportunity to express their "natural" sexuality. The distortions of sexuality do not come from lack of socialization or from repression, but from the attempt to socialize or to repress sexuality at all. The sex instinct is a good instinct, and by repressing it we turn it away from its "natural course." The release of sexuality would bring on a new kind of human being. Again, civilization is in opposition to human "nature," but this time the villian is civilization, which distorts and represses the innocent and beautiful sexual impulse.

This point of view, the position of such people as Wilhelm Reich, Paul Goodman, and A. S. Neill (who founded Summerhill School), turns the Freudian-Christian world upside down. The political consequences of this position would be social reconstruction, to bring societies into accord with "human nature." Herbert Marcuse and other neo-Marxists have taken a more moderate position, looking for a middle road between Freudian conservatism and the radical political tradition, but have not added much to the debate.

SIMPLE LEARNING MODEL

More recently, some people have chosen to give up the idea of a sex drive *per se* and move toward a position that the human being is an active, energetic system that will learn in various environments. As the organism grows up, its behavior is continuously shaped by its environments. Such learning models come in different and more or less complex forms; the crucial issue is that the shaping characteristics of the environment are the primary force, beginning early in life to develop a particular learning history for an organism.

The learning-model focus is on the contingencies offered by the environment. The sexual does not come from "nature," but from activities which the organism learns. Some versions of the learning model assume that the learner is essentially passive, becoming the result of its learning history. Mistakes in development are functions of incorrect learning environments, or environments that offer multiple and competing instructions.

CULTURAL LEARNING MODEL

Another view (the one taken in this book) is that there is no sex drive or instinct. When human beings are born into a culture or society, they begin a process of acquiring the symbols and meanings of that proximate world as they learn who they are, develop a self-identity, and actively participate in assembling that self. They are purposive, intentional, and sometimes reflexive creatures. That is, they begin to choose and make meaning themselves, to ask questions and choose paths of behavior. The domain of meaning and conduct called sexuality is accumulated through social learning, without the aid of a drive. People participate in shaping the environment around them, and are not merely passive objects of that environment. Cultures are part of the environment that creates and elicits sexuality. There is no innate sexual potential within the child; we create our own sexual "natures" by the meanings we give to sex.

This perspective argues that the kind of sexuality that members of a culture believe helps create the kind of sexuality they get. If they believe that sex is an anarchic and powerful drive and teach that view to young people, then they will get at least some who will behave as if they were possessed by an anarchic and powerful drive. If they offer sex as a calming and therapeutic truth, a friendly gesture (and if they create a good learning environment, not merely holding out a set of goals without giving instructions on how to get there), then the good learners will find that sex is indeed a calming and therapeutic experience. All of social life is a part of self-fulfilling prophecy — if we teach people to believe something and tell them that it is right, then they will tend to act in that direction. However, our control of learning is never complete; people behave reflexively, and often choose not to do what we want them to.

Sexuality is a domain of feeling, beliefs, and acts which change over the life cycle, with different content and relations from birth to death. It is in part a function of both local and distant cultural environments, and because of the relative looseness of the scripting of behavior, a domain in which the individual has a wide range of improvisational choices.

Role of Sex Researchers

As we have changed our theories, our purposes, and our justifications for sex, the sex researcher has played an important role in charting the directions of that change. The theories have been reformulated and the data reinterpreted, the purposes of sex have been widened, and research itself has become a justification for ordering our sexual lives one way or another. Sex research has become part of the process of social change, and its findings are part of the fuel for discussion and argument.

It was only relatively recently that sex research became possible. At one time it aroused the same disapproval as the sexual act itself. Research implied that sex could be studied just like anything else, that sex was not apart from the rest of life. Both the religious and the romantic thought that the meddling (and muddling) of science, particularly numerical science, could only do harm to the mysteries and values surrounding sex. By knowing about it people would either do it too much or lose interest because it had become commonplace. These attitudes are still common and often serve as the basis for criticism of sex research: sex is too spiritual or too material to be studied, and the researcher is either debasing it or promoting it.

We still know very little about sex, and what we do know has been accumulated over the past seventy years, especially the last twenty-five or thirty. (See Figure 2.) The rate of increase of knowledge, even the most rudimentary, is still quite slow and will probably remain so for some time, for reasons explored in Chapter 3.

The modern era in sex research began with the work of Sigmund Freud in Austria, Havelock Ellis in England, Albert Moll and Magnus Hirshfeld in Germany, and a host of others active in both research and sexual reform at the turn of the century. Particularly vital was the rising importance of the women's movement, including

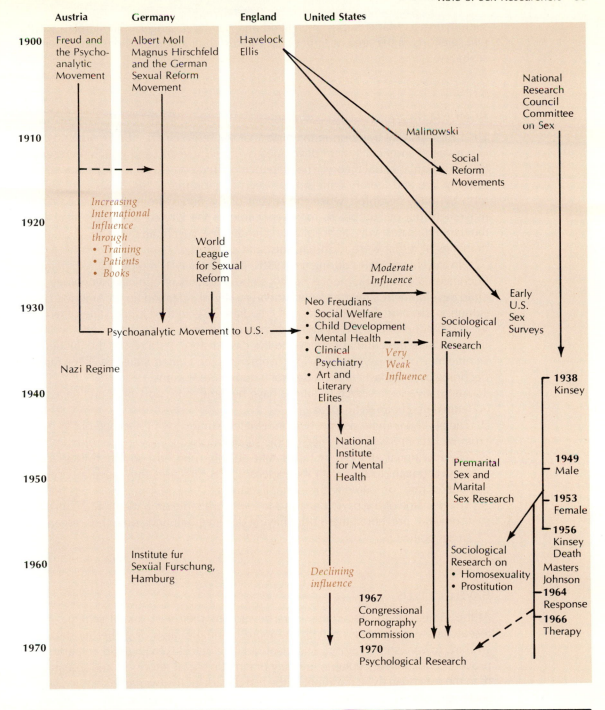

Figure 2.   Sex Research: Chronology and Patterns of Influence.

such figures as Marie Stopes in England and Margaret Sanger in the United States, whose efforts in the area of birth control focused attention on the issues of female sexuality.

SIGMUND FREUD

The first important tradition in the history of sex research was the Freudian, which was a vast theoretical system developed over many years, and which represented far more than a sexual theory. The influence of Freud on psychotherapy, social philosophy, art, and literary criticism has been extraordinary. His views were carried forth by many disciples; when the advent of the Nazis drove the psychoanalytic movement out of Europe, its members came to the United States. In many ways the United States was a hospitable climate for psychoanalysis, at least those branches of it that were most reformist and optimistic.

In the United States during the 1930s, psychoanalysis rapidly gained major influence on social work, mental health, some branches of clinical psychology, and child development. Freudian sexual theories, slightly cleaned up for American consumption, became the centerpiece of Freudian ideas in the United States. Freudian ideas did not produce any systematic body of research, since the analysts' primary interests were the clinical patient and the case history. As a result, the intellectual significance of the psychoanalytic movement in the United States has been rapidly declining over the last two decades, for a number of reasons:

1. Alternative sex research traditions have become more powerful, and have challenged psychoanalytic ideas.
2. The psychoanalytic perspective on female sexuality, which turned out to be extremely conservative, has been under steady attack.
3. The traditional analytic therapies take so long and cost so much they are no longer thought to be worth the expense. In some cases they have a very poor success rate compared with simpler therapies.
4. The decision of the psychoanalysts to focus primarily on patients and consulting rooms has prevented them from having decisive influence on either research or social policy.

HAVELOCK ELLIS

At the same time the Freudians were developing their vast sexual scheme, other researchers were getting on with the more mundane tasks of gathering data and working toward social reform. The ideas of Havelock Ellis in England, in particular, proved to be more acceptable to many pragmatic social reformers and researchers than the psychoanalytic tradition. In the first decade of the twentieth century, small-scale sex surveys and inquiries about sexual health occurred in many parts of Europe, including Scandinavia, Germany, Russia, and some countries of eastern Europe. Such research inquiries were used in discussions of homosexual law reform and the sex education of children, and were the basis for the rise of the World League for Sexual Reform after World War I.

In the United States the influence of Ellis was profound, particularly his interest in the sexual lives of "fairly normal" people. He recognized that a full understanding of sexuality depended on moving attention away from sexual criminals, lunatics, or people in therapy. Such people did not represent the "everyday" sexuality which ought to be the measure of normality. Ellis was reasoning against the kind of mistake made by nineteenth-century criminology in saying that all criminals have certain head shapes, which was only disproved when it turned out that university students had the same head shapes. Ellis proposed to survey what people actually did—a radical departure from the prescriptive approach of telling people what they "ought" to do.

In the period 1920–1938, a number of small surveys were made of sexuality in "normal" people and a series of small sociological studies was made of sexuality in marriage and of premarital intercourse. It was not until 1938 that a major national survey was begun to find out what "fairly normal" people did in their sex lives. When the results of this research were published a decade later, the sexual information blackout in the United States was truly over.

ALFRED KINSEY

In 1938 Alfred Kinsey was a well-known biologist at Indiana University, interested in evolutionary theory. He was asked to teach the sex part of a course in marriage. Upon finding that there was no information in the library, he developed a questionnaire and circulated it to the students in the class. He then reported the results back to them.

What Kinsey was doing, as Freud did before him, was to extend the normal procedures of scientific inquiry into a new and taboo area. The tradition of statistical surveys was already developed; what Kinsey did was to use the method to study sex. This is the major accomplishment of all the major sex researchers—they extended the limits rather than the methods of research.

Beginning on the Indiana University campus, and moving from it into the general society, Kinsey and three assistants interviewed approximately 17,000 people. The interviewing technique and the content of the interview was to some degree biased in the male direction, particularly in the study of sexual arousal and response. In 1946 Kinsey felt that he had a sufficient number of male cases to write up the findings. In 1948 he and his associates published their findings under the title, *Sexual Behavior in the Human Male*. It was a major sensation, perhaps the largest public event in science since the atomic bomb. Out of the massive publicity—the stories, editorials, jokes, cartoons, and Congressional inquiries—came a new public character, the sex researcher.

When all was said and done, Kinsey had, in his first book and the next, *Sexual Behavior in the Human Female,* held a mirror up to U.S. society, and opened the door to public discussion of sexuality. The two books were accepted to a remarkable degree. There was resistance and criticism, but they rapidly became the standard work on sexuality in the United States. Even with their limitations of method and analysis, they were and are monuments to a brave intellectual effort.

Kinsey's work stimulated sociological observational research of homosexuals and prostitutes, and the beginning of non-pathology-hunting psychological research work with homosexuals. The intent of these two types of research was to look at homosexuality and prostitution in a larger context, to see the former as people with complex life styles living in urban subcultures and the latter as people in an illegal occupation. Both of these research programs played down the role of the sexual, and played up the other organizing aspects of homosexual and prostitute life.

Also stimulated by Kinsey's research was an academic interest in premarital intercourse and female virgins, particularly on college campuses. There has been a steady stream of studies on collegiate attitudes toward and rates of premarital intercourse, including national samples as well as studies of local college campuses. As a result, there is probably more information on premarital intercourse on college campuses than on any other social aspect of human sexuality.

MASTERS AND JOHNSON

Just before Kinsey's death in 1956, William Masters (a gynecologist), and his research assistant, Virginia Johnson, began research on the physiological and anatomical aspects of sexual response, venturing into observational work in the laboratory. Kinsey and his group had done this kind of research from 1945 on, particularly making films of sex, but did not report that they had done it. Masters and Johnson began with prostitutes as subjects, but eventually switched to a middle-class population available at the medical school where they worked. For a decade they did research on various aspects of anatomy and physiology during sexual response, and then turned their attention to treatment of certain sexual inadequacies, displayed mostly by married couples. Their first publication, in 1966, *Human Sexual Response,* was greeted with some dismay, but has since been generally accepted as an important preliminary work on female sexual response.

The work of Masters and Johnson has been particularly influential in the treatment of sexual dysfunction, and has had some influence in legitimating the right of other laboratories to do basic research on sexual arousal. Equally influential has been the Congressional Commission on Obscenity and Pornography, which supported a series of studies by psychologists and sociologists on the impact and use of erotic materials. While the influence of the Commission on national policy was negligible, it did offer an opportunity for psychologists to do laboratory research on erotic materials, and it legitimated the use of such materials with subject populations. As a result of this work and an interest in the therapeutic techniques of behavior modification, an increasing number of psychologists have become involved with sex research.

With the increasing number of people involved in research on sexuality, there has been acceptance of the idea that sexual behavior can be studied by any competent professional oriented to the current interests and concerns of his or her field. Sex research can now be viewed as simply a subject matter specialty within a variety of scientific disciplines.

Conclusion: Science and Purpose

As the importance of science as an arbiter of purposes in human life has increased, so has the influence of the sex researcher on public attitudes toward sex. As standards have shifted, as religious values have weakened, science has become one of the justifications of normality and health. At the same time that science erects such ideas, its very process tends to tear them down—health for whom? normal says who? for what purposes? The skeptical tradition that characterizes much of modern science, combined with a strong dash of relativism, makes it a weak supporter of collective purposes and a stronger supporter of individualism. While individual scientists may be authoritarian, the tradition is not.

Our sexual purposes and the justifications that we have for them have generally grown less legitimate and enforceable over the last seventy years. We have made the move, or at least some of us have, from the divine to the mundane, from big purpose to little purpose, from sex as sin, crime, degeneracy, to the more modest term unconventional. We are still prisoners of our purposes, and we continue to justify what we do. We now have a whole new series of purposes, sex for joy, and personal. We have moved from collective metaphors to personal metaphors, and even those who still believe in the sacred traditions have to compete with the alternatives.

This is what the people who censured the sexual revolutionaries of the 1890s recognized was going to happen. If they allowed information and competing world views to be publicized, it was possible that the views would gain enough strength to undermine the current purposes and justifications. The censors were not foolish in those fears; what they feared did happen; and the world is not the same as it was.

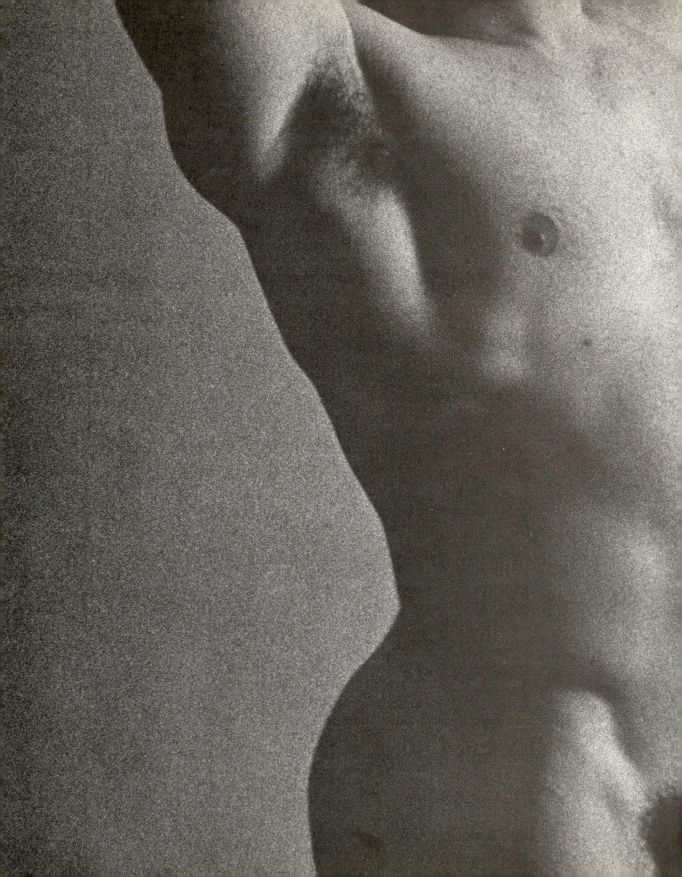

EVALUATING SEX RESEARCH

3

Nor can science itself rightly lay claim to finality or the complete comprehension of reality, but only to the honesty and accuracy of the additional facets it may be permitted to discover and report.
Alan Gregg, Preface to *Sexual Behavior in the Human Male*

EVEN THOUGH THE UNITED STATES IS INUNDATED WITH BOOKS AND MAGAZINES and newspaper articles about sexuality, this popular literature contains very little novel or substantial information. Moreover, these sources tend to simplify and distort the little reliable information that exists. This situation is the result of a number of interrelated factors. First of all, articles about sexuality help sell periodicals and books. Publishers want to make money; authors want to make money; there is a market for sex-related materials — the result is a flood of articles and books.

Second, the pace of publication of popular materials is very rapid. A journal must appear with some regularity, a newspaper every day, a magazine once a week or month; a book publisher should have a new sex book (and a new cook book) every year. Demand is what characterizes a mass media system: look at the number of hours of prime time television; many of the shows are similar because it is difficult to think of that many new ideas for that many hours of broadcasting.

Third, the rate of production of new information by scientists is very slow. This is in part a result of the way most competent scientists work. Careful research takes a long time to perform, sometimes many years, as the scientist designs instruments, gathers cases in some systematic way, analyzes the data, presents preliminary results to colleagues, and finally goes through the process of preparing an article or book manuscript that is once again reviewed before publication. If we include the sometimes long delays waiting for grant support for research, the time from first idea to final publication may be three to five years.

A high rate of production of new scientific information depends on a relatively large number of scientists working in a common area, so that they can exchange ideas and equipment and information, and train new scientists who begin their work with a head start over their teachers. However, very few persons do sex research as part of a career or established set of concerns. Sex research is still not very respectable, and sex researchers are viewed skeptically by their more conventional colleagues interested in more conventional research topics. It is often difficult to get funds to do sex research because granting agencies and foundations are fearful of being attacked for supporting sex research. Finally, since there is not a body of easily accessible background information and already developed techniques, scientists who wish to study human sexuality must learn a new body of information and adapt research techniques. These considerations make it unlikely that the best of young scientists will undertake research on human sexuality. They are often directed elsewhere by their teachers since they know that sex research is an area beset by social taboos and difficulites.

Finally, scientists are not robots who exist above everyday social life, motivated only by the desire to promote scientific truth. Scientists live in a culture with sexual values, act out the culture's sexual scripts, and themselves have histories of sexual conduct. The more taboo the topic, the more that personal and cultural factors play a role in research. Much of this book will record how people who have studied sex have been influenced by the time and place in which they did their work. It is not only that accepting the *status quo* influences scientific work; being opposed to the *status quo* also introduces biases.

All of these factors contribute to the low quantity of valid and reliable information about sexual conduct, and to the fact that it is being added slowly. As a result, most media articles say the same thing over and over again, from year to year. More daring opinions will be aired, both conservative (e.g., an article by a woman discounting the importance of orgasm) and radical (e.g., bisexuality is "in" and everyone ought to try it; anyone who is only heterosexual or homosexual is fixat-

The artist and scientist are creative voyeurs. They are not merely onlookers, but the inventors of a reality that is complex and shifting. The woman in the painting on the easel is an abstraction. The woman being painted seems more real, but we know that she is an abstraction as well. The young man—did he paint the abstraction, or is he the fantasy of the artist who made the lithograph we are looking at? The old man looking through the curtain—is he the artist? Is he looking at a current scene (the young artist having sex with the model whom he is painting), looking at his past (remembering when he was a young artist), or is this just a fantasy, either of the past or the present? All of us create as we look.

ed), but most of the references to scientific literature are limited to a small number of sources: the names Freud, Kinsey, and Masters and Johnson appear with regularity. This is a correct measure of their importance; however, it is also a measure of the tendency of the media to "personify" complex scientific processes. These names have recognition value; they are the "superstars" of sex research, whose opinions are valued and important in a media context.

Another result of the lack of continual new research is that journalists and publishers themselves often do a form of research—usually involving a set of unsystematic interviews with a small number of homosexuals, bisexuals, unmarried pregnant teenagers, etc., combined with telephone interviews of experts who may have done some research in the area. More recently, publishers have used either market research organizations or their own magazine pages to circulate questionnaires, and have published their results as "scientific findings" or "scientific surveys." Recent examples of this practice are found in the magazines *Psychology Today*, *Redbook*, and *Playboy*. Such material rarely reaches even a minimum level of scientific or social utility.

If we judge what we know by the number of pages printed or the number of trees that had to be cut down to print them, we would think ourselves remarkably well informed about sexuality. Yet if we examine our own personal lives and the lives of our friends, we find wrong choices made merely because of simplified, distorted, or incorrect information rather than "wrong" attitudes or values.

Theory and Data

Very little data exists on the sexual things that people do, what they feel about those sexual things, the ways in which sexual things are connected to other aspects of life, or the ways in which people acquire a culturally appropriate set of sexual scripts.

A result of this lack of systematically gathered data is leaps of the imagination in explaining what persons do, which means, in scientific terms, greater reliance on theory or explanations than on "the facts." We have only a very small number of facts, and some of them we are not too sure of. We must therefore rely on inferences, trying to make up in cautious speculation what we lack in solid information.

Another consequence of a lack of secure information is that introspection has a great influence on interpretations of data. *Introspection* is the use of personal experience to explain or judge data. With a small body of facts and a limited consensus about them, the biography of a scientist becomes important to him or her in judging the meaning of those facts. This is particularly true in assessing the feelings or motives people have about or for their actions, since even scientists tend to judge the feelings and motives of others by how they themselves might feel. Introspection is common in the behavioral sciences and often directly affects the interpretation of data. Such biographical influences on research also exist in the physical sciences, but they affect the process far less directly.

In research on sexuality, introspection may be even more of a factor than in, for instance, the study of voting, sibling rivalry, or violence on television. In these other areas we at least have the experiences and attitudes of our friends and acquaintances to compare ourselves with, information that can widen or alter our views. But in sexual matters, due to the limited and distorted communication discussed in Chapter 1, we do not even have that.

In the study of human sexual conduct, the explanations used to make sense of the world often have great influence. Even if "the facts" were unequivocal, we do not have the facts. Therefore, we are forced to rely on explanations; that is, we usually say, "It makes sense, given the other things that we know about both sexual and nonsexual conduct, that this is more likely that that." Further, we often say, "Given my general theoretical views about how people become sexual, even though I don't have any data, it is likely that the following things are going on." Thus a Freudian, who believes that all children go through a phase during which they masturbate (even though there is little data from observations of children to demonstrate such a finding), will say, "Of course all young women masturbate, because masturbation is a necessary part of psycho-sexual development. If they do not remember, they have repressed it."

Our problem lies in making sense of the little data that we have. We must have some way of judging the quality of the data that we have about human sexual conduct, and the quality of the explanations offered for this data.

Judging Data and Explanations

Data is probably easier to judge than explanations or theories. Explanations are so subtly interwoven into the whole process of deciding what is or is not data, the correct procedures for gathering it, and the ways of interpreting data that sometimes we do not even know that we are viewing the world in particular ways. Theories in part are "taken-for-granted" views of how the world works, or how people work, and they influence our selection and acceptance of the facts that we have. Take an example from the physical sciences: It was once believed that the earth was the center of the universe. Observations of the movements of the stars and the planets were thought to be correct or incorrect as they fitted with a geocentric view of the universe. As soon as a heliocentric (sun-centered) view was adopted (only after a long political, religious, and scientific struggle), some old observations were discarded, some were reinterpreted, and in other cases the theory directed observers to look for different "facts."

It is also true that a fairly large number of explanations can fit or explain any given set of facts. Which explanation is chosen is only in part determined by the facts (in some cases an explanation may have no relationship to the facts or may be in opposition to them). This relative independence of chosen theories from empirical data is an issue in the study of how science progresses, and an issue in the study of sexual conduct. Understanding why we are comfortable with one explanation for sexuality at one time and discard it for another explanation at some later point, in the absence of any new or different data, takes us outside the narrow study of sexuality. We must begin to examine the connections of the study of sexuality to other developments in the behavioral sciences, as well as to currents in the larger social world that surrounds science.

For instance, researchers are now at least as interested in the hostility or prejudice expressed against homosexuals by many heterosexuals (*homophobia*) as they once were in the part that hatred of the opposite sex (*heterophobia*) might play in the development of a homosexual object-choice. This change has resulted from the changed attitudes of the larger society toward homosexuality, and the increased militancy of gay activist groups both inside and outside the scientific community. An interesting topic in science has been created by conditions outside science.

History: When We Knew

Studies of human beings are done at particular moments in time. Ignoring that fact can cause problems in properly interpreting scientific research. One problem is that of changes in people's behavior over time. In some studies, explaining changes in conduct itself is a matter of interest, but in others scientists may be trying to establish that something is constant over time (e.g., that all historical periods have the same proportion of homosexuals). The problem is that different factors may be producing the same proportions (homosexuality may be rewarded at one historical moment; young men and women may be segregated at another).

This can be a problem over even very short periods—the subjects of similar studies may be selected in different ways or have different social histories, resulting in different findings. For example, research subjects are often college students, typically middle class. An increase in the number of college students from working class origins, who might have different attitudes toward the research topic (premarital sexual intercourse or homosexuality, for instance), can produce different results for apparently very similar experiments, done at different times.

Thus, the date a study was done is important in evaluating it, and its conclusions should not be uncritically applied to the present time. Circumstances may be the same; or they may have changed dramatically. In the absence of contemporary studies we are left to make judgments on how much significant change may have taken place.

Again we find ourselves in a situation where theories or explanations become more important than data. If people believe that rapid social or sexual change is possible, they will argue that older information does not accurately represent contemporary standards. If they believe that sexual change is slower, or if they believe that a given behavior always occurs for certain theoretical reasons, they will discount historical factors.

Sometimes such arguments are very complex and involve many factors with differing weights. For instance, if we believed that most young unmarried women really wanted to have sex and did not do so primarily because they were afraid of getting pregnant, we would predict that available effective birth control methods would lead to a higher incidence of intercourse before marriage. If we had no data on current rates of premarital intercourse, but we did know that effective birth control methods are available, we would argue that there is more intercourse now, and that older information on premarital sex does not apply to the present.

The historical period not only affects what topics the scientist studies, it also affects what factors scientists think are important, what methods they use, and what explanations they offer for their findings. These differences often make comparing research studies done at different times difficult. Thus, how a question was asked in a study on masturbation done in 1920 may be quite different from the way a question on masturbation was asked in 1940 or 1970. Comparisons across time of the percentage who say they did or did not masturbate become complicated as a result of a simple difference in wording. (They can also be complicated by possible changes in attitude toward both survey questionnaries and studies of sex — more people now than in the past may feel that they can answer honestly.)

Scientific explanations also change over time. If a sex researcher subscribes to trait theory, he may study the relation of aggression or dominance to sexual behavior. But then the study of traits as explanations for behavior becomes less popular in psychology, so later interpretations of his findings change.[1] He may have found that some subjects scored high on both a dominance scale and a scale of frequency of sexual activity. A later interpretation of his findings may conclude that a relationship between dominance and sexuality was found because dominant people are more likely to volunteer for experiments and more likely to violate social rules about sex.

Caution must also be taken in considering research whose data comes from historical records or records made by contemporary observers. Suppose, for example, that a researcher is investigating the historical incidence of rape, and finds records from a section of Germany in the nineteenth century. Police statistics collected in most countries even today are rife with error, from the moment of reporting to final compilation of tables. The level of error in most official statistics, even without particular biases (such as not reporting certain kinds of offenses), is very high. Thus, in looking at the nineteenth-century German data, our researcher must ask: Why did they keep these records? What cases were not reported? In what cases was no offense proven? What was the legal as well as the pragmatic definition of rape? What are the costs to the victim of reporting? All of these questions and more have to be satisfied before an "official statistic" (including one gathered only yesterday) can be used as a representation of reality.

Attempting to convert information gathered in the past into a form compatible with present knowledge has many pitfalls. This is particularly true in the study of sexuality, where information from the past is scarce and full of uninterpretable biases.

Location: Where We Get What We Know

Most of the cautions expressed about time can be extended to the place where research was done. The effects are quite similar. One effect is the definition of science in that place. Each country possesses a national tradition in various fields of what are acceptable and unacceptable kinds of research and explanations of data. For instance, studies of social mobility and stratification are common in the United States. The results are interpreted by the political left as proving that there is less mobility and therefore less opportunity (America is growing rigid), and by the political right as demonstrating the opposite (Everybody can get ahead in America). Mobility and social equality are part of the "American Dream," and everyone is interested in it. In Europe, such studies have been comparatively rare and their interpretations considerably different. "Social class" is not a dirty word to European social scientists.

---

1. Science, like clothing design, is sometimes the slave of fashion.

In addition, there are often greater or lesser restrictions on whether findings will be politically or socially acceptable. There are societies with no tradition of free inquiry, or where sexual facts are viewed as political facts. For some years the Soviet Union, for example, has reported no prostitution and no venereal disease, since they theoretically could not exist in a fully developed communist state.

Where there are social taboos against certain kinds of behavior, people will deny the behavior, under-report frequency, or report it as past behavior ("I don't masturbate any more, but I used to when I was young"). How much more constrained are people where there is legal pressure put on them to conform? Members of sexual minorities must feel such constraints when they are asked in research studies about illegal sexual activities.

In some cases cultural traditions prohibit certain kinds of questions, or traditions of privacy or courtesy distort the answers. In a society where public opinion polls are infrequent and viewed as an invasion of privacy, interpretation of poll results will differ from that of polls taken in the United States, where they are a common and expected source of knowledge. Alternatively, in some Asian countries the tradition of courtesy is so powerful that people who are asked questions search for the answer their questioner seems to want—they wish to be agreeable.

Scientists trained in cross-cultural research can work with such issues and produce fairly reliable explanations, but some barriers exist which cannot be surmounted. Thus, when we find research studies done in places which have different traditions, we must decide how much we trust the data, and how much it can tell us about what is going on elsewhere, as well as how well it applies to our own culture.

This is particularly true in dealing with research that looks very similar to research produced in the United States. Things that look the same may be caused by very different factors, and things that look different may be caused by similar factors. After World War II it was discovered that many young women in Scandinavia, particularly Denmark and Sweden, had premarital intercourse. There were those who said that such behavior was the result of a moral breakdown caused by having a socialist government. Other people thought that women in Denmark and Sweden must be very promiscuous. However, Scandinavian rates of premarital intercourse were in part a survival of previous rural traditions, and most of the young women were having intercourse only with the young man that they eventually married. In addition, there was no tradition of premarital petting with a number of "steadies" as there was in the United States.

In many ways the Scandinavian countries are like the United States—urban, modern, industrialized societies. A too easy interpretation of familiar features of these societies can lead to false conclusions, much like those false-friend words discovered in learning a foreign language. The fact that a word is spelled the same does not signify that it means the same.

Premarital intercourse takes its meaning from the cultural place in which it occurs and the role it plays in that culture. It is part of an extensive set of social and sexual scripts, scripts that have been learned in that place and for the purposes of that place. The act of intercourse is not merely organs grinding together, but an act linked to other acts, with precursors and consequences. To take premarital coitus out of its cultural context is a violation of the integrity and meaning of the idea of culture.

When major differences in sexual practices can be found even in societies which are similar to the United States, we should be even more cautious when we study modern societies with different traditions, or developing societies, or the small-scale human communities and cultures that have been the basic social units of interest to anthropologists. What might intercourse before "legal" marriage mean in an advanced Oriental nation such as Japan; or a rapidly industrializing nation like Brazil; or a developing nation such as Kenya, composed of rural tribes and urban city dwellers; or the small three-to-five-hundred-person language-cultural groups of the highlands of New Guinea?

The dilemma of using information from other human cultures and societies is that too often we simply compare their pattern with ours or use their pattern for purposes of praise or blame. If we like what they do more than what we do, we say "Look at this tribe, they have lots of premarital intercourse and very nice children; therefore, we should have more premarital sex." If we wish to blame, we say "Look at that tribe; they have lots of premarital intercourse and a high suicide rate, we don't want to have that." Even if we could establish a connection between premarital intercourse and anything else, we might not be able to replicate such a relationship in our own culture.

Probably the most helpful way to think about cross-cultural research, especially in the area of sexuality, is to use it as an opportunity to examine the ways in which other cultures have integrated different sexual patterns into a cultural whole. Once we have thought through that specific design, that specific set of scripts, both sexual and nonsexual, then we can begin to look for similar patterns in other cultures and in our own. Then, if we wish to go on to think about how our culture could be more or less like other cultures, we could *begin* to think about how our culture could be manipulated.

People: Who We Know

Once we have sorted out the problems of when and where research has been done, we then concern ourselves with how many subjects have been studied, and whether the subjects have been selected in such a way that inferences can be made about the behavior of people in general. The word *sample* is often used in research studies to label the persons who have been gathered together and questioned, or observed, or experimented on. The selection of a sample and the limitations of various procedures for sampling are relatively technical matters, but the importance of such procedures is that they give the researcher confidence that the findings can be generalized to populations larger than the sample itself.

For instance, to study opinions of persons in the United States requires a procedure by which the persons interviewed are, within certain limits, representative of the population of the United States. For practical reasons (money and time usually) most studies fall short of perfection in sampling, but in the best of research studies the reader is given an accurate picture of how the sample was gathered and the limitations on generalizing from the data.

Very few studies of sexual behavior meet even minimum criteria for sampling. Most of them depend on volunteers or patients, and thus have the weakness of self-selection built into them. Such groups should not be called "samples," because the procedures for getting them are often imprecise or even unknown to the researchers. They could be called "collections," or "chunks," or "bunches," but not samples. Such bunches of people often provide very useful data, sometimes the only data we have. We make inferences about behavior from that data, but we must be careful not to overestimate their generality. The Kinsey titles, *Sexual Behavior in the Human Male* and *Sexual Behavior in the Human Female,* or the Masters and Johnson title, *Human Sexual Response,* imply that the data gathered represented a true sample of humans (of all races, creeds, classes, nations) rather than collections of mostly white middle-class volunteers in the United States. It may be that these studies have in fact charted the behavior of most people (and we do have more confidence in physiological research not based on careful samples than we do in poorly sampled studies of social or psychological conduct, though this confidence may be misplaced), but in the absence of valid sampling we must infer cautiously.

We have very little data on sexuality that comes from people selected by moderately strict sampling rules. There are a number of studies of opinions about premarital intercourse and extramarital intercourse, and a few studies of general attitudes toward sex, that have used valid samples. There are even some studies of sexual behavior that have sampled from a single university or set of universities and colleges, or from a single state. In some cases we have data about marital sex from sampled populations which gives us confidence that we know roughly the frequencies of marital intercourse at various moments over the last twenty years.

It is likely that more data will be gathered in this manner in the future, but little of the data we have now on any of the taboo areas of sexuality comes from carefully gathered cases. There is not a good sample of homosexuals, either from the population at large or from the population of homosexuals themselves. We have tended to gather such cases from public locations (bars and toilets, for example), homophile organizations, individuals in therapy, or through a procedure called "snow-balling": beginning with one person and then interviewing others, a process that might be called interviewing friends of friends. As interesting as such procedures might be, they clearly do not gather together the entire network of persons with homosexual experiences or even persons with homosexual self-identities. In fact, the definition of "homosexuality" used may vary so much that the sampled cases may have no relation to the definition of the population itself.

When an author claims to be studying homosexuality, sex in marriage, or mate-swapping, we must ask: In what ways do the people the author has studied represent the class of persons that the author wants us to think about? Who could be missing from this study? In some cases a judgment is easy—the author has studied, say, homosexuals who come to therapists, and wishes to say that these cases represent all homosexuals. In other cases the biases are harder to find, especially when we like the findings. Other questions might be: Who is over-represented? Are there too many young people, old people, rich people, poor people, highly educated people? Do these categories have anything to do with sexuality? Essentially, we must ask whether the researcher has so gathered the cases that inferences can be trusted. This is not a mere exercise in method, it is one of the few ways in which we can get a careful picture of one study and compare it with another.

Another question related to sampling is, how many persons have been studied? Thus, if a study is of twenty college students, we might be uneasy about its findings, because it is unlikely that twenty students will represent all of the variability we might find in a college population. Can this number of people (even if they have been selected correctly or in a way that seems correct) represent all of the differences that might exist in a population? The variability may be sufficiently narrow that the first five people studied give an accurate picture of the behavior in question — but this is unlikely.

The problem of the number of cases and how the cases were gathered seriously afflicts psychological experiments in which students are given credit or money to participate. How students select themselves for particular kinds of experiments is presently unknown, though it is probably safe to assume that psychological studies about sex are likely to select students who are more sexually interested, if not experienced, than the students selected for studies on recall of nonsense syllables. The degree to which psychological experiments can be generalized beyond a part of the college student population may be very limited.

Most of our knowledge about human sexuality is in fact derived from studies of college students. The college student and the white rat have been our greatest sources of knowledge. As a laboratory subject, the college freshman or sophomore has generated more scientific information than any other human group. The college educated are also over-represented in most other studies of human sexuality: answering questionnaires about sex, participating in interviews, and as the guinea pigs in laboratory experiments on human sexual response. The people who do *not* participate are more likely to be religious, less educated, of ethnic and racial minorities, and of lower economic status. Our inferential leaps are even greater when we try to determine what the sexual conduct of these sections of society might be.

Methods: What We Can Know

To find something out it is best to have some kind of stable procedure, or what is commonly called a *method*. Methods are the agreed-upon practical procedures that many social scientists use when they go about trying to find out something. They have no sacred status — an agreement on practical methods means only that researchers can trust each other's findings because they have at least an outline of the way in which the data was gathered. They are a shared body of techniques and procedures for gathering information.

Sex research has been conducted largely through five methods. Such methods have a historical order, that is, some were used earlier in research than in others, but they all represent ways of knowing that have elicited data about both sexual and nonsexual forms of conduct.

CLINICAL RESEARCH

When people who are suffering from a physical or mental disorder are gathered together, and that disorder is studied through attempts to treat it, a clinical research program is going on. For instance, cancer patients are given a specific drug, and from the reactions to that drug, inferences are made about the nature of the disease. Researchers are using clinical procedures to find out about the development of cancer. Such techniques can also be used to infer patterns of healthy development. Control groups are sometimes used to determine if clinical treatment works; they are also used to infer differences between healthy and diseased conditions. Psychiatrists who study, say, child molesters in therapy and make inferences about the development of adult heterosexuality are doing clinical research — in the course of treatment the psychiatrist learns things which may illuminate the origins of the disorder being treated.

Clinical research has a long history in the study of sexuality, since so much of sex was considered "unhealthy" or criminal in the past. It focused largely on what were thought to be sexual deviates and criminals. This focus on those who were defined as deviants resulted in what can be called the "pathology-seeking" bias of sex research. Clinicians look for what went wrong or is wrong with these people. At present, the study and treatment of children with atypical gender identities (see Chapter 4) and the laboratory study of sexual dysfunction are the most common forms of clinical research into sexuality.

Major questions for evaluating clinical research are the following:

1. On what basis was it decided that a condition was unhealthy or healthy? Such a decision may seem easy for cancer or a broken leg, but it is not so easy for masturbation or shoe fetishism. The decision to view certain sexual preferences as disorders is a cultural decision. Unlike physical illness or injury, patterns of cultural behavior are not so properly judged as normal or abnormal, healthy or sick.
2. Can inferences actually be made from the behavior of sick people to that of healthy people? Even if it were agreed that A is sick and B is well, how can we be sure that we will really learn anything about B from studying A?
3. What evidence is there that those who come in for treatment are representative of the condition under study? Studying rapists in jail is clearly not studying a representative sample of all who have raped. (This is more a sampling question than one of method, but it is a curse of much of clinical research.)
4. Do the procedures used in treatment prevent finding out what is wanted? Using a drug to treat a disorder may so change things that the normal processes of the disease are permanently obscured. A sexual parallel occurs in psychoanalysis, where the conditions of treatment may distort the patient's recall of the experiences that the researcher thinks are critical.

OBSERVATIONAL RESEARCH

Clinical research seeks to change the course of events; observational research seeks to have as little effect on its subjects as possible. Much of anthropological and sociological research is observational in character, as is the research of those who study primate groups in the wild, and even those who merely observe events in a laboratory without attempting to change them.

This research involves watching from the sidelines, especially when studying, for instance, baboons in the wild. The observer sits and watches and makes more or less systematic notes about what is going on. This same procedure can be used in the study of human beings. The observer is an onlooker, the more unobtrusive (that is, not disturbing the normal flow of activity) the better. All kinds of methods can be used to gather observational data—looking from behind a one-way glass screen, taking photographs or videotapes for viewing later. The task is to get a systematic record of events.

Another technique can be used when being an unknown onlooker is not possible. The observer can participate, either disguised or known to be a scientist. In the latter case the observer can either disclose or conceal the purposes of the research. There are ethical and personal problems, however, in concealment of identity or purpose. Entering into the lives of other people involves a trust which is violated by covert participation. While people believe the researcher is a friend, helper, or onlooker, the researcher is using the relationship for other ends.

Observational procedures involve other serious questions of method:

1. How much does the presence of a known observer change the behavior of a group?
2. How can the conclusions of covert observational studies be checked against explanations that might be offered by subjects?
3. What methods can be used to record accurately but unobstructively the myriad events that may be going on?
4. Since the primary measuring tool in the observational study is the observer, how much can we depend on the reliability of observations? Would others see the same things? What are the effects of observer fatigue, boredom, etc.?
5. What are the effects of knowing too much about a particular subculture, being too well acquainted with the patterns of conduct? Knowing too much may be as dangerous for accurate, unbiased observation as knowing very little.

QUESTIONNAIRES AND INTERVIEWS

Probably the major source of data on human sexual conduct has been asking people about their sex lives. The researcher asks a person to tell about actions and feelings from the distant or recent past. This information can be asked for relatively directly, as in the questions, "How old were you the first time you masturbated?" or "How often have you had intercourse with your husband in the last month?" or "If you found out that a close friend of yours was homosexual, would you keep (him/her) as a friend?" The questions can be asked by an interviewer or through a questionnaire given to the subject. They can also be asked indirectly, as in using scales of attitude items that seem to measure sexual permissiveness, or authoritarianism, or masculinity (see Table 1, Chapter 9).

One job of the researcher is to increase the accuracy of what the subject recalls or reports. There are a number of techniques that appear to improve accuracy of reporting; the most important seems to be an interviewer who feels comfortable about sex and does not judge the reported behavior of the subject. Combined with suitable ways of asking the questions, this seems to make people able to report their own behavior accurately and calmly.

At times it is best to interview people alone and in private. When it is useful to interview other persons involved in the relationship (a spouse or lover) to get another perspective, they might be interviewed separately, or a couple might answer questions together. In other cases there might be a group of persons discussing the same topic or set of topics—Donald Marshall in his study on Mangaia (Chapter 1) got some of his data by gathering together groups of men who in the process of building a dictionary of their language also talked about sexual words and practices. Each of these procedures adds and subtracts information. Husbands and wives may have different versions of how often they have intercourse (and may tell different stories depending on whether each knows that the other is going to be interviewed). People in a group will tell different things depending on the nature of the group, their prestige in it, and the ease with which they talk.

People are, in general, rather poor reporters of their own sexual conduct. The ways in which most of them have learned to talk about sex will distort what they think is desirable and what they will remember.[2] Men often want to brag, women to dissemble; therefore, men may exaggerate their premarital sex experience, women may not want to tell about one-night stands. Also, people change, and in the process they change their pasts as well. A five-year-old's perception of its behavior in the last week will differ from that of a ten-year-old or twenty-year-old remembering (or trying to remember) that same week. The five-year-old's version of its feelings will differ from recollections when it is ten or twenty years old. The same person has different interests at different ages, and many of these interests have developed since the person was five years old. Such interests will make her or him add and subtract things from the age-five experience. This process often makes actual past experience inaccessible—what the researcher gets from subjects is what they think their past might have been as they talk about it in the present.

There are interview and questionnaire studies in which the researcher may be interested not in an accurate recollection of the "facts," but in a contemporary version of past feelings or the ways people have of talking about their past sex lives. Such a researcher might be interested in the gossip people exchange rather than the actual sex they have. This type of research interest would require using another set of techniques and procedures.

The interview method has its weaknesses:

1. If the interviewer wants to know accurately what occurred in the past and when, how can he or she be sure that subjects recall equally accurately? If there is data that the people who recall having an early puberty also recall masturbation around the same time, how do we know if this is a difference in the way people remember or a difference in the occurrence or relationship of actual events?

2. What are the differences among different kinds of techniques (questionnaires versus interviews, for example) in getting the same information? In filling

2. Gene Starbuck pointed out to me that being a subject in a sex research project may be arousing. I recall the sex history taken when I joined the staff of the Institute for Sex Research. The opportunity to think and talk about my own sexual past was arousing. Rereading that interview some years later, I do not feel that the arousal itself distorted the record, but I cannot be sure. Colleagues and students of mine, as well as research subjects, have reported the same experience. Does this arousal from the research context produce different responses to questions or stimuli? Do women and men respond differently to such context effects?

out a questionnaire, the person can be anonymous, but can make any answer; face-to-face the interviewer has greater control, but the presence of the interviewer can affect the replies.

3. What is the effect of different kinds of interviewers? Can women interview men about sex? Can old people interview young people? Can an interviewer be of a different racial or ethnic group?

4. Should there be many interviewers who are slightly trained or a few who are well trained? With a few, a large study would take a long time, bringing in the possible complications of time discussed earlier, as well as a possible common bias among so few researchers. On the other hand, it is difficult to train equally well a large number of interviewers.

EXPERIMENTAL RESEARCH

Experimental research, other than clinical experiments, is probably the most infrequent form of research on sexuality. An experiment requires that individuals be presented with various kinds of stimuli under various kinds of controlled conditions, and that the results be measured carefully. Experimental research can be powerful and precise, because it offers the researcher an opportunity to control many factors and to isolate the effect of specific variables.

Certain procedures can be used to narrow the focus of the study to a few particular variables or relationships: random assignment of subjects to various conditions (to control for different life histories); keeping the researcher ignorant of the condition of a subject (so that experimenter behavior does not influence the outcome); use of control groups (to study what happens when a particular stimulus is not presented, or the effects of simply being in an experimental situation). The experiment offers obvious advantages of control over other research procedures.

However, experiments are not always easy to design: selecting a control group may be difficult; and perhaps more difficult is creating an experimental situation that is a good analogue of the real-world situation under study. For instance, there have been many sex experiments presenting subjects with depictions of sexual activity, either in words or pictures, while measuring blood flow in the genitals as a measure of sexual arousal. Experimenters argue that such measurements reveal differences in reaction to real-world sexual situations. This may be so, but are the behaviors called forth by the experiment the same as those called forth by an actual sexual situation? Take one example: in an experiment the subject usually receives sexual stimuli through a single channel (seeing or hearing), while sitting passively or doing a simple task; in a real sexual situation a person is active, goal directed, and receiving information through many channels—sight, hearing, smell, taste, and touch.

All this is not to argue that experiments are useless, but that they must be carefully designed, with constant reference to the usual world in which people behave. All too often, experiments are performed to fit the convenience of the researcher, without reference to the experiences of subjects outside the experimental situation.

The best experiments are those that draw their design accurately from the non-laboratory world, and after the study refer to the meaning of the experiment in non-laboratory terms.

One of the main reasons that laboratory experimentation is only now occurring (and therefore it is only now that experimental psychologists are developing a professional interest in sex) is that until quite recently it was taboo to show people the stimulus materials and to do the measurements required in certain types of experiments. It was not until the early 1960s that what was considered pornography could be shown to subjects without a powerful reaction from the community, including other researchers. To show young men pictures of sexual activity was thought to be psychologically dangerous, and to show such pictures to young women even more terrible.

It is only as a result of social change outside the scientific community that experiments in sexual conduct now exist. Despite the original Masters and Johnson work, it is still not possible to do experiments with sexual behavior itself—that is, having a subject engage in a sex act in an experiment—except as part of clinical research under the guise of therapy.

Some of the limitations of experimental research can be summarized:

1. To what degree in an experiment can the complexities of everyday sexual conduct be modeled or emulated?
2. Do the measurements taken in the experiment affect subject responses, so that they are fundamentally different from sexual behavior outside the experimental chamber?
3. To what degree do responses of subjects in experiments depend on what they have learned in the past in a particular time and place? A specific stimulus (a woman's breast, for instance) may arouse, say, a U.S. male, but not be arousing to males in other cultures.

Science and Ideology:
Why Are We Talking About Sex?

One of the uses that has been made of research on sexuality is to offer us an opportunity to know more about ourselves, in more objective ways. One function of science is to debunk the old myths, to tell us that masturbation will not drive us crazy, that people with homosexual preferences are not necessarily neurotic, that premarital intercourse will not make us failures in marriage, that women do not mature by changing from clitoral to vaginal orgasms. This is a socially useful role for careful inquiries into sexual conduct, but the old myths served social and psychological purposes for those who believed them, and they guided the conduct of such people.

Science may appear to be an objective and detached way of knowing, a way that is sure and dependable; however, what scientists do know is that most of their findings will turn out to be wrong in fact, or to be true only for a limited time and place, or to be better explained by another theory offered by another person. Theories and findings are approximations, with limitations on their utility and generality. However, science now has a peculiar role in western societies — the discoveries of social science very quickly become part of the daily lives of people. Rather than using folklore, or religion, or community wisdom, many people now justify their conduct by reference to scientific findings. When the Kinsey studies reported that very large numbers of men had masturbated, other men who had done so felt better. Others argued that masturbation must be harmless, or even a natural and a good thing to do, because so many people did it. What was first an act of sexual bookkeeping became an opportunity to create new guidelines for sexual conduct itself. But such assertions are likely to form new social myths, new beliefs that will turn out not to be acceptable in the future.

The tendency to turn findings into rules should evoke a strong sense of caution. Findings may be wrong, and we must ask ourselves why we are prepared to believe certain findings one day, when we have not believed them in the past. What is it about the non-scientific part of the world that makes some findings more palatable and others less?

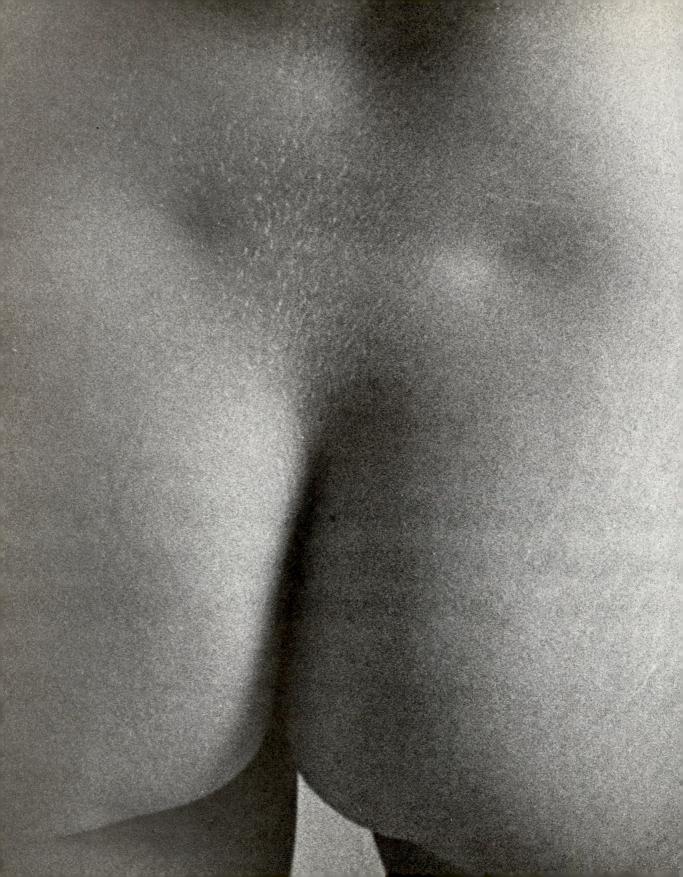

GENDER IDENTITIES AND ROLES

It is the bliss of childhood that we are
being warped most when we know it the least.
William Gaddis, *The Recognitions*

HOW DOES A PERSON ACQUIRE AN ONGOING BELIEF THAT HE OR SHE IS EITHER A boy or a girl, a man or a woman, masculine or feminine? Only a few years ago such a question would have been met by a wrinkled brow and a puzzled glance— "What kind of a question is that?" People are born little boy infants and little girl infants, and they grow up to be men and women and do what men and women do. We all know that things can go wrong, but the natural and orderly process is to become whatever our bodies seem to predict. Such a point of view has a certain naive and innocent appeal, but, as always, the world has turned out to be a complicated place.

Evidence for how complicated has been accumulating steadily over the last four decades, and the acceptability of that evidence has been reinforced in a variety of ways. The women's movement has questioned a whole range of gender-role stereotypes about what women and girls are *really like,* stereotypes that were widely held by scientists and which determined scientific research. The mass media have publicized the experiences of the transsexuals, and scientists have studied biological anomalies and patterns of social learning that have produced persons whose bodies and gender beliefs do not match. There now appears to be nothing automatic about the process of going from a fertilized egg of female or male chromosomal makeup to an adult who possesses a gender identity.[1]

Why is this important in terms of sexuality? First, in U.S. culture most sexual conduct is originally learned, coded, and performed on the basis of gender identity beliefs. We learn to be girls and boys and young women and men before we learn to be sexual in any specific ways. This society does not encourage sexual conduct among young people (until the late teens), but does emphasize from an early age sharp differences in gender identities and roles. When we do begin having sex in our society, our beliefs about woman/man strongly influence whom we have sex with, what sexual things we do, where and when we will have sex, the reasons we agree, and the feelings we have. Both the person who is being sexual and the people who know about it judge most sexual activity by the primary identifications of woman or man.

---

1. Conventionally, the general social and psychological aspects of male and female behavior are called *sex roles* and *sexual identity.* This leads to possible confusion between social and sexual behavior. In this book the words *gender identity* and *gender roles* refer to the nonsexual aspects of behavior—those things commonly linked to masculinity and femininity, to identity as men or women. The term *sexual* refers to roles and behaviors that are part of thinking about and doing sexual things.

A second reason for the importance of gender to sexuality is theoretical. There are a number of theories of the sources of gender identity, some of which give more weight to relatively inflexible biological processes, and others which emphasize a more flexible, social-learning approach. People adopt one or another of these views, or some mixed intermediate position, and it influences how they think about sexual conduct. If people believe that there is a natural gender identity, and that natural gender performances are based on that identity, then they believe that these natural gender performances will determine sexual performances. The biological program is thought to unfold in a relatively fixed and determined manner, culminating in particular patterns of sexual activity appropriate to women and to men.

In contrast, the more weight given to social learning, even in early infancy, and to the need for continuous environmental support for identities and performances, the more likely a looser and less determined program of development will be supported. In this perspective, sexuality among adults, no matter what script they might follow, must be understood not as the result of an unfolding process, but as a result of continuous construction, a result of interaction between the person and the environment.

These theoretical distinctions are often crucial, since they influence what a scientist will consider as relevant data. They also have certain ideological consequences. If development is a closed program expected to culminate in particular valued adult patterns of behavior (adult heterosexual genital maturity, for instance), then other forms of adult behavior must be considered anomalies, deviations, or perversions of that program. If it is an open program, then all sexual outcomes are equally possible, affected only by differences in cultural likelihood.[2]

The perspective of this book is that from birth to death, the environments we live in tell us that females and males are different—or should be different. Since children are born into societies that have existing role patterns for women and men, they must learn to understand and operate within the framework of these role differences. This process involves the creation of a belief about the self; and going from girl to woman, from boy to man requires social arrangements which continuously affirm and support that belief. The social and psychological differences between women and men (and the sexual conduct based on them) emerge only indirectly from hormonal or genetic states. The closer to conception, the greater the weight that should be given to these biological forces, but their influence steadily wanes with the buildup of widely different learning experiences, all of which have gender differences coded into them. The usual interactionist position is expressed in the following quotation:

The basic proposition should be not a dichotomization of genetics and environment, but their interaction. Interactionism as applied to the differentiation of gender identity can be best expressed by using the concept of a program. There are phyletically [biologically] written parts of the program. They exert their determining influence particularly before birth, and leave a permanent *imprimatur*. Even at that early time, however, the phyletic program may

2. The use of the labels "closed" and "open" for different programs is not meant ideologically, but it is certainly true that open is usually a more valued adjective than closed: it is better to have an *open* rather than a *closed* mind, to be *open* to new experiences rather than *closed* to them, to be *open*-hearted rather than *close*-fisted when giving. It is only a cultural prejudice that open is better than closed, but as long as I am open about it. . . .

When I grow up I want to be Barbie.

be altered by idiosyncrasies of personal history, such as the loss or gain of a chromosome during cell division, a deficiency or excess of maternal hormone, viral invasion, intrauterine trauma, nutritional deficiency or toxicity, and so forth. Other idiosyncratic modifications may be added by the biographical events of birth. All may impose their own imprimatur on the genetic program of sexual dimorphism that is normally expected on the basis of XX or XY chromosomal dimorphism.

Postnatally, the programming of psychosexual differentiation is, by phyletic decree, a function of biographical history, especially social biography. There is a close parallel here with the programming of language development. The social-biography program is not written independently of the phyletic program, but in conjunction with it, though on occasions there may be dysjunction between the two. Once written, the social-biography program leaves its imprimatur as surely as does the phyletic. The long-term effects of the two are equally fixed and enduring, and their different origins not easily recognizable. Aspects of human psychosexual differentiation attributable to the social-biography program are often mistakenly attributed to the phyletic program.[3]

Belief in an interaction between biological and environmental factors does not reduce the necessity of judging the weight to be given to them in any particular interaction, or determining the role of each in the variability of a person's behavior. It is important not to accept automatically that development is continuous, with permanently fixed and enduring imprints. There is a great deal of discontinuity in human development; past experiences rarely completely determine responses in

3. John Money and Anke Ehrhardt, *Man and Woman, Boy and Girl* (Johns Hopkins Press, 1972), pp. 1–2.

new circumstances. With both biological and environmental factors, there is interaction between the prior history of the organism and the demands of contemporary
and even future or desired environments. What "I will be" may be determined
more by what "I want to be" than what "I have been." In addition, there are very
few environments that are "surprise-free," that do not face people with demands
they did not expect and which therefore change what they are.

Gender identity grows more complex over time, and includes more domains
of behavior as the roles that are linked to gender also enlarge. At puberty, a second
surge of biological events occur. The impact of these physical changes is mediated
by both the gender identity of the child and the reactions of other people. By the
end of adolescence, during which elements of sexual conduct are usually assembled, a reasonably acceptable adult gender identity has been developed.

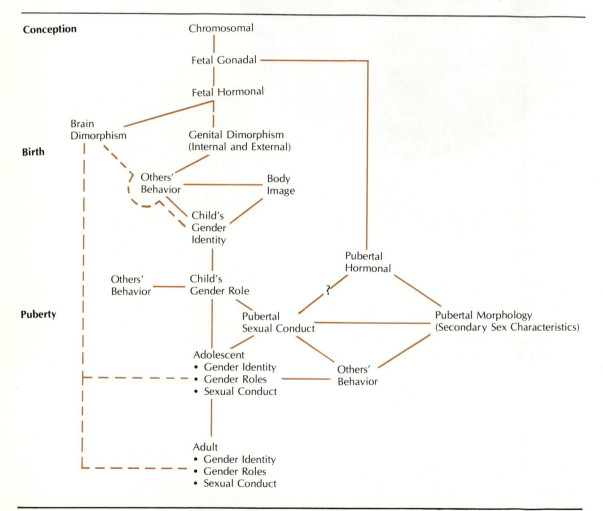

Figure 1.   Development of Gender Identities, Gender Roles, and Sexual Conduct. The
basis for this figure is in Money and Ehrhardt (p. 3), but the lines of influence are drawn
differently and other factors are added. The question mark signifies an effect not demonstrated (that hormonal changes produce sexual conduct or eroticism in any direct way)
and the dashed line suggests weak connections.

Definitions

The *biological sex* of an individual develops over time in two bursts of activity, pre-natal and pubertal (see Figure 1), and is based upon chromosomal makeup, external and internal genitals, ovaries or gonads, hormonal states, and secondary sex characteristics — body hair, voice pitch, and so on. We generally speak of a female as having 46XX chromosomes and female genitals, and a male as having 46 XY chromosomes and male genitals. However, there are within the two sexes variations in genetic and hormonal femaleness and maleness. An infant may be born with too many or too few X or Y chromosomes, giving it the genitals of one sex and the chromosomal makeup of the other. (This can be caused by excess hormonal secretions or injection of hormones into the pregnant mother.) Children may also be born who are true hermaphrodites, having the chromosomal pattern and genitals of both sexes.

Gender identity refers to the psychological state in which a person comes to believe "I am female" or "I am male." This is the first stage in gender development, and appears to be pretty well set by age three. In most instances, biological sex and gender identity correspond; that is, the child who is chromosomally female and has female genitals labels herself a girl, and the child who is chromosomally male and has male genitals labels himself a boy. However, there have been a number of cases of individuals whose gender identities do not match their genitals or chromosomes. In some of these cases the child was inaccurately labeled at birth because the child appeared to the doctor and parents to be a male, but turned out to be a female with an enlarged clitoris thought to be a penis. In other cases, a male child's penis was damaged (sometimes through faulty circumcision) and corrective surgery undertaken to remove all of the male genitalia; a vagina was created by plastic surgery later in life. *(See Box.)* What is important about these cases is that misassigned children appear to develop by age three a relatively stable gender identity, consistent with social labeling and not with biology.

The term *gender role* refers to learning and performing the socially accepted characteristics and behaviors for a given gender. In each society there are traits, interests, responsibilities, and actions defined as appropriate for females; others defined as appropriate for males; and some considered appropriate to both sexes. The first two sets of characteristics are called *sex-typed* behaviors, for they elicit different rewards and punishments when exhibited by males and females.

Theories of Gender Development

IMPACT OF FREUD

The psychoanalytic tradition of Sigmund Freud has been very influential in the study of gender, primarily in giving early direction to investigation and research. By focusing in part on biology, in part on cognition, and in part on social learning, it directs our attention to the main issues of child development, and stresses (perhaps too much) the priority of childhood in human development.

Case of the Unlucky Twin

In October 1963, a young couple took their identical twin boys to a physician to be circumcised. During the first operation, performed with an electric cauterizing needle, a surge of current burned off the baby's penis. Seeking a way to cope with this tragedy, the parents took the advice of sex experts: "Bring the baby up as a girl." The experiment has apparently succeeded. Aided by plastic surgery and reared as a daughter, the once normal baby boy has grown into a child who is psychologically, at least, a girl.

The change began at seventeen months with a girl's name and frilly clothes. An operation to make the child's genitals look more feminine was done, and plans were made to build a vagina and administer estrogen at a later age. The parents, counseled at the Johns Hopkins psychohormonal research unit, began to treat the child as if he were a girl. The effects of the parents' changed attitude and behavior were marked. "She doesn't like to be dirty," the mother told the clinic in one of her periodic reports. "My son is quite different. I can't wash his face for anything. She seems to be daintier. Maybe it's because I encourage it. She is very proud of herself when she puts on a new dress, and she just loves to have her hair set."

In another case, a newborn infant with only a rudimentary penis and other genital defects was "assigned" as a boy because he had two testes and the chromosome makeup of a male. With the realization that he could never be a normal man, experts decided when the boy was seventeen months old to give him a chance at happiness by reassigning him as a girl. A brother, two years older, was instrumental in helping the child develop a new feminine identity. To help the older boy accept the change, his parents explained that the doctors had made a mistake and that his little brother was really a little sister. Not long afterward, the big brother began to display a newly protective attitude. Reported the father: "Before, he was just as likely to stick his foot out and trip her as she went by; now he wants to hold her hand to make sure she doesn't fall."

[This case seems to offer strong evidence for the importance of social learning factors in the development of gender identity. It also illuminates elements of conventional gender role training—why should girls be daintier or cleaner, or want to wear cosmetics? Why should boys want to trip other boys and not girls? The cultural predisposition to gender-type young children strongly is at work, perhaps even more powerfully here because the parents are worried about male-type behavior emerging in the adolescent or adult gender identity or roles of their daughter.]

Biology was pivotal to Freudian theory of gender development, since the conduct of men and women was thought to originate in reproductive differences. Freud and his early followers thought the anatomical genital differences between men and women were the visible biological manifestation of their different reproductive and sexual purposes. This belief led to the phrase "anatomy is destiny." The Freudians also believed that the body itself had a certain wisdom or direction, that it knew in some mysterious way what it should turn out to be—the future gender role requirements of society were thus forecast in the anatomy of the child. (We must remember that practically nothing was known about genetics, hormones, or different cultures when Freudian theory was developed. It was therefore easy to generalize from middle-class life in central Europe to universal differences between men and women on the basis of the most obvious anatomical differences, and from the fact that only women could have children.)

A parallel psychological theory of gender role development was added to these biological factors by the early Freudians. The argument was that when an infant is born it is taken care of, fed, loved, and the like, by the mother. As a result, the child begins to identify with the mother. The mother is the first person to intrude into the self-centered egotism of infancy. The Freudians called this the *oral* stage of development (see Figure 2), and it happens to both male and female infants. In the second *(anal)* stage of early development, the role of the father becomes more important, and a significant set of emotional ties begins to be created, ties that often center around self control and discipline. Finally, in the last *(genital)* stage of early development, the child comes to identify itself with the same sex parent—young girls with mothers, young boys with fathers.

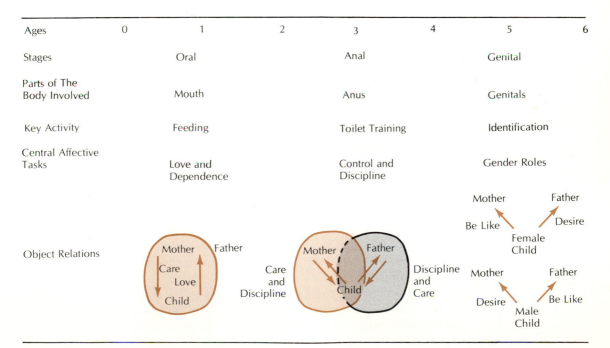

Ages	0	1	2	3	4	5	6
Stages		Oral		Anal		Genital	
Parts of The Body Involved		Mouth		Anus		Genitals	
Key Activity		Feeding		Toilet Training		Identification	
Central Affective Tasks		Love and Dependence		Control and Discipline		Gender Roles	

Figure 2. Freudian Model of Child Development.

The Freudians argued that the process of assuming gender roles is more difficult for boys than for girls, since a girl from the beginning learns to identify with her mother, an identification which is continuous into adulthood. A boy must detach himself from his mother and identify with his father—unlearning one attachment and forming a new one. A second difficulty in this process is that mothers commonly offer a great deal of affection and caring, while fathers are less affectionate and more authoritarian, making the transition more difficult.

The Oedipal crisis postulated by the Freudians is a critical stage, when males must learn to desire sex with women and to identify as a man with father. However, at the same time, the boy is also in competition with father for the affections of mother. The parallel (Electra) crisis for females was viewed as less traumatic, since, even though there is competition for father's affection, this competition does not have the added complication of gender identification.

The sexual aspects of Freudian theory are now largely unimportant, except among those still influenced by psychoanalytic theories. However, the process of gender-role modeling on the same-sex parent remains important to considerations of gender development.

BIOLOGICAL IMPERATIVE

One contemporary view of the way in which gender identities and gender roles develop is that men and women are fundamentally different as a function of biology. In this view, there has been over a long period of evolution a clear-cut division of labor between male and female nonhuman primates. In addition to differences in reproductive functions, there are different behaviors linked to biological differences. It would be very strange, the argument goes, if humans, given their long evolutionary history, escaped the processes which create innate sex differences.

This theory is based on the premise that since the appearance of the species, nearly all humanity has lived in hunting and gathering societies, with very differentiated roles between males and females: males were out in the wild chasing, attacking, and killing other animals; females were engaged largely in bearing and taking care of children, gathering ground nuts, and so on. After a few million years, a biological adaptation must have occurred, predisposing each sex to a different set of gender characteristics.

A natural corollary of this theory is that one sex is more "biologically fit" to do or be something than is the other sex. For example, men are perceived to be more dominant, more aggressive, more controlling, more managing; and women to be more passive, more reactive, more emotional. Margaret Mead, an influential anthropologist, uses the language of biological fitness (based on images of penis and vagina) when she says that men are more intrusive, and women more passive, receptive, and introspective.

In U.S. society, by and large, women have less sexual experience than men do, and are less responsive to certain erotic stimuli. In the biological determinism view, the explanation is that women have a lower sex drive because most of their energies are going into reproduction, and because sex is connected to male aggressiveness: The gender that approaches is more interested in sex than the gender being approached; among primates, males always or nearly always approach females.

According to this biological imperative view, innate structures condition the way in which male and female humans receive information from the world. They have different filtering systems for organizing and understanding information. It is as if the brain only lets in certain kinds of messages, so that, for example, being gentle with a boy is a different experience for him than being gentle with a girl is for her. Even treating male and female children exactly alike would not erase the differences between them. According to this theory, the organism possesses *before birth* a biological mechanism which directs it to become male or female, and which accounts for the later development of gender differences.

COGNITIVE SWITCH

Another perspective locates the information filter slightly later in life. It argues that children are born more or less neutral—that is, there are no important biological differences between boys and girls at birth which explain later gender differences. One of the central developmental tasks of early childhood, however, is to label oneself as either male or female. The point in time at which children learn "I am a boy" or "I am a girl" is a point after which self-identification seems fixed. The decision is cognitive, part of the pattern of growth in the organism. A mental filter of the sort discussed above is "inserted," and information from the social world is now coded in terms of a gender identity. Things, persons, and activities are labeled, "this is appropriate to whom I am" or "this is *not* appropriate to who I am." Messages coded in certain ways get through to boys, and those coded in other ways get through to girls.

By this view, the acquisition of a gender identity is a switching point in the child's life. The child is afterward less of a passive receptor, and becomes intentional in seeing the world in gender terms. The child cannot go back, because the process of acquiring gender identity is irreversible after age three or four. (Viewed as evidence of this is the apparent gender fixity of children assigned an incorrect biological sex at birth.) All gender-role performances that are socially coded as appropriate for men or women become thereafter more easily acquired by the child who possesses the "correct" filter. Because so many aspects of behavior depend on having a gender identity, an irreversible filter is considered a necessary part of human development, to be expected in all societies.

SOCIAL LEARNING AND LABELING

A third point of view, the one employed in this book, focuses on social learning, and the continuous construction and maintenance of gender roles throughout the life cycle. This perspective acknowledges that young children come to label themselves as "boy" or "girl" at an early age, that this is an important moment, and that often the child actively begins to use the label to organize its environment. However, it is clear that this label, demonstrated by the capacity to express the sentence "I am a boy (girl)" in a number of ways and situations, does not exhaust the content of gender roles or pick out unerringly the appropriate gender-typed stimuli. The child does not know most of the things that an adult knows, or believes or likes or feels. The two or three-year-old female does not know that a female is not likely to become President. She knows only that she uses the word "girl" to label herself, and that she is comfortable with that label.

Since there is no "natural" relationship between gender identity and gender-role performances, the child possesses a label with very little content. The label has a forward function, that is, it is used to organize the new things that happen. This is done by observing who works to earn the principal income, who is in charge of the housework, and who plays with cars or dolls. All of these activities are more or less gender typed, mostly by frequency rather than dramatic differences, and by verbal exhortations of what boys do and what girls do.

The stability of the sense of self as a male or female from this point of view does not depend only upon biological differences at birth, or a cognitive filter, but on the fact that the child's day-to-day situations continuously stabilize his/her sense of being male or female. Since males and females each have different social learning histories, we find gender differences in the behaviors and values of male and female children and adults. To understand our own sexuality, we must look at the kinds of arrangements we have made for the way men and women are supposed to behave in our society and the way they conceive of themselves. If you conceive of yourself as female, and you are put in circumstances where people in your society expect women to react in a certain way, the fact that you think of yourself as female shapes the way you react to those circumstances. Thus, in a society, there are always two factors that affect gender-role behavior: The demands of the social situation, and prior experience of being a girl or a boy.

Gender Identity and Social Change

What implications do the foregoing points of view have for social change? If male-female differences are basically innate, and biological differences account for the different psychological and social realities we daily observe among males and females, then attempts to change current patterns of male-female differences go against natural imperatives. That is, gender-role changes would violate natural tendencies and might create stress, anxiety, and physical and mental illness. Changing gender roles would "go against nature." By this view, women ought to be in the home taking care of babies and men ought to be out working, because these roles are thought to be continuations of our biological heritage. Tinkering with that heritage risks doing psychic damage to children. For example, it is considered risky for a father to take care of the children full-time while the mother works full-time, because fathers do not know how to "mother."

The view that people internalize a fixed gender identity (plus other things) early in life and that adult experiences are shaped by a gender-identity filter allows for some change, but says that action to change gender roles must focus on childhood. That is, efforts to alter socialization patterns must be presented to children before age three. Attempts at change later in life would be resisted by individuals because they have (1) a fixed self-identity, (2) internalized predispositions, or (3) a structured and integrated personality.

If what keeps us in our masculine-feminine roles is a combination of our beliefs and a system of labeled opportunities—that is, the sum of our ongoing social experience—then there is far more flexibility possible in our lives than we suppose. In order to produce change we do not need to go against biology or against our childhood or our personality, but against sets of socially visible arrangements. A woman could be a successful president of General Motors—neither nature nor early nurture is against it—the problem is that we do not let women be presidents of General Motors.

Socialization of Boys and Girls

How do parents influence gender differences in their children? Parents possess a set of gender-specific ideas of what their children need; that is, they were themselves socialized to some belief in what girls and boys of various ages are like. Through college courses and textbooks, the popular press, child-rearing manuals, "old wives' tales," admonitions from friends and relatives, reports from other parents, and adages (What are little girls made of? Sugar and spice and everything nice. What are little boys made of? Frogs and snails and puppy dogs' tails.), they have developed not only the construct "child," but the constructs "boy child" and "girl child," and they attach different expectations to them.

In addition, parents observe what they perceive as "typical behavior" of girls and boys their own child's age. They also have hopes, aspirations, and desires for what kinds of adults their children will be, what types of roles they hope they will play (however vaguely defined), and ideas about what types of adult "personality" characteristics are most valuable for effectively playing those roles.

BEFORE AND AT BIRTH

The different treatment of girls and boys can be viewed all along the age spectrum. Gender typing to some extent begins even before the child is born. Parents spend hours speculating about the sex of the as yet unborn child, often making guesses based upon the amount of kicking and other intrauterine behavior. Relatives and friends contribute, deciding whether the baby is "high" or "low," and making such comments as "With that much activity, it must be a boy!"

When the child arrives, the first characteristic noted is usually its gender. The doctor informs the mother and then the father, "It's a boy," or "It's a girl," before remarking on health, size, weight, and so on. This news is then transmitted to relatives or friends, either by word of mouth or through birth announcements which may say on the front in big letters, IT'S A GIRL! or IT'S A BOY! The relatives and friends respond with what they consider to be gender-appropriate gifts, such as frilly clothes for a girl and functional outfits for a boy.

The amused remarks of visitors during the first day echo the same sentiments—a boy is greeted with such comments as "Who knows, some day he may be President," or "With that size he'll grow up to be some football player." A girl is more likely to elicit such comments as "She's beautiful—she'll really knock the boys out when she grows up!" or "It won't be long before she's a mother too."

DURING INFANCY

During the first six months of life, mothers tend to look at and talk to girl infants more than boy infants, and mothers tend to respond to girls' irritability (crying) more immediately than they do to boys'. In fact, these behaviors tend to be greater for girls over the first two years of life. Boys, on the other hand, receive more touching, holding, rocking, and kissing than do girls in the first few months, but the situation is reversed by age six months. By one year, female infants are allowed and encouraged to spend significantly more time than males in touching and staying in close proximity to their mothers. The girls are encouraged to move away at later ages, but never as much as boys are.

Parents' interest in building autonomy or independence seems to explain this difference. As a function of societal stereotypes, mothers believe that boys rather than girls should be independent and encouraged to explore and master their world. They start to wean their sons from physical contact with them at an earlier age. Parents are more restrictive with their daughters and create more limits on their acceptable behavior from a very early age.

Parents' early treatment of their infants are usually not deliberate efforts to teach the child a "proper" gender role, but rather reflect the fact that the parents themselves accept the general societal roles for males and females. Sons are treated as though they are "naturally" sturdy and active; they are played with more roughly, and greeted with smiles and other indications of pleasure when they respond appropriately to this image. Girls are thought to be more delicate and sweet, and sweetness, docility, and lack of independence are likely to elicit parental approval.

AGE TWO AND UP

As the child moves from the infant to the toddler stage, somewhere around age two, gender-typing increases. Boys are told that "Boys don't cling to their mothers," and "Big boys don't cry." Boys' independence, aggression, and suppression of emotion are rewarded, and failure to comply brings increasing disapproval. Girls are encouraged to display opposite characteristics.

The toys children play with are also designed and labeled as being girls' toys or boys' toys. Girls are given dolls and dollhouses; boys get trucks and building blocks, and are told that they are "sissies" if they want to play with girls' toys. These labels come originally from adults, for it has been noted that at age two and a half, many boys prefer dolls and dollhouses, but are urged away from them because they are considered by parents to be girls' toys. The parental responses are quickly absorbed by the children, who shortly thereafter display quite different toy and game preferences.

Physical appearance is tied to social definitions of masculinity and femininity. Girls are rewarded for their looks and for appearing attractive, while boys are more frequently rewarded for physical performance. These differences continue well into adolescence. Girls are taught to capitalize on good looks, cuteness, and coyness, and learn to look in mirrors and seek reflections of themselves from others. Boys discover that athletic prowess is what counts for males.

Gender Differences in the World of Play

The general play activities of boys and girls differ more and more as children grow older. As a rule, most boys engage in adventurous group play with fairly elaborate rules—cops and robbers, war games, cowboys and Indians, and explorations in woods and old houses. With some exceptions, girls tend to play "house," jump rope, play hopscotch, color, play with paper dolls and real dolls—activities less adventuresome and more individual. Such girls' activities keep them in a safe place; the boys' activities described above involve more movement and exploration. Jump rope and hopscotch can be played on sidewalk or driveway, in view of mother's watchful eye. Baseball requires a baseball diamond, often blocks away, and cowboys and Indians may lead the players all around a neighborhood "Wild West."

The differences extent to sports: girls typically engage in dancing, swimming, skating, horseback riding—activities involving little team effort or competition. Typical boys' sports, such as baseball, football, and basketball, are competitive team games, with elaborate rules and strategy. In addition, girls' activities are toned down to protect them from dirt and sweat ("unladylike") and possible disfigurement (considered a more serious problem for girls than for boys). Because of these concerns, girls are "banned" from some sports and allowed to play others only under simpler rules (e.g., touch or flag football).

One result of these differences is that girls get less sports practice; over time, they become less adept in competition with their male peers. They are forced out of many sports activities defined as "for boys only" and pushed to "girls'" endeavors. Parents are often less willing to buy good sports equipment for girls, for example, a good baseball mitt or a home basketball net for practice. Even the sneakers designed for girls are less suitable for running and playing than those for boys.

The concern with sports which tends to engulf many young boys in the five to eleven age bracket divides them from young girls not only during the time they are actively at play. Many "quiet" at-home games for boys are sports related, and to the extent that girls are discouraged from the "real" play, they are less likely to be interested in observation or simulation. At home, boys may play with an electric basketball game or football game, or may read and discuss with friends the scores and standings of favorite teams. Boys collect and trade sports cards, while girls may collect and trade cards with pretty scenes or ballerinas or horses. Boys acquire the badges of successful adult sports heroes: baseball caps and football jackets, for example, which reinforce their sports-mindedness and separation from girls, whose success models, such as movie stars and models, tend to physical beauty and attractive clothes rather than athletic prowess.

The dolls for older girls are less "infant dolls" to be fed, burped, wrapped in a blanket, and put in a carriage, and more of the Barbie and Ken type: "hip" teenagers with lots of clothes to wear, beach buggies to drive, and dances to go to. When we give Barbie dolls to eight-year-old girls, we are telling them that a girl should look good cosmetically. Little girls get the idea, "This is what I ought to look like."

None of this is sexual knowledge in a strict sense, but it conditions the sexual. If we tell young girls that they really want to be mommies, then the social stereotype of "mommy" begins to shape all the other things a girl does and wants. But we do not tell them that they might want to choose the people they date, be autonomous, or enjoy sex and be good in bed. What happens is that children come to know that somewhere in the future they are going to be married, be a mommy or a daddy. They do not know what goes on between here and there. They have no knowledge of the process by which one gets from being five or ten years old to being an adult mother or father. What children get is the desire to be married parents, and it is that desire that is strongly encouraged.

Early gender distinctions are far from absolute. Some girls are "tomboys," preferring active sports to doll play, ballet, jump rope, and baking brownies. Many are "allowed" to play in informal neighborhood games when extra players are needed. But as sports become more formal and controlled and sponsored by adults (such as the Little League), the doors (until recently) close to females, whatever their skill level.

For boys, the opportunities to play at girls' games are rare; the label "sissy" is more negative than the label "tomboy." There is a series of boy things that are all right for girls to do. But, by and large, there is no transfer the other way. It does not seem to be the male role that is in question, but the female role. Both men and women regard the female role as less important than the male, and the implication is that women can get better by being like men. But it does not work the other way: men cannot get better by being like women. It is a one-way street.

Of course, little boys do play with special kinds of dolls—male-role dolls such as "GI Joe" and "Big Jim." Some people find these dolls disturbing because we seem to be saying, "Young man, we have a war for you in your future. So we're going to start teaching you how to kill by arming your dolls with submachine guns and grenades." Since the Viet Nam War there has been a great increase of these male-action dolls, which are almost invariably either military or paramilitary figures. There are no professionals who may, as a result of physical activity, do something virtuous that does not involve spilled blood: forest rangers, for example.

School and Media Influences on Gender Development

During the five to eleven age range, other influences in the child's life begin to assume greater importance. Until then parents control the child's life and are the salient figures in it. When the child enters school, the locus of control shifts. Other adults (teachers) and children outside the circle of neighborhood and family contribute to definitions of masculinity and femininity, and reward or punish the child for conformity or deviance. In addition, the child is exposed to media depictions which contain obvious and subtle messages about how to be a boy or girl, a man or woman.

In nursery schools and kindergarten classes, we often find the heavy blocks, truck, airplanes, and carpentry tools in one place, and the dolls and homemaking equipment in another. While they may be officially "open" to anyone for play, the areas are often sex-segregated by invisible but real boundaries. In the elementary school years, the informal play during out-of-school hours involves different sports, different rules, and different playground activities.

Field & Stream takes you to A Man's Place

All your senses are alive to enjoy a day like this in A Man's Place. You're ready to appreciate the easy taste and great outdoor aroma of Field & Stream pipe tobacco.

A quality product of Philip Morris U.S.A.

There are few real cowboys left, but "cowboy" continues to be one of our most pervasive media symbols of what it means to be a man.

In the classroom, girls may be taught home economics, while boys take shop and later auto mechanics. These curricular differences are justified on grounds of different interests ("We could let a girl take shop if she wanted to, but we find that the girls all prefer sewing") and the belief that boys eventually will be providers, and their home concerns will be repair and building, while girls eventually will be homemakers. The school activities are seen as appropriate preparation.

Teachers' attitudes are often much like those of parents. Many teachers perceive boys as active, capable of expressing anger, quarrelsome, punitive, alibi building, and exhibitionistic, and perceive girls as affectionate, obedient, responsive, and tenacious. When boys "put girls down," as they often do at that age, teachers (female usually) often say and do nothing to correct them, thus encouraging their notion of superiority. Many teachers assume that girls are likely to "love" reading and "hate" mathematics and sciences, and expect the opposite of boys.

Boys and girls are separated and treated differently in a variety of ways. They are often lined up separately for assemblies, separated in seating arrangements, and placed on opposing teams for spelling bees and other competitions. Such separation supports the desire of little boys for exclusiveness; they generally already understand their superior social status. Girls serve the cookies and punch during school parties while boys move the furniture and carry the books. Boys are permitted to engage in considerably more physical activity and make more noise in the classroom.

The sexes are probably most frequently separated throughout the school year for discussions of hygiene and sex education, a procedure likely to ensure poor communication later between the genders on the subject of sex.

The image of masculinity that develops during school days is one of increasing attachment to achievement, competition, winning, and desire for an occupation. In contrast, the image of femininity is one of being compliant, dependent, and passive. Are these images of the growing boy and girl really accurate? Girls actually do better in school than boys, until puberty. However, adults tend to discount the facts in order to support the view that males are more achievement-oriented than females. The good grades of girls are not seen as a result of hard work, desire to achieve, or competitiveness, but as a result of conformity to adult desire.

Children's Books

Early in the school years, children learn to read, thus opening a new source of influence. Do these materials counter sex typing? Until recently, studies of children's books and anthologies consistently reported traditional sex differences and pro-male biases. *(See Box.)* Females have been vastly under-represented in pictures, in titles, and as main characters, often being completely absent. In addition, female characters have usually been cast in insignificant or secondary roles. Their activities were limited to loving, watching, or helping, while males engaged in adventuring and solving problems. Women were not given a job or profession; motherhood was presented as a full-time, lifetime job. In autobiographies, the tendency has been to portray a woman as dependent — for instance, Madame Curie as a helpmate to her husband, rather than as a partner.

Among the Caldecott winners and runners-up in the period 1967 to 1971, there were eleven times as many males in pictures as females. For animals with obvious genders (e.g., Peter Rabbit, Brer Rabbit, The Little Hen) the male/female ratio was 95 to 1; in the titles, the ratio was 8 to 3.

In a 1971 review of textbooks that were adopted or recommended for second through sixth grade use in California, 75% of the stories' main characters were male, and more than 80% of the story space was devoted to male characters. In illustrations, only 15% of those shown were girls or women, most appearing only as background figures.

A Princeton-based group, Women on Words and Images, found the following ratios in 134 anthologies with 2760 stories:

	MALE:FEMALE
Boy-centered stories to girl-centered stories	5:2
Adult male main characters to adult female main characters	3:1
Male biographies to female biographies	6:1
Male animal stories to female animal stories	2:1
Male folk or fantasy stories to female folk or fantasy stories	4:1

Television

Television takes vast chunks of its time to deliver entertainment and commercial messages to younger children as well as to those in school. There are programs for pre-schoolers in the morning, for school children when they have returned from school, and for all children every Saturday morning. For many children this is one of their largest commitments of time; for parents it serves as a built-in baby sitter.

The presentation of gender roles on television has been quite similar to that of children's readers, the playground, and the schools. Boys are the centerpiece of a story; they do things and occupy the valued roles. Girls serve as backdrop, are helpful and caring, and occupy the less valued roles. Commercials for children on Saturday morning usually depict boys driving cars or playing with trucks and girls playing with dolls. There has been some pressure to eliminate gender stereotyping in both commercials and show content, but television shows are linked into a gender stereotyped system — the toy manufacturers sell gender-linked toys, parents buy gender-linked toys, and the writers often take their stories from already existing materials for children.

Television commercials are especially powerful, probably more powerful than the shows themselves, because they are designed to persuade. Commercials also link gender roles with the significant adult roles that the young will be playing in the future. The narrators are nearly all men — the authoritative voice advising you what to buy — which indicates who the experts are. Similarly, gender-role stereotypes are attached to consumption, one of the most valued activities in U.S. society. By linking material benefit to gender roles, the commercials teach a powerful lesson — if you consume this is the kind of man or woman you can be.

Beyond the children's hours, we find similar cartoon-like people in the evening programs that show men and women relating to each other. Even the characters in more contemporary shows, which show single or divorced women, are careful to watch their morals and make sure they marry for love. When a hard choice is made, love or children always come first. These shows offer us women who appear to be Mary Poppins in the singles scene, Mary Poppins divorced, or Mary Poppins teaching about sex — in contrast to the grim recital of parental and childhood disaster that occurs in the police and medical shows that take up the rest of prime time.

Consequences of the Various Media

Media presentations do not have an immediate effect. Most children possess a variety of gender ideas; they also must negotiate in a real world. Thus, media representations become just one more element in a child's process of organizing his or her own ideas of gender roles. Nor are media effects dramatic as a rule, for most of human learning is a steady accumulation of information, attitudes, and ways of responding. The media are simply another push toward accepting current arrangements as if they were natural, right, and preordained ways of doing things.

The bias in media presentations, however, is more complex than mere stereotyping, for the story roles of males are extraordinarily removed from reality. There are no stories about working in an office, nor any that explore the reality of the factory line or glorify the role of the salesman. Boys are encouraged to aim for the top, the levels of achievement most highly valued in U.S. society. The sad truth is that most males will have routine adulthoods, lacking any of the high adventures they have been taught to expect. The male roles depict independence, aggressiveness, courage, emotional control, and toughness. In contrast, the female roles emphasize dependence, conformity, nonaggression, and emotion.

The problem of emotional expression is especially important, since it is critical to intimate relations with others. Clearly not all young boys want to be like John Wayne, but that stereotype of male emotional control represents a constant limitation on the open expression of fear, indecision, or worry—or perhaps more important, joy, delight, and love. Yet the emotional role left to women is often more paralyzing than expressive. A woman's pleasure in life is supposed to depend on a man. Pleasing a man is seen as more important to a woman than pleasing herself; her emotions are to be connected to relations with men and with children, rather than to the other pleasures and pains of life.

Scientific Findings on Male-Female Differences

We observe in parental behavior, in toys, on playgrounds, in schools, in books, and on television a fairly consistent differentiation among children and young people on the basis of sex. The process is constant and cumulative, beginning early in life and continuing in nearly every social context. There are very few gender-neutral environments in U.S. society. Yet, when the young are studied in research situations, few of our stereotypes about gender behavior are confirmed. Males and females can be trained for a vast array of characteristics, and male-female distributions along this array overlap extensively. Since only small actual differences are found between girls and boys, how do we account for the relative ineffectiveness of socialization activities (toys, play, television, schools) in shaping the behavior of children in psychological experiments, and yet the continuing assignment to children and adults of roles on the basis of gender typing?

The question can only be given a speculative answer. It appears that most psychological experiments offer boys and girls an opportunity to perform similar tasks without labeling the tasks as gender-appropriate. In these contexts, males and females perform mostly alike. It would appear that the real strength of gender typing does not reside in the child, but in the environments in which the child finds itself. The social environment is full of both gender-typed messages and activity segregation. It may be that the child does not possess an internalized gender role, but that social arrangements continually reinforce gender differences. In a gender-neutral experiment, social requirements are removed, so the child does not behave in accord with a gender stereotype. Perhaps it is not internalized beliefs that keep us in place as men or women, but rather our interpersonal and social environments. As there is considerable variation in what men and women actually do, it may require the weight of social organization and constant reinforcement to maintain gender-role differences.

EARLY LEARNING
OF SEXUALITY

*The usual goal of socialization
is to make the future safe for the past.*
William Simon

FROM VERY EARLY ON, CHILDREN DO THINGS THAT ADULTS INTERPRET AS BEING sexual. An infant touches its genitals, a child repeats words it has overheard on the street (or at home), two children play "Show me yours and I'll show you mine," a child asks where babies come from—all of these are "sexual" occasions which usually provoke a response from adults. The kind of response produced will depend on the ideas that an adult has about children in general and about sexuality in particular. However, we should not expect the responses of most adults to be always consistent in tone or purpose. Even people with well-developed theories of sexuality and human development have a hard time applying their theories to concrete situations, particularly when those situations involve their own children.

Most adults base their judgments on the factors in individual situations, as well as what they think the relative merits might be of interfering or not interfering. If two children playing "show me" are very young, the adult may decide that the children do not know what they are doing, and that it is "cute." On the other hand, if the children are ten or eleven and they are two boys, the adult may react very strongly. If the activity looks like the more taboo forms of adult sex (children involved in pretend intercourse); if the activity involves a daughter; if the activity involves only children of the same sex; or if the activity can produce shame or embarrassment in the neighborhood, then adults usually react strongly. Activity in private, involving younger children of opposite sexes, often evokes only the mildest of admonitions, if any response at all.

Most adults want children to grow up heterosexual, get married, and have children of their own, yet parents and other caretakers are expected not to allow the children under their control to do anything bad or embarrassing sexually between the time they are born and the time they get married. At the same time caretakers are told that what they do and do not do with children (the "what" is rarely specified) will have a profound impact on the child's adult life. Adults are caught in an impossible situation. On the one hand, it is important that children *should not* do anything sexual before they are supposed to; on the other hand, adults *should* play some positive role in developing children's sexuality.

At the center of the parental dilemma is the fact that practically nothing sexual anyone does prior to getting married is overtly supported or approved by society.

Adults are required either to suppress or to keep under cover their children's "sexual" activities, to set limits in adolescence on sexual experimentation, and then hope that their children will have happy adult sex lives. It would take parents with a strong ideological commitment to a particular sexual viewpoint and profound self-confidence to teach their own children to be overtly sexual. To teach children to masturbate; to provide sexual learning by taking children into the parental bed during intercourse (not only as babies but also as older children); to approve of homosexual experiences their children may have; not only to approve but to celebrate sexual activity — the decisions to do these things are probably for most people beyond imagining, much less action. Even if parents wanted to teach their children about sex in these ways, few would be prepared to take the risk of going against social convention. Most parents, even revolutionaries, train their children to live in the society that exists, not the society they want to exist.

Traditional Views

The practical dilemma of adults is not improved by either the folkloristic sexual ideas that they have or the fragmentary versions of psycho-sexual theories of development that they might possess. Prior to the sexual revolution at the end of the nineteenth century, Christian views and medical versions of these views were the predominant set of ideas about the sexuality of children. These theories emphasized the naturally sinful character of children, including their sexual acts. Apparent sexual activity by children thus required repression and control to prevent it from going any further. The sexual instinct was dangerous and corrupting, and children required discipline and control to make sure that it did not appear. The sexual impulse was within the child, and without external repression would express itself. *This view is still common today among many people, and it guides their behavior when they are confronted with "sexuality" among children.*

A variant of this point of view puts the blame not on the internal impulses of the children, but on the corrupting character of the environment. Agreeing with the sex-is-evil theorists that sexual expression by the young is bad, they locate the problem not in the child, but in the interaction between corruptible humanity and evil society. By purifying the external world, innocence can be maintained and the child can grow up to become a proper sexual adult. The practical procedures are similar to the "sex is evil" perspective, but are usually less repressive toward children. Such a tradition requires careful information control over the environments of the child and suppression of sexual activity when it appears.

These points of view are shared by most contemporary U.S. adults, and are particularly important in justifying responses to disapproved forms of "sexual" activity among children. The two traditions view sex as at worst a basic evil, and at best a problem, so the way to deal with it in children is to keep them ignorant, busy, and punished.

What modern sex theorists in general and Freud in particular did was make sex central to development, to say that sexual energies were given meanings by and attached to real people in the family. The Victorians thought they could manage the information given to children to prevent their being corrupted sexually (even though they thought children could be corrupted very easily); Freud said that was not possible, that only through the expression of sexuality in development could children become adults at all.

Freud sexualized *all* of the experiences of childhood. The innocent activity of breast feeding, an expression of mother love, became a form of eroticism for both infant and mother. The attachment of adult men to the breast as a sex object could be traced to this innocent activity. Biting the nipple near the end of breast feeding was an early indicator of the sadistic impulse. Toilet training to control the bladder and sphincter was the basis for anal eroticism. At the genital stage, the family became a dark forest of confused and competing erotic desires. Incestuous desires of the child for the parent of the opposite sex were countered by fears of castration among boys and perhaps fantasized castrations among girls (the problem of penis envy). In these crises of sexual identification, the meanings of the genitals are fixed. For some years (from five to eleven, the latency period) these crises go underground, until the biological pressures of puberty push to the surface again the child's incestuous desires, which are then suppressed so that children can give up their parents as sexual objects and move on toward genital maturity.

All the things Victorians thought they could prevent their children from knowing — Freud said they happened to everyone. Everything was connected to sex, to perversion, to eroticism — sadism, masochism, homosexuality, incest, castration, lust — all were hidden behind the romanticized family. No wonder Freud was controversial in Europe, and no wonder the versions we read of him today are scrubbed up. The modern sex books for children usually bypass most of this erotic underpinning, and tell us that many of the "sexual" things we see children do and say are quite natural; as long as we do not make an issue of it, children will probably develop into adequate sexual adults.

Meaning of Childhood Sexuality

Most people assume that children give the same or similar meaning to activities that adults interpret as sexual. Nearly all theories of psycho-sexual development ignore the fundamental problem of how the organism learns to label, experience, and desire what it is doing as sexual. It is only *after* people have gone through the experiences of development that they come to believe that those experiences are sexual. Sexuality is a domain of connected activities and ideas that we accumulate and assemble through growing up in a particular time and place. To the actor, masturbation as an adult has quite different meaning than genital experimentation as an adolescent, or genital touching as a three-year-old. Most of the past meanings are probably lost, particularly those of children. All the observers can do is *watch and infer;* they cannot know what the child is experiencing or what meaning the child is giving to the activity.

Imputing an adult version of a sexual experience to a child is an error. It is equally an error to assume that the meanings given to the activity early in life have any simple or direct connection with what the activity will mean in the future. The meaning given to a sexual activity may change radically as we move from relationship to relationship, from age to age, from one time and place to another. The meanings are not fixed; if they were, we would feel like children all our lives.

From an adult point of view this appears to be very sexy; from the children's point of view it is a playful imitation of the mass media.

The supposed and actual significances of adult-child interaction are in ironic opposition. The way adults behave toward children affects their sexuality—not by suppressing or controlling it, but in *creating* it. When adults react or do not react to what children do "sexually," they are creating what sexuality *will be* for the child (not what it is). Thus, an adult who stops a child from touching its genitals is not suppressing some natural urge, but taking one activity among many others and giving it a particular meaning. Adults by their responses create and shape domains of activity, feelings, ideas, and beliefs that in adulthood become sexual (or political or economic) domains. When adults have acquired such beliefs, they look backward from the perspective of those beliefs and assume that they have had them all of their lives, and that children must feel that way as well.

That adults help create sexual meanings for children is not the whole story; most things that children do are not done where adults can see them. Children do have unsupervised spaces in which to improvise. Adults only supply certain cognitive elements to aid children in making sense of the world around them. Keeping the body covered, what to do with the genitals, how to feel about the opposite sex are all taught in separate circumstances—the assembly of these items of information and action into a primitive script is usually left to the child. Whether activities are noticed or ignored, children may go on with them in private; stop; or do something else because their attention wanders. The "sexual" activity of the child does not become sexual through a series of dramatic events (psychoanalysis often creates the impression of single traumatic events shaping people's lives forever), but rather through a slow process of gathering information, doing some experiments, and eventually coming up with a modestly consistent set of activities that the person and the people around him or her think are sexual.

Sex as Play, Play as Sex

The problem of meaning must be considered in examining the two major areas of overt activity among children that are labeled as sexual in U. S. culture. The first is relatively common among infants and young children — touching the genitals. At one time that activity was suppressed by adults on behalf of the general taboo against masturbation. Such activities are now often viewed as "natural," or expressing some normal aspect of childhood sexuality. Parents are often counseled not to interfere with such activities (either because they will go away or because they are a good thing). It is assumed that such activities have a sexual meaning to the child. In fact we do not know what such activities mean to the infant, or even to older children. When parents ask older children why they are doing such things, they often reply that it feels good, but that does not tell us if the child considers the activity as sexual in any adult sense.

Kinsey and other observers report that many events adults associate with the sexual response cycle occur to infants and young children:

Orgasm has been observed in boys of every age from 5 months to adolescence. Orgasm is in our records for a female babe of 4 months. The orgasm in an infant or other young male is, except for the lack of an ejaculation, a striking duplicate of orgasm in an older adult. The behavior involves a series of gradual physiologic changes, the development of rhythmic body movements with distinct penis throbs and pelvic thrusts, an obvious change in sensory capacities, a final tension of muscles, especially of the abdomen, hips, and back, a sudden release with convulsions, including rhythmic anal contractions — followed by the disappearance of all symptoms. A fretful babe quiets down under the initial sexual stimulation, is distracted from other activities, begins rhythmic pelvic thrusts, becomes tense as climax approaches, is thrown into convulsive action, often with violent arm and leg movements, sometimes with weeping at the moment of climax. After climax the child loses erection quickly and subsides into the calm and peace that typically follows adult orgasm. It may be some time before erection can be induced again after such an experience. There are observations of 16 males up to 11 months of age, with such typical orgasm reached in 7 cases. In 5 cases of young pre-adolescents, observations were continued over periods of months or years, until the individuals were old enough to make it certain that true orgasm was involved; and in all of these cases the later reactions were so similar to the earlier behavior that there could be no doubt of the orgastic nature of the first experience. (Kinsey et al. *Sexual Behavior in the Human Male*, 1948, p. 177.)

The typical reactions of a small girl in orgasm, seen by an intelligent mother who had frequently observed her three-year-old in masturbation, were described as follows: "Lying face down on the bed, with her knees drawn up, she started rhythmic pelvic thrusts, about one second or less apart. The thrusts were primarily pelvic, with the legs tensed in a fixed position. The forward components of the thrusts were in a smooth and perfect rhythm which was unbroken except for momentary pauses during which the genitalia were readjusted against the doll on which they were pressed; the return from each thrust was convulsive, jerky. There were 44 thrusts in unbroken rhythm, a slight momentary pause, 87 thrusts followed by a slight momentary pause, then 10 thrusts, and then a cessation of all movement. There was marked concentration and intense breathing with abrupt jerks as orgasm approached. She was completely oblivious to everything during these later stages of the activity. Her eyes were glassy and fixed in a vacant stare. There was noticeable relief and relaxation after orgasm. A second series of reactions began two minutes later with series of 48, 18, and 57 thrusts, with slight momentary pauses between each series. With the mounting tensions, there were audible gasps, but immediately following the cessation of pelvic thrusts there was complete relaxation and only desultory movements thereafter."

We have similar records of observations made by some of our other subjects on a total of 7 pre-adolescent girls and 27 pre-adolescent boys under four years of age (see our 1948: 175–181). These data indicate that the capacity to respond to the point of orgasm is certainly present in at least some young children, both female and male. (Kinsey et al., *Sexual Behavior in the Human Female*, 1953, pp. 104–105.)

What meaning is to be given to these events, in terms of the sexual history of the child? We have no evidence that children who have such experiences are more or less interested in sex than other children who do not have them, nor are we sure what the experiences mean to the child. Kinsey does report that some young boys who had had such experience were "aggressive in seeking contacts." The dilemma here is that much of this information comes from adults who were in active sexual contact with these boys and who were interested in producing orgasm in them.[1] The aggressive seeking by the boys may be an adult interpretation based on feelings of guilt (the boys really wanted it), along with adults having created a particular set of training experiences for the boys.

In any case, there does appear to be something that could be called a competence for orgasm that can be realized at a very early age. What is more important is determining what activities or social circumstances might sustain the interest and contribute to the desire of young boys or girls to continue the activity. The reasons offered by the young are unlikely to be the reasons offered by adults, which are learned somewhat later in life.

The ability to have orgasm does not seem to create a self-sustaining desire; that is, even if a child has had an orgasm it does not automatically seek another. Orgasm, like other activities, must be placed in a social and psychological context in which seeking it is part of socially scripted activity:

The record suggests that the physiologic mechanism of any emotional response (anger, fright, pain, etc.) may be the basic mechanism of sexual response. Originally the pre-adolescent boy erects indiscriminately to the whole array of emotional situations, whether they be sexual or non-sexual in nature. By his late teens the male has been so conditioned that he rarely responds to anything except a direct physical stimulation of genitalia, or to psychic situations that are specifically sexual. In the still older male even physical stimulation is rarely effective unless accompanied by such a psychologic atmosphere. *The picture is that of the*

1. A less neutral observer than Kinsey would have described these events as sex crimes, since they involved sexual contact between adults and children. Whether or not these observers were "scientifically trained," it seems advisable to use caution in interpreting their "findings." At the same time, the observations should not be ruled out simply because they emerged from illegal or stressful situations.

psycho-sexual emerging from a much more generalized and basic physiologic capacity which becomes sexual, as an adult knows it, through experience and conditioning. (Kinsey, 1948, p. 165; italics added.)

It is possible to imagine a social order that does make orgasm an early and constant activity on the part of the child, an activity as important as eating, running, jumping, getting good grades, learning to read and to smile. It could even be made gender-specific, through the mechanisms described in Chapter 4. In such a society it is likely that orgasm and orgasm seeking would be characteristic of most children; however, it would be so not because of the innate desire to have orgasm, but because the activity was socially highly valued. If orgasm were a natural phenomenon and the outcome of a strong drive, many more people should have it than there is any evidence for.

The second major overt activity defined as sexual that children engage in before puberty is same-gender and cross-gender sex play. About one in every two adults asked if they had any sex play before puberty will recall something of that sort. Such activities may involve showing their genitals to others, or being shown others' genitals, touching others' genitals, perhaps having simulated coitus, or sometimes oral-genital contacts.[2]

It is important to focus on the social-psychological nature of these experiences. Much of this experience, particularly among younger children, seems to result from curiosity about the forbidden, or from imitating the activities of adults or slightly older children. It occurs in the context of children's games and is commonly done for children's purposes: "The sexual nature of these games is not always understood by the child; and even when the small boy lies on the top of the small girl and makes what may resemble copulatory movement, there is often no realization that genital contact might be made, or that there might be an erotic reward in such activity." (Kinsey, 1953, p. 108.)

When we think of preadolescent activities that look sexual—we, as adults, looking back on it, or as parents looking at it in our children—we respond to the sexual aspect: the *sex* is very important; the *play* is unimportant. To the child, however, the balance is exactly the opposite. The play is the major part; whatever sex might be in it, is mainly interesting because it is forbidden, like mommy's jewel box or daddy's tool chest.

Children are active and curious, and if they live in a world where the sexual parts of the body are hidden, they wonder what the parts look like, and they wonder what happens when the parts are touched. Most children in various phases of development will take a look to see what is going on, not because they are interested in the sexual, but because they are curious about the forbidden. It is not that they are erotically aroused by one another's genitals, in the sense that adults are aroused, it is that the mysterious parts of other people's bodies are not otherwise visible.

2. In the Kinsey research, about forty-five percent of the adult women interviewed recalled engaging in some form of sex play by age twelve. About thirty percent of that group recalled sex-play experience with girls and a similar proportion with boys. The comparable figures for the adult males interviewed was fifty-seven percent, of which forty-eight percent recalled experience with boys and forty percent with girls. A study of early adolescent males in the 1940s increased the incidence of sex play for males to seven out of ten. The experiences ranged from casual exhibition to coitus and oral sex; most of the latter occurred about the age of puberty.

Adults should also note that sexual forms of childhood play are often vocational in character. That is, children give one another job labels when they do these things. Who, in this society, is allowed to look at someone else's naked body? A doctor. Who usually plays the doctor? The boy. Who usually plays the nurse? The girl. Vocational context plus gender-role rules are what script the activity.

The fact that children do not have sex play very often (adults recall rates of two or three times between ages six and twelve) indicates the low level of interest sex play has for most children, in comparison to the rewarded activities of this age period. In U. S. society, where children have a good deal of privacy and where there is a minimal amount of sexual information given, there is not a large amount of sex play among young children. Without specific social and psychological linking of activities to socially valued actions, such activity will not occur with any regularity. This suggests why there is a sudden upsurge of sexual activity in adolescence, when such activity becomes part of the overt social and covert sexual definitions of young people.

From all of the evidence we have, there is little effect of these sexual patterns on adulthood. Kinsey concluded that there is an important transition from pre-pubertal activity to post-pubertal activity among some males. However, Kinsey considered an activity (say, genital play) to be continuous and influential if it recurred within a two-year span (occurring at age twelve; first ejaculation at age thirteen; a similar activity occurring again during the thirteenth year). This is a remarkably weak connection. In addition, most of the continuity data was from that part of the Kinsey male sample who had had the most criminal experience. As a consequence, extreme caution must be used in interpreting this data. What seems most reasonable to argue is that for most young people pre-adolescent experience has no significant effect on post-adolescent sexual adjustment, and that the very nature of sexuality changes as it becomes linked to a new set of scripts. Kinsey himself said as much:

The sexual life of the younger boy is more or less a part of his other play; it is usually sporadic, and (under the restrictions imposed by our social structure) it may be without overt manifestation in a fair number of cases. The sexual life of the older male is, on the other hand, an end in itself, and (in spite of our social organization) in nearly all boys its overt manifestations become frequent and regular, soon after the onset of adolescence. (Kinsey, 1948, p. 182.)

Sources of Information

Prior to the twentieth century rise of the middle class and the increase in privacy, most people learned about sex in part by direct observation. This satisfies at least one of the conditions of effective learning—the opportunity to see what is done and observe admired people when they are doing it. In the same way, an admired teacher can interest a student in scholarship and learning by being a role model, by being scholarly and learned in front of the student.

A second condition of successful learning is the opportunity to learn without being constantly worried about failing. Fear of failure contributes to many sexual learning disasters. Young people learning about sex in U. S. society rarely see anyone they care about have sex, and even more rarely do they have an opportunity to practice sex in relaxed circumstances.

Children have a wide range of informational inputs to their behavior as they move from birth to puberty, acquiring some aspects of behavior (the most important of which are gender roles, as described in Chapter 4) that will be used in sexual activity when they are adults. The sources of information are varied, and enter at different moments in development. The movement is from parental dominance of information, to a shared parent-media information system, to the addition of peers, and then to the school. What occurs is a decline in parental information control as the child grows older, a decline that is accelerated by the progress of the child into the school system. It is not so much that the school supplies information, but rather that parental supervision is reduced. Each of these channels also contributes different messages and with different force.

Parents make major contributions to gender-role definitions, which serve as a primary way to organize new experience. They offer the first tilt toward heterosexuality by creating an adult pair model of man-woman rather than woman-woman or man-man. They are the primary models for affection and caring, though they are not specifically sexual models.

The media system first contributes by reinforcing conventional gender-role activities, and as children grow older it offers models for masculinity and femininity, male-female relations, male-male relations and female-female relations. The media tell children who is important and significant in the world.

Schools usually offer only an institutional context for children to act in. Rarely do they contribute sexual information to young people until around or after early adolescence. Most of them make no formal contribution at all. However, they do continue patterns of gender-role differentiation, reward particular kinds of female-male activity, and reinforce what women and men do. Children in school live in a world formally as asexual as that of the family.

Peers are the major information source for young people. They supply most of the sex information that young people have in whatever form it appears. They are the others that children have sex play with, talk to, tell jokes with, go out with, and share information with. It is the covert information system of peers that makes the critical contribution to whatever sexual knowledge most children get. Peers tend to fill in, as best they can, the actual concrete aspects of the doing of sex.

ROLE OF PARENTS

Parents offer younger children sexual information in part by the physical ways they relate to each other. Even though most parents do not talk about sex to their children, they do set an example for the ways in which women and men relate when they are supposed to care about each other. Children notice whether their parents touch each other, and how often. The hug and kiss, the affectionate gesture, the touch on the arm, the slightly erotic response, are all forms of information. None of them are very dramatic, but they are cues about what people enjoy. Children also notice if parents rarely touch each other, or if they are careful not to do so in front of their children. The meanings are not precise, such behavior does not hang a "don't touch me" label on one sex or another, but it offers a model for interaction.

Part of this information is linked to access to the parental bedroom, under what conditions and what time of day. Can children come and romp in the bed, sleep with parents, or come in without knocking? If parents are interrupted during inter-course, what do they do? How do they respond? Do they go on; stop; or pretend to be doing something else? Do they invite the child in, say what they are doing, or continue in front of the child? Each of these responses tells the child something about the world, and the exchanges between men and women, even when the child does not know what the actual content of that world is.

Part of this learning process is about exposure of the body. Most parents create sets of rules about modesty, rules that increase in severity as children come closer to puberty. Such rules set the limits on who is naked, when, and who can see. Who can share the bathroom? Who can take showers together? At what ages do these things stop? All of these events tell children what responses they should have to their bodies and to the bodies of others.

The problem the Freudians have raised about the dangers of the primal scene, that is, parents having sex in front of their children, is a problem created by the ris-ing affluence and housing practices of the middle classes all over the world. In the past most families lived in one room and children learned what their parents did sexually by hearing the activity at night, seeing it in early evening or morning, ob-serving activity in the city streets, parks, or in the countryside. In modern societies with a premium on privacy, children do not see their parents (or siblings or strang-ers) have sex together. The fact that they do not do so is neither good nor bad, it merely requires that they learn about it in other ways. At least some of our contem-porary problems with sex education result from the contemporary conditions of housing and privacy.

Most children do not make an automatic connection between nudity, sex play, and parental touching and sex. They are only learning things about what men and women do, what parts of the body are exposed and shielded. Such patterns of learning are consequential, not because they determine what happens in later life, but because they are responses that must be added to, or unlearned, or made more complex as they are fitted into sexual conduct later in life. Eventually people have to use their bodies if they have sex (not everyone does have sex, nor do they need to).

If parents create prohibitive attitudes about the body, whether or not the child attaches any sexual significance to them, then the child may have to unlearn and relearn as the child begins to deal with physical sex. If parts of the body are defined as bad or dirty or unclean or not to be shown to other people, then these attitudes must be revised when the time comes for sex. For some people the solution to the body problem is to turn out the lights, keep the touching to a minimum, and have sex with as little fuss as possible. It is entirely possible for some people to find this satisfactory, to have children and find happiness in marriage. However, if children have been taught that they should not look at other people's bodies, that certain body parts are bad, that touching parts of their own bodies and others' is wrong, then the sexual demands that they put on themselves and which others put on them will have to be negotiated differently later in life. It is not that these attitudes are sexual to begin with, it is that they become involved with sex in the future.

There are some people who have a very noticeable boundary around the body. They are the people who jump out of their skins when touched from behind. Such a jack-in-the-box response can be interpreted merely as being startled, but it also indicates how they have learned to trust or distrust being touched by others. The ability to accept being touched in an intimate way requires trust in what is going to happen; for many people the transition from highly restricted touching codes to the more intimate codes associated with sex may be very difficult. Even the experience of affection and love may not be sufficient to allow being touched. Body space limits are often set by parental example and parental style, not only between parents but between parents and children as well.

Much of the information that children get from their parents is observational and indirect because they do not get information from conversation. Many of the experiences that children have are not labeled by adults. Such "nonlabeling" is one of the commonest forms of adult response to what children do that the adults define as sexual. A typical example: Johnny is in the bathroom. His parent calls out, "Johnny, what are you doing?" "Nothing." "Well, quit it!" Parents do not want to talk to their children about sex, but they also do not want their children to do anything sexual. So they tell them not to, even though they do not want to confront what they are (or are not) doing. This can be very puzzling and confusing to the child.

Girls are less often the object of active nonlabeling — but are the victims of a more severe form of information control, passive nonlabeling. In the case of Johnny the parent's saying something does provide information, even though it may also produce anxiety; however, with a girl parents are scrupulously silent. Usually only a mighty transgression on the part of a daughter will produce a reaction.

Girls tend to learn more about sex from their mothers than boys do from their fathers, but the information is often restricted to menstruation and to pregnancy and birth. Information about intercourse is far more sketchy, as is information about the genitals, particularly the clitoris. In those cases where mothers do not volunteer information, the impending possibility of menstruation may precipitate questions about menstrual pads and tampons. Since the ads for such commodities are directed at women, and dispensers are located in girls' restrooms in school, it is obvious to a girl that she should ask her mother, but mothers often do not help a great deal. In a 1967 study of college women (most of whom were twelve or thirteen in 1960), fifteen percent reported that they first learned about menstruation when it happened to them.

Another pattern of information control involves mislabeling — calling things what they are not. Parents say many things to children that are simply not so, such as agricultural versions of birth and sex. No one ever had sex by planting seeds in a furrow or by working in a cabbage patch. Children's heads are filled with very odd notions about the world because parents mislabel many human experiences. A typical exchange is "Where do babies come from?" "Well, Mommy loves Daddy. . ." Such an answer may suffice, but it is likely to have nothing to do with the child's question. What does love have to do with babies? Can a girl get pregnant only if she is in love? Will falling in love make her pregnant? It is difficult for the child to decide what the correct answer is without asking more questions; however, because children possess so little information about sex and even less practice it is difficult for a parent to formulate any but the most odd answers.

One more pattern of information control is to give children words, but not tell them what they mean. This happens most commonly with the vulgar words for sex but also often happens with the "technical" words. It is not clear how "penis" and "vagina" and "clitoris" and "nipple" and "breast" got to be technical language or thought to be too explicit, but a fair number of people think they are. So children learn such words as "wee-wee" and "hot dog" and "boner" (mostly for penis) and wonder what all of the technical and vulgar words mean.

A child walks down the street and sees a vulgar word painted on a wall in four-foot-high dayglo paint. The child may not know what it means, or may know that it is not a nice word, but takes it home. Sometimes children think that such graffiti are advertisements. The child gets home and says the word, or asks what it means. If the child is very young and lisps the word, the parents may laugh and think it is cute, but most of the time they tell the child not to use that word here or there. The child then asks what it means, and is told only that it is a bad word. Puzzled, the child leaves it alone, having recognized that the word is not to be used in this place or in front of these adults.

Another of the sources of sex knowledge and attitudes is the dirty joke. Pre-adolescent boys tell many dirty jokes; girls, not so many. They tell pre-adolescents something about sexuality, what is expected of them as a sexual person, how they should feel about sex. Telling one another dirty jokes is part of the process by which children start defining who they might be sexually, what they are supposed to feel, who the cast of sexual characters are. It is part of the process of sexual learning that emerges from the covert, private, child sexual culture.

Growing up is a disorganized experience, which is one of the reasons why children make up fictions about the world. To a child, adults appear to have all the knowledge, but they are not talking. A child's peers, on the other hand, have a lot of misinformation, which they will talk about a good part of the time.

It's the real thing.

ROLE OF PEERS

The significance of the peer subculture in teaching children about sex is largely a function of what adults do *not* do. By restricting information about sex, not only concrete knowledge about sexual acts, but what it might mean or feel to be sexual, adults turn over to the peer group the critical informational role. The covert sexual culture of children and adolescents is rarely influenced by adults, particularly parents, except as restrainers of information and casual enforcers of behavior. Into this vacuum flows a whole range of language and ideas and curious notions that children have about the world.

What parents do is give up an important role in creating an effective and simple learning environment for sexuality. Fortunately it is possible for alternate ways of learning to exist, pathways which have been created by peers and to which peers serve as the primary guides.

There are studies, going back as far as 1917, in which both adults and young people reported on where they got their information about sexuality. For the past sixty years, in answer to the question, "Who taught you the most about sex?" ninety percent of the respondents say their friends did. No matter what social class, race, or religion they are, even whether they have taken sex-education courses in schools, children learn about sex mainly by talking with their friends, because such discussions, if not very accurate, are immediate, open, and real.

What young people learn from their peers is packaged in peculiar ways. Much of the information is technically incorrect, particularly about birth control, abortion, fertilization, and homosexuality and other unconventional conduct. Information about menstruation is more often understood by girls than by boys, but information about pregnancy and intercourse is sometimes relatively accurate and shared. Boys are more likely than girls to learn about intercourse, oral sex, and masturbation, and to learn it somewhat earlier than girls. Girls on the other hand may learn about intercourse and pregnancy and menstruation, but also somewhat later.

More important than technical information in many cases are the attitudes communicated about sex by peer groups. The peer group supplies attitudes toward women and attitudes toward men, attitudes toward homosexuality and other sexual acts, attitudes toward people who are different and people who are to be admired. The fragmentary sex information is coded in these terms. Its coding also reflects the degree that youthful peer groups are dominated by sexism and a peculiar, narrow morality.

There appears to be an increase of sexual information coming to children just before puberty at around ages ten and eleven. It comes from young people who are a year or two older than they are, and who are currently going through the experience. This information seems to stop with pre-adolescent children; not a great deal of knowledge seeps further down to still younger children.

Ten to thirteen seems to be the age range that sexual information "takes" with children. Younger children may be told the "facts of life" over and over again and still return with questions that appear to adults to be about the same or related matters. Children forget most of the things they are told; they are interested for a moment, perhaps, but if the information is not used by them, or connected with something of interest to them, it is lost.

The same thing happens to adults; we remember best what we think about often and in many circumstances. The sexual knowledge that adults think they are imparting to children must be relearned by the children in new circumstances later. Often parents honestly recall having given an extensive sex education lecture to a five-year-old who remembers nothing of it when he or she grows up. This may account in part for peer-dominated sources of sex knowledge—young people learn about sex from their peers when it is important to them.

It is critical for our understanding of the relationship between early sexual learning and the learning that goes on during adolescence to know that both periods are largely dominated by covert peer information systems. Further, it is usually after ages twelve or thirteen that any seriously considered information, that is, information that is going to be put into practice, is really taken in. Finally, very few young people know much at all about sex, even after they have developed a considerable range of experience.

There are a number of kinds of sexual knowledge: *how to* is relatively widespread, even though it sometimes seems difficult to come by; *knowledge about*, an understanding of the processes and sources of activity and how they relate to personal conduct, is far less often available, and is usually clouded with myth and error. It is possible to conduct a sex life successfully with only peer information, but it is not possible to understand what is being done. In sex as in other aspects of human activity, personal experience does not reveal all that there is to know.

ROLE OF THE SCHOOLS

Very few schools offer sex education or information to children under the age of fourteen. Most family life, health education, or sex education courses begin in the ninth grade and increase in number through the tenth and eleventh. For many young people it is the first time that they have had an opportunity to talk about sex or learn about various aspects of sexuality—yet they may well already have had intercourse or homosexual experience, they may have used a contraceptive of one type or another, or a young girl may have had an abortion.

It is unfortunate that sex education programs are so poorly timed. By the time young people are offered the opportunity to learn something about sex, major components of their sexual scripts have already been formed and reinforced by experience. Many young people are impervious even to useful information, because they have already passed the point when that information could be easily integrated into their ongoing sexual life styles. The decision of the schools, often forced by parents, to delay or deny sex education is to assure that the peer group remains the most powerful source of sex information and practice in the society, and to assure that sex will be experienced in anxious and guilty ways by young people—an anxiety and guilt that is only reduced through the manipulations of values and attitudes by the peer group.

The schools face the problems of deciding *what* to teach, *when* to teach, *who* teaches, and *how* to teach. The crucial decision is probably WHAT to teach, because if the information is dishonest or incomplete or authoritarian it will probably reach only a tiny audience. It is relatively easy to teach sexual plumbing, the tubes and the hormones and the sperm and the egg, and even the physiological aspects of the sexual response cycle. It is easy because it is far from what people experience; it is not the plumbing that makes people nervous, it is the doing of sexual things. Similarly it is possible to talk about social etiquette, which also exists at some remove from the actual doing of sex.

What most young people are interested in is how sex feels, what are its consequences, why can or cannot people do it, where do the rules come from. All of these questions are far more serious challenges to the *status quo* than kissing on the first date, the spasms in the vaginal barrel, or the gonadotropins. It is not that physiological information is not useful, it is that it is not central to the experiences young people are living. Understanding physiology is possible only after having faced the facts of experience and feeling. It is important for young people to understand as well as experience, and it is equally important for teachers to recognize that understanding cannot be communicated by ignoring the existance of experience.

WHEN to teach should probably be as early as possible, but most important in U. S. society is early puberty, ages ten to thirteen. The body is changing, and important changes are taking place in the ways children are treated by adults. Such changes in adult response seem very mysterious to most children. Around puberty a specifically sexual identity begins to form (out of cultural convention), and the more information children have about what is happening to them then, the better. In addition, adult-type sexual experiences are occurring. Children are developing secondary sexual characteristics; girls are menstruating; most boys and some girls are masturbating. It is probably at this point that the most sustained attempt should be made to impart sexual information. The ignorance of small children is unfortunate, but not nearly as potentially dangerous as the ignorance of children who are turning into potentially sexual adolescents.

WHO should teach is anybody who is able to tell young people about the role that sex plays in the many aspects of human life. There is a tendency to stick sex education in the hands of the health teacher, the biology teacher, or the coach because these areas supposedly have "something to do with" sex and the body. Health, biology, and sport have no more to do with sex than do politics, English, or social studies, and often less. Attention should be paid to the sexual dimension of human life wherever it appears in a significant way. Such general attention to sex is unlikely to occur in schools, so what is probably needed is a teacher who is interested, non-judgmental, cool, and collected; one who cares more about the sex life of young people than they do their own.

HOW to teach is informally, non-judgmentally, non-clinically, and non-therapeutically. Sex should be taught like anything else: nobody put on and nobody put down. Method is less important than content, timing, and teacher. Films, discussions, books — everything works if presented in a positive context.

Very few schools do it well. Most young people find out very little about sex in school, except as a consistent reinforcement of stereotypical gender-role values: girls do this and boys do that; sex is linked to achievement and to clique behavior. From first grade through college, the school teaches far more about sex in its own organization and structure than it does in the curriculum. As a result of gender-role stereotyping, the school reinforces socio-sexual patterns, and creates contexts for sexual experimentation which sustain contemporary patterns of association, emotional intimacy, and sexuality.

ROLE OF THE MEDIA

For younger children, the major contribution of the media (television and books) is to reinforce gender-role stereotypes. Prior to puberty, the media is probably most significant for what it does *not* present. The relationships between men and men, women and women, women and men follow quite conventional patterns without a significant amount of overt sexuality, realistic or not. Sex is used to move a plot forward: there are unfaithful wives (most of whom are punished in some way), some hookers, and otherwise sexy but sexless women. Strong themes of homosocial values are produced by groups of men working as police, firemen, or doctors, or as lone wolves setting the world morally straight. Women generally relate to each other through male figures rather than directly. Everyone knows what is important.

If a child were raised absolutely innocently, with only television versions of the world, it might grow up to be like the character Chance in *Being There,* by Jerzy Kosinski. Chance has been totally socialized by the television set, and by "chance" has fallen into the life of members of the political and economic elite. His ignorance they treat as knowledge, his cliches as wisdom. At one point in the novel he has the following exchange with his host's wife, who has fallen in love with him:

She sat down on the edge of the bed; Chance moved back to give her more room.

She brushed her hair from her forehead, and, looking at him quietly, put her hand on his arm. "Please don't . . . run away from me! Don't!" She sat motionless, her head resting against Chance's shoulder.

Chance was bewildered: there was clearly no place to which he could run away. He searched his memory and recalled situations on TV in which a woman advanced toward a man on a couch or a bed or inside a car. Usually, after a while, they would come very close to each other, and, often they would be partly undressed. They would then kiss and embrace. But on TV what happened next was always obscured: a brand-new image would appear on the screen: the embrace of man and woman was utterly forgotten. And yet, Chance knew, there could be other gestures and other kinds of closeness following such intimacies. Chance had just a fleeting memory of a maintenance man who, years ago, used to come to the Old Man's house to take care of the incinerator. On several occasions, after he was through with the work, he would come out into the garden and drink beer. Once he showed Chance a number of small photographs of a man and woman who were completely naked. In one of these photographs, a woman held the man's unnaturally long and thickened organ in her hand. In another, the organ was lost between her legs.

As the maintenance man talked about the photographs and what they portrayed, Chance scrutinized them closely. The images on paper were vaguely disturbing; on television he had never seen the unnaturally enlarged hidden parts of men and women, or these freakish embraces. When the maintenance man left, Chance stooped down to look over his own body. His organ was small and limp; it did not protrude in the slightest. The maintenance man insisted that in this organ hidden seeds grew, and that they came forth in a spurt whenever a man took his pleasure. Though Chance prodded and massaged his organ, he felt nothing; even in the early morning, when he woke up and often found it somewhat enlarged, his organ refused to stiffen out; it gave him no pleasure at all.

Later, Chance tried hard to figure out what connection there was — if any — between a woman's private parts and the birth of a child. In some of the TV series about doctors and hospitals and operations, Chance had often seen the mystery of birth depicted: the pain and agony of the mother, the joy of the father, the pink, wet body of the newborn infant. But he had never watched any show which explained why some women had babies and others did not. Once or twice Chance was tempted to ask Louise about it, but he decided against it. Instead, he watched TV, for a while, with closer attention. Eventually, he forgot about it.[3]

Before puberty, most children's versions of the sexual world are probably closer to Chance's view than to the moderately organized view that adults might possess. It takes the increase in consistency in scripts and the experience with concrete sexual conduct after puberty to make what is presented by X and R rated movies and the men's and women's magazines into a coherent picture of the world. What children possess before puberty is a fragmentary set of ideas which increase in coherence as they pass through puberty. Only after other sources of knowledge have been operating do available media materials (no matter how explicit they seem to adults) begin to make sense to young people in the way adults mean them to and understand them to.

3. Jerzy Kosinski, *Being There* (Harcourt, Brace, Jovanovich, 1970), pp. 75–77.

Conclusion

In U.S. society we teach our children, before age ten or eleven, about gender roles but not about sexuality. Almost all the information children receive that relates to sexual behavior is linked primarily to gender roles. The information they get later about sexuality is thus mediated by the gender-role stereotype they have acquired.

For the most part, adults tend to treat pre-adolescent children as if they were asexual. Children are left to accumulate sexual information nearly at random, any way they can, picking it up piece by piece. Adults rarely realize how fragmented it all is, since most adults have managed to put together a more or less coherent sexual world, in which some types of behavior are accepted and others are not. For the most part, adults know who they are supposed to be aroused by, and what they are supposed to do sexually. They have sexual scripts of one kind or another.

In contrast, children have simply a bundle of disconnected knowledge, none of which has been assembled in a way that makes sense. A child may know that babies come out of a mother, but know nothing about intercourse. A child down the street may know about intercourse, but know nothing of where babies come from. Another child may have a large vocabulary of dirty words and yet know nothing about sexuality.

At the beginning of puberty, what do most children actually know about sex? The answer must be "extremely little." While they may be able to tell you where babies come from, and that during intercourse the penis goes into the vagina, and that mommies and daddies (or, from liberal parents, women and men) enjoy it, they know very little else of those matters that will turn out to be important to them. They do know that men do some things and women do other things, that the typical living arrangement in U.S. society is two adults, male and female, husband and wife, and most often mother and father. They have a rough idea of what boys are supposed to do and feel, and what girls are supposed to do and feel, and they have learned and forgotten many of the "facts of life."

As children move into puberty, during which the adult expectations of their conduct will change, they possess primarily a world coded by what men do and what women do — and therefore what is appropriate to them is a result of wanting to be a man or a woman. They will have feelings about nudity and modesty, and shame and guilt about what is forbidden (even that which is nonsexually rule breaking can be exciting or frightening). Into a new world they go, willy nilly, being labeled as having certain kinds of feelings and desires and propensities.

A peer group will fill in the empty spaces left by the adult community — the content for activities associated with those feelings, desires, and propensities. *Who* should do sexual things to each other is usually men and women; *what* they should do involves touching and hugging and kissing, not done in public. Little else is very clear; it is surely not clear *why* it should be done. But the script will be filled in: do this with this kind of person, or do not do it all; do these sexual things and not those; you should want to get to first base or you should fall in love.

The fragments begin to coalesce around age twelve or thirteen; with physical practice and experience they become more consolidated, they change from patterns that are being created to guidance mechanisms. They change from creations into blueprints. The scripting of sexuality *as we know it as adults* occurs for most children after puberty, built on the divisions of gender-role learning.

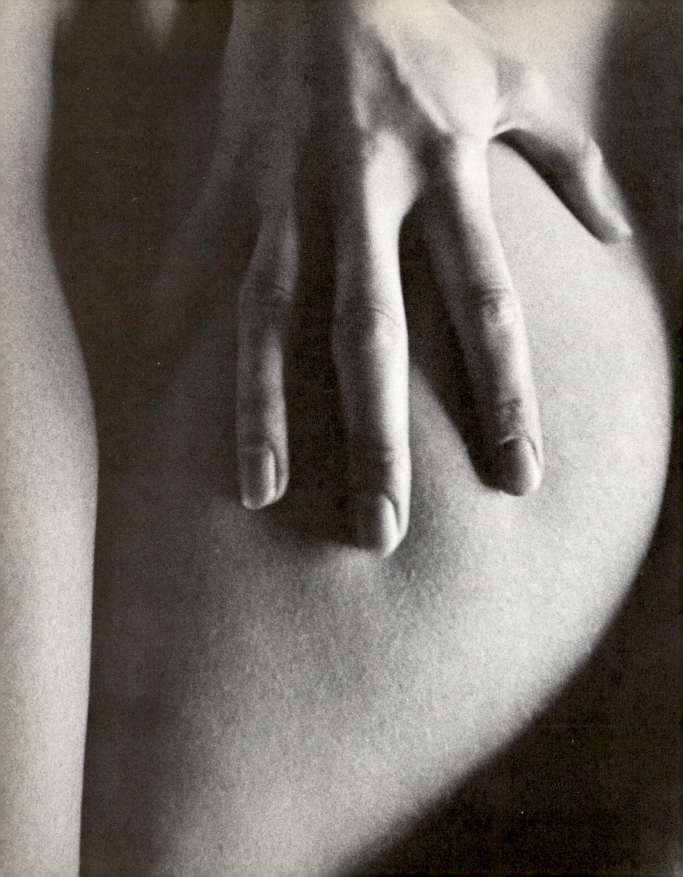

PUBERTY

Jeffrey and Matilda were beautiful, healthy babies; charming toddlers;
intelligent, lively, affectionate children. . . . Then last year, when
Jeffrey turned fourteen and Matilda twelve, they had begun to change;
to grow rude, coarse, selfish, insolent, nasty, brutish, and tall.
Alison Lurie, *The War Between the Tates*

TYPICALLY THE CONFUSED MELANGE OF INFORMATION CHILDREN HAVE ABOUT
sex does not bother very many adults. As long as children do not do anything sexual, or at least do not do anything adults notice and disapprove of, everyone leaves well enough alone. Children may not be interested, or if interested, have learned that they are unlikely to get much useful information from the adults around them.

However, much to the surprise of the child and the adults around him or her this calm state of affairs begins to change at about ages eleven or twelve. The bodies of children begin to change in rather obvious and sometimes alarming ways at the onset of puberty. These changes are signals both to the child and to adults that the period of reproductive maturity is approaching, and that this reproductive maturity is associated with doing at least some sexual things. As a result, changes begin to occur in the relations between children and adults. The activities of the child are taken more seriously, not only potentially sexual activities but all other aspects of the child's life as well.

What young people are losing is a "childhood exemption"; what they did in the past was protected by being a child, by not being responsible, by being innocent—both successes and failures were judged in terms of this exemption. However, with the passing of both chronological and biological markers—ages twelve, thirteen, fourteen; changes in the body and acquisition of secondary sex characteristics—the exemption lapses. We can see it in all kinds of ways. In the sixth grade everyone stays in one room at school; in the seventh they find their way through the corridors of the school from room to room. Permissiveness begins to disappear; now grades, manners, and rules assume a greater importance both for the future and for judging current conduct.

In the United States this transition between childhood and adulthood is stretched out in time, is publicly tied primarily to chronological age rather than to developmental age, and is linked to the development of various skills or the acquisition of different rights and obligations. However, while everyone may march through this period in chronological lockstep, the biological changes and sexual expectations associated with puberty are not nearly as neatly organized. This disjuncture between chronology and development, between overt expectations attached to age and informal definitions of self tied to body changes, is a major characteristic of most urban-industrial societies.

Nonurban Preindustrial Patterns of Transition

In societies with a relatively simple division of activities and a narrow range of adult roles, childhood can end relatively abruptly. When the child is recognized as being "of age"—often by evidence of menstruation among girls, and attainment of certain height and weight and other physical characteristics among boys—the transition may be marked by what anthropologists call a *rite of passage*. That is, the culture has as one of its social rituals a celebration, a test, a change in cosmetic or dress style, or sometimes a combination of all three, which attests to the existence of a new adult in the society. This tells the individual and other members of the society that he or she is now a different person than before. The "new adult" has new rights and opportunities for new experiences, but must take on new obligations, and is judged by a new set of standards.

Such a transition brings few surprises to the child, even though it occurs with relative rapidity, for in simpler societies the obligations and rights of adulthood are relatively visible, and the growing child has practiced many of his future adult activities in the form of play. Even the sexual dimensions of life are visible to children, who share housing arrangements with parents and who receive relatively direct information about what their sexual life will be like and when it will begin. In some small though not all societies there is an opportunity for observation, formal training, and experimentation before moving into adult status. Anthropologists rarely record the sexual dimensions of this change, but they do in the areas of work and sport and other important dimensions of life. The actual experience or the feelings of the actual experience are mimicked by the young before and during transitions into adulthood.

To mark the end-of-childhood/beginning-of-adulthood, family and relatives often gather to celebrate the change and affirm the adult status. In many places the rite is not performed for each young person as he or she "comes of age," but rather is performed at regular intervals (e.g., once every six months) for all those who have come of age since the last ritual. The gathering of several families at the same time becomes a gathering of the clan or village, and the occasion of collective celebration.

Urban Industrial Patterns of Transition

In complex urban societies the people, institutions, and activities that confirm the passage are diffuse. There are many aspects of adulthood, many roles to be performed, and sometimes a wide variety of skills to acquire. The transition from childhood to adulthood is not simple, recognized by the entire community and involving most aspects of life. There is no unanimity, no single celebration, but a number of smaller recognitions.

The rites of passage are generally tied to chronological age, and only some of them are required. Many are in the form of "you may" rather than "you must." New opportunities or responsibilities are often officially granted on a birthday, although there may be a period of practice (as in driving) or waiting (as in voting) before the new right can be fully exercised. Such events as the right to drive, to drink, to marry, to obtain working papers and a social security number, to vote, to be drafted into military service, and to be drafted into jury duty, are indications that childhood is over and adulthood has begun.

The rights reflect different *kinds* of adulthood as defined in modern societies, and tend to be given out piecemeal rather than all at once. The right to drive indicates a newly acquired independent responsibility for the control of property; the right to drink represents access to what adults define as pleasure; reaching the age of marriage offers legitimate sexuality and legitimate children; and the right to vote gives an opportunity for political participation.

In addition to the regulated rites of passage are those that are part of the youth subculture itself — those imposed by youth on youth. The wearing of cosmetics of various sorts, wearing a bra or not wearing one, dating, the testing of physical strength and courage in sports, and other peer-group activities are indicators of changing commitments, important both in themselves and as signs that some aspects of childhood have ended. Many of these activities are not the sole creation of the young, but are models of adult activities linked to future or expected life experiences.

However, the use and meaning of the activities by young people in their world is different from many of the adult meanings and purposes. Adults may promote and support high-school sports to build character, but the youthful participants may use them to promote status differences. Record companies may produce popular-music records for a profit motive, but the youthful purchasers use the knowledge and experience transmitted in them to express differences between their world and that of parents and other adults.

There is no sexual passage at all except as recognized by peers, and on occasion permitted by parents. Most of the sexual transitions that follow puberty are marked by ambivalence, anxiety, frustration, and satisfactions gained in a struggle against the adult community. This struggle creates a general tension between adults and young people (they ought to have fun, but not too much fun). For instance, the young person wants to use his or her money or a family car for dating and sexual adventure or cosmetic displays; parents think that the uses should be serious. The sexual transitions of adolescence — dating, love, petting, intercourse — are often unmarked and uncelebrated except by the people doing them. The adult community has withdrawn its support from the sexual dimensions of growing up, and indeed is usually against it.

The sexual practices of young people are often far removed from the nature of adult sexuality. The emotional content of chase and flight in dating or the experience of being popular is only marginally related to domestic affection and daily life in contemporary marriage. The acquisition of sexual experience often does not provide young people with closer ties to the adult world.

Not all of preadult life need be preparation for some distant future, for it has pleasures and accomplishments of its own. But the discontinuity of life-cycle experiences for people in contemporary industrial societies as compared to less complex societies, or to the United States of less than half a century ago, requires "unlearning" childhood patterns to learn adult ones, making the tasks of adulthood more difficult to perform.

Social Observance of Puberty

The body changes observed in children at puberty are only loosely linked to the formal adult system of privileges and obligations. They are more important to the informal world of youth culture and youthful development of sexuality. This detachment of sexuality from the formal, public movement into adulthood gives it a peculiar quality in western societies. As the bodies of these relatively uninformed young people begin to change, the people around them begin to react to them differently. The young people recognize that they are "growing up" and beginning to look like adults, but it is often obscure to them what is going to happen while they are physically changing.

At some distance away in time is the legitimate sexual transition of marriage. In between the moment when the body begins to change and marriage at age seventeen to age twenty-five (on the average, depending on social class, religion, education, pregnancy, love, and all that), young people must take what they already know and combine it with the experiences that lie before them in order to make sense of a world that will contain new opportunities for intimacy, affection, love, and sex.

When body changes signal that the young person is somehow different, the rules change. A preadolescent child is viewed as asexual. The physical signs of sexual maturity are viewed as a cue to respond to the child as a sexual or potentially sexual person. The tacit reasoning goes something like this: "If you *look* sexually mature, you must think and behave as if you are sexually mature, and therefore, we are going to treat you as sexually mature." The dilemma is that children are only rarely prepared for this change: Nothing much in their preadolescent, asexual world really equips them to deal effectively with their new sexual world.

It is a tricky and difficult transition, one in which what psychologists call *attribution* plays a major part. Adults attribute feelings to the child. They define for the child how it *should* feel, and the child learns to feel that way. The child begins to take on other people's definitions of itself very much as it learned the definitions of being male or female.

For example, any woman who developed large breasts at the age of twelve or thirteen remembers that, all of a sudden, people began to behave differently toward her. In U. S. society, large breasts signal "sexy" — although a large-breasted, early adolescent girl (and most boys around that age) probably have no clear idea what "sexy" is supposed to mean. But these girls cannot help but notice that older males, particularly, treat her differently.[1] It is a two-way street: the appearance of large breasts triggers a stock social response, which in turn reinforces the social-sexual consequences of having large breasts. At first, the girl may be baffled about what has happened. Nobody has ever told her, "Your breasts are a signal to these males that you are sexual and perhaps available," whether or not she thinks she wants or ought to be sexually available.

As part of the male social-learning process, boys have been taught that girls with large breasts are more sexually available than girls with small breasts. No

---

1. Her mother may react by being more protective ("those dirty men!") or by being more suspicious (girls with large breasts must be watched closely because they may be more sexy). Her father may react in equally strange ways.

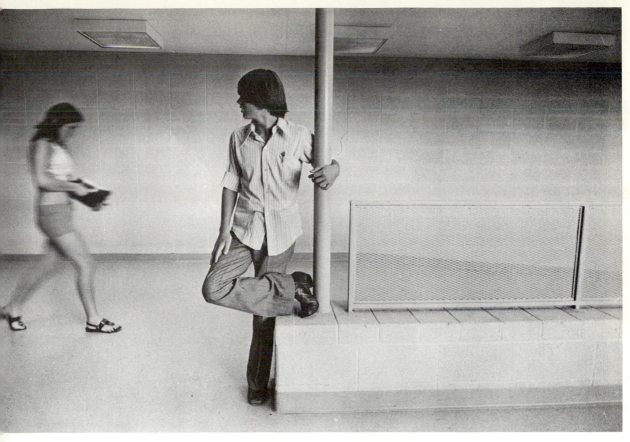

The newly pubescent boy fills his daydreams with the erotic images that pass him by.

doubt, popular culture—television, movies, newspapers, magazines, advertising, packaging—has a lot to do with a boy's conception of who is sexually available and who is not, who are "good" girls and who are "bad" girls. In American and European movies, there is a good deal of merchandising of actresses as good women or naughty women. Almost all the naughties have large busts. Some of the others have large busts too, but they wear clothes that disguise them. The notion is very strong in U.S. society that large breasts signal that a girl is grown up and sexually ready.

Boys, too, begin to be viewed sexually when they start to grow facial and body hair, when their voices deepen, when their carriage and musculature become more "masculine." Their sexuality begins to be taken more seriously: they, too, are thought to be sexually ready, which changes the way their parents and other adults treat them. It is as if adults decide that a post-pubescent boy can now be dangerous and needs to be watched more closely. This changed attitude does not necessarily reflect what is going on in the boy's mind, but only that his appearance is changing.

Biological Changes at Puberty

The physical changes in children at puberty (ages ten to fourteen) range from the dramatic external changes such as height gain, to internal anatomical and physiological changes linked to capacities for reproduction. Current research in endocrinology suggests that these visible and invisible changes result from changes in the activity of the central nervous system, which "trigger" the production of pituitary *gonadotrophins*, which in turn influence the production of hormones that produce growth and change. These hormones are often called "sex" hormones. The release of the hormones affects a wide range of tissues in the body, as can be seen in Figure 1(a). Figure 1(b) is a cross-sectional view of the mature sex organs.

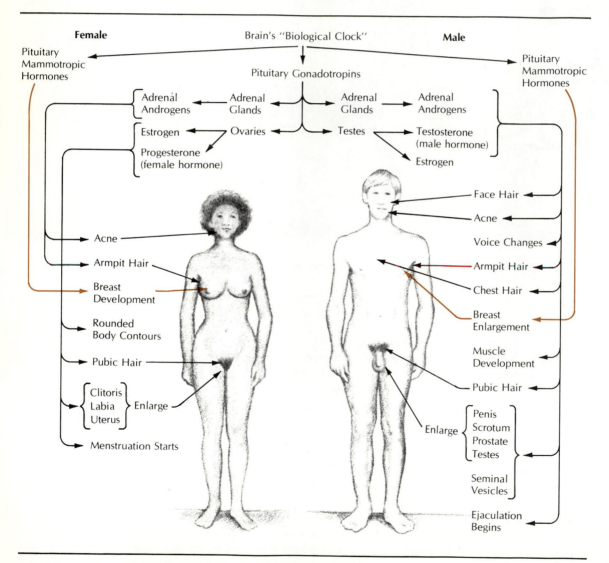

Figure 1(a)   Effects of Sex Hormones on Pubertal Development.

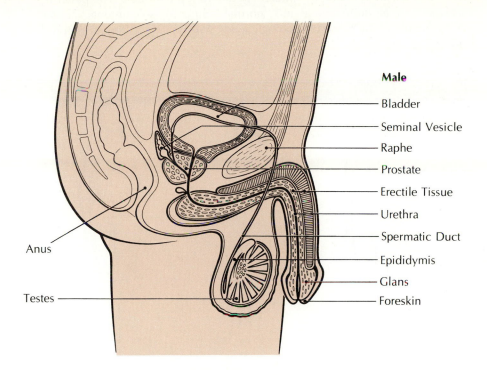

Male

— Bladder
— Seminal Vesicle
— Raphe
— Prostate
— Erectile Tissue
— Urethra
— Spermatic Duct
— Epididymis
— Glans
— Foreskin

Anus —

Testes —

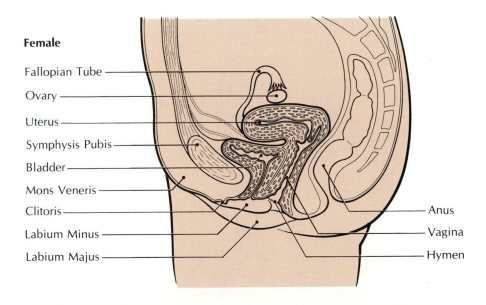

Female

Fallopian Tube —
Ovary —
Uterus —
Symphysis Pubis —
Bladder —
Mons Veneris —
Clitoris —
Labium Minus —
Labium Majus —

— Anus
— Vagina
— Hymen

Figure 1(b)   Male and Female Reproductive Organs.

The age at the beginning of puberty, the tempo of change, and the age at which it ends, are remarkably different in different individuals. The patterns shown in Table 1 are all quite typical and "normal." Since these elements vary so much, young people of the same chronological age will be very different in appearance. (See Figure 2.)

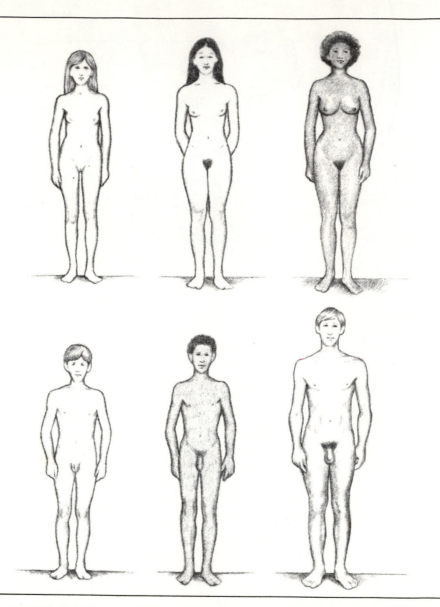

Figure 2   Different Degrees of Pubertal Development at the Same Age. The three boys in the lower row are all 14.75 years old. The three girls in the upper row are all 12.75 years old. (Based on Tanner, as Shown in Kagan and Coles, *Twelve to Sixteen*, 1972, p. 10.)

Table 1   Variations in Puberty

Beginning	Tempo (time from start to end)	End
age 12	1.5 years	age 13.5
age 12	6 years	age 17
age 11	6 years	age 16
age 14	2 years	age 16

Table 2   Physical Changes at Puberty

Females	Usual Ages begin	end	Males
Increase in height	9	15	Increase in height
Development of breast buds	10	16	Development of breast knots
Beginning of pubic hair	11	14	Beginning of pubic hair
Changes in uterus and vagina	—	—	
Enlargement of labia and clitoris	—	—	
	11	15	Changes in testes and prostate
	12	16	Enlargement of penis and scrotum
First menstruation	10	17	Production of motile sperm *(see photograph)*
Sweat glands	—	—	Sweat glands
		—	Voice changes

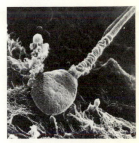

A sperm cell is only .06 mm long, but it contains the complete hereditary information from the father.

Whatever the age at beginning, the tempo, and the age at ending of puberty, there is a relatively common *order* of changes. First is an increase in height, followed by skeletal changes, followed by muscular development. Because not all the body parts change simultaneously, many young people spend a large part of this time period being and feeling out of proportion. Commonly the head, hands, and feet change first, then the legs, then body breadth, and finally shoulders. The feeling of gawkiness that young people often report is a real one, and the problems that arise in buying clothes contribute to this sense of uneasiness about the body and the body image projected to others.

In addition to the general "growth spurt" in height, skeleton, and muscles, the pattern of pubertal growth includes the changes described in Table 2. In general girls begin to change about two years earlier than boys; thus, some girls are taller than the boys in the same school year, and have more mature-looking bodies.

Experience of Puberty

The physical development of puberty is crucial in adolescence because it is directly linked to most aspects of social interaction—both competitive and cooperative—among peers and between adolescents and adults. Height and weight among males often determines participation in sports, the formal and informal order of selection for teams, and even whether peer-related athletic activities are available at all. For males the physical changes associated with puberty are part of a beginning sense of self as successfully masculine, at least along the dimension of physical achievement. Given the rewards attached to such success from both peers and adults, height and weight are a not very subtle basis of ranking among young men.

Girls reaching puberty have different pressures. While they are generally spared the comparative athletic ratings of boys, they are exposed to the importance of physical beauty to social success. Preteen and teen magazines stress ideal sizes, shapes, cosmetics, and so on, stressing the impact of good looks and positive presentation of self in "catching" a boy. Faced with "ideals" of size and shape, but finding themselves gawky and changing and unstable in form, many adolescent girls are likely to feel unsure of themselves. Worse yet, they often doubt whether they will *ever* emerge into a form that promises heterosexual popularity and success.

In the same manner, height and weight become markers in the interaction between young women and young men. There is a bias against short men, and the young man who grows later than his peers is at a disadvantage in dating relationships. Since some of the bias stems from the aesthetic norm of our society that the male should be taller than his female date, girls who experience the growth spurt early, and thus tower over the boys their age, are also at a disadvantage.

Similarly, changes in body shape among young women are taken by others as indicators that they are more mature, and may lead to their being defined earlier as eligible for dates. There is some risk in this, since too early presentation of self as "dateable" makes the younger, more developed, girl the target of exploitive adolescent male attitudes. On the other hand, the girl who experiences late development may feel deficient in social as well as physical attributes.

The onset of breast development and menstruation are the most significant indicators of change for young women. Breast development may be more important at first than menstruation, since it is visible, leading to different relationships to young men and potentially an increase in popularity and desirability. Concern about breast development pervades many a young girl's thought and nightmares:

I was about six months younger than everyone in my class, and so for about six months after my friends had begun to develop — that was the word we used, develop — I was not particularly worried. I would sit in the bathtub and look down at my breasts and know that any day now, any second now, they would start growing like everyone else's. They didn't.

I suppose that for most girls breasts, brassieres, that entire thing, has more trauma, more to do with the coming of adolescence, of becoming a woman, than anything else. Certainly more than getting your period, although that too was traumatic, symbolic. But you could see breasts, they were there, they were visible. Whereas a girl could claim to have her period for months before she actually got it and nobody would ever know the difference.

(Nora Ephron, "A Few Words About Breasts,"
Esquire, May 1972, p. 95.)

Although breasts are the most public aspect of female puberty, menstruation is significant because it involves feelings, experiences, and activities directly related to the genitals. Few parents direct their daughters' attention to the genitals before

Declining Age at Menarche

Menstruation is one of the pubertal changes that most dramatically calls attention to the changed reproductive status of young women. Although there is a variable period of sterility among some young women after *menarche* (first menstruation) — a period during which the ova that are produced cannot be fertilized — menstruation is the major signal to the young woman and the people around her that she can now become pregnant. The age at which this occurs begins a period of possible fertility, and the earlier it occurs the more years there are of possible childbearing.

Since about 1850 in Western Europe the age of menarche has been falling. This is called the "secular decline"; the age has probably dropped three to four years in the period between 1850 and 1960, as Figure 3 shows. The decline has significance for potential sexuality during adolescence as well as significance for reproduction. In the past, when the body changes of puberty took place later in life, young females looked like children longer, coitus during adolescence was less likely to result in pregnancy, and the total number of children born in the life of any woman was substantially lower (even in the absence of contraception).

Since puberty in males and females is produced by similar changes in the central nervous system, it is likely that male and female puberty has declined in similar ways for the last 100 years. Males in the past would have also shown signs of physical changes at a later age, been physically smaller, and not as strong in the age period twelve to seventeen as they are today. First ejaculation and the development of motile sperm was probably retarded as well.

The decline is usually attributed to the improvement of diet, beginning at the moment of conception (the mother's diet) and lasting until puberty. Since the diets of the poor have improved to a greater degree than the diets of the affluent, the secular decline of the age at menarche has been more dramatic among the poor.

Recent evidence from the Scandanavian countries suggests that the secular decline of menarche has stopped.

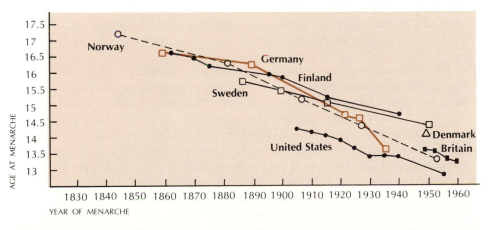

Figure 3   Historical Decline of Age at Menarche in Various Western Countries.

Menstrual Cycle

All female mammals experience cycles of ovulation *(estrus)*, but only human females and some nonhuman primates also experience menstruation, which is a periodic shedding, or bleeding, of the lining *(endometrium)* of the uterus. Most cycles are from twenty-six to thirty-four days, averaging twenty-eight days.

During the first phase of the menstrual cycle, lasting about fourteen days before *ovulation* (release of a mature egg from an ovary), the endometrium is regenerated. During this phase, the pituitary stimulates production of estrogen from the ovary, which causes the endometrium to regrow. The pituitary secretion also causes an ovarian follicle to mature and rupture, releasing the egg. The estrogen also stimulates changes in cervical mucosa; it becomes alkaline and nutrient for sperm. (One of the mechanisms of the birth control pill is to modify this effect, making the cervical mucus hostile to the sperm.)

During the second phase of menstruation following ovulation, the pituitary, stimulated by the estrogen in the blood stream, goes to work again, producing a secretion that in turn causes the remains of the ovarian follicle *(corpus luteum)* to produce progesterone and some estrogen. These chemicals in turn cause the glands of the endometrium to produce nutrients at about the time the egg, floating freely in the uterus, needs them (about the eighteenth day of a twenty-eight day cycle).

If sperm is not there to fertilize the egg, the pituitary responds to the high levels of estrogen and progesterone by shutting down, causing the corpus luteum to wither away. The fall in estrogen level then apparently triggers the shedding of the endometrium through the cervix and vagina — actual menstruation. As the estrogen level falls, the pituitary gland kicks in again and starts the cycle over.

Only about two ounces of blood are lost during an average menstrual period. However, inadequate diet coupled with fairly heavy menstrual bleeding can lead to anemia. The typical duration of menstrual bleeding is three to seven days.

menstruation, or do so only in preparation for the event. At the onset of menstruation, young women alone or in discussion with mother must confront the fact of the menstrual cycle, premenstrual tension, tampons or napkins, and so forth. *(See Boxes.)*

For many young women, menstruation means a significant change in their relation to their own body, depending on the ways in which they have learned about themselves, their bodies, and their sexuality. Menstruation may be felt to be a curse, an inhibitor of social and physical interaction, something dirty and disgusting, something to be surreptitious about (many girls report embarrassment at buying napkins or tampons). Or it may be defined as an experience which helps bring a girl into womanhood with feelings of greater control over her body. It is evident that a majority of young women view menstruation in negative terms, however.

Menstruation also involves comparison, since it is one way in which young women can compare their rates of growing up. While it is usually not sought, its absence may signify lack of maturity and lead to the pretense described by Nora Ephron.

Menstrual Cycle (cont.)

A woman's emotional states are intimately related to her menstrual cycle. Under severe stress, her cycle may not be regular. Just before her period begins, she may experience *premenstrual tension*, or feelings of fatigue and irritability. This may be related to her gaining weight because she retains fluids at this time. Some women also experience painful swelling of the breasts. Also, some women, usually younger women, experience abdominal pain during ovulation, lasting about a day.

In addition, many women experience what are usually called cramps, which seem to be related to spasms of the uterus. Cramps begin early; they are rarely experienced for the first time after age twenty. Sometimes they go away after childbirth. Some women also have severe "menstrual migraine" headaches during or just before their periods.

The experience of premenstrual tension and cramping during menstruation may or may not have a physiological basis. Clearly changes do take place — whether or not they necessarily are experienced as tension or cramps is currently under debate. An understanding of these events is social and political as well as psychological or biological. If the events are thought to be biologically related to menstruation, they become part of women's lot, a burden to be carried. On the other hand, if they are thought to be psychological, then (like all psychological problems) a woman ought to be able to gain control over them in some way. In this, as in many other instances, women cannot win. Until we change the way women and men learn about menstruation, even radically renovate our thinking about sex, hygiene, and women in general, we will not know the origins of these responses.

There is no physiological reason to avoid intercourse during menstruation, although many cultures prohibit it, and may restrict a woman's activities or ostracize her during her period. They may regard her as "unclean," or dangerous to her own fertility or to a man's virility during intercourse.

Social Aspects of Puberty

The physical changes in the years eleven to fourteen have significant *social meanings* built upon them. The changes in the body are important dimensions of the end of childhood because they are so often read as indicators that *other* changes have taken place. The dilemma for many young people is that the period of physical change is often not parallel with other changes. Some young people are socially or intellectually mature, but not physically mature. Others have changed physically but are not socially mature; they may nonetheless be treated as if they were older and more competent than they are. In some cases this may be fortunate; that is, a boy treated as mature and offered leadership may *become* a leader because of the opportunity to develop leadership skills and an enhanced sense of competence. But offering responsibility to the largest, most mature-appearing young person may lead to following poor leaders and to the scapegoating of smaller youth.

In any case, physical changes at puberty disrupt many of the social rankings of childhood. If for those who had relatively high social ranking in childhood the physical changes of adolescence are late, they find themselves moved downward in adolescent ranking, and many suddenly feel themselves outsiders in the new social world. For many whose childhoods were unhappy, adolescence may be second chance.

At the end of puberty there is greater variety of body size and shape among same-age boys or same-age girls than in childhood. There are also increasing differences between boys and girls, who until age ten or eleven were physically much the same in shape and development (this increasing difference is called *dimorphism*). *None of the physical changes themselves is responsible for what happens to young people during and after puberty; it is the social definitions of these changes, and the ways they are responded to, which begin the creation of sexual identity.*

It is commonly assumed that physical dimorphism leads to psychological dimorphism. Because women develop a female anatomy at puberty, they are expected "naturally" to organize their life plans around marriage and motherhood, as though the possession of a vagina, uterus, and breasts created penis envy, the desire to bear children, and the desire to breast feed. Increases in male musculature are commonly linked to social dominance, and having a penis is confused with the right to initiate sexual encounters.

Males generally do become stronger than females during adolescence; however, females in general rarely receive the physical training that males receive, and indeed are positively discouraged from many physical development activities (except ice-skating and dancing, for example, which are viewed as feminine). The disparity in physical ability between men and women might well be decreased by better female physical training in childhood and adolescence.

Adaptation is not a general concept; it is given its meaning by context. One cannot "adapt" in general, but must adapt to something. Physical strength may be important in situations without machinery, but in modern societies occasions calling for great physical strength are relatively rare, or not especially significant. Hunting is a sport, fighting a form of deviance, and manipulation of heavy objects without machinery a rare occurrence. The value given to hunting, fighting, and manipulating heavy objects is social in origin, not biological. Indeed, people who manipulate symbols such as words or numbers (e.g., advertising agents and bankers) make more money than those who manipulate heavy objects (e.g., piano movers and garbage collectors).

"Sex" Hormones and Sex Activity

In the United States puberty is a period accompanied by a major upsurge in sexual activity, particularly among males (see Figure 4). Most of this is masturbation, but it includes some social-sexual activity with persons of the same and the opposite sex. (An increase in sexual activity near the events of puberty is not nearly as marked among women in U.S. society.) This adolescent burst of sex is often attributed to an increase in the "sex drive" produced by an increase in "sex" hormones. As has been noted, the impact of these hormones on the bodies of young people are dramatic. Major changes do take place in the genitals and the reproductive system, as well as other changes in the body that signal that this is a "sexual" person.

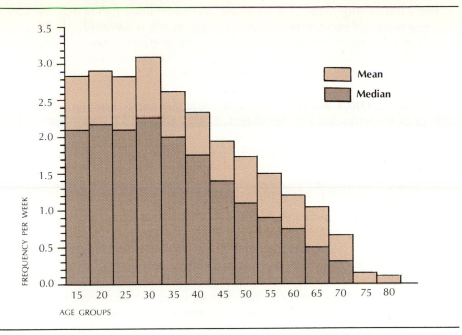

Figure 4   Frequency per Week of Male Orgasm from All Sources, by Five-Year Age Groups. Where median figures are not shown, they are zero. (Kinsey, 1948, p. 220.)

Our problem is to sort out the relationships of the changes in body chemistry, the consequent body changes, the changes in conception of self, and the associated increase in overt and psychological sexual conduct. A relatively simple biological-ly-oriented explanation is that increasing amounts of "sex" hormones somehow *make* the organism behave in a more sexual way. There are a number of ways to advance this view:

1. There is some *directional* force in the hormonal impact on psychological and social behavior of the organism. The chemicals themselves, by influencing body tissues, increase not only the amount of sexual activity, but also predispose the organism to choose as a sex object a member of the opposite sex. The hormones both potentiate and direct the activity of the organism down particular behavioral pathways. This is not a very widely accepted argument, but it does have some fans.

2. The hormones do not direct exactly what people will do, but they increase the likelihood of the organism doing something sexual, regardless of prior training. Thus, whether the organism chooses to have sex with a man or a woman, it will do something that observers call sexual. It is unclear how this works, but there are people who argue that hormones make the penis or clitoris more sensitive or the penis and vagina better able to fit together. There is little evidence for such specific effects, but in this view the hormones do have some sexual guidance effect on sexual conduct.

3. The hormones are interactive with prior social and psychological experience, and either increase the likelihood of sexual activity (the more hormone the more

likely the activity), lower the threshold to sexual effects (being touched may be more easily interpreted as sexual), or energize the organism so that the social and psychological components of sexual activity are effective. It is not that hormones determine what the organism will do, but varying amounts of hormone will increase or decrease the propensity or desire of a human being to do something sexual.

These biological points of view emphasize the direct or indirect influence of hormones on determining (1) sex-object choices, (2) sexual receptivity, and (3) sexual activity, either in puberty or later in the life cycle (particularly around the menstrual cycle or menopause). They are sometimes linked to the notion of a sex drive, an innate force located in the biology of the organism, a sex drive that knows its goal — a goal that may be heterosexuality (indicating a biological tilt) or the goal of sexual activity itself. A belief in the importance of biological forces in determining various aspects of sexual conduct has characterized most major sex researchers, from Freud and Ellis to Kinsey.

The impact of hormones on sexual behavior is a complex question, in which the predisposition of the researcher has a profound effect on what is thought to be strong or weak evidence. Kinsey reported that men during puberty have far higher rates of sexual activity than do women. It is sometimes argued that this results from higher levels of *androgens* (the male sex hormones which seem to be responsible for sexual activity in primates) in males than females. However, Kinsey did not find such a correlation:

Since we found a sudden upsurge of sexual responsiveness and overt sexual activity among human males at the beginning of adolescence, there may seem to be some correlation with the androgen picture; but the upsurge of sexual responsiveness in the male is much more abrupt than the steady rise in the levels of his androgens.

As for the female, there seems to be no correlation at all between the levels of her androgens and her slow and gradual development of sexual responsiveness and overt sexual activity. Although she has nearly as much androgenic hormone as the male in her pre-adolescent and early adolescent years, her levels of sexual response and overt sexual activity at that period are much lower than the levels in the average male. The near identity of the androgen levels in the female and male at the very age at which the two sexes develop such strikingly different patterns of behavior, makes it very doubtful whether there is any simple and direct relationship between androgens and patterns of pre-adolescent and adolescent sexual behavior in either sex. (Kinsey, 1953, pp. 730–731.)

What is most obvious is that women have very different social and psychological experiences when learning how to be sexual during puberty. The fact that women display less overt sexual activity than men during adolescence should be contrasted with the Masters and Johnson contention that all women have the capacity for orgasm. If Masters and Johnson are correct, and if women were allowed or encouraged to have sex early in life, they would have sex as often as men, and if multiple orgasm were taken into account, they would have orgasm more often than men.

The capacity-activity problem is a profound one in the absence of knowledge about the upper limits of sexual activity. As noted in Chapter 1, certain cultures have very high rates of activity for both males and females, some two or three times that of males in the United States. It seems improbable that such vast differences can be attributed to differences in hormone level.

There are equally startling low rates of sexual activity among certain male groups, particularly those with strong religious beliefs. There are a fair number of men who have very low levels of sexual activity prior to marriage. They do not masturbate, nor do they have premarital sex. The low rates of these men are unlikely to be attributable to variations in levels of hormones since their rates in marriage diverge only slightly from the more experienced.

There are differences in sexual capacity that might be due to biological forces; however, no human population has operated near the upper limits of sexual capacity or has selected itself genetically on this basis, and as a result, most of the variation in activity that we find may reasonably be attributed to social and psychological forces.

Biological arguments also confuse reproductive maturity and sexual activity. As noted, there is an apparent capacity to have orgasm, which is the important pleasure-related and biologically based accompaniment of sexual activity, long before puberty. Hormonal changes are not so much linked to sexual capacity as they are to reproductive capacity. While the hormones increase the size of the penis and scrotum, change aspects of the vagina, and increase breast size, none of these factors are directly related to capacity for orgasm. There is no systematic study which suggests that such hormonal events either enhance or inhibit the capacity for orgasm in either gender.

The changes which occur with reproductive maturity themselves require psychological interpretation. The experience of orgasm must be integrated into a sexual script; it is an event that is supposed to happen in a limited set of contexts. The same process of script integration occurs with the development of erotic sensitivity of the scrotum, the breasts in men and women, and other parts of the body. These body parts do not grow more or less sensitive to erotic arousal with variations in hormone levels.

The male sex hormones are called *androgens* and the female are called *estrogens*. It has been demonstrated empirically in monkeys that the male hormones are involved in the sexual receptivity of female nonhuman primates. Through an ingenious set of experiments it has been shown that the sexual receptivity of female monkeys can be eliminated by removing all sources of male hormones from their bodies, and then reactivated by replacement.

Such an important discovery would be significant for humans if there were any evidence that rising and falling levels of androgens significantly affected the sexuality of human females. There are a number of studies which suggest that women report different levels of arousal or sex activity during the menstrual cycle, but there are technical difficulties with such studies which make them difficult to accept. Further, none of the studies contain actual measures of the levels of hormones in the body. Also, these studies are contradictory in that they place the highest arousal levels at different points in the cycle.

Unlike any other primates, human female sexual interests are not regulated by the hormonal inputs of the estrual cycle. Among monkeys, sexual receptivity is governed quite directly by the hormones — however, human females choose to have sex on the basis of social and psychological factors. They act sexually out of an open genetic program.

From what evidence there is, it appears that the amount of hormone in the human body is not related directly to the amount of sexual activity. Even in animals where they are important, hormones seem to work primarily like a light switch; when there is *enough* chemical the animal is able to perform sexually. Adding more does not cause the animal to become more sexually active or receptive. What happens with female monkeys is that they remain equally receptive with increasing doses of hormone until the chemical suddenly changes its effect, producing aggressive behavior and not sexual receptivity. This suggests that hormones may create a threshold for sexual behavior (it takes a certain amount to get started) but does not have a variable effect on the amount or intensity of behavior (adding more does not increase the activity).

Conclusion: Puberty and Sexual Expectations

The impact of biology on sexuality in adolescence may be traced, not to physical events, but to the social meanings attributed to body changes. All the other elements for orgasmic experience are already there before puberty, but not named or elicited by the social world. When secondary sexual characteristics appear, they become the evidence for sexuality. As a result *reproductive* characteristics become the basis for defining sexuality.

There is nothing in the biological events of puberty that makes the organism act sexually or do sexual things. The hormones may generally energize the organism, create greater physical strength, change the mucosal characteristics of the vagina, and so on — all of which may facilitate sexuality, particularly the way we do it. However, none of these events automatically elicits sexual activity from a previously sexually inactive organism. Biological factors may contribute to the variability of human sexual activity, but only as they are shaped and controlled by social and psychological factors.

SEXUAL AROUSAL AND RESPONSE

IN THE COURSE OF A DAY PEOPLE DEFINE A WIDE RANGE OF STIMULI AS SEXUAL. IT may be the face of an attractive man or woman, a mysterious glance hidden by sun glasses, a passing scent, the sound of a voice or a song half heard, a touch on the arm, a swirl of wind around a loose-fitting garment, some forbidden flesh partially and inadvertently exposed—each of these events can cause a flicker of arousal by "mixing memory and desire" and setting off a chain of sexual thoughts. This response is usually short-lived, as other interests intervene and the regular (and usually nonsexual) course of the day resumes. In other cases such stimuli may be the cause of a quiet meditation in which the dreamer converts the fragment into a complex reverie, and may actually note changes in physiology—a slight hardening of the penis, a dampening of the vagina, perhaps an elevation and stabilization of the respiration and heart rates.

At first glance this description seems very simple, hiding practically nothing, exposing what happens to all of us at least some of the time. Is it really this simple? Is there only an event in the world (the sexual stimulus) followed by a response (sexual arousal) in the person? What is missing is the cultural history of the individual, a history composed of learning to define events as sexual and respond to them in correct ways. Our "responder" is a person with a culturally induced version of his or her own level of sexual interest in various contexts, as well as a publically shared and privately elaborated repertoire of people, events, and activities defined as sources of arousal. Thus a person may see himself or herself as "horny all the time" or "thinking about sex a lot," or say "sex is an important part of my life" (or the opposite of all of these, though it may be harder these days to make that admission), and may have a range of collectively shared sexual interests (if heterosexual and male, it is all right to be interested in female breasts, legs, hair) as well as a private set of interests (the odor of sweat, large penises).

People vary in the degree to which they define the world around them in sexual terms. Some go through a day without ever responding sexually; more accurately, *they do not actively perceive and define the stimuli around them as being appropriate to producing a sexual response.* Others exposed to the same events might have an incessant flow of internal erotic images, and a mild or intense physical response. In this case the person has *actively given sexual meaning to these events and has chosen to respond in a culturally appropriate manner*. In between the world of stimuli and the responses that people make is a long sequence and a wide variety of personal decisions.

Whenever a person makes what we simply call "a response," it is the result of a sequence of interdependent decisions. However, in most sexual situations that are not new to that person, this process is rarely experienced as a series of conscious choices. The response seems automatic, as a result of both practice (similar decisions have been made before) and cognitive preparation and organization (the stimulus is rapidly coded and organized into an entire sequence of ready-made scripts). For instance, a stewardess raises her hands above her head to get a coat down from the overhead rack, her breasts rise with the motion — a sexually interested passenger observes the event and codes it into a sexual fantasy of meeting her later and having sex. Once the original choice has been made to code the event as sexual, the resulting narrative carries on without apparent further decision. What is invisible is the history of the person who had to learn to code breasts as sexual, stewardesses as sexually accessible, being away from home as a context in which arousal is legitimate, knowing about intercourse, and all that. Previous practice and the organized channelling of information make the connection between stimulus and response appear to be involuntary.

The complexity of this process is considerable. It is never completely automatic, even among those who are very sexually experienced, and it usually requires an extended set of thoughtful decisions for those who are first learning how to be sexual. There is nothing in any particular event itself which produces sexual arousal — the classification of a stimulus as sexual and a response as sexual is the outcome of a history of decisions made by an individual in a particular society and culture. It is usually difficult for us to recall our first making the decisions to label and connect a stimulus and a response, partly because we often merely accepted the models provided for us.

It is common for heterosexually oriented men to be aroused by seeing women's breasts under clothing, by taking off a brassiere, by touching a woman's breasts with their hands or mouths. These activities are often accompanied by dramatic psychological and physiological changes in the man, experienced as appropriate to the sexual things he is doing. It is difficult for him as a participant or a product of socialization to recall the amount of learning that had to take place for all of these events to make sense as sexual events. There is no automatic connection between touching a woman's breasts and blood flow into the genitals.

A similar argument can be made concerning a woman's response to touching a man's genitals or accepting a penis into her vagina. There is nothing about handling a penis that invariably produces sexual arousal, nor does a penis in the vagina automatically produce vaginal lubrication, sexual excitement, or orgasm. Getting to the point where sexual activities can be combined together in a culturally appropriate sequence takes a substantial amount of learning, particularly under the conditions prevalent in U.S. society (see Chapter 9).

What makes these fragments of information, these stimuli, productive of different types and different levels of response? We have assumed a relatively passive subject, not thinking about sex, who in a moment of inattention is presented with a stimulus that in U.S. culture probably has a sexual meaning. There are variations in individual readiness to give a sexual meaning to specific stimuli: two people may see the same flesh; one may think it appropriate to respond sexually, the other may not. The difference in response may come from many sources: the object may not be preferred (a lesbian is unlikely to be aroused by attractive men); the object may not have any sexual meaning at all (few people see a nude child as erotic); or the subject may be overexposed to particular stimuli (a centerfold photographer or a person at a nudist camp may not be aroused by exposed breasts just because they are exposed).

There is constant interaction between a person's interests, the scripts that organize information from the environment, and the character of the environment itself. Similar acts will be experienced as sexual or nonsexual, depending on the script for that circumstance. A doctor examining a woman for breast cancer performs acts similar to a lover's. The doctor's manipulations are not officially defined as sexual in that situation; the lover's are — although a private sexual script might produce arousal in the doctor and/or his patient, just as one or both lovers might not feel aroused. People can feel one thing while doing another — in the extreme case, it is possible to put on a public sexual performance without the performers feeling any emotional involvement or arousal.[1]

The scripts we use mediate between us and the contexts around us. They serve to code incoming information and organize it; they can be plans for the future; and they serve as a device for recalling the past. As we use them to perform these three functions, our scripts do not remain static. They shift as we adapt to novel and changing environments and as we seek to make our environments conform to our wishes. In this sense scripts are guidance mechanisms through which we attempt to make the world conform — we seek to accomplish the goals we have through acting out the scripts we have.

How much more complicated sexual arousal now appears to be! When people say they are "turned on," when they display the physical signs of arousal, or when they do sexual things, it is not the automatic connection of some stimuli with some response. It is the decision process of an active, interested human being who has learned sexual scripts of a given time and place, trying to accomplish his or her reflective or unreflective purposes. What appears to be automatic is only that which has been well learned, and performed in stable contexts with stable goals.

Fortunately, the knowledge that sexual arousal is not automatic, but is the outcome of myriad experiences, does not seem to lessen most people's interest in or capacity to do sexual things. It is like finding out the physical principles of swimming after having learned to swim; it is interesting, but it does not make you so self-conscious that you are likely to drown. Similarly, most people learn to be sexual before they learn to analyze it.

---

1. The disjunction between the public and the private remains important all the way through our lives. It is common for privately induced sexual responses to intrude in nonsexual contexts, particularly among young people. A young person with a fever or with some other nonsexual but arousing state can misinterpret the arousal as sexual in certain contexts. Young males often have erections on buses, for example, which they have to conceal when they get to their stop.

A Fictitious Sexual Day

The chart that accompanies this section (Figure 1) shows the hypothetical but realistic sexual activity of a married man and wife over a period of a few hours, from about five in the afternoon until going to sleep at night. There is no way to verify the chart except to ask whether it seems to make sense, because attempting to record an experience interferes with the experience itself. Even if an external observer notes something which might be called sexual, there is no measure of subjective interest, except to ask the subject afterward. By then the experience is coded in talk and distorted by the scripts that intervene between the past and the present, as well as by the act of trying to describe what has happened. Measures of physiological changes will not help either, both because measuring devices create their own interference and because there is no one-to-one relation between the physiological events recorded and what the individual feels or thinks.

The problem is that our minds are not two-channel stereophonic; that is, it is difficult for us to observe what we are doing while we are doing it. We cannot record on a second tape, so to speak, exactly what we feel when we are having sex, and then replay that tape to get an accurate record. Even if we could we would face the problem of translating the tape into words. As we develop better research techniques we will be able to study parts of the experience, but we will never be able to record the entire experience as it is experienced. We can only study fragments of it and assemble them in a construction. The chart, then, is simply a device to call attention to various ways in which we experience ourselves and other people sexually.

The chart offers us an opportunity to approach four issues:

1. The scripted character of the sexual conduct which Mary and George have produced over the eight or nine-hour period.
2. The negotiated character of sexuality, negotiation not only with another person, but negotiation with the self about how appropriate, correct, or desirable it is to do certain sexual things.
3. The role of various sensory channels in providing information that can be defined as being sexual.
4. The relationship between a more extended and naturalistic view of sexual conduct and the researches of Masters and Johnson on the "sexual response cycle" as they studied it in the laboratory.

Scripts of Mary and George

The chart reflects many of the scripted elements of sexuality for both adult men and women. While our example is of a heterosexual married couple with children, some of these constraints (such as work, or caring for children) are felt by many people, male or female, married or single, homosexual or heterosexual. Our sexual acts and fantasies are shaped by our worlds, our scripts, and our willingness to manipulate both.

MARY

1. Watches talk show on TV, sees Robert Redford, has fantasy of meeting him, going out, having sex.
2. Children come home, talk about school, she gives them a snack.
3. Starts dinner, makes a batter, licks fingers, thinks the feeling is sexy.
4. Phone call about tennis date, fantasizes having affair with tennis pro.
5. George arrives, hug and kiss.
6. Finishes dinner, children watching TV.
7. George comes into kitchen, puts his arms around her; she pushes him away, muttering about the "kids and dinner."
8. Dinner.
9. Children leave table.
10. Clears table, does dishes, talk.
11. Leaves table, hugs George, says "take a shower when you go to bed."
12. Family TV viewing hour.
13. Prepares children for bed.
14. Washes her little boy's penis.
15. Children asleep.
16. Watches TV.
17. Tells George she'll "be there in a minute."
18. Goes to bedroom, undresses, waits for George.
19. Foreplay
20. Intromission.
21. Intercourse, no climax.
22. Rests.
23. Takes shower.
24. Reads.
25. Masturbates to orgasm while fantasizing love affair.
26. Sleeps.

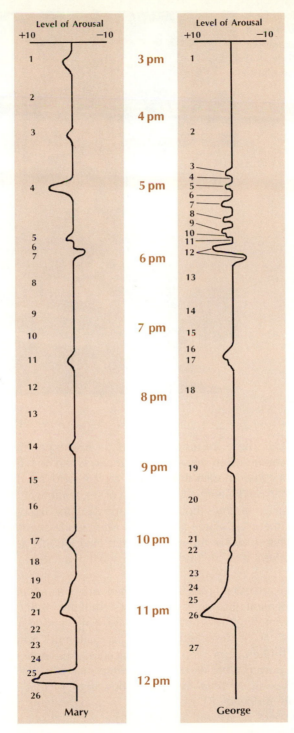

GEORGE

1. Working on final report, due at five pm.
2. Turns in report.
3. Walks back to office, smells perfume of a passing secretary, looks back at her.
4. Leaves office and walks to train.
5. Looks at women on the street.
6. Waits, boards train, reads paper.
7. Looks at X-rated film ads.
8. Looks at woman in train, fantasizes sex with her.
9. Arrives at station, walks home, looks at girl in passing car.
10. Enters house, greets children, walks into kitchen, kisses and hugs wife.
11. Gets drink.
12. Walks into kitchen, feeling very aroused, hugs and fondles wife, she rebuffs him, he walks out feeling annoyed.
13. Dinner, family talk.
14. Children leave table.
15. Clean up, do dishes, talk.
16. Reaches over, touches wife gently, kisses her.
17. Family TV viewing hour, looks at Raquel Welch, actress, aroused by her. Fantasizes having intercourse with her.
18. Reads paper and watches TV.
19. Daughter comes in, sits on his lap, hugs him and flirts with him.
20. Watches TV.
21. Show over, gets up, says he is going to take a shower.
22. Takes shower, goes to bedroom, gets into bed.
23. Foreplay.
24. Intromission.
25. Intercourse.
26. Orgasm.
27. Sleep.

Figure 1   The Erotic Day of George and Mary.

The exposure of forbidden flesh can catch the momentary interest of an onlooker. The amount required, however, will depend on the time and the place.

WHEN: There are long periods of time when neither Mary nor George think about sex at all: when she is making dinner; when he is finishing the report. Neither in the work environment nor in the scripts for work are there reasons to include the sexual. Mary and George usually think of sex while watching television, or walking to the train, or at times thought to be appropriate, like bedtime. There are inappropriate moments—George approaches Mary while she is cooking dinner and is rebuffed. This is one of those times when most people actively do not want to feel sexual, when it is an intrusion into what they think is more important at that moment.

There are other times when we think of sex as a break from what we are doing at the moment. Examples are Mary's thinking about sex while tasting batter; George's smelling a secretary's perfume. This "taking a break" aspect of thinking about sex can be described as an "escape attempt" from the demands of the present, much like taking a momentary vacation. The tendency to think about sex as a distraction from what we are doing often makes us believe that we would either think of sex all the time if we were allowed to, or that sexual thoughts are always waiting in our heads. These "random" sexual thoughts are more regulated than we might suspect, as we will find later. What we tend not to notice is how often non-sexual thoughts come into our minds when we are thinking about or doing sexual things—we think about work, or sport, or what we are going to do later.

WHO: Mary and George think sexually about a number of people, ranging from those they have direct sexual experience with (past or present lovers; each other); those they see in person (Mary's tennis pro; the woman on the train); and those presented by the media (television or movie actors). In some ways all these people have attributes that make them sexually accessible, in both fantasy and reality. Mary's tennis pro is one of those persons defined as sexual by virtue of an athletic occupation; Robert Redford, Raquel Welch, and X-rated film actresses are part of the galaxy of fantasy lovers offered by the media; the woman on the train is a stranger. Each of these people has different attributes that will produce different fantasies — and different activities in the real world. At the same time, there are people who should not elicit sexual responses, e.g., George's daughter from George. Feeling aroused by a child (even if it leads to sex with a spouse) can produce feelings of guilt and ambivalence. Even in fantasy there are limits on who can produce arousal without its common associate, guilt.

WHERE: Fantasy occurs nearly anywhere, but sexual activity is largely confined to the bedroom ("where" is closely associated with "when"). However, extended fantasies usually occur in those spaces that do not demand close attention — the train, watching television in a half-lighted room.

WHAT: Sexual fantasies include the usual activities — petting of all sorts, oral sex, intercourse — but what often makes the sexual act powerful are the other script elements, the persons and places and reasons for doing these things. For some people, particularly those who are relatively sexually inexperienced, just thinking about or doing the sexual acts themselves can be arousing. However, the context in which the sex takes place is more commonly what enhances the experience. In actual sexual activity George and Mary use the standard repertoire of hugging, kissing, general body touching, genital caresses, and intercourse. In fantasies and in love affairs they might both use more extensive and elaborate sexual techniques.

WHY: In a broad sense, "why" can be answered only by detailing the processes that got George and Mary to the point in life where they are. More practically speaking, it has to do with their sense of legitimacy for thinking or doing sexual things—their explanations and reasons. Mary may explain her fantasies about an affair by saying that George is an indifferent lover, that she wants romantic excitement, or that she has too much time on her hands. George will explain his fantasies in similar ways; he will talk about being horny, explain his sex with Mary by talking about love and intimacy and communication or about his rights as a husband and her duty as a wife. He will explain his uneasiness at feeling aroused by his daughter by saying that it is not right to have such feelings about one's own children.

We all have whys, but it is generally easier to be sexual than it is to talk about it. The whys we do produce are usually audience-specific; that is, we give a different set of reasons to different people. Mary, in explaining an affair to her best friend, to her mother, to George, or to a marriage counselor, would be likely to give very different reports to each.

Problem of Negotiation

Another dimension of sexual action observed in the chart is the degree of negotiation that must take place between people who are going to have sex. It is not a forgone conclusion that married Mary and George will have sex that night—the rebuff at dinner might turn him off, Mary might not signal by asking him to take a shower—many things can happen. It is perfectly possible for all this to go awry.

Negotiation is not only interpersonal, it is also intrapersonal. One must negotiate with oneself. George had to feel that he would not be too tired for work the following day—what if the report were due in the morning? At dinner time, Mary had to feel that it was more important to get dinner than to make love.

There is an extraordinary distance between stimulus and response, the degree to which our sexuality is limited by the structure of our lives as well as the scripts that are in our heads.

Channels of Information

Our various senses provide us with the information that we define as sexual. There is nothing in this information that automatically makes us respond sexually; we must assign the information a meaning which has an appropriate set of responses. In the process of learning the sexual stimuli and the sexual responses in our culture, we are actively constructing a sexual world. When we are correctly trained, these constructions will appear to us as a series of relatively rapid and sometimes fixed connections between what we believe are stimuli and responses.

The connection between events in the world and the responses of an individual is more variable in human beings than in any other species. The further we move away from the human species, the more connections between information from the world and the activity of the animal seem to be very fixed ("instinctual"). In some fish changes in coloration or display behavior on the part of the female almost invariably produces in the male a sequence of sexual activity leading commonly to reproduction. The reproductive act and the sexual act are bound together, and the behavior of the male animal is controlled by what some biologists call an *innate releasing mechanism* (IRM). The stimulus automatically produces the response. The biologist Ernst Mayr describes these relatively automatic processes as results of *closed* genetic programs; that is, the activities of animals are controlled very closely by genetic characteristics. As we get closer to the primate species, the weaker and less automatic these stimulus-response connections are.

The sexuality and the reproductive behavior of human beings are characterized by *open* genetic programs; that is, there is no evidence that one set of stimuli either from the world outside, or from inside the organism, will automatically and invariably produce sexual activity. There is very little evidence that human sexual conduct is strongly affected by *any* biological factors, except for those physically destructive—removing or damaging parts of the body can eliminate or distort sexual activity. In the intact human organism, sexual conduct is determined by the learning history of the organism, in interaction with the changing demands of the environment.

Humans are constantly modifying the meanings of events (both stimuli and responses) and creating connections between them in different contexts. The socialization history of an individual is a record of learning what things mean in a given culture and the ways meaning can be modified. Thus, being touched becomes a "sexual stimulus" to the person being touched only at the moment of deciding that touch is sexual. Then the person may decide (or not) to produce a correct "sexual response." That the touch could be defined as meaning something sexual and that the successive response activities mean something sexual had to be learned.

VISUAL STIMULI

If we examine the experience of Mary and George, who have already learned the right things to do—learned to connect the culturally appropriate stimuli with the culturally appropriate responses—we find that they get information from the world through a number of channels. Perhaps the most important of these is sight. George first sees most of the things that arouse him, in the real world, on the media, in his fantasies. The same is true of Mary. Visual inputs serve as a powerful source of information, including information defined as sexual. In the past it was thought that women do not define as sexual as much of the visual world as do men—that women do not respond to sexual stimuli as men do. This may have been true, but not for the reasons offered.

In the Kinsey research, both women and men were asked if they were aroused by seeing stag films, burlesque houses, stripteasers, or pornography. Fewer women than men reported high levels of arousal.[2] The most satisfactory explanation, other than assigning a biological meaning (women's brains are different), is that most women in 1950 did not see or see as much of these kinds of materials, that the materials were largely prepared for men (that is, they did not connect with women's sexual scripts), and finally, that women were trained to talk about such materials in a negative manner. The difference between men and women, then, could be partly that (1) some women who saw the materials did not define the materials as sexually arousing (no reason why they should); and that (2) some women did find the materials arousing, but did not want to say so.

More recent studies of visual arousal, conducted in the 1960s and 1970s, suggest that the differences between men and women are less than in earlier studies. More men were aroused by seeing pictures of naked women than women aroused by similar pictures of naked men, including ones with an erection. However, when offered pictures of sexual activity (petting or coitus) or a film showing extended sexual activity (petting through coitus), both men and women registered quite similar responses (erection in men; vaginal lubrication in women). In these later studies, measuring devices were attached to the genitals. Both sexes recorded blood-flow changes in the genitals when presented with erotic materials.

These studies suggest that there has been in the United States a separate learning track for men and women about sex, in rates of exposure to sexual materials, ways of talking about sexuality, and the script elements found to be particularly arousing. The studies also demonstrated that as men and women develop more common histories of exposure to sexual materials, are offered situations in which they are asked in a neutral or approving way about their sexual reactions, and are exposed to erotic materials that include both male and female sexual script elements, they will begin to report similar degrees of arousal by visual materials. The changes in findings were a result of both changes in the society and changes in the methods of the experiments.

AURAL STIMULI

Sound, like sight, offers information about the world which we can define as sexual without having to respond directly. However, unlike sight, which is a major source of information used for fantasy, sounds are less often defined as sexually exciting. Other animals cry out when they are in heat or make noises of one sort or another to signal sexual interest, but humans generally do not give each other vocalized sexual signals before performing a particular sexual act.

2. There is an important point to be made here. Often this finding is interpreted to mean that women are less aroused by pornography than men are—what the finding actually says is that fewer women reported being *highly* aroused than men reported being highly aroused, and more women reported not being aroused than men reported not being aroused. This is *not* a measure of intensity of arousal, and therefore we must assume that the women who said that they were highly aroused were just as highly aroused as the men who said so.

There are some people who are aroused by particular kinds of music (Rock, for example; in some recent albums the lyrics are expressly intended to arouse) or particular rhythms (people at one time reported being aroused by Ravel's *Bolero*), but these are largely an individual script element. More often music serves as a backdrop to passion, to get people into the mood, rather than being directly experienced as "arousing."

Sounds can be important during sexual activity itself. Most people do not give directions during sex (now do this, now do that, that feels good, keep it up); rather, they communicate nonverbally through touch and motions and vocally by making excitement sounds, using slang, making appreciative remarks ("that feels good," "you taste good"), calling out each other's names. (The cultural bias against directive speech during sex has some negative results, such as unwillingness to tell someone to stop doing something—often we simply accept certain sexual activities because we think that speaking will destroy the mood.) Vocalizations are usually experienced as exciting by the participants; some appear to be involuntary, but more often they are part of a learned set of signals to the other person of various levels of excitement and pleasure. The arousal power of such vocalization is not presently under study.

In addition are the sexual stories we tell ourselves as fantasies. There are many people who do not fantasize in visual images, but do so by telling themselves stories, "There I was sitting in this bar and this terrific looking girl (boy) came in and I walked over to her (him) and said . . . ," or, "We were having a glass of wine together, his hands were strong and beautiful and I wondered how they would feel . . . ." Script elements underlie these stories—the who, the what, the when, the where, and the why which legitimate the sexuality. Such narrative fantasies are often triggered by events in the world or are associated with masturbation, but they are stories listened to with an inner ear. The use of auditory fantasy and the character of those fantasies are only now being studied.

There is another source of auditory sexual stimulus, but most of us do not connect it directly to arousal. When we are with someone of sexual interest, we sometimes talk indirectly about sex ("You are beautiful"; "You turn me on"; "I find you very exciting"). How arousing such talk is physiologically is not known. However, such conversational gambits do serve to smooth the way to sexual activity, or set the stage for doing it, or legitimate doing it.

Some people tell each other their sexual fantasies or share sexual experiences. Adolescent boys tell each other stories of their sexual prowess, and some adolescent girls talk to each other about petting and necking. Such narratives are not only informational guides for behavior, but sources of sexual excitement as well. We tend also to underestimate the role of sexual narratives told as forms of gossip among adult men and women. Often such gossip is moralizing and negative, but to talk about affairs and sexual disasters may also be a source of sexual excitement for those listening.

This may be particularly true of conversations between men and women. Thus a young man may tell a young woman edited versions of his sexual exploits, hoping to interest and perhaps arouse her sexually. This practice is explicit among people who share the sexual aspects of their lives with each other. In these circumstances, such reports are often sources of sexual excitement for both listener and speaker, and serve as preliminaries to sexual activity.

OLFACTORY AND GUSTATORY STIMULI

Smell is an important part of the initiatory stages of sexuality among our nearest animal relatives; however, there is no evidence that particular smells have any direct sexual effect on humans. In the United States, with the heavy use of deodorant soaps, sprays, and roll-ons, vaginal sprays and douches, odorous shaving creams and shampoos, aftershave lotions, and perfumes for men and women, there are probably no natural odors left to smell. The nose must find its way through such a mist of artificial odors that arousal could not depend on natural odors.

Among nonhumans it appears that female primates excrete during their fertile period chemicals called *pheromones* that attract males. Such chemicals removed from females in estrus and painted on another, unreceptive female will produce sexually initiatory behavior in male animals similar to that toward females who are truly in heat. In other experiments, when the male's nose is anesthetized, he is not responsive to females in heat to whom he has been responsive in the past. In these animals the sense of smell has a highly specified role in making males initiate sexual activity. There is no evidence of this phenomenon in humans. The odors of unwashed or post-sexual male and female genitals are reported by some as repulsive; others find these odors highly arousing.

Taste is so intimately linked to smell that many of the same points can be made. Many erotic tastes, such as lipstick and body oils, are the products of cosmetic manufacturers. Excretions of the body—sweat, saliva, or genital secretions—are largely acquired sexual tastes, or (in some cases) aversions that have to be overcome by a sense of passion and desire. There does not appear to be any particular taste which is generally exciting to large numbers of people, again indicating a lack of direct predetermined connections between stimulus and response.

TACTILE STIMULI

Parallel to aspects of the taste experience are the experiences of touch. These are the experiences of texture, of things touched with the hands, body, mouth, or tongue, or the textures and shapes of things taken into the mouth. These textures are those of roughness and smoothness (of skin, of hair, of lips, of the genitals) and the thickness or slickness of fluids. Mary is aroused by the batter that she felt first on her fingers and then took into her mouth. This complex sight-touch-taste experience indicates the degree to which materials definable as sexual can be found in a wide range of experiences. At present we know practically nothing, except from personal anecdote, about the range of preferences, desires, and levels of arousal produced by taste sensations or touch experiences.

Along with sight, touch represents a major source of sexual excitement. The order in which the senses have been presented has moved from senses that can evoke at a distance to those that are more immediate to the body. This movement does not mean that the sense of touch is more important in sex than vision — sexual activity is a multi-channel experience. We look, listen, smell, taste, and touch. We move from one channel to another, using information from each to sustain our level of excitement. Nor are the distance senses more productive of fantasy — a touch on the arm can be as arousing as seeing a naked body.

Touch, however, is important, if only because of the notion of erogenous zones. Most men believe that there are particular parts of the body which when manipulated will automatically produce sexual arousal. Their own experience and the sex manuals tell them that the lips, the breasts, particularly the nipples, the areas around the genitals, the clitoris and the penis, the buttocks, sometimes the anus are places of particular sexual sensitivity. Women often share these beliefs (learned from the same manuals, from other women, and from experience, mostly with men). What are thought to be erogenous zones are those most abundantly supplied with nerve endings (except the buttocks, for instance), but this means that they are sensitive to any kind of touch — they are simply more sensitive in general.[3]

What makes zones erotic are the contexts in which they are touched and the meanings that are attributed to that touching. Extended touching of these areas usually only occurs in contexts defined as being sexual. For example, the clitoris is rarely touched (some young women do not know they have one), except for hygienic purposes, until either masturbation in early adolescence or attempts by young men to touch it somewhat later. Then the couple are in what they both define as a sexual situation, and when the young man touches the sensitive clitoris, the young woman has a series of sensations felt in the context of sexual meanings, so she defines the reactions of her clitoris as part of the sexual process.

Similarly, a young man must learn to associate his penis with sexual desires — for the earliest part of his life it is an excretory organ. As he enters puberty (in U.S. society) his penis is given a sexual meaning, and the feelings associated with touching it are defined as sexual.

Similar events occur with the breasts. Many women report no responsiveness at all in their breasts, even into adulthood. Other women report that they became aroused by having their breasts touched because the young men they went out with wanted so badly to touch them, and were so excited when they finally did. The female's reactions to this touching were then defined as sexual, and included in the repertoire of sexual stimuli and responses.

What is important is that we accumulate our erogenous zones. A current notion is that men's nipples are sensitive and can be an erogenous zone. Women are encouraged to kiss, fondle, and touch them — and men are now beginning to report wanting to have their nipples caressed as part of sexual activity. Here we observe the social creation of a new erogenous zone.

3. The hand and the fingers contain many touch receptors, but the hands are not defined as erogenous zones. Yet a lot of sexual touching is done with the hands. Does this mean that the part touched is erogenous, while the part touching is not? Perhaps this is another masculine version of sexuality — touching a woman's body arouses her; the feeling in the man's hands is not interpreted as arousal from touch, but arousal from accomplishing the touching of the woman's body. The question remains — are the hands an erogenous zone? They have enough nerve endings to qualify, but not the attributed meaning. If a woman were making the list, perhaps she would include her hands.

There are two other kinds of experience suggesting that the sexual consequences of being touched are determined by the contexts of touching and the meanings given to it. The first is being touched on "erogenous zones" in circumstances which do not result in sexual arousal. This is most common in medical examinations of the breast, the scrotum, the anus, the female genitals—while some people report arousal in these circumstances, most do not. A second circumstance is bathing—both men and women wash parts of their bodies that they will later use in sexual activity, but because the activity is hygienic, usually no sexual arousal is felt. It is the purpose in the script that makes the difference in interpreting the touch as erotic or hygienic.

The second kind of experience, reported by many, is being aroused by touches on parts of the body not usually considered erogenous zones. Touching the elbow or the back of the arm or knee, pressure on teeth, licking a palm or sucking fingers, have all produced orgasm, particularly in women, although men report a wide range of such arousing touches as well.

What are the practical consequences of this knowledge? One is that those of us who have been raised in U.S. society share a minimum conception of what to touch and how we want to be touched in order to produce arousal. For most of us, the sex-manual approach seems to work pretty well (the sex manual is merely our own experience written down and told back to us), so a couple who do not want to talk about what each wants may as well use the tried-and-true formulas. On the other hand, to be sexually effective with a particular individual might call for talking to each other about what each prefers to do and have done. This means exposing both how much and how little each has done sexually with others, or perhaps getting embarrassed or risking being turned down. For those who do not want to take that risk, the old formula may work just as well.

On a theoretical level, it is apparent that we must create our sexuality, that the links in humans between stimulus and response are not given even at the level of bodily experience. What we need to understand are the ways in which events in the world and responses in the self are labeled as being sexual and get connected to each other, until we get to the point that when we see, smell, touch, hear, or taste in given circumstances, our bodies respond in ways that we call sexual.

Sexual Response Cycle

If we return to Mary and George for a moment, we note that at the end of the day they went to bed together and had sex together—sex which (this time) resulted in orgasm for him and not for her. It is this part of sexual experience that Masters and Johnson have studied—those moments when the negotiation is over, the couple begins to touch each other in ways that they define as sexual, through a period of increasing arousal and sexual activity, until one or both reach sexual climax (one or a number of times) and then through that period which follows as they return psychologically and physiologically to a more restful state.[4]

4. The work of Masters and Johnson is built directly on the work of Kinsey and his associates. Many findings similar to those of Masters and Johnson were reported in the Kinsey publications of 1953; such findings were also the result of observation and filming of sexual activity by the Kinsey group. However,

The period from the beginnings of "effective sexual stimulation" back to an unaroused state has been divided by Masters and Johnson, for descriptive purposes, into the excitement phase, the plateau phase, the orgasmic phase, and the resolution phase. These phases correlate roughly with the subjective feelings people report that they have during sex—first they feel excited as they begin activity; for some time they continue activity; then at some point they come to climax; after which they rest and return to a nonexcited state. As Masters and Johnson point out, the periods are not meant to stand for any particular psychological set of events or to match psychological changes, but rather "the establishment of this purely arbitrary design provides anatomic structuring and assures inclusion and correct placement of specifics of physiologic response . . ." (p. 7).

Thus the charts that they reproduce do not describe actual psychological or physiological events, but serve as a device to characterize their findings. (See Figures 2 and 3.) These charts locate the phases of the sexual response cycle as well as the levels of intensity of reaction at each stage. The decision to represent the male response by a single chart is a result of the authors' judgment that most differences in the male response cycle are linked to duration (how long things take to happen) rather than intensity of response. For the female, there are three typical patterns presented (". . . representative of the infinite variety of female sexual response"). Unfortunately, Masters and Johnson offer no extended discussion of these charts and their meaning. They seem to have intended the following:

Trace line A for females is a pattern of steadily increasing excitement followed by a plateau period after which there is either a single orgasm (the solid line) or a multiple orgasm (the dotted line), followed by resolution. The return to orgasm from plateau could have been made a number of times, depending on the number of orgasms in the cycle.

In trace line B for females, the woman reaches plateau, there is a series of less intense orgasms than in A or C, followed by a long resolution period.

In trace line C for females, the female rises in a series of stages directly to orgasm without any plateau, and then drops very quickly back to an unexcited state.

The trace line for males looks much like line A for females, except that after the orgasm there is a refractory period during which the male seems unresponsive to sexual stimulation. If there is no renewed stimulation, the male falls back to an unexcited state. If stimulation begins again, the male usually falls below the plateau level and requires re-excitement to produce a new climax.

All of these patterns are normal—the trace lines are not evaluative, merely descriptive and organizing. Masters and Johnson have reported most of their findings in terms of these stages, so that the anatomical and physiological events that they have studied could be organized and understood.

To accumulate information about these aspects of sexual response, Masters and Johnson observed and performed measurements in a laboratory setting during a wide range of sexual activity, including masturbation (males and females), intercourse, and intercourse using a subject-controlled transparent phallus (females

---

these observations were not reported by the Kinsey group as the basis for many findings included in their publications. The social climate of 1953 would not permit them to admit that they observed and filmed sexual activity. As a result, findings which had already been made had no serious impact until they were joined by the research of Masters and Johnson a decade later.

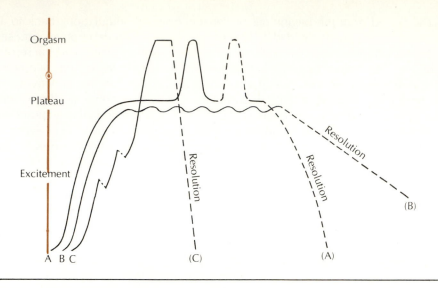

Figure 2   The Female Sexual Response Cycle. (Masters and Johnson, 1966.)

only). The subject population was 382 women and 312 men who volunteered for the research, many of whom were paid for their participation. Most of the subjects were recruited from the academic community surrounding a major medical center.

Although the study was based on a non-representative sample, it can be defended on two grounds: First, it is unlikely that certain measures would be directly affected by sample selection (acidity and alkalinity of the vagina; uterine contractions during sexual activity), though there would probably be more significant complications in evaluating whatever psycho-physiological or psychological evidence was collected. Second, the breakthrough in getting even a minimal amount of information was so significant, that even a skewed population could serve as a baseline for further research on sexual responsiveness during sexual activity.

Masters and Johnson estimate that they observed about 10,000 complete sexual response cycles (p. 15). About 7500 of these were performed by females, about 2500 by males. If every subject had been observed the same number of times, this would have meant an average of twenty-six cycles per female and eight cycles per male. However, this was not the case; it is clear from the report (though the numbers are not specified) that some subjects participated in many aspects of the study and were responsible for many of the cycles, while others performed less frequently. It is a weakness of the research record that an accurate count of these cycles, and which subjects were involved in which experiments, were not reported. In the absence of a detailed record of the research, caution must be used in interpreting the findings.

It is also important to note and stress—as Masters and Johnson do—that "the question of why men and women respond as they do to effective sexual stimulation is not answered" in their study (p. 8). This is so because all of the people who per-

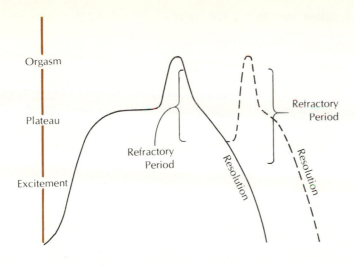

Figure 3   **The Male Sexual Response Cycle.** (Masters and Johnson, 1966.)

formed in their laboratory had already learned how to behave sexually. This fact was crucial, not only to how they performed in the laboratory, but to their ability to perform at all in the laboratory. Referring to female subjects, Masters and Johnson say, "it was from previously established levels of sexual response that the individual female was able to cope with and adapt to a laboratory situation." That is, the subjects knew how to have sex and, using this prior knowledge, were able to respond to the demands of the laboratory. In this sense, the origins of their ability are obscured because they already knew how.

The point here is that sex in a laboratory is remarkably different from usual sexual encounters. If we refer back to Mary and George, we find that, until the very last moment, the sex act is being negotiated; that the act is in private, at home, in legitimate circumstances. In contrast, the people who came to the Masters and Johnson laboratory knew that they were going to have sex at an appointed time, that they would be paid, that they would be observed, that they would take off their clothes *prior* to effective sexual stimulation (taking off each other's clothes can be part of the excitement), and that their activity was legitimated not by love, reproduction, or religion, but by the interests of science (and in some cases altruism, "this research will help other people").

These comments are not meant to disapprove of what was going on, but rather to point out that the laboratory study of the sexual response cycle demands people who know what they are expected to do in the laboratory. In those cases where the subject has never had an experience (orgasm in masturbation) or when an observation requires attaching an apparatus, the subject must be trained how to have sex in this new context. For instance, during the measurement of changes in vaginal pH (acidity), a speculum was inserted into the vagina before the response cycle, and measurements were taken from the vaginal walls using a probe. The subject had to be prepared to have orgasm through masturbation, with a speculum inserted in her vagina, and with a person standing between her legs taking a series of measurements on her vaginal walls.

In other cases the measurements required that the subject stay quite still during sexual excitement because large body movements would create disturbances in the polygraph record. Subjects must be taught to have orgasm quietly or without the large body movements which may characterize non-laboratory sexuality. This includes the involuntary body movements such as pelvic thrusting that may accompany orgasm.

Subjects are required to learn new skills, unlearn old responses, and in some cases act as if the laboratory apparatus and the experimenters are not there. How subjects adjust to this is not, and probably cannot, be known precisely. It is thus difficult to say whether what is being studied in the laboratory is like the experiences that occur outside of the laboratory.

This does not mean that many of the experiences are not similar. The pH of the vaginal fluids might not differ a great deal whether a woman was masturbating at home or in the laboratory, or having intercourse in various circumstances. However, the amount of lubrication might vary substantially, since we know that it does with various partners, in various circumstances, and at various times of the month and life cycle. Similarly, with a man, the scrotal reflex may appear similar from one sexual response cycle to another, but the degree of engorgement of the penis will vary from sexual circumstance to sexual circumstance.

When we move to the study of such systems as cardiovascular or total body response, or to the level of psychological response, we must expect increasing variability and increased difficulty of extrapolating beyond the laboratory. That is, within any individual, or among individuals who appear to have common attributes, we must expect substantial variations in the elements of the sexual response cycle. We might even conclude that some of the similarities we get in experiments emerge not from similarities in the subjects, but from similarities in the demands of the laboratory experience itself. In any case we may expect, as we move away from the laboratory, increasing variation in what happens to people as they perform sexually under different circumstances.

What is meant by "effective sexual stimulation" will vary from one life situation to another. Even the goal of effective sexual stimulation will differ from situation to situation, depending on the goals of the person or persons involved in the activity itself. Thus our research descriptions of the sexual response cycle are not descriptive of everyone in all sexual contexts, but rather an approximation of some of the processes that seem to be involved, some of which can be generalized to sex outside the laboratory and others probably cannot.

Relevance of Physiology to Satisfaction

The Masters and Johnson research has had a major impact on the study of sexuality in U.S. society. Perhaps most significantly it opened the door to further research using laboratory techniques: observation, measurement, and experiment in study-ing not only the sexual response cycle, but other aspects of sexuality as well. Not only did it supply some provisional answers, but like all useful research it has pro-voked a whole series of new questions as well.

What is the interaction between physiological events and psychological and social experience? The Masters and Johnson research identified a series of physio-logical and anatomical events that occur with some frequency (some nearly invari-ably) in a similar order in most people when they are in a socially defined sexual situation that will lead to orgasm. But few discrete sexual stimuli or moments of arousal lead to overt sexual activity, and not all overt sexual activity leads to or-gasm. Recall that Mary and George had many instances of arousal, some appro-priate, some inappropriate, some overt, most secret—but there was only one com-plete sexual response cycle between them, and she did not have orgasm.

During a wide range of sexual activity, one or the other of the persons involved may not have orgasm even though they may be pleasantly excited. Many episodes of adolescent or extramarital petting do not result in orgasm; many homosexual encounters result in orgasm for only one of the partners; some marital intercourse does not result in orgasm for the woman, and some does not for the man. These encounters should not be viewed as less valuable or pleasurable forms of sexuality than those that result in climax for both parties. Nonorgasmic sexuality has its own validities and delights.

Many of the biological events studied by Masters and Johnson are irrelevant to sexual satisfaction (e.g., vaginal acidity or alkalinity); others remain unnoticed and therefore also irrelevant. People with spinal injuries that prevent them from receiv-ing any sensation from their genitals report that they can "feel" an orgasm. These kinds of cases suggest the complexity of research into sexuality: some people can have the psychological experience of orgasm without the bodily events, while others who have all of the bodily events will not report having orgasm.

At a less complex level this is true also of the relation between the measured intensity of physiological events and the felt intensity of the orgasm. For instance, Masters and Johnson point out that certain measurements show a greater intensity during masturbation than during intercourse—but does the person doing these two different things have a different subjective experience of sexual pleasure? Higher heart rates, more contractions, more lubrication may not predict anything about the sense of pleasure in the act, either in the experience of the same person or among different persons. Women who lubricate very little and some who lubricate a great deal may both report being unhappy (or happy) with their levels of sexual response. As Masters and Johnson themselves point out, there is no single given relationship between any physiological event and subjective reports of intensity of response.

The relationships of physiological events to psychological events are the most complex and difficult to study in the laboratory, and research in this area of sexuali-ty is only beginning. Progress is likely to be slow. For instance, research into the psycho-physiology of such areas as pain and emotion has been underway much longer, and many of the problems of conceptualizing, designing, and analyzing such research remain to be solved.

Genital Sexual Responses, Female

Stages of Sexual Excitement	Excitement	Plateau	Orgasm	Resolution
Clitoris	Swells, elongates, and hardens as it fills with blood.	Withdraws to a position higher above vaginal opening.	No observed changes.	Returns to normal position 5–10 seconds after orgasm; size and hardness reduce slowly.
Vagina	Vaginal lubrication appears, vagina expands, and vaginal wall becomes distended with blood and purplish in color.	Outer third of vagina swells to form "orgasmic platform"; inner half increases in width and depth.	3–6 strong contractions in first 2.5–5 seconds, followed by 2–6 weaker, slower contractions.	Blood leaves vaginal tissues and walls relax; normal color returns in 10–15 minutes or less.
Labia majora	Flatten and separate away from vaginal opening.	Become congested and swollen with blood.	No observed changes.	Return to normal.
Labia minora	Thicken and expand to extend vagina outward by about 1 cm.	Color changes to a vivid red to deep wine as orgasm approaches.	No further changes.	Color fades to light pink within 10–15 seconds; size returns to normal.

Extragenital Sexual Responses, Female

Stages of Sexual Excitement	Excitement	Plateau	Orgasm	Resolution
Breasts	Breasts enlarge, nipples and aureoles swell, and veins become visible.	Breasts enlarge, aureoles swell further, and nipples become rigid.	No further change.	Breasts, nipples, and aureoles shrink in size and return to "normal."
Body color change	Red rash on chest and breasts in 25% of women.	Rash spreads, becoming a flush in 75% of women.	Flush reaches an intensity which may correlate with intensity of orgasm.	Flush fades.
Muscle tension	Increase in voluntary; minor increase in involuntary.	Increase in voluntary; involuntary changes in facial and abdominal muscles.	Loss of involuntary control; extensive involuntary muscle spasms.	Some muscle tension may last until five minutes after orgasm.
Breathing	————	Becomes deeper and faster late in stage.	May reach 40 breaths per minute. Rate indicates degree of sexual tension.	Rapid return to baseline.
Heart rate	Increases with level of activity and sexual tension.	Increases to 100–175 beats per minute.	May increase to 110–180 beats per minute; higher rates may be correlated with intensity of orgasm.	Rapid return to baseline.
Blood pressure	Increases with level of activity and sexual tension.	May increase by 20–60 mm Hg systolic, 10–20 mm Hg diastolic.	May increase by 30–80 mm Hg systolic, 20–40 mm Hg diastolic.	Rapid return to baseline.

These changes are not seen in all persons or in some persons all the time. They vary across individuals and within individuals across time. They are seen in the laboratory in approximately the order given in the table.

Genital Sexual Responses, Male

Stages of Sexual Excitement	Excitement	Plateau	Orgasm	Resolution
Penis	Rapid erection; degree may fluctuate.	Increase in circumference of penis at coronal ridge (rim of glans); occasionally change in color of coronal area.	3–4 pulsations of penile urethra at .8 second intervals; slower, less forceful pulsations continue for several seconds.	Rapid loss of rigidity followed by a slower shrinking to unaroused state.
Scrotum	Elevates and flattens; skin becomes "goose-bumpy."	No further changes.	No further changes.	Relaxes and returns to normal loose state, sometimes slowly.
Testes	Elevate.	Swell to 150% of normal size; further elevation as orgasm nears.	No further changes.	Return to normal size and elevation; speed depends on length of plateau stage.

Extragenital Sexual Responses, Male

Stages of Sexual Excitement	Excitement	Plateau	Orgasm	Resolution
Breasts	Nipples erect in 30% of men.	Nipples erect or remain erect in some men.	No change.	Nipple erection, when present, disappears.
Body color change	Rare.	Red rash on arms and chest in 25% of men.	Flush in 25% of men.	Flush, when present, disappears.
Muscle tension	Increase in voluntary; minor increase in involuntary.	Increase in voluntary; involuntary changes in facial and abdominal muscles.	Loss of involuntary control; extensive involuntary muscle spasms.	Some muscle tension may last until five minutes after orgasm.
Breathing	———	Becomes deeper and faster late in stage.	May reach 40 breaths per minute. Rate indicates degree of sexual tension.	Rapid return to baseline.
Heart rate	Increases with level of activity and sexual tension.	Increases to 100–175 beats per minute.	May increase to 110–180 beats per minute; little or no correlation with intensity of orgasm.	Rapid return to baseline.
Blood pressure	Increases with level of activity and sexual tension.	May increase by 20–80 mm Hg systolic, 10–40 mm Hg diastolic.	May increase by 40–100 mm Hg systolic, 20–50 mm Hg diastolic.	Rapid return to baseline.

These changes are not seen in all persons or in some persons all the time. They vary across individuals and within individuals across time. They are seen in the laboratory in approximately the order given in the table.

Female Orgasm

The nature of concern for the female orgasm has changed since the research of Kinsey and Masters and Johnson. Historically, the orgasm itself was misunderstood physiologically (it was, for instance, thought at one time that women ejaculated). Freud and the other sex researchers at the end of the nineteenth century took a renewed interest in the female orgasm, and it was Freud's formulation which became the predominant scientific view during the early years of the twentieth century.

SITE OF ORGASM

Freud's argument was as follows: Everyone goes through certain psycho-sexual stages, one of which involves masturbation as the important overt sexual activity. This stage occurs early in life as part of the parade of changes toward heterosexual genital maturity, that is, intercourse with a person of the opposite sex. Masturbation is infantile; intercourse is mature; being mature is better than being infantile. When women masturbate, they touch the clitoris; when women have intercourse, they have a penis in the vagina. Since masturbation is infantile, pleasures achieved by touching the clitoris are infantile. Sexual maturity requires that women move from having orgasms produced by touching the clitoris to having orgasms produced by the penis in the vagina. The site of sensation was supposed to move from clitoris to vagina.

When women reported (usually in therapy) that they felt sensation in the clitoris during intercourse, they were told that they were not mature; that they should have feelings in the vagina. But then Masters and Johnson and Kinsey reported that (in the words of Masters and Johnson) ". . . when any woman experiences orgasmic response to effective sexual stimulation, the vagina and clitoris react in consistent physiologic patterns. Thus, clitoral and vaginal orgasms are not separate biologic entities" (p. 67).

However, this finding has not ended the discussion, because women do report different subjective locations of sensation during masturbation, intercourse, or cunnilingus. Some women report that it seems to come from the vagina, and others from the clitoris. Many events occur in the body during sexual activity and at moments of orgasm. What is perceived by the subject depends on prior experience and training. (Ways of relocating the focus of such perceptions do exist, but are rarely used.) Each woman has an individual learning history in which she learns what sensations to have and where they appear to be coming from. Thus, different sources of sensation during sexual activity and at orgasm only become a problem when we label one or another of these experiences as better or worse, or more or less mature.

SINGLE AND MULTIPLE ORGASM

Another aspect of female sexual response that Masters and Johnson studied, following a large number of researchers, was multiple orgasm. This is the capacity in some women to experience orgasm a number of times during a single sexual response cycle. The intensities of orgasm vary from a minor series to more than one major orgasm. (See Figure 2, trace lines A and B.) How widespread is the phenomena is difficult to say. Kinsey reported in 1953 that thirteen to fifteen percent of the women he interviewed reported they had had more than one orgasm in marital intercourse (pp. 354, 719). The majority of these women had orgasm three or fewer times each intercourse; some who had multiple orgasm at times did not always have orgasm during intercourse. Similar information is not available on the masturbatory patterns of these women.

Kinsey also reported on multiple orgasm among men, especially prepubescent and early adolescent males. Even at age twenty a similar proportion of males and females (around twelve percent) reported multiple orgasm; however, these verbal reports may not correspond to the Masters and Johnson observations. At present it is not possible to determine if this capacity exists in males in the same way that it exists in some females.

Masters and Johnson incautiously describe multiple orgasm in the following way: "The human female is frequently not content with one orgasmic experience during episodes of automanipulation involving the clitoral body. If there is not psychosocial distraction to repress sexual tensions, many well-adjusted women enjoy a minimum of three or four orgasmic experiences before they reach apparent satiation" (p. 65).

The issue here is not that this happens, or that women who experience it are not well adjusted, but that it is not surely characteristic of *the human female*, meaning all women in all societies at all times. Since Masters and Johnson had selected these women for their ability to respond and had encouraged high rates of response in the laboratory, it would have been better to say that there are some women — how many we do not know — who are able to have multiple orgasm during sexual activity.

This incaution has led some commentators to decide that women are naturally sexually insatiable, and that female sexuality has been repressed by men in order to save themselves. It is clear that some women experience multiple orgasm at least some of the time. We do not know if all women are physiologically capable of multiple orgasm or whether under certain conditions any woman can learn to have multiple orgasm. It also should not be assumed that women who have multiple orgasms are more satisfied or more pleasured by their orgasms than women who only have one orgasm. It is an error to suppose that always "more is better."

Conclusion

Sexual arousal and the sexual response cycle exist at the margin of psycho-biological reality. Researchers have explored the biological aspects of this world because it is both simpler and more accessible to research. Because we know more about biology, it is easy for us to assume that it controls our lives.

What is more difficult to study is how we socially and psychologically create the meanings by which we experience, not only the world around us, but our bodies themselves. Modes of sexual arousal and the sexual response cycle are not given to us; they are constructed through our cultural experience. We learn to create sexual meaning, and to create connections between the stimuli and the responses that we define as sexual.

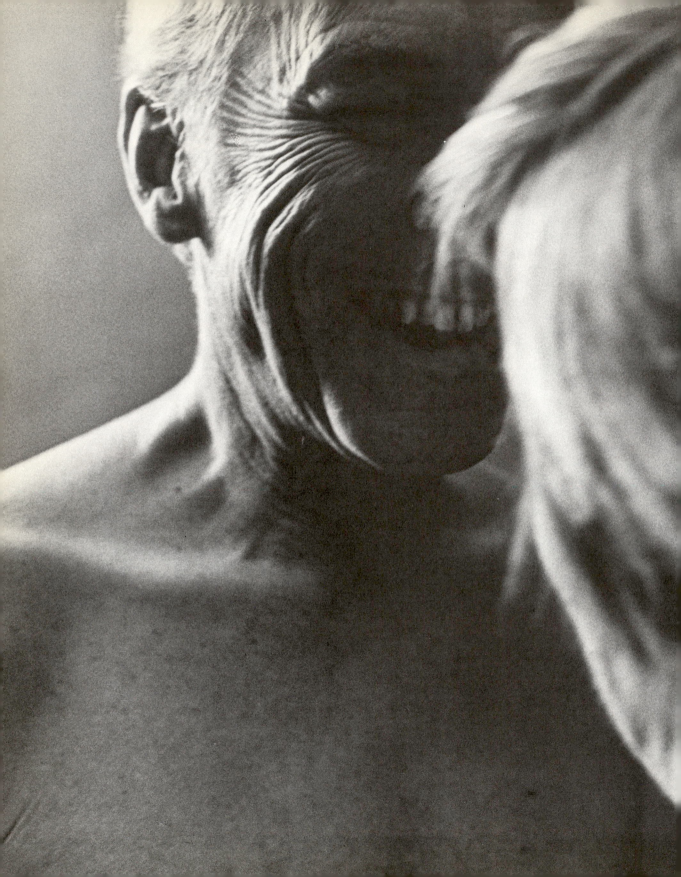

MASTURBATION

Countess: "You are a wonderful lover."
Boris: "I practice a lot when I am alone."
Woody Allen, *Love and Death*

IN THE UNITED STATES, WHERE IT IS INCREASINGLY POSSIBLE TO TALK FREELY about various forms of sexuality that have been forbidden, masturbation still retains many of its taboo aspects. Yet an understanding of the role of masturbation in psycho-sexual development, and its effect on our attitudes toward sexuality in general, is of great importance. Contemporary attitudes toward masturbation emerge from transmitted historical beliefs and from the conditions under which a person learns to masturbate; thus an understanding of them illuminates both the general processes of individual psycho-sexual development and the contemporary cultural contexts of sexuality.

The term "masturbation" commonly means manipulation by individuals of their own bodies, usually the genitals, for specific sexual pleasure.[1] It is possible for some people, usually women, to reach orgasm through nongenital stimulation, by touching either their breasts or other parts of their bodies which they find particularly pleasurable. It is also possible for a few people to reach orgasm through fantasy alone, without bodily manipulation. Again, women are more commonly able to do this than men, but it has been observed in both. In U.S. culture masturbation is largely a private solitary activity, although under some circumstances, often during adolescence, masturbation may be done in the presence of others.

Here the term will be used to mean self-induced sexual pleasure without another person being actively involved physically. This allows us to include as masturbation such activities as stimulating oneself (with or without orgasm) while looking at another person who may or may not be aware of what is going on.

Masturbation is often called "autoeroticism" — seeking of sexual pleasure with the self — and can be related to sexual fantasy, either when awake or during sleep. However, not all masturbation is necessarily accompanied by fantasy, and only a small part of sexual fantasy results in or is linked to masturbation. Further, the relationship between sexual dreams (both those that do and do not lead to orgasm) and masturbation is not well-defined. It is not clear whether persons who masturbate have more or fewer sexual dreams — or sexual dreams accompanied by sexual climax — than those who do not.

1. The term *masturbation* in this book will always refer to masturbation of self; touching, caressing, or manipulating the genitals of others is defined as a form of petting.

Attitudes on Masturbation

Discussions of masturbation often cause a certain uneasiness—even people who are quite comfortable discussing their heterosexual and homosexual experiences find it difficult to talk freely about masturbation. This uneasiness appears to have at least three sources. The first is our historical views about masturbation and its consequences for the individual. Such views, transmitted to young people by adults, help shape the folklore of children and young people about the meanings and consequences of masturbation. The sexual folklore of children is remarkably self-sustaining—it can remain quite stable over long periods of time.[2]

A second source of uneasiness is the period of life in which masturbation is learned and consolidated into a person's sexual life style. Masturbation is often one of the earliest forms of overt sexual conduct, and it is usually learned in secret. This covert aspect of masturbation means that feelings and activities cannot be checked against a common set of standards which affirm and support the activity itself. As a consequence it easily becomes a source of guilt and anxiety—guilt and anxiety that spread to other forms of sexual conduct.

A third source of discomfort about masturbation is the belief that it withdraws sexuality from approved socio-sexual relationships. We are a society that believes the best kinds of sexuality involve others, emotionally as well as physically. Masturbation appears to deny these social responsibilities. Masturbation can be understood, if not approved, for young people. For adults, especially those who have an accessible sexual partner, masturbation is thought to be immature—a selfish withholding of sex from a legitimate partner.

Science and Folklore

We possess very little information about the historical frequency of masturbation, the conditions under which it was learned, and the feelings of individuals in the past about its significance or importance in their lives. This lack of systematic knowledge extends to all forms of sexuality, but is particularly true of masturbation. Casanova recounted his sexual adventures with women, but there is no similar record of masturbation. Did persons masturbate in the past? The answer is certainly "yes," since we do possess religious documents that include taboos against it; what we do *not* possess are records of the frequency with which those taboos were violated. (The existence of a taboo is not a measure of what people actually do.) Further, the records we do possess are largely from the Judaeo-Christian tradition, which give us no information about masturbation among those who populated Europe for most of its pre-Christian history.

The history of Western societies, especially of religious beliefs, is replete with rules against masturbation. The "sin of Onan," spilling seed on barren ground, usually has been thought to mean masturbation, though it included a wide range of

2. The sexual folklore of childhood and its lack of congruence with adult versions of the sexual world is often seen, especially by Freudians, as a "necessary" component of child development. The "sex errors" of children—beliefs about the stork, babies coming out through navels, that girls are boys without penises—supposedly reflect a necessary developmental sequence of misinformation. Such a perspective is in error because it attributes to the child characteristics of the learning environment.

other sexual acts that could not result in reproduction. The commitment of Christianity to reproduction and not pleasure as the goal of sexuality clearly makes masturbation (as well as a wide variety of other sexual acts) immoral and sinful. Again, however, the history we possess of masturbation prior to the seventeenth and eighteenth centuries is largely a record of prohibitions, without evidence for actual practices and feelings.

Tissot on Masturbation

In the early part of the eighteenth century, books began to appear which focused on masturbation and its supposed dangers to physical and mental health. Probably the most influential book of the times was one written by the physician-economist Tissot. Tissot's position was based in part on the medical theory of his own day about body fluids, called humors. According to this theory, the various fluids of the body (blood and bile, for example) possessed certain powers, and too much or too little of one or another created imbalances in physical and hence mental states. This tradition accounted for the practice of bleeding people with certain ailments, on the theory that they were producing too much blood.

By extension and analogy, Tissot hypothesized that semen was an important fluid in maintaining bodily integrity, and that wasting it through masturbation, wet dreams, or even intercourse could weaken the body and produce illness. As a result of the theory, he argued that persons suffering from what would appear to a modern physician as tuberculosis, as well as a variety of other "weakening" diseases, re-

The Sleeper

sulted primarily from masturbation, but also from other forms of what was thought to be sexual excess. In addition, a multitude of what were then called nervous disorders, some of which seem related to what we now call neuroses, were also attributed to excessive sexual excitement, particularly during masturbation.

Tissot's view of semen as a fluid necessary for bodily health is a possible precursor of Freud's theory of sexual libido as a psychic force. In Tissot's terms, the physical fluid of sexuality was limited in amount, and if one expended it recklessly or too frequently it would not be replaced rapidly enough. This loss meant that energies would not be available to do useful work in the society. (This view has a parallel in male sexual folklore—some men believe a man has a limited number of ejaculations in a lifetime, and they are not to be squandered along the way.) The Freudian libido theory is more complex, but also suggests that humans have a limited psycho-sexual economy, and if people use up their libidinal energies in actual sexual activity, there will not be energy left to sublimate into socially useful and culturally creative work. The theories are not totally parallel, but there are important similarities—perhaps most important is the influential belief that the sexual energies of persons are limited and should not be wasted.

Tissot's short volume on onanism went through many editions, and was translated into all major European languages. There is no mistaking its general influence on thinking about sexuality. Why it was successful and acceptable is less clear. It is possible that this sexual dogma of the dangers of sexual excess found its acceptance as a result of the increasing importance of the new middle class throughout Europe, a middle class that had as its slogan "Waste not, want not." Indications of a rise in a restrained response to the sexual can be observed in this social group, which was to dominate the economic and political life of the West for the next two centuries. It is not unlikely that Tissot's "scientific" support for sexual restraint was easily acceptable to those people who believed that restraint was the key to the good life.[3]

During the next century and a half, it was official doctrine that masturbation would lead to severe physical and mental disorder. During the nineteenth century, most medical doctors and alienists (what we would call psychiatrists today) believed that masturbation was the source of a wide variety of ills. Near the end of the eighteenth century, the American physician Benjamin Rush said of masturbation, "The morbid effects of intemperance in sexual intercourse with women are feeble and of a transient nature compared to the strain of physical and moral evils which this solitary vice fixes upon the body and mind." Rush argued that masturbation caused such varied disorders as dimness of sight, epilepsy, loss of memory, and pulmonary tuberculosis.

Later, in the nineteenth century, the English physician Acton offered the following description of a boy who is a habitual masturbator:

The frame is stunted and weak, the muscles undeveloped, the eye is sunken and heavy, the complexion is sallow, pasty, or covered with spots of acne, the hands are damp and cold, and the skin moist. The boy shuns the society of others, creeps about alone, joins with repugnance in the amusements of his schoolfellows. He cannot look any one in the face, and be-

---

3. The end of the eighteenth century was a period in which there was a confluence of values that might have given support to Tissot's antisexual ideology. Concurrent with the economics of Benjamin Franklin (a penny saved is a penny earned) was the increased prestige and power of the medical profession (health and cleanliness) as well as the growth of "science" as a basis for belief.

comes careless in dress and uncleanly in person. His intellect has become sluggish and enfeebled, and if his evil habits are persisted in, he may end in becoming a drivelling idiot. Such boys are to be seen in all stages of degeneration, but what we have described is but the result towards which *they all* are tending.

Such descriptions appeared frequently during the nineteenth century, as part of the majority of the medical profession's stand against sexuality in general and masturbation in particular.

During the nineteenth century, the fear of masturbation and its consequences became so powerful in some sectors of the medical profession that extraordinary indignities and cruelties were visited on some young people who masturbated and then fell into the hands of such practitioners. Straps and restraining devices were developed to keep children's hands away from their genitals, and were advertised as proprietory devices in medical and popular magazines.

Parallels to these practices can be found in other programs of child discipline relating to posture and thumbsucking. One of Freud's most important cases, on which some early thinking about the causes of paranoia was based, concerned the son of a well-known German physician. The father so believed in good posture that he built devices and restraints to assure that children (particularly his son) would stand up straight. Freud interpreted the son's paranoia as indicating repressed homosexual wishes which resulted from an unresolved childhood sexual conflict. Freud then generalized this case to make the argument that paranoia and homosexuality are related disorders. A modern reinterpretation of this case argues that the paranoia of this man was the result of being persecuted by his own father through the use of such devices.

Dreams

Probably the most extreme case of such sexual oppression was the use of surgery to treat masturbation among young girls. In order to prevent masturbation and its presumed consequences, some doctors performed a cliterodectomy, an operation to remove the clitoris. Such extremes were probably rare, but they illustrate the fear of masturbation and the lengths people were prepared to go in order to prevent it.

At the end of the nineteenth century, many people, including such sexual revolutionaries as Freud and Havelock Ellis, reacted against these simple generalizations. As medicine advanced, it became clear that diseases thought to be caused by sexual excess were in fact the result of diagnosable organic conditions. At the same time, even as each disease was removed from the list, there remained mental disorders still thought to be linked to masturbation. Even Sigmund Freud and Havelock Ellis argued that masturbation in those with a "constitutional predisposition" could cause impotence, premature ejaculation, and perhaps an aversion to intercourse.

Even as advanced thinkers criticized the supposed connections between masturbation and illness, such views retained their power in popular thinking and were widely held throughout the middle classes of most Western societies. Until the 1940s, the Boy Scout Manual counseled against "self abuse"; medical journals reported on the dangers of *excessive* masturbation; and athletes were cautioned against sexual activity of any sort, especially before a game or match. Such conceptions still exist today, even though muted by the passage of time. Many people still think that masturbation causes physical harm and potential mental damage. *(See Box below.)*

Moreover, *not* masturbating is thought to be character building, since it is believed to represent a form of self-control over a strong sexual impulse. This view emerges largely from religious doctrines, which argue that sexual activity, including masturbation, is wrong — and that the sexual is a powerful impulse which tests a person's willingness to conform to religious values. Resisting such a powerful urge demonstrates religious commitment.

Feelings About Masturbation

In a 1967 national study, college students who said that they had masturbated in college (eighty-two percent of males and thirty-three percent of females) were asked if they felt guilty, anxious, or concerned about their masturbation. About two thirds of both males and females reported that they had had such feelings. When asked to specify the feelings, the same numbers of males and females reported having the following thoughts at one time or another:

— Four of ten had thought masturbation to be wrong or immoral.
— One of ten had thought it would affect their ability to study.
— Two of ten had thought it would affect their physical health.
— Two of ten had thought it would affect their mental health.
— Four to five of ten had thought it to be immature.
— One to two of ten had thought it would negatively affect their later sexual competence.

This religious point of view had for many years been supported by conventional doctrines of medical science: not only was masturbation regarded as sinful, it was believed that it would drive you mad. Although the negative elements of this medical point of view have at least subsided in the face of increasing knowledge about the sexual, the religious doctrines — whose validity as moral pronouncements are a separate issue — continue to exist without medical support. It is important to understand that moral and religious opposition to sexual practices cannot be overturned by "scientific facts." *(See Box on next page.)*

Resistance to abandoning rules against masturbation persists, now focusing on the potential dangers of *excessive* masturbation. The young person who is unsocial, who does not mix well, who spends too much time alone, may be suspected of masturbating excessively. Masturbation is sometimes thought to have a connection with being socially detached during adolescence, a period when one should be going out and having a good time. A connection between "the solitary vice" and failure to socialize is false; yet, it still appears as an argument against masturbation.

The influence of these doctrines about the mental and physical dangers of masturbation on actual rates of masturbation is largely unknown. Anti-masturbation publications did not circulate widely in Western societies in the early nineteenth century, and perhaps only had wide currency after the end of that century. Most people were not literate and did not share what was largely a middle class view of the world; they were probably not influenced by the scientific works themselves. However, popular books did abound, and the point of view they expressed was derived in part from sexual folklore and in part created sexual folklore, so they could not fail to be somewhat influential. The following quote is taken from a 1913

Her Phantom

Vatican Declaration on Masturbation

The traditional Catholic doctrine that masturbation constitutes a grave moral disorder is often called into doubt or expressly denied today. It is said that psychology and sociology show that it is a normal phenomenon of sexual development, especially among the young. It is stated that there is real and serious fault only in the measure that the subject deliberately indulges in solitary pleasure closed in on self ("ipsation"), because in this case the act would indeed be radically opposed to the loving communion between persons of different sex which some hold is what is principally sought in the use of the sexual faculty.

This opinion is contradictory to the teaching and pastoral practice of the Catholic Church. Whatever the force of certain arguments of a biological and philosophical nature, which have sometimes been used by theologians, in fact both the magisterium of the Church — in the course of a constant tradition — and the moral sense of the faithful have declared without hesitation that masturbation is an intrinsically and seriously disordered act.

The main reason is that, whatever the motive for acting in this way, the deliberate use of the sexual faculty outside normal conjugal relations essentially contradicts the finality of the faculty. For it lacks the sexual relationship called for by the moral order, namely the relationship which realizes "the full sense of mutual self-giving and human procreation in the context of true love."

All deliberate exercise of sexuality must be reserved to this regular relationship. Even if it cannot be proved that Scripture condemns this sin by name, the tradition of the Church has rightly understood it to be condemned in the New Testament when the latter speaks of "impurity," "unchasteness" and other vices contrary to chastity and continence.

book called *Sexual Knowledge.* Note the survival, unchanged from the eighteenth century, of Tissot's views:

We must also note the fact that every procreative act is performed at a sacrifice of some of the vital fluid on the part of the male. A wanton sacrifice of vital fluid, either in the act of self-abuse or excessive indulgence in the sexual act, is not justifiable under any consideration. In the light of these facts, every normal man will admit that frequent masturbation or excessive sexual intercourse, in wedlock or out, would certainly not be recommended as a method of developing the sex apparatus.

Young people today still joke about masturbation in ways that suggest that it will cause physical stigmata — young males talk about hair growing on the palm of the hand, drooping eyelids, fatigue that results from masturbation. Young women report the fear that masturbation distorts the shape of their external genitals. A distinguished American physician, whose work in sex research was an important precursor of Kinsey's, claimed that he could tell by examining a woman's external genitals whether she had masturbated — and which hand she had used. This point of view was held by an educated scientist as recently as the mid-1930s.

It is not difficult to see why young people should have feelings of guilt, anxiety, and fear about masturbation when all this is part of the climate in which they learn about it and how to do it.

Sociological surveys are able to show the frequency of this disorder according to the places, populations or circumstances studied. In this way facts are discovered, but facts do not constitute a criterion for judging the moral value of human acts. The frequency of the phenomenon in question is certainly to be linked with man's innate weakness following original sin; but it is also to be linked with the loss of a sense of God, with the corruption of morals engendered by the commercialization of vice, with the unrestrained licentiousness of so many public entertainments and publications, as well as with the neglect of modesty, which is the guardian of chastity.

On the subject of masturbation modern psychology provides much valid and useful information for formulating a more equitable judgment on moral responsibility and for orienting pastoral action. Psychology helps one to see how the immaturity of adolescence (which can sometimes persist after that age), psychological imbalance or habit can influence behavior, diminishing the deliberate character of the act and bringing about a situation whereby subjectively there may not always be serious fault. But in general, the absence of serious responsibility must not be presumed; this would be to misunderstand people's moral capacity.

In the pastoral ministry, in order to form an adequate judgment in concrete cases, the habitual behavior of people will be considered in its totality, not only with regard to the individual's practice of charity and of justice but also with regard to the individual's care in observing the particular precepts of chastity. In particular, one will have to examine whether the individual is using the necessary means, both natural and supernatural, which Christian asceticism from its long experience recommends for overcoming the passions and progressing in virtue.

From Vatican Declaration On Sexual Ethics, December 29, 1975.

Lover's

Learning About Masturbation

The older views of the danger of masturbation are now greatly reduced in significance and importance. Religious sanctions still remain, as do points of view that emphasize the possible dangers of excessive masturbation, with its supposed influence on social adjustment. There is also the fear that masturbation may lead to other forms of sexual experimentation, especially if indulged in too early in life. Unfortunately such notions as "excessive" and "too early" are unclear in their application to specific cases, so that whether sanctions are applied in any particular case depends on the fears and anxieties of adults rather than on any evidence.

The climate surrounding masturbation at present is that it is a necessary part of "growing up"; that many young people will do it; and that as long as it is not excessive, not done at the wrong times, and kept private, it is, if not a good thing, not a dangerous practice. It is also felt that the normal process of development will involve giving up masturbation when socio-sexual experience begins, especially after the onset of regular sexual activity in marriage. Thus, while masturbation is generally no longer believed to cause tuberculosis or trigger insanity, it is still regarded as an activity that should be restricted to adolescence.

Parents may not openly disapprove of masturbation, but, as with other forms of sexuality, they offer little or no information about it. The restricted channels of information that make other forms of sexuality difficult to learn and accept also affect the learning and acceptance of masturbation. Young people are left on their own to discover by themselves, to learn from peers or from books that it is possible to find sexual pleasure and sexual release by oneself.

Since sexual learning takes place in a peer-dominated environment, largely secret from or ignored by parents, the information and values of the peer world are critical in defining the meaning and importance of masturbation. Frequent masturbation usually begins in early adolescence. Prior to this time, most children have touched their genitals largely in the course of bathing or urinating. Clearly U. S. society does not celebrate or promote any self-inspection by children, much less body exploration that might be defined as sexual. Parents work at teaching their children to keep the genitals covered and self-exploration to a minimum. It is only recently that pictures of genitals in any detail have been readily available to adults, and then usually only in "men's" and "women's" magazines such as *Playboy*, *Playgirl*, *Penthouse*, *Viva*, and the like.

It is not known how many parents show themselves nude to their children, either spontaneously or in the course of dressing or bathing. Common access to the bathroom by many members of the family may promote children's knowledge, as does a declining anxiety about nudity. But as children approach puberty it is likely that in a majority of families any easy access to nudity diminishes. Knowledge about the body parts and their potential for sexual activity is probably still effectively screened by parents from a substantial majority of young children and early adolescents.

As a consequence, most young people, even those who do masturbate, have limited and often faulty information about it. As noted earlier, young people possess a wide variety of false beliefs about masturbation and its consequences. The culture of sexual joking among adolescent boys and calling each other names that are part of the slang argot of masturbation maintains a climate of ignorance and guilt. Boys may get their first intimations of masturbation by the name calling of early adolescence ("Joey is a jack-off"; "Charley pulls his pud"). Girls at this age are usually insulated from this pattern of joking, and the attitudes and information that it provides. Even though these male attitudes and information may be distorted, they do represent a recognition of the possibility of masturbation—females often do not even have that.

Boys and young men seem to learn about masturbation through a number of channels. Some young men report that they discovered it themselves, often as a result of touching their own genitals when their penises were erect or partially erect. A number of different events seem to bring this on. A young person may be stimulated by physical stress or activity. As a result of general arousal an orgasm may spontaneously occur (in either sex). Such orgasms can be surprising or even upsetting, since they are not expected. They may arouse curiosity about the genitals, and the young person may explore further. Other young people discover masturbation through body exploration, suggested by others or by their own curiosity. The first forms of specific sexual pleasuring tend to be fumbling and relatively inept. Later, after gaining skill and assurance, the masturbator tends to forget the clumsiness of these earlier attempts.

A second major source of discovery for males is discussion with peers. This can occur in non-sexual situations or in either direct or indirect discussions of masturbation; such discussions may then lead to private experimentation. Somewhat less common is a situation in which an experienced male in a group of younger and older males will boast of his ability to ejaculate faster or further than the others.

Touch

Such "sexual contests" may involve males in a "circle jerk," in which all of the males either race to ejaculate or see how far they can ejaculate. This situation supplies information to younger and less experienced males and permits them observation and peer-reinforced practice. The important dimension here is the *demonstration of prowess*, rather than the experience of sexual pleasure.

These sources of information about masturbation are less common for females, who do not engage in sexual contests and whose networks of peers often supply less directly sexual information about the body. Many young women's contacts with their genitals are largely hygienic, as a result of the onset of menstruation. The menses and the attention the genitals require is rarely experienced by females as sexual, but rather as one of a continuing series of responses to the genitals linked to cleanliness. Young women may know of masturbation, but not know *how* to masturbate—how to produce pleasure, or even what the pleasures of orgasm might be. They tend to learn about masturbation over the entire span of adolescence, but do not always follow immediately with practice. Some young women report that they learned how to masturbate after they had orgasm from intercourse and petting, and decided they could do it for themselves. Others learn from lovers or husbands who introduce the practice to assure that the woman reaches orgasm or because they like to watch.

Different patterns of initiation to masturbation for females and males can be a factor in different patterns of psychosexual development for the two sexes. Much of male learning and first experimentation occurs in early and middle adolescence. It is therefore associated with the feelings and values of males during that period. On the other hand, young women tend to move into masturbation more slowly. Some begin in early adolescence, others begin in later adolescence, and many begin in adulthood and middle age. (Kinsey's data suggests that half begin after age twenty.)

These ages provide different learning contexts, and people who begin at different points in the life cycle bring different social and sexual histories to the act. As a result, the role that masturbation plays in their lives is different. If masturbation is the first sexual activity, occurs frequently, and is accompanied by fantasy (as it is for some males), it can provide a pattern of expectation for the sexual response cycle in socio-sexual situations, and may limit (or enhance) some aspects of sexual preferences. If masturbation comes after socio-sexual experience (as it does for many females), fantasies are more likely to be based on previous sexual reality. Women who begin later in life often do so because a male partner is absent, as a result of separation, divorce, or death. Other women begin masturbation in the middle years because it offers freedom from unwanted or uninteresting heterosexuality. Thus, the meaning and importance of the act are influenced by the types, extent, and meaning of prior sexual activity.

In almost all cases, the learning conditions for masturbation for both men and women engender guilt and anxiety. It is a secret practice, ambivalently responded to by peers, and frowned upon in comparison to the "real" thing, which is socio-sexual behavior. Practice is secretive—males worry about stains on bed sheets or taking too long in the bathroom. Young women do not have these particular fears but they share the fear of discovery. Learning how to masturbate is a darker side of learning about sexuality in general, for it has far less social support, covert or not.

Contemporary Status of Masturbation

Masturbation is, at best, regarded as part of an adolescent stage people must go through, but a practice they ought to give up when they begin regular socio-sexual activity. Yet many people do not give it up after adolescence; in fact, many, mostly women, only begin during adulthood. How are these anomalies usually explained? A strict Freudian view is that adult masturbation is infantile or immature—a throwback to what the young do. A similar judgment is made in popular folklore—adults masturbate because they cannot get sex with other people. Masturbation is evidence of sexual immaturity or sexual incompetence. There is very little merit in such explanations, but they do express the fears and anxiety that adult masturbation causes.

People who masturbate in adulthood, when there are appropriate sexual partners around, seem to us to be withdrawing from social responsibility. They are denying the sexual rights of others, especially when they are married, since we believe that our sexuality belongs to our spouses. In addition to the fear that we are being deprived of our property rights in our partners' sexuality, we may also fear that our partners are masturbating because we are no longer sexually attractive. Thus one partner may say to another, "If I really turned you on, you wouldn't need to masturbate." This fear probably also animates the man who reports being afraid or angry if his wife buys a vibrator—he fears that she will come to like the vibrator more than she likes sex with him.

There seem to be three issues involved in contemporary views of adult masturbation. The first is property rights—a person's sexual resources are thought to belong to his or her sexual partner. Sexual potential is "scarce," and should be used only with the approved person. This view is linked to the belief that masturbation might be all right when spouses are absent, but never when they are accessible.

The second issue, allied to the belief that sexuality is property, involves efforts to control all solitary or private behavior. People are always inquiring about other people's behavior when they have been away or alone—mothers ask what children are doing; lovers ask where their beloved has been. Some of these inquiries involve affection, but others suggest a powerful need to know about and thus control the behavior of the cared-about person. In intimate relationships secrecy is taboo; everything must be shared. Masturbation is commonly secret and private, and therefore dangerous.

Finally, there is the suspicion that masturbation might be more interesting or less troublesome than having sex with a partner. For instance, masturbation does not require the interpersonal negotiation that socio-sexual behavior involves, even intercourse between a married couple. Since we are raised to believe that masturbation is second best, to choose it voluntarily as an adult seems to be a judgment on the sexual abilities of a partner.

At this moment in time, masturbation still evokes a sense of uneasiness. Our script assigns it to adolescence and to absences. However, it is far more than that for many people. What we have is that ambivalent compromise between approved scripts and private scripts and practice that characterizes so much of our sexuality.

Male Learning and Technique

As we have noted, masturbation seems to begin for most males around puberty, but for females at various points in the life cycle. Puberty is not an instant in time, but rather a period of changes in different parts of the body. For males, the "sexual" events that occur during this period are the ability to ejaculate, changes in genital anatomy, and the growth of pubic hair. In suitable learning environments, a boy notices these changes (or they are called to his attention) and they are linked to potential sexual activity, which is realized in a majority of cases. Beginning to masturbate is not a very orderly process—young men ejaculate spontaneously, in sexual dreams, or while washing the penis, as well as from direct manipulation stimulated by sexual interest or peer group instruction. It is not clear how much pleasure accompanies this early experience. Some men recall the discovery and practice of masturbation with considerable delight; for others, beginning to masturbate was troubling and difficult.

The most common male technique for masturbation is manual, stroking the penis with one or both hands, increasing the rapidity of movement as orgasm approaches. Another common practice, reported especially by adolescents, is lying face down and rubbing the penis against bedclothes, in a simulation of intercourse. There is a wide range of male techniques; however, it appears that only a minority of men use a wide range of practices. The majority tend to continue using whatever techniques of masturbation they learned in adolescence.

Many young men have trouble with logistics as well as with technique. The logistical matters largely involve privacy, which may be difficult to get in a large family, a shared bedroom, or behind a lockless bathroom door. Lack of privacy and fear of interruption can make masturbation a fleeting pleasure at best.

Given our focus on the moral value questions of sex, we tend not to spend much time thinking about how males learn to masturbate. It seems so obvious. However, when they begin to masturbate some boys are so excited, guilty, or anxious that they ejaculate after just touching the penis or after a few strokes. For others there may be considerable delay or difficulty because they do not know that climax is the goal they seek. Some males are shocked when orgasm and ejaculation occur. Others are inept, and chafe the penis. It is only with practice that techniques become refined, so that orgasm can be quickened or delayed as desired, and a set of reasonably coordinated activities can occur. Once these first attempts have become stabilized, perhaps after several practice trials, the male tends to forget how incompetent the first trials really were.

Female Learning and Technique

The issue of masturbatory techniques among women is more complex, especially since they begin masturbation at different points in the life cycle. Those women who begin in adolescence face the same socio-psychological problems as males, but the problem of "how to" seems to be more complex. The lack of information many young women have about their genitals, especially the clitoris, is extraordinary. A young woman must first begin to touch her genitals, find it pleasurable, and then continue self stimulation long enough for orgasm to occur. Males and females who are experienced can masturbate to orgasm at about the same speed; however, this is not necessarily true of those less experienced or unpracticed.

Many young women stop far short of orgasm, sometimes not knowing that it is the goal, or they may have orgasm and not realize what it is. Indeed, not all women identify the experience of orgasm as sexual (sometimes it is sought to reduce tension or menstrual cramps or headaches). Others identify it as sexual only after it happens in socio-sexual activity (petting, for example). For older women it is usually physically easier to begin masturbation. They know where the clitoris is, they have had the experience of sexual excitement, and they may have had orgasm — all this makes competent masturbation easier.

Female masturbatory techniques tend to be more variable than those of males. Women may use different parts of the body as locations for manual stimulation: the breasts, torso, legs, and lips, as well as the genitals. They also tend to use general body tension, and thigh pressure particularly, to produce arousal and orgasm. There is a lessened genital focus, which may be a result of a less specified content for masturbatory learning. A common technique is manual stimulation of the clitoris and the external genitals, with shallow insertion of fingers into the upper aspect of the vagina. Insertion of other objects may occur, but rarely; this is largely an extension of male fantasies about what women do. In recent years the electric vibrator has become a popular aid to female masturbation. There are a variety of types, including those shaped like penises, but even they are not often inserted. There are of course women who do masturbate by inserting penis-like objects into the vagina, and find it quite pleasurable. However, the external female genitals and the clitoris are more commonly involved.

Data About Masturbation

The data we possess of when people begin to masturbate, how often they masturbate, and the significance masturbation has in their lives relative to other forms of sexual activity derives largely from the Kinsey research, and from a few other smaller surveys and studies. We have less information on masturbation than on many other aspects of sexual conduct. A lack of findings that can be checked against one another has two consequences. First, the available numbers should be treated with caution, and should be regarded as approximations rather than precise measures. Secondly, when data is rare, and often only suggestive, interpretation of that data carries a great deal of weight. In the absence of secure information scientists do not cease to speculate, but they should speculate more circumspectly.

As you can see from Figure 1, there is a steady accumulation of women into masturbation over the life cycle. By age forty-five this reaches about six of every ten women. In contrast, there is a sudden surge of males, with about eighty percent masturbating by age fifteen. What is important are the differences in the timing of entry into masturbation. For males it is an adolescent phenomena; for females it is one of steady, unspectacular increases across the entire life cycle.

When we look at Table 1 we see other differences. Here the bars indicate the percentage of persons in different age groups who had masturbated in that five-year period. They are counted as having masturbated even if they did it only once in the five years. Again we see that the males tend to have far higher proportions

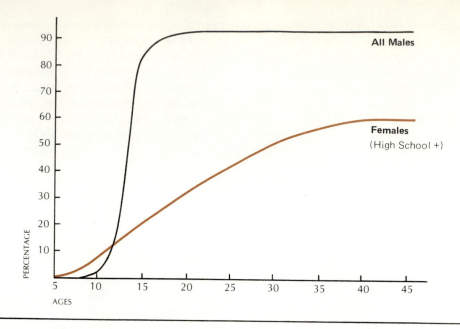

Figure 1   Accumulative Incidence of Masturbation to Orgasm. (Kinsey:1948, Fig. 135, p. 502; 1953, p. 149.)

who ever masturbated, both among those who were single and those who were married. However, as men and women get older, the incidence and frequency of activity tends to move closer together. Note, however, that during early adolescence through young adulthood, especially among the single, not only do two to three times as many males masturbate, but they do it from two to three times as often.

There is one interesting reversal in these figures for which the explanation is not clear. Though more men tend to masturbate during marriage, the women who do, do so more often.

There are a number of factors that affect rates of masturbation. Four seem to be critical:

1. Rates of masturbation go down with age, as do nearly all other forms of sexual activity. Male rates seem to go down further than female rates, perhaps because they start higher.
2. Persons who are conventionally religious (as measured by church attendance) are less likely to masturbate, or masturbate less frequently, than those who are not religious. These differences are not very large, but they are noticeable.
3. When persons marry or begin regular socio-sexual relationships, frequencies and incidence of masturbation drop.
4. It appears that more men who have attended college masturbate (and do so more often) than men who have attended only high school. This appears only among males, and is reflected primarily in increased frequencies of masturbation and in continued patterns of masturbation after marriage.

Table 1   Number of People Who Masturbated During Different Age Periods (Incidence) and Times Per Week for Those Who Did (Active Median Frequency).

Age	Never Married				Married			
	Men		Women		Men		Women	
	Incidence %	Median Frequency	Incidence %	Median Frequency	Incidence %	Median Frequency	Incidence %	Median Frequency
Adolescence to 15	85	1.8	20	.5	—	—	—	—
16–20	88	1.1	28	.4	39	.1	23	.4
21–25	81	.8	35	.4	48	.2	27	.2
26–30	77	.7	43	.3	48	.1	31	.2
31–35	71	.5	49	.4	46	.1	34	.2
36–40	63	.6	54	.3	37	.1	36	.2
41–45	61	.4	50	.3	33	.1	36	.2
46–50	54	.5	47	.3	31	.1	34	.2

Adapted from Kinsey: 1948, Table 51, pp. 240–241; 1953, Table 23, p. 178.

There is very little other data on national populations that focuses on masturbation. However, in 1967 a national sample of male and female college students were asked if they had masturbated in high school, and asked about their estimated frequencies.[4] In Table 2 we can see that the gender differences in the incidence and rates of masturbation found by Kinsey appear still to exist.

Table 2   Masturbation in College

Frequency	Males				Females			
	Fresh	Soph	Junior	Senior	Fresh	Soph	Junior	Senior
Daily	1%	4%	2%	4%	0%	0%	0%	0%
Twice/week	16	12	18	19	3	6	4	4
Once/week	19	19	20	14	6	3	4	5
Twice/month	21	16	15	17	10	0	8	8
Once/month	12	15	18	17	21	12	7	17
Less than once/month	17	17	17	18	25	28	41	47
Not in college	14	17	10	11	35	52	36	19

4. This data is from a study conducted by William Simon and John Gagnon, supported by Public Health Service grant HD04156.

Masturbation and Fantasy

For most persons masturbation is not merely the mechanical release of fluid (among males) or "sexual tension" (among females) from an overflowing sexual reservoir. It must be learned and practiced as any other social skill; it is influenced by social factors; and our culture provides us with a complex of attitudes about it.

The major importance of masturbation for many people is its association with the development and rehearsal of sexual fantasies or scripts. The word *association* is used quite deliberately in making this connection between masturbation and fantasy. While there is an increase in both during adolescence, there is no evidence that masturbation necessarily produces fantasy *or* that sexual fantasies necessarily produce masturbation.

It appears in Western societies, at least, that most people who develop complex sexual fantasies begin to do so around adolescence. Complex fantasies are those that have a narrative structure or order and which involve recognizable "adult" sexual acts, as well as adult versions of the persons, places, times, and motives for these acts. Such fantasies are apparently rare in younger children, and appear to be elicited by the changed psycho-sexual status of the child at puberty. It is not known whether such fantasies occur among children in societies where adequate sex knowledge or actual sexual activity is available to them.

When, as in Western societies, the development and rehearsal of sexual fantasies and masturbation occur at the same time in some individuals, there is an important interaction set in motion. The fantasy provokes the masturbation, and the physical pleasure and orgasm reinforces the fantasy. Thus the sexual scripts of adolescence are supported by physical sexual activity, *and* when fantasies produce arousal, masturbation can result.

The coordination of fantasies and physical activities is not automatic, and may contribute to difficulties in developing masturbatory competence. The young person is not only required to manipulate the body, but a series of words or images as well. The physical climax of orgasm must be coordinated with the progressive sequence of acts imagined in the head. For young people who are relatively ignorant of the usual sequence of sexual activity (or do not know at all what sexual activity involves), this coordination can be crude indeed. For some young boys, the fantasy can be composed simply of french kissing, looking up a girl's dress, or seeing a breast covered by a bra—only later do narratives involving intercourse, oral sex, and orgies develop. For some young girls, fantasies associated with masturbation may involve imagined dates, kissing and necking, and in some cases, weddings or engagements.

Many people do not fantasize before or during masturbation and are perfectly well able to have orgasm. These people report that they do not fantasize anything: they think only about the physical manipulation they are doing. This masturbatory style seems to characterize more women than men, and more less-educated men than well-educated men. We do not understand why these differences of fantasy occur. The differences between men and women may result from the different timing of entry into masturbation—those people who start early may fantasize more, although this is speculation. It may also be true that those people, male and female, who start early and masturbate frequently tend to fantasize more, but this is equally speculative.

In any case, for substantial numbers of men and women, masturbation is an activity accompanied by an explicitly sexual fantasy. Most such people report that they cannot masturbate without an associated fantasy—indeed, for them the very definition of masturbation includes fantasy. These fantasies are examples of sexual scripts—they are little stories which involve who, what, where, when, and why. Even as the adolescent boy masturbates while thinking of the girl with the "bad reputation" in school, or the girl with large breasts, or the *Playboy* picture, he is selecting a legitimate "who." He may try the fantasy with his mother or sister or the nice girl next door, but they are less acceptable sexual targets. He will select a social context, imagine a reason for the action going forward, devise one or more sexual activities and arrange them in order, consider the consequences of his actions (how excited she is with him, her orgasm, etc.), and bring the scenario to a close at orgasm. He may add other people, paraphernalia, harems, dress styles, movie actresses, current lovers—they are part of the movie in his head.

Among those males who fantasize, there seems to be a pattern of fantasizing far more than what they actually do or will ever do; there is more aggression and group sex in men's heads than in actual practice. Sometimes the fantasies wear out and need replacing, or new persons are added to the script as the life cycle changes. The married man may fantasize an affair, the winter-bound city dweller sex in Caribbean sun, the inexperienced adolescent removing the bra of the girl down the street.

If the fantasies of men are often expansive and aggressive, linked to the gender roles they are supposed to play and their roles in the initiation of sexuality, women's fantasies are often limited to what they have done, are less focused on the genital aspects of the act and more on the contexts and the person, and are often related to conventional gender role expectations. Women report fantasies of sexual activity in the context of romance and affection, often without genital detail, focusing on the social and psychological factors of a desired relationship. Women do fantasize group sex and other experimental sexual activities, but far less often than do men. Women also report fantasies of mild sexual coercion, sometimes rape, or sex with a stranger. Clearly few want these kinds of actual experiences, as do few men really wish to act out some of the fantasies that seem most arousing to them. In part the arousal lies in the transgression of social norms—doing the forbidden. At the same time there are even rules about the forbidden. The woman who might fantasize sex without preliminaries is unlikely to do so in reality, but the fantasy of being taken by a stranger slightly against her will allows for non-responsible sexuality.[5] The man who fantasizes having cruel sex with a "notorious woman" justifies it because of the bad things she may have done to him or other men on other occasions. Even sex in fantasy requires that we justify what we do.

Fantasy has a number of uses and consequences. For some young people it is a form of sexual rehearsal. They try out activities in their heads—speculating on what it might feel like and what they will do—and assemble a provisional plan which enables them to make the action go forward. This use of fantasy as rehearsal also occurs among older people, who fantasize having sex with someone else's spouse

---

5. This is what Erica Jong meant in *Fear of Flying* by the term "zipless fuck"—irresponsible, nonconsequential, and therefore erotic.

or with a famous actor as part of a tentative speculation about extramarital sex. Such fantasies can become practically logistic rehearsals, as the person excitedly manipulates a symbolic reality looking for a way to have an actual sexual encounter. Another use of fantasy is as escape attempts from the humdrum of daily life — one is working, or reading, or restless, and sets in motion a sexual fantasy that provides relief from the usual world. Sexual fantasies are also pleasurable in themselves; they can be played with as can any set of symbols. Reorganizing, reordering, or revaluing sexual scripts can offer as many delights as doing the same with other symbolic aspects of life. Sexual fantasies may also be used as a supplementary source of arousal during boring acts, when one or both partners may be thinking of someone or something else to make the physical sex work.

Adolescent Masturbation and Later Sexuality

The differences in adolescent sexuality between males and females can be consequential for their future socio-sexual encounters. Some males (mostly of working class and lower class origins) have early heterosexual experience; a few males of all classes have early regular or erratic homosexual experience; however, the majority of males begin their sexual lives with masturbation. Far fewer females than males have early socio-sexual experience, and the evidence is that fewer masturbate as well. Thus, while many young men are actively touching their own genitals, making up erotic stories, and excitedly looking around to see if they can catch a glimpse of exposed women's bodies, the majority of young women are not masturbating (and if they are, are doing it less frequently). They are making up romantic tales, and living in what is a more sexually neutral environment. This is not a biological difference, for there are young women who have extensive histories of masturbation and complex erotic fantasies. The difference resides in the different gender role expectations about sex that they bring into adolescence, and the different expectations about how they are to behave sexually at that time.

During adolescence, most young men are acquiring an image of their own sexuality, a fantasy about women's sexuality, and practice in relatively rapid, self-controlled, manually produced orgasms. It is a rare woman who shares this history — the majority have little experience of private experimentation in developing their own sexuality, have not explored their own bodies sexually, and have never (or rarely) experienced orgasm. Thus early, inept heterosexual encounters are made more clumsy by the male experiencing his sexuality as a chronic push ("I'm really horny") and the female being caught in an ambivalent situation — she should express a limited degree of arousal, yet is expected to prevent things from "going too far." Since she has not had much experience with her own sexuality, she often assumes that the male knows what he is doing and what she is feeling — an assumption that is usually in error.

Problems of mutual sexual satisfaction are also created by the strong genital focus of male masturbation — the constant manipulation of the penis makes it the primary site of male sexual pleasure. Young men (and many older men) often want only genital things done to them (and by transfer they make the same assumptions about women). The rest of the male body, except for the lips, may be erotically indifferent. Such a focus can result in a limited range of sensuality on the part of men, and male indifference to the non-genital eroticism of women.

One of the values of masturbation to orgasm for young women who do so is that they begin relatively easily to have orgasm in marital intercourse. From Kinsey's research, there is evidence that if premarital coitus, petting, or masturbation has led to orgasm, all are equally effective in increasing the frequency of female orgasm in the early years of marriage.

Masturbation and Female Sexual Autonomy

It has been argued that one of the ways women can begin to gain sexual autonomy is through masturbation. The argument proceeds as follows: Women tend to learn about sex through men, or as a result of the attentions of men. They are usually aroused only in socio-sexual contexts; their fantasies are usually linked to male versions of the world; and their sexuality is learned for the most part in a male-dominated system. Masturbation can offer women an opportunity for private sexual expression, the opportunity to explore their own bodies sexually without another person conditioning how they feel or what they will do.

Masturbation is the way we discover our eroticism, the way we learn to respond sexually, the way we learn to love ourselves and build self-esteem. Sex is like any other skill — it has to be learned and practiced. When a woman masturbates, she learns to like her own genitals, to enjoy sex and orgasm, and furthermore, to become proficient and independent about it.[6]

This issue has been raised both for adolescent and sexually inexperienced young women and for older women. In the case of younger women, it is argued that they will have an opportunity to learn about their bodies, to begin to have orgasms, to locate what is arousing to them. When they become involved in socio-sexual contacts, they will have more control over the situation, since they will know what gives them pleasure, they will be more aware of what is going on inside them and their own reactions, and they can fully participate in sexuality rather than being passive responders to male activity. For older women, married or not, masturbation offers an alternative source of satisfaction, decreases their sexual dependency on men, and offers a sure and rapid source of orgasm. For women who have difficulty having orgasm in coitus, masturbation may provide either an alternative source of orgasm or an opportunity to practice and perhaps improve the ease of coital orgasm. This search for liberation through masturbation can be seen as part of a movement among some women to increase the area of privacy and self control they have in their lives in general.

If such views about the role of masturbation became general or popular, they would have profound consequences for the role of masturbation in our sexual scripts. As has been noted before, our sexual learning system is largely covert, and

6. Betty Dodson, *Liberating Masturbation: A Meditation on Self Love* (Bodysex Designs, 1974).

our attitudes toward masturbation range from toleration to hostility. Such a shift in values would require that we become overt in our sexual teaching and perhaps move to a premasturbation curriculum which could offer instruction and practice in self-pleasuring. The impact of such a program of sexual learning (one that focuses on masturbation) would have outcomes unknown at this time.

The reactions we have to the idea that masturbation should be valued and taught can tell us something about how we actually feel, not only about masturbation, but about sexuality as well. It is unlikely that this kind of attitude shift will take place in U.S. society in the near future, but it is important to know that a whole new set of values and attitudes, a new set of sexual scripts, are under consideration. Knowing about them can offer us the opportunity to reflect upon what we currently do and think.

LEARNING HETEROSEXUALITY

Technique in art is much like that in lovemaking.
Heartfelt ineptitude has its appeal, as does heartless skill,
but what we want is passionate virtuosity.

John Barth

THE PHYSICAL CHANGES OF PUBERTY ALLOW YOUNG PEOPLE TO DISPLAY THEM-
selves to the world—and have the world treat them—as potentially socio-sexual
actors, yet most young people know little more about how to conduct themselves
sexually than they did before they had breasts, pubic hair, ejaculations, or menses.
In part this is because they did not know very much before puberty, in part because
they were not told very much while they were going through puberty, and finally
because what they knew must be thought through again because *they* are now going to begin sexual experimentation themselves. It is very well and good to be
exposed to a sex education book (or books) in childhood, even one that is quite
explicit about sexual activity, and it is useful for parents to recite how the penis and
the vagina get together and how everyone likes it very much. Little of this information is directly helpful in doing sex, or in dealing with the new feelings, commitments, and desires that are developing into heterosexual scripts.

At the beginning of adolescence, the model that most young people probably
have is the married heterosexual couple. (This model also influences quite directly
the lives of those who will never marry, since it cuts down on the number of possible sexual partners, and creates a sense of isolation, of not going along with the
crowd.) The concept of pair-bonded, loving husband-wife, even if it did not exist
in any reality known to the child, is a construct that influences the development of
patterns of sexuality for the entire period between puberty and the conventional
moment of marriage in U. S. society. Most children want to be a husband or a wife,
as loving or more loving than mommy and daddy.

Between ages twelve or thirteen and the moment of getting married lie adolescence and young adulthood. During that time young people learn how to associate in new ways with persons of the same or the opposite sex, how to experiment
with modes of affection and intimacy, how to have a variety of sexual experiences,
and how to tie all these elements into a rough set of guidance mechanisms called
scripts. The scripts offer blueprints for arrivals and departures, for the naming of the
self and of other people, and tell the participants what feelings they should have.

This is also a period of unlearning as well as learning. Most people must leave behind the values of childhood and early adolescence. All kinds of activities have to be revalued, made appropriate for the self, and feelings have to be accepted and labeled. The transition between childhood and adolescence is not a smooth period during which childhood is directly influential on adolescence. For many people adolescence is not joined to childhood; for some it can be a new life.

The period between the end of childhood and getting married is often very short, rarely longer than a decade. The physical changes of puberty are over for most people by age thirteen or fourteen; most of them are married by twenty-four or twenty-five, with a large number marrying at nineteen and twenty. Young women tend to marry earlier than young men, so the period of social and sexual experimentation may be very short for them. The length of this period is affected by social class and education—the working class and non-college young tend to marry early; those with middle class and upper middle class backgrounds who go on to college marry later. The importance of marriage in a society affects premarital sexual life, particularly for women, by giving it an organizing focus, and age at marriage determines the length of time that premarital sexual scripts can be played out. (Learning heterosexuality goes on in marriage, but the script is different.)

Premarital sexual conduct is not merely directed at getting married or practice for being married, though this may be the way many young people experience it. However, since marriage is the single legitimate institution for adult sexuality, it affects the sexual lives of the young. Many adult anxieties about the sexuality of young people focus not on the sex, but on the idea that the sex will make them unmarriageable. Premarital sex thus exists in a state of tension between the pleasures of the moment and the demands of the future; premarital sexual scripts offer love and passion versus the marital scripts of domestic affection. Most young people resolve this tension by using the script for love and passion to select the person with whom they will then live in domestic affection.

Conditions of Heterosexual Learning

The conditions of heterosexual learning before marriage remain largely in the control of peer groups. Information comes earlier and more graphically from peers than from parents or other official sources. Peer information is powerful because it is closest to a shared experience—peers are going through the same thing or have just gone through the same thing. The information may well be wrong, but it is valued, and says not only what is done but what ought to be done.

Until recently in U.S. society, a primary mechanism for adult control of premarital heterosexual activity has been to try to keep sex a secret. By restricting the channels of information and the content of those channels, adults have expected that young people would be less sexual. This is the purpose of excluding sex education from the schools. If young people do not know about sex they will not do it.

The change that has taken place in the past two decades has been principally a change in popular media treatment of sexuality. Most adolescents still learn the most important things about sexuality from peer group sources, but that is now reinforced by a more explicit media system (*Playboy*, *Cosmopolitan*, advice columns, movies, television) which offers a wide range of sexual knowledge. There may be some greater participation of parents in the informational process, but most significant information still comes from the covert and overt knowledge systems created by and for the youth culture.

Peer and media learning have a mutually reinforcing character. Both are committed to scripts for sexuality that are exciting or loving, attached to consuming both goods and time. There are scripts for sexuality that are recreational, attached to fun dating (*Gidget Goes To The Moon*) and scripts that are deeply emotional and passionate, the scripts for *Love Story* and *Romeo and Juliet*—but even in a sexually "advanced" film like *Shampoo* the hero is punished for being promiscuous by losing the woman that he loved the most. Most media versions of the world are morality tales, stories of virtue rewarded and vice punished—virtue may be more broadly defined, vice more narrowly, but media scripts still involve the justification of sexual activity.

The learning of restrictive values and attitudes associated with overt sexuality still comes from parents. In the earliest stages of adolescence, parents are usually silent about sex, perhaps hoping that matters will reverse themselves and go back to normal. Somewhat later, usually after large doses of peer input, parents may make an attempt to tell sons and daughters what they might do sexually and why they might do it. Usually the conversation is why they should not "do it" (especially for daughters), or if they do want to "do it" they should wait a while, and if they wait a while they should find someone that they care about, or best of all can fall in love with and want to marry. Males are usually left out of this morality-tale/information-session largely because it makes parents uneasy. The female remains the guardian of morality or at least of non-promiscuity, and the promoter of that association between love and sex which is the key to modern morality.

It is not that most parents want their adolescent children never to have sex, but rather that they want it staged or scripted in particular ways. Because they are fearful that any information may provoke activity, and that if their children start they will not be able to stop, they often take a very conservative line, appearing to be more antisexual than they really are.

The important issues are the degree of emotional attachment between parents and children and the congruity of their values. Even liberal parents and liberal children who do not like each other may fight over sex (as well as over other things). Similarly there may be grave differences in values mediated by interpersonal affection. The dilemma is that the values and information are always offered in contexts with many hidden emotional and personal agendas, that make even accurate information difficult to transmit and to receive.

The actual ways of doing sexual things are learned primarily in direct experimentation and pre- and post-experimental discussion sessions with peers. There can be discussions with some parents (particularly daughters with mothers), as well as some discussion of birth control and in some households directions about how to get it. However, the main source of knowledge remains peer-oriented, and parents are often excluded from all but the moral aspects of sexual learning.

Peer Structures: Homosociality and Heterosociality

By the end of childhood, again depending on social class and other traditions, many young children of both genders have played together. However, even with extensive coeducation there is, as has been noted, a division of roles between boys and girls. These differences have serious sexual consequences, both in the short and the long run. With the advent of puberty there is often a re-segregation of sexes, even in middle class communities, with an increase in female-female and male-male activities.

It is as if a signal were made by the changing bodies of young people telling them that there is a new and perhaps risky way of relating to each other not present in the past. This is not inherent in the changing bodies, but in the social and psychological responses to the changing bodies. Nudity now becomes more exclusive; children are not bathed together; single-sex activities increase (sports versus home economics).

The expectation that boys and girls are going to be like men and women in what they do, and how they look, and how they will treat each other is the central theme of the transition from childhood to early adolescence. This is less a sexual transition (since most of the sexual things will happen after the transition) as it is a change in gender-role expectations, a change in social relations to the same and opposite sex.

This period is not well understood from a social-psychological point of view. It has largely been lost between the innocence of childhood and the storms of adolescence. It is, as we have seen, chaotic from a physical and developmental point of view—this very chaotic quality means that it is difficult to study. What we can know is not very stable or accurate. Also, it is easy scientifically to justify doing research during this period, but very difficult socially, since most of the research itself is a form of sex education. Questions about sex provide information as well as elicit it. Parents feel very uneasy about letting young people be asked such questions, even though the young people may be knowledgeable and sexually active.

A central theme in adolescence is learning about sex in the context of social attachment to same-sex peers, *homosociality*, which is followed in later adolescence by cross-sex association (dating, going steady), or *heterosociality*. It is a movement from values attached to persons of the same sex to values characterizing relations between the sexes. Often crucial to this period is reinforcement of the sexist values of childhood—values that support the socially learned stereotypes of the differences between men and women. The socially constructed gender roles of childhood, which first create and then emphasize the differences between women and men, are part of a framework into which sexual information and values (which are already coded by the environment as gender-appropriate) must be fitted. Gender-role differences and differences in sexual conduct are assembled to form an essential part of the stereotyped identities of men and women.

In later adolescence young people do manage to get together—many by continuing to emphasize the stereotyped differences. Men are more aggressive sexually, women more passive; by playing these expected roles (and others) they manage

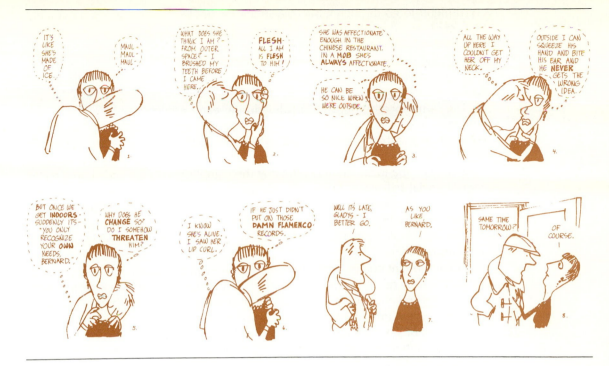

Our acceptance of the stereotyped versions of sexuality for men and for women may have us saying one thing to our partners while we are saying the opposite to ourselves.

to fit themselves together. Other young people try to avoid the stereotypes and attempt to share some common values. More often the result is a mixture, sometimes following the stereotyped patterns based on differences; other times looking for commonalities. Both of these strategies come into play in later adolescence and young adulthood.

In the all-male groups of early adolescence there is a pattern of learning and developing sexual attitudes toward the self and toward females which are quite explicitly sexual. Much male adolescent talk is sex talk about "boobs," and being "horny," and how girls look, and how far a girl will go. It is about the achievement aspects of gaining sexual access to females. At the same time there is a distinction between "good girls" and "bad girls"—scripts for sexual exploitation and sexual affection. All of these scripts are reinforced by experience and the qualities of masturbation. (In middle class groups, as was noted in Chapter 8, masturbation represents an important contribution to the content and structure of heterosexual scripts.)

How directly a young male is embedded in this information system depends on his attachment to peer and male life. There are many young men who are only on the periphery of such sources of information, but the effects are coercive. It is very difficult to go through a male adolescence in U.S. society and emerge without a set of sexual scripts influenced by the values of all-male groups. The mixture of dominance and sex, aggression and sex, guilt and sex, expectations of being "horny" and sex, is part and parcel of most male adolescence. Even religious values have specific injunctions on the need to suppress the powerful male sexual urge.

The homosocial groups of females during early adolescence are commonly learning a less sexual and more affectional version of the world. Like the males, they are learning that there are "good girls" and "bad girls" — girls who go all the way, or go all the way with many boys, or go all the way with boys they do not love (depending on the local morality). But that there are "good girls" and "bad girls" is a fact of social existence. Whatever may be done to deny this fact, it seems that prior to age sixteen the dichotomy remains real to both boys and girls — it is a source of moral judgment and moral inclusion or exclusion. It does not mean that some young people do not escape the judgment or that others do not ignore it, but it remains a reality.

The important component of female groups is an emphasis on love in emerging heterosocial relationships — like males, they distinguish between recreational relationships and affectional relationships, between a world of fun and world of seriousness, but the important dimension is not the erotic, it is the emotional. If men are prisoners of sex, women are prisoners of love. As prisoners both genders may seek escape, often successfully, but equally often they flee back into the custody of sex or love.

These themes inform the scripts of young people as they enter into the associational patterns of adolescence, the arena of asking for dates, being seen together, sharing activities, managing emotions, beginning to experiment sexually, reporting back to same-sex peers, and to parents. It is a world of learning how to get on with persons of the opposite sex in the contexts of emotion, attachment, and sexuality. It is a period of trying out homosocially derived scripts in heterosocial situations.

Early dating, particularly among those with middle class values, is often characterized by patterns of heterosocial association in which very small amounts of sexual experimentation go forward. The questions that were problematic for sixteen-year-olds in the 1950s (should we kiss on the first date?) are now questions that arise somewhat earlier, perhaps at thirteen. They also appear earlier for girls and later for boys, perhaps by a year or two.

It is important to remember that not all young people participate in the early dating game; some do not date successfully in high school at all. This does not mean that they might not have some heterosexual experience, but most often it will be connected to non-affectional relations. Lack of early heterosexual participation has both good and bad aspects. For some, to participate early means heterosexuality is experienced in its most conservative context (both in terms of sexism and morality). For others, early participation means actually learning something interesting about sex and perhaps growing beyond the conventional pattern. On the other hand, for some, not to have participated early means feeling left out and unpopular; and for others, not to have participated early means a chance to escape the more sexist aspects of early male-female sexual relationships.

Problem of Love

Contrary to appearances, young men are not uncommitted to love—they are firm believers in love with the "right" woman—but they are also committed to trying out sexual things, mostly because they are told that it is masculine to do so. Women are not told that it is feminine to try out sexual things; they are usually told that it is probably not a good idea to try them out unless they (and the man) are in love.

Love, the powerful feeling of attachment to an individual, is one of the great creations and consequences of heterosexual association in U.S. society, and when it is included in sexual scripts it often promotes sexual experimentation. (It can also prevent it, as in "If you really loved me you wouldn't ask me to do that.") Love is probably the most important emotion that people can expect to feel in U.S. society—it is obligatory for getting married, and lack of it can legitimate not being married, or getting out of a marriage. In 1930s' movies young women were always leaving rich young men to marry poor young men because they were in love (*Love Story* is a reversal—she is a poor young woman, he is a rich young man). "I don't love you anymore" is a classic exit line in every relationship. Donny Osmond assures us that we are not "too young to love" (though we may be too old?).

The incapacity to feel love or to fall in love is one of the central social crimes of the twentieth century. An unloving mother, a heartless child, a false lover—they are the contemporary villains. Not to have been loved leads to all kinds of complications: the unloved child grows up to be a bad person; the unloved wife pines away; the jilted lover shoots the one who deserted him or her. Love is probably the most advertised and sought-after emotion in society. It is a state of being, of delight, a moment of transformation.

Love is the emotional bond for many relationships. It is a feeling that operates as an explanation—I did it because I was (or am) in love. It is also linked to self disclosure and intimacy—if I am in love I can tell my lover all my hopes and fears and desires. Love makes certain kinds of communication legitimate—and even necessary; there are to be no secrets between lovers.

As people grow older they believe less strongly in love as the most important emotion in life, but during adolescence and mate selection love is central. Perhaps its most important use is in narrowing the mate-selection process, in being a criterion for sexual intimacy as well as interpersonal intimacy. Later in the life cycle people are often unhappy with what they call romantic love, but nearly everyone has a residual desire for the sense of commitment and pleasure involved in love relationships.

Association-Love-Sex

At around age thirteen or fourteen many young people begin to move into conventional heterosocial patterns of association, commonly called dating, out of which emerge a sense of intimacy and love which may facilitate forms of sexual experimentation. It is clear that some heterosexual young people do not begin these patterns until much later in life, and some of them never do so until the last years of college. Those people who develop heterosocial skills late usually have far less total experience in emotional or sexual love than those who begin early. The person they marry may be the only person with whom they have had a social, emotional, and sexual relationship.

The staging of entry into heterosociality and sexuality has three important dimensions. The first is age at the start, which affects the length of time taken to practice heterosocial relationships, falling in and out of love, and sexual contacts of varying sorts. Certain forms of sexual experimentation (as a result of lowered dating ages) have begun earlier in the life cycle, closer to the moment of puberty. Starting early means that "how far one can go" may be limited to hugging, kissing, and light petting. For many young people there is a ceiling on what they do, set by how old they are. It may take an early experimenter four years and a number of relationships to move from light petting to intercourse (say from age thirteen to age sixteen or seventeen). Someone who starts at twenty may move, in one relationship, all the way to intercourse within a year because that is appropriate for a twenty-year-old.

A second dimension of heterosociality is the approved female courtship structure. During the middle 1920s the expected courtship period extended from the mid-teens until marriage. The components were going out with a group of young people, selecting from that group a few special friends, finding among those special friends someone to fall in love with, making a private agreement with him, and then coming to terms with the two families. This took all of the time from age sixteen to age twenty-three or twenty-four.

This was a middle class pattern, but it had major similarities with patterns of working class and ethnic communities, where strong parental control was exerted over the behavior of young women, and young men adhered to the good-girl/bad-girl code. This meant sexually that a girl might be hugging and kissing and light petting with two or three young men, and perhaps heavy petting and intercourse with her fiancee. If that marriage arrangement did not work out she could go through part of the cycle again. Such a design for mate selection narrowed both the range of emotional and sexual experimentation and the numbers of people involved.

A transitional stage in this process began in the 1930s — going steady at various times between age sixteen and marriage. At that time (and until the early 1950s) going steady was viewed as a moral problem, which would lead to intercourse. What it did lead to was extended patterns of petting without intercourse among many young people, even including the persons they ultimately married. Going steady made heavy petting more likely, but also offered an increasing number of emotionally laden and sexually experimental relationships between the times dating began and marriage occurred. Going steady created the struggle in the car back seat, with young men attempting to increase sexual intimacy, while young women attempted to prevent it before the young man made assurances of affection and love. Going steady has now evolved into the general pattern in U. S. society.

Going steady can be described as selecting one person through dating, going through increasing levels of emotional and sexual intimacy, and then breaking up, followed by the same cycle over again. From the start of dating to marriage, many young people may go through five or ten such relationships. Some have only one, others have many. What this structure implies is that young people are going to meet a number of partners with whom they will associate with relative intimacy and increasing love commitments—and such commitments lead to increasing amounts of sexual activity.

They also give young men more opportunities to fall in love, and they are expected to fall in love. This may have the effect of breaking up the male-dominated aspects of premarital sex by creating emotionally laden relationships in which males participate. It may also affect the good-girl/bad-girl distinction by locking sex inside the legitimating context of love. At the same time it may inhibit early casual sex by taking young men out of all-male groups earlier in their lives.

A third dimension of heterosociality is location. Premarital sexual experimentation takes place in different locations depending on the age of the young people who are doing it. Places are not the same as ages, but tend to give ages a good deal of their meaning. The majority of young people start their heterosocial careers in high school. High school educational goals and social climate affect the structure of association, the persons thought to be valuable, and those not. Most high schools have relatively conservative sexual climates, and attempt to control the behavior of young people at least in their public activity. On the other hand, the school offers both an opportunity to get away from parents and more open spaces in which young people can be together. Probably critical to the high school and its sexual climate is the expectation of going on further in school. For those who do not expect to do so, the high school and the first years in the labor force afterward are the crucial period for mate selection. This means that the pace and intensity of sexual experimentation increase for the non-college person far faster than for those going on to college.

Those who go on to college engage in further emotional and sexual experimentation in the continuing cycle of "going steady" that went on in high school, only now in far more permissive sexual circumstances. Beginning in the middle and late 1960s, college dormitories were made coeducational—or at least greater access was allowed between male and female dorms. These events caused a great public outcry, since the college environment was a place from which sexual change could be extended into the larger society. Even though at that time only minor changes had taken place in premarital sex, the fact that they now took place among young people during college rather than after made everything seem very different. Many people thought a sex revolution was going on, but in the mid 1960s the increase in college sex was a joint function of younger age at marriage and value changes. However, when the age at marriage rose again in the 1970s, the practice of premarital experimentation remained part of the college institution. Since the late 1960s premarital heterosexuality has become a conventional part of the college experience for a majority of young people.

Experimentation in college is both more extensive in terms of what people do sexually and more emotionally charged. The intensity of relationships and the potential for cohabitation has increased. At some colleges the opportunity to live together has led many young people to set up living arrangements involving all the attributes of marriage. This pattern does not comprise a majority (estimates vary around fifteen percent); however, unlike in the past, the practice is visible and more or less legitimate.

The majority of young people select a mate sometime between ages nineteen and twenty-five. Those who do not move into the world of older singles, which offers another set of sexual scripts. When they do marry, they select a marital partner in different ways than those people who used the school, family, or neighborhood as a base. The longer the wait the more likely that mate selection will be characterized by a long sequence of sexual and emotional relationships.

Heterosocial Petting Script

Sexual experimentation is linked to patterns of association and the emotional character of the relationship. For most young people having conventional heterosocial relationships, who are following and learning the script, experimentation begins with hugging and kissing, moves on to tongue kissing, to his touching her breast, his touching her genitals, perhaps her touching his genitals, and then simulated intercourse (clothed or nude), and/or oral sex.[1] The extent of sexual activity depends on the definition of the relationship (from casual to planning marriage), the age of the participants, and the number of prior relationships.

The sequence above is, of course, what is or was called petting. It remains an important form of sexual conduct in the society, even though it may be called a wide variety of names other than petting. At one time petting was thought to be bad, by both sexual conservatives and liberals. The conservatives felt that petting was a sign of immorality and could lead to intercourse. Liberals felt that it was a perversion of the goals of sex, that people should not start sexual activity without being ready to go on to intercourse and orgasm. They saw a problem in having an erotic experience without a release of sexual tension, and believed that such inhibition of sexual release might affect marriage. Even Kinsey was quite ambivalent about premarital petting that did not involve intercourse. However, in his own research on females he discovered that marital sex was not affected (except positively) by premarital petting to orgasm. The fact was that many people did it, found it enjoyable, and learned about each other's bodies in this way.

From a practical point of view, petting is a useful activity prior to marriage in the absence of contraceptives, the situation under which such practices evolved. Getting pregnant was to be avoided, so petting served as an occasion for expressing sexual desire and general affection.

The connection between levels of petting and levels of affection is very important. What petting offered (and offers) is a gradient of physical intimacy that goes with a gradient of emotional intimacy. What you do sexually with someone depends on how you feel about them. So hugging and kissing may be all right in one relationship, while mouth-genital contact may be all right in another. Increasing levels of physical intimacy follow increasing levels of emotional intimacy across a series of relationships. Age interacts directly with levels of affection and sexual intimacy, largely by creating a ceiling on such intimacy. Thus a thirteen-year-old in love may pet above the waist; a twenty-year-old may have intercourse.

1. The place of oral sex in this sequence of events is ambiguous. In some cases it occurs as an alternative to intercourse among the premarital; in other cases it only occurs in a relationship after intercourse. It does not appear to be common until after high school for most young people. Oral sex is more frequent premaritally among the college educated.

Combining sexual activity with emotional response is the central script element which allows many forms of intimacy, including the sexual. At the beginning of adolescent petting, a beginning marked by social and sexual ineptitude, anxiety, and fears about general masculinity and femininity as well as peer-group standing, there is a relatively wide separation between the genders. The young males have a relatively advanced sexual script, reinforced by peer-group values, relatively coordinated with the experience of masturbatory orgasm, and integrated with general cultural prescriptions, now linked to the sexual, about male initiation and dominance.

The young females have a relatively more restricted sexual script, constrained by the female "gate-keeper" role; are less likely to have sought orgasm in masturbation; and are bound closely to marriage and motherhood as female goals, but with the script of falling in love as a potent basis for sexual experimentation.

Adolescent petting is a rhythm of increasing general intimacy which peaks at various kinds of sexual activities linked to age, the possibility of falling in love, and marriage. It is an activity of extraordinary subjective excitement, with each performance often extended over long periods of time, and commonly completed without orgasm. *(See Box.)*

This pattern is suggested in Figure 1, with the dotted line suggesting the possibility of declines in excitement and the rare possibility of orgasm. The plateau is long sustained, and in the absence of orgasm, the resolution is long drawn out, often with males and females feeling some pain or discomfort in the groin or genitals. What is important are the differences in cycles of excitement and in the conditions of sexual learning, as well as the difference between durations of various parts of the orgasmic cycle when compared with prior orgasmic practice on the part of the male.

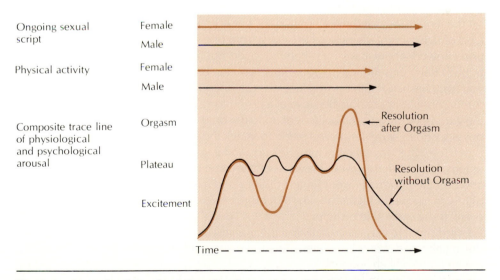

Figure 1   Example of Levels of Coordination and Possible Durations of Segments of the Orgasmic Cycle in Adolescent Petting. (Similar trace line for both genders.)

AN EXCERPT FROM
"The Socialized Penis"

BY JACK LITEWKA

In looking back on my sexual experiences and those of male friends, a very definite and sequential pattern was evident. I'm talking about actual (overt) sexual events, not subliminal or imagined or representational sexual experiences. I'm thinking of adolescent times in adolescent terms when males begin to experiment and develop their knowledge and expertise. I'm thinking about things you did sequentially as you got older. With a few total exceptions and an odd irregularity or two (like fucking a "whore" before you'd kissed a "girl") among the many men I have known and talked with, the sequence runs roughly as follows.

You kiss a girl. You kiss a girl a number of times. You kiss a girl continuously (make-out). You kiss a girl continuously and get your tongue into the act. All through this process you learn to use your hands to round out the orchestration, at first with simple clumsy chords and later with complex harmonies (with the woman, of course, being the instrument made to respond to the musician). You, as a young male, are told (or figure out) what sensitive spots you should seek, and learn more as the young female (hopefully) responds to your hands. First you just hug and grasp. Then you make little circles on her shoulders with your fingers. Then you go for the back of the neck, and run your fingers through her hair (music, please), and then over her face and throat. Then the outer ear (lobes especially). And middle ear. Then lower back (at which point your tongue might cover the ear as a stand-in for the absent hand). Then the tender sides of the waist above the (maybe-not-yet) hip bones. Then the belly. And after, the upper belly and the rib cage. Here let us take a deep breath before the great leap upward to the breast, which is a bold act broken into a number of ritualistic steps. First the hand over one breast, with blouse and bra between your hand and the female's flesh. This is a move that took special courage (balls?) and was very exciting for it seemed a new level of sensuality (which it was for the female, but for the male? no, only a new level of expectation). Then came a kind of figure-eight roving over the chest from one breast to the other (if your position allowed — how many right-handed lovers out there?). Then a sneaking between buttons (later unbuttoned) so your hand is on the breast with only the bra separating you from flesh. (Or if this procedure was too uncouth or too visible to others in the dusky room or impossible because of a no-button sweater, you worked underneath the garment from a fleshy belly right up to the bra.) Then, by means of gradually developed finger dexterity, you begin to attack the flesh of the breast itself, working down from the top of the bra into the cup. And if you hadn't yet picked up any signs of female complicity in your previous experience, it was often clear here. If she sat and breathed normally, your fingers didn't stand a chance (bras were worn very tightly in my junior high school so that nipples were always pointing up at your eyes). If she wanted to be helpful, she would deeply exhale and move her shoulder forward so there was space between the bra and the breast. (Women's cooperation during all these events is an interesting topic and really should be written about by a woman.) And here came the rainbow's gold — the assault on the nipple. While a kiss was exciting, and cupping a breast breath-taking, the conquest of the nipple was transcendent. Partly because it was the only part of a female's anatomy that we have dealt with so far that isn't normally seen or even partly exposed. Also because you knew that when this was achieved, the girl really liked you, and that getting the bra unhooked and off would not be far away. Maybe as soon as next week. When older, the same night. And you also sensed that you were getting closer to the core of sexuality (excuse the geographically mixed metaphor). Then began the assault on the crotch, in steps similar to those of the battle of the breast. You caressed her hip, worked around to her ass, pulled her close to announce (if it hadn't already been discovered) the existence of your penis and give it some pleasurable friction (and provide the girls with a topic of gossip later? if you were erect). Then you worked down to the side of her leg. Then the front of her thigh. Then with a deep breath, and microscopic steps, you slowly progressed toward the vaginal entrance (how many of you had imagined the entrance 4 inches higher than you found it to be?). Now here there are many variables: was it at a swim party when she only had on the bottom part of a two-piece suit, or was she wearing jeans, or did she have a skirt on? Whatever the case, you usually ended up rubbing her crotch through cloth and then worked down from her belly toward her crotch, getting your hand (as one variation of the phrase goes) in her pants. Then you sort of played around above or on top of her slit and eventually got a finger in it, and by accident or design (depending on your previous intelligence briefings) found the "magic button." And soon (usually), all hell broke loose and more than ever before, you didn't quite know what to do with yourself if fucking wasn't yet in the script.

And that pretty much covers the pre-coital scenario. Except it was described in a semi-humorous manner and, as a male, many of these events were terrifying. You, most often, had to take the first step. And you could be rejected. Refused. Denied. Cold and flat. And that could hurt. Hurt bad. In your own eyes and in your male friends' eyes. Being scared to try and therefore not trying could just as easily become the subject of psychological self-punishment and social ostracism. So there was always this elementary duality: while apparently the aggressor and conqueror, you were captive to a judgment by the female who would accept or reject you.

Also important to remember is how these events were reported to/discussed with male friends after the party or date. Or gone over in your own mind, again and again, detail by detail. How every step along the initiation route was stimulating and could/did cause an erection (remember the 4-hour erections and blue balls?). How we compared notes, made tactical suggestions, commented on important signs—heavier breathing, torso writhing, aggressive hands, a more daring tongue, involvement of teeth, goose bumps, erected nipples, and when menstruation occurred or was expected to occur. Which girls liked what, since in those days "relationships" were short-lived and you never knew which female you might be with another time. And if you were ever in doubt as to what came next in the scenario, your friends informed you of the specifics of the next escalation. And sometimes, if that wasn't possible, the female you were with (embarrassingly enough) let you know in any one of a number of subtle (or not-so-subtle) ways what was next on the agenda.

There were, in retrospect, many funny occasions that cropped up in this initiation process. I don't really need to talk about them because you probably have your own to tell. What stuns me now is that origins of the tragedy of sex emerge clearly from that process of socialized sexuality.

Liberation, Vol. 18, No. 7, March-April 1974, pp. 16–24. Copyright (c) 1972 by Jack Litewka. The original, full-length version of the essay appears in an anthology by Times Changes Press, and also in anthologies edited by John Gagnon and Eleanor Morrison.

The struggle in the back seat was a routine part of 1930s American courtship.

The petting cycle is repeated over and over again, and only as couples get older and closer to marriage is it likely to result in the scene of first coitus described later in this chapter. In these situations of petting, young people learn skillful kissing and develop other noncoital skills. Both males and females learn to tolerate (and enjoy) fairly high levels of physical and emotional excitement without orgasm.

Such restraint is sometimes difficult for males; they experience orgasm in masturbation, but there is no easy translation of the solitary, autonomous, fantasy-laden experience of such orgasm to the dual, dependent, exploratory situation of petting. By contrast, females — whose bodies take on erotic meaning derived from male reactions — learn that arousal is possible and pleasurable (as well as fearful, since it affects successful gatekeeping) through the sequence of petting activities that males attempt and in which females ultimately cooperate. They learn in the context of love a sense of the physical and its role in sexual gratification.

Early Homosocial Sexuality

There are other patterns of sexual experimentation which depend largely on other definitions of the moral worth of the participants, particularly the females. These patterns are linked to male sexual values and good-girl/bad-girl definitions. The petting theme described above has been linked to "good girls," or to girls who accept (and are acceptable for) emotional and social bonding. Even if the relationship breaks up, the sex was legitimated by the affection. However, if intercourse occurred at a young age, and the male is tied to his male friends, the girl becomes a "bad girl."

Casual sex with "bad girls" depends on male scripting of sexual activity. Male-dominated cultures are sexually exploitative, particularly youthful male cultures, and there is a good deal of trying to have intercourse with females, especially those with marginal moral reputations (based on looks, appearance, social class, and leisure style).

A marginal moral reputation scarcely involves any sin. A young girl with a large bust is defined by boys as "sexy"; if a man meets a woman in a bar and drives her home, she is thought to be available; student doctors like to believe that student nurses are good for sex but not to marry (not high enough social status); if a man has had sex with a woman once, he thinks he is entitled to it again.

In some all-male groups masculinity is supported by "scoring": counting up the number of females with whom a male has had sex. There are some communities in which all females are vulnerable (there are no "good girls" — similar to working class servants in the nineteenth century). This pattern is particularly common in very poor, lower class communities which have strong commitments to *machismo*, and where sexual scoring is one of the few ways in which men can subordinate other males. This is a homosocial sexual script. That is, the sex is performed not for the women, but in order to tell the other men about it. Sex is for status ranking among men, not for the pleasure of the act or for the pleasure of the woman.

Such patterns also characterize many middle class males, especially those with a strong commitment to all-male values (as members of fraternities, athletic teams, hunting clubs, and golf clubs). In these cases there is a search for relatively casual sex, the one-night stand, the pick up. Such sexual relationships may emerge from the *when* and *where* of the beginning of the relationship — a couple formally introduced defines the relationship one way; if they meet in a bar or other pickup place the definition of what can or will happen is different.

The evidence is that men have more single encounters or relationships that last a very short time than do women. It is possible for a young woman to rewrite her affection-based script by being "carried away," being drunk, or being in a particular place at a particular time, all of which can legitimate a brief, erotic encounter. More autonomous women less often use these script elements to justify or further a sexual encounter with a limited investment in emotion or time.

Permissiveness and Sex

The reality of a script in controlling patterns of sexual experimentation before marriage has been confirmed by studies on patterns of premarital permissiveness. Table 1 shows a scale (developed by Ira Reiss) for asking under what conditions it is appropriate for young people to have sex. The scale items were used with the instruction that they were to be answered in terms of the subject's own behavior and not tolerance of others. Men and women were asked their standards for the opposite sex as well. The scale has three dimensions: what is all right for men and women; what is all right in a certain type of relationship; and what kind of sexual activity is involved. The term "full sexual relations" means sexual intercourse.

The items were answered in expected ways: sex is more acceptable for men than women under conditions of less emotion; religious people are more conservative than non-religious; there were some differences by class, race, age, etc. All of the percentages are subject to change; what is important are the script elements implicit in the questionnaire. Without the ordering of a previously learned script, such a verbal sequence would be meaningless to the participants.

The general framework offered by the scale can be shifted to ask about particular persons (would it be all right for you, for your daughter, for your mother?) or to change the range of sexual acts. Such changes vary the character of the script. Reiss chose three dimensions; others might choose other aspects of the premarital script.

The relationship between such assertions and actual sexual behavior is not clear. Those with more sexual experience tend to be more liberal on the scale it-

Table 1   Premarital Sexual Permissiveness Scales

Agree	Disagree
Strong / Medium / Slight	Strong / Medium / Slight

One of the above choices to be made for each of the following:
1. I believe that (kissing; petting; full sexual relations) is acceptable for the male/female before marriage when he/she is engaged to be married.

2. I believe that (kissing; petting; full sexual relations) is acceptable for the male/female before marriage when he/she is in love.

3. I believe that (kissing; petting; full sexual relations) is acceptable for the male/female before marriage when he/she feels strong affection for his/her partner.

4. I believe that (kissing; petting; full sexual relations) is acceptable for the male/female before marriage even if he/she does not feel particularly affectionate toward his/her partner.

We use the words below to mean just what they do to most people but some may need definition:

Love means the emotional state which is more intense than strong affection and which you would define as love.

Strong affection means affection which is stronger than physical attraction, average fondness, or "liking" — but less strong than love.

Petting means sexually stimulating behavior more intimate than kissing and simple hugging, but not including full sexual relations.

self—we cannot tell from most studies whether greater liberality leads to more sex, or more sex leads to greater liberality. It is possible that there is a long-term drift toward more liberal responses with age (up until marriage), whether or not there is sexual activity, so that earlier in life sex comes before liberalism; later, sex comes after.

The Virginity Barricade

In the United States, sex that involves intercourse is considered to be different than sex that does not. Kinsey discussed this in relation to young people in the 1930s and 1940s:

It is amazing to observe the mixture of scientifically supported logic, and of utter illogic, which shapes the petting behavior of most of these youths. . . . They (young people in the 1940s) are particularly concerned with the avoidance of genital union. The fact that petting involves erotic contacts which are as effective as genital union, and that it may even involve contacts which have been more taboo than genital union, including some that have been considered perversions, does not disturb the youth so much as actual intercourse would. By petting, they preserve their virginities, even though they may achieve orgasm while doing so. They still value virginity, much as the previous generations valued it. Only the list of most other activities has had new values placed on it. (Kinsey, 1948, pp. 543–544.)

While fewer people today give such weight to virginity, the transition from nonvirgin to virgin still means a substantial change in self concept. The importance of the change varies by individual, but the fact of nonvirginity, particularly for females, remains an important step, only sometimes undertaken casually. The importance of the shift is reflected in the obsessive popular and scientific interest in the percentage of virgins among young people. This number and its change from the past is probably the most recorded statistic in all of sex research. The number of females who have had intercourse before marriage *is* the sexual revolution.

The importance of this number is related to two factors: the first is that in traditional patriarchal societies the marriage value of the female depends on the presence or absence of a hymen. Virginity was (and still is for some) the mark of new goods, the sign that this person has never been owned by anyone else. A woman's sexuality was treated like the new car that drops in value as soon as it is taken from the lot.

The second factor is that marriageability is more than an economic value; it is a moral category. It is a balance between good and evil, reflected in virginity. If women are to be given the burden of controlling the lustful male, the virginity rate is a measure of their success. The proportion of female virgins is thus a measure of the moral health of the society. When Kinsey put the proportion at fifty percent during the 1940s and 1950s, doom was thought to be at hand. Successive increments of change in that percentage remain of central importance to the moral bookkeepers of the society. *(See Box.)*

Decline in Premarital Virginity

The data on the incidence of premarital intercourse taken from the best studies (see Tables 2 and 3 for recent comparable data on males and females) suggests the following patterns of change. From the limited data that is available on the premarital sexual patterns of women who married before World War I, it appears that about one woman in four was having intercourse before marriage at that time. The rates are primarily from middle class white women in their fifties and sixties who were interviewed during the 1940s. (We have no information that can be converted in reliable estimates for any period prior to 1890.) From 1890 to 1920, patterns of

Table 2   Female Nonvirgins by Age (%)

Study	Ages:	13	14	15	16	17	18	19	20	21	22	23	24	25	Married
1953 Kinsey (includes single/ married)															
Total		0	2	3	7	10			20					33	50
grade school				18					25						
high school				5					26						
college				2					20						
1953 Burgess-Wallin (all married)															47
1967 Simon-Gagnon (national sample; all single, in college)						17	19	30	37	44					
1970 Veder (high school students) Three Michigan towns															
blue-collar		7	8	13	21	40									
mixed		10	11	13	23	27									
professional		1	2	9	7	12									
Total		7	7	12	18	26									
1972 Kantner-Zelnick (national sample; all single)				11		22	34								
1972 Illinois Youth Survey (state sample; 13–17)															
Total				10		27	38								
high school				11		40	40								
some college				12		20	27								
going to college				4		12	23								
1973 Veder Mixed town		10	17	24	31	35									

courtship were changing in the middle class, and modern patterns involving greater sexual intimacy between those intending to marry were developing.

This change can be observed in the incidence of premarital intercourse among women studied during the period 1920 to 1950. In a number of small studies, as well as in Kinsey's research, it appears that about one in two women were having intercourse before marriage. The rather large increase from women married before World War I to those married in the 1920s should arouse some caution, since most social changes do not seem to take place that rapidly. However, there was a substantial increase in nonvirginity before marriage during this period, and the figure one in two did characterize the incidence of premarital coitus among women until the early and middle 1960s. A number of studies (largely studies of women who had not yet married) indicate that in the 1960s one half of contemporary women were nonvirgins by about age twenty-one, and that about sixty-five to seventy-five percent of young women today have intercourse before marriage.

The data suggests that social class differences in age at marriage probably have a great deal to do with age at first intercourse. Young women who do not go to college begin coitus during and just after high school, while college women begin somewhat later. Women with working class origins or those who do not expect to go to college are about twice as likely to have had intercourse by age seventeen as college women. Major changes have taken place on the college scene, with a doubling of the proportion of women having intercourse by their senior year (compared to the Kinsey research). Similar changes are now occurring in the high schools, with an increase in the proportion of women having intercourse during their middle and later teens. Once again the middle class has less experience than the working class, particularly at early ages.

One of the major findings of the Kinsey research was that premarital intercourse for many women was prompted by how close they were to getting married. If they were in a secure relationship, which in their judgment was likely to result in marriage, they were more willing to have intercourse. This pattern was quite constant in the United States from the early 1920s through the 1950s. We can see from the data that there is some breakdown of the pattern, with the increase in the number of women having intercourse separated in time from the usual ages at marriage. However, the different proportions of working class and middle class young women engaging in premarital intercourse suggest that this pattern is still influential. Working class women show a sharp increase in premarital sex at ages sixteen to about nineteen, while among college women the rate of increase comes at ages nineteen to twenty-one (particularly during the sophomore and junior years).

The changing relationship between marriage and sex is reflected in the Kinsey data on numbers of sexual partners before marriage. Of those women who had premarital coitus, half had intercourse with only one man (the man they married) and another one-fourth had intercourse only with their fiance and one other man. Only five percent of the women in the Kinsey study had sex with five or more men before marriage. With an increase in the incidence of premarital intercourse and a gap between age at first coitus and the age at marriage, we can expect these figures to have risen somewhat over the last decade.

Decline in Premarital Virginity (cont.)

When we look at male data on premarital coitus (Table 3) we find that (1) there is less data and (2) the coital incidences are less strongly linked to getting married. The sexuality of young women seems to follow a pattern predictable from earlier training—linked to love and marriage. On the other hand, young males seem still attached more directly to sexuality outside the orbit of love, at least part of the time. In the 1940s, the proportion of premarital nonvirgins among college-going males was less than half by age twenty. In the middle 1960s, the proportion at age twenty had increased by sixteen percent. Most other studies support these figures, placing the proportion of coitally experienced single young men at thirty to forty percent of all seventeen-year-olds, and increasing to seventy or seventy-five percent by the end of college. As with women, this represents a major increase during the early adult years.

Table 3   Male Nonvirgins by Age (%)

Study	Ages:	13	14	15	16	17	18	19	20	21	22	23	24	25	Married
1948 Kinsey (includes single/ married)															
Total		14	28	39	52	61			73					83	
College				10					44					65	
1953 Burgess-Wallin (all married)															68
1967 Simon-Gagnon (all single; in college)						30	36	63	60	68					
1970 Veder (high school students) Three Michigan towns															
blue-collar		24	23	15	31	38									
mixed		25	21	26	32	38									
professional		8	7	19	21	31									
Total		20	18	21	28	33									
1973 Veder															
Mixed town		28	32	38	38	34									

Recent research suggests that some of the patterns observed in the past may be changing. The Illinois Youth Survey, reported by Miller and Simon, found a significant convergence of male and female rates of intercourse, especially among the college-bound, suggesting that the older dichotomy between "good girl" and "bad girl" may be declining as more young men seek emotional and sexual relationships with young women. At the same time, young women still have a good deal of difficulty integrating sexual identity into a high-school social climate, an integration that is much easier for them in college, although not yet as easy as it is for males. In sum, men and women are converging somewhat in terms of the kinds of situations in which they feel sex is appropriate, with the women changing faster than the men.

Script and Experience

Managing sexual experimentation is not merely a problem of dealing with the body, but coordinating scripts inside the head with the body. First intercourse at any age requires a substantial amount of interpersonal coordination before, during, and after the act. This coordination cannot be expressed in numbers, but rather in descriptions that seem to mirror reality.

The following is a description, in some detail and with marginal comments, of a heterosexual act of intercourse, the first for a young couple in their late teens, tracing the ways scripts elicit behavior. Most of the elements in the situation are conventions, only some of which are related to biological reproduction.

A young man and a young woman are in a social relationship that is going to result in intercourse. It is voluntary, and involves no direct exchange of money. It is the culmination of a series of experiences with each other that they both recognize as likely to lead to intercourse. They are the products of middle class and working class socialization for sexual performance in U.S. society. This implies that they both possess at least a fragmentary version of the sequence of activities that they are going to perform, even though they may have had little practice.

As the couple move beyond that tipping point when the conventionally sexual becomes salient, they are very likely to be alone together, in a private place, screened from the public — perhaps his home or hers, or a friend's. They are past the age for the couch in the living room or the back seat of a car. They will begin touching each other while still clothed, clothing appropriate to where they were and what they were doing publicly before going off to be alone. In public the couple will commonly conceal that they might be thinking of intercourse, even though they might be defined as in love or engaged; in public, sexual modesty needs to be preserved. The time could be afternoon or evening. The light in the room is more likely to be dim or even dark rather than bright, offering a certain privacy in the midst of mutual intimacy.

As they begin they are likely to talk in a slightly desultory manner, probably a little anxiously, given the danger, novelty, and forbidden nature of what they are going to do. The shyness of their talk and its unspecific reference demonstrate the difficulty of moving easily to physical activity from a public world in which the physical aspects of the sexual largely do not exist, and in which sexual talk between women and men is oblique. An easy transition from public to private sexuality may never be achieved — in part because we lack the words to say "this is it," even to an audience of one.

No matter how often they have made physical love short of intercourse, this moment is seen to be different. It is "going all the way" — a rite of passage, a moment of particular significance linked to historically specific ideas about what this sexual transition means. After coitus the couple will change, with reference to themselves, to each other, and to their surrounding social world. Some young women have reported an uneasy sense that after their first intercourse other people could see a change in their faces — that the private moment has somehow turned into a public stigma.

The couple will begin by kissing, and if they have had some physical contact before, they will perhaps move quickly to tongue kissing. His hands will touch her body outside her clothing, tentatively or more directly, depending on the history of their relationship. She may resist, at first more and then less, perhaps only because she has resisted such gestures so often before, but she reveals her own desire. They will kiss almost continuously, maintaining a sense of intimate contact and in some degree avoiding direct attention on what their hands may be doing.

They will begin to undress, or rather, parts of their clothing will be loosened, unbuttoned, unzipped, conventionally hers first and then his. There will be fumblings, slightly inept gestures; he may never have undressed anyone but himself before; she has rarely been undressed by others since childhood and perhaps never by a man. The initiative is still largely his; buttons turn out to be stubborn, removing her bra turns into a slightly tense ballet. Each of these moments represents a momentary stumble, a deflection of attention from the sense of passion that is part of managing the concrete activity.

As their clothing is finally completely removed, usually hers first and then his (from some obscure origin there is a convention that allows her to be nude before he is), there will be a slight clammy chill as the cool air of the room touches the bare, perhaps perspiring, bodies. To master these interruptions and transitions they may kiss more fiercely. She may straddle his leg or he may intrude it between hers and they will make movements which simulate coitis, giving the act both a genital focus and predicting its conclusion.

There will continue to be distractions, both internal and external. Footsteps in the hallway, the turning of keys in locks, the sounds of passing traffic—the external world continues to make its presence felt. There is also a lingering double sense of anticipation and risk. He wonders whether he will stay erect, whether she is enjoying what he is doing; she wonders how to keep him doing things that do feel good and how to stop him from doing other things that do not, whether she will have an orgasm, whether there is any danger of getting pregnant. There will be gentle grunts and moans and whispers of affectionate fragments, words, and sentences, which they can mutually interpret to be signs of pleasure and permission.

After some time the distractions lessen and the decision is made (except for nagging doubts): they test each other's readiness (more commonly he tests hers) and she opens her legs to let him enter. He may or may not have difficulty, for there is a tense moment as the erect penis begins to enter the vagina. The mechanics intrude; there may be pain for her and sometimes for him. If it is too difficult he may lose his erection; if he is too excited he may ejaculate too soon, sometimes before entry or at the moment when his penis touches her. If she feels too much pain she may close herself emotionally and endure the wanted and unwanted intrusion.

In these moments when what was subliminally coordinated fails, there is a sense of sadness, a resonance of personal failure, a hoped-for and often given, but necessarily inadequate, commiseration. He is apologetic, she is disheartened. Can the failure be repaired? Should they try again? They will talk, sometimes too much, seeking to heal the damage, to make sense of the failure, and perhaps to try again, if not now, then later.

But failure only occurs sometimes. The couple is joined together, there is a set of physical sensations on parts of their bodies that have been imagined, but never experienced. It may be fumbling, to be sure—are the limbs quite coordinated, does

You get a lot of help undressing before sex, but afterwards you have to get dressed again by yourself.

it hurt, is the rhythm of movement correct? She compares what is happening with literary or cinematic models while he tries to recall whatever sexological advice he has heard or read or picked up from his other sexual experiences about the arousal of women. They may, in a moment of inattention, become uncoupled, and this results in a spasm of activity—his hand, perhaps hers; there is an eruption of the physical into their dreaming life; the genital fluids make their undeodorized presence known. The romance in the head is confronted with a transient reminder of the reality of the regions below.

They continue, he more often active but also passive, she more often passive and sometimes active, as they move, largely apart, but seeking to be together, toward orgasm. It is a dumb show in which their private passions and excitements are coordinated through quickening movements, sounds, and vague tensions which anticipate culmination. Such inarticulate pleasures contain their own anxieties: if he has climax too soon he may lose his erection, she may remain unsatisfied. But in the best of circumstances, given our current cultural blueprint, they move relatively closely to climax, or at least they both will have orgasm. At this moment there may be exclamations, requests for activity, assurances of affection. The external world—the movement of the bed, the floor perhaps creaking, the sounds of a passing and disinterested world—is largely gone but even at this moment there can be that instant of double awareness: What if the neighbors are listening? What if a roommate returns?

When they are done—and the moment and quality of doneness is often difficult to define—there is the moment of separation and awareness. The coolness of the room, the stickiness of the flesh—the world intrudes, only to be held at bay by expressions of mutual affection, talking, touching, assurances of trust, gentle reminders of the social relationship that allows the sexual moment. There is a problem of reentry into that other world, even between themselves. There is mutual nudity, his body and hers without that protecting cloak of the erotic by which they have modified the boundaries of modesty. They must clean up, remove the evidence of physical intimacy, and dress in their cold and rumpled clothing, perhaps untangling hers from his; they must share or sequentially use the toilet, washbasin, or shower. They may smoke, have a cup of coffee, talk, sit across a table and look at each other.

In the end they must admit the claims of the external world, when they are together and when they are alone, when she is with her friends and he with his. There are the dilemmas of partial and total disclosure, to what audiences. For him there may be the crudities of adolescent male judgments and braggadocio about his conquest that will exist ambivalently with his sense of a betrayal of intimacy. For her there may be worries (more virtuous girls quietly moralizing) and justifications (she was in love, why else would she have done it?). For both of them the outcomes are ambiguous, and their scripts will be reordered and transformed to provide plans for the future and justifications for the past.

It is possible to create many such scenes which involve the sexual. This cryptic and incomplete description contains only a part of the reality of the specific act and suggests only one of a variety of circumstances under which first coitus can take place in U.S. society at a specific historical-social moment. One can vary the ages, the personal histories, the degrees of skill, the quality of assent, the legal circumstances, and the social status of the participants and produce differences in what might be called the conventional social situation for first coitus. But even in this simple form, the extraordinary complexity of the situation and the levels of coordination necessary for finding a successful conclusion are apparent.

Within the social and psychological fields of the two young people are a wide range of script elements that must be integrated, organized, and reassessed. These are scripts that have relevance at the physiological, psychological, and social and cultural levels. When sexual conduct (of which the physical aspects are only a small part) is viewed in this manner, its explanation is not simply a matter of determining a sequence through which a kind of biological mandate is expressed. Rather, the emphasis is on psychosocial processes and cultural-historical situations which provide meaning for behavior, allow for the integration and reorganization of information and skills learned at earlier stages in the life cycle, and elicit from an organism the culturally appropriate responses to novel situations.

Conclusion

There are a number of pathways by which we acquire one or another script for heterosexuality before marriage. These pathways represent the staging and timing of activities, offering us contexts in which to try out different scripts and their variations. We begin at different ages, and we conclude at different ages. Some people never stop being premarital in the sense that they do not marry, but they do stop being premarital in the sense that they become adult singles.

What happens is that we learn to integrate dating, affection, love, attitudes toward women and men, and sexuality into increasingly complex scripts. We try them out in concrete situations, find that they work or do not, and then try them again with the same or different people. We may try the one-night stand, the love affair, living together, and affectionate or passionate relationships. We can add and subtract the various sexual techniques we have learned and practice them in different combinations. We can have premarital sex dominated by female values or by male values.

There are many ways to be heterosexual in that narrow decade of singlehood between puberty and marriage. Some people try most of them, some try only a few.

The problem this period represents for young people is that they are left to their own sexual and social devices. While they may be covertly encouraged by peers and the media, there is no system which whole-heartedly endorses or condemns sexual experimentation. Society is fragmented and individuals are ambivalent on the question of premarital heterosexual experimentation. This situation will probably continue for many years, even though the drift of society in values and practice is in a more prosexual direction. In the interim, the costs of this system will continue to be carried by the young as they struggle to acquire sexual scripts and a sexual persona on a stage that is often barren of useful directions.

MARITAL SEXUALITY

Mel Funn (proposing to Bernadette Peters as Vilma Kaplan):
Marry me and you won't ever have to take off your clothes again.
Mel Brooks, *Silent Movie*

MOST PEOPLE WHO LIVE IN THE CONTEMPORARY UNITED STATES ARE GREAT
believers in being married. Even those who do not believe in it often do it, and
those who are disappointed in it often do it again. Thus upwards of eighty to
ninety percent of any generation marry, and a similar proportion who divorce
remarry. Being married is perhaps more characteristic of the way of life of the
United States than any other attribute. And regardless of recent changes in sexual
values, sex with spouse remains the most legitimate and approved form of sex
available in U.S. culture. All aspects of the marital relationship are affected by its
sexual aspects, and the sexual relationship of parents has consequences for their
children in later life.

The central role marriage plays in our society is reflected in the impact it has
on all other forms of sexuality. Much of premarital sex is organized around getting
married, as young people look for future marital partners in a cycle of heterosociality, intimacy, love, and sex. Even living together is often a form of trial marriage.
Also, extramarital sex is conditioned by the promises made in the marriage contract
and justified or vilified on the basis of that contract. The sex lives of those who remain single, or who are divorced or widowed, are affected by the availability of
potential sexual and marital partners—limited by the fact that so many people are
married in U.S. society. And a large part of the sex that occurs between marriages
leads to remarriage.

Even the sex of exclusively homosexual people is affected by the marriage institution—"good" relationships among homosexuals sound very much like what
we describe as "good" relationships among married heterosexuals. A warm, loving, faithful, emotionally close, stable, long-term relationship is what most homosexuals say that they are looking for, and is often reported by male homosexuals as
lacking in the male homosexual life style.

Given that marital sex is the sex most widely approved, and given that most
people get married, we might surmise that marital sex is frequent and even pleasurable. Yet in fact marital sex occurs with a relative infrequency that lessens even
more with age, and all around us is a constant outcry about the quality of sex in
marriage. Masters and Johnson have suggested that half of all marriages involve
some sexual dysfunction (although this seems an inflated estimate, perhaps encouraged by a utopian standard of sexual functioning). The popularity of sex therapy,
sex manuals, and the sex advice columns of men's and women's magazines suggests that many people seem dissatisfied with the current state of marital sexual life.

In part this dissatisfaction results from high expectations on the part of some contemporary people about sex: it is supposed to be joyous, delightful, fulfilling, etc., but for many people it turns out to be less exalting. In part this gap between reality and expectation is encouraged by the fact that we believe fulfilling sex should occur without practice. We think we should be able to enjoy sex without any skill or knowledge about it. In part the difficulty may be in technical preparation. Even though we do not like to think that sex requires practice, like tennis or driving or swimming or reading or doing arithmetic, many of the technical problems of sex may be resolved by doing things a number of times with some variety in procedure and partners.

Perhaps more important is our cultural ambivalence about sex and the pleasures we think we deserve from it. This ambivalence is part of a general cultural uneasiness about pleasure: who should have it, who deserves it and under what conditions, what tests should people go through to earn pleasure, and so on. We like to think people should earn their pleasures, or at least pay for them in some way, including the pleasures of marital sex.

Women are at a particular cultural disadvantage in terms of their right to practice sex as well as enjoy it. Any measure of the sexual activity experienced by men and women reveals that men simply do more sexual things than women do. Only recently has it become popular to argue that women have a right to sexual pleasure at all, or as much right as men to go beyond the marriage bed. We are not yet out of the Victorian era, a world in which female sexual pleasure (among good women) was not allowed. Denial of female sexual pleasure still exists in working class subcultures, and in Latin and Mediterranean societies where the cult of the Madonna and Motherhood is still powerful. Even in the United States, where there is some recognition of the sexual rights of women, permission is still often limited to sexual pleasure in marriage, usually as part of the property relationship between men and women.

It represents a major cultural revolution in U.S. consciousness to have accepted even to a limited degree the view that women have a right to sexual pleasure, a right to want sex on their own terms. This view represents a fundamental change in the sexual doctrine of U.S. society, as well as a change in the expectations of people when they are having sex. In the very recent past, female orgasm was a matter of indifference not only to men but to many women, who accepted or believed this male point of view. (In some cases it was more than that, since having an orgasm or expressing an interest in sexual pleasure was evidence of something "wrong" with a woman.) Of course there were women entitled and even expected to have orgasm, particularly prostitutes, who have long known how to fake sexual response for their clientele.

The shift in attitude—that women not only have the right, but should want to have orgasm—is now official doctrine. Many women who do not have orgasm now feel inferior. Their husbands or lovers also feel sexually inadequate. The female orgasm has become entangled with that other major theme of our society, the need for achievement. Female sexuality has once again become involved with male views of the sexual—orgasm has become an achievement to be strived for and something to be counted (and accounted for) in sexual relationships. As a result, many (particularly middle-class) men are very much concerned that their wives have orgasm since it is evidence that they are good lovers. Concern for a wife's pleasure is in part a concern for male self image.

The desire to control the sexual responses of women remains a powerful cultural force. That sexually responsive women are dangerous to the social order is a major theme of the movies of the 1920s and 1930s. In the 1920s German film, *The Blue Angel*, Marlene Dietrich plays a nightclub entertainer who seduces a middle-aged, respectable teacher infatuated with her. In his infatuation he loses his teaching post and ends up playing a rooster in a beer hall, crying out *cock-a-doodle-do* to drunken audiences. The myth of the erotic woman who is dangerous to men is inverted in the 1970s Hollywood movie *Jaws*. At the opening of that film a woman is consumed by a shark. What had she done just before that happened? She had sex with someone on the beach. Was she married to him? Were they in love? Were they swept away by passion? No, it was simply casual sex after a cocktail party. Willingness to engage in casual sex was sufficient script justification for the woman to be destroyed by a shark.

The picture we have of sex in marriage revolves around cultural ambivalences and practices—pleasure in sex and who deserves it, practice in sex and how to get it, and the problem of fitting the practice and pleasure of sex into our daily lives.

Frequency of Sex in Marriage

In recent years there have been a number of studies of the frequency of sexual intercourse in marriage, and they have all tended to show the same picture. The rate of sex for young married people is about three times a week; for older married people the rate drops off steadily throughout the life cycle. By the middle thirties and early forties, median and mean coital rates are one and a half to two times per week. Beyond age fifty, these figures drop to once a week and less. This means that married couples in their early twenties are, on the average, having sex together about 150 times per year, while married people in their forties are doing so about 100 or fewer times per year.

There are of course people who have sex much more often than this, both early in marriage and later. However, these numbers describe the mainstream experience. Whether these rates are "high" or "low" is a value judgment; "Compared to what?" would be a proper evaluative question. One answer would be, "Compared to the importance we place on sex in general and on sex in marriage." However, we may be fairly confident that these figures do locate the general tendency in U.S. society. *(See Box.)*

What can we judge from the rates reported in Figure 1? First we might think of other nonsexual activities that people perform in the course of a year, and their frequency: We eat regular meals about 1000 times per year, and go to and from work twice a day. Many housewives in the suburbs, it is said, run ten errands with the car each week day. By comparison marital sex does not occur with very great frequency.

Evaluating the Research

Four of the studies in Figure 1 are of nonsampled populations—that is, of volunteers who either responded to phone calls (Hunt), a magazine questionnaire (*Redbook*), a handed-out questionnaire (Bell and Bell), or a scientist asking for interviews in various ways (Kinsey). One study (Westoff) reports the results of two probability samples of the U.S. female population. (By "probability samples" is meant subjects carefully selected at random to represent accurately the total U.S. female population.) The first four studies report what can be judged as inflated figures, since their subjects were volunteers, who tend to come from the more sexually active portions of the population. Since we can also expect that these studies' subjects include more people with extremely high rates of activity, we can have more confidence in medians than in means—since means are affected more by exceptionally high rates (note the difference between the mean and medians in the Kinsey studies).

These studies, done at different times and reporting on both men and women, are remarkably consistent. The mean rates from the 1965 and 1970 Westoff studies are quite similar to the medians from the Kinsey study of 1953. The studies by Westoff report a rise in coital rates between 1965 and 1970, which Westoff attributes to effective contraception. If the Westoff figures are correct (and they are the best available), it would appear that the Kinsey figures for thirty years ago were probably high for that time, and that people then had even less intercourse than people do now. The Hunt, Bell and Bell, and *Redbook* studies probably report higher rates than the actual average because of their selective bias. What they can tell us, however, is that it is unlikely the true picture is any higher than they report and is likely to be substantially lower.

Second, we can consider the time involved. People report that marital intercourse commonly takes about ten to twenty minutes—if they do it 150 times per year (take twenty minutes per act to be the average) it will take up about fifty hours per year. We spend 2000 hours working (40 hours times 50 weeks), watch television about three hours per day (1000 hours per year), spend perhaps an hour per day commuting to and from work. Marital sex does not consume a great deal of our time.

Given that marital sex is both sought out by individuals and approved by society, and that much of our advertising (for cars, cosmetics, toothpaste, deodorants, floor cleaners) is linked to sex, why does it actually occupy so little of married life? The decline by age in the rates of intercourse cannot be explained only by biological aging, nor can the fact that these rates are, for example, about one third those of Polynesia be explained by differences in genetic constitution. The sources of the discrepancy must be in how we prepare ourselves for marital sex and the conditions in which we live sexually in marriage.

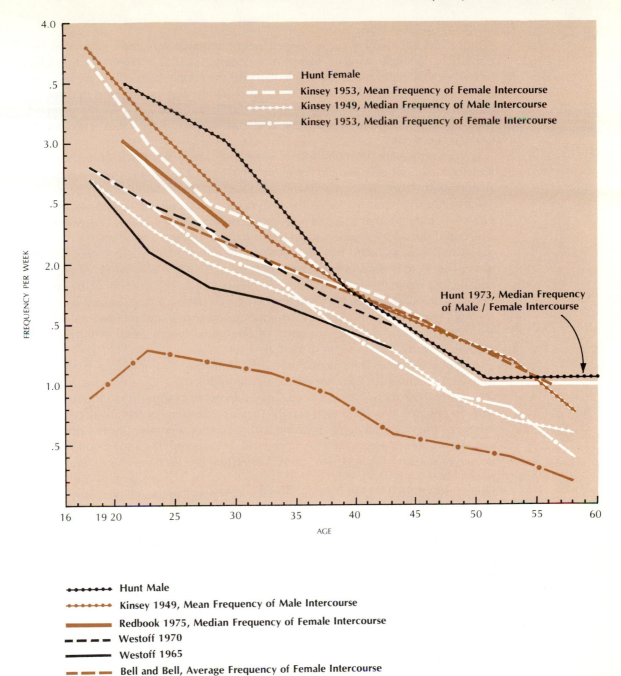

Premarital Practice

Historically, the moral standard for sex before marriage was "no" to anything for either sex—a single standard of sexual innocence until marriage. This norm has never been the norm practiced, particularly for the people from whom we received our sexual attitudes and values. The practical standard of the societies from which most of the voluntary immigrants to the United States came was a double standard. Men could be sexually experienced and still remain in the moral community; women could not.

Women usually learned most of what they knew about sex from men who were sexually innocent and did not know what to do, or from men who were experienced with "bad" women and who supposed that they should not do or feel the same things with their wives. Women who came from cultures or subcultures with close-knit communities of women (as most contemporary middle-class women do not) could still get information about sex from their mothers and others.

The double standard has been eroding for about a half century—but it is not gone. There are in the United States people who, by virtue of religion, ethnicity, or social class, retain the distinctions in their original form. The majority of the population still probably shares the corollary belief that men are more sexual by nature than women. Men have more opportunities to be sexual and more social support for their sexuality. However, in terms of premarital heterosexual activity we are moving toward a pattern of "yes" for both sexes.

Premarital coitus is a potential training ground for sex in marriage, particularly in terms of technique. Take, for example, the traditional couple entering marriage who are both sexually inexperienced. They start out with some idea about how, but with no practice. It is very much like the first time dancing, or the first time playing tennis, or the first time doing anything with a partner who also has not done it. A great deal of fumbling and stumbling goes on, because neither knows quite what to do—even if both have read *The Joy of Sex*. There is a fundamental difference between having a blueprint and building something, or looking at maps and finding your way in the real world. Anyone who cooks knows that the recipe is only a script that must be translated into activity. Moving from the printed page to personal action is the same with sex. No sex book can tell people how they are going to feel, or what exactly is going to happen to them next. Much of human behavior is improvisational. We improvise on our basic scripts all the time, because no set of instructions can prepare us for the reality of the action.

Even in the recent past, most marriages began with either both partners inexperienced in heterosexual activity or the woman less experienced than the man. At present, matters are more complex: both people may have had sexual experience, in different kinds of ways. One way is experience with each other, marital sex as a continuation of premarital sex. Couples have sex together, get married, and continue having sex together under "legitimate" and more comfortable circumstances. As more people live together before marriage, the structure of marriage itself becomes directly continuous with the structure of premarital life. That is, a couple already sets up a household before they get married.

From the evidence on changes in rates of premarital sexual experience, it appears that a relatively large proportion of young people (perhaps one third of females and one fifth of males) will be coitally inexperienced when they marry; a large proportion (perhaps half of women and two thirds of men) will have some coital experience with one or a few sexual partners; and perhaps twenty percent of men and fifteen percent of women will have cohabited or had extensive heterosexual experience before marriage. Although the opportunity to practice sex in a context somewhat more like marriage is now possible, it is not being practiced by a majority of young people.

Premarital Practice and Orgasm in Marriage

What is the effect of premarital sexual activity (intercourse, petting, masturbation) on marital sex? In the 1940s Kinsey studied the relationship between premarital sexual practice among women and their subsequent sexual responsiveness in marriage. The women he studied came into marriage with very different sexual histories (as do women today). One group of women never had coitus before marriage, and never had an orgasm. Another group of women never had intercourse, but had orgasm doing something else, such as masturbation, petting, nocturnal dreams, or homosexual contacts. A third group of women had coitus before marriage, but without climax. Finally, there were women who had intercourse accompanied by orgasm.

What was their sex life like when they got married? Did they have orgasm, and how often?

1. For women who had intercourse before marriage with orgasm one or more times, the transfer was quite direct to marital intercourse: 95 percent had orgasm the first year, and about half had orgasm 90–100 percent of the times they had intercourse.
2. Of those who had no coitus but had orgasm doing something else, 85 percent had orgasm the first year of marriage. This suggests that it is the experience of orgasm, not how it is achieved, which is effective for orgasm in later intercourse.
3. Of women with experience of orgasm from other sources but premarital coitus without orgasm, 62 percent had orgasm the first year of marriage.
4. Of women who had no coitus and no orgasm, 60 percent had orgasm the first year.
5. Of women who had intercourse before marriage, but no experience of orgasm, only 44 percent had orgasm the first year of marriage. They were in a sense worse off than the virgins at marriage. They had tried it and it did not work.

The percentage of intercourse to orgasm increased over the years of marriage for all groups, but the last category increased the slowest. Women who had intercourse without orgasm, and did not have orgasm any other way, appear to have had the greatest difficulty with marital orgasm.

What this study does not tell us is the quality of premarital intercourse for these women or how well their male sexual partners performed. Much of what at first appears to be female sexual inadequacy may be traced to the problems men have in dealing with sexuality. Often young women expect their first sexual intercourse to be a major success, and are profoundly disappointed by pain, ineptitude, and the like. If the mark of an early unsuccessful experience is not washed out by later, more successful practice, a woman may retain her first impressions and find future sex unpleasant. This may explain why women who have premarital orgasm outside intercourse, and premarital intercourse without orgasm, have lower rates of marital orgasm. This means that we need to enter into the equation the level of male competence (not only physical, but emotional).

If we can interpret present trends from a study this old, and assume that those relationships still hold, it is possible to suggest that with increasing successful premarital experience more women will find the transition to orgasm during marriage easier. Also, to the degree that premarital conditions are similar to marital conditions—intercourse in the context of affection, over some period of time, perhaps with a common residence—orgasm rates in marriage are likely to increase.

What seems to matter most in female orgasm rates is how long people have been married, and when they were born, relative to the time the Kinsey studies were done. *(See Box.)* A second factor is the one noted above—experience of orgasm prior to marriage. If more young women are having coital and noncoital orgasmic experience before marriage (particularly during the late 1960s and early 1970s), and they are growing up in a more permissive sexual climate, it is likely that the proportion of marital coitus leading to orgasm is increasing.

Orgasm and the Pleasures of Sex

There are a number of dilemmas hidden in the concern for female orgasm. Female sexual responsiveness has been, for the last century at least, the pawn of male sexual needs. It was denied and suppressed or promoted only in narrow circumstances. More recently female sexual responsiveness, at least in terms of orgasm, has become mixed up with forms of achievement and sexual success. The present obsessive concern with female orgasm has led some women, particularly intellectuals and writers, to argue that it might be more liberating to give up what appears to them to be an obsessive search for the orgasm. In part this position reflects a real concern and contains a real point: it probably is not helpful to women for the media to go on and on about the orgasm and the necessity that women have them, thus creating another standard for people to meet sexually. However, it also seems premature for one group of women (who may well have had orgasm) to advise other women (who may never have had orgasm) not to be concerned about it.

A stance that perhaps takes into consideration the interests of most women is to argue the following: It is a right of all women to have sexual pleasure, including orgasm, and they should have the information and opportunities to find what pleasure they wish. However, the orgasm should not be used as a way of keeping sexual score. Orgasm is not the only source of sexual pleasure; other physical and psychological events can also provide gratification. Touching and holding, sexual contact without orgasm, or only one person having orgasm are all legitimate forms of sex from which personal pleasure may be derived. On a psychological level a wide range of emotional responses can give the physical sexual act meaning and enhance the pleasure in it. Not all of these psychological states require orgasm.

It is perfectly legitimate to have physical sexual relations in which one person is offering another person sexual pleasure without being immediately concerned with his or her own. To make sexual pleasure between people a form of counting, "You just had an orgasm, so now I deserve an orgasm" creates a restricted emotional climate for sexuality. This does not mean that orgasm should not be sought, or that a partner should not be helpful in creating orgasmic circumstances. However, to make orgasm the be-all and end-all of sexual activity is as limiting as denying a person the right to have orgasm at all.

Another important point is that orgasm itself is not a guarantee of sexual pleasure. It is perfectly possible, as many men and women can testify, that one may feel depressed, sad, dysphoric, unpleasured, or guilty after orgasm. The events of the sexual response cycle do not automatically equal a sense of psychological well-being or joy. One can feel sorry that he or she has had sex with a particular person, can feel exploitative or exploited, angry or embarrassed after sexual encounters that have involved orgasm. People can even feel uninvolved or unhappy with what they are doing sexually at the very time that they are doing it. Orgasm is only part of sexual pleasure, and the subjective sense of pleasure is not always related to the strength of any set of physical responses.

We have focused on orgasm for women because it has historically been denied them, along with many other sources of sexual pleasure (perhaps the most important of which is the right to choose); as female pleasure becomes more widely available it is important not to narrow the focus too sharply. A second reason for the focus on orgasm is that it is more easily counted than subjective feelings of fulfillment or pleasure. Orgasm appears to many people as a real biological fact more important than psychological feelings. For Kinsey and others it became the key measure of sexual experience — the "outlet" for "sexual tensions."

However, it is likely that it is psychological context which tells us that we can have an orgasm, as well as supplies us with our ultimate sense of pleasure when we have one. Perhaps the best measure of the limited value of orgasm as the final arbiter of pleasure is that men ejaculate in nearly every sexual act, yet they experience very different levels of pleasure.

The Practice of Marital Sex

If marital sex is the most legitimate form of sex in U.S. society, the two people who are sharing the bed have chosen each other to love, and sex is an expression of that love, why do people not have more sex in marriage? There are those who may argue that the amount of sex reported in marriage is already excessive. They may be right, but the question as formulated results from strong social emphasis on the importance of sex, and particularly on the importance of sex in marriage.

TECHNIQUES OF SEX PLAY AND COITION

One of the reasons offered for why people do not get much pleasure out of sex is that they are not technically very competent. This is the presumption of nearly all

Female Orgasm in Marriage

The most substantial body of data we have about rates of female orgasm in marital intercourse remains the Kinsey data gathered in the 1940s. In the absence of more recent and more reliable information, it remains our best guide to the topic. If we assume that the social and psychological events affecting orgasm in marital intercourse at that time still operate, we can use the Kinsey figures to estimate the direction and amount of change since 1945. (If we take the amount of concern expressed in the popular media as a measure of rates of orgasm, we would be likely to believe there has been little change.)

The Kinsey data for coital orgasm in marriage is summarized in Table 1. This table organizes the information by birth year, and reports rates of coital orgasm by number of years married. The percentage figures are the proportion of acts of marital intercourse accompanied by at least one orgasm. The tables are not complete for women born after 1910 because the women were interviewed before their marriages had lasted ten or fifteen years.

Table 1   Decade of Birth and Percentage of Marital Coitus Accompanied by Orgasm

	% of coitus with orgasm	in 1st year of marriage	in 5th year of marriage	in 10th year of marriage	in 15th year of marriage
Born before 1900	None	33	23	19	15
	1–29	9	14	15	17
	30–59	10	14	13	13
	60–89	11	12	13	12
	90–100	37	37	40	43
	N	(331)	(302)	(261)	(219)
Born between 1900–1909	None	27	17	13	9
	1–29	13	15	14	14
	30–59	12	13	12	11
	60–89	11	13	17	20
	90–100	37	42	44	46
	N	(589)	(489)	(376)	(251)
Born between 1910–1919	None	23	12	10	
	1–29	12	13	13	
	30–59	15	16	14	
	60–89	12	17	19	
	90–100	38	42	44	
	N	(834)	(528)	(216)	
Born between 1920–1929	None	22	12		
	1–29	8	14		
	30–59	12	19		
	60–89	15	19		
	90–100	43	36		
	N	(484)	(130)		

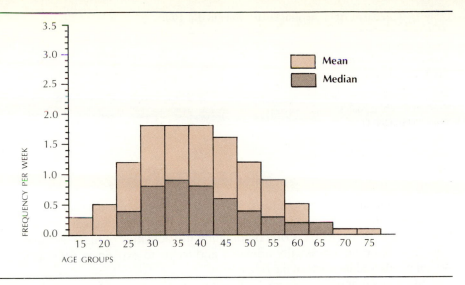

Figure 2   Frequency per Week of Female Orgasm from All Sources, by Five-Year Age Groups. Where median figures are not shown, they are zero. (Kinsey, 1953, p. 548.)

There are two important findings. The first is that women born later tend to begin having coital climax earlier in marriage. The differences are not very large, but they seem to be consistent. If this trend remained consistent for later generations (women born between 1930–39, 1940–49, and 1950–59) we could expect nine of ten women to be having orgasm in marital intercourse at least some of the time. This may seem hopeful, but it is tempered by the second finding, that only four or five of ten women had orgasm between 90 and 100 percent of the time, no matter when they were born and no matter what year of marriage they began. There is some improvement in women having orgasm some of the time, but little improvement in women having orgasm all of the time. Our projected trend would be only modest improvement in the proportion of women having coital orgasm all or nearly all of the time.

Kinsey estimated that on the average women had orgasm about seven to eight of every ten acts of marital intercourse. By the average rates of activity in Figure 2, this means that women are likely to climax seventy or so times per year if they are having intercourse twice a week. In Figure 2 the graph of the median orgasm rate for women in marital intercourse follows the downward slope of the coital rate, suggesting that improvement in orgasm rate is not very much as women age.

Remember that this data is *only* about orgasm in marital coitus. Women have orgasm noncoitally with their spouses and some have orgasm from masturbation. The felt necessity that orgasm should occur during coitus (the cult of "orgasm during penetration") *may be* subsiding, which may then legitimate orgasm during a wide range of "marital sexual activity."

Table 2   Popularity of Noncoital Sexual Acts in the 1940s

Simple kissing	everyone
Man touching woman's breast	98%
Man's mouth on woman's breast	93%
Man touching woman's genitals	95%
Woman touching man's genitals	91%
Extended-tongue kissing	87%
Man's mouth on woman's genitals	54%
Woman's mouth on man's genitals	49%

marriage manuals and sex manuals. They are largely about kinds of sexual things we can do, the order in which to do them, and the kinds of pleasure we can get from them. A major focus is on coordinating the activities of male and female (all such guides are heterosexually oriented) and trying to explain to each gender the sexual needs and interests of the other.

Many sex manuals make sex seem not so much a form of fun and relaxation as a new form of work. However, there are a fair number of people whose ignorance of technique makes sex difficult for them, and the technical information such books offer is useful. Perhaps more important, such books approve of the sexual activities they describe. People use them not only to learn how to do things, but as a justification for doing them. The books promote and validate sexual experimentation as self-improvement, by saying that experimentation will improve marriages, make life more exciting, or widen personal horizons. At the same time, they make it easier for spouses to communicate about what they desire. It is sometimes difficult to suggest to a marriage partner doing a certain thing, without disclosing that it has been done with other people—one can point to the marriage manual and say with some authority, "Let's try that."

The techniques validated by marriage manuals have been practiced for some time. Kinsey found that a large proportion of the married population as far back as the late 1940s engaged in a wide range of sexual techniques prior to coitus, or after coitus, or without coitus. (See Table 2.) How long these activities lasted and their effectiveness is a matter of debate. Given that marital intercourse often lasted from ten to twenty minutes, focus on any of these activities may well have been brief. There is evidence that over the past twenty-five years there has been an increase in oral sex, and perhaps an increase in the time spent on sexual activity without coitus. There is no reliable data to support this conclusion, but such activities have been strongly promoted by sex manuals, by such magazines as *Playboy* and *Cosmopolitan*, and by marriage manuals from various religious organizations.[1] Such increases in noncoital techniques are suggested largely to enhance female sexual response, and in some cases recommended for their own sake as sources of greater sensual focus. The more advanced manuals suggest that orgasm in oral and other noncoital sexual activities is appropriate.

1. The increase in oral sex was one of the main points made in Morton Hunt's book, *Sexual Behavior in the 1970s* (Playboy Press, 1974). Again, the case collection procedure was so biased toward the sexually active and liberal that the figures can only be treated as a measure of the upper limit.

The variety and extent of coital techniques have been reported and encouraged in the same way. (See Figure 3.) Once again from the Kinsey studies we find that the most common position is male above. In about fourteen percent of the cases it was reported that intercourse took place only with the male above. About fifty-eight percent reported the wife on top frequently; about one third frequently side-by-side facing each other; about fifteen percent frequently from behind; and only a few sitting on a chair or standing. It is likely that the proportion of the population who use most or all of these positions regularly has increased with moral approval from the sources cited above.

As with precoital techniques, it is argued that such coital variety enhances general sexual responsiveness, as well as improving the likelihood of female sexual response. It is pointed out that intercourse may not be physically the best way for women to have orgasm, and the male-above position may be less effective for female orgasm than other positions. It is possible to have intercourse without any part of the male's body touching the clitoris. For this reason people are often advised to try different positions to increase clitoral contact. A second problem is that if the man lies on top of the woman like a stone he can prevent her from being responsive. Many women report that it is easier to have orgasm while on top, where they can control the rate of stimulation and activity. In fact, this position is the one preferred during the treatment of most sexual dysfunctions.

FEELINGS ABOUT TECHNIQUE

We are just beginning to propose publicly the wide range of the things people can do with each other which are pleasant. But we must learn to define them as pleasant. There is nothing obvious about the pleasure of oral sex, for example. Why is it men or women want that? Is it better than coitus? Partly its pleasure has to do with the forbidden, but it is also an expression of erotic and emotional intimacy. For many people oral sex remains exotic and intimate, something that they would not do with just anyone. As it becomes more routine, it will become less charged with special emotions or meanings.

If we think about sexual acts as pornography, they become organ grinding—putting the organs together and rubbing them back and forth. But if we are concerned with how people feel and think, we discover that a person has a specific sense and feeling about particular sexual acts and what they mean, and whether or not he or she is willing to do that with someone.

If we think of the usual order of marital sexual acts we find that the sequence is hugging and kissing, fondling the breasts, touching the genitals, and then perhaps mutual or one way mouth-genital contact, followed by intercourse. Is there mouth-genital contact after intercourse? Is the man willing to put his mouth on the woman's vagina? Is the woman going to put her mouth on his penis? Should the woman swallow the semen? Would a man kiss her after she had? Should she wipe her mouth? These are the kinds of things we often think about—or do and try not to think about.

There is nothing natural or unnatural about any of these behaviors. They are all outcomes of social convention—what people believe is good and bad about the

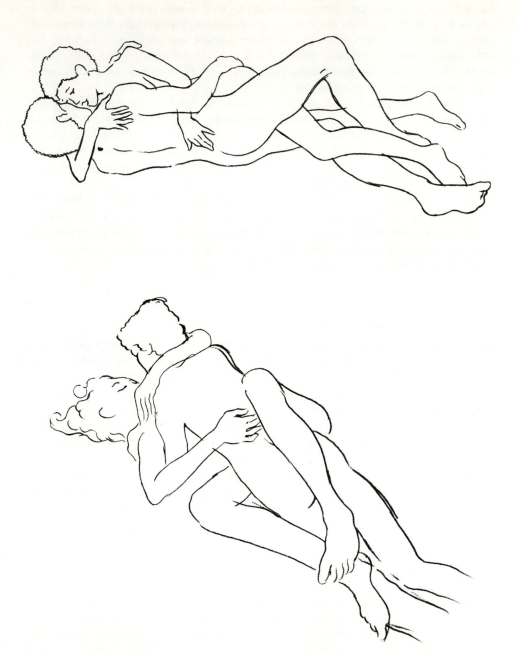

Figure 3 Typical Coital Positions: Side-by-Side; Face-to-Face, Male Above.

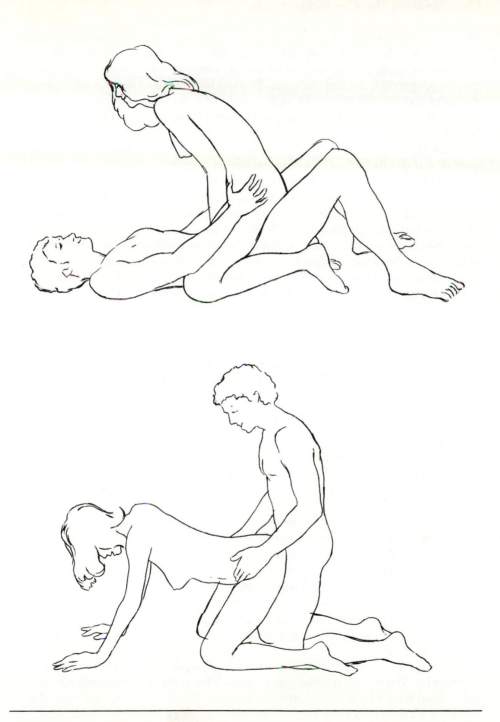

Figure 3   Typical Coital Positions: Face-to-Face, Female Above; Rear Entry.

Coordinating the Orgasmic Cycle

Figure 4 is an example of the two orgasmic cycles of a married couple, suggesting differences in the duration of their response to the sexual situation. The trace lines do not stand for quantitative measures, although there is some evidence that males become excited more rapidly than females, and there is some evidence of a rising and falling subjective sense of arousal in both partners. Where we put the moments of disrobing, penetration, and other events on this trace line depends on the situation.

The durations of the orgasmic cycle vary among individuals and in the lifetime of a single individual. Looking forward in time for this couple, it is possible to predict that coordination of the orgasmic cycle will become better; that is, it will meet the culturally specified definitions of good performance. Part of this improvement will result from practice together, and from greater assurance about the sequence of pleasing each other. Many aspects of the behavior become more or less automatic: the risk of losing an erection lessens; if she wishes something to be done she can indicate it by signs or words; elements of the behavior will be integrated as routine sequences. Such sequences of behavior become largely conventionalized, having a normal order and character between any couple.

sexual. There is no poison in semen and there is no poison in the vagina. There is nothing in those fluids which is dangerous to our health. But we say to ourselves, is this right or is this wrong? We have such doubts because we have been systematically trained to have ambivalent feelings about our genitals, what comes out of them, and the odors they have. (We now sell women sweet-smelling carcinogens to spray in their vaginas as well as those for their armpits.)

Kinsey once said when he was doing his research that middle-class people often tongue kissed and working class people usually did not. Yet middle-class people would not drink out of the same cup, and working class people would. We see that "hygiene" is a word that often stands for whatever social conventions we believe.

It is also all too easy to overestimate the value of technique and underestimate the role of psychological processes in choosing coital positions. If people learn that the male ought to be on top (he is more masculine in that position) and that the female ought to be below (more feminine), they may be able to have orgasm more easily in that position. On the other hand, if a woman feels it is more exciting and uninhibited to be on top or that she is more in control, then it will be a better position for her. If a couple feels that it is exciting to violate sexual taboos and erotic to have sex with the male in a rear-entry position, then that position will be very arousing to them.

Managing the body during sex is not only a physical exercise, it is also a mental exercise. The sexual activities we perform have symbolic meanings for us. Sexual arousal is not like rubbing two sticks together. It really does require mental acts: Is what I am doing right or wrong? Does it feel good? How do I justify it? What will the other person think of me if I do it? It may well be that only gross errors in physi-

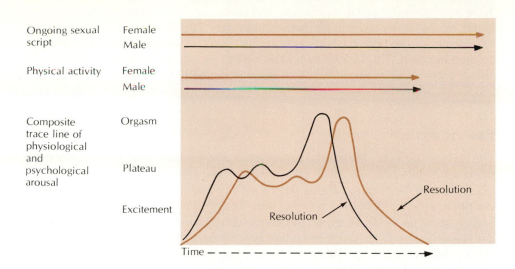

Figure 4   Example of the Orgasmic Cycle in Coitus. (Separate trace lines for each gender.)

cal technique result in difficulties, and that it is the psychological meaning given to specific sex acts that contributes to arousal and orgasm. Such meanings reside in the sexual scripts of individuals. There is no single relationship between event and arousal; the relation is mediated by the sexual scripts people act upon.

TIMING OF ORGASM

During the 1950s the belief was promoted that sexual partners should seek simultaneous orgasms as the ultimate in mutual sexual fulfillment. More recently there has been less emphasis on such close timing, but some coordination is necessary, since it is part of our current social script that both partners should, if possible, have orgasm. If a male comes too quickly he may be defined as sexually dysfunctional (premature ejaculation), since he has failed to coordinate his sexual response cycle with that of his partner.

Most people learn to time sexual arousal, and try to have their orgasms near each other. (See Box.) If a man has orgasm long before his partner does, he may lose his erection (some men do so immediately after orgasm). There are also people whose genitals become extremely sensitive after orgasm, and they do not wish to have continued stimulation. In these cases it is best if the person who is most sensitive has orgasm last. Often one partner's orgasm will be cued by the other partner's orgasm; excitement builds on excitement, and as one comes close to climax the other comes to climax as well. Such forms of coordination are often highly idiosyncratic, and there may not be much transfer of information from one relationship to another.

Coordinating the coital act requires relearning the timing for couples who have had little prior coital experience, and particularly for a man who has had only rapid masturbatory experience before marriage. The duration of his sexual response cycle is extremely short compared to that of a woman who is just learning to time her own. This lack of mutual as well as individual experience may be the major cause of low rates of female orgasm in the early years of marriage.

TIME OF DAY

The "when" aspect of the marital sexual script also contributes to problems of how often sex occurs and how much pleasure is derived from it. Frequently marital sex occurs late in the evening, after a day of activity and just before sleep. A working couple has spent eight hours at work, some hours commuting, some time cooking and cleaning up, and then expects to find a second wind for sex. Finding a time for sex is even more difficult for those who have children. Those without children have the weekends without any other people around; people with children have someone else around most of the time.

The felt necessity for privacy and quiet leads many adults to locate sex late in the day after they have expended most of their energy and interest on other things. As a result marital sex gets squeezed by the pressures of the day that has just gone by, as well as by anticipations of the day to follow. It is therefore not surprising that frequency and time spent may be very low. This may reflect level of psychological interest, but it also reflects the fact that the organization of social life relegates sex to a low priority of time allocation.

NEGOTIATING MARITAL SEX

Most bedrooms are very silent places. Many sexual partners find it difficult to talk to each other about sex. We often cannot tell the other person what feels good and what does not feel good; how often we like to do it; what would be fun to do. We are only beginning to get a public language about sex so that people can talk to each other about it. But many people still have no private language of sex.

Consider the kinds of talk that occurs before intercourse in most households. In some the husband or wife may say, "let's go do it," but such directness is rare. What usually happens is that the husband may say, "I think I will take a shower." What that really says is "I am going to be clean for you." In U. S. society the body must be clean before sex. The wife then says, "I will be upstairs in a few minutes." That is a "yes." Or she says, "I am too tired today; I have a headache; I have been to the hairdresser; the kids might wake up." Those are all "no." A man will say, "I am tired; I have got to get up early in the morning; I have some reading I have to do." There is a whole indirect language which people use to say "yes" or "no."

Even in marriage, when the sex is legitimate, negotiation occurs—including people married a long time. This is another reason why frequency of marital intercourse goes down with age—as we get older such negotiation gets more tiring. The immediacy of our interest in sexual gratification is reduced, and we say to ourselves "Well, maybe tomorrow" (even though we have fewer tomorrows). A person may feel aroused and interested in sex, but knows that it requires negotiation. That person may choose to masturbate—one does not have to negotiate as much with oneself. Being turned down for sex, even in marriage, is a bump to the ego—in part because that is how we felt before marriage, and in part because in marriage it is a right. To protect ourselves we wait for the other person to make the first move. This is particularly anxiety-provoking for men, because it is they who are usually expected to make the first move, and who run the risk of being turned down. At the same time, many men have difficulty letting their wives take the initiative.

Finding that negotiations are difficult to manage, we may ritualize sex, because we do not want to put ourselves on the line every time. Thursday night becomes the night. Knowing that it is going to happen on Thursday night makes it okay. A lot of effort is not required. But feeling amorous on Wednesday night starts negotiation all over again.

Marital Sex and Social Scripts

Restraints of various kinds on frequency and enthusiasm in marital relations arise from elements of our public scripts about marital sexuality.

HEALTH AND GOOD LOOKS

Although most people find a considerable number of reasons for getting married to someone, physical attraction remains an important source of sexual arousal in marriage. The decline in marital sexual activity with age results in part from standards of beauty modeled chiefly on youthful good looks. It is not that older people cannot have sex (even though the young are often shocked by the thought) but that the cues for arousal have been eroded by time. The process tends to affect women more than men because good looks are a major factor in female sex appeal. Men have other sources of sexual attractiveness (money, status, power) that compensate for appearance.

We not only lose our looks, we also throw them away—and reduce our ability to handle the physical demands of sex in the bargain. This is related to the fact that we teach children how *to get* married, but not how *to be* married. We tell them how to get to the point of being married, but we never talk about what it is going to be like afterward, that it is a continuing human relationship which may last thirty years. As a result young people are often highly skilled at the dating and getting married game, but know very little about sustaining a relationship. Children who rely on parental modeling rarely are informed of the role of the sexual in social conduct.

For many of us the important game is over when we get married. What made most of us attractive before we got married is not what we work at after we get married. Thus a young woman and a young man may keep themselves attractive while they are in the marriage market. Finally they get somebody. After the honeymoon she starts gaining weight or wearing curlers; he starts to get a paunch. They were on the hunt, but once the hunt is complete, they do not have to put up a front any more. They do not have to keep in shape; they feel that they do not have to make any sexual presentations of self. The majority of men who have been married for fifteen years are ten to twenty pounds overweight.[2] The reasons that made them stay in shape—organized sports and being attractive to women—have disappeared.

This physical neglect has very serious consequences which are more important than being attractive. Sexual activity involves the cardiovascular system extensively, in that blood pressure rises sharply during sexual activity. An overweight person's heart pumps blood through several miles of extra blood vessels. Also, high cholesterol and fatty deposits in the arteries make the heart work harder to move blood through them. Sexual competence is not only a function of how we look, it is also a function of how healthy we are.

KEEPING SCORE

Many men, particularly those whose sexual self-image depends strongly on peer group approval, affirm their sexuality by the *number* of women they have had. They keep count, a practice linked to the tradition of sex as a form of male conquest. When they get married, they can only count their wives once. The wedding night is it as far as peer group approval is concerned.

Such men may try to claim to their peers that they keep their wives sexually exhausted, but they are rarely believed since the tradition also produces a good deal of sexual bragging. One of the ways such a man *can* assert his manhood and be sexually faithful is to keep his wife pregnant. A catch phrase among working class men when their wives are pregnant is "I just dropped another one in the basket." The women often recognize that their husbands need this continuing public evidence of sexual competence, and are willing to get pregnant to help maintain the male self-image. This attitude may also account in part for resistance to birth control by some classes and cultures.

REPRODUCTION

The capacity to reproduce is a very important justification of sex for many men and women. To them sterilization (either male or female) represents a serious sexual threat. These men view reproduction as the central reason for sex, and are intensely opposed to their wives not being able to have children. "If I don't have a wife who can have babies I don't have a wife." Such men also have quite negative reactions to vasectomy. Without reproduction there is no justification for sexuality.

Menopause is an important moment in the decline of interest in sexuality among women who view sex primarily as a reproductive activity. Since they cannot reproduce anymore, they feel they should not be interested in sex. Decline in sexual activity may begin even earlier for such women when they feel they have had enough children.

2. There is no weight data for single men of comparable ages (late thirties and early forties), but casual observation of older single homosexual men suggests that their weight is under better control than married men.

EROTIC INTEREST AND MOTHERHOOD

One important difficulty that exists in some men's minds is continuing to find their wives erotic after they have had children. This is a continuation, though less extreme, of the Victorian image of the wife as nonsexual by virtue of being a wife. In this case women who are mothers are defined as nonsexual. This attitude also characterizes some women, who feel that when they have had children they have fulfilled their sexual purposes, and wonder why their husbands are still sexually interested.

CHILDREN

Not only are children important in redefining the members of the household in symbolic and role terms (wife becomes mother, husband becomes father), they also increase the time demands on (primarily) the woman, change the direction of her interests, and as the children grow older decrease the amount of casual sexual expression in the household. Men and women who fondle each other sexually in the privacy of a home without children commonly restrict such intimacies to the bedroom when children are around. The bedroom often becomes the only private place in the house for lovemaking, and even there children restrict the time available and the times of day for sexual activity.

Children also take up time, space, and money formerly used for the pleasures of the couple. Parents find that they cannot take vacations or go away as easily. Vacations were erotic and pleasurable events and allowed sex to be "like it was before marriage," exciting and detached from daily responsibility. Having sex with a spouse somewhere other than the bedroom also served to increase the erotic character of the relationship.

BOREDOM

Sex is supposed to be exciting and romantic. For many people having sex with the same person becomes boring. The partner does the same things again and again, as does the person who is bored. It is something like listening to the same piece of music over and over again—sooner or later even "our song" becomes uninteresting. It is difficult to prevent marital sexuality from drifting into a routine. Couples often make attempts to increase the variety in their sexual lives by taking vacations, reading sex manuals, learning massage, going to motels—such activities seek to relieve the pressure toward repetition that exists in most long-term human relationships.

Such repetition does not have to be a problem. There are many people who find real comfort and pleasure in making love to the same person over and over again. It is not novelty which turns them on, but the fulfillment of their expectations. Many people in the United States probably have this sort of sexual life. Sex as a form of mutual caring and interpersonal stability is probably far more common than is realized, but it does not receive as much attention.

Conclusion

Sex, even in marriage, can be a very lonely business for many people. Often we do not have any way to compare what we do with what other people do. We are isolated from others, so we do not have any sense of what their sexual lives are like. That may be why we have so much fantasy about the sexual. Inexperienced young people, for instance, usually think sex is going to be much more remarkable than it is. It is painted in such magical colors; young people are told, "Just hold out, wait a while, and this marvelous thing will happen to you." Then they do it the first time and discover it is something they have to practice.

Once people have mastered the mechanics of sex, the technology, they must come back to the fundamental question of feeling. How do you feel about the other person? Do you like yourself? Do you like what you are doing? These are much tougher questions than the questions of technique, because they are about how to experience life, not how to do sexual things. Ours is a culture that makes figuring out how to be physically sexual so complicated that many people never get to the question of how they feel about it.

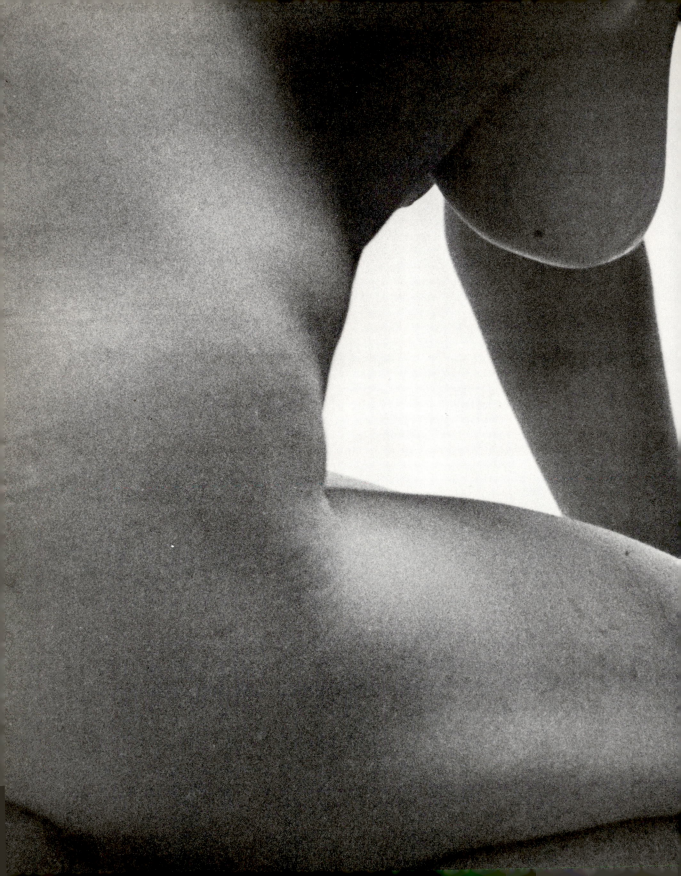

NONMARITAL SEXUALITY

Foxy: Adultery. It's so much *trouble*.
John Updike, *Couples*

IT IS NOT KNOWN HOW MANY PEOPLE ARE SATISFIED WITH THE KIND OF MARITAL sex life they have. Estimates of dissatisfaction range from one third to one half, but such figures are largely guesses, or more often figments of the imagination — satisfaction (or dissatisfaction) is an elusive concept, and it has been measured in many contradictory ways. For instance, how many people are positively satisfied with their sexual lives (in marriage or out)? That is, if offered more or different sex (without cost), would they do that in addition or in preference to the sex they are regularly having? In contrast, how many people are extremely dissatisfied with their sexual lives? That is, how many are actively seeking a new partner, a new life style, or a new script? Finally, how many people are neutral about their current sexuality? They do it; it affords them some satisfaction and they feel no great need to change, or the effort to change is seen to be greater than the prospective benefits. Such people have come to terms with whatever sexual adjustment they presently have.

The above may make people seem a great deal more rational than they really are, but it does begin to suggest some of the complications of talking about satisfaction. A further problem results from the fact that in most sexual relationships the satisfactions of two (or more) people are involved, not those of only one, and that changing or not changing depends on the choices, estimates, and desires of both. Changes do occur, for all the evidence we have suggests that not only does the rate of marital sex go down over the years, but so do many measures of non-sexual marital satisfaction. (Others have a U-shaped distribution, high in the beginning, a dip in the middle, going up after the children leave.) It is common to attribute declines of this kind solely to marriage and family life, but this is too simple. As people grow older, they must come to terms with the fact that they are not going to realize all their dreams, that many of their expectations are not going to be met, that they are going to settle for less than they may have wanted.

This is not true of everyone, nor is it true of all aspects of most people's lives. There are people whose lives have turned out far better than they expected, and there are others who find that some aspects of their lives (such as their work or the success of their children) have turned out very well. Most lives are like this, a mixed bag of expectations met and disappointments to cope with. It may well be that the disappointments thought to be associated with marriage are merely the disappointments of getting old in a society that values the young, of running out of time to do different or more things.

The disjunction between expectation and outcome, between what one expected and what one got in marriage or what one thinks one can get (sexual and otherwise), can lead to a number of alternative adaptations:

1. One can marry, engage in sex with people other than one's spouse, and remain married. This can be done with either heterosexual or homosexual partners, though the former is more common. Such adjustments may be simple or complex in terms of numbers of persons, types of relationships, and the like.

2. One can marry and then leave the marriage through separation and divorce, an increasingly common adaptation to marital dissatisfaction, sexual or otherwise. This plunges a person back into the world of singles, where the patterns of sexual conduct are more like premarital sexuality. Frequently people who divorce remarry, a second (or third, or more) attempt at getting a better match between expectation and outcome, often with a substantial downward adjustment in their expectations.

3. One can choose not to marry in the first place. While a minority of heterosexuals choose this adaptation, there seems to be a growing number of people who have decided not to test their expectations about marriage (which are often negative). The world of the permanently single intermixes with the world of the formerly married, and these two worlds look more and more alike the older the individuals get. For the formerly married, children are often a complication, and there is greater pressure to remarry for child care. This may represent a serious problem in relations between the permanently single and the formerly married. Many of the former do not want children and therefore are unavailable to those who either want children or want new partners who will share child care.

Still another world is that of the widowed, those involuntarily separated from spouses to whom they were still emotionally attached. The widowed may find more difficulty than the divorced in post-marital sexual adjustment. In part, this is because parents and children expect the period of mourning to be long and celibate (to have sex would defile the memory of the departed). Further, since the widowed were not necessarily disappointed in marriage, they commonly search for a relationship similar to the one they lost and are unwilling to "settle for less." (They also tend to see their marriage as having been more ideal than it was.) The divorced may want to remarry, but are more likely to find satisfaction in less permanent affectional relationships which may involve sex.

In recent years, after about age twenty-five, three quarters of the men and women in U.S. society have been married. Of the unmarried quarter, some are viewed as non-marriageable (the chronically, mentally or physically, ill; the physically handicapped; the institutionalized), while others do not wish to be married. The popularity of marriage limits the range of available sexual partners, since normally most people are moderately respectful of the marital bond as a limit on sexual activity. This is a continuation of a tradition set premaritally when young men and women feel that someone else's steady friend, lover, or affianced is off-limits to affectional or sexual approaches. It is generally considered poor form to approach a married person for affection or sex because of moral constraints, good manners, or respect for the institution of the family. This does not mean that it is not done, only that it requires a different script and different conditions than approaches involving unmarried people. Not being married indicates that a person may be in the marketplace—for association, affection, sexuality, or marriage. Married people are less often viewed in this way, or are viewed as having more limited purposes when they are approached.

It has been argued by some sociologists that we are moving toward a condition of universal availability in partner or mate selection, even after marriage, and with the divorce rate rising, a modified version of universal availability may in fact becoming institutionalized. Many people are more willing to recognize and act upon their marital dissatisfactions by looking for a new marital partner. A few may look around for a better marital partner even when they are happily married. In a sense, they see themselves and others as available for something better, even if they are married. This attitude is probably rare; it is more likely that most people who get married expect to stay married, yet for some reason (and there are many) find that they are dissatisfied, and then either become aware of or become interested in changing marital partners. This pattern of sequential monogamy tends to characterize both our contemporary premarital and marital scene. That is, people before and during marriage go through a series of relationships: they look around, find someone, become emotionally involved, get dissatisfied (or their partner does), and then break up and look for another relationship.

These cycles of sexual, emotional, and legal attachment, breaking up, and reattachment have not yet become a preferred societal pattern, but they certainly characterize the lives or part of the lives of a large number of people in U.S. society. During these periods of legal attachment, as expressed by marriage, divorce, and remarriage, people may also be going through a sequence of sexual relationships which may or may not coincide with official changes. Thus, people may have affairs while they are married or when they are between marriages: sexual relations may or may not result in major changes in marital partners or housing arrangements. In this way we are usually more available as sexual partners than we are as marital partners—however, after the mid-twenties these patterns of availability often begin to decline.

We do not yet have "universal availability" in sexual or affectional or marital arrangements, even though shifts in sexual attachment are becoming more common throughout the life cycle. Indeed, we can raise the question: Why should it really make any difference in our sexual, affectional, or potential marital relations with others, whether or not they are married or otherwise attached? If one is interested in them, one might just be the better person who has come along. Why should one deny them the opportunity to make another choice?

Extramarital Sexuality

"Extramarital" sex immediately brings to mind the thought of something dramatic like an "affair." But if we look at the data on the subject, it is clear that most people do not have many (if any) affairs, especially if "affair" means a relationship which has some significant emotional meaning sustained over a reasonably long period of time. We usually think of an affair as occurring between two people who are desperately in love but who cannot divorce and remarry because of other obligations (a sick child or spouse, or a spouse who will not accept divorce, or who would be

Kinsey Studies

In all matters of socially disapproved sex, the most comprehensive research is the Kinsey studies. They show that in the late 1940s a quarter to a third of married men had extramarital intercourse at least once in a five-year period. Of those who were doing so, the mean frequency ranged from five to fifty times per year. The median figures are lower, since the means are affected by those men who have a great deal of extramarital sex, men who are quite untypical in their life styles. For college men, there was a gradual increase in the proportion having intercourse with women other than their spouses, an increase which peaked sometime in their late thirties and early forties. Working class men (a much less well documented part of the population) seem to have begun extramarital sex earlier and decreased in their activity with age. This would conform to what we know about the amount of freedom and resources which characterize the life cycles of these two groups; with age, middle class men can afford to allocate more resources to nonmarital pursuits, while working class men cannot. Also, middle class men can gain position and sometimes affluence and power which can make them more attractive later in life.

too "hurt"). More often, however, extramarital sex is sporadic. On the average, most people who are doing it probably do not have the experience more than five times a year. It can be spread out over the year (the "traveling" pattern) or it can follow a "bunched" pattern, a burst of activity followed by a long period of quiet.

The reason for sporadic adultery is that extramarital sex is regulated by social context. The extramarital lover is married, he or she has many responsibilities, and it is difficult to find a way around those responsibilities. It is difficult for most married adults to find enough open space and time in their lives for extramarital sex (or many other things). Although many married people have thought seriously about having sex with someone besides their spouses, the logistics of carrying out even well-made plans are usually difficult and sometimes overwhelming. Potential lovers must explain whenever they depart from their regular schedule. It is often only when people travel away from home that they can feel at all free and unsupervised, and even then many people find this unexpected "lack of requirements" a source of great anxiety rather than an opportunity.

The consequence of regular schedules and self policing by most sexual pairs is that conventional extramarital sex usually happens in some kind of "open space" or "open time," such as a convention or a summer vacation—a new context in which people are detached from their habitual ways of life and in which sex can "just happen." When this kind of extramarital sex happens, both men and women rarely tell their spouses, because the sex (even if very intense) is a side issue to "normal" life, a temporary lapse or fling, and because each of the persons involved wants to protect himself or herself against too deep an involvement or commitment.

If we look at the forces which tend to restrain extramarital intercourse and at those which tend to increase it, we find that the former are weakening while the latter are becoming stronger. Rising rates of extramarital sex can be predicted from the contemporary decline in religious activity, since of all the sexual behaviors we

In contrast to these figures, the women Kinsey interviewed reported a pattern of increasing extramarital activity with age, from about ten percent in early marriage to twenty percent later in life. Of the women who had *not* had premarital intercourse, about twenty percent had extramarital intercourse by age forty. Of those who did have premarital intercourse, forty percent had sex outside marriage by age forty. This does not mean, however, that this proportion of women were having extramarital sex in any one year. The annual figure was between ten and fifteen percent. The annual *rates* for women were somewhat less than for men, from about five times per year to thirty times per year. Once again the mean figures are strongly influenced by those for whom extramarital sex was frequent and may have replaced marital sex as the primary source of heterosexual activity. In addition, women report somewhat higher proportions of orgasm in extramarital sex than in marital sex, probably because it is experienced as more passionate or more personally chosen than because of differences in sexual technique. The evidence from the Kinsey studies is that younger women were more likely to have extramarital intercourse at some time. The differences were not very large, but the trend toward a larger proportion of women becoming involved in extramarital activity was visible at that time.

know, extramarital intercourse is probably most restrained by religious commitment. For instance, devout people commonly do not report much lower rates of masturbation or premarital intercourse than do the non-devout. Their rates *are* lower, but not by much. However, there are large differences between the devout and the non-devout in the incidence of extramarital sex.

A second factor is the relationship between premarital and extramarital intercourse. In the Kinsey studies *(see box)*, if women had premarital intercourse, they were more likely to have extramarital intercourse. Premarital intercourse thus seems to predispose people to extramarital intercourse (or the factors that cause premarital sex also cause extramarital sex), and this is true of both men and women. If other data on premarital sex is correct and premarital intercourse is increasing in U.S. society, we would expect extramarital intercourse also to be rising.

A third factor may well be the large contemporary divorce rate. The more people there are who have been married a number of times in the society, the more common the view is that sex between and perhaps at the end of an unhappy marital relationship is morally neutral. On the other hand, extramarital intercourse is implicated in some divorces of couples who are unable to agree that sex is the exclusive possession of marital partners. In the Kinsey research there is a table, rather amusing because it is so self-serving. When people were asked "Did *your* extramarital intercourse figure in your divorce?" they answered one way. When they were asked "Did your *spouse's* extramarital intercourse have any effect on your divorce?" they answered another. When *they* had the sex, they said it had very little effect on their divorce (though it might have if their spouse had known), but when they knew their *spouse* was having extramarital sex, it was viewed as a very important factor, especially by men.

Effect of Extramarital Sex on Divorce

		Answer: It had			
		Major effect	Moderate effect	Minor effect	No effect at all
Question: Did *your* extramarital sex have any importance in causing your divorce?	(Women)	14%	15%	10%	61%
	(Men)	18%	9%	12%	61%
Question: Did your *spouse's* extramarital sex have any importance in causing your divorce?	(Women)	27%	49%	24%	0%
	(Men)	51%	32%	17%	0%

Extramarital sex is both cause and effect in divorce—it contributes to the divorce rate because it is viewed as a violation of the marriage contract and because it is part of the process of next-mate selection. In addition, more people getting divorced probably increases the proportion of the sexually experienced who are sexually available to the married.

Another source of extramarital activity may be that the interest of women in sex is changing, both in life cycle and historical terms. Many women in their late thirties apparently have an increased interest in sex at the very moment their husbands' interest may be declining. At the same time, women in general are apparently getting more interested in sex—and expect more from it. Both types of increase in interest can lead to sexual experimentation. The increasing interest of women in sex outside marriage is usually based on the idea of a woman at home whose husband has declining sexual interest in her. This dissatisfaction may be a reaction either to other women or to expectations about sexuality created by the mass media (particularly the women's magazines).

Another factor to be considered is affluence. The more money and personal resources a person has, the more able that person is to purchase the open spaces where extramarital sex can be done, and to support marital and family obligations without using limited resources from one for the other. Affluence can also pay for the consequences of being found out by an irate spouse, who may want a divorce. If the U.S. standard of living continues to rise as it has, extramarital sex could become more frequent just because people are richer.

More important than any of these factors may be the changing role of women in the labor force. Extramarital sex has probably always been easier for men because they have always had greater freedom than women (at work or at play) and often have had access to single women and married women at the work place. In contrast, the woman who works at home in domestic tasks and child care has a far more limited selection. As more women now join the labor force, the opportunity for extramarital sex increases—there are simply more eligible men around. Secondly, and just as important, is a greater feeling of personal autonomy produced by at least some jobs that women have. A sense of autonomy in economic and vocational life can lead to a heightened sense of right to sexual choice.

Redbook Survey

The *Redbook* survey (recall our cautions about the sampling) reports that slightly less than half of working women thirty-five to thirty-nine years old have had extramarital sex, in contrast to twenty-seven percent of wives not working and thirty-two percent of wives working as volunteers. These are probably high figures, and it must be pointed out that these women had had extramarital sex *sometime* in their lives; it may well have been before they went to work. In this case the extramarital sex may have caused the going back to work, or the sex and the work may have been caused by some other common factor. In any case, there is an association between working and extramarital sex for women.

The *Redbook* survey reported that among the twenty to twenty-five year old wives who answered their questionnaire, twenty-five percent had had extramarital sex (Kinsey reported nine percent). Among the thirty-five to thirty-nine year olds, the figure was thirty-eight percent (Kinsey reported twenty-six percent). We should remember, however, that the Kinsey studies also had a tendency to report higher figures than existed because of the volunteer bias, though the problems of getting accurate information after the person decided to cooperate were reduced by the Kinsey interview technique.

What we can say from this is that twenty-five percent represents the top figure for younger women (an increase of fifteen percent in thirty or more years) and that forty percent represents the top figure for older women (once again an increase of about fifteen percent). The true figures are probably lower—perhaps by a factor of five to ten percent.

How much extramarital sex is now going on is hard to estimate, since we have no satisfactory studies on the contemporary scene. The *Redbook* survey *(see box)* does allow us to identify the upper limits, even if it was based on reports from the more sexually active and was not controlled for sexual bragging. Clearly changes in U.S. society have been such as to produce more extramarital intercourse on the part of women. The problem is that contemporary studies have all tended to inflate the figures. Given the change that has occurred in other areas of society, even a fifteen-percent increase in extramarital sex on the part of women might not be called a revolutionary development.

Conventional Extramarital Sex

For most people, extramarital sex never escalates into an "affair." It is convention and bar and free-zone behavior, something which men and (less often) women do one or two times with a partner, stop, and then resume again two years later with somebody else. It follows this pattern because most people do not have enough time, energy, and resources for anything long-term.

Conducting a real "affair" presents a number of problems. An affair usually requires a certain amount of "dating," of courtship which takes time, especially if the affair is between a single woman and a married man. A single woman expects that at least some of the same things will happen to her that happen when she dates an unmarried man, even though she may know there are some constraints—such as a wife. After a while single women recognize a number of constraints; if they have an affair with a married man, they have to get used to not having a date on Saturday night; if they wear perfumes different than a wife's they may have to give up their favorite perfume for the duration.

The marital status of the extramarital couple is crucial for the people involved. First, it affects the different male and female expectations of whether the affair can or should escalate. Second, it affects the motives for the affair itself (what script are we following?). Third, it provides a set of external limits and constraints on expectations. There are three ways the heterosexual extramarital relationship can be shaped by marital status.

MARRIED MAN AND MARRIED WOMAN

This is a reasonably common situation. Both persons are restrained from escalating the amount of time involved in the relationship because of emotional expectations by and commitments to spouses and children. The script is often that of the film *Brief Encounter*, of ships passing in the night. Both understand the other's predicament and they can share with a third party their own family life and the successes of children. The relationship can have a significant and gratifying sexual component because both recognize the difficulties of being seen in public. Dangers occur when one or the other wants to get a divorce, thus destabilizing the relationship.

MARRIED MAN AND SINGLE WOMAN

This situation is also common, tending to involve an older man and a younger woman. It does, however, involve very unstable forces, since the woman often wishes to escalate the relationship. She often finds the relationship unsatisfactory because she has to be on his schedule; she cannot call him at home or at work—there is a major load of secrecy, and she may get less non-sexual time with him than she wants or needs. She may also be taken out of the marriage market for a number of years, which provokes a good deal of male guilt. Both recognize that divorce may break him economically and that, divorced, he might not be as interesting.

SINGLE MAN AND MARRIED WOMAN

This situation is less frequent than the above, but it does occur. Males may say they prefer such relationships because the restrictions on the woman limit the emotional claims that she can make. The relationship can be largely sexual without the male having to be responsible for the result. There are certain classes of males who appear vulnerable to this arrangement, often in athletic or other entertainment roles which involve both attractiveness and free time.

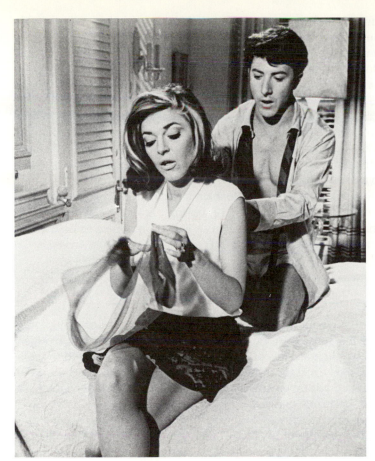

The Graduate (Dustin Hoffman) undressing Mrs. Robinson (Ann Bancroft) on an occasion when heartfelt ineptitude and heartless skill first meet.

Affective and Sexual Rewards

Most people find their extramarital relationships highly exciting, especially in the early stages. This is a result of psychological compression: the couple get together; they are both very aroused (desire, guilt, expectation); they have only three hours to be together; so they really try to fill those three hours with all the experience possible. Rarely do people do that with their spouses. Another source of attraction is that the other person is always seen when he or she looks good and is on best behavior, never when feeling tired and grubby, or when taking care of children, or when cooking dinner, or when doing other pedestrian things. Each time, all the minutes that the couple has together are special because they are stolen from all these other relationships. The resulting combination of guilt and excitement has a heightening effect, which tends to explain why people may claim that extramarital sex and orgasms are more intense.

These special features of the extramarital relationship are things people often do not have with their spouses. The familiarity of a day-to-day relationship fosters a certain lack of attentiveness to each other. In U.S. culture it may be that people who live together for a long time cannot sustain their erotic feelings because there are too many distractions, too many other significant things going on that erode the erotic commitment.

The first steps of an affair can be relatively casual and sporadic (fun), in contrast to the later stages, which may involve a strong mutual emotional commitment. It is these later developments which endanger marriages most, for they can be preparation for moving into another marriage. The novelty and excitement of the extramarital relationship makes people think that the level of intensity can be sustained. They never realize that marriage to the next person can turn into another pedestrian relationship. Their marital relationship may be boring because of living together and the extramarital relationship exciting because they do not have to be with the other person all the time.

Being Found Out

Extramarital sex in its conventional form always generates the risk of being found out. For some people this sense of risk may enhance the sexuality as part of a general commitment to the illicit aspects of sex and the excitement involved in violations of sexual taboo. However, for most people the risk of discovery is a burden which must be negotiated with the extramarital partner. The secretive character of the relationship often becomes particularly burdensome to single women, but it also affects the married man or woman who may be involved. The secrecy seems to be shameful, as the two people hide out, looking over each other's shoulders for friends of a spouse, and often it goes against the ideology of what they believe or have said about the importance of the relationship. The intimacy and mutual assurance of the lovers are violated when one partner says, "You must be ashamed of me," and the other declares, "There is nothing shameful about our love."

There are two pathways to discovery, or perhaps two major paths with some mixed motivations in the middle. One is accidental: the couple is discovered by the spouse or by a friend of the spouse who tells; an accident may occur, revealing the couple together under suspicious circumstances; the spouse who is having extramarital sex contracts and transfers a venereal disease. The probabilities of any of these single events are low, but they can add up to produce fairly paranoid feelings during an affair.

In the middle are forms of discovery to which one or the other member of the affair appears to contribute. Articles of clothing are left in cars or rooms, lipstick or perfume is in the wrong place, phone calls are accidentally intercepted, letters are left in pockets or purses. Such discoveries may be truly accidental, or a person's ambivalence may result in carelessness. Either partner may do it, and there are a multiplicity of possible motives. The careless partner may want to get out of the marriage *or* to get out of the affair but not be able to be direct, and so create the discovery to break off one or the other. Or they may want to injure their spouse, or their lover, or the lover's spouse.

A last way of being discovered involves self-disclosure. Self-disclosure can be either an announcement or a confession. One uses the form, "Dear, I have something I have to tell you. So and so and I are having an affair and we are in love and I am going to. . . ." The other sounds like, "Dear, I have something to tell you. So and so and I are having an affair, and I am sorry. . . ." The announcement may be the end of one marriage and the beginning of another, but this depends on the reaction of the spouse, who may wish to continue the marriage. The confession, which is often motivated by guilt, has the intent of putting the speaker in the hands of the partner, perhaps in hopes of shoring up the marital relationship.

Guilt

Guilt plays the same marvelously ambivalent role in extramarital sex that it does in all the other forms of sexual conduct. It can be *exciting* when people feel it and have not been caught, because they have performed a successful transgression. It can also be a crippling burden to those who have done things which they feel are morally wrong. At present, most sexual libertarians do not like to acknowledge guilt or talk about it because in the past it was argued that everyone did or at least was supposed to feel guilty. Since guilt feelings might restrict sexual activity, they are often called false guilt by those who are interested in promoting sexual "freedom." It is an unpopular topic, except with moralists, who tend to overplay its role.

A substantial number of people do, however, feel guilty when they have extramarital sex, and a smaller number have difficulty managing it. When we enter our first marriages, very few of us think that we may get divorced or that we will have an affair with someone else. Most of us believe that our marriages are going to survive and be pretty much like the good marriages we were raised to believe in. We are certainly not going to be *unfaithful*, which, though it is a less commonly used word today, has a correct psychological resonance. One had a lot of faith when one got married, expecting to have a faithful relationship; one's spouse is still being faithful, but one is not being faithful.

For some people, guilt does not appear to be a very important corollary of extramarital sex—they are capable of explaining their behavior and justifying the lack of fidelity on many grounds ("I need more sex than . . . " "I am/was in love . . . " "It was just a fling . . . "). Other persons carry a greater burden of guilt, especially as relationships come to involve emotional commitment and as the emotional commitment to the outside partner comes to overshadow the emotional and sexual attachment in the marriage. It is often this sense of guilt that produces the accidental or confessional disclosure.

Such discoveries, announcements, and confessions can often result in a welter of accusations and counteraccusations, claims and counterclaims, until the sex itself has receded into the background, obscured by complaints that have lain dormant until provoked. The meaning that is given to the knowledge and the sex depends on the character of the prior relationship between the man and the woman. The offending spouse can leave the marriage, can leave and go to the lover (often to begin another marriage), or the couple can agree on new terms. Such terms can be "no more outside sex" which is a return to the original contract, or outside sex can be allowed under particular conditions. This renegotiation can be accomplished by the couple alone or with the aid of professional help.

An important aspect of the impact of extramarital sex is that it is often experienced as a deep personal shock by the spouse who has been faithful to the contract. The offended partner often experiences a deep sense of rejection and inadequacy, and if the events become public, both men and women are profoundly ashamed in front of their friends. The depth of the sense of injury is often underestimated and can be the source of a rage which may appear as vindictiveness in divorce arrangements. Since men more often engage in extramarital sex and women are the injured parties, it appears that more women have these feelings than men—however, men may have an equal or greater sense of anger and shame when they discover that they have been faithful and their wives have had sex with other men.

As with guilt, the significance of this sense of injury is often underestimated by sexual libertarians. It is in the interest of sexual liberals to argue that marital partners are both adults and that the pains of broken contracts are more than made up for by the increase in personal sexual freedom. This would be perfectly true if everyone entering a relationship announced their future plans, or if both parties had equal access to joint resources when a marriage broke up. The right to extramarital intercourse, if it is not to be to the advantage only of men, also requires forms of economic and personal freedom for women, which would allow them access to the same choices. Under current circumstances, too easy an adherence to such freedoms without acknowledging the costs does not recognize the need to change other aspects of social life in order to assure equal sexual opportunity for men and women.

Sexual Jealousy and Sexual Property

Jealousy, like guilt, is a common feeling when people get involved sexually. Though some people may be immune to the emotion, most of us are susceptible. What is sexual jealousy? At root, it is the belief that your spouse or lover is giving away to someone else what belongs to you. Male jealousy is generally seen at least in part as a result of a sense of ownership, but wives very often feel the same way. That is, people feel that when they got married they received the property rights to this person, and this person's time and energy and resources, including sex, belong to them.

Rarely do people assess the degree to which they have this property relation to another person. A measure of the proprietary character of marriage is the degree to which people automatically expect things from their spouses without negotiation. If you want to have sex with someone you are not married to, it means you have to negotiate, unless you rape. If you want to have intercourse with your spouse, more limited negotiations may take place, and you usually expect at least to share a bed without discussion (sharing a bed is a real advantage in making a sexual approach).

What characterizes most marriages is how much is taken for granted, from going places together to sleeping in the same bed every night. One can imagine the furor that might be caused by saying, "I am having a hard time sleeping in the same bed with you. I am going to move into the next room." The furor might justly be regarded as unreasonable, since many people do not sleep very well with someone else in the same bed, but we are all prepared to be slightly less comfortable at night in order to show the solidarity of the married couple.

The problem of feeling "owned" or "owning" sexually is very real for many people. If a person's spouse has sex with someone else, the person feels the spouse has taken something away. It is a betrayal in two ways, partly a betrayal of trust, partly a betrayal of ownership.

The source of this sense of betrayal can be traced to the conditions of sexual attachment and love formalized in the marriage contract, which is one of the few contracts that is absolutely open-ended, "until death do us part." Most contracts—like a thirty-year mortgage—have an end-point built in. But a marriage contract is forever, and it specifies permanent sexual ownership, with no sharing. Extramarital sex amounts to abrogating the contract. People may continue to own a house together, raise their children together, call themselves Mr. and Mrs., and do all the other things a married couple do together, but if one or both does not keep sex for the other alone, he or she is not being "faithful" to the contract.

Rewriting the Marriage Contract

Most people approach problems in marriage by rewriting, in effect, their marriage contracts in an informal way, though few mutually revise the section on sex. However, a mutual and formal rewriting of the marriage contract in nonsexual ways is becoming popular in contemporary marriages. Couples sit down in the kitchen or living room, or perhaps even in a hotel conference room, and tell each other, "These are the kinds of things I would like to do for the next three years, so now we are going to write a new binding contract between the two of us." If they cannot come to terms, they may even agree to get a divorce.

Little is taken for granted in this kind of relationship, and no one assumes that anyone else is going to do something automatically just because they are there. This makes marriage different. It obviously changes the way spouses perceive each other, it decreases the automatic assumption of property value of the other person, but it also makes mental calculations about reciprocity more explicit. In this sense, formal contract rewriting makes the property character of marriage more obvious.

Most couples, however, do not mutually rewrite the sexual exclusivity part of the marriage contract until one of them has had an affair. The rewrite comes after the violation of the contract. Most people never rewrite the contract but merely assume that it has not been violated, or if they know it has, they choose to ignore it because the costs of raising the issue might be too high.

Even within sexually faithful marriages there are at least a few exemptions to fidelity which it is possible for couples to discuss. These "exemptions" to the contract are those people with whom one is unlikely to have sex, but if an opportunity did arise, it would be all right. Movie actors, actresses, and entertainers in sports and the media are the usual exemptions, and couples often joke about such opportunities, particularly if they are hypothesized to occur only once: "Would you object if I went to bed with Robert Redford (Raquel Welch)?" It is part of the sexual fantasy life of the society that under certain conditions there are exemptions. Men who are away at war (but not the wives left behind) may also have an exemption as long as they do not get emotionally involved. Exemptions as the result of exceptional opportunities which are long periods apart lead to relationships in which extramarital intercourse can be part of a covert agreement between spouses that serves to stabilize the other aspects of their relationship.

There are couples who have a fundamental difference in level of sexual interest, but who have a large number of other things in common. In some cases one member of the couple is not interested in sex, or is interested in a different kind of sex. In these cases extramarital activity, even if it has an emotional tone, may be helpful to the adjustment of the two people (there can also be an exploitative element here; the third party is sometimes used as an object to stabilize the marital relationship). Such differences in sexual interest can emerge from very different sources. While conventionally it is thought that the wife is the person less interested in sex, there are many men for whom sex is not very interesting or is not competitive with other things they want to do. It is not that they fear sex, but that they are indifferent to it, or rank it as being of less importance than other activities in their lives.

There are people who are driven workers, with responsibilities that stretch far beyond the eight-hour day. They travel a great deal, confer in endless hotel rooms and conference halls, are involved in apparently important activities. There is not much time or energy left over for sex—and perhaps little interest. It may be more interesting to make major political or economic decisions[1] than it is to have sexual intercourse (indeed, it can seem more interesting merely to watch television). If the spouse of such a person has sex with other people, it may relieve a burden which that person does not feel willing to shoulder. In other cases, one marriage partner may by virtue of handicap or illness be unable to have sex, in which case extramarital sex may be a solution for the nonhandicapped person.

In such cases the agreements are often covert, as long as there is no falling in love. In other cases such agreements may result from attempts to work through a conflict about sex in what may otherwise be a blissful relationship. Such solutions are probably not very common, but they may occur more frequently than is suspected.

Formal Rewriting: Mate-Swapping and Swinging in Marriage

A mutual response to the idea of extramarital sex can be the product of a desire for extramarital sex, of the guilt produced by doing it covertly, of an interest in sexual freedom or equality, or just of the problems of logistics (or of a mixture of all these and more). This mutual response, which has received a great deal of media attention, is relatively rare, but it can change the nature of extramarital intercourse drastically. Its usual expression is the phenomenon labeled as "swinging," and it includes mate-swapping.

---

1. Few people will sacrifice their career for their sex life; most sacrifice their sex life for their career—sex may, in fact, be a consolation for those who are settling for second best.

It is usually the man who, for any number of reasons and motivations, raises the issue of mutual extramarital sex. Bringing the topic into the open probably requires a good deal of finesse and tentative exploration, for to raise the issue at all may be to put the marriage at risk. It is likely that most wives respond by saying "no," and ask whether he is doing it, but a minority may agree to go along with it (again for a variety of reasons, of which sexual desire may be the least). As a result of that decision, various forms of "swinging in wedlock" emerge. One is the traditional mate-swapper, whose rule is basically, "You can have mine if I can have yours."

The structure of such relationships is usually two couples, sometimes more, who trade sexual partners for an evening or a night. This can be done on neutral ground, such as a hotel, or at home. The couples may be strangers or people who have come to know each other through letters and/or past nonsexual meetings. The encounter is largely limited to some prior discussion and then sexual activity. It is noteworthy that, regardless of the rhetoric of sexual freedom, these activities are almost always promoted by men: they are trading wives, allowing another man access to their sexual property. The presumption is that neither member of the marital couple will have any sex outside of such an arrangement.

In its more cheerful form, such an arrangement can be an extension of family leisure-time activities, done the way they play tennis, or go camping or to the beach or on vacation. They find a compatible couple and have sex with them. They may deny it any relationship to their marriage by denying its emotional significance, by calling it "just play" or they may be more positive in their reactions. Utopian swingers say "The fact we can do it indicates that we feel more strongly about each other than most couples do. We know none of our friends could have sex with anybody else without getting divorced. The fact that we do it demonstrates our maturity and understanding and caring for each other." Just as with other forms of leisure activity, they say it helps their marriage — it is shared time, shared activity, and fun.

For many people such relationships with more or less emotional strangers are personally limiting. They develop a more extensive ideology of extramarital sex, sometimes calling it "co-marital sex" to indicate that both persons are doing it with consent. They point out the increase in the range of emotional sexual relationships possible for people who follow this pathway. Co-marital sex becomes an opportunity to know more people, to increase the number of significant persons in their lives. This variation contains a great deal more emotional tone than does the swapping of mates in hotel rooms or with strangers picked up at bars. It is from "co-marital" arrangements that people are recruited into group marriages in which sex is shared.

The insistence on emotion raises the old issue of falling in love or getting attached to someone else's spouse. In the simple mate-swapping situation, where the other couple remain strangers, the risk is minimized. Since the couple is always there together, they can police each other's emotional responses. In the more ideological case, a solution to this problem is attempted by trying to separate sexuality from affection — that is, to make sex expressive of neither passion nor permanent commitment, but rather of friendship and liking. Sex is then a less powerful form of social bonding and can exist without the necessity for love and affection that it carries in most conventional relationships.

There may be a progression in these situations in terms of the content of the relationships and of the kind of sexuality expressed. In the mate-swapping context, there is a limitation on emotion, a limitation that is modified in a more utopian "swinger" posture, where some emotion may be expressed in the sex with other partners, but where the full commitment remains to the spouse. Sexually such relationships can begin with simple heterosexual sharing and then move on to forms of group sex.

One pathway that has created considerable difficulty for the mate-swapper, or even for the utopian swinger, is the decision by one or another member of the couple to have emotional or sexual relationships outside of shared relations, to "go single" again. Swapping and swinging are designed to make extramarital sex safe for marriage by defusing emotional involvement and exclusivity. In some cases the wife, who is usually the more valuable sexual commodity, decides that she does not want to share or be a token in a male-dominated sexual exchange. At that point she may decide to have extramarital sex with someone of her own choice and without her spouse along. This is totally disruptive to mate-swapping, whose primary premise is that the wife is the price for access to other men's wives, and it can have serious consequences for the ideology of co-marital sex, since it produces a non-shared component in the marriage.

Any kind of extramarital sex tends to complicate the relationship between husband and wife. Whether it is covert or mutual, or involves swapping or swinging, it requires that the couple (or at least one member) change the script that is guiding the marriage. In some cases this involves changes in only the "who" of sex. In others it involves changing the number of people involved, or the "why" (for freedom, fun, mutual sharing), or even the "where" and the "when." When the script changes from extramarital sex to co-marital, it implicates both persons by bringing formerly deviant behavior into the marriage contract. The contract between the two becomes the basis for new behavior. Extramarital sex is normalized by changing the agreement, but the marital unit then becomes "unconventional."

Single, Postmarital, and Intermarital Sexuality

The person who waits to get married until after age twenty-five enters a world of sexuality very different from that experienced during the late teens and early twenties. Much of that sexuality was in the context of mate selection. It was, so to speak, premarital sexuality as preparation for getting married. The definitions of the self as youthful, of heterosexual associations as fun, the contexts in which dating took place (the corner, the school, the college), all reinforced and structured encounters with other people and the opportunities to see them socially and sexually. In these contexts, the interests of parents remained an important and significant guide to who might be chosen.

Today, with an increasing number of people waiting until their middle twenties to marry for the first time, and with a larger proportion of the married population divorcing at all ages, there are more people than ever before living a single life style—that is, they are unmarried, with a job and income, defined as adult, not dependent on parents, and sometimes with children. The margin between a premarital adjustment and a single adjustment is a narrow one, since practically every-one in the single world is doing some looking for either a sexual or an emotional partner, commonly in marriage. However, there is a qualitative difference between these two worlds, depending on age. For many people around age twenty-five the single world is merely the premarital world with a slightly greater likelihood of having sex.

The singles world itself is stratified by age and expectation of getting married. As people get older, most of them still want to marry (or, more likely, remarry), but they now often live in circumstances in which meeting other people may be more difficult. Only a few people have made the decision at an early age not to marry, for it is only with age that marriage may lose its charm. Even so, while marriage may be less attractive sexually, it may come to be more attractive as a living and emotional arrangement.

The segment of the single world most visible to us, because of the media, is the "singles scene." This is the singles bar, the urban, detached middle-class world to which the magazines like *Cosmopolitan* and *Playboy* cater. For descriptive purposes, we may suggest that this scene has two main groups: one for the under-thirties, composed of the never-married and the divorced; and one for the over-thirties, composed mostly of divorced people. These groups are quite different from the premarital singles, who are usually under twenty-five. The age grades are flexible, however, so that slightly older men (up to about thirty-five) can be in the under-thirty group and women under forty-five can mix with thirty to thirty-five-year-old men. Singles above these age levels have a great deal of difficulty unless they are very attractive or have other resources (such as money) that can be brought into play. Age is a merciless enemy in the singles scene.

The goals of the participants in the singles scene are generally either remarriage or recreational sex, but because many of the participants have previous sexual experience and/or want to get married, the likelihood of sexual activity is relatively high. In the 1950s, it was estimated that seventy to eighty percent of people between marriages probably had sex during that time. Present figures should be very similar or somewhat higher (actually ninety percent may be a true ceiling for sex—ten percent may just not want to do it).

The contemporary institution which best seems to represent our image of the singles scene is the singles bar, a minority experience converted into a media majority. It is very much like a homosexual bar. That is, everybody is there for a very narrow purpose. The women are usually looking for Mr. Right (*Looking for Mr. Goodbar*), though they will settle for a date; the men are all looking for what Philip Roth, in *Portnoy's Complaint*, called "the real McCoy," but they too will settle for a date. During the week the bar is crowded, with a good deal of eye contact and walking up and down. Everybody is displaying themselves and writing down phone numbers. The bar is a dating roost where people pair off.

Unlike a gay bar, where men know that other men are interested in sex, the singles bar brings together people looking for sex and people who may be interested only in socializing. Conflicting interests produce a tense situation; most singles bars are appalling places if you are not very attractive, getting a little old, and do not know the local argot.

Many singles, however, take no part in the singles scene. This is particularly true for both men and women over forty, for people with children or low incomes, or for those isolated by community, geography, ethnicity, or religion. It is also true for those who find the dating and rating scene in the single world difficult to take or manage. For these people, sexuality and remarriage have to take place under the sponsorship of friends and family. Indeed, a traditional association and remarriage pattern is still characteristic of a very large proportion of the population.

Many people cannot successfully participate in the singles scene, while others do not want to (because they are too conservative *or* too radical). For them new forms of heterosocial association, intimacy, and sexual relations have to be invented. Under the best of conditions, people find that they have to do many things— call for dates, worry about sex, take people home—which have not concerned them since they were much younger. When a person is forty, it is difficult to call somebody up on the phone and go through the "Hi, how are you, would you like to go to the movie" routine he (or she) went through at sixteen. It cannot help but make people feel slightly infantile. The first problem for the postmarital is the whole problem of renegotiating how to meet people. Neither men nor women are necessarily good at it, and there is no evidence that dating is easier for one sex than for the other.

People do get together, however, some in the more contemporary ways of the singles bars and mixers and summer vacations—many in the traditional ways of meeting people at work or through family and friends. The difference is that sex is more likely to occur in the contemporary way, though it may be difficult to accomplish comfortably: people with children still have to worry about where to go; women often regard sex as something which involves at least some intimacy; and many men carry with them some aspects of the double standard.

Changes are occurring. Some divorced women are staying unmarried now that they can participate more fully in the labor force. Others are sharing houses with other people, men and women, in some cases with sexual relationships and in other cases not. These changes have not yet gone very far, and we have no institutional forms that seem to meet the needs of those who choose either to remain single or to go through a single period during their middle and later adult years.

As yet we do not know a great deal about this period and the sexual adjustments that characterize it. We particularly do not know anything about it as it occurs in small towns and middle-sized cities, in more religious parts of the population, or among poorer people. At this moment our images are limited to the larger cities and the middle-class world of singles there.

What we may be sure of even at this moment is that the majority of people who have been divorced and widowed are likely to be married again, and that their sexuality will once again be regulated by whatever form of the marriage contract they accept or, more rarely, choose.

Being "normal" is no more natural than being "queer."
All of us studied to be what we are.

Arnie Kantrowicz

IT IS A COMMON, BUT FALSE, BELIEF THAT IF WE KNOW THAT PERSONS choose same-gender sex partners, we can successfully make inferences about the kinds of families they come from; the kinds of sex lives they lead; their tastes in clothing, art, music, interior decoration; the way they talk; the kinds of work they prefer; and their religious or leisure orientations. We do not believe we can make such inferences about persons who choose opposite-gender sex partners. Homosexuality (unlike heterosexuality) is a significant label, since it elicits a sequence of interlocked beliefs or judgments which organize our responses to ourselves and to other people. Our responses to the word "homosexual" or "homosexuality" (or persons so labeled) are part of a culturally acquired pattern of beliefs about a cultural stereotype, and constitute what we mean by homosexual and homosexuality.

Many of our intellectual difficulties in thinking about homosexuality have centered on the choice between narrow and wide definitions of homosexuality. Narrow definitions have usually focused on homosexual "acts," while more inclusive definitions have focused on the whole person, and have ranged even more widely into society and culture. Very narrow, externally defined versions of homosexual acts — all we need is two persons of the same sex touching each other in ways we consider sexual — assume a meaning that is both simple and automatic. However, meaningful definitions of sexual acts between human beings always require that we concern ourselves with what people think and feel while they are doing things, and the contexts in which they do them. As has been pointed out, it is possible for people of the same sex to do sexual-appearing things with each other and not have it experienced as sexual (the doctor pushes his finger through the anus into the rectum, presses the prostate, and ejaculate comes out of the penis); for one person to experience an act as homosexual and the other not; and finally for both persons to experience an act as homosexual. It is also possible for people who have had no overt homosexual experience to define themselves as homosexual.

Problems of Definition

In the past, largely influenced by the "homosexual person" definitions of psychoanalytic tradition, it was believed that homosexuality was a powerful character trait; that to do homosexual things required a certain kind of psychological history and that this history combined with homosexual experience would be powerfully influential on a whole range of a person's nonsexual activities. The Freudians attempted to solve the problem of observable variety in homosexual conduct by creating such types as the latent homosexual (possessing the character, but not acting out); the true homosexual (a person possessing both the typical background history and present behavioral syndromes); and the obligatory homosexual (referring to people who were homosexual outside of prison and "had" to be homosexual in prison). It was believed that there was a homosexual pattern of conduct (always self-destructive, according to one analyst; usually with work-inhibitions, according to another) and a visible homosexual influence in other, nonsexual activities of the homosexual person: e.g., artists might paint pictures with homosexual symbols, conscious or unconscious; male homosexual writers could not write convincingly about women because they were hostile to them. The key notion was that the *sexual* adjustment was all-powerful, and had profound consequences for the entire life pattern of the individual.

In reaction to these kinds of definitions and typologies, Kinsey chose the narrow definition of homosexuality. Offended by anti-homosexual uses of these pejorative psychoanalytic and psychiatric labels, and unable to locate the homosexual stereotypes that the therapists and the medical profession found in their patients, he focused directly on the act and a limited time period around it. His argument was that homosexuality and heterosexuality were a continuum, that people were not one or the other but a combination of acts. Kinsey was attempting to break down the old stereotypes and find a way to show that homosexuality and heterosexuality shared a common domain; indeed, that they simply existed on a continuum, with no point being "better" than another. As long as we limit our perspective to the anatomical sex of the object, and limit the critical events to the time from the first to the last orgasmic spasm of the penis or vagina, such a definition might be workable, although not particularly useful in understanding what people do.

Perhaps the limitations of the homosexual-heterosexual continuum can be made clear in the following way. In U. S. culture the gender of one's sexual partner is crucial, and therefore leads to a key label; however, let us think of a society where gender does not matter, but where it is very important what emotions one feels during sex. People would then divide up by the kind of *feeler* that they are; they could be love-feelers or lust-feelers (the former obviously would be "better" people). In our studies we would find that there are many love-feelers in the society and only a few lust-feelers; in the middle we would find bi-feelers. Soon we would have theories about why people felt lust (and not love); their childhood would be studied; the fact that they were not able to feel correctly would tell us that they were immature, neurotic, perhaps even criminal. A more facetious dimension might be that of clothing — at one end would be those who are dressed while having sex; at the other end those who wear no clothing; in the middle the mixed types. If it were important to us we could build a psychology, a sociology, a criminology, even a sexuality around such categories.

Unfortunately for those who prefer the narrow definition, people do not experience themselves that way. They do use labels and experience various portions of their lives through such defining terms as homosexual and heterosexual; straight and gay; gay men and lesbian; queer, faggot, dyke, butch, fem. Such words are signs to themselves and to other people of who they think they are and what they are going to do in certain circumstances. The very wide definition is faulty as well — just because people call themselves homosexual or queen or dyke does not mean that everything they have been, are, or will be is affected by that label.

What needs to be understood is that there is not one homosexuality, but a multiplicity of ways of organizing a homosexual preference into other ongoing life styles and commitments. There are moments in people's lives when they are operating entirely within the limits expressed by "being homosexual," and other moments when their homosexuality (indeed any aspect of their sexuality) is irrelevant. For some people their sexuality is present, important, or eruptive in every circumstance, either for their entire lives or for a certain period in their lives; for others it is a matter of minimum significance in all circumstances.

The significance of types of sexual conduct, even of those sexual categories that loom as very important in our eyes, is that they are changing factors in a person's life rather than constants in a social and psychological reality. Any act may be defined as having a sexual meaning or connotation regardless of its distance from the usual cultural definitions, and any act that is well within the cultural definitions may be defined by the actors as nonsexual. Intellectual, athletic, or business events may be directly experienced as sexual in conventional cultural terms (having a good idea occurs with an orgasm), as sexually symbolic (winning is like orgasm), leading up to something sexual (when I get promoted I will be able to have an orgasm with . . .), or not have anything to do with sex at all. Inversely, the content of culturally defined sexuality can be experienced in the other direction: "When I have an orgasm I get a good idea," "Orgasm is like winning," "When I have an orgasm with . . . I will get promoted."

Our definitions reflect our interests and our concerns, both as individuals and as residents of a socio-historical moment in a given culture. Whether we have expansive or narrow definitions of heterosexuality and homosexuality, love and lust, or clothed and naked sex, depends on the cultural significance that these dimensions have in both our personal lives and the collective expressions of sexuality around us. Definitions should not be created to exhaust reality, to stand for all time, or to account for all meanings in all circumstances. The utility of a definition is the directions it gives us for looking at the world. The definition should not be confused with the world itself. The map is not the territory.

Assumptions of Research

Homosexuality and the homosexual have been allowed to stand in intellectual and moral opposition to heterosexuality and the heterosexual for a very long time. A person's preference for the gender of their sexual partner or partners seemed obviously to stand for a series of simple exclusions. Homosexuality and homosexuals were A, B, and C and heterosexuals were non A, non B, and non C. If one wanted to be slightly more complicated one could set up a series of oppositions between heterosexual men and homosexual men, between heterosexual women and homosexual women.

Unfortunately this perspective has a major fault. Its concern is to reinforce the moral and social superiority of heterosexuality, not to examine or understand the emergence and maintenance of alternative object choices in sexuality. Heterosexuality was viewed as the natural outcome of nearly all of the plans for human life—from the points of view of divinity, biology, society, and mental health it was not only preferred, it was what you got when the normal processes of development were not interfered with. Whatever was thought to be the normal process, a homosexual preference, particularly one that characterized someone's entire adult life, was either immoral, perverse, dysfunctional, or neurotic.

Having taken this position, researchers then began to search for reasons in the life histories of homosexuals for why they might have become perverted, what had bent them away from the normal pathways. It was generally understood by the most tolerant of such researchers that homosexuals were not "responsible" in some sense for their condition, but homosexuality was thought to be inferior to the rather better adaptation of heterosexuality. Comparative studies of the different past histories of homosexuals and heterosexuals have consumed a good deal of the time and energy of sex researchers, and a number of hypotheses have been generated on why a homosexual adaptation might have happened.

In the early days of this research, it was proposed that the difference might be the result of different genetic or biological factors (particularly hormones). There has never been a satisfactory demonstration of such a connection between "constitutional" or biological factors and the emergence of a homosexual object choice; however, such an argument did at one time have a certain political potency. Havelock Ellis, for instance, made such a proposal: if a homosexual preference were genetic, then those having it could not be accused of practicing a vicious or criminal habit; the fact that it was inherited would make it like color blindness, or (more positively) the ability to see colors that most people could not. Ellis came very close to claiming that homosexuality (particularly in men) might be a virtue, since it gave them access to a world of feelings and attachments heterosexuals could not have. Having a genetic condition implies that one is exempt from both sin and cure—freed from the attention of the church, the state, and the therapist. However, it was possible for those who disapproved of homosexuality to argue that even though it might be constitutional, it still represented a biologically inferior adaptation (after all, they do not reproduce) rather than a superior or equal adaptation compared to heterosexuality. The inferiority theorists have dominated the study of homosexuality, looking for biological abnormalities that might produce such an "anomaly."

More environmentally oriented researchers, following the psychoanalytic tradition, have looked back into the childhoods of homosexual adults, seeking the reasons for their "perversion." What they have wanted to find is a particular kind of family arrangement that might produce or at least predispose persons to homosexual object choices. Such studies have usually fallen prey to one or another sets of errors, but the most common ideological fault is the original decision to look for something that went wrong in development to result in a homosexual, in contrast to what went right in the development of heterosexuals. The decision has been made ahead of time that the outcome is pathological; therefore, any social or psychological commonalities found in the pasts of homosexuals must also be pathological. Even if researchers try not to make this distinction, the comparative method of looking at differences between the two groups often leads to the same results: the unpreferred outcome has unpreferred origins.

Such researchers usually report that they find differences in the parenting of homosexuals (both male and female) and the parenting of heterosexuals. Male homosexuals are reported to have mothers who are seductive and smothering, who arouse their sons' sexual desires but do not let them fulfill them, and who also keep them from normal "boyish and masculine pursuits" like baseball and getting dirty. The fathers are often reported to be detached, unavailable, or outright hostile. In contrast, the female homosexual is reported to be raised in a home where the mother is detached and hostile while the father is seductive, and she behaves in tomboyish and non-feminine ways. The argument is complex, but its outlines are that male homosexuals never develop an adequate masculine identification, that female homosexuals have difficulty with feminine identification, and that the sex-object preference emerges from these faulty gender-identification patterns.

Problems of Research

Most of the studies of the differences (either developmental or cross-sectional) between homosexual groups and heterosexual groups tend to focus on the dimension of masculinity and femininity, the sissy and the tomboy. In other cases these differences are correlated with other social and psychological measures designed to test whether homosexuals or heterosexuals are better adjusted socially or psychologically. In the past nearly all studies showed that homosexuals were more poorly adjusted; more recent studies have shown equal levels of adjustment or that heterosexuals are more poorly adjusted. These changed findings probably do not have anything to do with the social or psychological adjustment of people with different sex-object choices, but with sampling of cases, types of instruments, and the ideologies of researchers.

These retrospective developmental studies suffer from four very serious flaws. *First*, they assume that people who are adults can remember in any complete detail what their childhood was actually like. There is a growing body of social-science research suggesting that people actually remember very little of their past (try to remember all you can about when you were four years old and then think how much of your fourth year those memories represent). What people remember of the past is highly dependent on the context in which they are asked to remember (you remember different things for your women or men friends than for your mother or father). Finally, there are studies which suggest that we actively embellish and reorganize our past for different purposes. The further back things get in time, the more we use contemporary scripts to organize what must have happened to us.

You do not think of your own past as quite real; you dress it up, you gild it or blacken it, censor it, tinker with it, . . . fictionalize it in a word, and put it away on a shelf — your book, your romanced biography. (John Fowles, *The French Lieutenant's Woman*, p. 84.)

Take a nonsexual example. Mothers who have been observed in child-rearing practices (toilet training and feeding) during the first two years of life by a visitor who comes each month and watches, are asked some years later how they did these tasks. The mothers sound like Dr. Spock. Why? Because they do not remember, but they do have an acceptable version of the past they can use, Spock's handbook. This is a problem of all studies of humans that depend on recall, and people may not even know that they are telling a different story than what happened. Our versions of both our long-term and short-term pasts are highly variable in accuracy. The accuracy of what we remember may not matter if we are in therapy (everything is grist for the therapist's mill), but it certainly does if we are doing science.

Second, researchers often assume that their knowledge of whether the subject is or is not homosexual as well as of the subject's life experiences does not have an effect on how they interpret experimental or research instruments. During the 1950s a study showed that if researchers using a projective test called the Rorschach knew the respondent was homosexual, they found many more negative or damaging responses in their answers than they did in the answers of people they knew were heterosexuals. When the same responses were scored blind (that is, the researcher did not know if the person was homosexual or heterosexual) there was no difference in the comparative frequency of negative judgments. Thus, many studies do not tell us whether homosexuals or heterosexuals are "mentally healthy" or even "different." What they do tell us is that a researcher who already has certain facts about the respondent will tend to look for information that fits in with a stereotype. This tendency will occur whether a person is pro- or anti-homosexual, and will develop at all stages of the research, from the design of the questions to the use of the instruments to analysis of the data.

Third, in some cases the research subjects are in therapy, usually forms of therapy which focus on parental influences on the development of current conduct. In such cases the subjects are being trained to respond in appropriate ways by the people who think they are doing objective research. It is remarkably naive to assume that a patient in therapy for homosexuality would not be well aware of theories about homosexuality, and would not be influenced by them in producing information about the past. Since the same "versions" of the past are not expected of heterosexuals, there is no reason why they should emphasize them, or look for incidents that would support them.

Fourth, a factor often overlooked is that many of the responses scientists get to their instruments are thought to be related purely to a sexual attribute, and may in fact be a function of other aspects of a person's life style. For instance, it is sometimes thought that male homosexuals are more paranoid than other people, and there are studies suggesting that on some scales homosexuals may appear more suspicious than heterosexuals. The validity of such a finding depends on the belief that homosexuality and paranoia are "pure essences" inside a person. An alternative interpretation would be that since homosexuality is illegal and socially disvalued, that people can lose their jobs for it, and that they can be arrested for their sexual behavior, they have something to conceal. People with something to conceal are at risk and do not want to be found out. If they are suspicious, it is because they have something to fear, not because of some character fault or trait.

This problem is highlighted by the following fantasy, in which anxiety is substituted for homosexuality:

Imagine for a moment that you are an anxious person and that being anxious is against the law. You must try to hide your fears from others. Your own home may be a safe place to feel anxious, but a public display of apprehension can lead to arrest or at least to social ostracism. At work one day an associate looks at you suspiciously and says, "That's funny, for a crazy moment there I thought you were anxious." "Heck no," you exclaim a bit too loudly, *"not me!"* You begin to wonder if your fellow worker will report his suspicions to your boss. If he does, your boss may inform the police or will at least change your job to one that requires less contact with customers, especially with those who have children. (Davison and Neale, *Abnormal Psychology: An Experimental-Clinical Approach,* 1974, p. 293).

What this suggests is that the conditions under which the preference is learned and lived produces the associated behaviors (perhaps both good and bad), rather than the preference itself producing them.

Becoming "Homosexual"

The study of how people get to be homosexual or to do homosexual things is probably a fruitless enterprise, though it has occupied most of the attention of those who have studied homosexuality. Data has been obsessively searched to prove that there is a unique set of pathways or sequence of experiences (type of family, type of peer group, type of school experience, first homosexual experience, etc.) that will produce a homosexual.[1] But the meaning of being homosexual is not merely an accumulation from the past; it comes from the environments that await the child, environments where childhood labels and experiences are unrelated to the sexual preferences adults may want to make. The "meaning" of sexuality is continually evolving as people get older; an act at age fifteen is different than an act at age twenty; a deep emotional crush at age fourteen is fundamentally different than a one-night stand at age forty. The meanings of these acts often derive not from their sexual content but from other, more potent factors: emotion, age, and the like.

There are more reasons to be homosexual (or anything else) than there are ways to be homosexual. All through our lives we choose and are chosen. We may feel unhappy with our gender-role performances when we are twelve because we are too small or too large; by age fourteen, depending on what happens, we can forget our unhappiness or have built on it, either positively or negatively.

In part our response will depend on how we are grouped in nonsexual ways. Thus, many young people apply for medical school for very different reasons, from the desire to make 120,000 dollars a year to a desire to help humanity. They get in for different reasons than the ones they had when they applied. Similarities we see in them as interns and residents are a result of the homogenizing effects of the medical-school experience. After medical school, doctors are regrouped; some go on to teach and do research in medical schools, others go out to general practice or to specialties. Whether their salary is paid or whether they work for a fee does more to shape the kind of doctors they are than what they shared in medical school. So it is with our sexual preferences—we become heterosexuals or homosexuals, partly as recruits and partly as draftees. The kind of heterosexuals or homosexuals that we become depends on the stability of our relationships, our income, if we marry or have children, buy a house, or want to maintain a religious commitment.

1. The focus on the sources of homosexuality has obscured the sources of heterosexuality. Most researchers assume that the causes of heterosexuality are everything that does *not* cause homosexuality (or other undesirable outcomes). There is no adequate theory of heterosexual development, particularly not when viewed through the work of those who research homosexuality; and it is assumed that heterosexuality, in the absence of these disabling conditions, will flourish because it is "natural."

GENDER

The basis for most theories of becoming homosexual is that something has gone wrong with the process of gender-identity formation—that the connection has broken down between the development of manhood and a preference for women in the case of male homosexuality, and womanhood and a preference for men in the case of female homosexuality. The underlying argument is expressed primitively by saying that male homosexuals are basically effeminate men and female homosexuals are masculine women.

As a result there is a search for attributes which will demonstrate the case. The gay man is feminized and the lesbian is masculinized by researchers. We find in research reports that male homosexuals do not like sports; that lesbians do like sports; that gay men cried a lot when growing up; that lesbians liked trucks and chemistry sets; that in adulthood homosexual men like to cook and lesbians like to fix lamps. "Incorrect" behavior when young is tied to incorrect behavior when adult without any evidence of a connection between these earlier or later states except the decision of the researcher.

What is usually going on is the search for something wrong, a search for models of the homosexual experience which justify treating it as both a perversion and a parody of contemporary heterosexuality. As long as the heterosexual majority, including the scientific community, react to homosexuality in these terms, people who have a homosexual preference must take these reactions into account as part of their cultural reality. Some of them may even come to believe this majority view and become a parody of the "invert"; most others attempt to resist or evade becoming what the majority believes them to be.

Even though we learn about gender roles and label ourselves "girl" or "boy" before we learn a great deal about sex or before we experiment sexually, it is important not to view our gender roles as being permanently fashioned and complete, waiting for us to become sexual. Gender roles are not a mold into which we pour our sexuality. In the same way that our sexuality changes through the life cycle, so do the activities and performances we put into our gender roles. The middle-aged man and woman going through a personal crisis of aging not only have their familial or occupational lives under review, they are changing and working with their gender roles and sexuality as well. Thus children may have a whole series of gender-role conceptions which will change as they take on sexual roles and activities during adolescence. The fact that a male can say "I am a boy" does not mean that masturbation or dating or playing football will be automatic; they may be easier or more accessible for a male than a female, not because of individual pasts, but because of the adolescent social arrangements that are created for boys.

FAMILY

The importance that contemporary nuclear family patterns may have for the development of homosexuality at the present time (it is unclear what role the family may have played in the development of homosexuality, say, during Classical Greece) is to offer patterns of role differentiation. The contemporary family strongly emphasizes gender-role dimorphism by providing as primary role models an opposite-sex couple (usually heterosexual) with different tasks assigned to the different genders.

All children learn or observe these patterns in the home or in other areas of society, and, become either comfortable or uncomfortable with these models of what the future may hold. However, it is not clear that the "sissy" or the "tomboy" is in fact reacting solely to this family constellation. The boy who is weak, timid, and fearful may in fact be physically less apt or legitimately afraid of getting hurt. The tomboy may be highly rewarded by the peer group for her performances during much of her childhood.

What may be important developmentally is not whether children possess a particular set of stigmas or abilities or inabilities, only whether they feel some sense of alienation from the conventional gender roles offered by parents, peers, teachers, or television. There is no particular pattern of parent-child relations that will produce a "homosexual"; there are only many children more or less comfortable with the usual gender-role expectations. A lack of comfort, or alienation, can have different outcomes, depending on other aspects of the environment, present and future. Two examples: A small, physically weak boy is rejected by and rejects his aggressive working class peer group. In school he may find opportunities to be upwardly mobile, go to college, and become successful, while his classmates are still hanging around the corner tavern. In the same circumstances, the sense of alienation may influence the boy toward a homosexual preference. A girl who is a tomboy, and who is disvalued in a sex-stereotyped society because of her interests in "boys' " things, may become interested in homosexuality; or, in a society where female athletics are highly rewarded, she could become famous and the object of considerable heterosexual attention. In both of these examples there are expressions of values—between heterosexuality and homosexuality, between upward mobility and working class life styles, between fame and obscurity.

The family constellation of role models does not so much prepare the child for "homosexuality" as for a wide range of responses, the content of which are specified in the arena of adolescence. "Poorly adjusted" children may find many opportunities as well as problems, depending on the resources that become available to them as they move from period to period in their lives. Socialization patterns may produce discomfort; whether this discomfort is a potential for becoming different than what is expected (indeed most people do not realize this potential) is not as important as whether that "different" is defined as good or bad.

ADOLESCENCE

Young people uncomfortable with conventional gender-role expectations often find themselves also uncomfortable with the heterosociality and heterosexuality of adolescent social life. Only for a few of the most popular does youth culture approximate its television versions—most young people, those moving into heterosexual and those moving into homosexual preferences, find the period only sometimes pleasurable and joyous. However, the period is usually more comfortable for those who are moving or drifting into a heterosexual pattern. Even if they are heterosocially inept, it is possible to be carried by the general tide into a minimum heterosexual adaptation.

The adolescent period is commonly far less comfortable for young people who are moving into the beginnings of either a homosexual self-identification or homosexual experience, and who are looking for ways to validate an emerging sense of who they are sexually. The process is both positive and negative—the heterosexual and heterosocial world is often both rejecting and inadequate, but the homosexual life style has few outposts in the adolescent subculture. Because of the heterosexual tilt of adolescence, a heterosexual commitment is easier to accept or drift into, and tends to coalesce more rapidly.

Another reason it is easier is that a commitment to the opposite sex does not have to be *thought about* the same way a commitment to the same sex does. It is possible to go through the public rituals of heterosexuality and heterosociality without much conscious effort; the same rituals do not exist for the young people who have an alternative sense of what they want emotionally and physically. This period appears to be chaotic for adolescents with homosexual interests because there are no affirming public markers about what they are feeling and thinking.

The experience of being different, of being invisible or too visible, is profoundly demoralizing for many young people. All around them others appear to be "turning out right" (no matter how unhappy those others may be in fact), while they feel different. (Many of these feelings are shared by young people who become heterosexual later.) The search for an honest listener or companion or lover can be very difficult. Parents are rarely cooperative, teachers may be ignorant, doctors and counselors try to "straighten out" or treat the young person. The worries that these young people have about their masculinity or feminity during this period are often connected with believing the cultural myth that there is a necessary connection between gender-role conformity and sexual conformity. Because they are not participating, they feel uneasy.

GETTING THERE

Some homosexuals will say that they knew they were homosexual when they were five or six years old. It is unclear what this means—it may only mean that they felt different at that time; it may mean that they are more comfortable locating their "homosexuality" very early in life; it probably tells us something about how they relate now, and little about their pasts. What is likely is that most people who develop a same-sex object choice do so during adolescence, in a sequence of events which involves: recognition that they are "different" and that they might label themselves as "homosexual" or "gay" or "lesbian"; the beginnings of association with others who label themselves in the same way; beginning to have sex with others of the same sex; and finally at some point informing significant others (homosexual and heterosexual) of their preferences.

The sequence of these events has no "natural" order; some people think it first, other people do it first, still other people are told it by others first. The sexual information blackout during adolescence, the stigmatized status of homosexuality, the fears and terrors of being different, all can contribute to a tangled, painful, and disordering sequence of events. Some young people have a good deal of homosexual experience before they know what it is; others read about homosexuality and say, "My God, that's what I am!" (This was particularly true of a 1930s and 1940s generation of lesbians who read the novel, *The Well of Loneliness*.) Others come to the conclusion on their own and go to a gay bar to find out.

These experiences then begin to consolidate. Young people learn how to find people with similar sexual, emotional, and social interests. They begin to learn about the institutions, rituals, and structure of the gay subculture. They begin to deal with their important nonsexual relationships to people they believe (correctly or incorrectly) will react negatively to their sexual preferences. Unlike the young heterosexual, who can drift into adulthood, sex, marriage, and children with scarcely a thought, a homosexual preference requires a fairly high level of personal and emotional self-consciousness about sexuality.

The adolescent period can be quite different for males than for females who have emerging homosexual commitments. The influence of gender-role expectations about sexuality is quite important. Many young women move into strong emotional relationships with other young women without physical sexual commitments at all; some have sexual experiences without knowing what to call the experience; a few connect both the physical experience and the emotional commitment to a person of the same sex. These patterns of emotional and sexual self-identification also occur among males, as does sexuality without self-identification—however, males more often have a physical introduction, females an emotional one. As with heterosexual young women, the early period of development for young women who are developing a homosexual commitment is less physically focused than for most young men. Young women also move into overt homosexual experience at later ages, and many may marry before making a final commitment to homosexuality at some later point in life.

GAY WORLD

As young people move into a world of others who identify themselves as homosexual, they come into contact with the "gay world," the homosexual subculture itself. At one time the public gay world consisted nearly entirely of sexual meeting places of various kinds. The most common was the gay bar. Depending on the size and the density of the homosexual community, these bars ranged from a few to a large number. The number also depended on the intensity or corruptness of local law enforcement. Everywhere, the number of bars catering to men outnumbered those catering to women.

The more bars there were, the greater the number of separate groups or interests they tended to serve. For instance, in San Francisco, there were (and are) a wide variety of gay bars: places to find a pickup; places for dinner and conventional entertainment; bars with female impersonators and a mixed homosexual and heterosexual audience; neighborhood bars with regular customers looking for sociability; bars for particular sexual preferences.

In addition, there were bars where people could dance, be rowdy, be quiet—in other words, a range of institutions that paralleled most of the functions of the bars that heterosexuals go to. There were also other "pickup" locales: beaches, parks, Turkish baths, rest stops on the expressway, restaurants — all of which could be learned by the novice. In addition to bars, regions of cities could be gay residential areas, or leisure communities could develop largely a gay clientele. What most of these institutions had in common in the early 1950s and later was that the people who went to them had a common sexual interest.

Since that time new homosexually based organizations have appeared. Beginning with education programs in the 1950s, they have now turned into service organizations, educational organizations, therapeutic centers, and professional subsections of professional organizations (e.g., The American Gay Psychologists). This emergence of a number of organizations indicates and has been instrumental in the change in the status of the homosexual in U. S. society, and a change in relationship to the sexual majority in society. They also offer a different way of finding sympathetic common-interest groups than the bar, the bath, and the other primarily sexual institutions of the gay culture.

INFLUENCE OF GENDER STEREOTYPES

Historically, roles in the gay subculture were aligned along strongly differentiated gender-role lines. Particularly the male homosexual community, but also the female, tended to be modeled on *heterosexual* male-female stereotypes. Often this characteristic of the subculture was confused with the preferences of the members of that subculture. In the same way that the subculture of the Marine Corps is more *macho* than most individual marines, so the gay community is more strongly divided along butch-fem lines than are individual homosexuals. This public characteristic of the community has two effects: first, it offers the persons just coming into the community a set of roles that are more exaggerated or differentiated than are actually needed; second, it continues a tradition that is less and less fully adequate to meet the needs of its members.

As we have noted, many young people who are beginning to adopt an alternative sex-object preference feel very uneasy. Since the cultural stereotype of the gay male is effeminate and of the lesbian is masculine, it is hard to shake these imposed conceptions. At the same time, the young person is not receiving those nonsexual reinforcements of gender-role identity which are the automatic rewards of those who are heterosocial. Nonsexual association between men and women probably contributes more to gender-role comfort than does sexual association — if young people are cut off from these social supports there can be an uneasiness about the stability of their gender-role identity. The exaggerated roles offered by the gay community are accepted with rather more passion than reflection by many young people, some of whom find for the first time a sense of connection between gender and sexuality.

During the early days of a homosexual commitment, young men often engage in a good deal of casual sex, a sexual "honeymoon." This often occurs simply because the young person has finally found a variety of sexual partners, and the period of not knowing how or who is over. Among young women this period of casual sex seems far less likely to occur; more often they begin intense love affairs, affairs that may be transient. Traditional gender-role definitions still seem powerful; young men are interested in sex and then in love; young women are often interested in love and then in sex. After this rather chaotic early period, most young people begin to develop stable patterns of homosexual conduct organized around friends, lovers, public and private places.

We should not overlook the fact that most young people, heterosexual or homosexual, are also spending this period until the early twenties either going to school or developing a work career. The fact that the occupational distribution of homosexuals parallels the distribution of heterosexuals is in some ways more important than their sexual differences. While we commonly think of homosexuals primarily in terms of their sexuality, only some of them go through in any exaggerated form the patterns outlined above. For most young people sex occupies only part of their lives. They are getting into a wide range of interests that will shape the kind of sexuality they will have in the future.

Coming Out and Being Open

Because of the significance of a homosexual label in U. S. society, most homosexuals have to manage tensions between their preferences for sexual partners, the public stigma attached to that preference, and their relationships to a world divided into straight and gay. This division of the world can extend into their relations to work and career, their commitment to religion, their attachments to their parents and siblings, their activity in the political and social life of the community, their desires for love, intimacy, and friendship, their future as possible parents, and the ways in which they spend their leisure time. What they choose to do in any of these arenas of life, arenas of choice shared by all heterosexuals as well, interacts with the choices they will make about how to manage their sexual lives. What a person does sexually depends on what he or she wants to do with the rest of life. For instance, someone with a strong homosexual preference who wants to be President of the United States or president of General Motors might well marry and have children and stay in the "closet" in order to achieve this occupational ambition. Similarly, a heterosexual man will conceal his extramarital sex life to achieve the same set of goals.

Other social interests interact powerfully with a homosexual object preference; out of this interaction emerges specific homosexual life styles. These life styles involve a wide range of disclosures. For some people the fear, shame, or possible consequences of being known as a homosexual may keep them entirely "in the closet," that is, sexually inactive. Guilt, fear that a parent might find out, having a job as teacher of the young, are all reasons why some people conceal a preferred sexual activity.

Some men emerge from the closet only momentarily, to have sex with other men in impersonal circumstances. (This pattern has never been true of women.) Such men only appear in gay baths, public toilets, bus stops, and parks to engage in brief, anonymous encounters. Some of these men might like to have more to do with their sexual partners, but out of fear remain silent, even when approached. Such casual, impersonal sex is not always motivated by fear or shame; in some cases a man may prefer it because it is uninvolved and uninvolving. There are heterosexual men who go to female prostitutes because they do not want the responsibility or emotional contact required in sexual relationships. Further, such men may have little in common socially with their momentary partners, and do not see their common homosexuality as a significant basis on which to build a more complex or longer relationship.

Many homosexuals "come out" in some fashion, that is, their homosexuality is known to a number of other people: their parents, their friends, some people at work, some people in the gay subculture. Critical to being "out" is who knows, as well as the level of participation in the traditional gay subculture. In many cases only some of the people at work may know; one parent might know rather than another. At the same time the person may be living with a lover, seeing gay or lesbian friends, and participating regularly in a largely homosexual social world. Most homosexuals move back and forth between concealment and openness — it is this combination, this balancing act, that is the essence of being "out" rather than "open."

The tension between a concealed identity in some worlds and an open identity in others can be difficult to endure. One solution of many homosexuals is slowly to detach themselves from all but a very few emotional and social contacts in the straight world. Their homosexuality has become sufficiently important to them to become an identity, a way of describing themselves and a way of making sense of the world around them. Because becoming homosexual is so often filled with trials and difficulties, being homosexual becomes a central way of labeling oneself and giving meaning to life. This is not a necessary transition; many people of different sexual persuasions and interests never organize much of their lives around their sexuality (or around their politics or their jobs, for that matter). Because of its disvalued status, affirmation of homosexuality (or disclaiming it) becomes a more significant act than the same would be for a heterosexual, with significant consequences for a life style.

It is at this point that the gay subculture can become extremely important, since it can supply the cultural materials for a homosexual identity. It provides places for people to meet, to find lovers and sexual partners, to talk about themselves openly, to have fun and spend leisure time. The problem with that subculture is that its members are there for very different individual reasons, and they may have very little in common other than sex-object choices. Because people are "out" in various ways, there are people in gay bars looking for a one-night stand; some looking for a new lover; others looking for conversation; still others looking for friends or companions. All of these things can be found, but it requires a lot of sorting out. In the male gay bar you can always at least have sex; in the female gay bar priorities are placed on emotion and attachment as precursors of sexuality.

The public gay culture is often limited in its social and emotional diversity; however, an emotionally serious and satisfying private gay world exists offstage. It is in this private world that homosexuals have lovers, set up households, choose friends, travel together, and build a world of common interests. For males this world may be more unstable than the private worlds of heterosexual or female homosexual couples, but it is likely to be as satisfying as most alternative life styles in society.

The problem of this life style is still the problem of being "out" — open here, concealed there. The problem exists within a person, wanting to share what is important to them with others (parents, straight friends, casual acquaintances), and within the gay subculture itself, since it often does not contain all of the people or interests someone may want to know or have. Like a circle of heterosexuals in a suburban neighborhood, the gay subculture has its limits, and many people have to go outside of it for work and pleasure and politics and leisure.

They also have to deal with the heterosexual majority. Many heterosexuals would argue that there is no big problem: why don't they just do things with their heterosexual friends and not bring up their sexual preferences; after all, heterosexuals do not publicize their preferences. However, this is not so. Members of the heterosexual majority *are* constantly affirming their heterosexuality in a multitude of ways — men and women gossip about sex, they tell jokes, they talk about their children, they sexually admire actors and actresses and passersby on the street. There is a volume of casual sex talk rarely noticed by heterosexuals that affirms their sexual preferences. For many homosexuals their preference is very important (it is an identity), but it has to be concealed.

Some homosexuals solve this problem by moving into the gay subculture entirely. They get jobs in and around gay institutions — the bar, the bath, the gay movie house, the gay boutique. They cut as best they can their ties with the majority of the straight world and its work institutions. By moving into the gay subculture, they become the carriers of that subculture, they become "open" homosexuals but in a very special way. Their openness depends upon committing most of their lives solely to a gay milieu.

A variant of this pattern is opening a business or playing an occupational role where society expects a homosexual — the hairdresser, the interior decorator, the antique shop owner, the dress designer (primarily service occupations to women). These are roles where someone can be openly homosexual, but open in a stereotypical way that requires effeminization, "camping" for a straight audience. Even heterosexual members of these occupations may develop what they think are homosexual mannerisms because of the demands of the audience to which they cater. The traditional gay subculture or traditional gay service occupations allow people to express their homosexuality, but in ways that cut them off from social and emotional contacts outside the gay culture, and which can make the sexual side of their lives dominant.

Since the middle 1960s alternative forms of openness have been created by other homosexuals. It has been such people with commitments to the dominant institutions of society (work, politics, church, family) who have sought to change the homophobic biases of these institutions and the heterosexist majority who inhabit them. For these homosexuals, the homosexual identity is an important way to shape their relationships to others, and the ability to express love and caring for people of the same sex is a positive aspect of that identity.

Openness means keeping a job in the institutions dominated by heterosexuals, talking about one's own sexual preferences when other people are talking about theirs, disclosing that preference to parents and continuing to see them, keeping heterosexual friends and educating them, working in politics for gay purposes as well as for general political goals, and retaining a religious commitment if wanted.

In some cases this requires confrontation (the anti-homosexual joke, the problem of bias), in some cases political action (working for anti-discrimination laws or reform of laws on homosexuality), and in some cases counseling or education (for people in trouble, or for heterosexuals who want to understand more about homosexuality).

This form of openness is quite different in its goals and purposes than being "out" in the traditional gay community; it involves continued contact with the sexual majority in society, it focuses on gay pride, and it affirms homosexuality as a positive sexual preference in the society. The goals of gay activists are similar to the goals of activists of other minorities in society—to achieve equality in all aspects of life. In achieving that goal they may create a situation in which sex-object preferences cease to be a significant label of discrimination in society. As sex-partner choice becomes more a casual matter, so it will become less a problem of identity and ideology.

Such openness is not achieved cheaply, and many homosexuals who are open in this way have found that they have had to fight against discrimination in their professions. The consequences have probably been different, depending on what sector of the society they are confronting. It may be easier for psychologists than for medical doctors, and easier for medical doctors than for bankers. It may be easier for a Unitarian than for a Roman Catholic or a Southern Baptist. Different social locations will have different responses to openness; some will welcome it, others will resist. At the same time openness is not without its personal problems as well—often someone who chooses to be open has friends or lovers who are not open. Openness may have consequences for parents and others who may be injured. All of these factors must be considered in a decision to be open.

Homosexuals and the Law

Even though there have been extensive changes in the social position of homosexuals in U.S. society, particularly in some major urban centers, and in the extent of media coverage and general knowledge, campaigns to change the law or change the stigma attached to homosexuality have not been very successful. The effort to decriminalize homosexuality began in Illinois in 1961 when homosexual contacts between adults in private became noncriminal as part of a general revision of the criminal code. Since 1961 in four other states decriminalization has occurred on an *ad hoc* basis.

Even with this shift toward decriminalization in a few states, conventional police practices continue in other jurisdictions, and from some reports there is harassment of the homosexual in those states where the private act is not against the law. Changes in this section of the statute (acts in private) offer only the mildest form of reform, since the largest proportion of homosexual offenders are arrested in public or quasi-public situations in which they are looking for sexual partners (e.g., in a homosexual bar or meeting place) or as the result of a sexual contact with a slightly underage male. It is not uncommon in these cases for the police to use *agent provocateurs* to elicit a homosexual approach before the arrest is made, but the frequency of this practice varies in the same jurisdiction and from jurisdiction to jurisdiction.

The police response to homosexuality in any community is commonly confined nearly exclusively to male homosexuals, since the style of life of female homosexuals largely keeps them outside of the orbit of police activity. The female homosexual rarely gets involved in disputes in public; there are crimes of passion that have been linked to female homosexual relationships, but these are perhaps as rare as crimes of passion always are. Even in the female gay bars there is a sedateness and calm that is disturbed only by the presence of heterosexual males who find the lesbian a problem for their masculinity. Even when adolescent young women are attracted to older women, there is rarely an overt situation which would bring their preferences to the attention of the police. Women with a sexual preference for other women rarely fall afoul of the police, and when they do so it is largely in connection with other kinds of behavior that are defined as criminal.

The response of the criminal legal process to male homosexuality normally emerges from about five circumstances:

1. The police operate at the margins of the homosexual community and keep its more overt aspects invisible to the conventional community. This involves the policing of public toilets frequented by homosexuals, sporadic raids on homosexual bars, beaches, and parks, and the harassment of street hustling or "outrageous" behavior in public places.

2. Law-enforcement agencies use information from people arrested in the above circumstances to arrest others who might be implicated, and exploit household searches that reveal letters, photographs, and other materials that may implicate other homosexuals.

3. Anti-homosexual crusades can be set off by a sudden community discovery of homosexuals. Such crusades begin when relatively innocent communities discover the homosexual "menace," and a concerted effort is made to put the homosexual community under surveillance. These attempts can be community- or institution-wide (e.g., universities, government agencies, towns). Such homosexual hunts usually collapse when the extent of the behavior is discovered or when a child or relative of a major figure in the community is caught in the net.

4. Another source of police involvement with the homosexual community is through criminal offenses associated with homosexuality. There are two dimensions: first is preference for certain sexual partners among some homosexual males (that may, in part, be derived from the legal status of homosexuality); second is the vulnerability of the homosexual to criminals because of the social and legal status of homosexuality. Some male homosexuals have well-developed preferences for males who give the appearance of excessive masculinity, or young males who appear new to the homosexual marketplace, or for a different male in nearly every sexual encounter. Whether these particular preferences are rooted in the stigmatized status of the homosexual is unclear, since these same preferences (the desire for cosmetically erotic females, younger females, or for many different females) on the part of heterosexual males are generally only ambivalently disapproved, if at all.

There exist in the larger cities and in some smaller communities specific locations in which such males can be found either for affection or for pay. Many of these young men are recruited from delinquent or quasi-delinquent communities, and the homosexual can be victimized either through theft or blackmail by these young men. Other homosexuals who present themselves as heterosexual to the conventional world or who are heterosexually married are often driven to the use of these males or these locations in order to find sexual contacts. Such males are easily blackmailed by either their homosexual partners or by the police if they are arrested in the most marginally suspicious circumstances.

The legal status of homosexuality makes the homosexual vulnerable to victimization and makes a law-enforcement response to that victimization, even if well intended, extremely difficult. Homicides, robberies, and assaults that arise out of homosexual relationships are concealed or badly investigated because the victim is unable to feel trust in the police. If the homosexual has been involved in what is considered to be a sexual crime, he is unlikely to report being robbed during a criminal act. Further, there is no guarantee to the victim that there will not be further reprisals against him or his friends.

5. The least police activity results from public reports of specific criminal offenses which involve homosexual activity. While the policing of public manifestations of homosexuality may be elicited by complaints from well-placed moral entrepreneurs, reports of single homosexual offenses come mainly from parents charging that their children or young adolescents have had a homosexual contact with an adult (for example, the proverbial Boy Scout master; or they have been picked up by a homosexual while hitchhiking). These situations are quite different from paragraph 4 and involve the intersection of adults with younger people (see Chapter 16).

In a homosexual career there are periods when the homosexual is particularly vulnerable to the police. Young homosexual males can be arrested if they enter places of usual homosexual congregation, since they are vulnerable both as adolescents and as homosexuals. Since most homosexual congregating places are those that serve liquor, and there are only now emerging recreational locations for the younger homosexual, the bars serve as risky points of entry. These younger males are attractive to older males since they are new faces on the scene, but these relationships are dangerous since the young male may live at home, or setting up a cohabitation may result in legal trouble for both males.

Congruent with entry into public homosexual life styles is a period during which a large number of homosexual males affirm their new-found and released sexuality through large amounts of sexual activity. These males often embark on an endless search for new sexual partners in highly vulnerable locations (bars, baths, parks) with a low degree of discrimination about the characteristics of their partners or the situation in which they find themselves. Their naivete and their desire combine to put them at considerable risk. Most males pass through this phase, but some retain a strong commitment to sexual adventure, and these males often find themselves in legal or other trouble because of the places and ways in which they seek sexual activity. During periods of sexual monogamy many homosexual males are less vulnerable, but at the breakup of relationships there is sometimes either a burst of sexual activity or a search for another partner, which increases risk.

It is presently estimated that about three to four percent of adult males are largely or exclusively homosexual. If these males are having homosexual experiences on an average of two times per week, it is apparent that there are some two to three million homosexual acts committed per week in the United States. Clearly the criminal legal process intersects this activity only on the most sporadic basis, existing as a trap for the unwary, the foolish, the unlucky, and the uninitiated. Decriminalization will obviously remove a substantial number of potential sex offenders. If homosexual groups achieve their goals (nonstigma of homosexual preferences), there will surely be a reduction in the age of consent parallel to that for heterosexuality.

The removal of homosexuality as a contributing or significant factor in criminal statistics or involvement in the criminal legal process depends as much on destigmatizing the behavior as it does on decriminalization. When the stigma is removed (1) criminal offenses against homosexuals can be reported to the police, (2) men may have both families and homosexual outlets, and (3) homosexual meeting places will be more accessible and open. What impact this would have on the ways in which gay life styles are currently organized is unknown. To the degree that being gay is no longer stigmatized, the defensive character of the gay subculture may fade, as might the need for a distinct gay male or lesbian identity.

How Many Are There?

Until the Kinsey research it was not possible to make even a guesstimate about the numbers of people in U. S. society with either homosexual preferences or experiences. This lack of knowledge allowed the heterosexual majority to assume that homosexuality was a rare disease — no one they knew ever did it. On the other hand, homosexuals could entertain fantasies that behind every father wheeling a baby carriage lurked a potential homosexual.

Kinsey reported that of the men he had interviewed, thirty-seven percent of the total (including all educational levels) had had sex experience, including orgasm, with a person of the same sex. However, this figure included men who had such an experience at any time in their lives and it took only one experience to be included. There are at least two reasons to believe that even this rather modest version of homosexuality (once in a lifetime) was inflated. First, Kinsey had included in his total sample a considerable number of men who had not gone beyond the twelfth grade, had been imprisoned, and who came from poverty-stricken and disorganized sectors of the society, a number far greater than would have been included in any random sample.[2] There was therefore an upward bias in the homosexuality figure. Second, interviewed in the study were men from groups nearly entirely homosexual in composition.

If we exclude these cases (the homosexual subgroups and the men with no college experience), there is a major drop in the figures:

1. Thirty percent of the college men interviewed had ever had a homosexual contact with or without orgasm. This varies from the Kinsey definition, which required an orgasm — it is estimated that five out of the six men with a homosexual experience had an orgasm.

2. It is difficult to be accurate about this figure, but it appears that there were about 1300 men in the Kinsey report of 1948 with educations of twelve years or less. Somewhere between 900 and 1000 of these cases had had some prison experience. An examination of a later study of the Institute for Sex Research, published in *Sex Offenders* (1965), shows that twenty-six percent of men in the control group in that study (men with no prison experience and less than college educations) had had a homosexual experience by age twenty, compared to fifty percent of the men with prison experience (not as sex offenders) having had homosexual experiences outside of prison.

2. Sixteen percent had their homosexual experience only between puberty and age sixteen.

3. Nine percent had homosexual experience between puberty and age sixteen, and/or between ages sixteen and eighteen.

4. Six percent had extensive homosexual experience after age twenty (regardless of what had happened earlier).

5. Of the six percent, three percent had been exclusively homosexual, and three percent had had a mixture of both homosexual and heterosexual experiences.

These figures are from a college-attending population of 2900 men under the age of thirty, which restricts our knowledge about later moves into homosexuality. But it does provide a more adequate representation of the data by removing those cases where there is a known bias. We can estimate that there are probably something like three to four percent of the adult male population with exclusively homosexual preferences. This is probably the best estimate we are going to have for a long time. This is *not* anywhere near an estimate such as one in ten or one in six, but it is a large absolute number of people.

In contrast to the figures for men, the Kinsey data on women was never as contaminated by biased groups. The comparable figures for women suggest that about two percent of women had had homosexual experience and orgasm by age twelve, with the proportion having homosexual experience increasing to about ten percent and staying at that level by age twenty, and the proportion having orgasm in homosexual experience rising to six to eight percent and stabilizing about there by age twenty. The rates are higher for women who remain single.

This data suggests about two to three percent of the female population who may be exclusively homosexual and a similar percentage with mixed experience. Of the women in the sample who had had homosexual contact, half had it for one year or less and a quarter for two to three years, suggesting that for many women homosexual experience was often probably transient in frequency and duration, but it was not concentrated in adolescence. Homosexual experimentation, like most other forms of sexual experimentation, appears to occur later in the life cycle for women than it does for men.

The problem of numbers has a certain interest, both from a scientific and from an ideological point of view. However, scientific concern must be tempered by an awareness that the numbers we observe are an outcome of the peculiar conditions of sexual learning and development in U. S. culture, and not some natural "rate" from which there are deviations or corrections. The number of people with homosexual preferences or experience could rise and fall by a large amount and not affect the other processes of the society at all.

As has been noted, the proportion of the population who are homosexual cannot be viewed as evidence for the "breakdown" of the family structure, because there is no unequivocal evidence that certain kinds of families produce sons and daughters with such preferences. Further it must be noted that heterosexuals produce the majority of homosexuals in society, since (particularly among males) there tend to be very few exclusive homosexuals with large numbers of children. Further, what evidence we have about lesbian mothers does not demonstrate that their children become homosexual in any greater numbers than children of non-lesbian

mothers (even if they all did, it would make a miniscule contribution to the homosexual population).

The ideological problem of number is that the more people of a certain kind
there are in society, the easier it is to argue that they are normal or virtuous or necessary. It is far easier for a majority to persecute a tiny minority than a larger minority, all other things being equal. However, the status of the homosexual in society
should not depend on numerical questions as opposed to questions of equity.

Directions of Change

The claim of homosexuality to be just another minority in the United States is still
not a strong one, but it is real. The efforts of gay activists, increasing acceptance in
the media as a form of entertainment or topic of information, increases in openness
between people with sexual commitments who share the same social, psychological, economic, political, and religious spaces, are all lowering the barrier between
the two worlds, merging the straight and the gay, at least at the edges. The results
are hard to imagine, but one sensitive observer has reported on the change:

"The gay world is succumbing to its own revolution. Once invisible, it is now
being publicly examined as a curiosity. But the more it shows itself, the less reason
it has to exist, because it was the creation of a people in hiding, a people who had
to develop a private language and secret rituals and obscure places to survive. The
laws haven't changed yet, but open gays are slowly being accepted into the life of
the city.

"The charm of the gay world is fast becoming nostalgia. The characters who
people it are yielding to a variety of forces. The drag queen and the diesel dyke are
being transformed by women's liberation and its challenge to gender roles. The
pathetic, lonely caricature called the auntie, who ages in a panic over each new
wrinkle in his sexual desirability, is giving way to new respect for the sexuality of
old people and new validation of the single life-style. The dizzy faggot is being
challenged by the seriousness of gay liberation itself. The superstud is waiting for
men's liberation, which is taking its own sweet time about abandoning male privi-
lege. Hiding together in the confines of the gay world, these people convinced each
other that they were not "queer," but "special," which served as compensation for
having been excluded from the rest of the human race. If they were special, it is
because they dared to manifest a part of themselves that most people suppress.
Some, perhaps most, remain hidden in their daily lives, but as a group we are becoming visible. The gay world has begun to overcome both its fear of exposure and
its fear of equality. Homosexuals remain different, but less mysterious to the public
and less illicit to themselves.

"Like the Old South, the charming myth of the gay world is being swept into
history by the truth. Gay liberation had no Gettysburg, but it did stir up a couple of
nifty riots back when rioting was the thing to do, and it did present America with an
idea: *Being "normal" is no more natural than being "queer." All of us studied to be
what we are* [emphasis added]. Call it cooptation, call it victory. The gay world's
fragile construct of make-believe, its sexual exploits, and its sociological charm are
rightfully and inevitably giving way to the same facts of life everyone else lives

with. There will still be places for gay people to go to meet each other, but more and more, the cruising, the dancing, the shopping and eating out and partying, and even the sex, will happen with straight people present. We will have to endure the awkwardness of parties where ideological attempts to mix the gay and straight worlds frequently result in separate camps on different sides of the living room and perplexed hosts relaying messages of goodwill back and forth. We will have to do without our protective bubble. Although I will mourn its passing, it has to go.

"As a member of the movement generation, I was seduced into a ghettoized freedom in front of straight visitors, which is still not acceptable everywhere I go, not for example, in front of a crowd of ball-scratching construction workers. It was hard to maintain a sense of proportion on Christopher Street, hard to make the transition to the harsher realities of Staten Island or Herald Square, where I was in the minority as usual, often the minority of one. I ended the paranoia by moving uptown, where the traffic is a little more mixed and a lot less self-conscious.

"For the time being, there remains a large group who still believe themselves inferior to straights, and to balance it a small group who consider themselves superior. But most of us fall somewhere in between and simply consider ourselves people. And so it remains before us to make ourselves real. From conservatives we still face some open hostility, but it is beginning to give way to bored tolerance. We should be able to maintain at least the liberal acceptance we have won, even if it is still socially uncomfortable. If repression does not force blacks back to the ghetto and women back to the kitchen, it probably will not force gays back into the closet.

"For those of us who have unscrewed our doors from their hinges, there is no course but to go forward, continuing to sacrifice our privacy in favor of honesty, and to insist in public on our right to freedom of sexual choice. Whether the straight world abandons its marital family structure or resuscitates it, there ought to be enough room for homosexuals to lead their lives openly among the rest. But it means changes for both worlds. Like the gay world, the straight world is defined by whom it excludes, and the borders are blurring already. As the gay world dies, paying the price of its own honesty, the straight world, as the single framework admitted by society, must die as well, and acknowledge the validity of alternate ways of love. Gays may not be understood or loved in spite of themselves, but with enough exposure, they should soon cease to be treated as the pernicious threat to the community they were once thought to be. The memory of the gay world will be absorbed into the history of Western culture, probably with legends more glittering than the actual facts.

"As for me, I'm moving on to plain reality. If we have to wake up from our nightmares, we have to wake up from our dreams as well."[3]

3. Arnie Kantrowitz, "A Gay Struggles with the New Acceptance," *The Village Voice*, November 17, 1975, pp. 39–40.

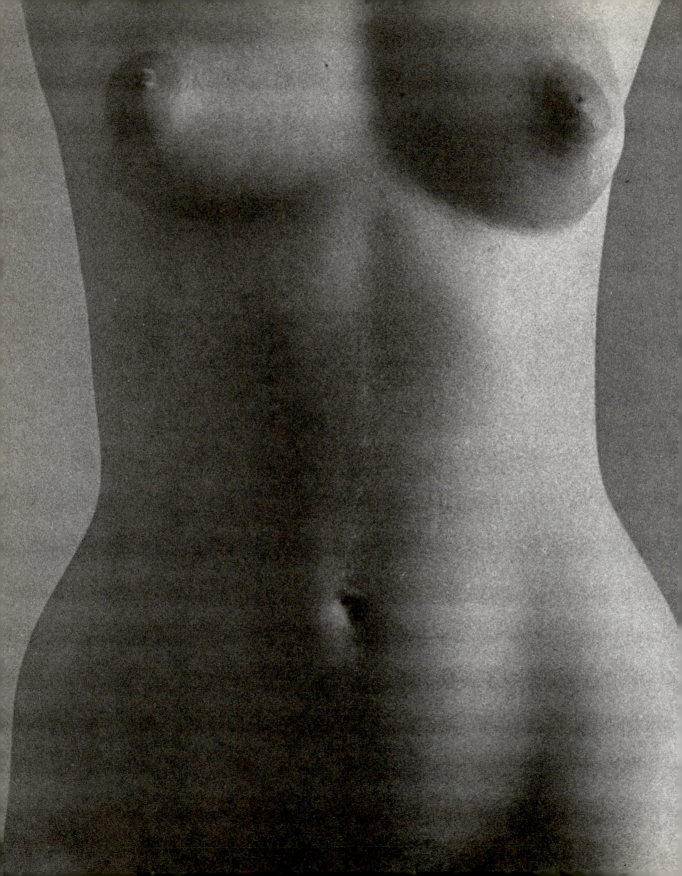

BISEXUALITY

*Well, it's not quite the same as six of one
and a half dozen of the other.*

Anonymous

PEOPLE WHO HAVE SEXUAL PARTNERS OF THE SAME AND OPPOSITE GENDER during their lives seem to represent a serious intellectual and scientific problem for those trying to understand human sexual conduct. In part this problem arises because one of the main axes along which we allocate people sexually is the gender of their sex-object choices. Men interested in men, and women interested in women are called homosexual; women interested in men, and men interested in women are called heterosexual; women and men interested in both sexes are usually called bisexual or ambisexual. This would be adequate if the only important factor in the kind of sexuality that people have were the gender of the sex object.

However, people have different ways of being sexual, even if they have sex only with men or only with women; different relations require different scripts. Those who have sex with both women and men rarely simply do (or feel) the same things with both women and men. Using the same script and revising it only by substituting one gender for the other is rarely done. There are many scripts associated with having sex with both men and women, scripts that are quite variable in all their elements. The patterns often observed are the following:

1. Young people have not yet committed themselves to a fixed sex-object preference and do some experimenting with both.
2. People use various rescripting devices to have sex with one gender when their regular preference is the opposite one.
3. People use two separate scripts, with an ambivalent attachment to either men or women. Sometimes these people are moving from one preferred attachment to another.
4. People by virtue of context or of individual history do not care about the source of stimulation (in part a form of reducing the importance of gender elements in the sexual script).
5. People have a positive preference for both men and women, sometimes at the same time, more often sequentially, a preference that can be mediated by strong emotional attachment.

The fact that people can have sex with both genders at various points in the life cycle, under various conditions, at the same time or in some sequence not only suggests the possible variety in sexuality, but also illuminates some of the assumptions of research into sexuality. Havelock Ellis thought that homosexuality was congenital, that is, acquired not through learning but through an innate predisposition. The existence of bisexual people is a problem for those holding this view. If homosexuality is innate, then to make the theory consistent heterosexuality should be innate, and the bisexual must be explained as something other than a mixture of homosexual and heterosexual preferences.

Ellis handled this problem largely by shifting his ground toward the Freudian position: the infantile sexual potential is not gender-specific; that is, under different learning conditions the sexual energies of the child can be attached to either a male or female sexual object. However, at no point did either Freud or Ellis entirely give up a constitutional or predispositional view of homosexuality. They both held to the possibility that some people with partial or complete homosexual commitments acquired them through biological pathways.

From Freud's point of view, homosexuality was a perversion, a term which he felt carried no moral onus, but rather described homosexuality as a deviation from the normal biological path of human development, which was to become heterosexual as an adult. Ellis, on the other hand, saw homosexuality as an abnormality or an anomaly (words which he also believed carried no moral content), as a condition that was statistically rare, but within the range of normal species variation. Both Ellis and Freud were seeking to link sex acts seen in the nineteenth century as immoral and criminal to the range of sexuality then acceptable. Freud focused on the role of sex in the developmental process and on the circumstances of learning about sex as people grew up; Ellis argued that the normal variation of genetic constitution was broad enough to include homosexuality and heterosexuality.

Kinsey also attempted to link homosexuality and heterosexuality by creating a continuum of sexual activity from one to the other. One only needed to count up the sexual acts with each gender in some period of time, divide by their total, and multiply by 100 to get the percentage of each. This percentage could then be located on a continuum from 1 to 100. What Kinsey was doing was political as well as scientific. He, like Ellis and Freud, was making the world safe for sexuality. By creating a link between homosexuality and heterosexuality he could reduce the differences and change public attitudes. Such an attempt required a theoretical basis, and Kinsey found it by both agreeing and disagreeing with various ideas set forth by Freud and Ellis. For example, he agreed with Freud that sexuality emerged through a learning process (disagreeing with the early Ellis position on congenital factors), but he agreed with Ellis that homosexuality (and hence bisexuality) was part of the normal responses of the organism (disagreeing with Freud that it was a perversion of normal development).

Kinsey was committed to the notion that sex is primarily physiological and that it is therefore measurable by adding up orgasms (later, after finding that women and many male homosexuals did not always have orgasm, he substituted sexual contacts). He was prepared to carry this position to its logical conclusion by arguing that there were no homosexual people (no homosexual identity, personality, or self-conception), only homosexual acts, and that there were no heterosexual people, only heterosexual acts. The act (sometimes the orgasm) exhausted the reality of the conduct. Bisexuality was then a statistical combination of the heterosexual and homosexual acts committed by the same person. Once the orgasms and/or acts with men and women had been counted up and divided, the person could be located on a scale from 0 to 6, a continuum from people who had histories of only homosexual acts (6) to people with only heterosexual acts (0). (See Figure 1.)

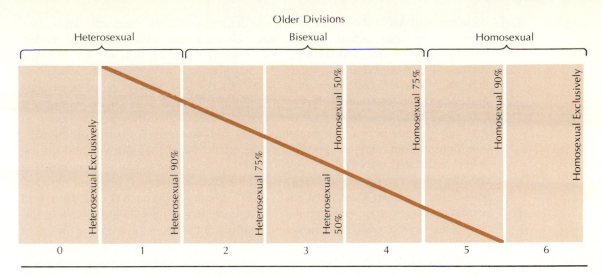

Older Divisions

Heterosexual   Bisexual   Homosexual

Heterosexual Exclusively

Heterosexual 90%

Heterosexual 75%

Heterosexual 50%

Homosexual 50%

Homosexual 75%

Homosexual 90%

Homosexual Exclusively

0   1   2   3   4   5   6

Figure 1   Kinsey Heterosexual-Homosexual Continuum.

Kinsey's continuum, however, merely stretches out the homosexual-bisexual-heterosexual model into seven instead of three groups. The narrowness (even futility) of trying to sum up human sexual conduct through counting physiological events is illustrated by the very existence of bisexuality. The physiological events are no more (and often less) important as indicators of what people are experiencing than the statements people make about what they feel or think. The biological prejudices of Kinsey led him to decide that physiological events both determine and are more important than the felt experiences of individuals.

Some limitations of orgasm or act counting to create ratios can be suggested in the following ways (in each case assume that the same period of time is involved):

1. Comparing different amounts of activity: If a person has sex ninety times with a woman and ninety times with a man, is it the same as a person who has sex nine times with a woman and nine times with a man?

2. Comparing different mixtures of people and activities: What if a person has sex twenty times each with five different women and five times each with twenty different men?

3. Comparing motivation with acts: What if a person has sex with ninety men one time each for money and ninety times with one woman for love?

4. Comparing fantasies with sex acts: What if someone masturbates to orgasm fifty times thinking of one woman and has sex with five men each ten times?

5. Thinking about one thing and doing another: What if a person has sex twenty times with twenty people and thinks of the opposite sex half the time?

6. Sex acts with and without orgasm: What if a person has sex twenty times with twenty people and has orgasm half the time, and another person has sex twenty times with twenty people and has no orgasms?

Depending on how you count, it may all look like bisexuality. But what results is adding up apples and oranges, mangos, cucumbers, carrots, and artichokes. Furthermore, the theory is faulty, in two ways: First, it assumes that sexuality is merely the capacity to respond to stimuli, without recognizing the scripted nature of the sexual experience. What is needed is to examine the conditions under which certain kinds of people become eligible as sex objects. Second, we do not experience ourselves or the world around us as a continuum, but rather as a series of discrete categories. People do label their behavior and themselves; they do not count up acts, but call themselves gay, straight, or bisexual, and the world around them offers them opportunities for sex depending on the label they present and on the scripts associated with it. People who think of themselves as gay may approach a specific sex act in one way; those who think of themselves as bisexual may approach the same act in another; male prostitutes may approach it in a third; and people at an orgy may approach it in still a fourth way. These differences in scripting for the same act will determine the meaning of the act in the personal history of the individual.

We can look at the Kinsey data and ask ourselves how many people have sex with both women and men in the same five years. (*See box.*) Remember, however, that the answer is a number which locates only the most obvious aspects of the issue; indeed, it may suggest to us a further series of questions, not solutions. The question that needs to be asked is what kinds of learning histories and contexts offer scripts to people at various moments in the life cycle which make sex with both genders possible. In some cases, the person must operate with quite different scripts. In others, only a single script element may need to be changed to legitimate what happens sexually and how the person feels about it afterwards.

Scripts in Formation: Adolescent Sexual Experimentation

The largest number of people with homosexual experience in the Kinsey studies acquired that experience in early and middle adolescence. This is true for more young men than young women. In a society that offers little guidance to young people during this period of transition, it is likely that even though the general pattern is one of increasing heterosexual experimentation, there can be occasion for some (or much) parallel homosexual activity. It is thus possible for young people of the same sex to engage in mutual masturbation, oral-genital sex, or merely rubbing bodies together, with varying degrees of affection and caring, while at the same time they are beginning to associate with members of the opposite sex and to experiment sexually with them. For most young people, early sexual experimentation is linked to the motivational content of adolescence rather than to the more complete and fixed sexual commitments of adults.

A mixed pattern of sexual commitment is vastly reduced as young people are required to choose (or drift into) a commitment to one pattern or another. Many young people in adolescence may make a substantial commitment to affectional and sexual life with someone of their own sex, and then find that the object of their affection has fallen in love with someone of the opposite sex and begun to move toward a heterosexual pattern. For a young person moving toward a homosexual

Kinsey Data on Bisexuality

In order correctly to interpret the Kinsey figures we must note the large differences between men and women in the population who did nothing sexual (at least nothing measurable at the threshold Kinsey was interested in) in any given year. There were, among the single, three to four times as many women as men in this category. If these cases are removed and only single people who were actively sexual are examined, the proportions of women and men who were exclusively heterosexual at various ages are as shown in Table 1. The increase with age in the proportion with homosexual experience is largely a function of heterosexual men moving into marriage, leaving a residual number who had homosexual preferences.

Between ages fifteen and twenty-five, seventy-five to eighty-five percent of men and eighty to ninety percent of women were exclusively heterosexual. Both those with mixed sex-object preferences and those with exclusive preferences then must be drawn from the remainder. If Kinsey was correct that about two percent of women and four percent of men are exclusively homosexual, then there are about fifteen percent of men and ten percent of women with mixed histories. It is from this ten to fifteen percent that we can draw those people who are involved in the various types of mixed sex-object preferences. These numbers express the limits on how many people may be drawn from the various age, sex, and marital status groups (see Table 2).

Table 1

Age	M	F
15	76%	85%
20	84	87
25	78	84
30	68	79

Table 2   Heterosexual-Homosexual Ratings for Males and Females by Marital Status and Age (Kinsey, 1948; 1953).

Scale Category:		Age	0 M	0 F	1 M	1 F	2 M	2 F	3 M	3 F	4 M	4 F	5 M	5 F	6 M	6 F	Not Sexually Active M	Not Sexually Active F
									Single										
(2856)	5714	15	59	34	3	2	3	1	3	1	3	0	1	0	6	2	22	60
2306	3746	20	81	72	6	5	3	2	1	1	2	1	2	1	2	1	3	17
687	1315	25	76	72	6	4	2	3	1	1	3	3	4	1	5	2	3	14
179	622	30	65	67	4	5	.6	4	.6	2	3	3	10	2	13	2	4	15
									Married										
330	1331	25	91	90	5	6	2	1	1	0	2	0	.3	0	.3	0	0	2
386	1215	30	90	90	7	6	1	2	.8	0	.8	0	.5	0	.5	0	0	1
300	908	35	90	89	6	7	3	2	.7	0	.7	0	0	0	0	0	0	1
205	569	40	89	89	5	6	3	2	2	0	1	0	0	0	0	0	0	1

People are assigned to various categories based on (a) overt sexual contact accompanied by orgasm, (b) overt sexual contact not accompanied by orgasm, (c) masturbation accompanied by orgasm, (d) dreams with and without orgasm, and (e) fantasy alone. The first factors are most likely to have been weighted more heavily in the assigners' decisions than the later ones. The later ones were used if there were no overt or orgasmic experiences.

commitment, the loss of this adolescent lover is often deeply shocking because it may have involved overt sexuality for both of them and deep affection on the part of at least one of them. Another pattern also occurs, though less frequently: a heterosexual pair may break apart because of the increasing homosexual commitment of one member of the pair.

Very few adolescents resolve such conflicts by making a strong commitment to both homosexuality and heterosexuality, and the capacity of these few to sustain a dual commitment is weakened by increasing societal emphasis on heterosocial or heterosexual commitment during later adolescence and young adulthood. Also, there is probably some difference in scripting for the heterosexual and the homosexual commitments—one or the other can come first in time, be more important emotionally, be defined as more (or less) socially acceptable, or be largely a physical interest in contrast to an emotional one.

It is not entirely clear to what degree such experiences during adolescence with persons of both sexes might be integrated into a bisexual script later in life. It is also not known how many of the young people involved in adolescent homosexuality and heterosexuality at the same time would continue a bisexual or a major or exclusive homosexual commitment if a homosexual life style were viewed as acceptable as the heterosexual. At present, the mixed or homosexual patterns are not equally competitive with the heterosexual pattern during adolescence.

Separate Scripts: Hustling

Among adolescent and young adult delinquent and military groups, and among young men detached from family life, there are some who have sex with homosexual men for favors. Such favors can involve money, housing, food, drink, or any other things which socially unattached young men often need. At no point before, during, or after the sexual act do these young men define themselves as homosexual or as experiencing or performing a homosexual act. Even though they become erect and ejaculate (following all the events of the sexual response cycle), they do not consider that they are responding to a homosexual stimulus.

There are a number of revisions of script elements that allow them to define their experience in this way. The first is that the act may occur only a few times, with different men and for money—the activity is "playing the queers," not homosexuality. Even when they are involved over a longer period with a number of events or people, other script changes are possible. Commonly such young men refuse to allow hugging or kissing or anything sexual above the waist. As long as the partner's head is below the belly button and contact is on the penis, it is the other person who is *being* homosexual. Without affection (such as there might be in heterosexual activity) and reciprocity (the young man is not active) there is no reason to define the self as homosexual. The money, the genital focus, the lack of affection, and the physical inactivity are all components which offer a different script for the act. Further, it is possible for the young man to think about his girl friend or other women while the act is going on—some do, in fact, report that they cannot become aroused unless they have another scenario in their heads.

The person having sex with such a young man is often running a grave physi-

The Midnight Cowboy Joe Buck (Jon Voight) and his instructor in the arts of Times Square hustling, Ratso Rizzo (Dustin Hoffman) suffer in the cold when customers are scarce.

cal risk since not all young men have equal scripting skills. Some of them, particularly those with little experience, may find it very difficult to manage the experience in these limited terms, and they may feel the need to beat up or rob the homosexual in order to bolster their belief in their masculinity and heterosexuality. In some cases the customer makes a mistake by trying for more than a purely genital relationship and seeking a more affectional contact. This sometimes provokes a violent reaction on the part of the young man, who has defined the situation more narrowly.

These reactions suggest a basic theme in such encounters. The young man is able to revise the script because he believes that homosexual men are or have the attributes of women. They are defined as weak, inferior, and submissive. If a person is active in certain sexual acts (fellatio), or passive in others (the object of anal intercourse), or responds to the sexual acts that are being performed, he violates the masculine image. To do these things indicates that a person is weak and therefore homosexual. The boundary being defended is the boundary between brave, strong, violent men and cowardly, passive, weak men, the boundary between heterosexual men and homosexual men, and ultimately the boundary between men and women. Symbolic manipulations are required for *why* the sex goes forward, *who* the other person is defined to be, and *what* the permitted sex acts are.

There are probably many young men who have had this kind of homosexual experience one or two times in their lives. Some of them may do it more frequently and earn the label "male prostitute." Such young men seek the bright lights of the major cities (Times Square in New York, for example), or hang around the hotels of small cities and towns offering their services to homosexual men. They often act and look conventionally masculine, perhaps even tough and delinquent, for this version of "machismo" has a certain appeal to some homosexual clients (who have also been taken in by the imagery of masculinity). Such young men are often called "trade," and the young men with the roughest exteriors are called "butch," while those who appear likely to beat clients are called "rough trade."

There is a saying in the homosexual community that "this year's trade is next year's competition"—meaning that the "heterosexual" young man you pay this year will want to pay someone else next year. What this suggests is that the script breaks down, that the continued contact with homosexual acts and experiences is seductive, and that young men who begin for money will eventually continue for pleasure. Given the transitory nature of the prostitute role, however, it is unlikely that this happens to many young men. What may contribute to this impression is that some of these young men have homosexual preferences but conceal their homosexuality because clients want "real" heterosexuals as well as masculine-appearing young men. As these young men move into more open homosexual commitments, they may produce the impression of a regular movement of young men from heterosexual to homosexual life styles.

Substitutive Scripts: Effects of Sex Segregation

Groups of healthy and active people of one sex may sometimes be effectively iso-lated from people of the opposite sex. Such groups may contain a mix of people with histories of homosexual and heterosexual interests. When the isolation in-volves a great deal of effort and commitment (an army in combat), a relatively brief separation (a submarine cruise or an expedition to a mountain), or starvation and isolation (a concentration camp, a forced labor camp, or a POW camp), very little sexual activity occurs. However, in peacetime armies, in one-sex schools, or in pri-sons, where little else goes on, sexual segregation can result in both short- and long-term homosexual experimentation.

MEN AND WOMEN IN PRISON

The prison situation contains the common forms of script manipulation. Homosex-ual activity occurs fairly often in some prisons and less often in others. It does not happen to everyone, even in loosely administered institutions where homosexual subcultures have existed over a number of years. Even among long-term felons only about half have had overt homosexual experience, and this experience tends to be sporadic rather than continuous. Interviews with 700 prisoners by members of the Institute for Sex Research showed that, taking all sources of sexual activity into ac-count, very few of the men had levels of sexual activity that reached even ten per-cent of what they experienced outside prison.

The prison is an antisexual environment, both for those who have a rigid prior commitment to heterosexuality (or what we might call limited rescripting abilities) and for those who have homosexual histories. Sex occurs, but it is often without choice and in degrading and violent circumstances. The prison also rarely contains stimulus materials that can be used to provoke sexual scripts, particularly for men who do not have strong symbolic sexual commitments.

The problem is not one of orgasms or sex acts, but rather of the meanings of the sex acts. Many heterosexual male prisoners view the sexual world very much as do male prostitutes. That is, the homosexual act in prison is defined as being heterosexual for one person and homosexual for the other. One man is defined as masculine, strong, powerful, and controlling, while the other is feminine, weak, subordinate, and controlled. The stronger inserts his penis into the weaker—the act of penetration parallels the act with women, and assures a symbolic continuity with experiences in the world outside the prison.

These parallels begin in reform schools and other institutions for young men in which the stronger and more powerful induce or threaten the physically weaker or more feminine appearing into sexual activity as the "female" partner. Once this process of seduction or coercion has occurred, the "female" partner can go from relationship to relationship with men (and from institution to institution) having been categorized and defined as a "punk" or "sissy" by the other men in the institution. In some cases men with homosexual preferences find themselves in this role in prison and are coerced into sex by aggressive heterosexual males.

Most male homosexual experience in prison does not involve affection. It is usually motivated by aggression, violence, and control, and is often less important in terms of the ejaculation it produces than the way it enhances the dominant partner's masculinity. The ability to dominate and control, to make someone else do what you want is extremely important in male status ranking. Homosexuality is one of the few ways to achieve status in prison. Many men in prison are aggressive and assertive outside, but in prison their capacity to be aggressive or assertive is highly restricted. The guards, walls, guns, and marching, working, eating, and showering to the ringing of bells deny them the freedom to affirm their masculinity in the ways they are used to: with sex, aggression, and assertion. By including sex in their domination of other men (becoming "wolves" or "jockers"), they give a different meaning to homosexual acts and make them serve the same purposes as heterosexuality.

The men who are coerced have a very different experience. Some of them, because they are fearful and physically weak, drift into a transitory homosexual adaptation for the sake of protection by their lovers from other aggressive men. Men with heterosexual or homosexual preferences may be forced to comply in order to protect themselves from rape. Such men often suffer the same degradation as women who are raped: because they are unable to protect themselves sexually, prison officials see them as weaklings, as not "manly" enough to protect themselves. Having the attitude that masculinity requires a capacity for physical violence, prison officials and guards do not do much to safeguard the peaceful, weak, and unprotected.

Affectionate relationships are possible in male prisons, but they are not as frequent as in the outside community. The submissive member of the pair may develop an emotional commitment to the dominant one, but this pattern is often not reciprocated. Emotional misunderstandings can occur when one man with casual emotional standards has had sex with someone who wants love, and violence can occur when the dominant male changes sexual partners. In long-term prisons, the release of a man who has developed a long-term relationship with another can result in a period of emotional crisis.

Women also respond to prison life by having sex with each other, but where men model themselves on the heterosexual couple, the women often recreate the family dimensions of heterosexuality. In adolescent institutions, this may mean recreating the extended family. Where the dominant, sex-initiating men are called jocks and wolves and their submissive partners are called punks and sissies, the female parallels are "poppas" and "mamas." In adolescent institutions, there are even brothers and sisters, aunts and uncles, imitating the traditional kinship patterns of the family.

Prison homosexuality among women appears to be slightly less common than it is among men, but it does tend to involve much higher levels of emotional commitment. Since women's prisons contain women with extensive criminal histories as well as women who have committed serious offenses but who lack a prior criminal career, prior sexual histories are mixed. Getting an affair started may take a long courtship, both because this is what most women expect and because they lack practice in initiating sexual contact of any kind. If the prison population includes women who have had homosexual experience in the community, starting up an affair is easier. The amount of sex in these relationships is often minimal, out of preference or lack of privacy, but they may be quite emotional and long-term, which produces trauma when one partner is released.

Many people in prison are attempting to resist the institution and trying to maintain their identities, despite all the coercive forces around them. Their prison sexuality may thus be interpreted as a form of social and psychological resistance to a threatened destruction of identity. They fight the prison's efforts to drive individuals apart, by attempting to form sexual relationships. For men, this means exploiting and using other men, creating an informal status ladder which the institution says should not exist. For women, it means attempting to create a family where one does not exist. For both, sex becomes a vehicle of resistance to depersonalization.

Most prisoners involved in such contacts who did not have prior strong commitments to others of the same sex apparently do not continue their prison adaptation in the outside community. It is less clear whether the prison experience can move adolescents toward an easier acceptance of homosexual or prostitute roles in the outside world. Prisoners who are homosexual only in prison commonly do not seek to imitate their prison experience in the outside community; they return to the sexual life style scripts they chose outside. In these cases, the object choice is substituted into their existing model of sexual relationships. The script is kept as unchanged as possible while it is applied to a new situation, and is still available when they are freed.

MEN IN THE MILITARY

A situation relatively similar to prison, but one without some of its negative aspects, is the old-style military encampment with large numbers of isolated men. Here men are also without women of their own, but they do have some access to prostitutes. The homosexual activity which appears in these institutions is less aggressive and coercive than in prisons, usually occurring between predominantly heterosexual men and predominantly homosexual men. In this context, identities are less threatened, and the heterosexual men can legitimate their homosexual activities more easily. "I'm not queer," they may say, "there are just no women here, and I have a sex drive, so it's okay."

Soldiers in combat are less likely to seek homosexual partners—they are too concerned with other things, like staying alive—but there is one telling scene in James Jones' novel, *The Thin Red Line*, set in World War II. Two men have survived a day of combat in which people they cared about were killed all around them. It has probably been the worst day of their lives, and they reach out to each other sexually. They are lonely and terrified, and the homosexual act affirms their humanity.

Parallel Scripts: Heterosexuality Versus Homosexuality

It is not rare for people of both sexes to find themselves in a heterosexual marriage and to discover either in the process of that marriage or as a result of premarital experiences that their sex lives conflict with how they feel about themselves. This does not mean that they always define themselves as something which they would call "really homosexual," but rather that they feel uneasy, unhappy, or unable to deal with the demands of heterosexuality without some sort of homosexual attachment.

Most people in this situation are men. Such men, who often have families, may feel a strong need for some homosexual experience—it is often such men who have homosexual contacts away from home or in public rest rooms and parks. Their homosexuality is a source of guilt and fear, and they wish to keep it secret from their wives and children, who may not understand. Because the man does not have extensive experience with conventionally scripted homosexual relations, his homosexual conduct is largely impersonal. It tends to have a genital and impulsive focus, and it seems to the man to be a force, or power, or compulsion (many other socially unsupported strong feelings have this aspect) over which he has limited control. The sexual act is often conducted under difficult circumstances and with great anxiety. These patterns of secret homosexuality combined with marital heterosexuality are poorly understood, but there are likely to be complications arising from the interaction of the two sexualities.

Such men are often under considerable risk of arrest and/or discovery and exposure by the police, or of blackmail by their homosexual partners. It is a risky adaptation, for these men are caught not merely between two sexual preferences, but also between two social preferences. They are similar in some ways to heterosexual men who go to prostitutes or one-night stands, and who are thus risking marriage and family. The latter's risk is smaller in terms of social stigma, but many of the psychological problems remain the same. In the case of bisexual men, it is not clear that they prefer homosexual acts to heterosexual acts; rather the two domains seem to be serving different purposes for the sexual.

Rescripting: Discovery of the "True" Self

Patterns of bisexuality may be observed in people who have married and had children and then discovered or recalled a prior homosexual relationship which seemed to them much more satisfying emotionally and sexually than the relationship with a spouse. In many cases these people may have far less opportunity to find homosexual companions (just as they may have difficulty finding heterosexual lovers), and must either suppress what they want or break off the marriage. There are many women and men who have entered into a heterosexual marriage because it was the thing to do, but then found that it did not satisfy their emotional and sexual desires.

These men and women have found themselves in a marriage where there is a conflict between marriage, family, and sexuality. However, unlike the men who find that they have two scripts, these people know what they want their script to be; they are in the wrong one, and they want to move into another one. For them the heterosexual period was a mistake. (Fewer people go the other way, but it does happen.)

This kind of self-discovery often creates difficulties in rearing children. People who have made the transition often have children living with them or with their ex-spouses. In many cases, the children of a lesbian mother continue to live with her and the woman she loves in a common household. There is no difficulty as long as the husband does not try to get the courts to take the children away by defining the woman as unfit, and there may even be no difficulty even if he does try. Court decisions have been split about fifty-fifty, for the issue is usually whether the children will be more likely to turn out homosexual if they are raised by a homosexual mother. We do not have any definite, "scientific" answer to this question, but the best guess of the liberally minded is that the children of heterosexuals are probably just as likely to turn out homosexual. It is unlikely that most homosexual parents would be any more successful in the sexual socialization of their children than are heterosexuals.

Another approach to the problem would be to ask whether the child's sexual orientation made any difference, as long as he or she grew up as a happy, productive, and decent person. It matters to the courts, though, and it is worth noting that they have been much more concerned with how boys turn out than with how girls turn out, an indication of the greater social importance of male sexuality. The courts have also been more restrictive on the visiting rights of homosexual fathers than lesbian mothers, and worries are often expressed about the father meeting the children in the house he may share with his lover.

It is this tangled postmarital world that often dissuades people who wish to transfer their sexual interests exclusively to the same sex. There are probably substantial numbers of heterosexuals and bisexuals in society who would prefer to move entirely into the homosexual domain. This transition has now been made easier for many by the existence of the Gay Liberation movement, which has served to legitimate publicly the image of the homosexual in society.

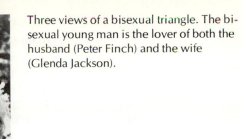

Three views of a bisexual triangle. The bisexual young man is the lover of both the husband (Peter Finch) and the wife (Glenda Jackson).

Single Script: A Matter of Indifference

There are sexual situations in which people are simply not aware of or interested in who is doing what to whom sexually. This is usually a result of either heightened excitement or the legitimating context of group sex. Much of group sex in society continues to involve either heterosexual couples or all-male homosexual groups. In group sex with a mixture of men and women and gender contact, anxieties often arise—more commonly with men than with women—about homosexual contact. The reasons are not clear, but women do seem better able than men to manage the sexual script involved. For some women it may be doing what men want to see that produces the rescripting; for others it may be an autonomous interest in finding out what happens.

In such group-sex situations, people find themselves touching others of the same and opposite sex with equal or nearly equal interest. It turns out that some skin is hairy, and some is not, that mouths are often very similar, and that the general excitement of the activity subdues the differences in gender. Such rescripting is often transitory, lasting only during the event and not transferring to other circumstances. Only a few people use the occasion to begin a longer term sexual commitment.

Another form of sexual indifference is more individual and less contextual. There are people who have sex with both men and women, and who do not care about gender. It is not that they are positively attracted to both, but rather that their script requires just another body.[1] They will do very much the same things with both men and women; the rescripting is private and the critical element becomes the activity, not the gender. This adaptation is more common among men than among women, although it is rare among both. It is as if the script did not contain a gender differentiation. Sometimes other usual script elements may be reduced in significance as well.

Scripting the "Why"

There are people whom ideological bisexuals prefer to call "true" bisexuals. These are people emotionally and sexually attracted to both men and women, and who have relations with them accompanied by all the "correct" emotions. Unlike the indifferent bisexual, there is positive response to men and women, one that is affectionately caring and desiring. It would appear that such people are rarer than most other kinds, even given the prestige offered to people who can define the world in such terms.

In the 1950s, the psychologist Albert Ellis argued that people unable to have sex with both genders were being psychologically and sexually rigid and cutting themselves off from half the world. Bisexuality was not only psychologically healthy, but compulsive homosexuality and heterosexuality were illnesses, or at least less healthy. Ellis has since changed his views in this matter and now regards exclusive homosexuality as an illness, but there are people still committed to his

---

1. I recall a man who might be called a "monosexual" bisexual. He had sex with men and women, but was so entranced by the size of his penis (it was larger than average) that he described his sex simply as "sticking his good old thing in and touching bottom."

earlier line of reasoning. They believe, and announce, that the capacity for such bisexual experiences is the mark of mental health and that bisexuality is the sex of the future. Such a prescription for sexual health seems similar to the hetero-sexual prescriptions of the past: tyranny masking as freedom. However many such people there are, they represent a minority of all people who have had sex with both genders.

Another ideological pathway to sexual experience with the same gender has emerged from the women's movement, as part of the attempt of women to get in touch with each other, to try to relate as women to women rather than as com-petitors for men or as appendages to men both socially and sexually. An extension of this political position has been the increased possibility of sexual love among women. This has ideological support from women who believe that any sexual re-lationship between a woman and a man in a sexist society will result in oppression of the woman.

As a result of the increased emotional warmth that women experienced with each other in the movement and as a result of intellectual persuasion, a number of women have undoubtedly tried homosexual experience. Some have discovered that they preferred contact with women, others have maintained a partial commit-ment to both men and women, while still others did it only as an experiment. For many lesbian women, this experimentation was an affront, since they felt they were being used.

Pressure to Choose

People who have sex with both genders often find themselves under great pressure to "be one thing or the other." This is not so true of people who maintain secret or sequential commitments, or whose heterosexual or homosexual activities are tran-sitional and impersonal, but it is true of those whose sexuality is marked by emo-tional or ideological commitment. In these cases, there is great pressure from het-erosexuals on the one side and homosexuals on the other to make up their minds.

This occurs for a number of reasons. If a person is likable, affectionate, and a decent lover, then most people that he or she is with will want to have him or her around most of the time. The pressure on them is similar to that on a person with two lovers of the same sex. There is insistence that the person choose one or the other. The fact that the other lover or lovers is of the opposite sex merely provides a greater incentive for complaint. Accusations of not really being heterosexual or of not really being homosexual abound from both sides.

Further, the preferential bisexual makes everyone nervous because he or she is not in anyone's camp. The bisexual does not believe that heterosexuality is better than homosexuality, or vice versa. Such an independent posture makes people with fixed positions uneasy.

Conclusion

The less culturally structured a particular sexual preference is, the greater the vari-ety of scripts that will begin to emerge around it. Thus heterosexuality may be more constrained in its expression because it is locked into so many regular social contexts and institutions. Homosexuality is less so, but it has a long and complex social history and a chain of subcultural institutions which structure scripts. Bisexuality is only now beginning to receive both publicity and support, so bisexual scripts show great variability. They illustrate that sexual scripts can be modified in many ways to justify sexual contact. Because the variations include changes in the reasons for doing sex (for love, lust, or resistance to social pressure) and in the person (by using partners in a sequence of symbolic substitutions), it is clear that sex serves many purposes and motives.

It is not accurate to say that the fairly large numbers of people who have had sex with both genders are sexually somewhere in between heterosexuals and homosexuals. Our conventional view of bisexuality is a very limited perspective, and Kinsey was naive in merely counting up same-sex/opposite-sex orgasms and contacts. Though such a procedure does call our attention to one dimension of the sexual variations among people, it ignores the other meanings of their experiences. Some orgasms may be more equal than others, and one event may be more (or less) significant and memorable than the average of all events. A useful picture of human sexuality depends on moving beyond a simple quantitative vision to a vision of how people think and live emotionally with what they do, which sees people as trying to manage a world rather than as mechanisms experiencing so many orgasms per week, month, or year.

The quantities expressed by orgasms are only a limited approximation of the world in which people live, think, and feel. This world is a complicated place to do research — people are far more willing to reveal frequencies than feelings. The fact that bisexuality cannot be comprehended solely by counting suggests that neither can heterosexuality and homosexuality.

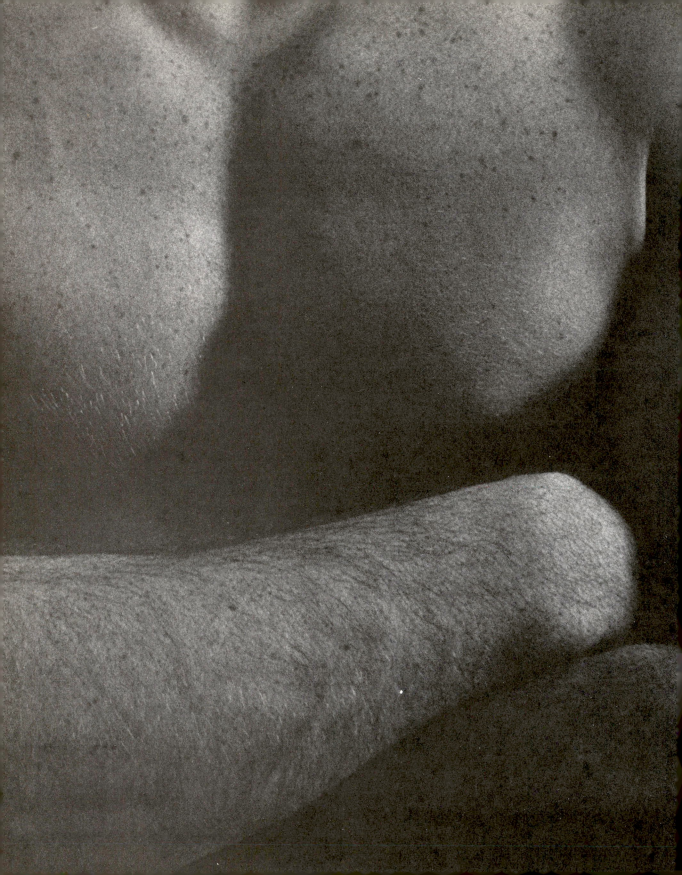

PROSTITUTION OF WOMEN

14

Woman's virtue is man's greatest invention.
Cornelia Otis Skinner

MANY ASPECTS OF THE SEXUAL ARE FOR SALE EITHER CRASSLY OR SUBTLY, BUT THE aspect that usually attracts our attention is the woman prostitute for sale to men.[1] The cliché about the world's "second oldest profession" reflects the popular stereotype about the universality of prostitution, but tends to obscure the fact that the prostitution of women is a different activity in different cultures and eras. The temple prostitute in ancient India, the child prostitute in nineteenth-century England, and the modern-day prostitute in midtown Manhattan all share a common label, but not a common life-style, nor a common relationship to the larger society in which they live, nor the same sense of who they are and the meaning of what they are doing.

The existence of an occupational label like "prostitute" tells us as little as the occupational label "banker" or "lawyer." To compare a lawyer in ecclesiastical courts or a Florentine banker of the sixteenth century with a small-town district attorney or the head of the Chase Manhattan Bank is a remarkable simplification. So it is with the prostitute. Our contemporary versions of the prostitution of women emerge from the current economic and political status of women, combined with the sexual scripts that allow for and demand their existence as well as our cultural stereotypes about the prostitute as a sexual heroine or erotic object.

The conventional definition of prostitution is sex for money. No matter how elaborate or simple the setting or the service, payment is immediate, and understood by the participants to be limited to a specific occurrence. The contrast is like that between a meal at a restaurant and eating at home with a spouse; in the former the payment is expected at the time, and the responsibility of the parties is limited to the meal itself; in the latter there is an ongoing and more complex relationship, financial and otherwise, between the parties. The above definition highlights the limited social and economic character of the customer-prostitute contact. Actually, if we highlight only economic functions, focusing on the economic transfers for sexual services, we can find many relationships in U. S. society in which one person gives another goods, services, money, or gifts for sexual access. Examined this way, as purely an economic exchange, we can move as some feminists have done to define as prostitutes married women who provide sexual access, children, and housekeeping services to men in return for economic security. Noting such similar-

---

1. A useful question to ask is why there is no prostitution of men to women in our society. The gigolo or male escort commonly supplies social rather than sexual services — they are SOCIO-sexual relationships rather than socio-SEXUAL relationships. There does not seem to be any female equivalent to the busy male executive who uses female prostitutes because their services require little negotiation and offer a period of sexual relaxation limited in its emotional, social, and economic consequences.

ities between marriage and prostitution is done to attack marriage (which we value) by comparing it to prostitution (which we disvalue). The phrase "marriage is just like prostitution" assumes that prostitution is a bad thing to begin with.

Nevertheless, it is "cash on the barrelhead" that distinguishes prostitution from other forms of heterosexual relations—with the mistress, the sexual friend, the wife. Clients purchase only the act. Indeed, the attempts of some mistresses to stabilize the economic aspects of their relationships meet with strong psychological resistance. A man may give gifts and pay bills, but he resists paying a mistress a salary. The intrusion of money as an expected element into a relationship defined as companionate or erotic forces either a redefinition of the relationship or a recognition of elements that the parties might wish to ignore. The mistress, unlike the wife, cannot insist on getting her mate's paycheck on the grounds that he might drink it up or otherwise waste it.

There are other erotic occupations for women in the society, some of them marginal to the world of prostitution, others more distant. To the degree that any of them involve men and women in open social spaces without the requirements of conventional courtship, they increase the probability of casual sexual activity and the intrusion of money in unconcealed ways. Thus strip-teasing, go-go dancing, and modeling are occupations either marginally or directly related to prostitution. These roles all contain certain elements of sexual allure and erotic manipulation— they are sexually suggestive ways of entertaining men. The women who occupy such roles are often attractive, and are the targets of men with money to spend. Also, transitions from these occupations to prostitution are linked to economic conditions—in affluent times, a woman may work as a "clothes rack" and also may be having non-commercial sex with buyers and others in the clothing industry to keep her job, or for other rewards. In hard times, this experience makes it fairly easy for her to drift into high-level prostitution. At less affluent levels, we can also find transitions of go-go dancers into bar prostitutes.

Prostitute as a Fantasy Type

The "hooker," the "playboy," the "queer," the "philanderer" are all significant sexual labels—they mobilize and organize our ways of dealing with people we label as such (including ourselves). In the nineteenth century there were very few social roles in which the sexual component was a central and organizing aspect of conduct—one that provided a significant sexual label, a label that organized a response or set of responses. The prostitute, however, was particularly important at the end of the nineteenth century because she was a pivotal figure in the moral demarcation of good women and bad. The existence of the prostitute could be construed by sexual conservatives as evidence of individual moral failure—the lost woman. As such she could be drawn into morality plays of sin and redemption (the harlot reclaimed) or of corruption of the innocent. Each of these morality plays provided occasions for sexual excitement; like people interested in suppressing pornography at the present time, those interested in suppressing prostitution often found excitement both in their own purity and in considerations of the impure.

Social critics viewed the existence of the prostitute as evidence of the moral corruption of the society. The prostitute was not an individual sinner, but a victim of the inequities of the society, inequities that existed between men and women and between social classes. The prostitute as either sinner or victim was a pivotal character in the economic-political struggles at the end of the nineteenth century. At the same time she remained an erotic character since as sin chosen or innocence corrupted she was one of the few erotic types available to nineteenth century sexual thinking.

These images of "the soiled dove," "the whore with the heart of gold," "the woman with a past" are our inheritance from the nineteenth century. They are the categories of mind with which we approach the fact of prostitution, and they were the principal rhetoric about prostitution well into the 1960s. They still appear in the mass media presentation of the prostitute and in the memoirs of ex-prostitutes. The cultural rhetoric about an activity becomes in retrospect more real than the activity was itself; the cultural rhetoric both shapes the experience while it is going on and organizes the memory of the past. These rhetorical labels are the stereotypes which both the public and the prostitute share of what the latter might have experienced.

In the twentieth century the odd place that sex has occupied in our psychic lives means that the people we know who are probably having the most sex, our parents when we are younger or our married friends, are rarely judged by us to be sexual (unless we fantasize about them sexually or have concrete interest in one of the spouses). Even when we are interested in other people sexually we often do not want to know all about their sex lives. We often consciously screen out the fact that the persons we are going out with or have married have had sexual experiences with other people. Usually only the prostitute has been faced with the question, "How did a nice girl like you get into a job like this. . .?"

The prostitute was one of the few people we could legitimately talk about when we talked about sex. The prostitute used to loom very large in the psychic life of society — largely because there was no one else to loom sexually. However, now that we can think about people having other kinds of sex, in marriage and out, the prostitute and the sex offender have a smaller moral and psychological significance to society. Now that we can worry and fantasize about swingers and mate swappers and orgies, we have added to the sexual cast of characters, to the heroes villains and fools of the sexual drama. The prostitute, like the sex offender, has been submerged by a rising tide of alternative sexual types. It is not so much that we have changed our views of prostitution as that it has assumed less significance in the collective sexual dramas of the society. The prostitute is a less important figure in the drama of good and evil, of good women and bad, and as a result there is less collective interest either in enforcing the law or in the welfare of the prostitute. It has become a marginal service occupation informally regulated by the police — largely a problem (as far as the community is concerned) of public order.

Who Uses Prostitutes

In the data gathered by Kinsey some twenty-five years ago we can find the origins of a substantial shift in the pattern of the way men use the services of prostitutes. Over the last seventy-odd years since the turn of the century, there has been a steady de-

Hollywood confronts the prostitute. The fallen woman (Greta Garbo as Anna Christie); the loose woman with a heart of gold (Shirley MacLaine in Can Can); and modern pseudo realism — the prostitute redeemed by a good man, at least for a time (Jane Fonda in Klute).

cline in the frequency with which men have gone to prostitutes. Between the two world wars the proportion of men who had gone to a prostitute at least once remained between sixty and seventy percent. However, men were going less and less often. And after World War II, not only did the frequency continue to decline but the incidence of men who had gone to a prostitute began to decline as well.

A number of processes — some sexual, some not — seem to be at work. Probably the most important factors have been (1) the steady decline in the proportion of single and never-married men, and (2) changes in the patterns of courtship and marriage in the society. In the nineteenth century, regular visits to a brothel or to a prostitute characterized the lives of many men, both middle and working class, old and young, married and unmarried. Going to a prostitute was a form of male recreation, often part of an "outing" or celebration. In some cases (probably exaggerated in numbers and perhaps limited to Europe) prostitutes functioned as sex educators for the sons of middle class families. The major support of the prostitute, however, was a regular clientele of unmarried men who viewed sex as a regular necessity rather than as a leisure activity. Such regulars supported the working class brothels of cities all over the United States in the late nineteenth and early twentieth century.

For many years these conditions assured a steady stream of both regular and irregular customers for the prostitute, customers of all social classes; but three major processes began to intervene. The first of these was the steady decline of mari-

tally unattached men in the United States — at the present time we can expect that eighty-five to ninety percent of all men will marry once. This decline in unattached men has eroded the "regular" customer of the prostitute.

A second major force has been the change in the sexual habits of the middle class male — as we have moved into the twentieth century there has been a steady shift in the sexual values of the middle class away from paid sexual relationships. In part this is a result of the changed conditions of courtship, which now provide increased opportunity for heterosexual access and intimacy during adolescence and young adulthood. Young men who have become increasingly heterosocial during adolescence now find more and more sexual opportunity with "good" women. As a result, prostitutes are no longer as much in demand either for all-male sexual entertainments or for youthful sex education.

As this shift took place in middle class populations, a similar but delayed shift (the third major change) took place among the working class after World War II. Immigrant and working class populations during and after World War I used the services of prostitutes about two to three times as frequently as middle class men. During the Depression large numbers of working class men moved about the country, unattached from families, and they continued going to prostitutes. It was with the affluence after World War II and the accommodation of working class courtship patterns to middle class standards that the use of prostitutes declined for these men.

At the present time there are only a few men who resort to prostitutes regularly. Even in the Kinsey data of some twenty-five years ago, the contacts of single men from twenty to twenty-five years of age with prostitutes accounted only for five percent of their sexual activity. For some men, contacts with prostitutes remain an important ingredient in their sexual lives; for most men, however, contact with a prostitute is a rare experience.

Reasons for Using Prostitutes

Why do men go to prostitutes at the present time? There is a wide range of reasons, but the chief explanations seem to be the following.

SEX WITHOUT NEGOTIATION

There are men, both working class and middle class, who for a variety of reasons find the negotiation that is involved in present day heterosociality more complex than they can tolerate. Some of these men simply do not possess the social skills to court a woman sexually, and find that contact with a prostitute is both simple and uncomplicated. Other men, who have a limited interest in sex and a major interest in other affairs, dislike the expenditure of time involved in sexual courtship. Calling for a date, taking her out for dinner, dealing with the waiter and the check, deciding whether sex is going to occur afterward (even when it is assured) takes up too much time and energy. Further, there is always the possibility that the time and the money will be misspent, for the woman could very well say "No." With a prostitute a man knows what is going to happen: he gives her the money; she knows why; there is no mixup in communication. The social organization that provides for prostitution (the institutionalization of a role in which negotiation is eliminated) allows a man to escape the risk of a negative outcome.[2]

SEX WITHOUT RESPONSIBILITY

Contact with a prostitute not only saves time and often money, but it also reduces the man's obligation to the woman. Most sex under current conditions requires some minimum personal or emotional commitment. Sex with a prostitute is limited by its very definition. Contacts without a past or a future allow a person to create a fantasy around the activity and to walk away from it at the end without any sense of obligation or commitment.

Such sex offers the opportunity to be purely erotic without mixtures of the sentimental or emotional. The woman can be used as an object because the money and the context limit any other appeal that she might have. This bounding makes the sex act of primary importance, thus allowing many men to act more effectively sexually.

---

2. A parallel negotiation system that has no risk for the woman is the arranged marriage. In this case the woman's sexual virtue is preserved and non-negotiable. In circumstances where the man is interested in sex and the woman in marriage, the man feels exploited because "I spent fifty bucks and she shook my hand," but when the woman has sex and the man never returns, she feels exploited. Negotiations involving risk—either of money or of virtue—leave everyone feeling uneasy.

SEX FOR EROTICISM AND VARIETY

Contact with prostitutes offers a number of other services. For men who are ambivalent about their wives' sexual responsiveness or the sex techniques appropriate for them, the prostitute is the prototypical "bad" woman who can be expected to do "dirty" sex. The fact that wives may now be willing to do many things (particularly oral sex) that men at one time went to prostitutes for may not change things much, however, because many men cannot accept or enjoy their wives doing such things.

Prostitutes also supply variety, simply by adding to the number of persons a man may have sex with. The desire for a wider range of bodies may be sufficient motive. Also, there are some men who want sexual experiences which cannot be expected with most conventional women. Men interested in bondage, discipline, sadomasochism, and other sexual rituals turn to prostitutes. The payment of money eliminates much of the embarrassment connected with such activities. However, many prostitutes find such unconventional sex offensive, so there is a subgroup of specialists available for these clients.

Another dimension of eroticism is that prostitutes supply the commodity of youth to older men. Past fifty, many men find that young women are sexually inaccessible. Usually only men with wealth, power, or charisma retain a strong sexual attractiveness after fifty. For them, there is a substantial number of young women who are the "groupies" of power and wealth. As we have seen, Washington D.C. has perhaps more than its share of political groupies; Henry Kissinger is reported to have once said, "Power is the ultimate aphrodisiac." For other men past fifty, access to the attractive, the youthful, the erotic can usually be achieved only through payment.

PROSTITUTION AS SOCIABILITY

In the past the brothel was a place of sociability for many men, sometimes rivaling the poolroom and the barroom. While this service is now gone, there are some men who are interested in sociability with a woman, but not in dating in a conventional sense. These men may use the service of a call girl as a public escort as well as a prostitute. Such arrangements offer pleasant company for an evening—and an automatic sexual experience.

SEX AWAY FROM HOME

The greatest contemporary incidence of prostitution probably occurs when men are not connected to or living in their usual environments, particularly when they are in all-male groups such as the military. Prostitution is always frequent near military installations, both in the United States and abroad. Military personnel from the United States have been stationed over much of the world during the last thirty years, and most of them were probably introduced to prostitution during their tours of service.

Undercover agent arrests undercover agent. The problem is that you cannot tell the players without a score card.

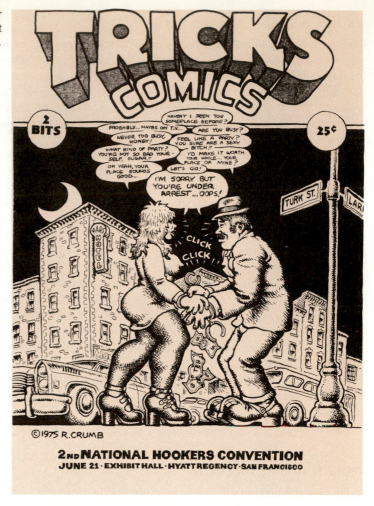

Such supportive all-male groups also exist at conventions and other usually all-male activities in the United States. Conventions, particularly those related to commercial enterprises, and arenas for gambling or sports are common locations for prostitution. Men in these circumstances (away from home, in all-male groups) often get involved with prostitutes. When these conditions are complicated by heavy drinking and the striving for masculinity associated with commerce, gambling, or sports, the pressure to indulge in sexual adventure is often overwhelming.

SEX FOR THE INEFFECTIVE

Because of a variety of physical or mental handicaps, some men are unable to promote sex in conventional ways. They may be physically deformed, very ugly, mentally deficient, or visibly crippled. As a result, they do not approach conventional women, believing that they will be turned down. Often such men go to prostitutes, thinking they are unlikely to refuse anyone who is able to pay. But even though prostitutes are usually willing to take on all clients, some prostitutes will charge these men a higher rate or refuse them service.

Prostitution as Law and Economics

At the present time, the most influential factor shaping the life of the prostitute is that what she does is illegal. In only one state (Nevada) is prostitution legal, and there it is regulated for the profit of the state. Legalizing and regulating prostitution have been widely discussed, but such actions have only taken place informally (brothel districts of the nineteenth century or tolerated zones controlled by the police) or organized by the military services for civilian or military personnel outside of the United States. For instance, the U. S. military quietly supervised the prostitution of local women in certain locations in Indochina.

The fact that the act is illegal makes the prostitute vulnerable both to the police and to criminal groups, who may have an informal alliance with the police. The police, through vice and morals squads, engage in containing prostitution, but rarely is containment an attempt to stamp it out. The point of containment is to shield prostitution from public view, to locate it in parts of the city where it improves certain kinds of business and does not damage others, and to exploit the prostitute as a source of information about the criminal underworld and sometimes as a source of illicit income.

In some communities which depend on conventions, sports, and gambling, the police restrict who works in an area and attempt to control robbery and associated crimes that may accompany prostitution. Young prostitutes who work in these locations are often arrested in order to give them a record, and then are allowed to work only if they associate themselves with a criminal "management organization." The women are part of the entertainment requirements of such communities, and their behavior is regulated for the overall economic health of the tourism and convention industry.

Because prostitution is about money (and illegal money) there grows up around the woman a large number of men and male-dominated institutions making a living from her earnings. (See Figure 1.) In most jurisdictions, living off "immoral" earnings is a crime, yet there is a large number of both criminal and conventional people whose well being depends at least in part upon the activity of the prostitute. A wide range of criminal and quasi-criminal "personnel" promote prostitution, work in its facilities, guide people to prostitutes, and operate as managers, drivers, and links to law enforcement agencies. A figure that largely disappeared in the past together with the brothel, but who seems to be reappearing in the new apartment-type brothels in the large cities is the madam. Formerly a controller, she now seems to be, particularly among the better educated and more self-sufficient women who share a working location, only a household manager. In addition there are pimps, men who live directly on the earnings of prostitutes. They supply what appears to be affection and caring, raise bail bonds, offer prostitutes status on the street, and take most of their money. Through cajolery, threats, and violence, they assure that the women will be working. The pimp is necessary for women who work in public

Figure 1   The World of the Female Prostitute.

locations where they need protection from "street people," local small-time criminals, police, and other prostitutes and pimps. Street and bar prostitution requires a great deal of territorial control; the pimp is supposed to supply protection for the woman in these situations as well as deal with the police and courts.

In addition to the pimp, there are the suppliers of information about prostitution, the steerers—the bellboy, the desk clerk, the cabdriver, the bartender—all of whom serve as sources of information and direction for the customer, and all of whom will close their eyes to the prostitute who works the hotel, the bar, and the street corner. In addition, there are the managers of the prostitution hotel, the bar, the motel, and the massage parlor—as well as the "muscle" who are hired to control unruly guests.

Another major sector that profits from the prostitute is the criminal justice system, composed of bail bondsmen, defense attorneys, police, prosecutors, judges, bailiffs of the court, jailers, and wardens. The illegal status of prostitution assures them a steady income, paid either by the state in order to control the activity or by the prostitute in order to stay in business. The major revenue from prostitution probably comes through attempts to suppress it; that is, the public funding that goes to suppression and control agencies is probably far larger than the income prostitutes earn.

A source of unintentional profiteering from prostitution is the moral reformer, for without moral degenerates, moral reformers would have little demand for their moral indignation. Moral indignation goes hand in hand with moral publicity, particularly that of the daily press and the magazines who write steadily about the "problem of prostitution." In addition to the reformers and publicists are the professionals who unintentionally profit from prostitution: mental health professionals who give therapy to prostitutes; sex researchers who study them; medical doctors who treat their diseases; and social workers who sympathize with them and try to find them other occupations.

Finally, there are the large-scale profiteers: the owners of the facilities in which prostitution occurs, the hotels or convention centers or gambling locations or tourist attractions. These owners are doctors and politicians and civic leaders, people whose assets are hidden in the trust departments of major banks. They are the good people of the community, even the bankers, legitimate people, people you might meet at parties if you are rich enough.

There are even bordellos in Nevada (where prostitution is legal) that will accept credit cards. The receipt does not say "Mustang Bordello," and it shows a dummy charge (jewelry or entertainment). But the charge-card companies take their seven percent overhead on every transaction. If it is thirty dollars for a trick, someone is making two dollars and ten cents off the top—another legal profiteer from prostitution.

If prostitution is viewed as a legal-economic enterprise, it is no wonder that few want a change in its status. If it were decriminalized, most of the people shown in Figure 1 could not make money from it, not even the good people in the community. Any analysis of criminality suggests that someone is making a good deal of money out of it, and that most of the money is made by the "respectable" people.

That this is an old connection is expressed in the words of Sir George Croft in Bernard Shaw's long-banned play of the early 1890s, *Mrs. Warren's Profession.*[3] Croft, in suggesting marriage to Mrs. Warren's daughter, is not aware that she knows that her mother's profession is managing the brothels that Croft has financed. When confronted with the facts, Croft says: "Why the devil shouldn't I invest my money that way? I take the interest on my capital like other people: I hope you don't think I dirty my hands with the work. . . . How do you expect me to turn my back on thirty-five percent when the rest are pocketing what they can like sensible men? . . . If you want to pick and choose your acquaintances on moral principles, you'd better clear out of this country, unless you want to cut yourself out of decent society." And then Croft goes on to define "decent society" in this way: "As long as you don't fly openly in the face of society, society doesn't ask any inconvenient questions . . . there are no secrets better kept than the secrets everybody

---

3. Written in 1894, *Mrs. Warren's Profession* was first presented as a theater club performance in January 1895 but did not receive a public first night in England until March 1926.

guesses. In the class of people I can introduce you to, no lady or gentleman would so far forget themselves as to discuss my business affairs.''

Shaw, in order to draw his archetype of Victorian hypocrisy with hard edges, probably makes Croft too knowing and too cynical. But to see that the same situation of respectable profit from society's dirty work still exists, we need only to examine an essay by Gail Sheehy in *New York* magazine (1972) which exposes the ownership of the hotels that profit from the recent boom in prostitution: "No one in city government was willing to talk about the *owners* of prostitution hotels. It was all very embarrassing . . . a little research turned up the names of immaculate East Side Wasps [White Anglo-Saxon Protestants], . . ., *bona fide* members of the Association for a Better New York and the Mayor's own Times Square Development Council . . . [as well as] several Park Avenue Banks. . . .''

Subculture of Prostitution

The criminal status of prostitution, its profitability to a large number of people, and its status as erotic and degraded sex[4] shape the subculture of prostitution and the life of the prostitute. Particularly important is the criminal status of the prostitute, for it creates a barrier between the prostitute as a member of a deviant group and people who have a more conventional sexual status. As a woman moves into "the life," she begins to lose many of her relationships with more conventional people. Contacts with family and church and with conventional work and occupations begin to dissolve and are replaced by associations with the people who share the subculture of prostitution.

It is a subculture with its own set of codes and values, many of which are antithetical to the values of noncriminal communities. Since prostitution is stigmatized, it is only in this subculture that a woman can find friends who do not view her as a freak, or immoral or dangerous. Most people tend to associate with others who have common experiences, who understand them, who treat them well — the prostitute is no different. The only members of the conventional community that many prostitutes meet, particularly if they are deeply involved in the subculture, are clients, policemen, bail bondsmen, and lawyers. Such contacts are scarcely the stuff of which enduring human attachments are made.

The subculture of prostitution is in part a set of occupational skills and techniques. Like most occupations it possesses a private language, a set of training procedures for new members, a set of values for members to adhere to (a professional code of conduct), a set of human relationships which are valued. In addition, it is a moral community, which exists in part to defend its members against the stigma attached to them. The strength of this community is double edged, however: it is required in order to recruit and train members and to sustain them during their activities, but it is also a factor in discouraging members from leaving the profession.

---

4. It is important to point out that for many working class men who went to prostitutes on a regular basis as their primary source of sexual contact, the sex was not a major erotic experience; it was viewed as possibly wrong, but a necessity, like having regular bowel movements.

RECRUITING AND TRAINING

Recruitment of women into prostitution has changed over the last hundred years. Under the hardships of urban industrial life during the middle and end of the nineteenth century, prostitution was often a realistic option for women who worked in factories and as servants. It was not that women wanted to be prostitutes, but that the conditions of conventional life for poor women, particularly during economic recessions, often represented only a minor moral advantage over the conditions of prostitution. This was an era when many young women went to work in a factory when they were twelve years old and worked ten to twelve hours a day, six days a week, for a few dollars a week. The work was often dangerous and unhealthy.

In European cities there were many brothels, considerable street prostitution, and a flourishing trade in children bought from parents and sold to brothel owners. These were "normal" conditions until the end of the nineteenth century. Under these conditions fairly large numbers of sexually inexperienced young women ended up as prostitutes because of economic problems, because they had been sexually exploited by their employers, or because of accidents in their lives (deaths of fathers, mothers, disruptions of families).

At the present time, in a world of greater opportunity, the factors of poverty and exploitation are still significant. Most prostitutes are not recruited from the suburbs or from fine women's colleges, much to the disappointment of those whose fantasies run in these directions, but rather from the poor, the uneducated, the ethnic minorities of society. However, unlike the past, few of them are seduced or sold into a life of prostitution; it is more a process of drift and chance. Often they are unskilled young women who are physically attractive and who have found that men are interested in such physical attributes. Indeed, what they have learned is what many young women learn in U. S. society, but these other young women, by good fortune and social status, end up getting married.

It is the sexually active young woman who lives in a sexually exploitative environment, who is unskilled in other ways, who develops a "bad" reputation, who falls afoul of the juvenile court for being incorrigible, who is particularly at risk.[5] The plans and values of these young women are quite conventional: they believe in marriage and hope for all of the same things that other young women hope for; however, the forces of circumstance accumulate. Prostitution is not a career that is planned for; women are not volunteers, they are recruits, or draftees. What women often do is move from a sexually active young adulthood into sexual activity for money. This transition can be abrupt (falling in with a pimp) or slow (taking money from a friend or having money left by a pickup). At the present time, there are only a few women who were seduced and abandoned, who came to view themselves as

5. The nature of the margin between "good" and "bad" women is important here. If there is a very narrow margin between being a good woman and marriageable and a bad woman and a prostitute, then the slightest misstep can cause someone to become totally stigmatized. In small rural villages in Thailand, a young woman can be identified as morally bad and hence unmarriageable. Since marriages are arranged within a small number of communities, her unmarriageable status is known to everyone. In such communities there may be no alternative roles between wife/mother and prostitute. The woman then has no choice other than prostitution or suicide. In large urban cities and societies, the margin of "error" is much greater: (1) women may move from community to community and start a new life; (2) there is a considerable gray area between good and bad; and (3) there is a wide range of moral audiences for one's behavior, with some approving and others not. These are very different conditions governing the sexual conduct of women.

lost women, and so became prostitutes. It probably still does happen that a few women are innocents betrayed, but such events are far less common than in the past.

Becoming a prostitute involves a number of levels of learning, only some of which concern sex. Further, what has to be learned depends upon the level or location where the prostitution is practiced. Young women in training to be street or bar prostitutes, to work in brothels or massage parlors, or to be call girls are all operating with different kinds of clientele, need different kinds of skills, will be differently embedded in the criminal network, and will have different vulnerabilities to the police and pimps. There is some migration between levels and locales, but not nearly as much as one might expect, primarily because of social class skills and education. At the very top of the profession are those courtesans who possess the image and often the reality of intelligence and education which allow them to associate with a wide range of sophisticated clients. At the bottom are the occupationally and socially unskilled, who have only the transient bloom of youth for sale.

MANAGING THE MONEY AND THE ACT

One of the things any beginning prostitute must learn is the conscious management of money with reference to sex. Sex, like justice and love, is not supposed to be for sale, but in the world of prostitution, it has to be sold. Indeed, the bargaining must take place before the sex: get the money before anything else happens. If there is a sliding scale for different sex acts, the customer's sexual desires have to be determined and an amount settled on. When this is over, the sex begins.

The exchange of money serves a number of purposes. Payment provides access, it eliminates negotiation and affection, it enhances eroticism for the male, it legitimates the act for the woman. The fact of money hardens the line between the conventional customer and the prostitute. By having to pay, he is the "john," the "trick," the "square"; by taking the money, she is the "whore," the "hooker," the "slut." The symbolic mediation of mutual degradation, a degradation that must be kept secret while the act is going on, is critical to the maintenance of the ephemeral goodwill that allows the sex to occur.

Another element that has to be managed is the sexual interests of the clients. Young women are often recruited from social classes where more adventurous sexual techniques are looked down on. Thus a young woman may have to increase the range of her tolerated sexual acts. Certain acts, such as anal intercourse, may be performed never or only for a very high price. Oral sex, which might have been taboo, is actually something women may wish to do because it takes less time and effort than coitus. In the past, many prostitutes recruited from working class backgrounds had a wide range of "perverted" sexual acts which they would perform with clients, but which they would never perform with men that they liked or loved.

MANAGING THE LOCATION

The prostitute must learn to manage the location in which she works. The working class brothel prostitute of the turn of the century worked in a high turnover environment where the price was relatively fixed, and where she was fairly well protected from the police by the madam and by the existence of a tolerated brothel zone. Client management, income levels, and the kind of life were established by the location. With the suppression of brothels in the United States during the 1920s and 1930s, most of these working environments disappeared. The massage parlor has some of these elements, but negotiation is now more often in the hands of individual females on the street and in the bar, vulnerable to the police and to the stigma of the conventional community. These young women must actively solicit customers, accept the turndowns, accept the hostility of conventional women, and run from the police, but they still require the services of the pimp for protection and the hotel or motel for a working site. They are often the least skilled young women, the ones who are most driven and controlled by the police-pimp axis. The police are forcing them off the streets; the pimp is forcing them out to work.

The usually most protected of prostitutes is the call girl. Once a young woman has developed a clientele and a range of contacts, she can partly opt out of the world of prostitution except for patterns of friendship. At the present time, as police relax their pressure on off-the-street prostitution, the brothel-apartment is appearing in large urban centers. Often located in respectable neighborhoods, it is used for work by a number of women. Relatively affluent clients, making appointments by phone, come in the evening or during the day to be entertained. There are sometimes managers of the apartment, but rarely pimps: these women are in business for themselves.

GETTING OUT

Except for a very few women who work at the top of the profession, most young women who move into prostitution do not begin with a large repertoire of non-sexual skills, and the world of prostitution rarely operates to enhance those few skills. It is a life that increasingly detaches many young women from conventional opportunities by creating values that are contemptuous of those opportunities, and by creating a life style of consumption and living at off times (getting up late and working late — the leisure/service-occupation cycle). Since their market value is transient and few are economically prudent, most women do not get rich from the life. Some of them rationally and carefully save money while working hard for a number of years, and then move out of the profession. This is possible only for a few, since the exploitative pressures of the police, criminal organizations, lawyers, and pimps work to take their money away from them. Even if a woman is prudent economically (and this is not the basis for becoming a prostitute), she will often be unable to save.[6]

Ways out of the life are more common than they were in the past, though it must be noted that even in the nineteenth century most prostitutes, as they aged, probably moved out into more or less conventional roles in the society. Most prostitutes eventually marry, some directly out of the profession, marrying either clients or nonclients they have met in their role as a prostitute. Some such marriages are

---

6. This is less true in European countries with older cultural values about prostitution. There, particularly in smaller cities without a criminal underworld, prostitutes may save their money and in their thirties move into conventional occupations.

upwardly mobile, particularly for working class women who have worked at the upper edges of prostitution. Often, a woman who remained marginal to prostitution finds a conventional husband who does not know about her past.

Most women simply move out of prostitution into occupational levels suitable to their education or skill level, and find husbands during this period. There is a minority who cannot or will not leave prostitution. Often these women drift downward as their looks decline, working more and more for less and less money. In large cities there are zones which differentiate street prostitutes by their value and attractiveness. Some women stay in the occupation until they are very old, but most drift out of it, being replaced by younger bodies with greater energy and higher market value. Prostitution for most women is youth bound—somewhat like being a professional athlete (the body can take the beating only for a while) or a theoretical physicist (be smart while you are young; all creative work in physics has been done by physicists under the age of twenty-seven). However, most athletes make more money, and academic physicists get tenure.

Decriminalization and Unionization

When a change in the legal status of prostitution is discussed, the solutions usually proposed are licensing or other forms of regulation. The analogy is made to liquor and bars: they are controlled by the state, severely taxed, and limited in times of service, age of clientele, and who can get a license. Regulators point to the experience of prostitute registration in France and the existence of prostitution districts in such cities as Amsterdam and Hamburg. These districts, in addition to being cordoned off from the city, double as tourist attractions.

Another option (different from legalization) is decriminalization, which would make sex of consenting men and women not an offense, paid for or not. Such a decision would probably not decrease the social stigma of prostitution and would not "get the girls off the streets," but it would remove from the prostitute the necessity of supporting certain components of the criminal justice system. In addition, it would make the prostitute less vulnerable to the criminal underclass of the city, giving her the opportunity to claim police protection if she were being threatened or exploited. It is unlikely, however, that certain other conditions of prostitution would disappear—the need for a place to work and for a network of contacts to get clients, the association between money and sex, or the alienation from the conventional social world.

The prostitution of women represents a difficult issue for the women's movement. The movement cannot approve of prostitution since it is a commercial use of a woman's body, a commercial use that largely profits men. In addition, the fact that prostitution exists represents a major critique of the economic status of minority and poor women in the society, a status that recruits them into criminal life styles. At the same time, it would be very difficult to argue for a continuation of laws against prostitution since these limit the control that women have over their own bodies. The problem is how to be opposed to prostitution without being opposed to the prostitute.

COYOTE GROWLS

The Newsletter of
a Loose Woman's Organization

JUNE/JULY 1975
Volume 1 Number 3

Published irregularly by Coyote
P.O. Box 26354
San Francisco, CA 94126

Dedicated to exposing and eliminating
current laws against prostitution and
other non-crime crimes

The newspaper of the prostitute's union, COYOTE, which means Cast Out Your Old Tired Ethics.

A major source of original thinking on the issue of prostitution has been the new prostitute's union organized in California. Named *Coyote,* this union is dedicated to self-help, consciousness raising, political change, and social protection. The political problem of organizing a union in an illegal occupation is obvious, but the social power of the prostitute is weakened by economic as well as political factors. Since prostitutes do not supply a service that people depend upon (like medical services or heroin), it is pointless for them to threaten to withdraw their services. The strength of the prostitute's union is then in its moral appeal (much like the farm workers under Cesar Chavez) as an exploited underclass. Its future will depend on its ability to find allies in the women's movement, law reform groups, and other sectors of the society which are committed to opposing the oppression of minorities.

SEXUAL OFFENSES AND OFFENDERS

15

The only purpose for which power can be rightfully exercised over any member of a civilized community, against his will, is to prevent harm to others. His own good, either physical or moral, is not a sufficient warrant.

John Stuart Mill

AT THE PRESENT TIME IN THE UNITED STATES NEARLY ALL FORMS OF SEXUAL conduct could be viewed as part of the "sex-crime problem," and a large number of people labeled as sex offenders. The sex crime laws in the United States are a relatively direct outgrowth of Judaeo-Christian sexual prohibitions, prohibitions that have been added to, regularized, and rationalized in secular terms over the past two centuries. In nearly all jurisdictions prior to the 1950s, and in nearly as many today, *legal* sexual conduct is largely limited to heterosexual hugging, kissing, mouth-body (but not oral-genital), and hand-body contacts and coitus, all within marriage. Of all other forms of sexual conduct, only masturbation has escaped legal prohibition, though it has been used as "evidence" of mental illness and sexual psychopathy, particularly in people accused of illegal sex acts. In the state of Indiana it was not criminal to masturbate, but it was illegal to encourage someone else to do so. Even at the present time, unmarried hetero-sexual intercourse is illegal in thirty-one states under one or another set of laws that forbid fornication, habitual fornication, or cohabitation.

From what we know about what people do sexually, it is clear the sex laws in many jurisdictions do not coincide with the personal sexual standards or sexual practices of a majority of people. We also know that some of the sex laws are not enforced, other sex laws are only occasionally enforced, and only rarely are there systematic and efficient attempts by law enforcement agencies to suppress even the disapproved sex crimes. This uneven and inefficient enforcement of sex-crime laws is not a modern development, but has been characteristic of law enforcement for as long as there have been equivalents to the modern criminal justice system, begin-ning in the middle of the nineteenth century.

At the same time that the law does not match what people do, and is enforced unevenly if at all, there is a great deal of anxiety about the "sex criminal" among a few people most of the time and among more people when a major crime is publi-cized in the media. This anxiety is exacerbated by what is seen by some as the leni-ency of the criminal justice system and as danger from the offenders. This response contrasts with the activity of other people, who are attempting to change the sex laws so that they coincide to a greater extent with what most people do—attempts that have not met with great success. In the middle is the vast majority of society, who are largely unconcerned with the "sex-crime problem" until and unless it touches them personally. This majority is also often blissfully unaware that many of the things they are doing sexually are either misdemeanors or felonies in the states where they live.

What has produced this tangled situation, in which there is a fundamental lack of congruence between the law, the institutions of criminal justice, and the activities of people in U.S. society? Mostly it has resulted from our inability to decide in any clear way what we are talking about when we talk about sex crimes, what role we want the police and other criminal-justice agencies to play in controlling our own sex lives (as opposed to controlling other people's), and what forms of sexuality we are prepared to approve or disapprove. Sex law and sex crime represent the public end of the sex debate, a debate that most people wish to ignore because it forces them to confront the relationship of their private lives to collective sexual values and to the institutions that embody those values.

Sex Against the Law

From one point of view, the criminal law on sex could be considered the major approved sexual script in U.S. society. Primarily through exclusion, a series of *do nots*, it sets up boundaries around what is approved. There is no provision in the school curriculum or in the home for teaching this particular script—sex law is not part of our formal sexual learning. However, it hovers in the background, transmitted by folklore, by conversations with family and peers, and by the mass media. The sex law works largely through excluding *who* you may have sex with and *what* you may do with them. The first four categories below specify *who*, although in many cases, the *what* limits the *who*.

GENDER RULES

There are laws restricting homosexual activity in forty-four of the fifty states. Gender exclusion is usually based on laws against sodomy or "crimes against nature"—homosexuality is forbidden usually by laws against mouth-genital or anal-genital sex, where there are not specific statutes against homosexual solicitation. The latter offense, however, accounts for most arrests of homosexuals in the United States. It is in the preliminaries of the approach that the homosexual (particularly a male) is most vulnerable to the police.

The hedging of legal language on sex has resulted in such curiosities as an Ohio decision which construed female homosexuality as not against the sodomy law because sodomy required that an "unnatural object" be placed in an "unnatural orifice." Since female homosexuality does not involve a penis in the mouth or anus, it did not qualify as sodomy.

The sodomy and "crime against nature" statutes, along with specific bestiality statutes, also forbid sex between humans and nonhuman animals.

AGE RULES

Age restrictions are sometimes specified by an age-of-consent rule, but can also be part of statutes that prohibit acts labeled as lewd and lascivious conduct or as sodomy. The latter two statutes can be used when adult-child sex involves oral-genital or hand-genital contacts. The age statutes specify only lower limits (there is no age at which people are too old for sex, except by custom), and normally at two age ranges. Children ages eleven to twelve or younger cannot give consent; offenses at these ages are child molestation. Adolescents up to the legal age to marry (fourteen to eighteen) might give qualified consent; this distinguishes voluntary fornication from statutory rape. Offenses at these ages usually involve sex between adolescents or between an older male and a young female.

Age laws are sometimes used to deal with homosexual contacts with children, but homosexual contacts during adolescence are commonly treated under statutes more directly related to homosexual activity or solicitation, although the age of the partner may be used in the charge as an aggravating element of the offense.

Using age-of-consent statutes as the basis for charges of statutory rape against young men (say, ages fourteen to seventeen) seems less frequent than it has been in the past; however, juvenile court proceedings against sexually active young women are still very common. Even with increased sexual activity among adolescents, there has been no reduction of the ages in U.S. consent laws. In European countries the age of consent is being lowered, and is now approaching (in the most liberal countries) ages fourteen and fifteen for both homosexual and heterosexual consent.

KINSHIP RULES

It is illegal in all jurisdictions for sex to occur (regardless of age) between parents and children, between brothers and sisters, between uncles/aunts and nieces/nephews, and in some states between cousins of various degrees. Many states include step-parents and stepchildren.

One justification of the incest statutes has been to assert the dangers of genetic damage through inbreeding; a more important contemporary reason is the danger of sexual exploitation of children by parents. However, while there seems to be a widespread cultural prohibition of father-daughter and mother-son incest, it is not clear whether these were originally sexual prohibitions or property prohibitions. Incest was not so much a sexual threat as a threat against the property rights of the future husband (father-daughter) or the property rights of the father (mother-son).

MARRIAGE RULES

Probably the most restrictive rules for heterosexuals are those that link legal sex to marriage. Premarital and postmarital sex is restricted by fornication and cohabitation laws, while sex during marriage is constrained by adultery statutes. For heterosexuals in many jurisdictions this restricts *legal* sex, other than petting, to their current marital partners.

There have been laws forbidding sex as well as intermarriage between racial groups (until very recently in the southeastern part of the United States, and at the present time in South Africa) as well as religious groups (in Nazi Germany as a result of the Nurenburg laws). In the United States these laws forbade sex and intermarriage between people of European-American descent and people of Afro-American or (in some cases) American Indian descent. When not part of the law, such rules were bitterly and often ferociously upheld by custom. The murder and lynching of blacks often centered on some "slight" to white womanhood. In Germany the laws forbade relations of all kinds between Aryans and Jews as part of the process of social exclusion and genocide. South Africa prohibits sex and marriage between those of European descent and native Africans or those of Asian and mixed parentage.

Restrictions of sexuality on the basis of religion, social class origin (caste rules), tribal affiliation, or family status have long been matters of custom and law over most of the world. Sexuality, marriage, and children serve as the channels through which power and resources flow in many societies. There is no reason to be surprised that such restrictions would emerge, given the processes of social differentiation and social subordination that have characterized most of recorded social life. The current decline in the power of such marriage/sex laws may be a result of the declining role of the family in the transmission of material resources.

The following categories of prohibition on sexual conduct focus on *what* people do, and as pointed out before the *what* may affect the *who*.

TECHNIQUE RULES

By restricting what parts of bodies may be juxtaposed (oral-genital and anal sex) as well as other techniques (hand-genital and general body contact, hugging and kissing) when used by people of the same sex, laws that preclude homosexuality also preclude a great deal of heterosexual noncoital sex. In the past judges in some jurisdictions have ruled on whether rates of marital intercourse and whether masturbating in front of one's spouse is actionable in civil cases and in judgments of mental illness, but most of the law relating to *what* persons may do during sex is included in marriage law, which specifies the right of spouses to sexual intercourse.

ACCESS RULES

Certain types of sexual access or approach are forbidden, although only one is presently illegal in the United States: the use of force or threat of force. Forcible rape (and attempted rape) is at this moment probably the most significant sex offense in the United States. Rape is not in most cases an offense that can be legally committed between husband and wife; therefore, the fact of rape must depend in part on the two parties being unmarried. Such nonmarital sexual activity might be illegal in any case; force or threat of force makes the offense the responsibility of the male.

The fact that rape cannot occur between husband and wife focuses on the property origins of the offense. Rape in the past has been considered an offense against the property rights of a father, brothers, or husband of a raped woman. A man taking by force something that belonged to other men was the offense. It is only recently that the offense has come to be viewed as an offense against the woman.

Two other modes of sexual access are illegal in some countries—seduction and breach of promise. Seduction is the corruption of the innocent or dependent through promises or favors. Such offenses have never been against the law in the United States except where "innocents" were induced to become prostitutes, or in cases of "contributing to the delinquency of a minor." A similar civil wrong is breach of promise, in which a man promises to marry a woman and then backs out. Even if there were no intercourse, a woman could start civil procedures to gain damages for her loss of reputation (her marriageability or property value) due to the breach of promise to marry.

A number of sexual relationships are not forbidden by law, but are considered aggravating circumstances to a sex offense (such as fornication) and may be used as a basis for losing a job or professional standing: sexual activity between doctor and patient; psychotherapist and patient; teacher and student; lawyer and client; judge and defendant; military officer and enlisted person; executive and secretary; or any superior and subordinate in other circumstances. Most commonly these events involve the exploitation of women by men. There is some evidence that such exploitations are also erotic fantasies for men: the casting couch, the doctor's office, the sex therapist, are all part of the erotic landscape of pornography.

PUBLIC DECENCY AND PERSONAL PRIVACY

Two other classes of offenses are common, and involve violations of public decency or modesty, or intrusions on a person's sexual and personal privacy. *Exhibitionism* is exposure of male genitals to women. (Genital exposure by women to men may also be labeled exhibitionism—police do raid massage parlors, burlesques, and the like—but men are rarely complainants.) The voyeur or peeping tom peers through windows at people in their own homes. Both of these acts involve intrusions into personal privacy, the first by intruding the sexual into a public place, the other by seeking to see acts which usually occur in privacy.

PROSTITUTION AND PORNOGRAPHY

Prostitution is the sale of sexual services, most commonly by women to men. Prostitution is both fostered and suppressed by contemporary societies, often by the same institutions. It is illegal in most jurisdictions, even those where it flourishes most openly. (See Chapter 14.)

The other major intersection of sex and money is pornography, the sale of sexual depictions or live sexual displays. The struggle between those who defend the current statutes on pornography and those who oppose them has been largely fought out in the courts. The national attitude has become more liberal toward pornography and prostitution, reflected not in legal change but in lessened intensity of enforcement. (See Chapter 17.)

Table 1 Classifications of Sexual Offenses

	Types of Sexual Conduct	Legal Labels	Incidences in the Population
Heterosexual			
illegal conventional	1) pre-marital sex (1) between youths and (2) between adults and youths (victim?)	sex delinquency incorrigibility contributing to delinquency statutory rape	common
	2) pre-marital, post-marital, extra-marital sex	fornication, cohabitation, adultery	very common
	3) sex techniques	sodomy, crimes against nature	very common
illegal unconventional	4) female prostitution	prostitution, soliciting, loitering, disorderly conduct	many consumers, few sellers
	5) pornography	obscenity, pornography	many consumers
	6) forced sex adults (victim) youth (victim)	rape, indecent assault, attempted rape	somewhat common
	7) voyeurism (victim)	voyeurism	uncommon
	8) exhibitionism (victim)	exhibitionism	
	9) sex with children (victim)	child molesting, lewd and lascivious, indecent assault, sodomy	to
	10) incest child and youth (victim) adult (victim?)	incest (and all of 9 above)	
	11) forced sex children (victim)	rape (see 6)	very rare
Homosexual	12) with adults	crime against nature, lewd conduct, sodomy, soliciting	fairly common
	youth (victim)	see 9, 1	somewhat common
	children (victim)	see 9	uncommon
	13) male prostitution	sodomy, see 4	somewhat common
	14) pornography	see 5	many customers
Animal Contacts	15) animal contacts	bestiality, crime against nature, sodomy	rare

Proportion of Events Reported to Police	Police Activity	Effectiveness of Legal Control on Rates of Behavior		See Chapter
rare	(1) only against sexually active young women (2) some older males arrested	nil		9
nil	extremely rare, usually for non-sexual reasons	nil		9 10
nil	harassment, particular circumstances			11
rare—by moral entrepreneurs, not participants	sporadic campaigns, keeping public order, often involves police corruption	low	could be effective due to public nature of offenses	14
rare—by moral entrepreneurs, not participants	sporadic campaigns, now limited by court decisions	low		17
some	limited by sexism, often unresponsive to victims	low	could be somewhat more effective	
few	minimum reaction to reports, unlikely to make arrest	very low		
few to some	minimum reaction unless children are involved	low		
few to some	react strongly to reports	low		
few	react to reports, particularly with children	low		
many	very strong reaction			
	sporadic campaign, harassment	low	could be more effective	
few/few some				
see (4)	strong reaction to reports			
see (5)				
nil	may react to report	nil		15

Sex Crime and Sex Theory

It is difficult for anyone who did not grow up before the Kinsey reports were published to understand the degree of sexual ignorance and evasion that existed in U.S. society. Most people did not have a clue about how one another lived sexually. In most sectors of the society, the most conservative sexual views were affirmed and supported in public. People who did sexual things that seemed to go beyond the bounds of the "normal" did not admit or discuss them with friends or neighbors for fear of being treated as perverts or sexual deviants.

At the same time, as has been pointed out, the only information supplied about sex derived from the clinical practice of psychiatrists or psychoanalysts who focused on the neurotic and the maladjusted, from the studies of criminologists about sex crime, or from newspaper and magazine reports of the sexually dramatic, perverted, exotic, or unusual. Information about "fairly normal" people was difficult to find and rarely believed when it was made available.

The sex offender and his variants, the sex moron, the sex fiend, the sex psychopath, were among the most important socio-sexual types in society. Their representation in the media was both a form of pornography and a form of moral education. The sex offender depicted as a sexual beast reaffirmed the public view that the sexual impulse was both dangerous and explosive, that it needed to be repressed and controlled to prevent its destructive consequences. The typical reported case was the rape murder of a child by a sex offender with many previous sex convictions who had been released to prey upon the community by an incompetent parole board. Such newspaper reports could fascinate and thrill a population living in sexual ignorance and tension. Like an earthquake in a foreign country or a flood in another state, the sex offender was one of a number of natural disasters, usually occurring to other people, which populated the pages of the tabloid press.

Since no one knew exactly how much "sexual perversion" was going on, it was possible to believe that the police were catching most of the "perverts" or criminals, and that the community was being constantly cleansed by law enforcement. In this state of ignorance the public could be frightened by reports of hundreds of uncaught criminals seeking to molest their children (therefore the public would agree to increase the enforcement budget), or of many sex criminals who had been caught and sent to prison for a long time (thus convincing the public that the criminal justice system was doing "a good job").

Studies of sex offenders from the turn of the century until the 1940s focused on what made the sex offender different from everyone else. The search was for the cause of sex-offense behavior, a search that led most researchers into studying the "differences" between imprisoned sex offenders and what it was assumed normal people were like. This usually involved one of three strategies: (1) comparing different kinds of sex offenders (the exhibitionist with the rapist), (2) looking for a single attribute common to many different offenders, or (3) comparing the sex offender with people outside of prison. These research strategies suffered from significant flaws:

1. They rarely involved adequate control groups. The researchers took a group of people in prison who had been charged with a sex offense (usually disregarding such factors as age, prior criminal records, or periods of imprisonment) and studied their IQ, or hormones, or body type, or chromosomes, and then announced their

findings. From such studies sex offenders were found to have lower IQs, different hormones, different body types, defective chromosomes — none of which were checked against other populations who were not sex offenders. From this research the public was told that there were "sex morons" who had defective intelligence and that is why they committed sex offenses, or that sex offenders were defective hormonally or genetically, or that sex offenses were caused by a body type. As soon as adequate control groups were designed, all of these theories collapsed scientifically, if not in the media.

2. They assumed that there was a social or psychological category of people who could be defined by their legal status. Most studies of sex offenders (even quite modern ones) make the assumption that because there is a set of legal categories defining sex offenses, the people who commit them are all alike. For instance, because a group of men exhibit themselves to women and because the behavior has a common legal label, it is assumed that there is a common cause of the act.

3. They assumed that people in prison were representative of similar people not in prison. The man in prison for adultery was assumed to be like all other adulterers, and the same assumptions were made for rapists, prostitutes, and homosexuals. The researchers reasoned from those in prison to people who might perform similar acts in the community, never thinking that the system by which their cases were selected might not be the same as a random sample of the population. People who are in prison for adultery or homosexuality may have got there for reasons unrelated to their sexuality.

4. The researchers defined the activities they were looking at as abnormal, immoral, or perverted, as well as being criminal. Once this assumption has been made, attention is focused on finding something wrong in the subject. This happens in everyday life — if you are told that a person is going to be aggressive and nasty you are ready to judge them negatively before they begin to speak.

Changing Conceptions of the Sex Offender

After the publication of the Kinsey reports and a series of studies of sex offenders during the 1940s and 1950s, knowledge about the sexuality of both fairly normal people and the sex offender was greatly expanded. The Kinsey research "normalized" many kinds of sexual conduct, particularly the behavior of conventional heterosexuals. With the revelation that so many people had premarital, postmarital, and extramarital sex, and practiced a wide variety of forbidden sex techniques, it was difficult to continue believing that they represented a moral or psychological minority. It was apparent that such conduct was common, and part of the pattern of heterosexual growing up in U.S. society. In addition, the Kinsey research opened up discussion of homosexuality, prostitution, and pornography, which were found to be sufficiently widespread that it became more difficult to argue their abnormality.

The Kinsey studies stimulated further research into unconventional sex, which confirmed the connections between these forms of sexual conduct and conventional heterosexuality. Criminological studies undermined the belief that there was some single type called the "sex offender." The major publication of the Institute for Sex Research during the 1960s was titled *Sex Offenders* in an attempt to under-line the diversity that had been found. Most sex offenders were not "sex fiends," and only a few of them were violent or dangerous, or likely to repeat their crimes.

A more modest and less violent image of the sex offender began to appear in the public press. Rather than focusing on rare violent events, attention began to be paid to the majority of people whose offenses were occasional, who had noncri-minal pasts, and who were responsive to treatment. Such research into sex offend-ers characterized the 1950s, and was followed in the 1960s by research into homo-sexuality, prostitution, and pornography, which undermined the stereotypes of these offenses as well. With an increase in public sexual knowledge about people who have and have not fallen afoul of sex law, new ways of thinking about the rela-tionship between sex and law began to emerge. Fewer influential people thought that all sexual problems could be solved by the law and law enforcement. Both le-gal change and redefinition of sex offenses began to emerge.

Pivotal to these conceptions was the distinction between victim and victimless crimes. This distinction had been latent in criminology for some time, but applica-tion to sexual offenses began in the 1950s. The distinction is between violating per-sons or their property against their will, and illegal acts involving people who have sought out the activity. The distinction is one of consent. Prostitution, consenting homosexuality, pornography, adultery, fornication, and cohabitation are crimes without victims. Unless the participants were coerced or were in any way unwilling it was argued that the act should not be a crime.

This distinction contains grey areas, but if we restrict the concept of harm to the persons directly involved, then they are crimes without victims. Crimes without victims are crimes without complainants; that is, the police have to discover the events. But practically none of these events are discovered by the police; only those publicly visible (the porno shop or theater, the massage parlor, the prostitute on the street, the gay bar) make participants vulnerable to the police.

Sexual conduct that might be more properly construed as crimes because they do have unwilling victims are child molestation; rape; incest; and violations of public decency. These offenses have victims, people who will complain about what has been done to them if the circumstances are right. They often do not, but there is a real someone who is offended, not some abstract principle such as saving the family (reasons for laws against adultery) or social corruption of the innocent (laws against prostitution and pornography).

The attempt to redefine the category "sex offender" is directly tied to a change in the relation between the criminal law and the institutions of criminal justice and sexual conduct. Historically the sex statutes embodied the bulk of conservative Christian sexual morality. The police and the courts were assigned the role of en-forcing that morality. For a majority of people in the nineteenth century and for many people today, the decision to have the law and the institutions of justice en-force a dominant religious sexual morality is both obvious and correct.

The process of societal secularization has included an increase in the criticism of the police, the courts, and the prisons for enforcing sexual morality. Many peo-ple, for a variety of reasons, no longer accept that the interests of the state are the same as the interests of particular religious groups. This has resulted in an attempt to separate what the state disapproves of sexually and what major religious groups

The current sex law, combined with present-day electronic surveillance, could create the real possibility of a sexual Big Brother.

disapprove of sexually. However, while sex law still represents traditional Christian sexual values in the United States, it is being criticized from the following points of view:

1. Criminal law in general and the laws concerning sexual conduct in particular should be enacted only when it can be shown that a victim has been harmed. Harm to a third party (a spouse or child of an adulterer, for example) is not enough; harm must be local and proximate. As long as the behavior involves people who are capable of consent, the state has no legitimate interest in the act. One can of course object to such a limited definition of harm and point out, for instance, potential harm to society from the results of sexual activity.

2. There is no longer a single dominant sexual morality in society. The existence of a wide variety of sexual practices shows that few people pay more than lip service to traditional values. In addition, subgroups of the population have different sets of sexual values, and the views of these groups should not be infringed by a majority.

3. It is possible to make a basic distinction between morality and legality. Although in the past laws were often based on moral values, the law and morality do not necessarily overlap. The illegal and the immoral are not common domains;

not everything that is illegal is also immoral, and not everything that is immoral is also illegal.

4. One important criterion of illegality is whether many people agree with or conform with the law. This is a tricky point, but is often raised with reference to sexuality. If many people have extramarital intercourse, a change in the adultery laws could be justified. Clearly one might not want to apply this criterion to a majority wanting to kill a minority; however, in many societies such decisions about morality and legality are often made on the basis of the majority point of view. Numbers do count.

5. Linked to the majority question is the efficiency question. Many sex laws are not enforced and not enforceable, because the acts are performed in private. Such unenforceable laws breed erratic and unfair enforcement, police corruption, and contempt for the law itself. On the other hand, unpopular laws may be morally right (school desegregation); also, the law has a symbolic function — even if unenforceable, it is a signal to society of correct values.

6. The issue of privacy poses one value against another — while the state may have some interest in the consequences of people's sex lives, the laws infringe on individual rights to personal privacy. The privacy argument appeals to higher values.

The foregoing arguments urge a major change in the sexual climate of society, a change that is liberal and libertarian in direction. However, proponents of these views have not been effective in producing legislative change. Only in Illinois has there been a major liberalizing change in the sex laws; in most other states there have been only minor revisions in the criminal codes. In many states proposals to change the sex laws have been defeated regularly. In New York State attempts to change the sodomy statutes have been defeated on the traditional moral grounds of suppressing homosexuality; in Pennsylvania the state legislature recently enacted a new fornication statute on the grounds that it symbolizes moral support for the family.

Even though legislative changes in the sex laws are uncommon, there are administrative changes in the activities of the criminal justice system in a somewhat more libertarian direction. This has been particularly applicable to crimes without victims: pornography, prostitution, and public aspects of homosexuality. This is largely because the police are overwhelmed by other kinds of offenses about which the public is more fearful. Crime in the streets and crimes of violence occupy more public attention than most sex crimes, and the police are responsive to differential pressure from the public. At the same time, members of a legislature who wish to be reelected are responsive to citizens with conservative sexual views who resist legal change vigorously and are probably as numerous as people preferring changes in sex laws.

Contemporary Sex Offenders

When we study sex offenders we are often studying the efficiency or inefficiency of the criminal justice system rather than people who share attributes in common. (See Figure 1.) Thus, limiting the domain of sex offenders to events involving force

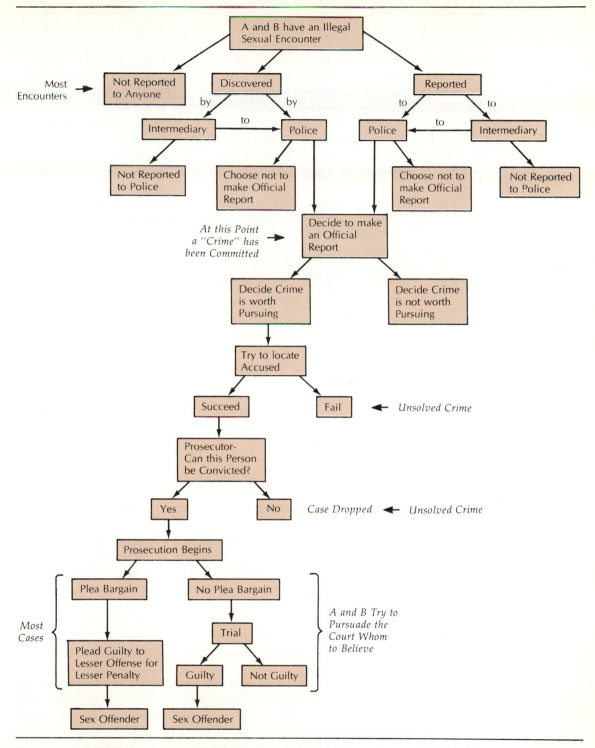

Figure 1   How to Become a Convicted Sex Offender.

or the threat of force, offenses against children and young adolescents, offenses against kin, and offenses involving breach of sexual privacy (voyeurism and exhibitionism) is based on the following kinds of considerations:

1. There is considerable collective agreement that these activities should remain against the law, and that the criminal justice system has a role in their control, no matter how inefficient it might be.
2. These activities have participants who are unwilling; that is, they have victims.
3. There is agreement that these activities call forth a strong negative reaction from both enforcement agencies and the public.
4. These offenses are relatively uncommon, and are not usually psychologically or socially linked to any substantial majority or minority forms of sexual conduct.

Not all the listed activities meet all of the criteria set forth above, but they do share enough common features that they can be treated together.

Heterosexual Offenses Involving Force and Violence

The offenses receiving the most attention in the past five years have been those of rape and attempted rape. This has largely been the result of a systematic campaign by the woman's movement to encourage better enforcement, to change male attitudes toward rape and its victims, to increase penalties, and to raise the consciousness of women about the rape question.

Rape is the critical contemporary sex offense because it is at the center of the current conflict between women and men, a conflict that is far wider than the sexual, but which the sexual symbolizes and expresses. A violent sexual encounter between a man and a woman expresses such diverse social elements as the differential power of men and women in society, the attitudes of women and men toward themselves and each other as individuals and genders, and the historical commitments of social institutions. The use of force to gain sexual access mobilizes these different groups to mitigate, exacerbate, dramatize, symbolize, praise, or blame one or another of the participants.

Only recently has it been recognized that rape is a crime, not against the men associated with the woman, but to the woman herself (a change that has not yet occurred in some societies). Women who are victims of rape often wonder what they did to provoke the crime, worry about the effect on men they know ("What will my husband's friends say?"), or worry about their own moral reputation ("What will other women think?" "What will my husband or lover think?"). These responses are the result of female-male differential power in the society—continuations of the property value of women in marriage and the social allocation of shame.

In part this expresses the attitudes of men toward women. The woman who has been raped is defined as either pure and innocent *or* complicit and thus deserving what happened to her. Again we find ourselves in the world of the "good" woman and the "bad" woman—for a woman to be a legitimate victim of rape she must be sexually pure. This attitude also accounts for our view of the offender—in one case he is a mad beast who attacks innocents, in the other he is a normal man whose sex drive has been aroused, and his use of force is understandable because the woman did not "come across." As a result the victim must demonstrate her right to be a victim, by her manner as a victim and by her prior moral status.

The status of a raped woman as victim is made more uncertain by other women, who have assimilated many of their attitudes from men. They often ask how a victim could have been so stupid or so complicit as to allow the event to occur— what did *she* do? In part this is a morality play in which "good" women (those not victims) define themselves as morally better than victimized women.

Another dimension of the rape problem is that force in heterosexual encounters is in part the outgrowth of the way most people are trained to be sexual together. The current sex-role assignments are for the woman to resist and control and for the man to initiate and press forward. There can be a verbal expression of mutual desire, so that both parties are clear about what they are doing, but so much sexual communication is ambiguous and distorted that it is not always clear what people mean when they say "yes" or "no" or "maybe" or "later." Because a woman's moral and property image is so often compromised by sexual assent (a man's interest is in conquest; he believes she is too "easy" if she says "yes" too quickly, or he worries about how many others she has said "yes" to) she learns to resist. Miscommunication can result in the use of force, even in ongoing relations. On one college campus a quarter of the young women reported that they had been the victims of force at various stages of socio-sexual relations with young men: coerced to do something sexual that they did not want to do.

REPORTING RAPE

The rape event can emerge from a relatively conventional socio-sexual encounter (meeting in a bar or at the beach; a continued dating relationship; being driven home by a friend) or can be an attack by a stranger. It is more difficult to establish victim status under current legal conditions if the offender was previously known to the victim, or if the victim had sex with the offender under other circumstances. When the offender is a stranger it is easier to report, since the onus falls more directly on him. The rape victim, in deciding to report the event, is in a dilemma, knowing that she will be required to publicize her sexuality and participate in a moral drama of blame. Only recently have police departments begun to try to deal with rape as a crime of violence rather than as part of the general moral struggle between men and women.

As a result of these conditions, a low percentage of rapes are reported to the police. In 1967 the Uniform Crime Reports, based on police department reports to the FBI, fixed the rape rate at 11.6 per 100,000 population; however, a study in which a sample of households was asked whether someone in the house had been raped increased the rate to 42.5 per 100,000. This study, in which someone who answered the door was simply asked whether such a thing had happened to someone in the household, increased the reported rate fourfold.

Given that such studies themselves involve under-reporting (if it happened to the person who answered the door they might not say so; if it happened to others in the household, they may not have told the person who answered the door) and that people often interpret rape in a very narrow sense (solely forced intercourse or other extensive sexual intimacy), the rape rate is probably double the victim study rate (somewhere between 70 and 90 per 100,000), and the general experience of force in sex is probably double that rate (140 to 160 per 100,000). This base figure of 100,000 includes men; since only women get raped, if we are calculating risk the rate should be doubled again.

If a woman decides to take legal action, she often finds herself involved in a long contest in which her version of reality is contrasted with the man's version of reality. Many women find the experience so degrading that they are unwilling to begin, or to continue the process after it has begun. There are attempts underway to change this system by using female police officers or by changing the attitudes of men in the criminal justice system, but it is a long and slow process.

Rape is difficult to prove legally. Some rape laws are very narrowly construed, requiring both penetration and/or specific proof of penetration; the New York law at one time required corroboration, requiring the woman to bring a witness to her rape! The laws are designed to protect the accused, so very few rapes are reported, and few of those reported are processed through the criminal justice system to imprisonment of the offender. The men who are in prison for rape are thus not representative of all of the men in society who have forced or raped women.

RAPISTS IN PRISON

Most imprisoned rapists are men who are social incompetents in many more ways than the sexual. Given current enforcement conditions and a moderate level of personal skill, a man could rape many women and never or rarely be arrested. The cards are stacked in the perpetrator's favor. The men in prison are those whose offenses involved alcohol, personal ineptitude, a belief that they would not be reported, fantasies that the women "liked it," or who impulsively raped a woman in much the same way they engaged in other violence. These are the characteristics of most of the men who are imprisoned for rape; few of them are men who engaged in systematic careers of sexual violence.

A study by Paul Gebhard and others (1965) offers the best description of the subclass of sex offenders using force who are in prison. While the categories developed by these researchers depart from usual classification systems, they do seem to relate to the elements of behavior that characterize the nonsexual conduct of these men. The authors identify a series of subclasses, the most common of which were men whose sexual contacts with women regularly included threat or violence (about one-third of this study's cases) combined with a history of generalized violence. The expression of violence emerged as the central theme in these males' behavior, perhaps indicating that they well represent men who were committed to violence rather than to sex.

The second largest class was the "amoral delinquent," that is, males whose general life styles involved aggressive self-seeking; their approach to sexuality is the same as their approach to other desires. The third group were males whose judgment seems to be blunted by drunkenness, or whose sensibilities and ability to cope with sexual situations are distorted. A last group were men whose behavior was termed explosive, that is, there was nothing in the accessible history of the individual to predict any behaviors of this kind (he is not a "normal" rapist); in these cases the male seems unable to interpret the appropriate signs of assent and, captivated by his own internal states, uses force.

What is most interesting about the categories developed by Gebhard et al. is that they place sexual behavior in the context of other forms of behavior. The sexual act is shaped by the existence of other factors: general aggressivity; a heedless life style; the confusions of alcohol; as well as problems of sexual repression. In consequence, it is difficult to settle on a series of categories that exhaustively describe the offender, indicating that different kinds of males are collected by the legal criminal process, but not altogether randomly since those with records appear more often, as do those who have a general predisposition to violence. What is required to understand them is a knowledge of the way in which the conventional sexual script which exists for males seeking sexual activity contains many of the same elements that contribute to these crimes. Aggression, drinking, and sexual ignorance are involved in many sexual encounters in this society, but only in some of them is excessive force used, and few of these ultimately become the basis of the charge of and conviction for rape.

PROTECTION AGAINST RAPE

Preventing the use of force in sexual relations is made difficult by the uneven processes of conventional socio-sexual change. Even though women are becoming more open to sexuality in nonmarital relationships, the patriarchal attitudes of men and women toward sexuality have changed only slightly. Because sexuality remains covert and has some moral taint, women are still vulnerable to aggression in socio-sexual encounters. The capacity to transmit sexual interest accurately and clearly by women and the capacity to receive it in the same spirit by men has not kept pace with changes in courtship practices. There are now more chances for things to go wrong. By becoming more open sexually, women may have given up an older protection while not yet gaining autonomous sexual status.

In these kinds of conventional socio-sexual relationships there are only three protections that seem feasible. The first is a clear-cut decision point when fair notice is given about sexual intent — the promise of sex should not be used by women to hold on to a potential partner. Since desire changes throughout a relationship or encounter, and sex is often used as a counter in bargains between men and women, or people want to be "spontaneous" (a "bad" woman thinks about sex ahead of time), the potential for error and resulting force is very high.

A second protection is for men to view "no" or "maybe" as "no," to abandon the rule of initiator — when a woman says "no" to believe her. As long as women and men cooperate in stereotyped sex-role performances, they will be constantly involved in potentially dangerous relationships. The problem is that such miscommunication is often important to us as sexual actors; women do not want to define themselves as sexually interested or autonomous, they want to be overwhelmed or spontaneous or swept away. Men want to feel a sense of conquest, that sex is a victory. How can a man "score" when he has a partner rather than an opponent?

A third protective change that might be made is to reduce the importance of the sex aspect of rape and focus on the violence and coercion. No one ever asked the victims of mugging whether they should have been on the street at night, why they were carrying money, whether they attracted the mugger — it is assumed that the mugger was in the wrong. The point is that if the use of force in human relationships is wrong, then the legal key to the rape question is the use of violence — rape is assault. Such a view of rape gets rid of the question of good woman/bad woman and focuses on the violence. The question comes down to "Was this person attacked or threatened?" If the answer is "yes" (one does not have to prove that there was intercourse, or semen in the vagina, or any of that) then the police could proceed. If this were the signal to men — just do not attack women (sexually or otherwise) then the potential for rape might decrease.

At this time we really do not know how to deal with or treat the rapist or aggressive sexual offender. This is true in part because the population in prison is not typical, and in part because aggression for sexual purposes characterizes a very large number of conventional men. It might be possible to explore such topics as hostility to women as a major source of rape rather than focusing on the physical characteristics of the offense. Also, it would be useful to increase the rate of reporting by changing the police and judicial system to make reports both psychologically easier and convictions legally more likely. A general increase in the efficiency of criminal justice might be more productive than specific changes in rape penalties. On the legal side, punishment that is swift and sure is more effective than that which is delayed, unlikely, and unevenly severe.

Offenses Against Young Adolescents and Children

Going from childhood to early adolescence is a difficult transition in this society. Sexually ignorant adolescents are given sexual definition and a potential sexual status by adults. During the period between ages twelve to fifteen, many young females are vulnerable to the sexual attentions of older males, and many of these encounters are marked by ignorance and the possibility of exploitation. At one time such events were viewed with considerable concern, and resulted in charges against the males involved, ranging from contributing to the delinquency of a minor to statutory rape. At present such charges are rarer, as the sexual status of young people is more widely accepted.

However, this has been a one-sided solution which has left a fairly large number of young women as the only population of female sex offenders (other than prostitutes) in the United States. Because of the intervention of juvenile courts, many young women who are sexually active early in life have become defined as delinquent or incorrigible. Nearly all young women who are taken into the custody of juvenile courts for whatever reasons are routinely given vaginal examinations to see if they are virgins (as well as to check for venereal disease). Young men's genitals are not examined when they are arrested, even when they are arrested for a sex offense.

The intervention of the court system in the lives of these young women, when they become pregnant, when they run away from home, or when they are caught with a young man, is not particularly constructive. The juvenile courts often further demoralize them (particularly since they are doing things that many other young women are also doing) with genital examinations, incarceration for shorter or greater lengths of time, and a strong focus on their sexual "immorality." These young women are victims of sex offenses, but they are offenses committed by agencies originally designed to aid them.

CHARACTERIZING THE CHILD MOLESTER

Few men are true *pedophiles;* that is, men who prefer to have sex with children. Such men represent perhaps no more than five or ten percent of men who commit offenses against children, but it is among pedophiles that we find men with long histories of child molesting, who have never been arrested or convicted. A few such men are extremely skillful in their approach to children and reduce the risk of arrest by exercising great caution. Among them we also find those offenders who are most likely to have sex with both female and male children.

Most men in prison for child molesting were substituting sexual contact with children for contacts they were unable to manage with adults. They are usually alcoholic, senile, emotionally unstable, or mentally disabled — generally socially inadequate and impulsive. It is their social inadequacy and impulsive behavior that gets them caught and put into prison. However, most police and therapists operate on theories that attribute specific sexual motives and characteristics to child molesters. Sometimes such offenders go ahead and assume these characteristics, since it may improve their chances of being treated or released from prison. To "get better" they must pretend to be what they are expected to be.

Men known to the children they molest are far more likely to be reported and apprehended than are strangers. The more extensive the sexual activity, the more likely the child will say something, the parents be alarmed, and the police energetic. The vast majority of physical sex offenses against children (as opposed to exhibitionism) involve only casual touching and fondling; few involve oral-genital or coital contacts. Rarely do they involve violence, or death of the victim; however, these acts are the ones that generate the greatest public outcry. The latter types of contacts create far greater risks of an active enforcement response. The longer the duration of the offense, the more likely an arrest, if only by accident. Many offenders against children act impulsively, as if not in control of what they are doing; they often report feeling "compelled." Such men are often quickly arrested, since they take few or no precautions. The prison population of such offenders is thus representative only of their own behavioral strategies.

REPORTING AND EFFECT ON THE VICTIM

Another factor that influences who is reported, caught, and imprisoned is the child's attitude. The reporting process is usually in two steps: children report to their parents; their parents report to the police. (See Figure 1.) At both these points there is loss of reporting, but for different reasons. Whether or not children report the event to their parents depends in some measure on how implicated the children are in the offense (did they enjoy it? do they feel complicit?) and how free they are to talk to their parents about sexual matters.

Children do not interpret the offense behavior of adults in the same way that adults do. What is perceived to be sexual by adults is perceived by children as unpleasant, or immodest, or anxiety-provoking. The child's description of the event, both in objective and motivational terms, is vastly different from that of the adult's. This disparity is greater the younger the child, for while young children may know that something is happening, they are often not sure what. It is this sense of discomfort that the child reports to parents — who then convert the ambiguous report into a sexual offense. Prior parental responses to other kinds of ambiguous events will condition the child's capacities to report others to them. These reports will be offered in proportion to the extent that lines of communication to parents are open, that the event occurred with a stranger, that the event was frightening, and that it does not leave the child feeling implicated. Being implicated is often difficult for children to understand; they may feel guilty because it occurred while they were in a forbidden place, or because they were doing something else that they were warned against.

Parents must decide whether or not they wish to expose their child to the police and the courts, an experience that they know will be unpleasant for the child. If the child is not implicated in the offense and it was not frightening, the parent might well report it. Counterbalancing this tendency is the parents' knowledge that the possibility of arrest and conviction is relatively poor. Perhaps the crucial element in reporting is the use of police to protect the safety of children from persons in the environment of the child (janitors, shopkeepers, casually known neighbors) who are identified by the child in such offenses.

Parents recognize that their children may be negatively affected by contacts with police and the courts, so they often do not report offenses their children tell them about. Other countries have adopted new systems for handling child victims which involve a "child examiner" who interviews the child, and serves as a surrogate for the child in the courtroom with the permission of the prosecution and the defense. Such a procedure would change the rules of evidence in the United States, which require that the child be cross-examined; such procedure is thus unlikely to be adopted here.

Except for those offenses that involve force and violence or coercion, children seem resilient and remain largely undamaged in their future adjustment. There are some adults who report long-term uneasiness or fear about sex resulting from being a child victim but even in these cases there are rarely gross defects in social functioning. Such a minimum long-term impact of the offense is true of children who both do and do not tell their parents — though there is evidence that children are sometimes more affected by the strength of the parental reaction than by the event itself. If the parent reacts strongly or emotionally and begins cross-examining the child, the child may think that he or she has done something wrong. Often children do not interpret these experiences as being sexual unless they occur near puberty or are extended over time.

HOMOSEXUAL OFFENSES

Homosexual contacts by adults with adolescents or children present an extremely mixed picture. Some contacts with adolescent males can result from normal mistakes about the age of consent (a sixteen year old really looks eighteen), but there are a minority of persons who have strong attachments to males around the age of puberty. The existence of homosexual photo magazines of young boys, some of them prepubescent, indicates at least a fantasy interest in boys and nubile adolescents in some proportion of the male homosexual population. It is doubtful whether this fantasy activity is converted to overt activity in any large measure.

Studies of homosexual offenses against adolescents and young children are relatively rare. Research suggests that the contacts with children are largely substitutes for contacts with slightly older boys (normally around 14 and over), but that there is a certain amount of generalized pedophilia, regardless of gender, represented in a few of these offenses. While this particular group of offenders was more homosexually experienced than other offender groups (other than those who had offended homosexually against adults), they offered a substantial picture of heterosexual activity as well. In some cases this heterosexuality also included a pedophilic interest in female children.

These contacts with younger males also result from a homosexual interest concealed inside other adult-child roles (teacher, older friend, guide). The legal categories mask as many differences in motivation and development among offenders as it exposes. One can estimate that a larger number of these kinds of offenses occur than are reported, with young males not telling their parents about transient homosexual contacts or approaches. The impact of these offenses on conventional sexual development is currently unclear, since most of the studies of child victimization are of females.

A substantial number of homosexuals report in adulthood that they had a homosexual experience with an older male (perhaps only an older adolescent) early in life which would indicate that there is some significance at least for those males who have other predisposing experiences. Studies of adolescent male sex offenders, however, report that few males continued their offense behavior into adulthood, indicating a low level of predictability from adolescent to adult experiences. A review of the Kinsey data on the homosexual experience of college-going males suggests that about twenty-five percent of all college-entering males (about eighty percent of those having homosexual experiences) have their homosexual experiences mostly sporadically and prior to age eighteen, and five to seven percent of all such males (about twenty percent of those with homosexual experience) have homosexual experience thereafter. It is possible to suggest that only a minority of males who have homosexual experiences in adolescence continue homosexual activity into adulthood.

Incest Offenses

An understanding of incest, what causes it and what allows it to continue, requires examination of the family in which it occurs. The majority of known cases involve fathers and daughters (or stepdaughters), or brothers and sisters. The incidence of brother-sister incest seems to be low, but this impression may result from the fact that few cases are known to the police. Most of those that are known involve intellectually limited young people drawn from isolated rural pockets of society. Some cases are reported to therapists, but it is difficult to estimate how many cases there are or to predict what the outcomes might be.

The majority of men in prison for incest are fathers, many of whom come from rural, isolated communities or who migrated from such communities to urban areas. These offenders are often characterized by limited intellectual ability and environments that offer limited social or sexual opportunities. This has led to the assumption that incest is uncommon among middle-class families. However, a recent program of treatment for unconvicted people in California has led to the conclusion that such offenses may be more common in the middle class than was supposed. In this study many of the patient families were middle class, yet many of the same patterns of family dynamics appeared that are described below.

Father-daughter incest seems to arise in families in which the father is under considerable stress outside the family, the wife has withdrawn her emotional and sexual support, and the father turns to a particular daughter for emotional and then sexual fulfillment. It is the intersection of an available daughter, a weak or absent mother, and a chronic or transitory stress that seems to predispose men to incest. Whether it continues depends on a pattern of collusion developing in the family — father and daughter against the mother, or the father and mother in secret collusion against the daughter.

Incest can occur with one preferred daughter, or can, in some families, become a pattern which involves a number of daughters. As each daughter leaves, the father switches his attention to a younger child. In these cases there is complicity between wife and husband, since the relationships between father and daughter may continue for years.

A pattern of family complicity in incest depends largely on the responses of both the wife and the daughter to the father's activities. The daughter may cooperate in the relationship to please her father, particularly if it begins when she is young, before puberty. She may even be pleased to be a substitute wife, replacing her mother. If the mother knows what is going on, she may ignore even the most obvious evidence in an attempt to keep the family together. In this case the daughter is trapped by both her parents. In a few cases the daughter may report her father to school or friends, hoping to end the relationship. Often during adolescence girls who are involved in incest or who are approached by a father run away from home in order to avoid it. Such girls are often treated as "runaways" and delinquents. When the mother reacts early, or when the daughter can get help, the incest is interrupted. How often these various outcomes actually occur is unknown.

There is little evidence about the long-term effects of incest on the daughter, and little evidence about appropriate modes of treatment for the offender and the family. Most modern treatment programs are focusing on the dynamics of the family rather than on the single individuals involved.

Voyeurism and Exhibitionism

Both voyeurism and exhibitionism are violations of the sexual privacy of others, so they have victims who report them. However, they are committed by quite different kinds of people and are linked to conventional sexual conduct in different ways.

VOYEURISM

Most men walking down the street will glance in a lit window, look out of a train or car window, or look into the wall of windows in a hotel or apartment building nearby. Many apartments in high-rise buildings now have telescopes or binoculars near the windows, suggesting that the residents may window look. In some communities of high-rise buildings there is a tendency to keep the shades up, thoughtfully or thoughtlessly providing sexual stimuli for a stranger.

What differentiates the offender from the casual onlooker is willingness to "walk on the lawn," to leave the sidewalk, so to speak, and go up and look in. Instead of taking a casual opportunity, the voyeur makes opportunities. If the activity is carefully done, is not constant, does not involve entry or making noise, then rarely is the voyeur noticed or reported.

As far as we know most voyeurs simply want to look. The looking fulfills a sense of sexual adventure and participation, a heightened sense of novelty which many of them are not socially competent to manage in real life. Such men are rarely dangerous; however, there are offenders with mixed patterns of behavior, such as the peeper-burglar or the peeper-rapist. Danger to others is introduced by willingness to enter the house and willingness to assault a victim. Such patterns can develop in a number of ways: the man can begin as a peeper, go on to burglarize houses, and then rape a woman during a burglary. What may distinguish the peeper from the onlooker is the willingness to walk up to the window; what distinguishes the dangerous from the non-dangerous is willingness to crawl in the window.

We know very little about voyeurism. Because it is so closely linked to what most men do, passive onlooking, it is difficult to trace particular patterns of conduct. It appears to be mostly a transient activity of young men, though there are cases of men who continue the practice for many years as part of a general repertoire of sexual activity.

EXHIBITIONISM

Exhibitionism is quite different from voyeurism. Wearing tight clothing or bathing suits to display a "basket" or bulge is not uncommon among male homosexuals, as is the display of the penis in a public restroom or bath. However, it is uncommon for a man to display his penis in approaching a woman sexually; it is not part of the usual script.

Probably the best distinctions that can be made are (1) between men who expose themselves to adults and men who expose themselves to children, and (2) between men who expose themselves because of some transitory stress and men who have consistent and systematic patterns of exposure. Exposure to adults is commonly an expression of anger and hostility; it represents the desire to shock women, who are simply unaware of or indifferent to the man. This desire to shock often occurs among men who are suffering from transitory stress or sexual deprivation (a pregnant wife, a lost job, a slight from a woman) — the resultant anger is directed toward a passerby, toward uncaring people. It is an attempt to reaffirm or display potency. The shock that women show is an integral part of the "erotic" character of the act. Often when the stress is removed, such men stop exhibiting and return to regular life. Most men who exhibit themselves do so for very short periods of time and most are not arrested.

Men who exhibit regularly to adult women are also seeking sexual reparations, saying angrily, "Look at me!" However, men who expose to children are often looking for a nonjudgmental response and such men also may have histories of child molestation. This tends to be an uncommon link, but is represented in prison fairly often because the potential for arrest and conviction is very high; that is, an exhibitionist who is also a molester is more likely to be arrested than one who is only an exhibitionist.

Studies of the exhibitionist suggest that among those who are arrested many seem to be shy, inhibited, overcontrolled men who have very limited sexual experience. Few seem to be particularly dangerous, nor is there any evidence that many of them increase the seriousness of their offenses, except for the minority who also molest children. This pattern is usually the child molester becoming an exhibitionist rather than going the other direction.

Conclusion

Recent research about the sex offender no longer supports the older sex research and criminological images of the sex offender as the unrepressed sex drive gone wrong. The evidence is strong that in most cases these men are socially inadequate, and that their inability to deal with the usual stresses and strains of life (sexual and otherwise) results in their behavior. This is particularly true of offenders against children, incest cases, and exhibitionists. Rarely are they violent; more often they are ineffectual.

It may well be that people under stress have various ways of dealing with it. Some men get drunk, some go to a prostitute, some go hunting or fishing — perhaps many kinds of sex offenses are similar ways of dealing with the stress of life. In specific circumstances they seem to be a way of dealing with anger, discomfort, irritation, or fear. In other cases the offense may be deeply motivated by loneliness or by an attempt to get in touch with another person who will not judge them as inadequate. It is useful to search for the nonsexual as well as the sexual motivations for what people do sexually.

It is not that such offenses are harmless or inconsequential, or that they should not be controlled, particularly where violence or force is used; the dilemma is that many of the patterns of behavior we wish to control, particularly violence, are learned by conventional socialization, not as a result of rare or strange early lives.

Our problem is unwillingness to recognize that certain normal patterns are more dangerous than those we believe are abnormal. This is so because, as noted in the case of homosexuality, the origins are considered abnormal only after it has been decided that the outcomes are abnormal. Violence has not yet been determined as abnormal in the United States.

Our understanding of these patterns of conduct is remarkably inadequate, and at the present time there is little evidence that attempts to understand them are going forward particularly rapidly. We seem to be at a midway point; the sex offender no longer stands at the head of our list of public enemies, but we have not yet decided we need to understand his patterns of sexual conduct, or the light they may shed on "conventional" sexuality.

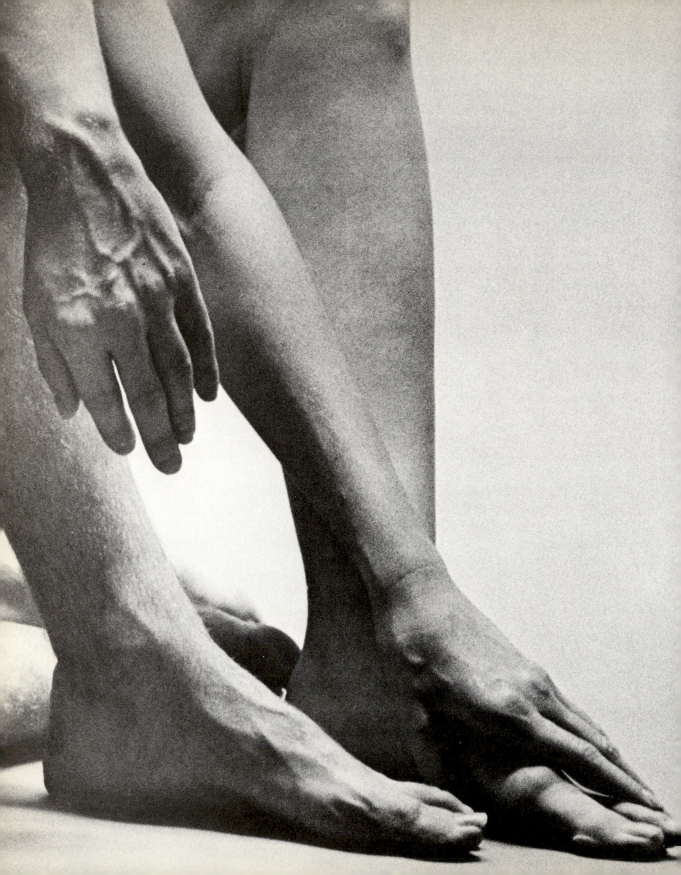

"Curiouser and curiouser," said Alice.
Lewis Carroll, *Alice in Wonderland*

THE STRUGGLE FOR CONTROL OVER THE MEANING OF SEXUAL CONDUCT, OF THE boundaries between approved and disapproved sexuality, can be illustrated in the choice of new labels to describe various forms of sexuality. The tendency by the media and libertarian groups to call certain forms of sexuality "new sexual life-styles," and the people who participate in them members of "sexual minorities" is a shift in rhetoric that has both political and scientific consequences. To label conduct that was once thought to be the ultimate of perversion, immorality, and criminality as simply one of a multiplicity of "life styles" is a significant comment on changes in U.S. culture over the last two decades. However, just because there are new options offered, there will not necessarily be a large number of takers nor will many people necessarily join the ranks of the sexual minorities. Even so, to describe these people as members of a minority group rather than as pathological and perverted is to record a major change in cultural emphasis.

The long history of political change and increased toleration of cultural diversity in Western societies has focused on the rights of minorities. The right to dissent from the majority and to practice minority activities and recruit people to them has been one of the primary fruits of pluralistic social orders. The recognition of the rights of religious and political minorities has been the core achievement of democracy, and recently, this umbrella of minority rights has been extended to such groups as national and cultural minorities. Extending this umbrella to sexual minorities in the United States is a conscious attempt to redefine the limits of legitimate and approved sexuality.

Viewed in this way, there is probably a sexual plurality in the United States, though probably not a sexual majority. That is, most people are probably practicing heterosexuality in marriage with a moderate range of positions and techniques in and around the marital bed and have intercourse a moderate number of times each month. At the same time, large numbers of people who practice majority sex also practice minority sex—that is, some are adulterers, and some have sex with people for pay, while others have group sex or anal intercourse, and still others have had some bisexual experience. Clearly sex between men and women (along with masturbation) is the majority practice, both in numbers and in frequency, but as we have seen there are a variety of kinds of sex between men and women, free and for pay, in marriage and out, for love and for lust, in pairs and in groups, all of which reduce the simple majority nature of the experience.

From this point of view a number of the sexualities we have discussed could be considered as minorities. Homosexuality, bisexuality, prostitution, child molesting, rape, and incest are all minority phenomena. Bisexuality, homosexuality, and prostitution have been treated more fully, because they are conventionally major aspects of the sexual conduct in society. Homosexuality and bisexuality reflect quite directly on heterosexuality, since understanding them makes our understanding of majority sex more precise. The dimension of sex-object choice is a key label which organizes our thinking, perhaps more than any other sexual label we possess. Prostitution involves a minority of women (but perhaps a majority of men), yet it illustrates the problem of the status of women in society and the complexity of law and economics as they intersect with what people do sexually.

Sex offenders can also be considered minorities. Indeed, it has been suggested that society could provide, for the exhibitionist and the voyeur, locations in which they might practice their interests with persons who would not be offended or disturbed. This drift has already begun in some societies where the indifference, at least to exhibitionism, has resulted in a dramatic decline in reports to the police. Most young women in Denmark, for instance, no longer find the exhibitionist sufficiently disturbing to bother calling the police; the impact of this indifference on the offender is unknown. The reason not to apply the minority label to most offenders is that the people they practice on are not volunteers. The child molester and the rapist may indeed be members of a sexual minority, but there is little willingness to extend to them the protections of minority "status."

Any list of minorities is thus arbitrary. There can be no final or ultimate list, for as we add dimensions to the sexual, new minorities may well appear. Any subset of activities or beliefs or preferences could become the basis for the claim for minority status. There are, for instance, people who are interested in sex with the dead (necrophiles) as well as persons who find sexual excitement in feces and urine.

There are, however, four sexual minorities which have a greater claim on our attention; first, because they have the capacity to strongly organize the sex life of some people, and second, because their organizing themes illuminate some of our understandings of similar elements that are important to members of the erotic majority. These minorities are sadomasochism (the mixing of pain with sexuality), animal contacts (sex with animals other than humans), fetishism (sexual arousal from objects detached from the human person), and transvestism and transsexualism.

Most of these minority sexual behaviors are more characteristic of men than of women—indeed men tend to predominate in most forms of unconventional sexual conduct and represent a majority of the customers for unconventional sexual services—from pornography to incest, the bulk of the appeal is to men. It is unclear why this should be so, but it may have to do with male sex-role requirements, requirements which offer opportunities both to initiate and to fail sexually. Perhaps as women find increasing social and sexual opportunities and roles to perform they will begin to show up as sexual minorities in increasing numbers. Another aspect of this phenomenon may well be that women have always had forms of minority sexual conduct which were never noticed, conduct which was both positive and negative. We are just reaching the point where the non-orgasmic woman can be defined as a negative sexual minority, while the multi-orgasmic woman can be defined as a member of an elite minority.

All of these minorities raise serious moral and psychological questions about the limits of the "normal" and our capacity to understand others, to move ourselves inside someone else and experience the world as that person does. We often ask people to do this in anthropology and sociology—to take the role of a cultural stranger. For example, there is a high school human-cultures program supported by the National Science Foundation which asks students to try to see the Arctic world as an Eskimo of forty years ago might have seen it. The program includes a film which shows Eskimos killing an elk and eating its eyeballs, passing them around as delicacies. Most of us would not find elk eyeballs appetizing, but if we try to see the behavior from the Eskimo's point of view, rather than from our own, we may end up with an understanding of the human environment which makes such conduct culturally "normal." We may still not want to do it ourselves, we may disapprove of it, or we may even want it to be against the law; thus, the process of trying to understand a form of conduct and the process of judging it may be at least partially independent of each other.

Sadomasochism

The word "sadomasochism" comes from the names of two men: the Marquis de Sade (1740–1814), a French nobleman and writer, and Leopold Sacher-Masoch (1836–1895), a German novelist of the nineteenth century. The word was invented by the German "sexologist" Richard von Krafft-Ebing as a name for behavior which links sexual conduct to pain. Those who inflict pain are called sadists; those who have it inflicted upon them are called masochists.

The Marquis de Sade was not primarily interested in combining sexuality and pain; his fundamental interest was in using cruelty and eroticism as vehicles for social criticism: he was primarily a political revolutionary, not a sexual one, and his treatment was traditionally repressive. He was imprisoned both by the king of France and after the Revolution by Napoleon, and he died in a mental hospital.

De Sade's tales of eroticism, cruelty, torture, excrement—the destruction of innocence by obscenity—were an attempt at cultural vandalism. This strategy of social change through obscenity is echoed in the words of Mark Rudd in the student revolt of the 1960s:

The obscenity helped define our struggle. Finally, we could say in public what we had been saying among ourselves. We could use our own language. All forms of authority, tradition, respect (you show respect, obviously, by not using your own language) had broken down.[1]

In contrast, Sacher-Masoch was probably the most widely read writer in Germany after Goethe. It has been observed that his novels contain most of the sexual themes that appear in Freud's case histories. His most important erotic novel was *Venus in Furs,* which focused on the theme of the erotic degradation of a man by a woman.

Our problem in understanding sadomasochism is one of clarifying the relation between such labels as initiation, assertion, and aggression in sexual preliminaries and the role of pain or the fear of pain in sexual response. Conventionally, sadism and masochism are often thought to be at the extreme ends of a continuum, a scale

1. Jerry L. Avorn et al., *Up Against the Ivy Wall* (Atheneum Publishers, 1968), p. 292.

that is somehow the same as the scale that ranges from assertiveness to passivity. Sadism is thus assertive, active, controlling, and aggressive, while masochism is passive, reactive, controlled, and submissive. These two polar opposites are often linked to masculinity and femininity as well.

Sadism and masochism appear in this scheme as extensions of conventional conduct. As we have seen, such a continuous model has not been helpful in the study of same-sex/opposite-sex relations, and it is of limited use in this case. As with homosexuality, there is a confusion of sadomasochism with conventional versions of gender-role differences. Since men are thought to be assertive, initiatory, and aggressive in sex, while women are passive, reactive, and submissive, it is thought that there is something particularly wrong with masochistic men or sadistic women. Some masochism in women and some sadism in men, however, is considered as within the limits of normal behavior. It may be more profitable to realize that some men who are interested in being hurt as part of sex may well develop role confusions that result from their sexual interests (If I want to be hurt, I must be feminine), but their sexual interests are not always a consequence of role confusions (I am a weakling, someone should beat me).

At present the status of the different behaviors classified as sadomasochism is unclear; they may not even have any relation to each other. There are some modest "sadomasochistic" activities (biting, scratching) that seem to enhance sexual activity among sexually conventional people, and there are other activities which seem to take on more elaborate and painful ritual forms. The connection between a little pain among conventional people and much pain among sadomasochists may, however, be false, the result of looking too closely at the inflicting of pain and not at other elements.

There is evidence from the Kinsey research that many people (perhaps a quarter of the men and women studied) are aroused by mild biting or being bitten (not enough to draw blood) during sexual activity. Slightly aggressive, tension-inducing behavior seems to characterize the sexuality of a large number of people. Sexual arousal produces higher thresholds to sensory stimuli (including pain) and often after sex people have bruises they do not remember getting or giving. Such levels of stimulation are hardly necessary for either arousal or orgasm, but they are well within the usual range of most people's scripts for sexual activity. If this is taken as the center point on a continuum, we could argue that inflicting pain is merely an extension of animal good spirits, but it may well be that important symbolic transitions are required before pain or fear of pain can be translated into pleasure.

FANTASY AND REALITY

It is at the level of fantasy that we find the most profitable entry into an understanding of the role of sadomasochism in sexuality. Again from the Kinsey data, about twenty percent of the men and twelve percent of the women interviewed reported that they were aroused by being told stories involving rape, bondage, chains, whips, and discipline. While it does appear that more women than men tended to link themselves to the masochistic role in these fantasies, a minority of men were aroused by the masochistic role as well. Women (and some men) have fantasies of bondage, of being tied up, of having sex with a stranger—a faceless, invisible person—who does sexual things to them and forces them to do sexual things. None of these fantasies, however, involves actual injury. It is as if they are really fantasies of having sex without responsibility or guilt. People can thus fantasize sexual activity which they would never do in reality. The thought of being tied up or held down during sex relieves guilt related to personal responsibility and offers an occasion in fantasy for sexual experimentation. Such fantasies can also produce guilt, particularly in the sexually inexperienced or those who view their fantasies as reflecting their desires. These are *symbolic* ways of tinkering with our sexual scripts.

What makes the picture complicated is that most *overt* masochists are men. That is, those people whose interests in sex are mixed in with a desire to be subjugated or tied up or injured are predominately men. There are a number of possible explanations, none of which are particularly satisfying in the sense that they account for very many cases. Indeed, as with other forms of sexual conduct in which a particular combination of sexual and nonsexual elements is uncommon, and how people learned the combination is not obvious, people with overt sadomasochistic histories appear to have very little in common in *concrete* observable terms. This messy data results in having a "theory" which is very abstract and for which there are many exceptions.

One possible explanation is that because of cultural role definitions those women who wish to be sexually submissive, reactive, and controlled (for whatever reasons) can do so in conventional sexual activity. The very character of conventional heterosexual scripts offers this role and may satisfy the fantasy and fact of domination. Extended slightly, the female component of such scripts often contains minimal elements of role-specific sadism and masochism. On the other hand, since men are expected to play the dominant, initiatory role, a male wish (for whatever reasons) to be submissive, controlled, and subjugated requires a powerful counter script. Conventional sex cannot express these needs for most men, and therefore there is a tendency either to fantasize or to act out in what are perceived as extreme ways. It is this role-reversal problem that produces the whips, chains, leather and rubber, the images of bondage and discipline that characterize the behavior or fantasies of some men. At the same time, the actual experiences of masochism may free some people from guilt about forms of sexuality which appear quite conventional to other people. Such symbolic transformations, as well as acting out the roles, can serve a wide number of purposes for the people who use them. What people are doing is using the resources of the culture around them to organize and stabilize their own experiences. It is important to point out that the way they currently perform is often uninformative about how or why they are now doing it.

MALE HOMOSEXUAL FANTASY

An example of using a particular sexual symbolism to express other, nonsexual conflicts may be seen in the large numbers of heterosexual men who have dreams in which they are involved in homosexual activity. These men have exclusively heterosexual histories, they have never had sex with men, and they have never thought or fantasized about having sex with men, but they tell their psychothera-pists that they have had these dreams. The usual way to interpret these dreams is to assume that the dreamer is latently homosexual and is working out a hidden homo-sexual conflict. An alternative approach is to ask what is happening in his daily life, and the therapist who does this finds that in many cases men who suddenly begin to have homosexual dreams report some prior injury to their masculinity. The boss has given them a hard time, or they have had a bad sexual experience with a wom-an and they blame themselves for it. They think their masculinity has been at-tacked, and they symbolically transform this attack into a question about their manhood. The failure to achieve is translated into "I must be weak, not strong," and then, because of the conventional cultural connection of male homosexuality with weakness, passivity, and femininity, into "I must be homosexual." They re-spond with the symbolic equipment they have acquired from their culture.

This also may explain the frequent homosexual fantasies of male paranoids. Freud said the sources of paranoia and homosexuality in males were the same be-cause male paranoids commonly report that other men are trying to do something homosexual to them. This happens in hospitals and with private patients, and con-ventionally it is assumed that the man is somehow homosexual (concealed, latent, repressed, or unconscious), but another way to interpret it is to stay at the symbolic level and note that the fear of other men may include a fear of physical rape. The paranoid man is saying, "Everybody's against me, including other men, and among the fears I have of them are sexual fears." He then makes a symbolic conversion to attribute homosexual characteristics to himself.[2]

The adaptive explanation of homosexual dreams and fantasies seems more plausible than the historical-analytic one. The fantasies emerge from the context of current living rather than from childhood, and this suggests the ways in which we convert and rearrange and set up new scripts for ourselves. If men are raised with an image of the world as rigidly dichotomized into men and women, masculine and feminine, with their sexuality connected to that dichotomy, then men who de-fine themselves as weak, dependent, or controlled will attempt to use the opposite elements to explain, understand, act out, or resist these definitions.

ROLE OF RITUAL

Most sadomasochistic conduct (fantasized and overt) involves extended symbolic transformations and ritualizations, particularly on the part of the masochist, who must convert what are objectively painful events into experientially erotic events. Such ritualizations are often less important for sadists (particularly where there is an unwilling victim), but in those cases where there is a cooperative pair the sadist must play at least a minimal role.[3]

The importance of these ritualizations is best displayed in what is one of the

2. The sexual danger from men is recognized by both men and women. The fear of homosexual rape among men is probably not as common, however, as heterosexual rape fear in women, although it is quite a common reaction (along with rage) in men who have masculinity conflicts.
3. The writer Alexander Trocchi, when asked why he only wrote about masochists, once said, "What can you possibly say about the sadist? His arm got tired?"

most important erotic dramas of the twentieth century, *The Balcony*, by Jean Genet. The scene is a vast brothel in which nonsexual fantasies of power and domination are mixed with the sexual. Genet's comment seems to be that there is little difference between the desires of people in the world outside the brothel-theater and those of the actors within.

TWO CASE HISTORIES

The highly ritualized characters of Genet's play are reflected in actual case histories, such as that of one man who was a success in his profession and in other conventional roles. He was also a masochist in most senses of that label, though he did not want to be physically hurt. To act out his fantasies, he had an arrangement with a woman prostitute who specialized in such clientele. About once a month he went to her place, and to satisfy his masochism took off all his clothes and had a sheet pinned around him like a diaper. Wearing a nursemaid's uniform and looking very demure she sat next to him, pretending to be in the park, and they engaged in child-nurse talk during which she instructed him not to have bad thoughts, not to talk to strangers, and to be a good little boy. After some time, she said, "I'm going to have to go away and you must not talk to anybody while I'm gone. You must be a very good little boy." He always promised her that he would.

About fifteen minutes later, she returned wearing a sexually "alluring" costume (a short black dress, garters, and sexy makeup, his image of the erotic woman). Sitting beside him, she tried to engage him in conversation and get him to talk "dirty" and touch her. After the appropriate dithering refusals, she took his hand and put it on her breast, while he sat there very aroused.

After that she left, to return wearing her white nursemaid's uniform and to ask him if he had behaved as she had told him. He denied any wrong-doing, of course, but then she slowly and aggressively wormed it out of him as if she were his mother. Finally he confessed all, and she struck him (not very hard) three or four times. After a tearful reconciliation in which he promised never to do it again, he got dressed, paid her, and went back to continue his very conventional life.

Involved in this extraordinary drama is a complex set of emotions: guilt, fear, and anxiety, all tied to a particular vision of the sexual. The important themes appear to be the fears (and excitement) generated by doing or thinking "dirty and wrong" things and by overpowering women. There are "dirty" women who make you do bad things and "pure" women who make you confess. Partly this expresses an underlying anger at women (which is not exclusively masochistic) and partly it expresses the theme of humiliation and degradation. In the process of degradation, it is possible to do two things: to experience sexuality and to get rid of the guilt involved in the experience.

This kind of masochistic phenomenon tends to occur disproportionately among men. Such dramas do not occur every day, and masochists are not being beaten all the time. What is important in these cases are the ritual components which organize the humiliation and the sexuality. It simply is not someone with a strong arm and a whip and someone else with a willing backside. Instead it is a collaborative enterprise between two people.

A second case history is that of a man who about once every six weeks had himself beaten by his wife, apparently as a punishment for his "weak" or "feminine" characteristics. In the conventional world, he was aggressive and controlling, but underneath he had a fantasy of wanting to be controlled. He therefore felt he needed to be punished because it was wrong to have such feelings (the fantasy of being controlled is both frightening and exciting for many men), and he would dress up and let his wife tie him to a rack in the basement. Then, with his buttocks in the air, wearing a schoolgirl's costume, he would have her give him an enema. If he could not control his bowels, then he had done something awful and she could legitimately beat him. Of course, he could not control himself, so she would beat him and leave him tied up for a few hours.

His wife did not like this activity very much, but they had an otherwise conventional relationship with a big house, children, cars, and a mortgage, so she viewed it as his curious aberration. She was not psychologically involved, nor did she find sexual pleasure in the activity. It was not quite the same as cooking dinner for him, but she did not hate it as much as some women do the intercourse they have with their husbands simply because they are married.

People's sexual behavior often has only a limited connection to the rest of their lives. People walk through a door and close it, and inside this space they do sexual things. When they walk out again, the door closes, and all or most of the conduct is left there. The bedroom is insulated in very important ways from the rest of their lives. Not everyone treats sex in this way, of course, but for substantial numbers of people there is a barrier around sexual conduct. This is particularly true of sexual minorities, who may feel a strong sense of guilt about things they feel and do.

An understanding of highly ritualized and symbolized kinds of sexual conduct may require an appeal to symbolic aspects of psychoanalytic thought. However, using such ideas does not require that we accept the whole of Freud's psychology or biology. What is important and living in psychoanalytic thinking, particularly for contemporary psychology, is the emphasis on cognition and symbolic processes. Freud was seeking to give his symbols permanent meaning by grounding them in the biology of the person, particularly in sexual and reproductive biology. Although these biological components may remain constant (penises, vaginas, etc.) the meanings given to them are located in the culture and not in the body.

SADOMASOCHISM AND HOMOSEXUALITY

Sadomasochistic conduct may be somewhat more frequent among homosexual males than among heterosexuals, at least in proportional terms. This is probably a function of the fact that this is an all-male group, and of certain cultural factors in the gay culture. Often gay men desire a sharp symbolic dichotomy between the two partners, due in part to the conventional stereotypes about the opposition between maleness and femaleness in sex. Since the sadist is "male" and the masochist is "female," such role playing by two men can enhance the differentiation between them. This is expressed in the sadomasochistic homosexual media as a taste for uniforms, cowboy motifs, and bikers, and enhanced in the public culture of some gay bars. Such dress standards are ritual modes of presentation which signal sexual preferences, but which do not always predict the kind of sex that will take place. The actual sex may not differ much from most homosexual sex. It is the drama of meeting and pairing that is arousing, and a gay bar is often far more sadomasochistic in appearance than the individuals who come to it or the sex they have afterward.

SADOMASOCHISM AND HETEROSEXUALITY

The formalization of the sadomasochistic aspects of the gay community has been paralleled by the creation of "clubs" for heterosexual masochists and sadists. Such sites offer opportunities for people with common sexual preferences to meet. Where once the problems of meeting were solved through word of mouth and through advertisements of various sorts, there is now a more public "velvet underground" in various cities which offers an opportunity for more interaction, and the creation of a local sadomasochistic culture. The city in this case provides for sexual minorities what it provided for literary minorities in the past.

The existence of these cultural resources and ways of manipulating sexual scripts to include themes of humiliation, degradation, and pain probably conceals their origins and the reasons why people use them. The recent publication of *The Joy of Sex* and *More Joy of Sex*, which both contain explicit scripts for acting out bondage, discipline, and "light" sadomasochistic themes, offers a public opportunity for people to shape and express their own uncoordinated interests. These two books spell out the stage settings and props required and the dramatic overtones which can help isolate the scene from reality and submerge self-consciousness. They also point out how "acceptable and normal" mild sadomasochistic role-playing can be.

Sadomasochistic themes are important for both men and women, although their dominant "experiential" components are for the masochists. Indeed, it may be that the themes of masochism are far more important and significant than those of sadism — and that the activity of the sadist is shaped more by the masochist than vice versa. The dramatic and sexual tension between masochist and sadist is expressed by the sadist's seeking to press the limits of the masochist's capacity to eroticize the pain, while the masochist sets the limit where eroticism becomes cruelty.

Whether the sadism category should include violence and cruelty against uncooperative partners rests on definitional decisions of various sorts. Mass murderers such as Gilles de Rais or Jack the Ripper have been called "sadists," but because we understand so little about the connections of aggressive and violent behavior to sexuality, it is difficult to locate the definitional boundaries. We must expect that we may never have culturally acceptable explanations of many human behaviors and their origins.

Animal Contacts

Animal contacts (or bestiality) occur when a human has sex with a nonhuman animal. The only body of behavioral data we have on this phenomenon is Kinsey's, though sex with animals has been of considerable mythological significance

throughout human history. Leda and the swan, Europa and the bull, the Japanese octopus and the fisherman's wife offer us the theme of an animal (usually a god in disguise) having sex with a woman. The significant point of such tales may be either impregnation and the creation of progeny with particular virtues or the heightening of sexual pleasure. The latter, more erotic, theme can be found in the myth of Danae and Zeus, the tale of the Japanese octopus, or the "excessive machine" (a modern version of the octopus) in the French erotic cartoon book *Barbarella*. The creation of special progeny can be found in the myths of Leda and Europa and in the American Indian creation myths, in which a god descends to Earth as an animal and fathers a particular tribe (or the "human" race).

The merging of nature and humanity is a common theme in myth, and it may be the source of many of the totemic animals, for the earliest myths usually emphasized creation. More recent ones tend to emphasize erotic values: probably the most important contemporary source of our images of such sexual relations derives from pornography or sexual exhibitions in which women have sex with various animals. This activity, like much of pornography, is created for an all-male market, and its meanings to its consumers are probably remarkably diverse. The theme of female degradation, as well as fantasies about penis size (the symbolic identification with the phallus of a large animal), play an important role.

Kinsey found that about eight percent of the men he interviewed had had orgasm and about three percent of the women had had an erotic experience (less than half a percent had had orgasm) while in bodily contact with an animal. The men were mostly from rural areas, and their experiences were usually with farm animals during adolescence. The women's experiences, on the other hand, tended to involve household pets. Kinsey's explanation for the males was based on opportunity. He suggested that boys in the country see animals having sex, but often do not have much socio-sexual contact with girls. The religious and conservative values of rural people tend to be highly protective of girls, so the animals become a substitute for the restricted heterosexual contact. His explanation for women was obscure, though a lack of socio-sexual opportunities was offered as explanation for older women.

About half the women who reported animal contacts had had them before the age of twenty, with the rest occurring later in life. Extremely few of them reported extended or frequent animal contacts. Nearly all the animal contacts of men occurred between the ages of ten and fourteen. Some men continued it for longer periods, but it appears to resemble masturbation in that it occurs among relatively socially restricted males living in a particular environment. It is interesting to note that according to Kinsey's data more men from rural areas who went to college reported animal contacts during adolescence than did those with more limited educations. This does parallel social class findings about masturbation.

Some histories of sex between rural boys and animals involve strong emotional attachment and love, so that some boys feel a great sense of sadness when they and their animals are separated. Before we discount or mislabel such feelings, we should remember that many people feel sad about dogs and cats and horses when they die or run away — we often establish such passionate (and nonsexual) relationships with animals that we are desolate when they are gone. People leave their money to animals, bury them in cemeteries, and reorganize their lives to feed and exercise them. There is no reason to assume that the feelings people develop about animal companions are any less deep than those they develop about other people.

While there may be transitional heartbreak for those who are sexually and emotionally involved with animals, there does not seem to be any long-term consequence. The adolescents, male and female, go on to standard heterosexual experience afterward, and only among some lonely or experimental adults do animal contacts supply either a socio-sexual source of arousal and sex or an opportunity for experimentation.

It is a crime in most jurisdictions to have sex with an animal, so that being caught is usually the most serious thing that can happen. Though legislators are often prepared to change the law for certain consenting sexual relationships, they are usually loath to change this one. There is also some difficulty in ascertaining just what a consenting sexual relationship between a human and another animal might be.

Fetishism and Partialism

Fetishism refers to being erotically aroused by objects, commonly by articles of clothing while they are being worn, when they are separated from their owner's body, or when they are represented in the media. Partialism is the same phenomenon but referring to a part of the body which has assumed fetishistic qualities. Thus a shoe fetishist may be aroused by a foot wearing a shoe, by the shoe alone, or by a picture or drawing of a shoe. In some cases, the fetishist is capable of being aroused by a person who is not wearing such an object, but there are also cases where the fetish object must be present before more conventional stimuli can have any arousing effect. Partialisms may operate in the same way. There are men who are strongly aroused by women with large breasts, but who are able to perform sexually with women with small breasts. There are also, however, men who can only perform sexually with women whose breasts are larger than a certain size.

Fetishisms and partialisms may be best approached by considering how our definitions of sexual stimuli are accumulated over time (see Chapter 9). There exists a preferred set of culturally approved stimulus objects, a list which develops in an interaction between a general gender preference and certain aspects of the preferred gender's body and associated paraphernalia. This is not a neat process where we begin with a general label and then fill in the parts, but rather an accumulation of experience in which the whole affects the parts and the parts affect the whole. It is important to remember that we do not begin by developing preferences for naked body parts, since most of the bodies we see in childhood and early adolescence are clothed (or were in the very recent past). It is worth noting that conventional men aroused by female breasts or buttocks are usually responding to the shape or look of clothed and concealed breasts and buttocks, and that bathing suits serve primarily to outline the parts of the body defined as erotic, by providing concealment patterns when worn and differences between tanned and lighter skin when naked. It should not be surprising that articles of clothing become fetishes.

Fetishes and partialisms of the type we are describing occur almost entirely among men. The sign stimuli that seem to arouse women involve a far wider range of items and contexts, and are diffuse rather than specific and limited. Thus a woman may have a range of arousing stimuli (such as a singer's voice) with limitations on some dimensions (such as weight) but without any extreme restrictions. Indeed, this is what characterizes most people. They have preferences, and find other people more or less attractive. They may prefer brown eyes to blue eyes, or red hair to blonde, but they can come to like other combinations as well.

The clothing objects which are conventionally converted into fetishes include corsets, brassieres, women's panties, negligees, garters, stockings, shoes, and gloves. Some of these are erotic paraphernalia which conventional people use and which are part of an eroticizing sexual script. The husband who likes his wife in sexy underwear or stockings before or during sex, but who also enjoys sex without the accoutrements, is not quite a fetishist. The fetish begins to emerge when the underwear is required for him to perform or when the underwear becomes a separate object of arousal.

This is what seems to have happened to corsets and shoes, particularly for an older generation. The advertisements in the 1930s Sears Roebuck catalog corset ads were quite asexual from a modern standpoint, but against the general backdrop of society then, they often took on strong erotic overtones. Shoes and corsets often have other overtones—particularly for those fetishists attracted to very high heels and tight corsets. In these cases there is considerable overlap with the sadomasochism of bondage and discipline, in which the corset is a form of restraint and the very high-heeled shoe is a disciplinary device. The source of this connection is not well understood, but it certainly exists.

Some fetishists often have masochistic fantasies of being stepped on by women in high heels or dominated by women in specific fetish costumes. In post-World War I Germany, women prostitutes advertised their sadomasochistic specialties by

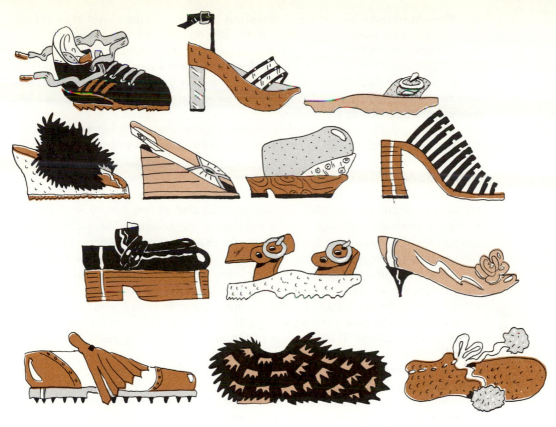

In fetishism and partialism the article of clothing or part of the body must take on sexual significance in order to elicit a response.

wearing high-heeled boots and shoes. With the increase in the availability of depictions of nudity and increased public body exposure such fetishes may begin to disappear. It is possible that they have been only a transient response to particular cultural learning conditions, a response that cannot be duplicated because of changed cultural conditions.

A number of fetishists are aroused by the objects independently of the person, or even more distantly by pictures of such objects as underwear, corsets, boots, or shoes. In one case, I met a man with a shoe and boot fetish who, in trunks in his musty basement, kept a collection of 15–20,000 photographs of shoes and boots. Some showed women's feet as well, but rarely was there a picture of a complete human being. This man, however, was overtly relatively asexual. He was generally pleasured by the ambience of shoes and boots and by the extent of his collection, and any erotic impulse had long been defused. It is often true of erotica collectors that they are no longer aroused by what they collect, only by the collection's extensiveness or its particular items. Human beings collect nearly everything, and there is no reason why they should not collect pictures of boots and shoes. Psychologically, what is collected may be far less significant than collecting it.

Partialisms seem less odd than fetishisms because they are closer to most people's preferences. Men who are powerfully affected by particular bodily attributes such as hands or feet (the most distant from conventional erotic cues), the color or texture of hair (less distant), or breasts, legs, or buttocks (well within the conventional range) are less immediately recognizable than the fetishist. Too, partialisms may be satisfied or unlearned in conventional sexual activity, so that they are less likely to call attention to themselves.

Many partialisms or strong preferences characterize both heterosexual men and homosexual men. Homosexual men may prefer partners with a certain degree of body hair or a certain physique, penis size (such men are called "size queens"), buttock shape, or skin coloration. They may even prefer partners who have or have not been circumcized. Heterosexual men, however, show just as many preferences, and ultimately partialisms. Their strength and variety can be noted in the erotic or pornographic materials offered over the counter. The large-breasted woman and the muscular boy are both media exaggerations of preferred types, but they do represent real preferences which can in some cases become fixations.

Both fetishisms and partialisms are clearly linked to normal sexual stimuli. In their full expression, however, they represent a powerful sign or stimulus capable of releasing an entire sexual script and the arousal that goes with it, and they represent a fixity in the individual's script, an inability to be flexible or responsive to a wide range of sign objects. Their domain of the sexual is severely restricted, and the number of signals that can serve for arousal is unduly limited.

As has been noted, the degree to which such strong preferences are learned and modifiable is not clear. We do not know from the preferences themselves why they developed or whether under different sexual learning conditions they would continue to occur. There is, however, some evidence in the reports of clothing fetishes that they may have something to do with strong attachments to mothers, with histories of being excited by contact with articles of female clothing, and perhaps with being caught and punished for either wearing or touching such articles. If this is so (and some men recall such events), it may be that fetishisms and partialisms have some common origins with transvestism and other gender-role variants.

Gender-Role Minorities: Transvestism and Transsexualism

Paralleling the sexual minorities are a set of people who find that they are profoundly uncomfortable with the gender identity and roles into which they were born. Despite the continuous forces that differentiate and support male-female gender-role expectations, there are some people for whom the connection never becomes automatic. These people are not genetically or hormonally out of kilter, but their sense of gender, the psychosocial component of masculinity or femininity, does not match their anatomy. In one sense these are not "sexual" problems, but gender-role problems. Since the development of gender roles and the development of sexuality are interlocked in this culture, however, an unconventional outcome with one has a profound effect upon the other.

TRANSVESTISM

At present, there are different adaptations people with gender-identity problems can make, depending upon how important to them is their choice of a sexual partner. Some adolescents resolve their gender-identity conflicts by making homosexual adaptations. They decide that they are men or women who are homosexual and that their preference for people of the same sex does not have any consequence for their views of themselves as male or female. The conflict is located in the culture's stereotyped view of the connection between conventional masculinity and femininity and sex-object choices. It disappears when the stereotype is denied. For other homosexuals the conflict over gender role is less transient. They may have histories of transvestism or cross-dressing (commonly young boys dressing as girls), and they may accept a feminine image of themselves. Some of them may become homosexual female impersonators, but only a few female impersonators have such conflicts.

In contrast to the homosexual pathway, there are people with heterosexual adaptations who also find themselves with gender-identity problems. Such people also often remember patterns of cross-dressing well back into childhood, but they have a preference for the opposite sex as a sex object. Their adaptations may take two forms. The first is shown by those people who both cross-dress and dress conventionally and who wish to retain their genitals. These people are transvestites. In some cases they appear to have only mild fetishistic histories, and the cross-dressing satisfies the fetish. More commonly they believe that they in fact have two personalities, that they are both male and female within one body. The female personality appears when they cross-dress, the male personality the rest of the time. Such people rarely have more than a minimal homosexual history (sometimes the result of encouragement by therapists who believe they are "really" homosexual), and they are often married.

In those cases that are free of marginal fetishistic interests there is a clear-cut demarcation between the two personalities, even to the point of having a separate name for each one. Such people are quite conventional in all other aspects of their lives. Their preferences in female clothing are often relatively unstylish, and sometimes they appear quite awkward in their clothing. Most often they have male body configurations and the female clothing they buy fits poorly, unless it is remade. Often transvestites have worked out an arrangement with their wives and sometimes with their children so that they can cross-dress at home daily or occasionally. In many cases, transvestites subscribe to interest group magazines and meet each other to exchange information and social support. Many transvestites move about in the community, and even those who are not convincing as "women" usually go unnoticed. Cross-dressing is against the law in most jurisdictions, but the law is rarely enforced except against homosexual male prostitutes who solicit in female clothing.

Heterosexual transvestites have solved the complexities of cross-dressing, identity discomfort, and heterosexuality by accepting the belief that cross-dressing expresses an important aspect of their personality, an aspect which involves both femininity and the interest and excitement of being a woman. The problem is "solved" by creating two discrete worlds and two discrete selves. They remain heterosexual and masculine in one guise, while in the other they express their feminine selves and are usually asexual.

TRANSSEXUALISM

The gender-identity conflicts of transsexuals are more profound than those of transvestites. Their anatomy-identity discontinuity produces a belief on the part of males that they are women trapped in a man's body, and on the part of females that they are men trapped in a woman's body. The sense of discontinuity can be so severe as to lead an unsophisticated observer to believe that they are psychotic, since they have normal physical equipment. It is difficult for many people to believe someone with a penis who says, "Don't believe the evidence of your eyes. Believe what I say. I am really a woman!" They are likely to call "him" crazy, and this was indeed the usual judgment in the past. However, many such people have existed, and some of them have made reasonable adaptations. They rarely married, but joined the ranks of single men and women.

In extreme cases, transsexuals may decide that they wish to change their genitals. The males feel they are really women, and they want to have sex with men (but not homosexual sex). Some are essentially transsexuals with homosexual histories (the homosexual transsexual). Others are transsexuals with heterosexual histories. The decision to remove the penis is a decision to rid themselves of the masculinity and heterosexuality. When the surgery is completed, there is congruity between genital appearance and self-identity. Unlike the transvestite solution, transsexuals (both homosexual and heterosexual) give up their historical past as either male or female and become the opposite sex.

Transsexualism is one of those rare psychological conditions that has found its solution in modern medical technology. There are now about 2500 people in the United States who have had treatment. It is remarkable that what was considered a mental disorder as recently as fifteen years ago could turn out to have a relatively straightforward medical solution. Once hormonal treatments to change secondary sex characteristics and surgical techniques for genital conversion were developed, the operations, while not simple, became nearly routine for males (who represent the majority of the cases). The penis and scrotum are removed and a vagina is constructed. A similar technology for the construction of a penis that will erect is not available, so the success with women who wish to be men is more limited.

After sex-change surgery there appear to be a number of possible outcomes. These outcomes, however, do often depend on the characteristics of the person before the surgery. Richard Green has identified several people who came in for sex-change surgery as societal misfits. Their desire for the surgery results from the fact that so many things have gone wrong with their lives that they believe sex-change surgery might help. It probably will not. If a person has an unstable past with a great many conflicts, he or she will have a similar range of problems after surgery, though perhaps not the gender-identity problem.

On the other hand, transsexuals with very stable histories often marry after surgery and, although they are infertile, make an adaptation as conventional married people. Indeed, many male heterosexual transsexuals wish to be the most conventional of heterosexual women. Their version of womanhood is quite traditional, and few of them appear to be potential recruits to the women's movement. This is probably because they have lived so long idealizing female gender identity without experiencing its problems and conflicts that they cannot help but identify with the most acceptable model.

DEVELOPMENT OF GENDER-IDENTITY CONFLICT

Studies of the developmental histories of transsexuals have been conducted through adult recall and through the study of children who exhibit what are called gender-identity conflicts. The childhood data is nearly exclusively on males rather than females. It appears that between ages four and six, some males begin to adopt female gender-role performance for a range of activities. They prefer to play with girls, they wear female clothing, and they like to do what women do around the house. Clearly, these adaptations can only occur with the tacit consent and support of the parents, who often go along believing the child will "grow out of it." When these parents are asked how often such behavior occurred, they usually reply "as often as he could." In addition, nearly all of these families possess photographs of their male children dressed as girls, or wearing wigs or cosmetics.

Such children find the world to be difficult when they enter the gender-role stereotyped school. As long as the boy is at home, it is not a problem. He cross-dresses and the parents believe it is cute and part of a passing phase. But when the boy gets to school the parents suddenly discover that his preferred view of the world is female. He might want to play with girls or be treated like a girl. In some cases he might want to wear a dress or have a toy pocketbook with toy cosmetics. At some point, these boys have learned a sense of gender that says, "I prefer female things." As far as is known, if this sense of self is allowed to survive publicly, these children have absolutely desperate childhoods. There seems to be no way they can fit into an early school peer group unless they are allowed to play with girls. The girls feel uneasy, however, because the child is clearly a boy but is rejected by boys. Such children can lead very lonely lives.

At this moment we do not have a systematic set of explanations for how such patterns start, or if all persons with such histories turn out to be transsexuals, transvestites, or homosexuals. The retrospective reports of both transsexuals and transvestites, both with homosexual and heterosexual histories, often have elements that also appear among the children studied who have gender-identity conflicts.[4] There are strong attachments to women in the household and frequent modeling of cosmetics, female dress, and women's activities. There is a strong sense of having been rewarded for cross-gender role performances. At the same time many young boys report being repelled by the male peer groups of childhood, with their emphasis on sports and aggression. The timid boy or the boy who prefers girls will quickly attract the animosity of the boys, who view him as a wonderful opportunity to prove their nascent masculinity. Some of their families resemble the traditional versions of the

---

4. The children do *not* automatically feel conflict. Most feel quite happy as long as the demands of school and peer group are not applied, or as long as their parents do not become disturbed.

"homosexual"- predisposing families with strong mothers and absent-weak fathers.

The problem with all this is that we do not know the outcome of these cases, or whether there is a disproportionate number of people with early gender-identity conflicts among those who become transsexuals or transvestites. For instance, in a recent book by a heterosexual transsexual, the author writes that he had no trouble as a male child or as an adult playing a male role. At a certain point in his life, he decided to express the female part of him (that which he had felt was the true part since childhood) and simply changed his sex. In this case there does not appear to be any childhood trauma or difficulty. The studies of children have been of those who were "problems," and most of the data came from a gender-identity clinic, a source which may conceal from us other less troubled pathways to transvestism and transsexualism.

The justification for the "treatment" or modification of these particular children to align gender identity with anatomy is something of a political matter. Treatment seems difficult and often unrewarding, so that several rather punitive strategies have been adopted, along with rewards for playing with toy submachine guns in order to reinforce masculine behaviors. A number of people have suggested that this provides a limited perspective on masculinity.

Many of these children are very uncomfortable in their current circumstances, so that treatment of some kind would seem essential. Choosing to "treat" them as individual deviants, however, may be in error. A better alternative may be to give such children the opportunity to grow up, freed from the oppressive gender-role divisions of the typical school, by placing them in less gender-typed school environments where the other children are less likely to stigmatize them. What the outcome of such a procedure might be is unknown, but it would appear to be more humane than those currently attempted or than the usual school experience of children who stand outside approved gender-role performances.

The problems discussed here—transvestism and transsexualism—are sexual only in part. They are largely problems of gender-identity formation and gender-role performance. However, if they are properly understood, they might throw light on the various pathways to conventional outcomes. As with other outcomes of development, we need to keep in mind the complex relationship between the history of the person and the power of the contemporary environment. In many cases people with very different sets of predispositions are changed by new opportunities as they grow up. Even with the transvestite and the transsexual, whose basic scripts appear to be fixed in childhood, we must be cautious about how we interpret our knowledge.

Conclusion

The problem of sexual majorities and minorities is one of beginning to sort out the multiplicity of pathways and potential character of human beings, not only when they are young, but also when they are older. Further, it is the symbolic character of life that we must keep in view if we are to avoid limiting reality or possibility too soon. Human life is ambiguous and loose, and the existence of sexual minorities suggests that people use the resources they have available in attempting to construct meaningful ways of living. Part of the issue is surely that among the problems they face looms the social reaction to what they are—the "sissy" suffers the reaction of all the potential John Waynes; people aroused by shoes suffer the reactions of those who like legs and breasts; the boy with his lamb suffers the reactions of the urban puritan. Seeing what they do as minority behavior rather than moral or mental illness means that our responses may be very different.

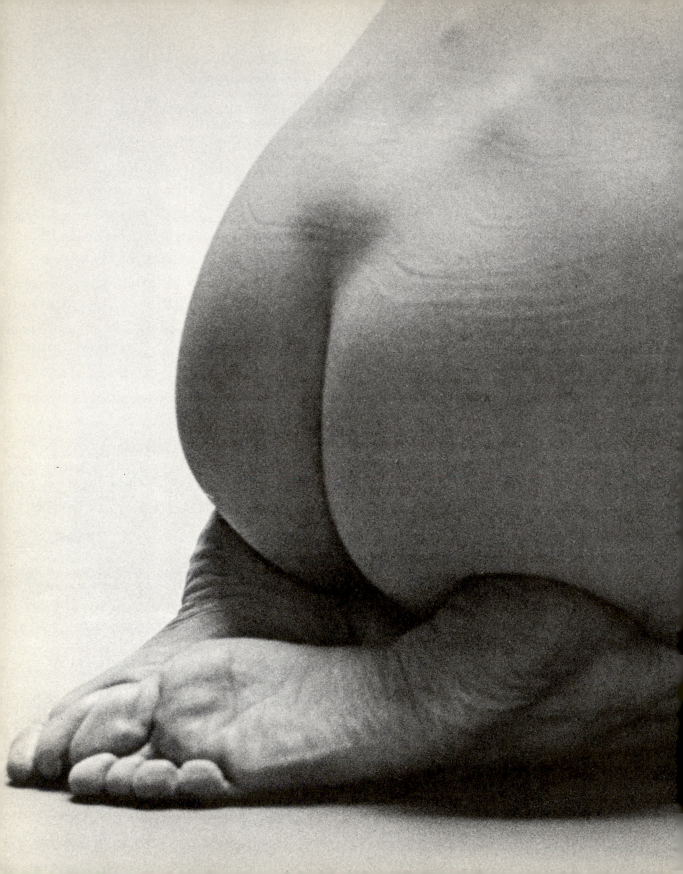

There is nothing wrong with being a sex object (unless you suffer
from some sexual disorder), for if people were not objects to each other,
then who would they be objects for?

Suzanne Brogger, *Deliver Us From Love*

IT IS A COMMONPLACE OBSERVATION TO SAY THAT THERE HAVE BEEN DEPICTIONS
of sexual activity, in whatever media forms were available, in most of the major
cultures of which there are records. Equally commonplace are the conclusions
that this availability proves the universality of the sexual instinct, or the universality of artistic interest in the sexual beauty of the human body or the universality
of an interest in depicting people doing sexual things. The illustrated coffee-table
books that summarize the history of erotic art do seem to support both the observation and the conclusions drawn from it.

These books provide what until very recent times only a few people had seen:
depictions of sexuality from the hands of accomplished artists, which contrasted
with the crude erotica available to most people. The erotic art of China or Japan or
India, or the fragmentary materials created by individual Western artists, from
Rembrandt to Picasso, show us what skilled artisans can do with explicitly sexual
materials. Most people are frankly startled, for instance, by the beauty of the Japanese wood-block print, compared with the crude eight-page cartoon books or
the blue movies that have been standard fare for most customers of erotica in the
United States. When works of erotic art are collected together, carefully reproduced, and bound in an expensive volume, it is easy to be seduced into believing
that erotic art can be found anywhere, and would be common if only people were
not prevented from making it.

Not so. There were long periods of time in many major cultures when the production of erotic materials of any quality was rare and ephemeral, not because it
was censored, but because the culture did not provide for it. The great Indian tem-
ples often reproduced in our modern displays of erotic sculpture represent only a few
buildings, constructed in a brief span of time. The history of erotic art in China has
been a history of periods of great production (in quality and quantity) contrasted
with periods of drought. Not only has the volume of materials changed over time
and place, but the content, the consumers, and the modes of production and distribution have differed as well.

It is fairly easy to take a wide variety of depictions of the naked human body or
depictions of sexual activity and arrange them in some order (by date, culture, content, or quality) to give them a particular meaning. However, these orders and
meanings are often arbitrary, an attempt to arrange a set of objects into a new

reality. Nothing is especially wrong with doing that, but the decision to select and arrange them in particular ways may reflect more about the culture in which the objects are put together than about the cultures from which they are taken. The meaning given a work in the present may have little or nothing to do with the way the creator of the work or various audiences at that time (or intervening times) understood the work.

Even in Western societies over the last few centuries, the connections between erotic materials of the past and the present must be understood as weak and often broken. Botticelli's *Birth of Venus* did not elicit the same emotional or psychological or aesthetic responses in its Renaissance audience that it does today. It also does not elicit the same responses in us as are elicited by present-day pop-culture nudes or present-day "high" art.

Many of the coffee-table art books and the bibliographies of "dirty" books and the filmographies of the blue movie tend to reproduce the same items, particularly if the material is pre-World War II. The volume of original erotic productions over the last two hundred years, no matter at what cultural level, has been small, accelerating only in certain periods and actually taking off in a meaningful way only in the last thirty years.

In painting his Venus, Botticelli was not engaged in creating an erotic picture for a rich patron, but rather using the rediscovered Platonic ideals of ancient Greece to create an image of the essence of perfect beauty for an educated Renaissance audience.

The library of the Institute for Sex Research, taken together with all other libraries of erotic book collections starting with the beginning of printing, probably can list only 5000 separate titles up until the 1950s. While there were many books published, they were often the same texts reprinted again and again; most of the materials available in the 1950s were written in the 1850s or earlier. The filmographies of the blue movie, until the upsurge of materials from the Scandinavian countries in the 1960s and the production of X-rated porno films in the 1970s in the United States, numbered something less than 2000 identifiable titles. Even though there has been substantial repression and destruction of such materials, particularly in the United States where the images of sex crime and pornography have been closely bound together, these numbers are neither impressive nor extraordinary.

Media of Expression

Several factors seem to be significant in understanding Western erotic materials. One is the particular medium in question. Frequently, discussions of the erotic only include books, though sexually explicit materials exist in all of the art forms (at least in fragments), including painting, sculpture, drawings, and graphics of various sorts, as well as photographs, films, and videotape. The repertoire of the erotic has grown with the widening and changing of technologies that produce what we call art. The history of erotica is a movement from medium to medium as they appeared in Western societies.

The medium in which erotica is created produces a particular set of constraints on the artisan and on the consumer. Some of these constraints are aesthetic and formal. What is of interest to painters or writers at any given moment in history may have great importance for the kinds of erotic materials that are created. Tom Wesselman's series of nudes have a great deal to do with the concerns of many modern painters: an interest in flat surfaces of paint arranged in certain ways. Our first impression is of naked women; a more reflective second response is with the decisions to paint in a certain tradition. John Cleland's erotic novel *Fanny Hill, The Memoirs of a Woman of Pleasure* parallels in form other non-erotic or non-sexual memoirs or novels written at the same time. Wesselman is primarily a painter of the 1960s; Clelland was primarily a novelist of the 1740s.

Constraints on Depictions of the Sexual

There has been a pattern of censorship or control by legal means of various kinds of erotic materials for a very long time, but the forms of censorship we know today are more systematic and skillful than those in the past. The enforcement agencies of the past were never efficient and technologically sophisticated; even the creation in England of a stable law-enforcement agency such as the police only came to pass in the early 1800s. However, in earlier societies fewer people lived in cities; even fewer were consumers of books or paintings or engravings; and even fewer were producers of such materials. The large-scale production of books in general had to await the rise of literacy and habits of reading, along with the technologies of mass

In this painting of an erotic nude, Tom Wesselman exploits the tension between form and content—a very cool, flat technique combined with warm colors and a heated topic.

book production and distribution. It is therefore not surprising that so few erotic books were produced between the rise of the printing press and the nineteenth century—actually very few books were produced at all, compared to modern standards. Acceptable levels of control of these limited materials could therefore proceed in a relatively slipshod fashion.

The construction of extensive statutory and enforcement practices for the control of sexual obscenity (what we call *pornography*, originally meaning stories about prostitutes) began in the nineteenth century. Prior to that century much of what we call censorship was directed at political and anti-religious publications; the transfer of the right to censor the seditious to the right to censor the sexual came in the middle of the nineteenth century. There was a modest but flourishing trade in erotic books and photographs for the newly literate working and middle classes in the early to middle nineteenth century, particularly in England. The discovery of this traffic by Lord Justice Campbell resulted in a systematic program to wipe it out. Popular erotica in the form of photographs, cheap novels, and erotic magazines and handbooks were seized in many of the countries of Western Europe.

The campaign against materials that could "deprave and corrupt" was headed in the United States by Anthony Comstock, who prevailed on the United States federal government in 1873 to pass a law that provided fines and imprisonment for mailing any "obscene, lewd, lascivious, indecent, filthy or vile article, matter, thing, device or substance." One of Comstock's stratagems was to have a "Chamber of Horrors" collection of pornography on display in the office of the Vice President of the United States to show members of Congress—a strategy that was repeated in the 1950s by the Post Office Department to acquire support for new anti-obscenity legislation.

Comstock traveled around the United States promoting state legislation to prohibit the manufacture or consumption of such materials. Until his death in 1915, Comstock claimed to have destroyed huge volumes of obscene materials—though it is unclear what these materials actually were and what made them obscene. Comstock was only a personification of the rising levels of control over sex information that came with a more literate population. As we have moved toward mass information systems, limits have been systematically placed on each new media form as it appears. Film and television have both been hedged with controls on sexual content since their inception.

These legal regulations created an underground production and supply system for erotic materials, a system that has shaped who makes the materials, what artistic and cultural quality they may have, the forms that they will take, the way they are distributed, and the conditions under which they are consumed. In the decade 1965-1975 this older underground system of supply and consumption broke down, as the barriers between the underground and the overground steadily eroded.

Constraints of Technology and Economics

The consumption of erotic materials is shaped by the technology that is required to produce, distribute, or consume it. Books must be written, transferred to type, printed, bound, taken to distributors and sold to customers. At each stage the producers are constrained by the technologies of printing and distribution systems. Following purchase, consumers are constrained by conditions of consumption: places to read them in privacy (reading erotica aloud is not common) and places to store them after they are read.

Such constraints also exist on such media as photography (where are the pictures developed?) or film (who has a sixteen-millimeter projector?) or videotape. Once a new technology is developed, an enterprising producer may create erotic materials, but both the producer and the consumer are bound by the technological and economic processes that affect all nonsexual users of that technology. The producers of erotic material often use the same firms (printing, developing, and retail outlets) as do producers of conventional materials.

Constraints on Erotic Content

Erotic materials must be about or show something that an audience has learned is sexual, to which they will have a conventional erotic response. This does not mean that they are going to do something sexual as a result of what they read or see or hear, but that they respond appropriately to an erotic book or film or record. This is quite different than responding to a concrete erotic situation involving another person, even though these responses to a media object have to be learned in much the same ways. When to feel aroused, what to do with the physiological evidence of arousal (erections or vaginal lubrication), whether or not to masturbate, whether to talk to other people about it—all are part of the learned scripts for consuming erotic materials.

At the same time the materials themselves may require internal scripting. Most of us learn that the pictures we see or the stories we read should have a narrative content. The characters go through a story in words (and maybe pictures)—their behavior is scripted, and they talk in different ways to each other. Most people come to expect such a minimum narrative organization in the materials they consume. Part of this organization is served by the conventions of the particular medium. Books and films have a movement in time, a sequence of actions, persons with names and roles which operate as elements of the scripts that organize their meaning.

However, erotic materials vary in their level of scripting. In many cases, particularly with photographs and drawings, it is possible to have a single picture of an erotic event, say two persons in intercourse, an event without a history or a future, without characters or roles (other than naked bodies of identifiable gender doing a specific sexual act—actually a good deal of information). In these cases the viewer brings to the picture or drawing scripts derived from other circumstances; the picture fits into a moment of time in an already created erotic script. The arousal results from the ability of the viewer to place the picture in a meaningful context. This is why children are so often bewildered by erotic photographs when they see them; they do not possess a script that can give meaning to the fragment they have seen.

A distinction can be made between materials that are *scripted* by the producer for the consumer and nearly unscripted materials that are simply erotic catalogues, a geography of the body and an atlas of activities arranged with all the intelligence of a laundry list, without any sense of character, plot, or action. It is a measure of the level of sexual ignorance in the population and the poverty of the erotic environment that the latter materials continue to have a market. In these cases the entire burden of scripting is placed on the audience.

A second distinction can be made between materials scripted by the rules of what is considered high culture and those scripted in terms of low, popular, or folk culture. The majority of scripted pornography derives its scripts from sexual folklore. It tells a simple story based on the dirty joke (in the case of the blue movie, the short erotic story or the eight-page comic book), or based on an erotic theme which seems popular with an audience in a given time and place (incest, adultery, seduction, or childhood sexual experimentation, lodged in a given social context that makes the sex plausible and meaningful). Such low cultural erotica is ritualistic in character; it fits with and reinforces the pre-existing social and sexual scripts of the consumer. The sexual activity is easily understandable in terms of who, what, where, why, and when.

What makes the material exciting is that it may be a violation of one of these categories, but a violation that reinforces conventional conduct in other spheres. If an author writes about incest, for example, he may create a set of motives that can make incest plausible without implicating the consumer to an uncomfortable degree. The father can be painted as an evil person; the daughter enjoys the sex only under duress; and she is eventually redeemed by a good man. Alternative scripts can be created to justify the daughter's enjoyment of the incest, but they may have to incorporate the theme of the lustful woman. The erotic tale locates its moral dimensions in conventional stereotypes of the violation of trust, the acting out of the forbidden, and the sexuality of men and women.

Less common than stereotypic and ritualistic forms are sexual depictions drawing on the implications of a particular art form or a particular nonsexual concern at a given time. The erotic engravings of Picasso do not so much affirm ritualistic views of sex as they make us uncomfortable, forcing us to think differently about sex (as well as the definitions and limits of art). They disturb rather than soothe. Most erotic materials arouse us sexually, but soothe us socially — however, erotica connected to the concerns of high art have the potential to disrupt both our erotic and social interests. Our ability to feel aroused in a usual sense is complicated because we are offered sexual information in ways we cannot understand automatically. This may be why most cultural materials, erotic and non-erotic, are conventional and ritualistic — why the novels of Jacqueline Susann and Irving Wallace are best sellers, and those of James Joyce and Marcel Proust are not. Materials of a high cultural level do not meet our expectations. Perhaps the key to successful erotica is not to disturb audience expectations.

We now see why erotica is usually socially and sexually conservative. The roles that men and women play in erotica, the kinds of sex that they have, and the reasons they have for doing it, fit into our cultural stereotypes about men, women, and sexuality. Pornography depends on previously acquired scripts for *disapproved* sexual conduct in order to make sense, and in most cases also reinforces the conventional elements of such scripts.

Repression and Creation of the Erotic Underground

Censors of erotic materials have struggled off and on with its producers for a long time. The early history of this struggle (1450–1800) was quite different than it is at present. Production levels were low, the amount of materials relatively small, the audience tiny, the objects expensive. The production of erotic paintings, for instance, has always been relatively small simply because there is such a limited market. Most pictures until 1600 were painted for display in churches and public buildings; the idea of a private erotic painting to hang in a study or library simply did not exist. While artists may have made erotic drawings, they would not have produced a major erotic work because they did not have a market for it. These conditions have continued until today; only with the willingness of museums and galleries to show erotic painting and sculpture will artists spend time creating it.

Uses of Pornography

Two themes lie at the heart of erotica: the definition of situations and actors that make sexual action possible (in particular, how such scripts facilitate the management of guilt deriving from unconventional behavior); and somewhat related to the first, the nonsexual themes that shape the sexual activity.

The basic question in the integration of the sexual element in the social script is: Who does what to whom in what kind of relationship, to what consequence? Here it is evident that of the five key terms — who, what, whom, relationship, and consequence — only one (the what) is essentially sexual, and that the other four, frequently in a rather complex interrelationship, determine the fifth.

This may be seen more clearly by briefly describing a pornographic novel, *Sin Struck*, which is organized around what appears to be a major theme in the land of pornographic prose — sex and social mobility. All societies must establish norms for social mobility that not only restrict ways of getting ahead but that also provide potential sources of consolation for those who do not make it. The common phrase: "I could get ahead if only I . . . ." appears, followed by some opportunity or offer that makes our hero feel extremely virtuous for having rejected it. It could have been cheating or stealing or being dishonest or ignoring the basic virtues and joys of family life or being ruthless and exploitative in relations with other people. Using sex is clearly part of this group. It appears to be a possible way of getting ahead, even if most people are perceptive enough to avoid a genuine test.

The initial question of the story *Sin Struck* is whether a young, aspiring, and untalented actor from a small mining town in Pennsylvania can find happiness and success by being a stud for an aging and insatiable actress. The answer very clearly is no.

The character in *Sin Struck* will suffer for his use of sex to achieve his goal by failing as an actor, his punishment for several explicitly described sexual encounters. Next, he will move into a world of crime in collaboration with a professional thief whom we know is untrustworthy because of his consistent abuse of prostitutes. The persons to be robbed are a wealthy Broadway producer and his nymphomaniac wife, who deserve to be robbed because they use their wealth to sponsor orgies at which all kinds of aspiring young actors and

BOOKS

Even after the advent of printing and engraving, and the beginnings of a mass production system for information, a real increase in the amounts of printed erotic materials had to wait until the nineteenth century. There were a few erotic books published in the two centuries after the beginning of printing (Gutenberg dates from 1448, Boccaccio from 1497), but most of them began to appear in the period after 1650. They began as stories about prostitutes or family incest, and by the middle of the eighteenth century the modern erotic novel with accompanying illustrations was born.

actresses will be misused. Already, the suggestion of easy expiation for our hero is suggested by the social justice implicit in the crime.

Enter a female in crisis; she has been deserted on her honeymoon by her upper-class husband who is unable to face his own impotence. The husband promptly dies in flight, making our heroine both sexually and morally available. Our hero services our heroine, convincing her that sex can be fun, and, at the same time, he reestablishes his dominant masculinity which was called into question by his subservience to the aging actress. His partner in crime is promptly killed by the police while trying to double-cross our hero. He goes to his death without implicating our hero—which will make our hero's ultimate atonement for crime psychological rather than penal. The hero's positive act of rehabilitation will be to rescue our heroine, who, while languishing in a highly suspect hotel, has been seduced by a multi-millionaire lesbian from Alaska who wants to take her away to a life of depraved comfort in her wilderness empire. The novel ends with our hero, now safe in his masculinity, walking into the sunset with our heroine who is now equally secure in her femininity; they are walking in the direction of a secure and exclusively heterosexual life among the working class of some small town. They have "found their place in the order of things."

The plot is trite; so is the sex. But the social environment of the sexual action is not incidental. Nor is it merely a flimsy attempt at meeting the requirement of having redeeming social content: the social plot is necessary to a more unambiguous enjoyment of the detailed sex.

Historically, it was the materials on the fringe that contained the most evidence of social scripts. However, evidence for minimal social scripting can be found in nearly all pornographic materials, and, with the decreasing boundary between the two, more rather than fewer elements of social scripts are to be found. Indeed, boredom with stag films when they are viewed without other people present probably derives from the absence of sufficient social cues in the film for integrating the presented materials and motivating arousal.

Adapted from pp. 273–275 of *Sexual Conduct: The Social Sources of Human Sexuality*, by John H. Gagnon and William Simon (Aldine, 1973).

It was in the nineteenth century that the production of cheap erotic books began in many places in Europe, particularly in Paris, London, and Amsterdam. In the 1830s and through the 1860s in England there was an active trade in cheap paper jokebooks, some erotic magazines, and engravings of sexual activity. The level of this trade seems to have dropped off dramatically in the last half of the nineteenth century due to legal repression, leaving only a relatively affluent middle class market for erotic novels. We do not know for sure that it dropped off, however, we only know that nearly all of the erotic materials that have *survived* have been the more expensive or middle class in content and quality. A tendency for the artifacts of the middle class to survive can be observed in other areas. For instance, most of the houses and family artifacts that have survived from the past belonged to the affluent or stable classes (often the same thing). The cheap, the jerry-built, the transient have fallen down, or been torn down or thrown away — therefore we believe the past was full of big white houses with columns. The erotic materials for the poor have always been ephemeral and easily lost, so it is only a presumption that the volume of such materials declined at the end of the nineteenth century.

PHOTOGRAPHS

The early increase in printed materials was complemented by the invention of photography. Within a few years after Daguerre's discovery in 1832, producers of erotica were photographing people in the statue-like stances required to expose a successful image using his process. There are surviving copies and reproductions of such daguerrotypes dating from the middle and late 1840s. With the development of better film, cameras, and methods of reproduction, erotic photographs became common. Like the cheap books, they were seized and burned all over Western Europe and the United States; however, most of those burned were not pictures of sexual activity, but pictures of women in various states of nudity. The erotic photograph of the nineteenth century and of the twentieth was largely produced in continental brothels using as models the prostitutes and the various men who hung around them. In the nineteenth century such pictures were made in series to tell a story, commonly an erotic theme peculiar to the country where it was made. For example, anti-clericalism was a popular theme in France, where the participants were dressed in the costumes of nuns and priests.

The tradition of using prostitutes as models has continued to the present time. Erotic photographs produced in the United States during the 1920s and 1930s often show brothel locations; in the 1950s and 1960s individual prostitutes posed for photographs in such diverse locations as Florida, California, Texas, Detroit, and New York City. Non-prostitute photographs do show up in the illegal trade; they are usually private erotica that has accidentally got into the illegal trade. The older pictures are now disappearing, since there is a steady stream of new pictures being made in Western Europe and the United States and sold in magazine form rather than as individual pictures.

MOVIES

The invention of primitive moving pictures at the turn of the century was the next breakthrough in the development of the arts, and rather quickly legitimate films began to be made that showed at least heterosexual affection and cheesecake. In the early 1900s erotic films made in brothels (from Buenos Aires to Havana to Paris) were the precursors of the blue and stag films produced in the United States from the beginning of World War I to the upsurge of "porno" films shown in regular movie houses today.

The stag film and most of the porno movies record the predictable arrangements of outline figures within the limits of the screen.

Production and consumption of stag films was heavily restricted by available technologies. The actors and actresses were gathered from brothels, and the developing and printing of films had to be done in film laboratories during off hours or in private laboratories. Film projectors were relatively rare and expensive until the introduction of eight-millimeter film and equipment in the 1950s and 1960s. As a result of these constraints the blue-movie business took on one form in the United States, in contrast to the forms it took in Europe. In Europe where the house of prostitution still existed the blue movie was used as part of the entertainment. In the United States the blue movie became the property of all-male organizations and the traveling blue-movie salesman. All over the United States the blue-movie man would come to college fraternities and men's clubs (the American Legion, the Moose, etc.) for smokers or stag parties (so-called because they were all-male; hence, the term "stag" film). The salesman supplied the films, the screen, and the projector. In more urban locales it was possible to rent films and projectors.

The evolution of the stag film in the United States went through three stages. First were the films that reflected local sexual folklore based on the dirty joke; these films dominated until the mid 1930s. The second-stage films which began in the 1930s had no story line; they merely displayed sexual activity. The third stage began when eight-millimeter film became widespread, and cheap films (once again without plot or story line) were sold to individual collectors and used in arcades. In the 1960s actors and actresses were no longer exclusively selected from the prostitute population. Also with the advent of the 1960s, similar eight-millimeter films were made in Denmark and Germany and dominated the United States home sales market. At the present time the "pornos," hour-long large-screen films, have come to replace the older stags as the primary source of erotic movie experiences in the United States.

The stag film had three major limitations. First, it was designed to be shown to all-male audiences, so it retained basically male ritualistic form. Second, it was one reel (400 feet) or twenty minutes long, which limited the story line. Third, it was easier to copy an old film than make a new one (at least until the 1960s); as a result the same old films were copied and recopied, until only the faded ghosts of long-deceased actors were flickering in darkened rooms.

PORNOGRAPHY SHOPS

The sale of erotic materials has until recently been only through pornography shops, which are more open now in certain districts of the cities; in the past they sold their wares in plain brown wrappers. The prototypical pornography shop was described in Joseph Conrad's novel, *The Secret Agent*, published in 1907:

The shop was a square box of a place, with the front glazed in small panes. In the daytime the door remained closed; in the evening it stood discreetly but suspiciously ajar.

The window contained photographs of more or less undressed dancing girls; nondescript packages in wrappers like patent medicines; closed yellow paper envelopes, very flimsy, and marked two-and-six in heavy black figures; a few numbers of ancient French comic publications hung across a string as if to dry; a dingy blue china bowl, a casket of black wood, bottles of marking ink, and rubber stamps; a few books, with titles hinting at impropriety; a few apparently old copies of obscure newspapers, badly printed, with titles like *The Torch*, *The Gong*—rousing titles. And the two gas-jets inside the panes were always turned low, either for economy's sake or for the sake of the customers.

These customers were either very young men, who hung about the window for a time before slipping in suddenly; or men of a more mature age. . . . Some of that last kind had the collars of their overcoats turned right up to their moustaches. . . . With their hands plunged deep in the side pockets of their coats, they dodged in sideways, one shoulder first, as if afraid to start the bell going. . . .

[The owner] would proceed to sell over the counter some object looking obviously and scandalously not worth the money which passed in the transaction: a small cardboard box with apparently nothing inside, for instance, or one of those carefully closed yellow flimsy envelopes, or a soiled volume in paper covers with a promising title. Now and then it happened that one of the faded, yellow dancing girls would get sold to an amateur, as though she had been alive and young.

Underground erotica was created by censorship: the back-street bookshop, the traveling dirty movie salesman, the men's smokers with stag films, the deck of playing cards with pictures from all eras (you could be sure to see a picture that your great grandfather might have seen), the books hidden behind others in the family library, the cheap typescript passed from hand to hand, the dirty picture kept in the wallet next to the condom — all appurtenances of a male erotic world that lasted at least until the 1950s.

Repression of the Erotic Overground

After the end of World War I, there was a steady escalation of the censorship of sexual materials in the United States. This escalation was a result of a number of forces. At the end of the nineteenth century, along with the rise of the new sexual theorists such as Freud and Ellis and Hirschfeld, there was a powerful renewal of interest in the use of sexual themes and sexual problems in the arts, particularly in serious literature and theater. This did not occur in painting and sculpture to nearly the same extent, in part for the reasons of production and consumption noted before, but also because the major thrust of Western European painting moved in the direction of the abstract. There were artists (painters and sculptors) who tackled sexually explicit works, but they were and are not common, and often not those considered to be the most important and influential.

With the increase in overground works which dealt explicitly with sex, there was a powerful reaction that attempted to stamp it out through censorship, to drive the works underground. This reaction in the United States took the form of banning an endless list of books by either the federal government (through customs or mail regulations) or by municipal and state agencies. This attempt to suppress sexual materials paralleled the expansion of sexual materials or themes in significant literature. In 1890 Leo Tolstoy's *The Kruetzer Sonata* was declared obscene when published in a newspaper; later, various censors suppressed *The Decameron*, *The Golden Ass of Apulieus*, and *The Temptation of Saint Anthony*. Also suppressed was *The Sex Side of Life* (a feminist book about the rights of women to sexuality), and in 1907 the *American Journal of Eugenics* was banned from the mails because it had an article on the treatment of unwed mothers.

By the 1920s the list of banned books included James Joyce's *Ulysses* and D. H. Lawrence's *Women in Love* and *Lady Chatterly's Lover;* and only expurgated versions of *The Arabian Nights*, the works of Rabelais, and the war novel *All Quiet on the Western Front* were allowed to be published in the United States. The Bible and Shakespeare were edited for the young; the Bible lost the Song of Solomon and Shakespeare lost the bawdy parts of the plays. Young people grew up never knowing what the original text of a great work might be, even missing its point, because it had been edited. Such practices were far more systematic than current programs to razor out the sex and reproduction sections of textbooks in biology — at least young people now know that something might be missing.

There were reversals in this process, slight victories over the censor, particularly with the admission of *Ulysses* into the United States under a judicial ruling that a work had to be judged as a whole and not with sections taken out of context (usually in obscenity trials the prosecutor would read the "dirty" part to the jury and ask, "would you want your teenage daughter to read that?" never noting that it would have to be a very literate and energetic teenager even to find that section of the book and understand it).

The general position of the courts then and now is that if something is judged obscene (using whatever tests are available), if it "serves no useful social function or psychological function in the development of ideas or art or the development of the intellectual heritage of men [women are not included] it is not protected by the Constitution." This position creates a special class of speech which is different than all other classes of speech—speech about sex. It declares that sexual speech, unless directed toward some "useful" social end (or if it is only directed at making people respond sexually), is bad, and therefore not protected by the First Amendment to the Constitution.

Given this background, books were suppressed using such language as "obscene in every sense of the word." "Thoroughly rotten and putrid. We can conceive of no calamity so appallingly disastrous to the nation as to make available to its youth such vile obscenity." Politicians were likely to make such statements as, "I appeal to the Senate of the United States to throw the arm of protection around the army of boys and girls who must constitute the citizenship of our country." Between 1930 and 1945 Lillian Smith's *Strange Fruit*, John O'Hara's *Appointment in Samarra*, and Ernest Hemingway's *For Whom the Bell Tolls* were banned in various places. The mailing privileges of *Esquire* magazine were revoked during World War II because it pictured partly clad women, the precursor of the *Playboy* centerfold. All this was done for the "public good."

Movies were also caught in the censorship net. After some sexual themes and nudity occurred in the 1920s, there was a major outcry, and the movie industry set up a code of what could and could not be shown sexually. The codes were both general and specific; the general themes prohibited were such things as white slavery and prolonged passionate love making (as well as scenes that might instruct the weak in methods of committing crime and that ridiculed public officials). The producer's code also restricted profanity, nudity, drugs, miscegenation, venereal disease, childbirth, and ridicule of the clergy. The Roman Catholic Church created the Legion of Decency in the 1930s, and by 1934 the standards of this group were strongly reflected in the production code used by Hollywood.

This surge of censorship as the majority response to all aspects of sex information (we are *not* talking about movies showing intercourse or homosexuality or oral sex—only movies with explicit references to premarital sex or venereal disease or childbirth) rapidly retreated after World War II. The rapidity of this transition makes it difficult to understand, but it may be related to the fundamental shift in power in the United States from a conservative, rural, single-minded protestant-puritan domination of the politics, economics, and morality of the United States to a more polycentric and plural society, particularly in its moral perspectives. The Anglo-Saxon Protestant reaction of the late nineteenth and early twentieth century, which was anti-immigration, anti-black, anti-communist and anti-foreign, also supported the prohibition amendment, the struggle against women's rights, the anti-drug and anti-prostitution campaigns of the 1920s and 1930s, and the censorship of books and magazines and films.

These efforts may have been the last gasp of the puritan hold on the morality of a new national society. No longer was the United States a nation of farms and villages, of a Protestant majority in power if not in numbers, a place where social control was within the grasp of a morals police. Now the society was urban and industrial, full of foreign-speaking immigrants, bound together by radio, the automobile, time payments, the movies, and the press. The Depression, World War II, postwar affluence, and mass education have all moved the society in a more liberal direction, a direction reflected in the changed power centers of the society.

It was in the postwar period that the courts became society's sexual censors, with the senior censor being the Supreme Court of the United States. In 1945 a series of landmark anti-censorship decisions were made. The State of New York law that banned crime comics on the grounds that they produced criminal behavior among the young was struck down by the State Supreme Court of New York. The State of Texas had suppressed the movie *The Miracle* (in which a woman thought that she had a virgin birth) using a law forbidding sacrilege. That conviction was reversed by a higher court.

The struggle between libertarians and conservatives about what was obscene, the effects of obscenity, and who should be considered when making such decisions continued in the courts from 1952 to 1965. As the balance shifted in the libertarian direction, it was apparent that the courts were often more liberal than some localities or social groups in society. The Warren Supreme Court produced many of the landmark decisions changing the legal climate of restrictions on the erotic in literature, film, and magazines during this period.

The struggle over suppression of sexual information in legitimate publications was fierce and prolonged. Hidden in this struggle was a theory of the sexual and beliefs about the impact of sexual materials on sexual conduct, as well as ideas about who could decide what other people could see.

Theory of Censorship

The legal struggle over the control of erotic materials has rested largely on the question of what impact pornography or erotica would have on society or particular individuals in it. The conservative position has been that nearly any non-condemnatory public discussion of sexuality is likely to lead to sexual activity—that sexual knowledge disposes people to sexual action. This is an obvious expression of a belief in a powerful and dangerous sex urge which would automatically express itself in people presented with sexual stimuli. This belief in a powerful sex drive is coupled to another set of beliefs about the ease with which people can be corrupted and led astray. The theory has two levels, one about sex and how it works, the second about people and how they work. Sex is dangerous and people are weak—therefore sex must be controlled and people protected.

The earliest censors emphasized that any obscenity could immediately and irretrievably corrupt. Thus the censors wanted to focus on the selected passages of a work taken "out of context." The court decisions after the 1930s reasoned that the selected passages should be judged in terms of the total literary intent of the work. The courts said, "Let us look at the work as a whole as the artist sees it"; the censors said, "If you look at how people read these books, look for the heavily thumbed parts of the books; those will be the obscene parts. That is what people are really reading." The censors were probably more right than the judges; for example, the soliloquy of Molly Bloom at the end of *Ulysses* has been far more often read than the book as a whole. However, the censor's error was more fundamental; even reading just the "dirty" sections still does not deprave and corrupt.

The struggle of censors to provide an underlying theory in face of social change has led them to focus first on this danger and then on that danger, from one stimulus to another. In the beginning pornography was considered an absolute incentive to sex crime—like the crime comic book which was supposed to make children into criminals. Depictions of sexual action supposedly made men mad with lust, resulting in rape and other terrible sex crimes. The connection between sex crime and pornography was believed to be proved, particularly after someone was arrested for a sex offense. The newspaper report always said, " . . . and the police found pornography in his possession."

When this argument failed to persuade, the censors then argued that they were attempting to protect the innocence of womanhood, and through women the integrity of the family. "What if your wife saw something like this?" they asked. Women were seen as more corruptible and innocent than men, and children even more corruptible and innocent than women. What should be read or seen should then be judged by the common denominator of a child's potential reaction. The corruption of the weak was the necessary consequence of even minimal exposure to pornography.

The censors' problem was compounded by the fact that the definition of pornography continued to change. What was the stimulus object the censors were referring to? For many years the nudity of women was sufficient—a bare back, the side of a breast, a revealing costume, the hint of a nipple was the margin between the obscene and the non-obscene. During the late 1940s girlie magazines showed nude female backs, then in the 1950s the sides of breasts, and finally in the 1960s nipples. At each of these stages of exposure the next sexual stimulus was represented as likely to overturn everything. During the 1950s the nudist magazines showed nude men with flaccid penises and nude women with pubic hair, but they were sold under the counter or through the mails in plain brown wrappers, with much ideological discussion of health and the uses of sunshine. Finally in the 1960s the pubic hair of women appeared in *Playboy*; in the 1970s flaccid penises appeared in *Viva* and *Playgirl*, and a hint of the labia of women peeking through pubic hair in *Penthouse* and *Playboy*. By the 1970s the raunchier sex magazines depicted erections and full-color labias. At this point the censorship battle was lost, for each time there was a further extreme the censors cried out that disaster immediately awaited. They had fallen into the position of crying wolf too often, and have simply ceased to be believed, much like anyone who preaches the end of the world and whose prophecy fails again and again.

The courts have been unable to make up their minds during this period. The decisions of the Warren Court chose three criteria for defining obscenity: (1) the standards of the community (taking the United States as a national community); (2) the work must be taken as a whole to see whether it has redeeming social purpose; and (3) the work must not be advertised to enhance its prurient appeal. These were roughly the national standards for judging pornography and obscenity. However, the Burger Court has been more limited in obscenity cases, upholding the rights of privacy against exposure to erotic materials, as well as more limited community standards. The federal government is now using the Comstock Act (passed in 1873) and is soliciting erotic materials to be mailed to postal inspectors in small towns and conservative parts of the United States, basing its prosecutions on the community standards of these locations. A sex magazine produced in New York or a porno film made in Miami thus may be judged in terms of the standards of a judge or jury in Memphis, Tennessee. While this strategy may not imprison the publishers or producers, it can certainly bankrupt them. (They may have to make more erotica in order to pay their legal fees.)

Effects of Pornography

There is no evidence that erotic materials have any deep or profound or lasting negative effects on the vast majority of the population. The theoretical presumption of a powerful sex drive released by simple stimuli mistakes the character of sexuality and the functions of pornography. Pornography is fantasy sex, consumed by people who know it is fantasy. Few adults go to pornographic movies or read pornographic books because they want sex instruction; they go or read because they want to participate in a fantasy experience. In the fantasy world of the book or theater they are released from responsibility, from the realness of life. Unlike real life they do not have to perform or succeed, they are having a momentary and pleasant escape from daily constraints, from sexual victory or defeat.

Erotic films and erotic books are sexual rituals, and as rituals they supply relief from normal social life. Many people report that they find pornography boring, but anything which is taken too often may become boring. Reading too many detective novels or too many science fiction stories can produce the same effects. Also, most people go to sex movies or read sex books thinking that something terrific is going to happen, because they have overestimated the potency of sexuality. They have high expectations, and find them dashed in the reality. Finally, pornography is *meant* to be boring in that it is not meant to disturb anything but the genitals. Some people may become aficionados or "addicts," but they are rare—as are people who become addicted to any specific art form. The people who watch *Days of Our Lives* or *Kojak* on television or went to movies twice a week in the 1930s and 1940s are and were equally addicted, equally interested in escaping from daily life. It is just that we judge these forms of escape more leniently than sexual escapes.

Most people's lives are more demanding of their attention (if less interesting) than pornography. As we have seen, sex as an activity, because of the unlimited promises and limited enactments, seems overrated. For most adults most of the time, sex and its representations in pornography appear subjectively important, but objectively may make only a marginal contribution to their life styles.

There is little systematic data on the reactions of adolescents to pornography; the data we have suggests that young males use it for masturbation fantasies (as they did the female movie stars of the 1930s and 1940s). Young females to whom it is offered may look at it for information. Among both middle class and working class young people it is the socially active and competent who have seen the most pornography. This does not suggest that pornography makes them more socially active or competent, but that the socially more active and competent do more things (date, fall in love, have drinks, get good grades, have many friends) than those young people who are late starters in developing interpersonal skills.

To younger children pornography does not make a great deal of sense since it does not refer to anything in their existing scripts. Even as more explicit sex instruction books are produced for children, books with photographs or drawings of intercourse and the genitals, it is unlikely that children so instructed would be shocked by pornography. They may even have considerable difficulty making the transition from sex information to pornography. It is unlikely that very many young children will ever be exposed to much erotic material, and whatever reaction they do have to it will be colored by how their parents act.

Experiment in Denmark

During the 1960s in Denmark a remarkable natural experiment was carried out— pornography was legalized, in two stages. The Danes allowed pornography to be produced and sold to people age sixteen and older, beginning at first with literary pornography in 1967 and then photographic pornography in 1969. Many porno shops were opened during the two "porno waves," first of literary and then of visual pornography: waves that produced a flood of books and then photographs, magazines, and films. The porno producers believed in the existence of a powerful sexual drive or instinct, and were sure that they had an endless market in sight. The opponents of legalization shared this belief and foretold the destruction of Danish society.

However, studies have shown that a majority of Danes sampled the pornography as it became available, and then either stopped buying it at all, or bought some only every once in a while.[1] Some people may have developed a collector's interest, but they were not sufficient in number to sustain a native Danish market for erotica. Within a few years after legalization, the porno shops disappeared from the residential areas of Copenhagen, and are now concentrated in only two areas of the city. The customers are no longer Danes, but tourists from other countries with more repressive laws. Tourists and the export market are what have saved the Danish porno producers from bankruptcy. This is what we would expect from social learning, that people have many interests, of which sex is only one, and pornography is only a minor aspect of sex. Few people will make sex a major interest in their lives, and even fewer will make pornography their major sexual interest.

A second major finding of the Danish research is the apparent impact of legalization of erotic material on certain kinds of sex crimes. (Crime rates in Denmark have always been relatively low compared to the United States.) The general rate of sex crimes in Denmark has declined, but the decline is due to different factors relating to different offenses. The child-molesting rate declined about eighty percent, that is, of 100 offenses reported before the legalization, about 20 are reported

1. This information about the Danish experiments, including sex crimes, is from an impressive and convincing body of work by the social psychologist Berl Kutchinsky.

now. This seems to be a real reduction, not merely a result of changes in the willingness of children or parents to call the police or the police to act.

There was also a major reduction in exhibitionism; however, this seems to have happened because women are less often reporting it to the police — particularly younger women, who find the exhibitionist more pathetic than disturbing. Finally, there are fewer reports of indecent assaults (which include all forcible physical approaches to women, including rape), with the largest reduction in reports of the less serious offenses. Young women, especially, are less likely to report minor annoyances (being physically touched while riding a streetcar, for example); however, the more serious offenses involving force are still being reported.

The Danish data also provides some insight into kinds of sex offenders — distinguishing even more clearly between the substitutive behavior of most child molesters (pornography can substitute for children) versus exhibitionism and aggression. The aggressive sex offender's behavior involves anger and hostility (pornography does not substitute for aggression).

Would we have the same results in the United States if we legalized pornography for all persons over age eighteen? (Keep in mind, many people are married by eighteen, and if eighteen year olds can buy it, both sixteen and seventeen year olds will have easy access to it.) There are many differences between the United States and Denmark. Denmark is a country of five million people, highly literate, relatively affluent, homogeneous in race, ethnicity, and cultural history. It has a low crime rate, an excellent social welfare system, and a fairly rational approach to social problems. All this makes Denmark quite different from the United States. However, it is unlikely that we would have very different effects from legalizing pornography in the United States; in fact, we may already be performing the Danish experiment without changing the law. In most large cities in the United States there are stores and arcades that sell pornography much like that available in Denmark. There are X-rated movie theaters in many cities and towns. There is considerable evidence that pornography no longer occupies the significant role it did for law enforcement in the 1950s and 1960s. The declining interest of the police in prostitution is paralleled by their declining interest in pornography. The public and police are far more concerned with violence and theft.

It is too early to tell for sure, but there is some evidence that the first surge of U.S. interest in pornography is wearing off. The clearest evidence comes from the X-rated movie houses which now play to only modest audiences (in contrast to the early 1970s) and the fact that in some suburbs admission to a double porno feature is now only $1.50. What impact availability of pornography has on sex crimes in the United States is unknown, but research parallel to the Danish studies is being undertaken in West Germany, which has recently legalized pornography.

Contemporary U.S. Scene

Since 1965 a series of major shifts have occurred in the United States in all media; they are more sexually explicit in some cases and more often deal with sexual themes and characters in others.

BOOKS AND MAGAZINES

Now available in editions of varying quality are nearly all of the books once locked up in the cabinets of erotica at the Kinsey Institute. In addition, publishers of cheap paperbacks have commissioned an enormous volume of new erotic books which are typed (more than written) by authors paid on a per word or per book basis. Conventional works of fiction can include explicit descriptions of sex acts without legal trouble or difficulty. Women's magazines and men's magazines come closer and closer in their content to the erotic picture magazines, and within a few years will probably show actual sex acts. A recent issue of *Playboy* showed Sara Miles and Kris Kristofferson (who is married to someone else) in what appears to be inter-course—if the intercourse was not simulated then it was both erotic and adulter-ous.[2]

MOTION PICTURES

The cinema through a rating system can now show any sexual activity in particular theaters in many jurisdictions. The hour-long "pornos" are part of the urban scene, and very large numbers of people have seen at least one of them. The R-rated films have also grown more sexually explicit, and often include vast amounts of violence associated with the sexuality. The rating system has effectively licensed the erotic film. Sexual themes of various sorts, nudity, and soft-core versions of sexuality are now common in regular theatrical releases, as they seek to compete with the "por-nos" for an audience.

TELEVISION

Restrictions on sexual conduct on television are still severe, since it is the primary form of "family entertainment" in U.S. society—entertainment in the home. There is *no* explicit sex on television (except perhaps for some cable programs); indeed, the amount of physical affection expressed between people is minimal, and even sexual innuendos are rare, except for the talk shows. However, television shows have dealt, often in a medical or crime context, with a variety of sexual issues, such as impotence, homosexuality, venereal disease, nonmarital pregnancy, prostitu-tion, and extramarital sex. The focus is usually on sex as a social problem. In the situation comedies, single women may now have sex (very discreetly); the formerly married may go out of town with a friend; a divorced husband and wife may sleep together; a gay male couple may be shown in a series. In the fall of 1976, two series had characters on a continuing basis identified as homosexual.

2. There is an interesting question to be raised about the actual or simulated sex that takes place be-tween performers in X- and R-rated films. What about their spouses? How do they feel? Perhaps they treat it like the husband of a woman who works in a massage parlor; he views her masturbating her clients as "part of the job," but he is enraged by the idea that she might have an affair. His attitude is part of the theme of a short story by the French author Colette, about a young prostitute whose lover does not mind her profession—so long as she does not enjoy it. One night she enjoys sex with a customer, and she is in terror, convinced that her lover will know as soon as he sees her and kill her for it.

What was formerly underground eroticism can now be found in chic living rooms as furniture. An elegant life-size statue of a woman in a sexually exposed position wearing a fetish and bondage costume is adorned with a cushion.

There is a powerful minority outcry against sex on television (often associated with an outcry against violence), even though television usually treats sexual themes in a stereotyped way. However, it must be understood that television, like pornography, is essentially a soothing medium — a mental tranquilizer — so this stereotyping must be expected.

EROTIC PERSONALITIES

Part of the erotic environment is media treatment of the sexuality of notorious personalities in society. The rock singer David Bowie, a favorite of what was called glamour rock, talks about his bisexuality, using elements from the gay culture and "decadent" heterosexuality to sell his act and manipulate the media. The media report on actresses having children out of wedlock, people living with others without being married, and the affairs of non-political public figures. Publicity on such activities was at one time sufficient to destroy the reputation and work of a performer. A slightly tainted sexual reputation or sexual celebrity is now part of "making it" in certain media or media-associated businesses. Athletic and rock groupies are part of our way of life. To be sexually outrageous is part of hyping the media. However much public-relations fakery there is to all of this media coverage, it does add a sexual dimension to many well-known people in various sectors of society.

These changes show the erosion of old distinctions. The newsstands and the movie theaters were once the point of conflict in most obscenity cases; it was *over the counter* versus *under the counter* sales. It now is possible in many cities to buy openly printed erotica at newsstands and book stores. Photographic and cinematic erotica are still restricted to specialized stores and theaters, but they are common and in some cities ubiquitous.

Another distinction that has eroded is between *art* and *pornography*. It is now possible to treat any sexual theme in serious art—the margin between erotica and serious art has nearly disappeared. The distinction created in the 1950s between pornography (bad and not art) and erotic realism (artistic and therefore good) is no longer useful, since the difference between the two realms is difficult to locate.

A final distinction to fall is that between *hard core* and *soft core*. The latter form, particularly in magazines and films, once drew the line at simple nudity or stopped just after, "No, Charley, don't . . . ." It has moved in a more explicit direction in the last few years. The soft core becomes hard core—only advertisements remain soft core. If television ever begins to show openly explicit materials, the advertisers will deal with it as they have in *Playboy* and *Penthouse*, putting their ads next to or in between the erotic offerings (or perhaps making their ads more sexual than the shows, as many are at present).

What is the impact of all this on what people do sexually? It probably facilitates or quickens certain aspects of sexual experimentation—e.g., people who would eventually have oral sex may do it sooner or in different circumstances. It provides information about sexuality, particularly to adolescents, or it simply makes the sexual world and its images available. The media now serve along with the peer group as primary sources of explicit sex information in society.

However, the media, like the peer group, provides a certain kind of information, which is packaged in traditional ways. These packages are often heavily stereotyped in a number of directions. One aspect of media stereotyping is to show the world as being more sexual than it really is—it makes the same promises about sex that the Top-Forty pop songs make about love. This is particularly true of erotic celebrity personalities who play up the exotic, the different, and the sensational rather than the pedestrian and the mundane. The X-rated movies and erotic books often use the standard stereotypes of male-oriented pornography: cast of characters (the stewardess, the divorcee, the nymphomaniac, the horny housewife, the baby sitter); erotic equipment (the deep throat and the big penis); and gender-role stereotypes (aggressive stud men, oversexed compliant women).

However stereotyped media presentations may be, and they would not be as erotically effective if they were not, they do increase the level of sexual information in society. It would be difficult to grow up as ignorant about homosexuality now as it was in the past — *Time* magazine tells all about it in a cover story — and it would be difficult to be as ignorant about birth — Channel Five in New York showed a Caesarian section on the late news in August, 1976. Sexuality may not make any more sense than it did before, or be put together any more effectively in terms of a person's daily environment, but the pieces are at least more visible. Sexual learning in the United States used to be like crime detection: trying to solve a puzzle whose pieces are missing. The detective, like the sexual neophyte before the 1970s, must first find the pieces before the puzzle can be assembled and solved. Perhaps the main benefit of the change in the erotic environment has been that now many more of the pieces of the sexuality puzzle are available.

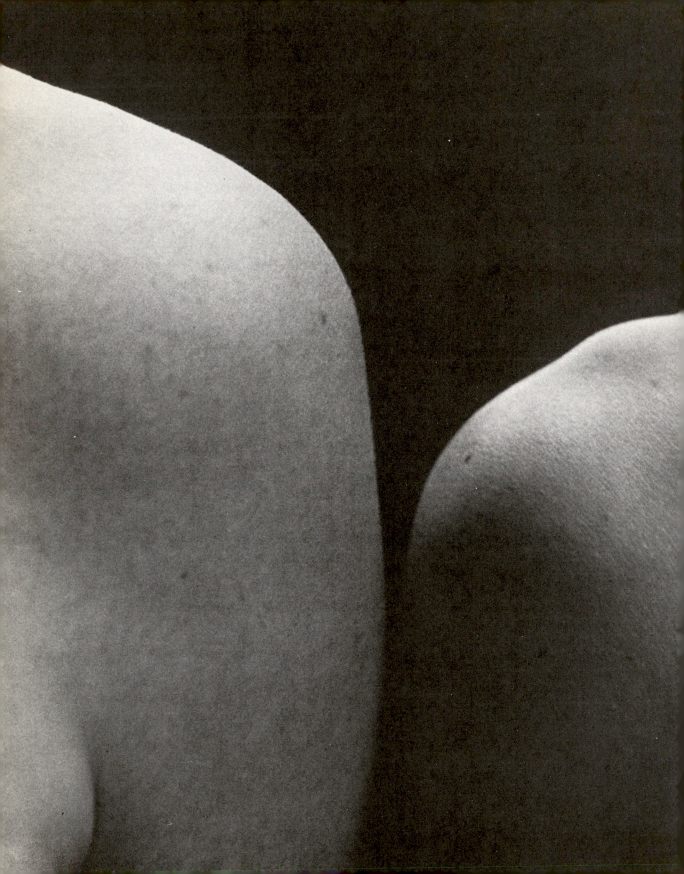

SEXUAL THERAPIES

We social workers of the twentieth century cannot
ignore sex; what we can do is to make it a burden.
E. M. Forster, *Abinger Harvest*

MOST OF THE INFLUENTIAL SEXUAL LEARNING THAT GOES ON IN THE UNITED States is covert and unofficial (we learn most from our friends and the media rather than from parents, doctors, preachers, and teachers), and the conditions under which we get our early practice in sexual conduct are full of fear, anxiety, and incompetence. These two conditions often follow people through their entire sexual lives, despite our cultural rhetoric that sex should be important and significant. As a consequence, we want very much to do things about which we know very little and for which we are badly trained.

Two consequences of this dilemma are sex information manuals and sex therapy for adults (as well as sex textbooks for college students). Sex information manuals (formerly called marriage manuals) have a history which goes back to the 1890s, culminating in such explicit picture books as *The Joy of Sex*. They have been a significant form of resistance to censorship and suppression of information about sex techniques, sexual pleasure, birth control, abortion, and venereal disease. Direct sex therapies, despite some verbal attempts to treat specific sexual problems such as impotence, or cure "perversions" such as fetishism and homosexuality, are relatively recent.

Nearly all sex therapy depends upon changing either *what* people do or *whom* they do it with, or upon changing the feelings that people have about what or whom. Thus people may be doing some undesirable things (exposing themselves in public), or doing some desirable things ineptly (not having orgasm during intercourse); or they may be doing what are thought to be the right things with the wrong people (intercourse with twelve year olds), or they may feel guilty or ashamed of both conventional (masturbation) or unconventional (homosexuality) forms of sexual conduct. In therapy we are always dealing with the problem of desirability, since the goal of therapy is to change people from what is undesirable to what is desirable.

One of the keys to the question of desirability is knowing to whom the behavior is desirable or undesirable. For instance, a pedophilic man may be absolutely delighted to have sex with children and feel no guilt about it and provide excellent reasons for doing it; however, the majority of the people in society, and most therapists, want him to change, and are willing to imprison him to make sure that he does. In some cases, a therapist may say, "I don't mind what you are doing (perhaps the person is a transvestite) but your wife and children are upset and going to leave you if you don't change. The choice is up to you, but you can't have both." Sometimes people may want to change something about themselves that a thera- pist may think is perfectly all right and probably does not need to be changed (an adult homosexual who wants to become a married exclusive heterosexual) but the patient wants to change. In other cases (the easiest to evaluate) people are simply unable to do something that they and everyone else wants them to be able to do (a woman having orgasm). In order to do therapy, a decision has to be made of what is good and what is bad — or at least what is preferred and what is not.

An important dilemma of the contemporary therapist is that the rules of what is sexually approved and disapproved are changing. For instance, early ejaculation is now being defined as a sexual dysfunction, as *premature* ejaculation. If a man ejac- ulates before entry into the vagina or after only a few strokes of his penis, it is be- lieved there is something wrong with him. Implicit in this decision, however, is that the man's inadequacy is in not satisfying his partner, not because he does not enjoy himself. It may well be that the man is perfectly satisfied with his own orgasm, and there is evidence that a fairly large number of men are perfectly happy with inter- course lasting less than a minute. In a time when women were not supposed to en- joy intercourse, or when their enjoyment was a matter of social indifference, early ejaculation was not a dysfunction. Ejaculation outside the vagina might have been a dysfunction if pregnancy were the point of intercourse, but not ejaculation after penetration. What has happened is that the definition has changed — women now have the right to sexual pleasure, and a man is supposed to keep an erection in the vagina long enough that the woman can have as many orgasms as she wishes. (It can be seen that vaginal intercourse is defined as better than oral- or manual-geni- tal sex.)

While new "problems" are being identified, what were sexual deviancies become defined as the rights of sexual minorities. As part of the shift from collective to personal standards of conduct, conduct is increasingly defined as problematic only when it becomes a problem for individuals — as long as they are defined as consenting and adult. If people are unhappy with what they are doing, treatment may be justified. However, viewed from a more radical perspective, part of the treatment process should be an attempt to find out *why* people are unhappy with what they are doing; if they are unhappy for the wrong reasons (social pressure) it may be appropriate to attempt to dissuade them from changing. For instance, agreeing to attempt to change a homosexual to a heterosexual preference, even if the person wants to be changed, may be giving in to social pressure (like a Jew be- ing forced to become a Christian by the Inquisition) rather than to a truly personal desire for change.

Sexual Difficulties: Physical or Psychological?

The role of physical disabilities in producing either dysfunctions in sexual perfor- mance or other forms of disapproved sexual conduct is minimal. This does not mean that certain physical problems cannot limit sexual functioning or interact with psychological processes to produce a sexual dysfunction; however, they represent a minority of cases. In part, physical limitations become a problem only when the sexual actors have a narrow view of "normality" in sex. A man who cannot get an erection for purely physical reasons (say a prostatectomy) can still be a competent lover, even for a woman who wants a phallus-like object in her vagina, as long as it does not have to be his penis. Even in those cases where the source of coital dysfunction is purely psychological, it is possible for the couple to choose other techniques for sexual pleasure.

There can be extensive damage to the body without impairing many aspects of sexual ability. Many people whose spinal cords have been injured remain able to have erections and orgasms, even though there are no longer nerve connections between their brains and their genitals. Erection and ejaculation are triggered by local spinal reflexes, and the orgasm is produced without direct neurological feedback from the genitals. In fact, many people with spinal injuries are now encouraged to undertake exercises in "sensate focus" to improve their ability to define the sensations they have as sexual, as well as building up a greater psychological awareness of sex.

Other than permanent physical limitations, transitory physical factors may become the basis for psychological problems. A diabetic who cannot get erect because of fatigue or other causes, or a man who fails to get erect because he has been drinking, can develop impotence because he begins to worry about performing the next time. As long as particular kinds of performances, especially erections and orgasms, are important, not "achieving" them can produce important side effects. The problem is usually not physical, but results from the mismanagement of the consequences of intermittent physical problems. This does not mean that the physical side, particularly of certain dysfunctions, should not be explored; however, they should not be routinely expected.

An overemphasis on the physical dimensions or sources of sexual problems can have two negative consequences, one for the patient, the other for the therapist. The consequence for patients is that the search for an immediate physical cause of the disorder allows them to deny any psychological basis for the problem. The patient may want to blame a physical inability (like homosexuals or their parents who want to believe that homosexuality is a genetically based preference in order to get rid of guilt, or feelings of incompetence, or pressure to change. The patient can transfer the responsibility for change to the medical profession which has not yet discovered a "cure."

The consequence for the therapist is more complex, since it rests on a belief in what might be called the *medical model* for the treatment of disapproved forms of social and psychological functioning, a model based on some success in the treatment of physical ailments. From this perspective, the patient's condition represents a deviation from approximate normal functioning of body, and treatment is designed to get the patient back to a normal state. We believe that doctors know how to treat a diseased kidney to make it act like a normal kidney, or how to set a bone so that it will knit and perform as well (or nearly as well) as it did before it was broken. As long as our interests remain with physical systems, and we do not expand them to the social and psychological functioning of the individual, the medical model seems to work.[1]

As we have seen, however, definitions of what are appropriate or inappropriate standards for social and psychological functioning rest upon standards different than those used to justify the treatment of a broken leg. The changing of conduct runs into conflicting values and morals. For example, is homosexuality a mental illness? For many years the American Psychiatric Association (which had accepted and promoted the cultural stereotype) believed that it was, and classified it as such. Then a committee of the APA, as the body with the social right to define mental illness, decided (under considerable pressure from gay activists) to reclassify it as not an illness. This change in classification resulted in a referendum among the entire membership, who decided by vote that homosexuality is not a disease, though it is still called a sexual identity problem. The changing attitudes of U.S. society toward homosexuality worked to change its status from more disapproved to less disapproved.

Whether or how to "treat" the homosexual is thus quite unlike whether or how to set a broken leg. Yet therapists often believe they have the same mandate to treat disapproved forms of sexual conduct that they do to treat physical ailments, and that the same medical model can be used. The sexual problem is an ailment, it can be treated to return the person to sexual health—however, central to the problem of treatment is the *definition* of illness and health. The question is rarely, "*Should* we treat this or that?" but is more often, "*How* should we treat this or that?"

Kinds of Sexual Therapy

In the last decade what appears to be a wide variety of sexual therapies has been developed; as a result of the work of Masters and Johnson there has been a dramatic break with the techniques of treating sexual problems typical of the last half century. For nearly fifty years sexual problems were defined and treated by a combination of the criminal law and psychiatry, acting either separately or together. On one hand were people who had committed some kind of sex offense and who were treated for their conduct by imprisonment. On the other hand were people whose sexual problems were not a crime, or who had access to psychiatric treatment either before or after arrest. In some cases people were committed to psychiatrically oriented prisons for having committed a sex offense and having been labeled a sexual psychopath or a mentally disordered sex offender.

The treatment of these people was heavily influenced by theories and therapies developed from traditional psychoanalysis. The presumption of traditional

---

1. The limits of the medical model, even in physical medicine, can be suggested by the following case: A quarry worker came to a physician with a badly crushed forefinger. The physician, an excellent orthopedic surgeon, reconstructed the mangled finger into a cosmetically satisfactory but functionally limited finger. Later, some time after the finger had healed, the man returned to the doctor and asked when it would work like it had before. The doctor explained that it would never be the same, although he had saved the finger and the man still had all ten of them. The man said, "Cut it off." The stiff finger got in his way at work, and he had none of the middle class investment in a complete body image. Even in medical cases the question of what is health is a variable question.

psychoanalysis was that any display of unconventional sexual conduct in adult-hood was symptomatic of a trauma suffered in childhood. What the patient was complaining of (exhibitionism, lack of orgasm, impotence) was only a symptom of an underlying conflict, which was the real disease. It was this underlying conflict that had to be treated, since if it were not cured new symptoms would appear. (Note here the medical model again—do not treat the symptoms of an infection, treat the infection.)

The treatment mechanism (psychoanalysis) is a period of time in a one-to-one relationship with a specially trained therapist exploring under set conditions aspects of past relationships, particularly those with parents. It is a technique that depends on learning to talk about the present problem in terms of the past, while developing a strong emotional attachment to the therapist. For many people, particularly those with sexual difficulties in their day-to-day living, talking about the past can be extremely frustrating, since the problems may continue to occur four or five times a week (e.g., impotence or lack of orgasm or the impulse to expose oneself). After many treatment sessions many patients are still suffering from the presenting problem, and have only an apparent understanding of what happened with Mom and Dad.[2]

Traditional psychoanalysis has had very little success in the treatment of most sexual problems. The successes it has had appear to be related to the emotional attachment between patient and therapist, a dependency that helps the patient re-shape behavior in a direction that the therapist approves. However, because the rule in psychoanalysis is that the therapist not give advice or be a direct guide, discovery by patients of how to cure themselves is rare.

As the lack of results from psychoanalysis became more apparent (as well as the fact that there were very few analysts, and they were very expensive), there was an increase in the number and variety of talking therapists for sexual problems. Freudian theory remained important in defining problems and identifying solutions, but patients began to be treated in more directive situations, sometimes as individuals, sometimes as couples, sometimes in groups. Therapists still seemed to avoid the presenting problem (the patient cannot keep an erection or cannot have an orgasm), and looked for causes in family relationships or in the past of the individual or in the realm of feelings. It was as if the therapists wanted to avoid talking about the sexual problems themselves.

Further, many therapists were dealing with isolated individuals removed for a few hours a week from their usual environment. It was against the rules to go outside the office to look at the actual situation the patient lived in, and the other people who were important to the patient. The sexual problem belonged only to the person in treatment. At the end of World War II the focus in the general practice of therapy began slowly to move away from the individual to the family or to the local context in which the patient lived. Even then, the application of this "discovery" to sexual issues was belated and difficult.

2. There is a good deal of evidence that nobody really knows what their parents did to them. As mentioned in an earlier chapter, we remember only a small part of what happened to us as children. What seems to be going on in psychoanalysis is that people are *inventing* their past. They are learning to talk about themselves and their conduct in certain kinds of ways, and rewriting their personal histories.

Masters and Johnson Break Through

In the late 1950s and early 1960s, as part of their research program, William Masters and Virginia Johnson began to develop what would become known as direct sexual therapy. Their previous research on the anatomy and physiology of sexual response would be the legitimation for the program of therapy they were developing. Their program offered a number of significant breaks with the majority of sexual therapies of the past. First, they engaged in an act of cultural relabeling. They distinguished the problems they would treat by labeling them sexual dysfunctions (rather than neuroses or diseases), and limited the dysfunctions to a small set of problems that plagued primarily heterosexual couples. They explicitly adopted a medical model and assumed that a function (an approved sexual activity) was interfered with by a dysfunction (some limitation in sexual ability). This medical model gave them the opportunity to appeal to a belief in a set of natural sexual responses which they said they were restoring by treatment. This appeal was extraordinarily helpful with patients who wanted to be sexually natural, healthy, and functional. Further, this appeal to medicine and natural sexuality tended to defuse criticism of their actual therapeutic techniques.

Their second major decision was to engage in direct sexual behavior modification with patients. If a patient came to them who could not have an erection or could not have an orgasm, Masters and Johnson proceeded through education, instruction, authoritative pronouncement, and (most important) sexual practice sessions to help them to do it. Although Masters and Johnson continued the practice of talking to patients, they used the talk to attack the problem, they were active and directive, they told patients how to do sexual things in a systematic and supportive manner.

Their third major departure was that they attempted to treat people as sexual couples rather than individuals. It was apparent to Masters and Johnson that the problem was sustained (if it had not been created) by the couples, not by the individual. The husband who failed first by being impotent or the wife who failed first by being nonorgasmic were often suffering a symptom of something amiss with the couple. Often one spouse was sabotaging the attempts of the other to get better without outside help.

Most of the couples who went to Masters and Johnson were in their thirties and forties. Some of them had not had successful sexual relations for five or six years; their problems often went back to or before the beginning of marriage, and many times they had been in therapy before. The duration of the problem was actually the basis for some hope, given that the marriages had lasted so long despite the sexual dysfunction. There was a commitment to going into therapy, as well as a willingness to spend nearly 3000 dollars for the treatment program.

The sexual dysfunctions of women were usually the inability to have orgasm at all, or inability with a current partner (they may have had orgasm with others or in masturbation). Some of the women suffered from *vaginismus*—when a penis or some other object is introduced into the vagina there is a spasm of the vaginal muscles.

The men they treated suffered from primary impotence (they had never had an erection in a sexual context, that they recalled) or secondary impotence (they had been able to have erections in a sexual context in the past, but were unable to become erect with a particular woman—a situational problem—or with any woman—an absolute problem) and from early or premature ejaculation. There were also a few men with a relatively rare disorder called ejaculatory impotence who could get erect and maintain erection for a long time, but who could not ejaculate.

The Masters and Johnson method involved a male and female therapy team who worked mostly with married heterosexual couples. Each couple would come to St. Louis and live in a motel near the treatment center for two weeks. The therapy began on the first morning, when each member of the couple was interviewed by the therapist of the same sex. The same afternoon, each one would be interviewed by the other therapist. In each case, a relatively elaborate history of sexual experience, preference, and previous therapy was taken, as well as the patient's own opinion of the problem bringing the couple into therapy. The cross-sex interview allowed the therapists jointly to determine the problem, so that they could then sit down with each other and then with the two people together and discuss with them what they thought was happening.

Masters and Johnson tell their clients that there is no dysfunctional individual, there is only a dysfunctional pair. They blame neither one, but they do try to locate in the couple's interaction what makes one or the other of them not have the experiences they wish. The issues may range from mutual ignorance to relatively deep-seated interpersonal sabotage. That is, the woman may want to have an impotent husband, or the man a non-orgasmic wife, because it is a way to control the spouse. She or he says, in effect, "That's the kind of weakling you are," or "You can't even come."

Relationships often stabilize around that kind of negative interaction, because people may not want their spouses to have good sexual experiences. Even in the therapeutic situation there is a good deal of ambivalence, and people are not always whole-heartedly interested in changing themselves; they believe the problem is completely their partner's and not shared. For instance, a husband who is technically incompetent in bed, who ejaculates so quickly that his wife has no chance to have orgasm, may say to Masters and Johnson, "My wife has a problem." The problem is partly his, but he does not want to hear about that. Masters and Johnson try to get both members of a couple to take responsibility for what they are doing to each other, to share responsibility for the problem. Only then can they generate the kind of communication that will allow them to solve it.

Impotence

The process of treating impotence involves both verbal and physical therapies. Both are based on the view that an impotent man is looking over his own shoulder all the time. He is self-conscious, and this prevents his arousal—when he has sex, he thinks about his erection, reflects on it, wonders how it happens, or wonders if it will happen—and either fails to become erect or loses his erection.

Because impotence is a severe threat to a man's masculinity, the man who is impotent once may begin to worry so much about doing it right the next time that he turns himself off. Having turned himself off a second time, he tries even harder the third time, without success. He locks himself into a descending spiral of self-

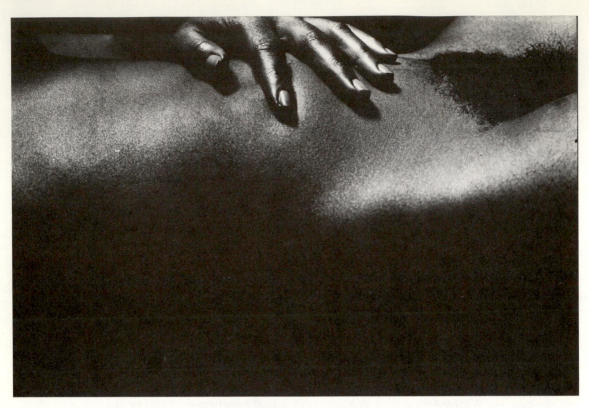

Learning to touch and be touched sexually, to desire without making demands, seems to be the major goal of modern sexual therapy.

criticism and failure to perform. This spiral can be specifically linked to the person with whom it started, so that in the presence of this one person the impotent man cannot get erect, though he may be able to with others. After a few such failures, he may well decide that sex, at least with this one person, is just not worth it; it is too self-defeating.

The Masters and Johnson approach is to tell the partner to forget about having intercourse, about having an orgasm or getting an erection. Instead, they teach him and his partner other things about sex. The couple is told to go back to the motel and simply pleasure each other—massage each other, feel good being together, take a bath together, rub oils on each other's body—but not touch the genitals.

Masters and Johnson understood that patients were beginning to get phobic about their genitals being touched. Genital tactile cues had become messages of failure, not of pleasure, and when their genitals were touched they simply turned off. Avoiding the genitals thus avoids any sense of likely failure, and as the pleasuring proceeds, the man often gets an erection. The therapists tell him, however, not to try intercourse. He and his partner should first become thoroughly aroused without experiencing failure. Eventually, as they continue to practice this nongenital arousal and meet daily with the therapists to talk about what they have done, there may be a spontaneous attempt to have intercourse. If it works, the couple will come in all aglow—they have succeeded. If the attempt fails, the failure can be blamed on not following directions ("You weren't supposed to try that yet") rather than on a more basic problem.

Masters and Johnson also instruct their clients in certain helpful sexual behaviors. They recommend that intercourse first be attempted with the woman on top, or in the side position, or in any position where the man does not have to do anything, where he does not have to perform. This is important because many impotent men are suffering from a great deal of performance anxiety. Early in this kind of therapy, the woman must take an active role. This is why Masters and Johnson and many of the therapists who have followed them, especially in California, at first used surrogates, usually women, who served as partners for single clients. (Often single women are less able to deal with male surrogates in a therapeutic situation, because of their sexual scripts.)

Masters and Johnson regard their treatment for impotence as successful if the penis remains erect in the vagina for twenty minutes. If this can be achieved consistently, there is a good chance of stabilizing the man's response to intercourse. Their success rates are fairly good. Two thirds to three quarters of their secondary impotence patients recover, and stay recovered for over five years. They also do not find that impotence, once successfully treated, crops up again later in another form.

There are impotence cases with which therapists have less success. It seems, for instance, extremely difficult to train an adult male who has never had an erection to have one. Such men do exist, and there appears to be nothing physically wrong with them, but they have never masturbated or got an erection with someone. They may not even be viewed as having a problem until relatively late in life. Parents do not notice their sons' erections, and the patient may feel that he does not need an erection in order to ejaculate—it is possible to ejaculate when limp. Masters and Johnson have called this latter condition *primary impotence* to distinguish it from the *secondary impotence* of men who have problems having erection after a previously successful history.

Early (Premature) Ejaculation

The second major complaint of men in sex therapy is an inability to control or delay the moment of ejaculation. Since most men who have ejaculated are unable to maintain an erection afterward, this complaint may result in sexual difficulty for a spouse. However, there are marriages in which the rapidity of male ejaculation is not a cause for complaint on the part of wife or the husband. This may result from cultural considerations (it is not expected that the wife have pleasure in sex), from attitudes about sex possessed by the couple (they may view the situation as normal), or because the wife is as rapidly responsive as her husband, or because they use other mutually satisfactory techniques for her orgasm.

When early ejaculation is a problem, it is because the male feels he should perform "better," or because his early loss of erection causes problems for his wife. Treatment of this phenomenon follows the pattern set in the treatment of impotence. There is an attempt to shift the focus of attention away from the anxiety- creating moment, to teach a wider variety of sexual skills, and to increase the activity of the woman. Specific to this dysfunction is the use of a technique in which the woman arouses the man manually, and just before he is about to ejaculate either reduces stimulation or squeezes his penis by pressing her thumb firmly just below the corona. The woman and man are encouraged to engage in a sequence of increases and reductions in stimulation so that the man can become aware of the sign of ejaculation and develop voluntary control. Most men develop such techniques in conventional sexual activity, either by reducing the rate of activity or thinking of something else. Men who are early ejaculators have to be taught these techniques. The couple can then go on to intercourse, with the man regulating the rate of stimulation both verbally and physically.

All of these techniques require much greater levels of verbal communication between sexual partners, since they are required to report to each other on the sexual sensations that they are feeling. Just this fact of enhanced communication is often helpful in the treatment of the problem. Success rates for the treatment of premature ejaculation are quite high using these techniques, paralleling those for impotence.

Lack of Orgasm

The treatment of women who have never had an orgasm with any sexual partner, who have never had an orgasm in a heterosexual relationship, or who have difficulty having orgasm with a specific partner (but who have had orgasm either with other persons or using other techniques) tends to follow the techniques described for the treatment of male dysfunctions. Once again the joint responsibility for the problem is emphasized, the couple is asked to focus on noncoital and non-orgasm-seeking sexual techniques, and the woman is asked to become more active. The couple are given instructions on what sexual activities to practice as well as meeting with therapists about communication difficulties. There is a shift away from the "awful test" — "If I don't come this time it's a disaster" — to a more leisurely, less anxious, less achievement-oriented sexual encounter. Again, massage, intimacy, feedback, support, and directive instructions are central to learning how to have orgasm.

This strategy seems to be quite successful, particularly with women who have had orgasm in other circumstances and who have reasonably good relations with their spouses. Often what is discovered in the process is that the male is an early ejaculator or his regular sexual repertoire is not arousing to the woman. If she fails to have orgasm she may come to believe that it is only her fault, which will further reduce her ability to have orgasm. This technique is less successful with women who have never had an orgasm in any way (women who are *preorgasmic*). It is not known exactly why this is so, but it may be that the more sexual experience without orgasm a woman has, the more difficult it becomes to make orgasm part of her script. Recall from the Kinsey data that women who had tried premarital coitus and had not had climax had the most difficulty in having orgasm in marital sex — women who had experienced orgasm (no matter how or how often) found it far easier to have orgasm in marriage.

A wide variety of techniques has been developed by other therapists in dealing with preorgasmic women, particularly the use of masturbation with and without a vibrator. These techniques emphasize the autonomy of individual women in seeking sexual pleasure, and emphasize the role of self pleasuring among women in developing general interpersonal autonomy.[3] There is no systematic data to suggest that these techniques are or are not as effective as the couple-oriented therapy developed by Masters and Johnson. From impressionistic evidence they seem to be very effective with preorgasmic women, particularly for women who dislike the couple-oriented therapeutic situation.

Vaginismus

A rare, but relatively dramatic, problem is of women who are unable to tolerate objects inserted into the vagina. In some cases merely touching the external genitals can result in a spasmodic contraction of the vagina. In most cases this dysfunction seems to respond quite well to a form of systematic desensitization. Under very relaxed conditions inserts of increasing size are placed in the vagina. As the patient grows accustomed to one size without spasm, a larger size is introduced (again under very relaxed conditions). This technique, in association with those mentioned above, seems quite efficient in eliminating this problem. There are, however, some patients (especially those with traumatic sexual histories), who do not seem responsive to such techniques.

Successes and Limitations

Directive sex therapy of the kind pioneered by Masters and Johnson and the variants of many sorts that have followed have been remarkably successful in reducing certain forms of sexual distress among married couples. Patients with long histories of impotence, premature ejaculation, and lack of orgasm seem to be aided by the process of emotional support, anxiety reduction, sex education, directed sexual practice, and increased interpersonal communication. The fact that so many things are being manipulated at once makes it difficult to determine exactly which factor is accounting for most of the change, but it is possible to hypothesize that anxiety reduction and the opportunity to practice sexually are extremely important, and may facilitate the other changes. One reason for this hypothesis is that these two factors are what is novel about the new sex therapy—talking about sex and improving communication have been for many years part of therapy. What was missing was the movement of the therapist into the sexual situation, at least via instruction and "homework."

The therapy has been particularly successful with patients who have traditional sexual histories, many of whom had inhibitions about talking about sex or doing different sexual things. Such people also have strong commitments to their marriages, and to their spouses, even if there are some emotional or interpersonal prob-

---

3. The willingness to seek autonomous sexual pleasure in masturbation is viewed as having an influence on the general level of assertiveness in women's conduct. Autonomy in sex helps lead to autonomy in other spheres.

lems in the marriage. It is possible for couple-oriented therapy to be quite success-ful for people who are committed to heterosexuality, marriage, and this spouse, but who are inept in some way. These patients can often be treated with quick results while living at home by weekly therapeutic sessions with nonmedical practitioners.

As has been noted, there are some difficult problems. One is spouses who do not like each other. In these cases the sexual problem is part of a marriage problem. The focus has to be on the marriage problem, since the sexual interaction may be a symptom of other marital conflict. In some cases the sex life of a couple may be excellent, but they still may hate each other. There is not a one-to-one fit between sexual adjustment and marital adjustment.

There are also the sexual problems of those who are not involved in a one-couple relationship (the singles), as well as those (women particularly) who do not wish their problem solved within a couple relationship. In these former cases the use of sex surrogates may be appropriate, and in the latter masturbation may be a helpful therapeutic aid.

Finally, there are cases which seem very difficult—primary impotence and women with long-term histories of sexual experience without orgasm. Rescripting in these cases does not seem easily done through conventional directive sex thera-py, although certain elements of that type of therapy may be useful.

"Treating" Sexual Offenders and Sexual Minorities

Until very recently it was assumed that conventional heterosexuality in marriage is so preferable to all other kinds of sexual conduct that it is appropriate to use the power of the state to make people change their ways. This opinion is still held by many, although in general there is not the will to enforce laws or to coerce change in the many people involved in minority or unconventional sexual conduct.

A fairly large number of people have been imprisoned and a still larger number have gone into therapy (either in prisons or in the outside community), voluntarily or coerced, to stop or change their disapproved sexual conduct. The history of therapeutic treatment of the sexually different in penal institutions has been, except in a few instances, a history of error, incompetence, and failure. It is not that people so treated went out and repeated their acts; it is that the treatment was irrele-vant (most of them did not repeat their acts in any case, treated or not, imprisoned or not), serving largely as window dressing for institutions charged with the goal of "protecting" the community.

Most of the therapies (in and out of institutions) followed the psychoanalytic model or variants of it, seeking to locate in the past of the offender the roots of his behavior, and by getting him to understand its causes and prevent it in the future. They were therefore talking therapies. With the rise of directive sex therapy and its association with that branch of psychological therapy called *behavior modification*, there has been a movement toward adopting these techniques for inducing sexual behavior change. A number of issues are related to the use of behavioral change techniques.

LEVELS OF DISAPPROVAL

We must first decide whether or not our level of disapproval of a specific form of sexual conduct is sufficiently high for us to be willing to use or make available behavioral change techniques. Do we sufficiently disapprove of rape, child molesting, homosexuality, fetishism, oral sex, or premarital intercourse to utilize various forms of behavioral change or control to modify or eliminate the activity? Does our disapproval reach the level that we would coerce people to be treated for one or another of these behaviors, or is it low enough so that we might make the technique available, but not mandatory?

Recall that all decisions to use behavioral change, from imprisonment to good advice, rest on the assumption that the conduct to be changed is undesirable from some point of view. In some cases there is collective agreement on the desirability of change (on the part of the larger community, the community of treatment, and the community to be treated). In other cases there is conflict both between and within these various groups. Many homosexuals do not want to be treated; some do. Some therapists think that all homosexuals should be treated; others think that volunteers might be; other people think that treatment should not be given in any case; the general society is equally divided in their views.

VOLUNTEER VERSUS COERCION

A crucial dimension of the problem of treatment is whether or not techniques should be applied to everyone, or whether they should only be used with people who desire them. This is a serious question, particularly among prisoners, who may be required to have therapy in order to be released from prison. For instance, "successful" participation in a therapy program may be used as evidence that a prisoner is cooperative and eligible for release on parole. In other cases, prisoners may volunteer even for castration in order to be released from a very long prison sentence. The question remains, "How voluntary can treatment be if a person's freedom depends on a show of cooperation?" There is evidence that coerced psychotherapy probably only promotes a cynical display of change (often skillfully produced) which disappears when the prisoner is released. The attempt to distinguish between the punitive purposes of imprisonment and the rehabilitating uses of therapy is still a matter of serious and recurrent debate in correctional agencies.

In a sense, the distinction between coercion and volunteering is clearer in the prison situation where the rewards and penalties are obvious, than it is in the outside community where there are subtle and unsubtle pressures on people to change their conduct. This is the point made by those who oppose all therapy aimed at changing homosexuals into heterosexuals, even when requested by a potential patient. The argument is that it is not possible to determine in U.S. society, where homosexuality is stigmatized, whether or not the patient truly has come for therapy voluntarily. An important corollary of this argument is that homosexuality ought to be tolerated or approved, and the use of therapy undermines the status of all homosexuals.

Goals and Techniques of Change

There are a number of different goals that exist and therapeutic techniques that seem to go with them when dealing with the modification of sexual conduct.

SUPPRESSION

Disapproving certain behavior and attempting to suppress it is essentially the strategy used in most punishment strategies to control behavior. There is no attempt to substitute positive activities to replace what is disapproved. This has been the most common strategy of dealing with disapproved sexual conduct, from children in the home to the patients on the psychotherapist's couch. It is also at the core of what is called *aversion therapy*. The therapist may show a patient, say a homosexual, pictures of naked men and make him vomit or give him an electric shock if he shows signs of arousal (the cues for arousal may be the widening of the pupils or the first twitch of an erection). The therapist may want the patient to develop a heterosexual commitment, but this is assumed to occur when the homosexuality is eliminated. The assumption is that heterosexuality is "natural" and will flower when the impediment of homosexuality is removed.

SUPPRESSION AND REWARD

A therapist may use aversion techniques to suppress one kind of behavior and reward responses to a preferred stimuli or conduct. In the laboratory these two techniques might be put together—if an erection begins in response to a male stimulus object there is shock; if it begins in response to a female stimulus object there is a reward of some kind. How well this pairing transfers to the real world is unknown, but the model is fairly clear. In some cases the patient-subject may be moved from the laboratory to be taught social and sexual skills with real sexual partners, often following the techniques of Masters and Johnson. A homosexual would be given practice in heterosociality and heterosexuality. It is unlikely that a therapist would attempt to engineer negative experiences with homosexual contexts in the real world, but it might happen.

REWARD ONLY

A therapist, either in a laboratory or in actual social practice, can offer rewards for approved conduct and ignore disapproved conduct. What is disapproved, it is hoped, will disappear or fade to a minor role in the life of the patient. One laboratory form of therapy which utilized masturbatory techniques focused on the use of pictures of women as a source of arousal for a homosexual man. He was instructed to masturbate using his conventional imagery and then switch to pictures of women near the point of orgasm. The pictures of women were introduced earlier and earlier in the masturbation cycle, and the man eventually became able to masturbate from the beginning to pictures of women. The assumption was that the capacity to be aroused by pictures of women would transfer to nonlaboratory experiences in which he would be aroused and able to have sex with women. A variant of this would be to offer homosexuals an opportunity to practice heterosexuality as part of a training program of some sort.[4]

MODIFICATION

To modify a disapproved aspect of behavior to result in approved conduct is essentially the strategy of Masters and Johnson. They disapprove of early ejaculation, and work to modify it so that heterosexual performance can be enhanced. A similar strategy has been adopted by therapists seeking to treat men who sexually molest children. Having decided that most such men would prefer to have sex with adults rather than children, the therapist teaches the patient how to approach and have sex with adult women. Therapists may do some aversion therapy as well (notice that we may be more willing to punish pedophilia than premarital intercourse or homosexuality). This strategy has been extended to homosexuals who prefer sex with children, by offering them an opportunity to develop the skills and preferences necessary to operate satisfactorily as homosexuals with adult partners.

RELABELING

The last example above demonstrates relabeling. The decision is made to approve of adult homosexuality, at least as a preference over homosexuality with children. This is what has happened with such formerly disapproved behaviors as oral sex, which are now approved and taught by some sex manuals.

The strategies outlined above do not exhaust the relationship between the goals of therapy and the techniques that can be brought to bear, but they do suggest the necessity of clearly defining the goals of behavior change, and realizing the implications of choosing any set of techniques or any set of goals.

Who Chooses?

A final important dimension of the treatment of sexual problems is who defines what the patient wants from the therapy. Most often this decision is made by the therapist: "So and so is an X; people who are Xs have the following kinds of problems; it would be better if so and so were a Y." Therapists already have in their heads both a diagnosis and a program of treatment (again the medical model) when the patient comes in.

A complication in the treatment of sexual problems (or of patients with unconventional sexual conduct who come in with a nonsexual problem) is that therapists often reduce the complexity of a person's life to a sexual label—so and so is a "homosexual," or so and so is "pre-orgasmic," or so and so is a "rapist." The sex

4. It is clear that these techniques are violating some of the traditional sexual rules of society in order to produce change in sexual conduct. Therapists may provide sexual partners or sexual stimuli under unconventional conditions in order to produce conventional sexual conduct.

label drives all other thoughts out of the therapist's mind; they see the patient only in sexual terms, and look for a sexual cause and a sexual cure. However, not all sexual problems have sexual causes, and not all members of sexual minorities have sexual problems.

To the degree that the therapist wishes to work "with" instead of "on" a patient, he or she should be careful to determine the real problem as the patient sees it, and to attack that problem, not some other one. The criterion of success in therapy should not be "Was this the result the therapist wanted?" but "Was this the result the patient wanted?"

There must be a serious pretreatment assessment. Only then can the variation in outcomes *desired by patients* be noted. Consider, for example, a single twenty-year-old man who went into therapy because he was unable to work. During the preliminary discussion the patient mentioned a modest homosexual history, and the therapist focused on this aspect of his report. It was determined that he had no heterosexual experience beyond petting, with a few homosexual episodes five years in his past. The therapeutic problem was conceived in terms of a choice between heterosexuality and homosexuality, and a preliminary proposal of aversion therapy was made.

It should be immediately apparent that this patient had a minimal history of *any* kind of sexuality, and only after considerable exploration did it emerge that he had interpreted his asexual status and his absence of sexual interest in women as "homosexuality." After further discussion it was determined that what he really wanted was to live with someone (which sex was not very clear) under conditions of mutual affection and caring, and that he had practically no interest in sexuality.

A minimal interest in sex is not an uncommon preference for some women and not a few men — sexuality is for them simply a vehicle for gaining social and emotional security. In this case, the patient had not learned that sexual activity might be a major part of the emotional bargain he wished to make, and his therapy should have been directed toward clarifying the decision and helping him make the decision.

In another case, a male patient with a well-developed homosexual history and without any heterosexual interest went into therapy because he and his male sexual partner went to group sex parties with a mixed-gender membership. The patient felt inadequate in these situations; his partner was capable of having sex with women and he was not. He wanted the therapist to help him develop the capacity to have heterosexual activity, including coitus, but in the party situations only. He did not want to become heterosocial in the sense of getting married and having children.

In both these cases the patients wanted only a part of the conventional heterosexual-heterosocial package. They had quite dissimilar histories, and required different strategies of helping them get what they desired. In the first case, there was a serious question of whether, given the underdeveloped character of the sexual pattern, the patient knew what his choices were. The therapist could attempt to enhance either a heterosexual, a homosexual, or a mixed pattern, but the patient wanted a stable emotional relationship far more than sexual activity. In the second case, the issue was quite different: the patient wanted simply the capacity to perform sexually with women — no love, dating, or conversation, merely heterosexual capacity.

However one might judge these goals, either therapeutically *or* ideologically, they were a patient's goals. Neither wanted a revision of personality, but help in dealing with a limited problem. Traditional psychosexual therapy insists on finding connections between any presenting sexual problem and most other dimensions of a patient's life adjustment. Because of the theoretical primacy given to sexuality in "personality development," it is difficult for the traditional therapist to view sexual problems as having the same limited implications for total functioning as phobias and other modifiable behavior problems.

Conclusion

The breakthrough in the treatment of sexual dysfunctions among heterosexuals is an extremely important one, since it emphasizes the learned character of sexual conduct. Following Masters and Johnson most therapists have tried to reorient the therapeutic enterprise, from merely talking about the past or the present to doing something about the present. To change sexually requires instruction and practice, exactly reflecting how most people got to be sexual in the first place. Many therapists still cling to the idea that they are like farmers, helping natural sexual plants to grow; however, they are more like architects, taking human beings and rebuilding them to fit the plans offered by the culture in which we live.

The way people change sexually (for good or ill) is a function of the conditions under which they learn. Perhaps recognition of that fact offers some insight into the learning environments in which children acquire their sexuality. If we want our children to live lives in which sex is important and fulfilling (and not everyone wants that) then we may have to change the ways in which they learn about sex. We may have to·become more directive, more informative, more positive—we may have to promote sexual activity—if we want to change the current processes of sexual learning and their outcome. (Again, many people may not want that.)

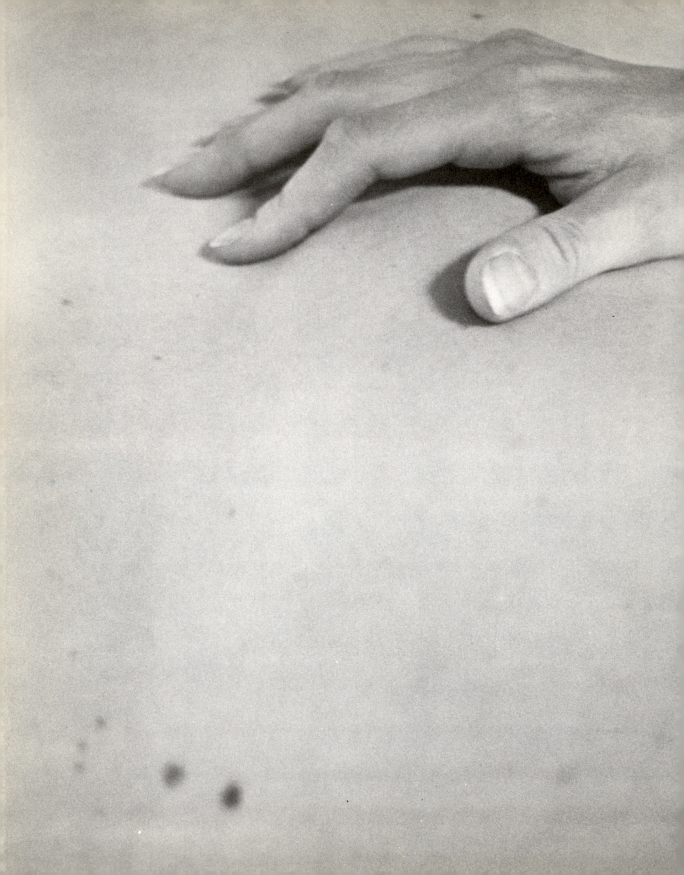

PHYSICAL HEALTH
AND SEXUAL CONDUCT

19

We need to love our bodies and treat them well.
Where would we be without them?
  Boston Women's Health Book Collective, *Our Bodies, Ourselves*

PHYSICAL HEALTH AS IT RELATES TO SEX IS FUNDAMENTALLY ENTANGLED WITH the cultural purposes and goals of sexuality. Physical capacity and physical function are not absolutes, but find their meaning and definition in specific social and historical circumstances with concrete environmental demands. The physical health or the capacities for physical performance demanded of a world-class athlete would scarcely be appropriate for the sedentary office worker or even the hard-hat construction worker whose labor is assisted by mechanical devices. Thus we cannot settle simply for a phrase like "healthy" sexuality since we do not even know what that might be—anyone can list under "healthy" any set of either practical or utopian sexual goals and expect other people to meet them.

Physical health has many aspects in common with mental health, in that there can be no absolute standards for performance, and the kinds of things that we expect people to do will define whether they are considered healthy or not. If we lived in a hunting society where it was very important that people be able to see clearly at a distance (and the society had no corrective lenses), being nearsighted would be unhealthy. On the other hand, even in such a society being nearsighted might relieve one of the risk of getting injured in the hunt, allowing time to study with the local priest and perhaps become Shaman of the tribe. Health then depends on what the demands are, how stringent they are, and how many alternatives there might be (what if there were no Shaman?). What may appear to be handicapping conditions in one society are dealt with in others by the use of appropriate social and environmental designs.

Issues and Goals

Physical health as it relates to sex depends on a number of issues in U.S. culture. One of the most important is the sources of information we have about physical sexual functioning and how to take care of our bodies. The information and values given to us about our bodies and the care of our bodies, particularly the specifically sexual parts, and what we are told about sexual activity influence our sexual health. A second issue is the changing sexual demands and expectations that are placed on people as they move through the life cycle. There are critical moments in the life cycle when bodily changes and social expectations change, placing new demands on people.

Third is the distinction between sexual health and reproductive health—many of the substances we ingest or use really have to do with our reproductive roles and only in part with our sexual roles. Contraception, abortion, fertility, and childbirth are reproductive issues linked to our views of sexual health.

Fourth is the level of knowledge and skill of the medical system in dealing with problems of sexual health, not only in the specific functioning of organ systems, but in a concern for the general functioning of individuals. Part of that problem resides in the values and the organization of the health-care system, with its monopoly on knowledge and techniques, but another is the lack of autonomy and control on the part of patients who fail to assert a joint responsibility for their own health.

At the very minimum it is useful for people in a society to have knowledge about sexual phenomena (physical, psychological, and social), an awareness of their own attitudes toward sex, a set of sexual values (and an understanding of where they come from) that can serve as guidance mechanisms for behavior, and a sense of emotional comfort with regard to sexual activities they engage in. Further, this knowledge ought to be sufficient to create a sense of personal autonomy and self control, so that the normal changes of the life cycle, as well as those problems which result from disease and illness, are understandable and manageable.

The concern of this chapter is with the physical side of sexual health, those issues that we commonly assume are the proper domain of the medical profession. The physical aspects of sexual health are those concerns which we might take to a physician—seeking freedom from disease and physical disorders. This may appear to be a restricted view of sexual health, focusing narrowly on the body, its workings and its problems. It is not as utopian as many sexual idealists would like, particularly those whose standards are based on sexual goals. Utopians on the left may argue that the sexually healthy person should be bisexual, or have at least two orgasms a day, or maintain an erection for forty minutes, or always have multiple orgasm, or whatever else is fashionable. On the other hand, this concern for physical health as it affects sexuality is wider than the concern of utopians of the right who define sexual health by the limited goals of marriage and reproduction.

What we need is a more pragmatic and use-oriented view of the body and physical health as it affects our sexual functioning: A cool-headed view that allows us to take into account the cultural demands and the physical facts with less guilt and embarrassment, so that we can try to maintain a sexuality free of physical problems, treat them if they occur, and face up to them when we cannot treat them successfully.

Sexual Ignorance and the Sexual Body Parts

Probably one of the central contributions of parents to physical sexual health is the communication of attitudes that restrict either hygiene or curiosity about how the "private" body parts work. Many parents do not instruct their children to wash their

Many women's genitals were once as far away to them as the other side of the moon. Self examination as well as looking at the genitals of other women is a way of learning about and sharing what was once a mystery.

genitals briskly and carefully, and those who do often provide instructions in such a way that the washing is done with eyes averted. There is a double edge in these instructions: There are parents who do not want their children to touch their genitals (or at least do not instruct them to do so) because it might feel good. The result is unwashed genitals. There are other parents who so carefully make the washing hygienic (wash, but it should not feel good) that children often have only a sanitary image of their genitals. Such a lack of information about the genitals is what results in young women not knowing that they have a clitoris, or many young men, even if they have masturbated for a number of years, never having looked at their genitals very carefully. It is difficult for most people to examine their genitals casually (without erotic or guilty overtones) just to see how they are getting along.

The need for hygiene must be stressed because many people—as pointed out above—deny the sexual aspects of their bodies. They wash under their arms and behind their ears regularly with soap and water, but they do not do a very good job on their genitals. Their genitals thus often smell, and if they notice it they may reach for genital deodorants which may do more harm than good. Certainly a genital deodorant is not needed if the genitals are kept clean—and it may well be carcinogenic for women. Douches advertised for women are easy to misuse. Under normal conditions a woman should use only plain tap water or a solution of two tablespoons of vinegar in a quart of water. Alkaline (soda) douches and many of the

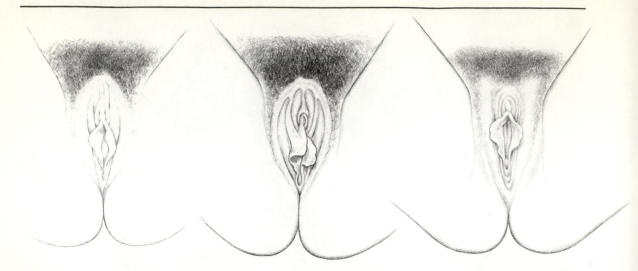

The genitals of women and men show a wide variety of shapes, textures, colors, and sizes. Here are some variations of normal genitals. Two facts: (1) contrary to most anatomical drawings, there is no ''hole'' in the female vulva; there are layers of flesh that part like leaves when something is inserted; (2) the flaccid size of the penis does not predict how large it will be when it is erect.

other kinds (when they are not chemically dangerous) can disrupt the normal chemical balance and bacterial population of the vagina, and make the vagina susceptible to serious and annoying infections. Washing the genitals can be fun, and it might help if people saw their sexual parts as beautiful rather than as ugly.

This is one reason why genital self-examinations by women are valuable. If a woman looks at her own genitals in a mirror or examines the interior of her vagina she may develop a calmer and more relaxed attitude toward her own body. Examining the genitals of other women is often helpful in showing a woman that there are substantial differences in the shape, coloration, and anatomy of the genitals and that their bodies are within the normal range. Such practices would also be helpful for men as well, since the casual side glance in the locker room is rarely informative about the variety of genital types that might exist. Many males' exaggerated fears about the size of their penises comes from observations of differences in flaccid size, which is not very predictive of erect size.

Lack of cleanliness can lead to odors and infections, but ignorance of the parts of the body labeled as sexual can result in other physical and sexual problems. Certain diseases are evidenced by changes in breasts, genitals, and anus, so an aversion to examining them can leave symptoms undetected. Failure to notice the signs of venereal disease, or infections, or growths, lumps, and bleeding may all result from negative attitudes toward these body parts. Not only do such attitudes prevent people from finding out that something might be wrong, but also prevents them from taking the problem to a physician because they believe that such disorders are shameful.

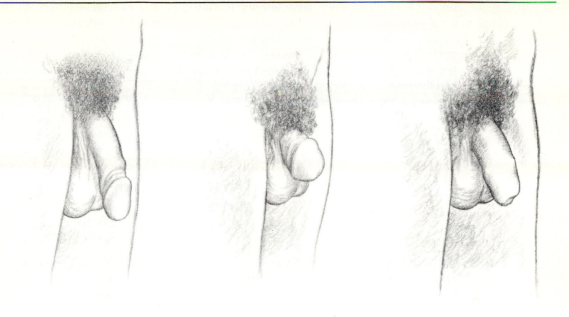

The shame and fear we associate with sexual activity begins with our attitudes toward the "sexual" parts of the body. It is a shame and fear that follows many people for their entire lives — it affects their attitudes toward infections or diseases, toward surgery on the genitals or surgery that may have sexual side effects, toward changes of the body in aging, toward such conventional aspects of life as menstruation, childbirth, and contraception, and toward such lethal diseases as cancer.

Adolescent Learning

Young people are informed about sexual health from a number of sources as they grow up, few of which are particularly helpful. Even with the best will in the world, those who try to teach the young about the physical aspects of sexual health have an uphill task. They are often obstructed by parents who do not want their children (or the children of other people) to know about sexuality, since these parents think that it will result in the children doing or thinking something sexual. As important as the restrictions, however, is the timing of such programs. Normally they occur either after the fact (females often are told about menstruation after it has happened to them) or when the young are interested in something else. Thus, a discussion of venereal disease or pregnancy in U.S. culture occurs at the very moment when young people are more interested in the pleasant aspects of sex.

Venereal disease and other physical side effects are presented or seem to be presented as reasons for not having sex rather than as controllable byproducts of sexuality. High-schoolers are interested in how to have sex and how they feel about it rather than in the physical equipment, which seems to be working in a perfectly satisfactory manner. This youthful response to sex conceals a vast ignorance which, since they are so much "on the line," they do not want to expose. Much of youthful sex is doing it without noticing the parts involved. Of interest are the mental plans and the emotional responses, not the organs.

Since experimenting with sex remains covert, when something goes wrong there are few people to turn to who do not consider it a moral rather than a health issue. This moral response contributes to difficulties in communicating about, understanding, and treating such matters as serious venereal infections (gonorrhea and syphilis), and minor vaginal disorders such as trichomonas and yeast infections.

Venereal Diseases and Genital Infections

The word "venereal" has its roots in Latin and means "pertaining to Venus," the Roman goddess of sexual love. Venereal diseases are thus any disease transmitted by sexual contact (oral, genital, and anal), and they can get established in any orifice of the body. They are relatively common, and if untreated their effects can be serious, but fortunately the venereal diseases can be easily and effectively treated. Before turning to those diseases which are literally "venereal," though, we should have a brief look at two common genital infections. They are marked, as is gonorrhea, by a whitish discharge from the vagina, and it is possible that they could be confused with it.

These two vaginal disorders are very common. Nearly every woman has or will experience them, some quite often. One is an infection by *Trichomonas vaginalis*. These organisms live on the surface of the vaginal membranes, and they can cause severe itching and soreness. They can also live on the surface of the penis under the foreskin or in the prostate gland, and both people in a relationship will usually have it if either does. For this reason, it is useless to treat only the woman—she will be promptly reinfected by her partner. The treatment of choice is a drug called Flagyl which is administered to both man and woman. The main drawback of Flagyl is that it acts like antabuse, so that the patients must not drink alcoholic beverages while being treated.

The second major vaginal infection is a yeast-like organism called *Candida albicans*. It also produces vaginal irritation and discharge, and it is often found in women using oral contraceptives, who have diabetes, who are pregnant, or who are undergoing prolonged antibiotic treatment for some other condition. *Candida* is ordinarily present in the vagina, and it multiplies when the chemical balance or other bacterial populations of the vagina are disturbed. It can be controlled by the antibiotic mystatin.

Other relatively minor disorders of the sexual organs include herpes infections ("cold sores") on the penis or vulva, venereal warts, and cystitis. Only the last is at all common, and it is virtually inescapable for women (men, because of their long urethra, are less vulnerable). It is a bladder infection caused when the bacteria normally present on the genital surface migrate to the bladder, sometimes pro-

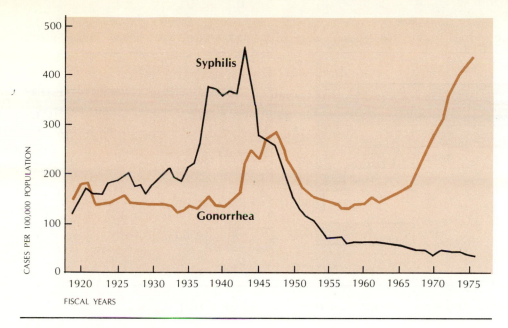

Figure 1 Reported Syphilis and Gonorrhea Cases per 100,000 Population in the United States, 1919–1975. (Beginning in 1939, all states are included in the reporting area. Military cases included for 1919–1940, excluded thereafter.)

pelled by the massaging effect of sexual intercourse. The main symptom is frequent and stinging urination, and the disorder can be treated effectively with antibiotics.

The above disorders are innocuous compared to the venereal diseases, the best known of which are syphilis and gonorrhea. Gonorrhea in particular is common, and both diseases if not treated can be very serious in their effects. The incidence of syphilis in the United States has been declining, but that of gonorrhea has been rising for the past twenty years (see Figure 1), despite the fact that we spend about twelve million dollars per year on attempts to prevent it.

It is worth noting that most cases of gonorrhea and syphilis occur in the fifteen to twenty-nine age group, and that about ten percent of all young people in this country have had a case of one or both of these diseases by age twenty-five (see Figures 2 and 3).

Of the diseases reported to the U.S. Public Health Service, gonorrhea now ranks first, ahead of both measles and mumps, and syphilis fourth. Gonorrhea is second only to the common cold, whether we take the 620,000 cases actually reported (1971 figures) or the two and a half million cases estimated.

The mission of the Public Health Service is prevention, and it requires doctors to report to it all cases of infectious diseases so that public health workers can track down all persons who have been in contact with an infected person and treat them before they have a chance to pass the disease further. This method has worked well for many diseases, but it has been only moderately successful with the venereal

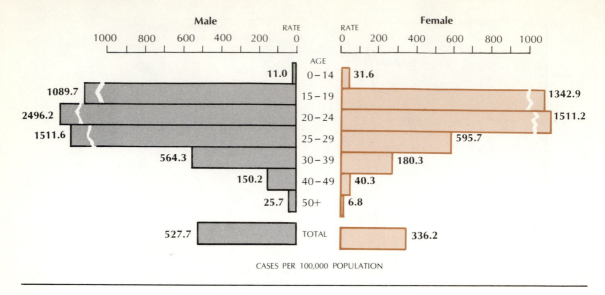

Figure 2 Gonorrhea Age-Specific Case Rates per 100,000 Population in the United States, 1974.

diseases. Many people are reluctant to name their sexual partners to the authorities because of embarrassment or fear of prosecution for fornication or homosexuality where these activities are regarded as crimes.

If the moral dimensions of venereal diseases could be faced down, it would be relatively easy to eliminate both gonorrhea and syphilis completely. Both respond well to antibiotics such as penicillin, and there is a possibility that vaccines may be developed, particularly for gonorrhea. There are other problems, however. The amounts spent on venereal disease control are quite moderate, and there is some ambivalence about its complete control. There are those who view VD as not really serious (it is so easy to treat, after all) and others who see fear of VD as a way of preventing sexual immorality. When penicillin first proved effective against syphilis, some members of the medical profession were opposed to its use, saying that fear of disease was a way of keeping people sexually moral, that VD was a punishment for those who violated the rules. This perspective is aggravated by the fact that increases in gonorrhea are mainly among minorities, the poor, and the young, which are not notably effective pressure groups.

GONORRHEA

Gonorrhea has been with us since the dawn of history. It was described nearly 5000 years ago by the Chinese, and later by the Egyptians. There are even references to it in the Bible. Its modern name was coined in the second century A.D. by the Greek physician Galen, and this name, which means "flow of seed," has persisted despite modern colloquial alternatives—"the clap," "the drip," "a dose," "strain," "the whites," or "morning drop." The gonococcus which causes gonor-

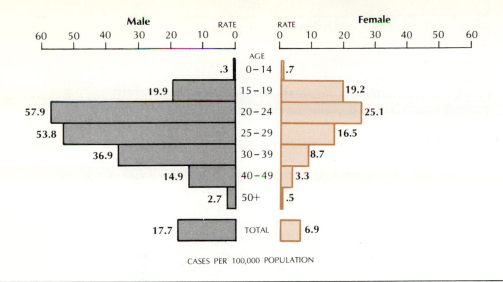

| Male | RATE | RATE | Female |

| 60 | 50 | 40 | 30 | 20 | 10 | 0 | AGE | 0 | 10 | 20 | 30 | 40 | 50 | 60 |

						.3	0–14	.7						
			19.9				15–19		19.2					
57.9							20–24			25.1				
53.8							25–29		16.5					
		36.9					30–39	8.7						
			14.9				40–49	3.3						
					2.7		50+	.5						
			17.7				TOTAL	6.9						

CASES PER 100,000 POPULATION

Figure 3   Primary and Secondary Syphilis Age-Specific Case Rates per 100,000 Population in the United States, 1974.

rhea, a bacterium called *Neisseria gonorrhoeae,* was identified in 1879, and the antibiotics which alone can kill it effectively were developed in this century.

Gonorrhea is communicated by sexual contact, and there is no sure way to tell whether your partner has it. About eighty percent of women and twenty percent of men with the disease show no symptoms.

Most men who have it, however, show symptoms within two weeks of exposure. The primary symptom is a pussy yellow discharge from the tip of the penis, accompanied by a burning sensation when urinating and a persistent itch within the urethra. Heterosexual women and men may catch gonorrhea of the mouth from fellating an infected person or of the rectum from anal intercourse. Pharyngeal gonorrhea is marked by a sore throat and swollen glands, while rectal gonorrhea is marked by itching and an anal discharge. Gonorrhea in any of these forms can be avoided by a condom and by washing the genitals thoroughly with a bactericidal soap, or by prophylactic use of penicillin or some other suitable antibiotic within a few hours of exposure. Gonorrhea can be treated with penicillin, tetracycline, or erythromycin.

In women, the infection usually settles in the cervix, where it may cause inflammation and a vaginal discharge. Because such discharges are not necessarily due to gonorrhea, however, a microscopic examination of bacterial culture, or the newer blood or "fluorescent antibody" tests, must be used for accurate diagnosis.

If left untreated, gonorrhea can have severe consequences. In males, it can spread to the prostate gland, seminal vesicles, bladder, and kidneys. It may even spread to the joints of the arms and legs, causing the very painful *gonorrheal arthritis.* In women, it can spread through the uterus to the fallopian tubes and other pelvic organs, causing severe abdominal pain, vomiting, and fever, often

Strategies for the Control of Gonorrhea

More than 1 million cases of gonorrhea were reported last year, and at least three times that many are estimated to have occurred. More cases of gonorrhea are reported each year to the U.S. Public Health Service than cases of all other communicable diseases combined, including chicken pox, syphilis, mumps, hepatitis, tuberculosis, and measles.

Most disturbing to public health officials is the fact that the incidence of gonorrhea in the United States keeps increasing each year despite the fact that effective antibiotics to treat this infection are readily available. The number of reported cases has tripled in the past 10 years and, according to investigators at the Center for Disease Control (CDC) in Atlanta, these increases represent changes in incidences rather than changes in the proportion of cases reported.

To combat this epidemic, the CDC began, in 1972, a nationwide gonorrhea screening program. Last year, about 8 million people were screened, and those infected were treated. In the past year, the rate of increase in the number of gonorrhea cases in the United States leveled off. The screening program, however, may not be solely responsible for this effect. European countries with good health statistics, such as Norway, Finland, Denmark, and Great Britain, report similar slowdowns in their gonorrhea epidemics, although they started no new gonorrhea control programs in recent years. And Sweden witnessed a remarkable decline in gonorrhea incidences over the past 6 years. The number of cases reported in Sweden last year was only about half the number reported in 1969.

Kondom

Since Sweden is showing that gonorrhea epidemics can be controlled, the reasons for Sweden's success are currently a subject of much speculation and interest. Lennart Juhlin of the University of Uppsala and others believe that an increased use of condoms in Sweden is a major reason why gonorrhea rates are falling there. The Swedish government has successfully promoted condoms by widely displaying a national condom symbol (see figure) and by making condoms attractive and easily available. Gonorrhea rates declined as condom sales increased, and the changes occurred in the same proportions. However, Finland, Norway, and Denmark did not promote condoms and do not report decreases in their gonorrhea rates.

Some critics point out that, among the Swedish university students surveyed, many claim they do not use condoms, and hence the young people most at risk for gonorrhea may not be using these devices. These critics postulate that other events, such as changes in social mores, may have been of greater importance in causing

during or just after menstruation. By causing a chronic inflammation of the fallopian tubes (*salpingitis*), it may even produce sterility.

An infected woman can also give gonorrhea to her child as it passes through the birth canal. The infection usually settles in the eyes, causing *ophthalmia neonatorum*, which was once the cause of a third of all childhood blindness. To prevent this, it is now required that all newborns have their eyes treated with silver nitrate or penicillin ointment.

Sweden's decline in gonorrhea cases. Yet many investigators recognize that these other events also occurred in Finland, Norway, and Denmark. Only the condom promotion is unique to Sweden.

Ralph Henderson of the CDC and others believe that the worldwide economic recession probably affected the gonorrhea epidemic in Sweden and also in the United States and other countries. Restriction of the amount of free time, mobility, and the spending money that people have is thought to be a factor in limiting sexual contact. If the recession did play such a role in reducing the number of cases of gonorrhea in the United States, then the effects of the CDC's screening program may have been minimal at best.

The CDC evaluation of the dynamics of gonorrhea epidemics in other countries and its analysis of its own gonorrhea control program led officials at the CDC to change their strategies. They are now focusing their screen on groups likely to have high incidences of gonorrhea, such as people between the ages of 20 and 24, and are retesting infected people 4 to 6 weeks after they are cured of their original infections.

The reason for retesting was derived in part from a mathematical model developed by James Yorke of the University of Maryland. Yorke argued that the dynamics of gonorrhea are controlled by a small "core" of sexually active people. At least 20 percent of this core population is infected at any time, and the core represents the main source of gonorrhea cases. Thus, the only way to decrease gonorrhea rates would be to decrease the number of people in the core. Since these people are likely to become reinfected once cured, members of the core would be detected and the number in the core would be reduced by rescreening infected people.

About 6 months ago, the CDC put its new program into operation, and already it seems to be more effective than its former program. Henderson reports that they are detecting more people with gonorrhea and are apparently finding some core members since 15 to 20 percent of retested patients have gonorrhea. Only 4 percent of all those tested in the previous program had gonorrhea. Thus as the epidemiology of gonorrhea becomes better understood, it seems increasingly likely that the disease may be brought under control in the United States.

From *Science*, April 16, 1976, p. 245.

SYPHILIS

Syphilis has been a disease of humans as long as gonorrhea has, although some scholars believe it did not reach Europe until Columbus and his crew brought it there from the New World. Certainly, shortly after the date of Columbus' return, a virulent strain of syphilis roared through Europe like wildfire and reached China within fifteen years. This particular lethal version of syphilis subsided, perhaps due to developing immunities, but it remained an important disease until the modern era. Known colloquially as "siff," "pox," "lues," "bad blood," and "Old Joe," it is communicated primarily among the young but the effects can last a lifetime. Perhaps half a million people have it but do not know it (they were either never treated or not cured). Even though the spiral-shaped organism *(Treponema pallidum)* which causes the disease can be killed by a large dose of penicillin, some people may be doomed to the deterioration, psychosis, and death which mark the late stages of the disease.

Like gonorrhea, syphilis is communicated by sexual contact and can be avoided by use of a condom. If it is caught, its first sign is usually a sore (or *chancre*) in the area of the genitals (usually on the penis or labia, at the site where the bacteria first entered the body) or occasionally on the fingers, lips, breast, or anus. The sore appears from ten to forty days after infection. It begins as a small red papule which soon becomes eroded and moist and may become ulcerated. The sore vanishes in one to five weeks whether treated or not, but as long as it lasts it is a potent source of infection to others. Once the sore is gone, however, the disease remains, now well established in the body and ready for its secondary stage.

Secondary syphilis begins between one week and six months after the end of the primary stage. It may last as little as three months or as long as several years. It is the period when the bacteria have spread throughout the body, and it may be marked by a generalized rash, sores in the mouth, painful joints and bones, sore throat, fever, headache, loss of hair, and other symptoms. The victim is highly infectious, since the bacteria are not only present in any sores but can also pass through the pores in the skin.

The third stage is called the *latent* stage, and it may last ten to twenty years with no symptoms, although the bacteria are still present, settling into internal organs such as the heart and brain. The victim ceases being infectious after a few years, but he or she is hardly well. The last stage is called *late* syphilis, and during it the bacteria attack the heart, brain, and other organs. It is marked by heart disease, crippling, blindness, insanity, and ultimately death. However, there is some evidence that among some people there is an immunity to this stage of the disease.

It is important to detect and treat syphilis before the late stage, and the earlier the better, in order to stop its spread to other people. It is most easily treated (by massive doses of penicillin, tetracycline, or erythromycin) in the primary and secondary stages, and every effort should be made to detect it at that point, whether by observation of the symptoms or by use of the simple and effective Wasserman blood test. This test is now required of anyone who applies for a marriage license, both to catch and treat cases of syphilis and to prevent congenital syphilis in the newborn.

Congenital syphilis is acquired by the fetus from the mother while still in the womb. It can result in such developmental defects as hydrocephalus or brain atrophy as well as in such neurological problems as convulsions and mental deficiency, although many syphilitic women who become pregnant either miscarry or have a stillborn child. The incidence of congenital syphilis has dropped dramatically in recent years—from 13,600 cases in 1941 to 300 in 1970—largely due to improved routine prenatal care and treatment of mothers. Treatment of the newborn with penicillin can also help greatly.

OTHER VENEREAL DISEASES

Nonspecific urethritis resembles gonorrhea, but its causative microorganism is not known. It does, however, respond readily to tetracycline. *Chancroid* is a bacterial infection marked by ulcerous lesions at the points of physical contact with the source of infection. It is painful, and the infection spreads quickly from the initial site, but it responds quickly to the sulfonamide drugs.

Lymphogranuloma venereum is caused by a rickettsia (an organism midway between a bacterium and a virus; another rickettsia causes Rocky Mountain Spotted Fever). The symptoms are enlarged painful lymph glands in the groin (or in the neck, if contracted through oral contact) and fever, chills, and headache. It eventually progresses, if left untreated, to enlargement of the penis, scrotum, or vulva, but it responds well to the sulfonamides and to broad-spectrum antibiotics. It is most common in the tropics and American South.

Granuloma inguinale is a chronic infection which can also be transmitted nonsexually. It begins as a small red papule, usually on the penis or labia, which turns into a bleeding, ulcerous lesion which may spread to encompass the entire genital region in a red, moist, bad-smelling mass. If left untreated, the ulcer will destroy a great deal of tissue before being replaced by thick scar tissue, but treatment is possible with the mycin antibiotics. This infection may be transmitted by anal intercourse, particularly when anal intercourse is followed by vaginal intercourse without washing the penis.

Crabs (pubic lice) are more of a nuisance than a threat, although they can carry typhus. They are tiny arthropods which infect the pubic hair and are passed from person to person during intercourse (and occasionally, unlike most other venereal diseases, from infected bedding, towels, or toilet seats). They produce intense itching because they feed by grasping the shaft of a hair with their legs and inserting their mouth-parts through the skin at the base of the hair to suck their victim's blood. They are about the size of a pinhead and a bluish gray in color. They can be removed only with a pesticidal cream, lotion, or shampoo.

Reproductive Health

The capacity to reproduce carries with it a series of health management decisions (or non-decisions), particularly for women, since it is they who bear the health consequences of conception, childbearing, childbirth, and most of child rearing. No matter how much the man may share in the experience from conception to childbirth, the events occur in and to the woman.

MENSTRUATION

As was noted in Chapter 6, menstruation begins around the twelfth year, though it may vary in time around that date. However, the fact of menstruation (a period of regular or irregular monthly vaginal bleeding), the conditions under which it is learned about, and the responses of men and women to its existence make it a complicated experience in the lives of many women.

The facts that many young women are ignorant about menstruation when it first occurs, that they are taught they should restrict their activities while it is going on, and that it should be called "the curse" may produce life-long confusions. The unseemly, unhygienic, and bloody image of menstruation promoted by "sanitary" product manufacturers adds to women's fears and anxieties. Having a "period" calls attention to a part of the body that many young women wish to conceal, and about which they may already have strong feelings of ambivalence.

While there may be hormonal changes in women's bodies and psyches during, before, and after menstruation, we are not at all sure that the psychological experience is associated with the chemical changes. Psychological studies suggest that women who report the most symptoms associated with menstruation are also women who report many psychosomatic symptoms when they are not menstruating. A second factor seems to be that women are responding to the actual level of and duration of blood flow — women who have less flow and for fewer days report that they are less apprehensive and anxious about menstruation. The amount and duration of flow may well be the signal to a woman trained in U.S. culture about whether menstruation is a serious problem.

At this time we do not know in any detail what produces different responses of women to menstruation. In part it must be the context in which menstruation is first experienced and how young women are taught to experience it. A second factor is likely to be whether women believe that menstrual pain or discomfort is part of "woman's lot," or whether they have a less stereotyped version of the woman's role.

Menstruation also has its political side. Since it has been used as a reason for not hiring women for certain kinds of work or as an explanation of why women are supposedly absent more often than men from work, it has a role in discrimination against women. The dilemma is that the response to menstruation is a cultural response — no matter whether the cramps and other symptoms are physical in origin or not. If we say that the problems are psychological, women will be told to get themselves together and get over them — if they are physical, they will be used to support the position that women are weaker than men. As we can see, there are no purely "physical" health problems.

CONTRACEPTION

One important aspect of sexual health is the need for control over the reproductive consequences of sexual activity. No one can have an anxiety-free sex life if she or he is worried about pregnancy. Freedom involves control over one's life.

Contraception is the act of preventing conception, the union of sperm and egg within the fallopian tube which produces a fetus. The sperm are contained in the male ejaculate (the semen) and when released at orgasm they swim through the woman's cervix and uterus and into the fallopian tube, where if the woman has ovulated within the last three days — or if she ovulates during the four or five days the sperm remain alive within her — they can fertilize the egg. Once fertilized, the egg travels down the tube to the uterus, in whose wall it becomes implanted. Once this has happened, the woman is pregnant and the fetus will develop, if all goes well, into a baby.

Conception can be prevented in several ways, with varying rates of failure (see Table 1). The two oldest—and least reliable—methods are coitus interruptus and the rhythm method. *Coitus interruptus* involves withdrawal of the male's penis from the vagina before ejaculation, but this method may fail because some sperm escape the penis before orgasm (in the pre-ejaculatory fluid). The *rhythm method* depends on the fact that a woman is not continuously fertile, but ovulates in about the middle of her monthly cycle and is fertile for only a few days on either side of ovulation. It may fail because ovulation is not sufficiently predictable.

The *condom*, which first appeared in the late nineteenth century, although sheaths of pig and sheep intestine were used occasionally earlier, is a rubber sheath for the penis. It is put on before intercourse and acts to trap the ejaculated semen and keep it from the cervical opening. It must be replaced before each act of intercourse, and if used properly it is very effective.

The *diaphragm*, which appeared at about the same time as the condom, is a circular rubber membrane with a spring-loaded rim. It is used to cover the dome of the cervix, with its rim pressed snugly against the vaginal wall, to block the passage of sperm. It should be used in combination with spermicidal creams or jellies which will kill any sperm which might get past it, and it should not be removed until all the sperm in the vagina are dead. This means it must be left in place for over

Table 1   Approximate Failure Rate of Contraceptive Methods (Pregnancies per 100 Woman Years)

	Theoretical Failure Rate	Actual Use Failure Rate
Abortion	0+	0+
Abstinence	0	?
Hysterectomy	0.0001	0.0001
Tubal Ligation	0.04	0.04
Vasectomy	Less than 0.15	0.15
Oral Contraceptives (combined)	Less than 1.0	2–5
I.M. Long Acting Progestin	Less than 1.0	5–10
Condom + Spermicidal Agent	1.0	5
Low-Dose Oral Progestin	1–4	5–10
IUD	1–5	6
Condom	3	15–20
Diaphragm	3	20–25
Spermicidal Foam	3	30
Coitus Interruptus	15	20–25
Rhythm (calendar)	15	35
Lactation for 12 months	15	40
Chance (sexually active)	80	80

Emory University Family Planning Program, *Contraceptive Technology 1974-1975*.

eight hours after intercourse without a spermicide (sperm can survive the vaginal acidity for only about that length of time) or six hours with a spermicide. Like the condom, the diaphragm is very effective if used properly. More recently, it has become possible to use only a *spermicidal foam,* without a rubber shield of any kind. The foam is inserted within the vagina just prior to intercourse with an applicator syringe. It promptly kills all sperm which come into contact with it.

Each of the above methods has a drawback—they involve an interruption in the sex act which may have a certain "interference effect," although they can also be incorporated into foreplay. Methods of contraception that met this objection did not appear until the 1950s, first with the Pill, and later with the intrauterine device (IUD). These were also the first contraceptives to become widely available, and both because of this and because they do not distract from the sex act, they have changed rates of intercourse in marriage and in stable premarital relationships. They have *not* produced the casual, multi-partner sexuality that many at first feared. Their main drawbacks are that they put all the responsibility for contraception on the woman (which may produce feelings of resentment on her part) and they have undesirable side effects in some women.

Very little work has been done on an unobtrusive male contraceptive. While it is often argued that the female reproductive system is more accessible to interruption than is the male (the latter "appears" very simple, it is constantly producing sperm, it seems less regulated by hormonal factors), it is likely that these objections conceal a fundamental male bias. If as much work and money went into an unobtrusive male contraceptive as went into the Pill or the IUD, there is no question that one could have been developed. At present, however, there is little incentive to discover such devices, since women are now taking all the medical risks and the economic investments have already been made for the manufacture and sale of female contraceptives. Also, men might not be willing to take the same risks that women currently take with the Pill.

The *Pill* works by making the woman's body act as if it is already pregnant. It supplies a carefully measured dosage of the female hormones estrogen and progesterone which makes the blood levels of these hormones resemble those of a pregnant woman. As a result, the ovaries do not release eggs; if they do the uterus will not allow the fertilized egg to implant. Since the Pill is taken only for three of the four weeks of the average menstrual cycle, it does not interfere with menstrual periods. It can, however, produce irregular bleeding, headaches, cramps, weight gain, and possible blood clots. Whether these dangers are made up by the sexual convenience of the method (other methods are equally effective) requires very serious thought on the part of most women. It is often noted that there is a greater risk of death from pregnancy than from the Pill; however, it should be noted that the maternal death rate in the United States is also quite high and could be substantially reduced with better prenatal care. One should always be careful what is being compared to what.

The *IUD* (intrauterine device) is a plastic device inserted into the uterus and left there indefinitely. A thread attached to the IUD hangs outside the cervix and serves both to check that the device remains in place and to remove it when its user decides to become pregnant or if a side effect develops. An IUD should, however, be inserted or removed only by a physician.

How the IUD works is not yet well understood. The current idea is that it causes a mild inflammation of the uterus which prevents implantation of a fertilized egg. IUDs which contain copper may interfere with certain enzymes necessary for implantation and with intrauterine sperm transport. For whatever reason, however, IUDs are very effective, with a failure rate of only one to seven percent, depending on type. As side effects, IUDs may cause perforation of the uterus (in one case in a thousand), increase the user's susceptibility to uterine or tubal infection, make VD harder to cure, cause pain during intercourse and orgasm, or produce bleeding and pain. Any of these side effects is reason for a visit to the doctor.

The most effective contraceptive method for either men or women is surgical *sterilization;* however, it is permanent. For men it is done by cutting the vas deferens *(vasectomy);* for women by tying the fallopian tubes *(tubal ligation).* Before undergoing such surgery, a person should be able to answer the following questions with little or no doubt:

1. Do you want any or any more children?
2. If one or more of the children you currently have were to die, would you want a replacement?
3. If your spouse died or you were divorced and remarried, would you want to have children in a new marriage?
4. If you suddenly became very rich and the cost of child care from birth through college became unimportant, would you want more children?
5. Are you at all afraid that when you have been sterilized (that is, when you are unable to reproduce) you will not be sexually responsive?
6. (For men only) Does it make you very anxious to think about someone cutting on your scrotum with a sharp knife?
7. (For women only) Does it make you very anxious to think about someone performing surgery on your sexual parts?

If people can answer all of these questions with an unhesitating "no," then they are reasonable risks for sterilization.

Sterilization may not be advisable for (1) anyone below a certain age, (2) someone with no or few children, or (3) someone whose spouse does not consent. There are few legal rules in this area, so decisions are matters of medical custom rather than statutory law.

PREGNANCY

When conception occurs, pregnancy begins. The fertilized egg—now the fetus— becomes implanted in the uterine wall, divides into cells, and begins to grow. Some of the fetal cells combine with a portion of the uterine wall to form the placenta, the organ which provides the fetus with oxygen and nutrients from the mother's bloodstream. Others form the membranes which enclose and protect the fetus. Most form the fetus itself, and as the nine months of the average pregnancy pass, they grow and differentiate to form a human infant.

One of the first signs of pregnancy is that menstruation stops. This sign should send a woman to her doctor, who will test her urine to confirm the pregnancy, give her a physical exam, and counsel her about what to expect and do. During the first twelve weeks of pregnancy, the woman may find that her breasts swell as her milk glands develop, her bladder needs emptying more often as the enlarging uterus crowds it, and her tissues may swell as they retain more water. Some women may feel nauseated, especially in the morning, and tire easily. During the second twelve weeks, her abdomen will swell noticeably, the areas around her nipples may darken, her breasts will get swollen and heavy and may leak fluid, and she may experience some side effects such as leg cramps, increased sweating, indigestion, constipation, and hemorrhoids. She should probably avoid alcohol, caffeine, tobacco, and any drugs, since these substances may harm the fetus. During the last third of pregnancy, fetal movements are very noticeable and in a few cases can be painful.

Women tolerate the physical side effects of pregnancy quite differently, depending on other psychological and social factors in their environment. The better physical condition a woman is in, the fewer side effects there will be. In any case, such side effects rarely turn into anything that might endanger the woman.

What is the effect of pregnancy on sexual activity? Here we enter a rather vague area. The traditional medical advice has been to avoid intercourse during the four to six weeks before and six weeks after childbirth, but this advice is not based on the findings of research studies. What a woman's gynecologist or obstetrician tells her seems to depend mostly on his own personal attitudes and experience. All that can really be said is that intercourse should be avoided if it is painful, if there is uterine bleeding, if membranes have ruptured, or if the woman has reason to fear a miscarriage. Otherwise, intercourse during pregnancy is usually harmless. It may be uncomfortable as delivery nears, but the discomfort can be avoided or reduced by care, tenderness, and the right choice of position.

CHILDBIRTH

After about nine months of pregnancy, the fetus is complete and ready to be born and the mother's body is ready to deliver it. This readiness is expressed in changes in the levels of various hormones which cause the uterus to begin to contract, or to go into labor. These contractions push the fetus to and through the cervix and vagina; although they can be painful, there are mental and physical exercises which can not only minimize and in some cases eliminate the pain but also help the woman manage the process more effectively. These exercises are presented as various systems of childbirth, such as the Lamaze method, and can be very helpful to most couples.

Childbirth is basically a simple and natural process. A hospital setting is necessary in only about four percent of births where complications may arise, such as a breech delivery (the fetus tries to leave the womb rear-end first, instead of head first) or a caesarean section (surgical delivery through the abdominal wall). Most births can be handled well at home, often with only a midwife in attendance. It often helps — whether in the hospital or at home — if a properly trained father is present to comfort the mother and help her relax.

Once the baby has been born, the mother's body begins to return to its pre-pregnancy state. The uterus shrinks to its normal size and position in about ten days. The hormone levels and other changed factors return to normal in about two weeks. Only the breasts do not return to their prior state — they remain enlarged, to

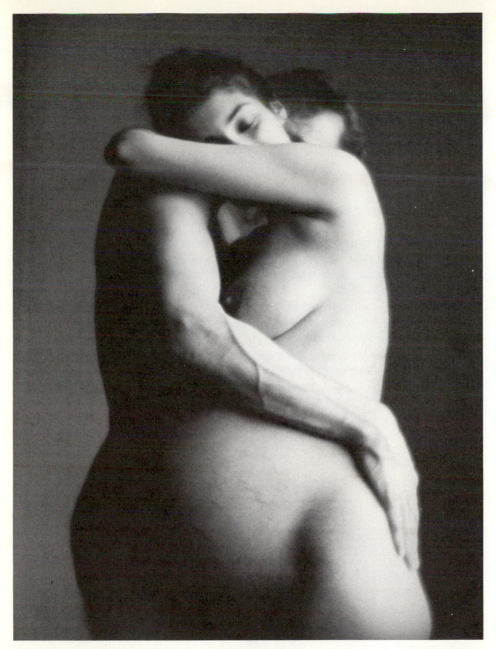

Many women and men find, without being sentimental, that a decision to share as equally as possible in all of the moments of conception, childbearing, and child rearing adds to the quality of their own relationship.

provide milk for the infant; only when nursing stops does the milk supply dry up and the breasts return to a non-pregnancy size.

The new mother can have intercourse as soon as she wishes. She may not wish to immediately, for some new mothers suffer a "postpartum depression," a state of mind based on the sudden change that has just occurred, and that may last from two days to as much as several months in some cases. This depression may affect a woman's interest in sex, but more extensive effects may follow from the changes in a couple's life that a baby produces.

ABORTION

If pregnancy is unwanted, it can be terminated by abortion, removing the fetus from the womb. Abortion is safest and simplest during the first three months of pregnancy, but it can be performed at any point up to six months. There are several techniques that can be used, each one best suited to a different stage of pregnancy.

Endometrial aspiration can be performed even before a positive pregnancy test is obtained. It is also known as "menstrual regulation" and can be used to get a late menstrual period started. It is done by inserting a flexible plastic tube through the cervix into the uterus and drawing out the uterine lining, along with the small amount of fetal tissue. It can be used up to the sixth week of pregnancy. *Early uterine evacuation* may be used up to the eighth week after a positive pregnancy test. The method is the same as that of endometrial aspiration.

Ages of Consent

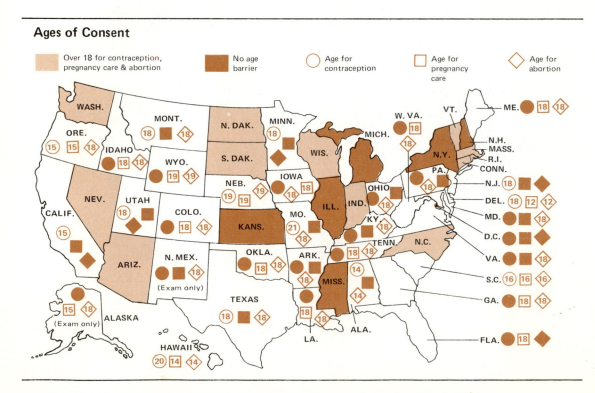

Dilation and evacuation (or *vacuum curettage*) may be done from the seventh through the twelfth week by dilating the cervix and inserting a nonflexible tube into the uterus. The size of the tube depends on the length of pregnancy, since it must be large enough to draw out all the fetal material.

Induced labor is used from the sixteenth through the twenty-fourth weeks. In this period the fetus is too large and well-developed for the simpler methods, and the woman's body must be made to help remove the fetus. Uterine contractions (labor) are induced by injecting salt solution or another drug (a prostaglandin) into the membranous bag surrounding the fetus.

Hysterotomy is also used, but rarely, from the sixteenth through the twenty-fourth weeks. It is major surgery, essentially an abortion by caesarean section.

Each of these procedures involves certain side effects and risks, greater at each later stage of pregnancy. They range from anxiety, cramps, scarring, uterine perforations, infections, bleeding, and shock to death.

The U.S. Supreme Court has declared that abortions are up to the woman and her doctor, at least through the first twelve weeks of pregnancy, but anti-abortion groups are trying to outlaw or limit abortion.

Sex in the Middle Years and After

Among women there is a biological signal (beginning in the mid to late forties, over in the mid fifties) that the reproductive years are over, called the "menopause." It appears that it is occurring later in life principally as a result of improved diet (which has also lowered age at puberty). The ovaries begin to produce less of the hormone progesterone (which prepares the uterine lining to receive the fertilized egg) as well as less ovarian estrogen. Menopause may be marked by erratic and irregularly spaced menstrual periods. The lowered output of estrogen can affect water and calcium balance, increase tenderness of the breasts, and the like. These biological changes are restricted to the reproductive system and have nothing to do with sexual responsiveness. Some women confuse these two domains and no longer feel sexual; other women feel sexually released from the fear of pregnancy and from having a menstrual period.

There is no similar biological set of events for men, but a male psycho-sexual crisis may occur in this period, which has consequences for male physical health. Many men in the early forties find themselves reassessing their lives: Have they been successful? Was it all worth it? Many men feel that they have not become what they wanted to be, or have failed in some fundamental way. They find they have lost their youthful vigor and attractiveness and drifted into middle age. This can produce a severe psychological crisis, as severe as the crisis that some women find themselves in during menopause. Unlike women, however, men do not have an experience comparable to no longer menstruating.

Other physical effects of age affect sexuality. As a woman ages, she has a tendency to less lubrication in her vagina. This can be treated by replacing the hormones her body no longer produces after menopause (either by injection or, preferably, by an estrogen-containing cream). It can also be avoided simply by maintaining frequent intercourse. Two factors affect sexual activity among older women. One is the amount of sexual activity they had earlier in life—if they had a fair amount of intercourse, if they masturbated, if they had orgasms, they tend to continue. The other is the age of the husband—the older he is relative to his wife, the sooner they slow down and stop, for it is usually the man who sets the rate of sexual activity in a marriage, not the wife. With men, the primary effect of age is that it usually takes longer to get erections, though older men usually can stay erect longer. (Younger males tend to ejaculate more rapidly.)

Overall, physical sexual changes with age in both sexes are remarkably small. Their biological systems do begin to run down at about sixty or sixty-five, but if people have been relatively healthy and if women take a certain amount of hormone, the physical problems of maintaining sexual activity are minimal. The real problems are psychological or social—the aged must deal with the fact that others, including doctors, do not approve of sex after a certain age.

It often makes children—especially thirty-year-old children—nervous to know that their sixty-five-year-old parents are sexually active. There is a tendency for younger people to be unnerved by the idea of old people walking around sun cities holding hands or kissing each other. Sexuality is being displayed by people who in the eyes of the young really should not be sexual. They are old, and they have wrinkles, and they do not have the wonderful, beautiful bodies we all believe in so much. Sexuality among older people creates a lot of anxiety.

The anxiety is made worse by society in forcing the aged to be sexual in "illicit" ways. The Social Security laws make it inappropriate for older people to get married, because the wife then loses her benefits. As a result many of the aged simply live together, an adjustment that those who visit them often find disturbing. Perhaps it is hardest for the married forty-year-olds in the middle, whose parents and children both may be cohabiting illegally.

A Modest Proposal for Maintaining Sexual Health

1. Keep your physical machinery in moderately good physical condition, particularly the cardio-vascular system. Men and women should jog, do yoga, do the Canadian Air Force exercises, ride bicycles, play tennis—anything that keeps up muscle tone and improves vascularization, heart capacity, and the like.

2. Keep your weight down near normal. It is very difficult if you are overweight to maintain the levels of physical activity sex may involve, although it is possible to have sex quietly and with low levels of effort (a useful change of pace for many people). Stay away from junk foods; they are bad for your weight and for cholesterol levels.

Both points above are physical, but they have psychological consequences. Like it or not, being overweight and out of shape makes other people view you as a less desirable sexual partner. This may be an unfortunate cultural prejudice, but there it is.

3. Spend some free time being sexual, or make some free time if you do not have it. "I would like to do that, but I do not have the time," is merely expressing a preference—I like what I am doing more than being sexual. Few of us are actually

so busy that we cannot add something to our schedules—or subtract something else to make time. If you want to be good at anything you find a time and place to practice, and you protect that time and place. Time for sex usually gets squeezed into the odd moment or at the end of the day—if you like it and want to do well, then do it when you have energy and time.

4. Try to have sex under conditions of as little anxiety, guilt, and shame as possible. Often anxiety seems to heighten sexual functioning, particularly anxiety about forbidden acts or people, but unless you are an anxiety addict, it can interfere with what you are doing sexually, particularly if you have a regular partner. Take the worry out of sex by planning for its reproductive consequences, the problems of disease, the issue of feelings—talk it over with your partner so that you know what you are doing together. Some surprises are fun, others simply complicate life.

5. Variety is often a useful aspect of maintaining sexual interest. However, many people like the ritual and expected. There is some difference between men and women in this regard, but you can have variety and stability either within a single relationship or among a number of relationships, depending on how you manage your sexual scripts. If either variety or stability, which can be incompatible, is especially important to you, it is best to signal the people you are having sex with so they are not surprised. Many of the interpersonal disagreements over sexual variety result from unwillingness to confront the consequences of what we want, as it conflicts with what other people want.

There are no guarantees—you may follow all of the rules (be they conservative, liberal, radical) and still have a lousy sex life. But the more you know about yourself and the world around you, the more you can exercise autonomy and control over your own life, and the better you can recognize the situations where you do not have autonomy and control.

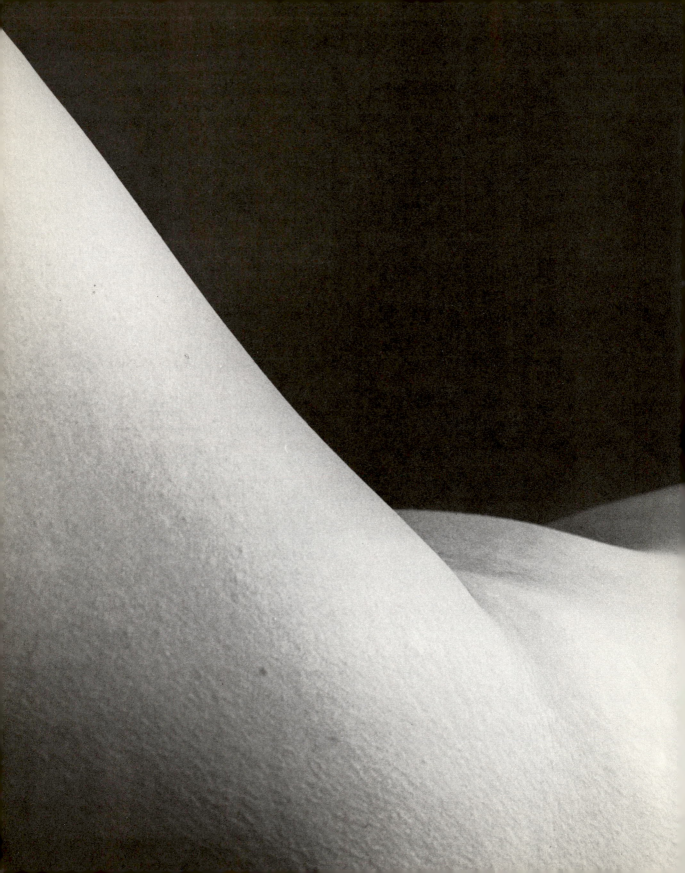

EPILOGUE: FUTURE OF SEXUALITY

Life is what happens to you while you are making other plans.
William Gaddis, *J. R.*

HOW WILL WE MANAGE OUR SEXUALITY IN THE FUTURE? NOT IN THE FAR DISTANT, science-fiction future, but in the twenty-odd years between now and the year 2000? The best answer is that the main contours of sexuality will remain much the same, that we will manage our sexual lives in somewhat the same ways as we manage them now. However, there will be changes resulting from tendencies that we can observe in U.S. society at the moment, and these tendencies result from both what we plan to do and the unintended consequences of what we plan to do.

Whenever something new is created in one or another sector of society, it has unintended ramifications which may be far more important than the intended effect. Often it is possible to judge what such second and third order effects might be, because society has an institutional structure which channels, directs, moderates, or accelerates such changes. However, many of the changes are unpredictable, since people grasp the elements of change and turn them to their own purposes.

In the 1920s and the 1930s the mass-produced automobile was widely introduced into U.S. society. Many people worried that the car would provide young people with all kinds of opportunities for premarital intercourse that they did not have before. Clearly Henry Ford did not invent the assembly-line automobile to promote the sex life of the young. In fact it only had a minor direct effect on the premarital intercourse of young people. The car did provide some youth a place to neck and pet, an escape from the supervision of adults, and became part of the sexual status hierarchy of high school and college. Boys who had cars dated more easily.

The real significance of the automobile for sexuality in the United States was the prosperity it represented and the suburbs it created along the freeways and expressways built for it. The movement to suburbs created the isolated middle class family, which changed marital sexuality and the rearing of children, and segregated adolescents. The affluence symbolized and partly created by the automobile supported the youth movements of the 1960s, with their emphasis on such pleasures as drugs and increased sexual freedom. The fundamental impact of the auto on sexuality was not in lovers' lanes and illegitimacy, but in long-term effects mediated by other social institutions.

Another social change was the introduction of the birth-control pill, primarily directed at family planning of the numbers of children and their spacing. It has had that effect over the last ten years in nearly all sectors of society. It also seems to have increased the rates of marital coitus somewhat, had a series of negative health side effects on some women, and perhaps most important has freed women to go into the labor force in larger numbers and in a less interrupted fashion. Effective contraception which is sexually unobtrusive provides for both sexual and economic autonomy, effects that were not part of the original idea. The effect that was feared, that the young would run sexually amuck when they could get an effective contraceptive, did not occur because the social and psychological climate of premarital sex is still primarily one of affection and intimacy, and not eroticism.

Yet another example of social change is the construction of singles housing complexes, the original intention of which was to cater to the large number of unmarried young people.[1] With a rising divorce rate, previously married people moved into singles complexes in larger numbers. This injected not only a more sexually experienced population into the premarital group, but a group who were less optimistic about marriage. The young marrieds who moved into these same complexes found a more sexually charged environment than they would have found in a conventional suburban housing development or in a more anonymous urban neighborhood. The housing complex for young adult unmarrieds provides a different social and psychological environment for socio-sexual encounters than do more traditional social locations that emphasize remarriage and traditional sexual values. The same change produced the singles vacation and the singles bar, which are primarily looking and dating locations, but which have the secondary effect of increasing at least the possibility of sexual adventure.

The impact on sexuality of change must be understood through the ways change fits into, facilitates, or conflicts with the ways people already relate to each other and the meanings they give to current conduct. No technological intervention will totally overturn the organization of social life. Sexuality is between people, and the changes that affect these human networks and social institutions are the ones that will most influence sexuality of the future.

Changing Purposes of Sexuality

In less than a century we have moved from sexuality as reproduction and a pivotal form of conduct in our judgments of good and evil to more diversified and pluralistic versions of its meanings and goals. In the 1970s the emerging purposes of sex are those related to the role of sex and love in the choice of sexual partners, sex as an expression of emotional intimacy, sex as interpersonal competence, and sex as passion and rebellion. The older sacred and collective versions of the purposes of sexuality are still around and have their defenders, who are often in powerful positions in prestigious institutions, but the new options are more visible and less costly to try.

The role of sexuality in the affirmation or confirmation of partner selection has gone hand in hand with the cult of romantic love. While there are those who argue for a separation of love and sex on the grounds that you do not have to desire everyone you love or love everyone you desire, sex (particularly for women) is something you do under conditions of affection, given as a measure of emotional com-

1. The college dormitory that houses both sexes as well as cohabitors is a pre-singles-housing complex.

mitment. To have sex with someone is a step in an attachment/choice process, a step which escalates the intensity of relations, particularly in premarital sexual life. Love and sex are techniques for convincing oneself that the correct choice had been made—willingness "to go all the way" affirms in action a set of choices. This is a powerful purpose of sexuality, be it premarital, extramarital, heterosexual, homosexual, or bisexual. Sex is part of "really" being in love for many people. Love justifies sex, sex justifies love.

A more recent goal that has been placed on sexuality is that it be a vital force in forging bonds of intimacy, especially between men and women in marriage. Sex is a form of communication for the couple, and good sex is especially useful in expressing closeness and attachment. This role of sexuality seems particularly important in societies where the external pressures for couples to remain together have eased somewhat, and couple stability increasingly rests upon the emotional attachments that they can sustain. An interest in increasing the amount and quality of marital sex is a way of creating another tie between two married people. The marriage bed, which is now only intermittently procreational, is required to take on an intimacy-enhancing (not quite recreational) role. It is not always sure that sex can perform the task which has been assigned it, since it is often not expressive of intimacy, but of exploitation and domination, both in and out of marriage. However, sex as intimacy/intimacy as sex follows rather directly the connection made between love and sex.

One of the new purposes for sex is the ways in which it is used as an indicator of competence. This association between interpersonal competence and sexual conduct already exists for men. However, in a society that gives at least lip service to equality between women and men, we can expect to find sexual competence becoming an aspect of personal competence for women as well. This is now visible in the arena of mate selection (dating, rating, sociability), but is also true in most sexual relations. People's comfort with the elements of various sexual scripts, their ability to play various roles, become measures or additions to their identities. "Being a good lover" is no longer immoral or wrong, but a positive label for both men and women. No longer is it sufficient merely to be (or potentially to be) a good provider or good spouse or caretaker for children, one must also have the socio-emotional skills that go with being a good sexual partner. What used to be a secret sexual ranking affirmed only by gossip is now a more public dimension. More information not only gets out about people's sex lives and their abilities to manage them, but such information becomes part of their accumulated persona.

Sex as a form of rebellion has an old and honorable history. The ability to transgress sexually could call down the wrath of the gods, or of their representatives here below. One could be dramatically evil sexually in contrast to being dramatically good. For many people an authentic sense of damnation was sought as ardently as an authentic sense of salvation. As a result of the marginal moral status of sexuality, sexual misconduct could be used in attacks on the Establishment (whatever it might be) or as symbolic acts to oppose values or institutions. Thus, in D. H. Lawrence's novel, *Lady Chatterly's Lover*, the theme of the physically crippled and impotent upper class lord of the manor being replaced sexually by an earthy gamekeeper is part of class warfare as well as of sexual warfare. The use of such sexual themes as a form of rebellion or complaint can be found again and again in the lit-

This picture represents a male version of a woman's dream of having every erotic desire fulfilled. It has nothing to do with the text at this point, but a number of pages have passed without illustration, and I like this particular woodcut.

erature of the United States from the 1920s on, and is still vividly exemplified in the work of such novelists as Erica Jong and Norman Mailer.

Sex as rebellion is particularly important at the present time in the relations between parents and children. While the temperature of the combat between the young and their parents has been declining since the 1960s, young people can still aggravate or enrage their parents by their sexual activities (having sex at all, having sex with the wrong people, having sex in a public way). Sex in this case becomes a form of interpersonal rebellion, a mode of revenge across the generations.

The symbolic use of sexuality and its use in interpersonal rebellion require that people feel strongly about sex itself. To the degree that sex does not express very powerful emotions or is a recreational act, it cannot call upon very powerful emotions and institutional responses. Sex is more significant (if not more important) than sport to many people, but its recreational character is increasing. Do parents (except a very few sport-fanatic moms and dads) really care if their children play a sport? Do most husbands and wives worry about whom their spouse plays golf or tennis with? We have not reached that point of casualness in our sexual lives and judgments, but we are drifting in that direction. If sex in marriage affirms the pleasure bond of the couple (rather than the sacredness of the promise of marriage), or sex is used as a part of making up your mind in mate selection, or sex is primarily a measure of personal competence (rather than moral worth), then it is hard to create a powerful emotional response to forms of sexual misconduct.

A decline in the emotional and political significance of sexual conduct has not resulted in a purely recreational morality for sex. However, the purpose of some sexual conduct is now defined as enjoyment—transitory pleasure without serious psychological or social consequences. The significant public purposes of sexual conduct reflect serious individual purposes, if not quite such fateful purposes as salvation or damnation. Pleasure, however, now has a place as one of the purposes of sex—perhaps the polar secular opposite to the sacred purposes of the religious tradition.

The fact that a pleasure purpose for sex has emerged, existing in parallel (some things are fun, others are serious) as well as in opposition to other sexual purposes (all sex is serious, or one should be serious about sex) is a further indication of the increasing coolness of the sexual world. The old purposes of sex were hotter, in the sense that they called for strong reactions, individually and collectively, to what people did sexually. Even if strong reactions did not always happen, they were in the scripts of hellfire, jealousy, the woman scorned, innocence defiled, the sex fiend. These are hot words and strong phrases. There has evolved in the second half of the century a cooling of the sexual climate; it is still warm, but no longer boiling.

It is this shift in cultural temperature that is most significant for our understanding of the changes in what people will do sexually over the next twenty years. Sexual conduct has two dimensions, presently operating in opposite directions: as the amount and variety of sexuality in the society slowly increases, there is steady decline in the individual and collective significance attributed to it. The decline in cultural significance is also associated with an overlapping of what used to be different sexual careers as well as domains and styles of sexual conduct. We have noted the commonalities between what were thought to be totally different forms of sexuality, but the very ability to make this comment is evidence of a changing focus on sexuality.

The choice of viewpoint is, in part, one of emphasis, depending on whether one looks at the differences or the similarities. In the past the differences between the supposed heterosexual majority and everyone else were important—the majority assumed that they themselves were all alike. A different perspective focuses on how the heterosexual majority resembles the sexual minorities, as well as on the ways in which the members of the heterosexual majority differ from one another. For instance, the partner selection patterns of heterosexual singles resemble those of homosexual men, and the passionate love affairs of both heterosexual and homosexual adolescents have major similarities. At the same time, the patterns of heterosexual marriage (from permanent fidelity to co-marital sex) appear to be as various as the patterns once labeled sexually "normal" and sexually "perverted." It all depends on what dimensions of conduct are thought to be significant—if we consider how people get together and how they feel, rather than think only of organs and orifices, the sexual world like a kaleidoscope falls into a different set of arrangements.

Formerly separate sexual worlds overlap, as things in common are both *dis-*

covered and *invented.* By changing our focus we discover things in common; in the process we create and invent similarities, or take over elements from other groups. Thus one major change in the last quarter of the century is likely to be a breakdown in the barriers between types of sexuality based on traditional distinctions (technique, gender, legal status) and an increase in sexualities based on affection, intimacy, and competence. All forms of sexuality are likely to become infused with the latter purposes, a process of cultural homogenization and interpenetration.

Changes in Sexual Conduct

If there is a general increase in the amount of sexual activity in society concurrent with a decrease in the cultural significance of sexuality, particularly at the collective but also at the individual level, and formerly disparate forms of sexual conduct come to be treated and experienced as more alike, the following changes seem to be probable.

HETEROSEXUALITY

It is likely that there will be a steady increase in the incidence of premarital intercourse to about eighty to ninety percent of young men and women, as part of heterosexual partner selection involving a sequence of relationships of various durations, with marriage the usual outcome. There will be a greater incidence of approval (or at least less active disapproval) by adults, more privacy, and more extensive sexual techniques used earlier. We can expect more sexual activity in high schools, but with the availability of birth-control technologies perhaps a reduction in unwanted pregnancies and births. This has not happened as yet, but as premarital sex comes to be institutionalized, the use of contraception will become more commonplace. The serial nature of relationships will call attention to the possibilities of changing sex and love partners, increasing the ease of partner transition.

The proportion of the population who marry will stay high. Coupling will remain the majority form of personal association for at least the next half century. The rate of couple dissolution will also increase, however, to well above the current rates. People will marry and they will marry more often. Both the increased involvement of women in the labor force and the probability of some form of guaranteed income will result in lower external constraints on marriage, resulting in more transitions, more intermarital periods, and more children who have had several parents or who have lived in households where parents are divorced.

Because of increased participation in the labor force by women, as well as other changes, there will be an increase in rates of extramarital coitus for both men and women. Much of this intercourse will accompany transitions of people from couple to couple. More complex forms of extramarital arrangements will emerge, but group marriage, communes, group sex, and co-marital sex will remain mostly experimental.

BISEXUALITY

The number of people in society who have had sexual experience with both sexes may increase somewhat. This will result from such factors as experimentation with group sex, some coerced heterosexuals coming out, and some women experimenting with homosexual adaptations as a function of a commitment to the women's movement. The majority of cross-sex experiences will remain largely sequential, and there will be some but not a great increase in the number of preferential bisexuals. An increase in bisexual experiences rather than an increase in bisexual identities is a function of multiple pathways. There are many reasons to have the experience, but fewer reasons to assume the identity.

HOMOSEXUALITY

It is possible that more access to heterosexuality in adolescence may cut into the numbers of young people who for various reasons have homosexual interests. However, at the same time the number of coerced heterosexuals or those with a homosexual preference who have not emerged may find themselves more comfortable with an exclusively homosexual life style as a result of the more open social climate and the existence of homosexual social institutions.

If gender becomes a less important dimension of sexual choice, two changes might occur: there may be fewer persons with exclusively homosexual histories (as well as fewer with exclusively heterosexual histories) because it will be easier to find people of both sexes with important emotional qualities that can be tied to sexuality. At the same time, those who are exclusively committed to one sex or another may feel better about maintaining permanent or more permanent relations because there is less stigma on their choices. If present societal patterns of defining and learning gender roles change, male homosexuals may become less sexually active and promiscuous, while female homosexuals may become less monogamous and pursue more sequential relationships. Male and female homosexual patterns may tend to become more alike.

PROSTITUTION OF WOMEN

If U.S. society chooses to decriminalize prostitution, and if transitory unpaid heterosexuality becomes more common, the market for prostitution among many men will be reduced. However, while the number may decline it is unlikely that all customers will disappear—the busy man, the inept man, the erotic man, the member of a sexual minority may well still have to pay for sex. Decriminalization of prostitution would result in changed patterns of recruitment (more women would do it a few times for money), a changed relationship to the conventional community and to the criminal justice system, and a greater opportunity for women to move in and out of the occupation with less stigma.

SEX OFFENSES

If the sex laws are changed there will be fewer sex crimes, obviously. But the real criminological problems will remain—offenses against children and offenses involving violence. It can be hoped that, if the general emotional climate surrounding sex cools off and there is a better environment in which to learn what the society thinks is sexually appropriate, fewer men will molest or rape children or women.

The offenses against children may decline as opportunities increase for contacts with adults, both heterosexual and homosexual. It is difficult to speculate about offenses involving force because the changing status of women may attract more rather than less male hostility. At the same time, if sex becomes less important in the struggle between men and women it may be possible to defuse this hostility. It is possible to argue that rape rates may rise (largely by men socialized in a tradition of female inferiority) during the period when women are achieving political, economic, and social goals, and that the rates will decline as young women and men are brought up in a more sexually permissive and egalitarian economic and social world.

SEXUAL MINORITIES

It is likely that there will be more publicity given to sexual minorities, and certain minority practices may be picked up by other groups. *The Joy of Sex* is evidence of this tendency for minority techniques or scripts to become available to other groups. Thus, mild bondage and discipline, the use of mechanical aids, and group sex will become wider spread, but few people will make these activities the central focus of their sex lives. There are some who will commit a little time to them, others who will commit all of their sexual interest to them. However, this latter group will experience their sex lives as being less compulsive, since there is now a continuum between what they do and what others do, rather than a sharp dividing line. There will not be the same sense of social and psychological isolation that produces most of the anxiety and pathology in such isolated minority groups.

EROTIC ENVIRONMENT

As pornography becomes more widespread and accessible, its use is likely to decline substantially. Most people will look at it every once in a while, and only a few will collect it. It will remain largely an object of popular culture serving as an escape rather than a route for new social inventions or the creation of art. There will continue to be more pornography than in the past (it was really all suppressed); however, at no point will pornography become a major enterprise.

THERAPY AND HEALTH

The future of sexual therapy is unclear. Sexual problems are cultural problems; as the culture changes there will be new cultural disorders. It has often been observed that no one has ever seen a case like one of Freud's cases after World War I, because the conditions that produced those problems were gone and new conditions produced new problems. Will directive sex therapy work in the future? Probably so, simply because there will always be problems in the system of transmitting information from one generation to another, and always the problem of getting it wrong. As a result people will have various kinds of sexual complaints. However, they may not be the same complaints we hear today, nor will the same techniques necessarily work in the future.

The ability to achieve physical health as it relates to sexuality depends in part on a changed climate of attitudes about the body and the willingness of people to treat the sexual parts more coolly and calmly. This will improve the practice of self examination and also improve the knowledge and control that people have over their own bodies. It might be possible, though it is less likely, that the doctor-patient relationship will become more of a partnership—in this way improving efforts toward maintaining health and preventing disease.

Conclusion

How probable are the changes discussed above? Barring a nuclear war or a major biological or social catastrophe, they look like the shape of things to come. If the contours of society remain the same, the sexuality that people will acquire and practice will remain much the same. Whatever the changes, the majority of people in U.S. society will become sexual through the same processes of acquiring a cultural identity that were used in the past. Most of the time people accept without a great deal of reflection or serious conflict the social and sexual arrangements of their culture.

The new generations will accept a social landscape with fewer gender stereotypes, with more sexual activity, with a greater number of significant emotional partners in a lifetime, as if the world had always been that way. They will accept the dominant sexual practices of their society the way we have accepted our beliefs that, for example, masturbation or premarital intercourse are wrong. At the same time there will be people unwilling to accept the new social order—who will wish to turn the clock back to the present (we will be the golden age of the past), or turn it forward toward a further future where a sexual utopia awaits. However, if the prospective cooling of sexual concerns does occur, debate about sex will be far less passionate and divisive than it is at the present.

It is difficult to judge whether the future world will be any better or worse than the present one, just as it is difficult to judge whether the present is better or worse than the past. It all depends on what your purposes are. Once you have them, you can always find arguments to support or deny them.

REFERENCES

General

Works of particular interest which have had an important influence on the author's ideas:

Burke, Kenneth, *A Rhetoric of Motives*. University of California Press, 1969.

——, *Language as Symbolic Action*. University of California Press, 1966.

Cohen, Stanley, and Laurie Taylor, *Escape Attempts: The Theory and Practice of Resistance to Everyday Life*. London: Penguin Books, 1976.

Mischel, Walter, *Personality and Assessment*. Wiley, 1968.

Peckham, Morse, *Man's Rage for Chaos: Biology, Behavior and the Arts*. Shocken Books, 1965.

Rappaport, Roy A., *Pigs for the Ancestors: Ritual in the Ecology of a New Guinea People*. Yale University Press, 1968.

Steiner, George, *After Babel*. Oxford University Press, 1975.

Turbayne, Colin M., *The Myth of Metaphor*, Revised Edition. University of South Carolina Press, 1970.

Wallace, Anthony, *Culture and Personality*, 2nd ed. Random House, 1970.

Chapter 1

Robinson, Paul, *Modernization of Sex*. Harper & Row, 1976.

Chapter 2

Bateson, Mary Katherine, *Our Own Metaphor*. Knopf, 1972.

Ellis, Havelock, *Studies in the Psychology of Sex*. Random House, 1936.

Hill, Christopher, *The World Turned Upside Down*. Temple Smith, 1972.

Kinsey, Alfred C., Wardell Pomeroy, and C. Martin. *Sexual Behavior in the Human Male*. Saunders, 1948.

——, and Paul Gebhard. *Sexual Behavior in the Human Female*. Saunders, 1953.

Madge, J., *The Origins of Scientific Sociology*. Free Press, 1962.

Masters, William H., and Virginia E. Johnson, *Human Sexual Response*. Little, Brown, 1966.

——, *Human Sexual Inadequacy*. Little, Brown, 1970.

Rieff, Philip, *The Triumph of the Therapeutic*. Harper & Row, 1966.

Robinson, Paul, *Modernization of Sex*.

Chapter 4

Goslin, D. A., editor, *Handbook of Socialization Theory and Research*. Rand McNally, 1969.

Green, Richard, *Sexual Identity Conflict in Children and Adults*. Basic Books, 1974.

——, and John Money, editors, *Transsexualism and Sex Reassignment*. Johns Hopkins Press, 1969.

Maccoby, E. E., *The Development of Sex Differences*. Stanford University Press, 1966.

——, and C. N. Jacklin, *The Psychology of Sex differences*. Stanford University Press, 1974.

Money, John, and Anke Erhardt, *Man Woman/Boy Girl*. Johns Hopkins Press, 1972.

Stoller, R. J., *Sex and Gender*. Science House, 1968.

Chapter 5

Freud, Sigmund, "Three Essays on the Theory of Sexuality," Standard Edition of the *Complete Psychological Works of Sigmund Freud,* Volume VII. Hogarth Press, 1953.

Gagnon, John H., "Sexuality and Sexual Learning in the Child," *Psychiatry,* Volume 28, Number III, August 1965, pp. 222–228.

Kinsey, et al., 1948, Chapter 5.

Kinsey, et al., 1953, Chapter 4.

Chapter 6

Kagan, Jerome, and Robert Coles, *Twelve to Sixteen: Early Adolescence.* Norton, 1971.

Kinsey, et al., 1948, Chapters 5 and 7.

Kinsey, et al., 1953, Chapter 4.

Chapter 7

Gagnon, J. H., "Scripts and the Coordination of Sexual Conduct," in J. K. Cole and Richard Deinstbier, editors, *Nebraska Symposium on Motivation.* University of Nebraska Press, 1974, pp. 27–59.

————, and William Simon, *Sexual Conduct.* Aldine, 1973.

Kinsey, et al., 1953, Chapters 14–18.

Masters and Johnson, *Human Sexual Response.* Little Brown, 1966.

Chapter 8

Kinsey et al., 1948, Chapter 14.

Kinsey, et al., 1953, Chapter 5.

Marcus, Steven, *The Other Victorians.* Basic Books, rev. ed., 1974.

Schatzman, Morton, "Paranoia or Persecution: Freud's Schreber Revisited." *Salmagundi,* Number 19, Spring 1972, pp. 38–65.

Chapter 9

Kinsey, et al., 1948, Chapters 16 and 17.

Kinsey, et al., 1953, Chapters 7 and 8.

Reese, I. L., *The Social Context of Sexual Permissiveness.* Holt, Rinehart and Winston, 1967.

Simon, William, A. S. Berger, and John H. Gagnon, "Beyond Anxiety and Fantasy: The Coital Experiences of College Youth." *Journal of Youth and Adolescence,* Volume I, 1972, p. 203.

Chapter 10

Bell, Robert, and Phyllis Bell, "Sexual Satisfaction Among Married Women," *Medical Aspects of Human Sexuality,* December 1972, Vol. 6, No. 12, pp. 136–144.

Hunt, Morton, *Sexual Behavior in the Seventies.* Playboy Press, 1974.

Kinsey, et al., 1948, Chapter 18.

Kinsey, et al., 1953, Chapter 9.

Levin, Robert, and Amy Levin, "A Redbook Report: Sexual Pleasure: The Surprising Preferences of 100,000 Women." *Redbook Magazine,* September 1975.

Westoff, Charles, "Coital Frequency and Contraception," *Family Planning Perspectives,* Vol. 6, No. 3, Summer 1974, pp. 136–141.

Chapter 11

Farber, Bernard, *Family: Organization and Interaction.* Chandler, 1964.

Hunt, Morton, *The Affair.* World, 1969.

Kinsey, et al., 1948, Chapter 19.

Kinsey, et al., 1953, Chapter 10.
Libby, Roger, and Robert N. Whitehurst, *Marriage and Alternatives: Exploring Intimate Relationships.* Scott, Foresman, 1977.
Neubeck, Gerhard, *Extramarital Relations.* Prentice-Hall, 1969.
Stein, Peter, *Singles.* Prentice-Hall, 1976.

Chapter 12
Bieber, Irving, et al., *Homosexuality, a Psychoanalytic Study.* Basic Books, 1962.
Dank, Barry M., "Coming Out in the Gay World," *Psychiatry,* Volume 34, May, 1971.
Davison, Gerald, and John Neale, *Abnormal Psychology.* Wiley, 1974.
Gagnon, John H., "Sexual Conduct and Crime," in Daniel Glaser, editor, *Handbook of Criminology.* Rand McNally, 1974.
―――― and Simon, *Sexual Conduct,* Chapters 5 and 6.
Gerassi, John, *The Boys of Boise.* Macmillan, 1966.
Hoffman, Martin, *The Gay World.* Basic Books, 1968.
Hooker, Evelyn, "The Homosexual Community," in J. C. Palmer and M. J. Goldstein, editors, *Perspectives in Psychopathology.* Oxford University Press, 1966, pp. 354 – 364.
Humphreys, Laud, *Tearoom Trade: Impersonal Sex in Public Places.* Aldine, 1970.
Kinsey, et al., 1948, Chapter 21.
Kinsey et al., 1953, Chapter 11.
Leznoff, M. and W. A. Westley, "The Homosexual Community," *Social Problems,* Vol. III, April 1956, pp. 257 – 263.
Reiss, Albert J., "The Social Integration of Queers and Peers," *Social Problems,* Vol. IX, Fall 1961, pp. 102 – 120.
Saghir, M. T., and E. Robins, *Male and Female Homosexuality.* Williams and Wilkins, 1973.

Chapter 13
Blake, James, "Letters from an American Prisoner," *The Paris Review,* Volume XIII, 1956.
Cantine, Holley, and Dachine Rainier, editors, *Prison Etiquette.* Retort Press, 1950.
Davis, Alan J., "Sexual Assault in the Philadelphia Prisons and Sheriff Vans," *Transaction,* Volume VI, December 1968, pp. 8 – 16.
Duberman, Martin, "The Bisexual Debate," *New Times Magazine,* June 28, 1974, pp. 34 – 41.
Gagnon and Simon, *Sexual Conduct,* Chapter 8.
Giallombardo, Rose, *Society of Women: A Study of a Women's Prison.* Wiley, 1966.
Kinsey, et al., 1953, Chapter 11.
Rechy, John, *City of Night.* Grove Press, 1962.
Robinson, Paul, *Modernization of Sex.* Harper & Row, 1976.
Ward, David, and Jean Kassebaum, *Women's Prison: Sex and Social Structure.* Aldine, 1965.
Williams, Colin, and Martin Weinberg, *Homosexuals in the Military.* Harper & Row, 1971.
―――― , *Homosexuals.* Oxford University Press, 1974.

Chapter 14
Gagnon and Simon, *Sexual Conduct,* Chapter 7.
Kinsey, et al., 1948, Chapter 20.

Chapter 15
Ennis, P. H., Field Survey 2: Criminal Victimization in the United States; Report of a National Survey. Report of Research Studies submitted to the President's Commission on Law Enforcement and Administration of Justice. U.S. Government Printing Office, 1967.

Gagnon, John H., "Female Child Victims of Sex Offenses," *Social Problems,* Volume 2, Fall 1965, pp. 176–192.

Gebhard, Paul, John H. Gagnon, Wardell Pomeroy, C. V. Christenson, *Sex Offenders.* Harper & Row, 1965.

Kinsey, et al., 1948.

Kinsey, et al., 1953.

Kirkpatrick, Clifford, and F. Kanin, "Male Sex Aggression on a University Campus," *American Sociological Review,* Volume XXII, February 1957, pp. 52–58.

Reifen, D., "Sexual Offenses Against Children—A New Method of Investigation in Israel," *World Mental Health,* Volume IX, May 1957, pp. 74–82.

Chapter 16

Green, Richard, *Sexual Identity Conflict in Children and Adults.* Basic Books, 1974.

———— and John Money, editors, *Transsexualism and Sex Reassignment.* Johns Hopkins, 1969.

Kinsey, et al., 1948, Chapter 22.

Kinsey, et al., 1953, Chapter 12.

Morris, Jan, *Conundrum.* Harcourt Brace Jovanovich, 1974.

Chapter 17

Gagnon and Simon, *Sexual Conduct,* Chapter 9.

Kinsey, et al., 1953, Chapter 16.

Kutchinsky, Berl, *Pornography and Sex Crimes in Denmark: Early Research Findings.* London: Martin Robertson, 1972.

Marcus, Steven, *The Other Victorians.* Basic Books, rev. ed., 1974.

Peckham, Morse, *Art and Pornography.* Basic Books, 1969.

U.S. Commission on Obscenity and Pornography, *Technical Reports,* Volumes I-VII. U.S. Government Printing Office, 1971.

Chapter 18

Green, Richard, editor, *Human Sexuality: A Health Practitioner's Text.* Williams and Wilkins, 1975.

"Removing the Plain Brown Wrapper from Sexuality and Sexual Health," *Postgraduate Medicine,* Volume 58, No. 1, July 1975.

The Boston Women's Health Book Collective, *Our Bodies, Ourselves: A Book by and for Women,* Second Edition. Simon and Schuster, 1976.

Chapter 19

Comfort, Alex, *The Joy of Sex.* Crown, 1972.

Dodson, Betty, *Liberating Masturbation.* Bodysex Designs, 1974.

Gagnon, John H., and Gerald C. Davison, "The Enhancement of Sexual Responsiveness in Behavior Therapy," A Symposium Paper Presented at the Annual Meetings of the American Sociological Association, New Orleans, August 30, 1974.

Higgins, Glen E., Jr., *Aspects of Sexual Response in Spinal Cord Injured Adults: A Review of the Literature.* Unpublished manuscript, 84 pages.

Kaplan, Helen, *The New Sex Therapy: Active Treatment of Sexual Dysfunctions.* Quadrangle Books, 1974.

Masters and Johnson, *Human Sexual Inadequacy.* Little, Brown, 1970.

GLOSSARY

abortion. The termination of pregnancy by human intervention.

abortifacient. Something used to cause an abortion, usually referring to a drug or similar agent.

amenorrhea. The absence of menstruation. Can be the result of either physical or psychological processes or events that affect the hormonal system.

anal intercourse. A form of sexual activity in which the penis is inserted into the sexual partner's anus. It is sometimes called *buggery* or **sodomy** (particularly in its legal definition), and can occur either in homosexual or heterosexual relationships. It is a criminal offense in many jurisdictions.

anaphrodisiac. Chemicals that reduce the level of sexual interest or response.

androgen. The "male" sex hormone, produced in both men and women in increased amounts at puberty. The principal hormone affecting secondary sexual development in males. In nonhuman primates, largely responsible for sexual initiation on the part of male animals and receptivity on the part of females.

anomaly. A deviation from the normal type, used by Havelock Ellis as a neutral word to describe homosexuality as an irregular biological type.

aphrodisiac. Chemicals that purportedly increase the level of sexual interest or desire. By analogy, used to refer to other sexually arousing substances or circumstances. There is little evidence that such chemicals have more than a psychological effect. The best "aphrodisiac" for most people is good health, rest, low anxiety, and an interesting sexual partner.

Bartholin's glands. Two tiny glands on either side of entry to the vagina which at one time were thought to produce a substantial amount of the vaginal lubrication. Masters and Johnson found evidence that they secrete only very tiny amounts of fluid.

bestiality. Sexual contact by a human being with an animal of another species. Also referred to as *zooarastia* or *zoophilia.* Kinsey uses the neutral term "animal contacts."

bisexual. In biology, an individual specifically having the sexual characteristics of both male and female, the equivalent of a **hermaphrodite.** When used with reference to humans, means having sex with persons of both genders, either in sequence or at the same period of time. The specific types of cross-sex/same-sex patterns of sexual contact that can be called bisexual are in dispute.

castration. Removal of the gonads, organs that secrete the majority of the sex hormones in both males and females. In females the ovaries, in males the testes. Removal prior to puberty has powerful effects on secondary sexual and reproductive development; after puberty the effects on sexuality are less dramatic.

castration complex. A key idea in psychoanalytic theory which refers to fears on the part of males that their genitals will be cut off because they have forbidden sexual desires. Particularly important to the Oedipus Complex, in which the male child is afraid that his father will castrate him because of his incestuous desires for his mother.

celibacy. Originally meaning a decision to remain unmarried, because sexuality was linked only to marriage. Now is used to refer to a decision to remain sexually abstinent.

cervix. Literally translated, means "neck." In the female genital anatomy, the narrow extension of the uterus that opens into the rear upper aspect of the vagina. The cervical opening is the entry into the uterus through which sperm enters the uterus during a woman's fertile period.

chancre. The first symptom of syphilis, a sore or ulcer that appears either in the genital regions or other soft tissues of the body, such as the mouth.

chromosome. One of several rod-shaped bodies found in the nucleus of all body cells. The chromosomal bodies contain the genes.

circumcision. The surgical removal of the foreskin or prepuce of the male penis. Ostensibly done for health purposes at the present time, though it is an outgrowth of religious practices. The impact of circumcision on either genital cleanliness or sexual response is unknown. In some primitive tribes, female circumcision is practiced by removing the hood or foreskin over the clitoris.

climacteric.   See **menopause.**

climax.   See **orgasm.**

clitoris.   A body of sensitive tissue located in the upper part of the vulva just above the urethral opening. The distance of the clitoris from the vaginal entry varies considerably among women. The clitoris is the embryological analog of the penis, and varies considerably in size, both when at rest and during sexual excitement. It is a primary site for tactile stimulation during masturbation and intercourse; hence, the term "clitoral orgasm."

coitus.   Sexual activity between male and female, specifically referring to entry of the penis into the vagina.

coitus interruptus.   A conception control practice involving withdrawal of the penis from the vagina before ejaculation. Apparently a relatively common practice in the nineteenth century prior to the development and widespread use of other contraceptives.

coitus reservatus.   The intentional suppression of ejaculation during sexual intercourse. Often used as a form of birth control; also a practice used to prolong intercourse by preventing the loss of erection which comes with ejaculation.

condom.   A male contraceptive device which involves drawing a sheath of material over the erect penis before intercourse. Originally made of animal intestines, now made of rubber. Very effective when used carefully, and has the secondary benefit of reducing the probability of transmission of venereal disease.

contraception.   The use of various techniques to prevent conception during sexual intercourse. Can include the use of mechanical devices (condom), chemicals (the birth-control pill), or controlled patterns of sexual activity to avoid conception (the rhythm method).

coprophilia.   A condition in which sexual arousal or response is associated with the act of defecation or feces themselves. May be associated with some forms of masochism.

corona glandis.   The rim of tissue surrounding the base of the glans of the penis.

Cowper's glands.   Two small glands in the male on either side of the urethra near the prostate. These glands secrete a mucous material which appears as part of the seminal fluid.

cunnilingus.   The use of the tongue or the mouth on the external female genitals for sexual arousal or orgasm. Contact may be on the labia, on the clitoris, or the tongue may be inserted into the vaginal entry.

cystitis.   Inflammation of the bladder, usually caused by bacterial infection. The major symptom of cystitis is a burning sensation during urination.

defloration.   Has come to mean the rupture of the hymen, whatever its cause (intercourse, vaginal examination, exercise), but originally meant the deflowering of a virgin in intercourse.

detumescence.   Generally meaning reduction in swelling. As a sexual term, refers to reduction in vasocongestion in the genitals and other parts of the body, following either orgasm(s) or the end of sexual stimulation.

diaphragm.   A mechanical contraceptive for women made of rubber and hemispherical in shape. Designed to fit like a cap over the neck of the uterus and prevent sperm from entering the cervical opening. Should be fitted by a physician, and is most effective when used in conjunction with a contraceptive foam.

douche.   The use of water or other liquid solutions to rinse out the vagina for sanitary, medical, or contraceptive purposes. In general, should be used sparingly unless prescribed by a physician. Ineffective as a method of contraception.

dysmenorrhea.   Painful contractions occurring during menstruation.

dyspareunia.   Painful or difficult coitus. Can happen to either men or women but is usually experienced only by women.

ejaculation.   The expulsion of semen from the penis, usually occurring at the same time as orgasm during sexual activity.

Electra complex.   A condition posited by psychoanalytical theory which is parallel to the Oedipus complex in males. Involves excessive emotional attachment of daughters to their fathers and a corollary fear of their mothers.

emission.   In the nineteenth century a term parallel to "ejaculation," occurring usually at the moment of orgasm. At the present time, more commonly refers to ejaculations that occur when there is little or no sexual activity, such as the involuntary ejaculations during sleep called *nocturnal emissions.*

endocrine glands.   Glands that are part of the hormonal system and which secrete their chemical products directly into the bloodstream.

erection.   The enlarging and hardening of the penis and clitoris as a result of vasocongestion produced by sexual excitement.

erogenous zones.   Areas of the body which are culturally defined as having a particular sexual meaning or sexual sensitivity. Include such areas as the mouth, lips, breasts, buttocks, genitals, nipples, clitoris, and penis. Although it is usually believed that these zones have automatic sexual meaning, cultural conditioning is required for people to experience them as sexual in character.

estrogen.   The "female" sex hormone, produced in both men and women in increased amounts during puberty. Much larger amounts are produced in women than in men, and it is responsible for secondary sexual development in females. Its secretion regulates the menstrual cycle.

estrus.   Periods of increased sexual receptivity in nonhuman animals, regulated by the hormonal system. Controlled in primates by androgens and in other mammals by estrogen. Associated with periods of fertility.

eunuch. A male who has been castrated. Castration prior to puberty prevents the masculinizing effects of androgen; therefore, the voice remains high-pitched and the body does not develop heavy male musculature. Castration after puberty tends to produce infertile but not necessarily sexually inactive men.

excitement phase. The initial stage of the Masters and Johnson description of the human sexual response cycle, meaning those physiological and anatomical responses that follow the beginning of effective sexual stimulation as defined by the person being excited.

exhibitionism. A sex offense in which an individual exposes his genitals publicly. Only men are charged with this offense, and only when they display to women and children. Exhibitionism also refers to the psychological conditions which appear to predispose persons to expose their genitals.

extramarital. When used in connection with sexuality, commonly refers to sexual activity, coitus or otherwise, with persons other than one's spouse. Sometimes but infrequently used to include both heterosexual and homosexual sexual contact.

fellatio. Kissing, licking, or sucking the penis and other parts of the male genitals. A limited meaning is taking the penis into the mouth and sucking it.

femininity. The traits of appearance and behavior which, on the average, seem to differentiate women from men in a society. They are culturally accepted patterns of conduct, and are not directly determined by the biological sex of a woman.

fetishism. A condition in which sexual responsiveness or orgasm requires the presence of an object such as an article of clothing (glove, shoe, underwear). Without this particular object the person is unable to respond sexually.

fornication. Sexual intercourse between two unmarried persons. Kinsey referred to this activity as "premarital intercourse."

frigidity. A quasi-medical term referring either to the inability of a woman to have orgasm or to her lack of interest in sexual activity. With its connotations of coldness, indifference, and insensitivity, often used as a negative label.

gay. Formerly a slang term applied to prostitution in the nineteenth century, and which now refers either to homosexuals or to the homosexual subculture. Politically active homosexual men now use the word gay (as in gay pride or gay liberation or gay activism) as a chosen label.

gender identity. A term used to describe the psychological sense of self as male or female. Young children acquire a relatively fixed internal sense that they are either a boy or a girl. Such a self-label seems to determine their future preferences and the ease with which they adapt to new circumstances.

gender role. The activities of a person which are linked to his or her gender identity. These activities are those which a culture defines as appropriate to a particular gender identity.

genitals (genitalia or **genital organs).** Those parts of the reproductive system specifically used for sexual activity, such as the penis, the scrotum, the external female genitals, and the vagina.

glans penis or **glans clitoridis.** The head of the penis or the clitoris.

gonadotropin. A chemical substance which stimulates the production of hormones in the gonads, the testes, and the ovaries.

gonorrhea. A venereal infection transmitted primarily through intercourse, though it can be transmitted through oral and anal sex. Involves inflammation of the mucous membrane. Untreated, can have serious consequences from secondary infections. Relatively easy to identify and treat in the male, somewhat more difficult to diagnose and treat in the female.

granuloma inguinale. A disease which affects the genitals and which involves widespread ulceration and scarring of the skin as well as underlying tissue. Can be transmitted by anal intercourse.

gynecologist. A physician who specializes in the treatment of the female sexual and reproductive organs.

hermaphrodite. A biologically intersexed individual who possesses both male and female gonads (ovary and testicle) as well as rudimentary sex organs of both sexes.

heterosexuality. Sexual preference for or sexual activity with persons of the opposite sex.

homosexuality. Sexual preference for or sexual activity with persons of the same sex.

hormones. Chemical substances secreted by endocrine glands that have specific effects on the activities or growth of other organs in the body. Thus, the hormone estrogen has specific effects on the growth of the breasts in the female, and regulates the activity of the menstrual cycle.

hymen. A fold of tissue that partly closes the external opening of the vagina in some virgin females. Has often been used as evidence for virginity, even though some women are born without hymens or with only rudimentary hymens, and the hymen is often broken by vigorous physical activity, as well as by non-sexual insertions into the vagina.

hysterectomy. The physical removal of the uterus, sometimes including the ovaries, either through the abdominal wall or through the vagina.

impotence. The inability of a male to achieve or sustain an erection during sexual activity. *Primary* impotence, a rare condition, is when a man has never had an erection. *Secondary* or situational impotence is when a man is unable to have an erection either with a specific sexual partner or after having had a history of sexual erections. Impotence may occur in any form of sexual activity.

impregnation. The act of fertilization or making a female pregnant.

incest. Sexual relations between close relatives, usually treated as a criminal offense within defined kinship limits. Commonly prohibited are sexual activity between fathers and daughters, mothers and sons, brothers and sisters, and step-parents and step-children.

insemination. The deposit of semen within the vagina.

intrauterine device (IUD). A contraceptive device for women which involves the insertion of a small plastic or metal device into the uterus. How it works is not completely understood, but it may prevent implantation of the fertilized egg by causing a mild inflammation of the uterine lining.

intromission. The vagina accepting the insertion of the penis.

invert. A term frequently used in the past to refer to homosexuals, but less often used today. Still used to refer to nonhuman animals showing sexual patterns of the opposite sex.

Klinefelter's syndrome. A general abnormality in males in which the sex-determining chromosomes are XXY rather than the normal XY. In this case the ovum contributes an extra X at the time of fertilization which affects the hormonal system, producing small testicles, sterility, and sometimes a distinctly feminine physical appearance.

labia majora. The outer and larger lips of the female external genitals.

labia minora. The inner and smaller lips of the female external genitals.

lesbian. The Greek island of Lesbos was the home of the classic poet Sappho. Sappho's poetry concerned the love of women for women; hence, the term lesbianism came to be applied to female homosexuality. Politically active female homosexuals call themselves lesbians as a chosen label.

libido. The psychoanalytic term for the sexual drive or urge, which the Freudians thought was innate in the organism.

lymphogranuloma venereum. A disease of the lymph glands of the genitals, which is produced by a virus.

masculinity. The traits of appearance and behavior which, on the average, seem to differentiate men from women in a society. They are culturally accepted patterns of conduct, and are not directly determined by the biological sex of a man.

masochism. A sexual preference in which pain is associated with or becomes the source of sexual arousal. Sometimes a necessary part of sexual gratification.

masturbation. The production of sexual response and orgasm through self-stimulation. The stimulation may be manual, rubbing against other objects, or through the use

of fantasy. May involve direct contact with the genitals or be purely psychological activity.

menarche. The beginning of menstruation in human females, occurring at some moment during puberty and serving as a major signal of reproductive readiness.

menopause. The period during which menstruation stops, usually occurring between the ages of 35 and 55. As reproductive capability ceases a relatively wide range of physical and psychological changes occur, and hormone production drops.

menstruation. A discharge from the uterus of blood, which contains the uterine lining and the egg which has not been fertilized. This discharge through the vagina normally occurs at intervals of about 28 days between the ages of puberty and menopause.

mons veneris. A mound of fatty tissue shaped like a triangle found just above the vulva and covering the pubic bone.

mucosa. The mucous membranes or tissues that have a moist surface through which mucus may be secreted.

mucus. The thick, slippery fluid secreted by the mucous membranes (for example, saliva or vaginal fluid).

necrophilia. A strong sexual response or strong attraction to the dead.

nocturnal emission. The involuntary orgasm and ejaculation of semen during sleep. The slang term is "wet dream." It may occur with relative frequency during adolescence and decline rapidly during adulthood.

nymphomania. A pejorative psychiatric term used to describe women who are highly sexually active. Also used to refer to women who are highly sexually active but who report getting no sexual pleasure from the activity itself. Not used to refer to women who have a great deal of sexual activity with their husbands and do not get sexual pleasure from it, only to women who have a lot of sex with men who are not their husbands.

obscene. In legal definitions of pornography, refers to sexual activity which is negatively defined according to certain standards of morality. Also often used negatively to describe erotic materials, along with the terms disgusting, filthy, or repulsive.

obstetrician. A physician who specializes in the care of women during pregnancy and childbirth and the period immediately following delivery.

Oedipus complex. See **castration.**

onanism. Taken from the Biblical sin of Onan, which involved the withdrawal of the penis from the vagina just before ejaculation. Expanded in the eighteenth century to include masturbation.

orgasm. The moments of climax or peak experience during sexual activity. Associated in post-pubescent males with ejaculation.

orgasmic phase. A term used by Masters and Johnson to describe what they call the third stage of the human sexual response cycle. Includes a set of genital and extra-genital responses specific to that moment.

ovulation. The release from the ovary of a mature, unimpregnated ovum.

partialism. The condition of a person who is only able to be sexually responsive and receive sexual gratification with another person when the second person has some specific and required body attribute (large breasts, red hair, a missing limb).

pederasty. Usually refers to sexual contact between an adult male and a young boy. Also refers to anal intercourse.

pedophilia. Sexual activity of an adult with a child. In a few cases the pedophilia is preferential; that is, the adult prefers sexual activity with children. In the majority of cases the sexual contacts are substitutive for adult contacts which are not available.

penis. The male sexual organ which is used both for activity and urination.

penis captivus. A condition in which the erect penis is clamped into the vagina by a spasm of the vaginal musculature during intercourse and results in the inability to withdraw the penis. It is not certain that this condition actually occurs in humans but it does occur in other animals, particularly dogs.

perversion. A psychiatric term that has come to have primarily pejorative meanings, referring to sexual activities which are thought to be different from a "normal" course of sexual development.

phallus. Usually refers to the erect penis or to "phallic objects," that is, objects that look like the erect penis, such as skyscrapers, baseball bats, or broom handles.

pituitary. A gland located in the head, whose secretions regulate the functioning of the other glands in the hormonal system, particularly the gonads, the thyroid, and the adrenals.

pituitary gonadotropins. Hormones secreted from the pituitary that stimulate the gonads.

plateau phase. The second phase of the Masters and Johnson description of the human sexual response cycle which includes those anatomical and physiological events that precede orgasm.

polyandry. A marriage form in which one woman has more than one husband at a time.

polygamy. A marriage form in which either spouse may have more than one mate at the same time.

polygyny. A marriage form in which a man has more than one wife at the same time.

pornography. Literally means stories about prostitutes, but has come to include all forms of erotic or sexually arousing materials in such media as literature, art, film. Has been used interchangeably with such expressions as obscenity.

precoital fluid. Drops of fluid secreted by the Cowper's gland that some men notice as the first few drops of clear liquid coming out of the penis during the early stages of sexual excitement.

premature ejaculation. Ejaculation which occurs either prior to, just before, or just after intromission of the penis into the vagina. It has come to include any form of rapid ejaculation which occurs prior to female sexual response.

priapism. A persistent erection of the penis which will not subside. This usually occurs without sexual desire and in chronic cases may require surgery to reduce vasocongestion.

progesterone. A female hormone with the principal function of causing changes in the lining of the uterus to make it ready to receive and develop a fertilized egg (ovum).

promiscuous. A usually pejorative term used to refer to individuals who have sexual activity with many other people. Also used to refer to people who engage in sexual activity either casually or with low emotional response. Difficult to define quantitatively.

prophylactic. Any drug or device used to prevent disease. With respect to sexuality, refers to devices (e.g., condoms) used to prevent venereal disease.

prostate. A male gland located in the neck of the bladder which produces an alkaline, milky colored fluid, the transport medium for sperm and the major part of male ejaculate.

pudendum. The external genitalia of the female, including the mons veneris, the labia majora, the labia minora, the clitoris, and the entry into the vagina.

refractory period. A temporary state following orgasm and ejaculation in the male, in which there appears to be a specific resistance to additional sexual stimulation.

resolution phase. The term used by Masters and Johnson to refer to their fourth and last stage in the human sexual response cycle, during which the body returns to a sexually unexcited state.

sadism. The preference for or the necessity of inflicting physical or psychological pain upon a sexual partner in order to achieve sexual arousal or gratification.

satyriasis. Usually used to refer to excessive sexual desire in men; a close parallel to the label **nymphomania** in women. Largely a pejorative term.

scrotum. The pouch of skin under the penis which contains the male testicles and accessory organs.

secondary sex characteristics. The physical characteristics (breasts, hair, body shape, etc.) normally appearing in puberty that distinguish male and female. The primary sex characteristics are the genitals.

semen (or **seminal emission** or **seminal fluid**). A fluid secreted by the male reproductive organs, composed of sperm and secretions from the epididymis, seminal vesicles, prostate gland, and Cowper's glands. Ejaculated by the male during orgasm.

sex flush. A term used by Masters and Johnson to describe the skin-color changes resulting from vasocongestive events which are associated with increasing sexual tension.

sex hormone. A chemical, including androgens and estrogens, secreted primarily by the ovaries and testes.

sexual dysfunction. See **sexual inadequacy.**

sexual inadequacy. A failure in sexual response, either on a temporary basis or as a chronic inability to respond to sexual stimuli. Masters and Johnson include in this group primary and secondary impotence, primary and secondary lack of orgasm, vaginismus, and premature ejaculation.

sexual outlet. A term coined by Kinsey to refer to various socially defined sources of or conditions of orgasm or ejaculation.

smegma. Thick, whitish, and odorous secretions which accumulate under the foreskin of the penis or the clitoris.

sodomy. A legal term, which includes sexual intercourse with animals and mouth-genital and genital-anal contact between humans.

sperm. The mature male reproductive cell which has the capacity to impregnate and fertilize the female ovum.

syphilis. A venereal disease transmitted usually by sexual intercourse when one partner is in the infectious stage of the disease. Caused by the invasion of a spirochete, and readily cured with antibiotics in its early stages. The disease can have serious consequences if left untreated.

taboo. A prohibition based upon various cultural standards related to religion, traditions, or other forms of social usage.

testicle (or **testis**). The male gonad which produces both testosterone and sperm.

testosterone. A hormone produced by the male testicle that induces male secondary sexual characteristics at puberty.

transsexualism. A belief that one is a person of the opposite sex who has been trapped in the body of the wrong sex. This often results in a desire to change one's genitals and secondary sexual characteristics to make them conform with one's psychological gender identity. This can now be done through a combination of surgical and hormonal procedures.

transvestism. A preference for wearing the clothes of the opposite sex. In some cases this is cross-dressing for entertainment or prostitution. In others it is based on the belief by the cross-dresser that he (or she) is in fact two personalities in the same body, a man and a woman, and the cross-dressing allows expression of both aspects of the self.

tumescence. Refers sexually to the processes of vasocongestion which produce swelling of the breasts and the genitals.

urethra. a tube through which urine passes out of the bladder and is excreted outside the body. In the male,

also the tube through which the seminal fluid is ejaculated at orgasm.

uterus. Female organ in which impregnation occurs and within which the fetus develops.

vagina. The opening in the female that extends from the vulva to the cervix and that accepts the penis during coitus. It is also the canal through which an infant passes at birth.

vaginal lubrication. A clear fluid which sweats through the vaginal mucosa after the onset of effective sexual stimulaton.

vaginal orgasm. Refers to the subjective sense of women that the sensations associated with orgasm are coming from the interior of the vagina. Freudians believe that women have two kinds of orgasm, one clitoral and the other vaginal, and that when women mature, they should have vaginal orgasms. The difference between clitoral and vaginal orgasms appears to be in the subjective sense of where the sensation is coming from, rather than from differences in neurophysiological processes.

vaginismus. Spasms by the vaginal musculature which prevent entry of the penis or other objects.

vaginitis. Inflammation of the vaginal mucosa, commonly the result of infection, but can also be produced by frequent, poorly lubricated intercourse.

vas deferens. Sperm ducts which lead from the epididymis to the seminal vesicles and to the urethra.

vasectomy. A surgical procedure for sterilizing the male which involves removing the vas deferens. A permanent form of contraception, which is rarely reversible.

vasocongestion. When used in connection with sexuality, refers to the congestion of the blood vessels, particularly the veins in the genital area, resulting in swelling or erection.

venereal disease. A contagious disease communicated by sexual activity.

voyeurism. A sexual preference in which a person achieves sexual gratification by looking at other people in the nude or during sexual activity.

vulva. The external sex organs of the female, including the mons veneris, the labia majora, the labia minora, the clitoris, and the entry to the vagina.

X chromosome. The sex-determining chromosome present in all of a female's ova and in one-half of a male's sperm. The fertilization of an ovum by a sperm containing an X chromosome will result in the conception of a female.

Y chromosome. A sex-determining chromosome which is present in one-half of a male's sperm. The fertilization of an ovum by a sperm containing a Y chromosome will result in the conception of a male.

zoophilia. See **bestiality.**

ACKNOWLEDGMENTS

ILLUSTRATION ACKNOWLEDGMENTS

7 "Him," 1964, Roy Lichtenstein. Print courtesy Leo Castelli Gallery. Private collection.

15 "I know how you must feel, Brad!" 1963, Roy Lichtenstein. Print courtesy Leo Castelli Gallery. Collection of Mrs. Vera List, N.Y.

25 © Barbara Jaffee

30 Ralph Gibson

42 Etching by Pablo Picasso from "The Voyeur" series, © S.P.A.D.E.M., Paris, 1977

61 Joanne Leonard

73 Courtesy Philip Morris

82 Catherine Ursillo

90 "American Nude," 1963, Charles Frazier. Courtesy Kornblee Gallery.

101 David Brill

103, 105 Drawings by Bernt Forsblad, electron micrograph by Lennart Nilsson: both from BEHOLD MAN, Little, Brown and Co.

122 U.P.I.

123 Elliot Erwitt/MAGNUM

143, 145, 147, 149, 151, 187 Duane Michals

169 From SICK, SICK, SICK by Jules Feiffer. Copyright © 1956, 1957, 1958 by Jules Feiffer. Reprinted by permission.

178 "The Back Seat Dodge '38," 1964, Edward Kienholz. Collection of Lyn Kienholz, L.A.

223 The Bettmann Archive

265, 280 Culver Pictures

271 (t), (b) The Bettmann Archive (m) Culver Pictures

281 Movie Star News (2)

284, 293 Reprinted courtesy COYOTE, copyright 1975 by Margo St. James.

305 Cartoon by Don Wright, © 1976 Miami News. Distributed by The New York Times Special Features.

330 François Lalanne

333 Drawing by Patricia Lenihan-Barbee

342 Art Reference Bureau

344 *Great American Nude, No. 57,* 1964, Tom Wesselmann. Courtesy Whitney Museum of American Art

351 "Home Movies," David Wilton.

361 "Chair," sculpture 1969, Allen Jones, painted resin and glass-fiber with accessories, life size. Courtesy The Waddington Galleries, London.

372 © 1977 Adger W. Cowans

385 Abigail Heyman/MAGNUM

401 John Brook

402 Reprinted by permission from TIME, The Weekly Newsmagazine; Copyright Time Inc.

410 *The Dream of the Fisherman's Wife,* Hokusai, © 1820. Courtesy of the Trustees of The British Museum.

LITERARY ACKNOWLEDGMENTS

32 From "Sexual Behavior" by Kingsley Davis in CONTEMPORARY SOCIAL PROBLEMS, 3rd Edition, edited by R. K. Merton and R. Nisbet. Published by Harcourt Brace Jovanovich, Inc., 1971. Reprinted by permission.

61 From MAN AND WOMAN, BOY AND GIRL by John Money and Anke Ehrhardt. Copyright © 1972 The Johns Hopkins University Press. Reprinted by permission.

64 From "Biological Imperatives" in TIME, January 8, 1973. Reprinted by permission from TIME, The Weekly Newsmagazine; Copyright Time Inc.

83, 85–6, 181 SEXUAL BEHAVIOR IN THE HUMAN MALE by Alfred C. Kinsey et al., from pp. 165, 177, 182, 543–4. Copyright © 1948 by W. B. Saunders Company. Reprinted by permission of Institute for Sex Research, Inc.

85, 112 SEXUAL BEHAVIOR IN THE HUMAN FEMALE by Alfred C. Kinsey et al., from pp. 104–5, 730–1. Copyright © 1953 by W. B. Saunders Company. Reprinted by permission of Institute for Sex Research, Inc.

94 From BEING THERE by Jerzy N. Kosinski. Copyright © 1970, 1971 by Jerzy N. Kosinski. Reprinted by permission of Harcourt Brace Jovanovich, Inc., and the author.

106 From "Crazy Salad: Some Things About Women" by Nora Ephron, as it appeared in ESQUIRE MAGAZINE (May 1972). Copyright © 1972, 1973, 1974, 1975 by Nora Ephron. Reprinted by permission of Alfred A. Knopf, Inc.

149 From DECLARATION ON CERTAIN QUESTIONS CONCERNING SEXUAL ETHICS. Published by Sacred Congregation for the Doctrine of the Faith with the approval of Pope Paul IV. Released by Vatican Press Office January 15, 1976.

161 Betty Dodson. LIBERATING MASTURBATION. (New York: Bodysex Designs), 1974

239 John Fowles. THE FRENCH LIEUTENANT'S WOMAN. (Boston: Little, Brown and Company), 1969

241 From ABNORMAL PSYCHOLOGY: AN EXPERIMENTAL-CLINICAL APPROACH by G. C. Davison and J. M. Neale, p. 293. Copyright © 1974 by John Wiley & Sons, Inc. Reprinted by permission.

256 From "A Gay Struggles with the New Acceptance" by Arnie Kantrowitz, THE VILLAGE VOICE, Nov. 17, 1975. Reprinted by permission of The Village Voice. Copyright © The Village Voice, Inc., 1975.

287 From MRS. WARREN'S PROFESSION by George Bernard Shaw. Reprinted by permission of The Society of Authors on behalf of the Bernard Shaw Estate.

288 From HUSTLING, *Prostitution in our Wide Open Society* by Gail Sheehy. Published by Delacorte Press, 1973. Copyright © 1971, 1972, 1973 by Gail Sheehy. Originally appeared in *New York Magazine,* November 13 and 20, 1972. Reprinted by permission of the author.

323 From UP AGAINST THE IVY WALL by Jerry L. Avorn et al., p. 292. Copyright © 1968 by Atheneum Publishers. Reprinted by permission.

349 From SEXUAL CONDUCT: THE SOCIAL SOURCES OF HUMAN SEXUALITY by John H. Gagnon and William Simon, pp. 273–5. Copyright 1973. Reprinted by permission of Aldine Publishing Company and Hutchinson Publishing Group Ltd.

393 From "Strategies for the Control of Gonorrhea" by G. B. Kolata, SCIENCE, 192:245, April 16 1976. Copyright © 1976 by the American Association for the Advancement of Science. Reprinted by permission.

397 Reprinted courtesy of Robert A. Hatcher, M.D., Contraceptive Technology, 1974–75.

INDEX